Scriptures of the World's Religions

SIXTH EDITION

edited by

James Fieser
University of Tennessee at Martin

John Powers
Deakin University

Mc Graw Hill Education

SCRIPTURES OF THE WORLD'S RELIGIONS, SIXTH EDITION

Published by McGraw-Hill Education, 2 Penn Plaza, New York, NY 10121. Copyright © 2018 by McGraw-Hill Education. All rights reserved. Printed in the United States of America. Previous editions © 2015, 2012, and 2008. No part of this publication may be reproduced or distributed in any form or by any means, or stored in a database or retrieval system, without the prior written consent of McGraw-Hill Education, including, but not limited to, in any network or other electronic storage or transmission, or broadcast for distance learning.

Some ancillaries, including electronic and print components, may not be available to customers outside the United States.

This book is printed on acid-free paper.

1 2 3 4 5 6 7 8 9 LCR 21 20 19 18 17

ISBN 978-1-259-90792-0
MHID 1-259-90792-9

Managing Director: *David Patterson*
Brand Managers: *Penina Braffman/Jamie Laferrera*
Product Developer: *Jamie Laferrera*
Editorial Coordinator: *Colin Balcarek*
Marketing Manager: *Meredith Leo*
Content, Design & Delivery: *Terri Schiesl*
Program Manager: *Jennifer Shekleton*
Content Project Managers: *Mary Jane Lampe / Jodi Banowetz*
Buyer: *Sandy Ludovissy*
Cover Designer: *Studio Montage, St. Louis, MO*
Cover Credits: *The entrance to an Asian temple.* © image100/Corbis [front – middle/left]; *Israel, Jerusalen, Western Wall and the Dome of The Rock.* © Medioimages/Photodisc [front – top/center]; *Golden Temple, Amritsar in golden morning light.* © Adrian Pope/Getty Images [front – bottom/right]; *Masjid Al Haram.* © Rabi Karim Photography/Getty Images [front – top/left]; *St Basils Cathedral on Red Square in Moscow.* © Aleksander Vrzalski/Getty Images [front – bottom/right]; *Ancient Buddha Statue at Borobudur temple in Yogyakarta, Java, Indonesia.* © Shutterstock/R.M. Nunes [front – bottom/left]; *Reflection of an illuminated temple in water, Confucian Temple, Nanjing, Jiangsu Province, China.* © Glow Images [back cover]
Compositor: *MPS Limited*
Typeface: *10/12 DejaVu Serif Book*
Printer: *LSC Communications - Crawfordsville*

Library of Congress Cataloging-in-Publication Data

Fieser, James, editor. | Powers, John, 1957- editor.
  Scriptures of the world's religions / edited by James Fieser,
  University of Tennessee at Martin; John Powers, Australian National University.
  Sixth edition. | Dubuque : McGraw-Hill Education, 2018.
  LCCN 2016051728 | ISBN 9781259907920 (alk. paper)
  LCSH: Sacred books.
  LCC BL70 .S37 2017 | DDC 208/.2—dc23 LC record available at
  https://lccn.loc.gov/2016051728

The Internet addresses listed in the text were accurate at the time of publication. The inclusion of a website does not indicate an endorsement by the authors or McGraw-Hill Education, and McGraw-Hill Education does not guarantee the accuracy of the information presented at these sites.

mheducation.com/highered

About the Authors

JOHN POWERS is Professor of Asian Studies in the College of Asia and the Pacific, Australian National University, and a Fellow of the Australian Academy of Humanities. He specializes in Buddhist philosophy and history, particularly of India and Tibet. He has published seventeen books and more than ninety articles, including *A Bull of a Man: Images of Masculinity, Sex, and the Body in Indian Buddhism* (Harvard, 2009) and *The Buddha Party: How China Works to Define and Control Tibetan Buddhism* (Oxford, 2016).

JAMES FIESER is a Research Professor in the Alfred Deakin Institute for Citizenship and Globalisation, Deakin University. He received his B.A. from Berea College, and his M.A. and Ph.D. in philosophy from Purdue University. He is author, co-author or editor of ten textbooks, including *Ethics: Discovering Right and Wrong* (8/e 2016), *Business Ethics* (2/e 2016), *Philosophy: A Historical Survey with Essential Readings* (9/e 2014), *Scriptures of the World's Religions* (6/e 2016), *A Historical Introduction to Philosophy* (2003), and *Moral Philosophy through the Ages* (2001). He has edited and annotated the ten-volume *Early Responses to Hume* (2/e 2005) and the five-volume *Scottish Common Sense Philosophy* (2000). He is the founder and general editor of the *Internet Encyclopedia of Philosophy* web site (www.iep.utm.edu).

Contents

Preface

Religion is one of the most complex phenomena of world civilization, and several avenues are open for understanding the major faith traditions. We could attempt to have firsthand encounters with those religions by talking with their believers, visiting their sacred sites, and attending classes for converts. Alternatively, we could attempt a more arm's length approach by reading surveys of the various religions, some written by believers defending their faith, others by critics, and even more by academic historians or anthropologists. Yet another avenue is to examine the collected sacred texts revered by these religions themselves.

This book takes the last approach. There are special benefits to exploring the world's religions through selections from their scriptures. In most cases the sacred texts are the oldest written documents in the tradition, and we gain a sense of immediate connection with these religions by studying the same documents that followers have been reading for millennia. The texts are also foundational to a religion's most important doctrines, rituals, and social and ethical positions. In this way, they explain the authoritative basis of traditions that might otherwise seem incomprehensible or even groundless. Finally, the texts have become the most sacred symbols of these traditions, which conveys the sense that we are on holy ground each time we read from them.

Since very few scriptures were originally written in the English language, these are selections of *translated* scriptures and to that end we have tried to find the most recent and readable translations. Some scriptures are still available only in older translation, and we have modernized these in view of recent scholarship. Unique to this anthology are several scriptures in Asian languages newly translated by John Powers.

An exhaustive collection of world scriptures would be over a thousand volumes in length; the challenge was selecting the right ones to fit into an anthology of this limited size. The first difficult choice was to confine the texts to those of religions that are practiced today. This excludes dead traditions that are mainly of academic interest, such as ancient Greek, Mesopotamian, and Egyptian religions. Second, we gave preference to texts that discuss the lives and teachings of religious founders and present central doctrines. These are not only of greater intrinsic interest, but including them ensures that the essential differences between religions emerge. Third, we tried to select scriptures that are accessible to lay practitioners, and not just theologians or scholars. Finally, we placed emphasis on religions that have a wide sphere of influence; specifically Hinduism, Buddhism, Judaism, Christianity, and Islam. We cover less influential religions more briefly; specifically Jainism, Shinto, Sikhism, Zoroastrianism, and the Baha'i Faith.

In spite of the above boundaries of inclusion, the notion of *scripture* that we use here is sufficiently broad to include three strata of religious texts. The first stratum involves texts that the religions themselves consider most sacred. The term *protocanonical* typically denotes this level, and it includes works such as the Buddhist *Pali Canon*, the Muslim *Qur'an*, and the Jewish *Tanakh*. The second stratum involves more peripheral sacred texts, often termed *deuterocanonical*. This includes collections of oral law, such as the Jewish *Talmud* and the Muslim *Hadith*, as well as texts on the lives of religious founders, such as the Sikh *Janam-sakhi*. The third stratum involves sectarian texts that at some time in the history of that religion were considered scripture by members of that sect. Examples are the Jewish *Zohar* and the Christian *Book of Mormon*.

The readings within each religion are categorized according to the inherent structure of the scriptural canons themselves, following either their original dates of composition or their historically structured narratives. We prefer this historical approach to alternative arrangements that categorize texts by topic because the former is more harmonious with the way each religion understands its own canon. It also enables readers to gain a sense of the historical development of ideas and practices, which is often lost in topical arrangements.

The most visible changes to this new edition are the inclusion of the following new selections:

Judaism
New selection from Talmud on why God is jealous of idols
New selection of stories about Baal Shem Tov
New selection by Moses Mendelssohn on revealed law
New selection by Solomon Schechter on Jewish dogmas
Christianity
New selection from the Gospel of Judas
New selection by Thomas Campbell on the Restoration Movement

Islam:
    New selection from the Koran on the birth of Jesus
    New selection from the Hadith on the essence of Islam
    New selection of stores about Rabi'a
Indigenous Religions
    New selection from Melanesian mythology
    New selection from Polynesian mythology
    New selection from Micronesian mythology

Other minor changes have been made throughout.

We thank friends and colleagues who have generously offered advice on this book. Alphabetically, they are Stephen Benin, Ronald C. Bluming, Christopher Buck, Stevan L. Davies, Richard Detweiler, James Findlay, Timothy Fobbs, Richard Elliot Friedman, Edwin Hostetter, Jennifer Jesse, Charles Johnson, Norman Lillegard, William Magee, Rochelle Millen, Robert J. Miller, Moojan Momen, Henry Munson, Randall Nadeau, Joseph H. Peterson, Richard Pilgrim, David Prejsnar, Habib Riazati, Kenneth Rose, Betty Rosian, Aziz Sachedina, Chaim E. Schertz, Robert Stockman, Mark Towfiq, and Mark Tyson.

PRONUNCIATION OF TERMS IN INDIAN LANGUAGES

The scriptures of India's religions are written in a variety of languages and dialects. Sanskrit was the *lingua franca* of intellectuals and religious authors in ancient India, much like Latin in medieval Europe. Most important Hindu scriptures were written in Sanskrit, and Jain and Buddhist texts are written in Sanskrit or related languages such as Pāli, the language of the Theravāda canon. Virtually all secondary literature by scholars uses diacritical spellings, and these often vary considerably from phonetic ones; in many cases, letters are pronounced similarly to Roman letters, but many letters marked by diacritics are not.

i. Vowels and Diphthongs Used in This Book:

Letter	*Pronunciation*
a	uh, as in fun
ā	ah, as in charm
i	ih, as in pin
ī	ee, as in seek
u	oo, as in sue
ū	ooh, as in school
e	ey, as in prey
o	oh, as in phone

ai	aye, as in time
au	ow, as in cow
ṛ	er, as in fur

Long vowels should take approximately twice as long to speak as short vowels; thus ā is slightly lengthened and emphasized when pronounced. In addition, emphasis is often different from what English speakers expect, so maṇḍala, for example, is pronounced MUHN duh luh, and not mahn DAH la, as English speakers unfamiliar with Sanskrit often pronounce it.

ii. Consonants

Sanskrit and Pāli have several types of consonants, which are divided into five classes: guttural, palatal, lingual, dental, and labial. These classes are based on where in the mouth the sound is made. Gutturals are made in the throat, palatals are made by touching the tongue to the palate, linguals are retroflex sounds made by curling the tongue inside the mouth and touching the bottom of the tip to the palate, dentals are made by touching the tongue to the teeth, and labials are made with the lips. The gutturals are ka, kha, ga, gha, and ṅa. The palatals are ca, cha, ja, jha, and ña. The linguals are ṭa, ṭha, ḍa, ḍha, and ṇa. The labials are pa, pha, ba, bha, and ma. Some other letters should be mentioned: (1) the "sibilants" śa and ṣa, both of which are pronounced "sh," as in usher or shine; (2) *anusvāra* ṃ, which is pronounced either as m, as in saṃsāra, or as ng, as in saṃgha; and (3) *visarga* ḥ, which is silent. Ca is pronounced cha, as in chair (so Yogācāra is pronounced "Yogahchahra"). The palatal ña is pronounced nya; other letters are pronounced like their English equivalents.

connect

The sixth edition of *Scriptures of the World's Religions* is now available online with Connect, McGraw-Hill Education's integrated assignment and assessment platform. Connect also offers SmartBook for the new edition, which is the first adaptive reading experience proven to improve grades and help students study more effectively.

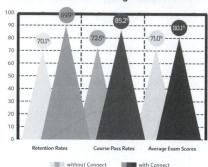
©Getty Images/iStockphoto

McGraw-Hill Connect®
Learn Without Limits

Connect is a teaching and learning platform that is proven to deliver better results for students and instructors.

Connect empowers students by continually adapting to deliver precisely what they need, when they need it, and how they need it, so your class time is more engaging and effective.

Connect's Impact on Retention Rates, Pass Rates, and Average Exam Scores

Bar chart showing:
- Retention Rates: 70.1% (without Connect), 89.9% (with Connect)
- Course Pass Rates: 72.5% (without Connect), 85.2% (with Connect)
- Average Exam Scores: 71.0% (without Connect), 80.1% (with Connect)

without Connect / with Connect

73% of instructors who use **Connect** require it; instructor satisfaction **increases** by 28% when **Connect** is required.

Using **Connect** improves retention rates by **19.8%**, passing rates by **12.7%**, and exam scores by **9.1%**.

Analytics ———

Connect Insight®

Connect Insight is Connect's new one-of-a-kind visual analytics dashboard—now available for both instructors and students—that provides at-a-glance information regarding student performance, which is immediately actionable. By presenting assignment, assessment, and topical performance results together with a time metric that is easily visible for aggregate or individual results, Connect Insight gives the user the ability to take a just-in-time approach to teaching and learning, which was never before available. Connect Insight presents data that empowers students and helps instructors improve class performance in a way that is efficient and effective.

Impact on Final Course Grade Distribution

without Connect		with Connect
22.9%	A	31.0%
27.4%	B	34.3%
22.9%	C	18.7%
11.5%	D	6.1%
15.4%	F	9.9%

Students can view their results for any **Connect** course.

Mobile ———

Connect's new, intuitive mobile interface gives students and instructors flexible and convenient, anytime–anywhere access to all components of the Connect platform.

Adaptive

THE **ADAPTIVE**
READING EXPERIENCE
DESIGNED TO TRANSFORM
THE WAY STUDENTS READ

> More students earn **A's** and
> **B's** when they use McGraw-Hill
> Education **Adaptive** products.

SmartBook®

Proven to help students improve grades and study more efficiently, SmartBook contains the same content within the print book, but actively tailors that content to the needs of the individual. SmartBook's adaptive technology provides precise, personalized instruction on what the student should do next, guiding the student to master and remember key concepts, targeting gaps in knowledge and offering customized feedback, and driving the student toward comprehension and retention of the subject matter. Available on tablets, SmartBook puts learning at the student's fingertips—anywhere, anytime.

> Over **8 billion questions** have been
> answered, making McGraw-Hill
> Education products more intelligent,
> reliable, and precise.

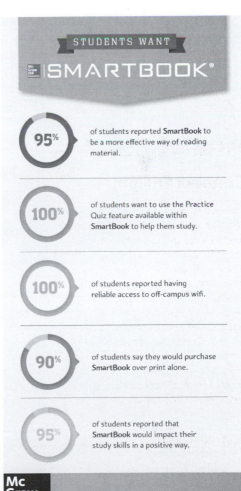

STUDENTS WANT

SMARTBOOK®

95% of students reported **SmartBook** to be a more effective way of reading material.

100% of students want to use the Practice Quiz feature available within **SmartBook** to help them study.

100% of students reported having reliable access to off-campus wifi.

90% of students say they would purchase **SmartBook** over print alone.

95% of students reported that **SmartBook** would impact their study skills in a positive way.

Mc Graw Hill Education

*Findings based on 2015 focus group results administered by McGraw-Hill Education

www.mheducation.com

Hinduism

INTRODUCTION

Contemporary Hindus commonly refer to their religion as "universal truth" *(sanātana-dharma)*, implying that it is a meta-tradition that is able to embrace the truths of all other systems of thought while transcending them through its expansive capacity to embrace truth in multiple manifestations. Hinduism is the dominant religious tradition of the Indian subcontinent, and currently more than 700 million people consider themselves Hindus.

Hinduism is, however, a difficult tradition to define. Its dominant feature is diversity, and its adherents are not required to accept any doctrine or set of doctrines, to perform any particular practices, or to accept any text or system as uniquely authoritative. Many Hindus, for example, are monotheists and believe there is only one God, despite the proliferation of gods in Hinduism. They assert that God has many manifestations and that God may appear differently to different people and different cultures.

Other Hindus are polytheists who believe that the various gods they worship are distinct entities, whereas pantheistic Hindus perceive the divine in the world around them as a principle that manifests in natural phenomena, particular places, flora and fauna, or other humans. Some Hindus consider themselves to be agnostic, contending that God is in principle unknown and unknowable. Other Hindus are atheists who do not believe in the existence of any gods; this position does not lead to their excommunication by their fellow Hindus. Even more confusing, in daily practice it is common to see one person or community sequentially manifesting combinations of these attitudes in different circumstances.

Hinduism has a plethora of doctrines and systems, but no collection of tenets constitutes a universally binding Hindu creed, nor is there any core belief that is so fundamental that it would be accepted by all Hindus. Hinduism has produced a vast collection of sacred texts, but no one text has the authority of the Christian Bible, the Jewish Torah, or the Muslim Qur'an. Perhaps the most widely revered sacred texts are the Vedas ("Wisdom Texts"), most of which were written more than 2,000 years ago. But despite their generally accepted authoritativeness, few Hindus today are even able to read them, and the brahmins (priests) whose sacred task is to memorize and recite them generally are unable to explain what they mean.

In searching for a way to define the boundaries of Hinduism, the term *Hindu* may provide some help. It was originally coined by Persians who used it to refer to the people they encountered in northern India in the Indus Valley. Thus Hindu referred to the inhabitants of a geographical area, and in later centuries it was adopted by people of India who identified themselves with the dominant religious tradition of the subcontinent.

Contemporary Hinduism is still delimited more by geography than by belief or practice: A Hindu is someone who lives on the Indian subcontinent or is descended from people of the region, who considers himself or herself a Hindu, and who is accepted as such by other Hindus. There are no distinctive doctrines whose acceptance would serve as a litmus test of orthodoxy, no ecclesiastical authority that is able to declare some to be Hindus in good standing or label others heretics, and no ceremony whose performance would serve as a definitive rite of passage into the tradition. There is no founder of the tradition, and no dominant system of theology or single moral code.

Contemporary Hinduism embraces groups whose respective faiths and practices have virtually nothing in common with one another. This is not to say, however, that Hinduism lacks distinctive doctrines, practices, or scriptures; in fact, the opposite is the case. Hinduism has developed a plethora of philosophical schools, rituals, and sacred texts, and its adherents commonly assert a belief in a shared heritage, historical continuity, and family relationships among the multiple manifestations of their tradition. The selections provided here represent only a small sampling of the vast corpus of Hindu religious literature. In addition, it should be noted that this literature represents only a tiny part of the Hindu tradition and primarily reflects the views and practices of a small intellectual elite. The vast majority of Hindus have been—and continue to be—primarily illiterate agricultural workers with little if any knowledge of the sacred scriptures. Their practices generally are derived from local cults and beliefs that may have little in common with the religion and philosophy of the authors of the scriptures. Furthermore, these texts do not form a coherent system but instead are as diverse as Hinduism itself. They were written over the course of millennia and reflect shifting paradigms and divergent political, religious, and social agendas, geographical differences, and varying ideas about how people should worship, think, live, and interact.

HISTORY OF HINDUISM AND HINDU SCRIPTURES

Hinduism can be compared to a complex symphony in which new themes are introduced as the piece develops, while old ones continue to be woven into its texture. Nothing is ever truly lost, and elements of the distant past may return to prominence at unexpected times, although often in forms that are altered in accordance with the intellectual and religious currents of a particular time and place. The scriptures of Hinduism reflect its diversity and its complex history. They include ancient hymns to anthropomorphic gods and liturgical texts detailing how priests should prepare sacrifices, mystical texts that speculate on the nature of ultimate reality, devotional literature in praise of a variety of deities, philosophical texts of great subtlety and insight, and combinations of these and related themes.

The earliest stratum of Indian sacred literature accessible today is found in the Vedas, which evolved into their present form between 1400 and 400 BCE. The earliest of these were codified around 1300 BCE by people who referred to themselves as Āryans, meaning "noble" or "wise." They referred to other residents of northern India as "slaves" *(dāsa* or *dasyu)*, but the actual relation between these groups is unclear.

The Vedas are referred to by Hindus as "revelation" (*śruti*; literally, "what is heard"), in contrast to other scriptures referred to as "tradition" (*smṛti*; literally, "what is remembered"). Both classes are regarded as canonical, but the latter is not considered to have the same level of authoritativeness as the Vedas. According to tradition, the Vedas are not the product of human composition (*apauruṣeya*) but are a part of the very fabric of reality. They were directly perceived by "seers" (*ṛṣi*), whose mystical contemplations—aided by ingestion of an intoxicating beverage called *soma*—enabled them to intuit primordial sounds reverberating throughout the universe and render them into human language as the books of the Vedas.

There are four Vedas: (1) the *Ṛg Veda*, so named because it is composed of stanzas (*ṛk*); (2) the *Sāma Veda* (composed mostly of hymns taken from the *Ṛg Veda* and set to various melodies, or *sāman*); (3) the *Yajur Veda* (composed of *yajus*, selected ritual prayers, mostly taken from the *Ṛg Veda*); and (4) the *Atharva Veda* (a collection of ritual texts named after the sage Atharvan). The Vedas contain several primary types of literature: (1) chants or hymns (*saṃhitā*), generally directed toward the gods *(deva)* of the Vedic pantheon; (2) ritual texts *(brāhmaṇa)*, which detail the sacrifices performed by brahmins;

and (3) mystical texts concerned with the quest for ultimate truth (*āraṇyaka*s and *upaniṣad*s).[1]

INDO-ĀRYAN RELIGION AND SOCIETY

The origins of the Indo-Āryans are a matter of considerable controversy among scholars. Early European Indologists, basing their analysis on obscure passages in Vedic texts, speculated that the Āryans were invaders from central Europe who entered the subcontinent, where they encountered indigenous inhabitants (commonly referred to as Dravidians) and conquered them with superior military technology. In recent years most of these assumptions have been debunked, and a consensus has developed that there is no real evidence to support the "Āryan invasion" theory.

It now appears that the Indo-Āryans may have been indigenous to the subcontinent and that they distinguished themselves from other peoples as the holders of the sacred Vedic scriptures and performers of Vedic rituals. Archaeological evidence from Dravidian cities in the Indus Valley region suggests that the inhabitants attained a high degree of social development, although their society probably was in decline by 1300 BCE. Little is known with any certainty about their civilization, but there appears to have been interaction between them and the Indo-Āryans, which may have led to cross-cultural influences.

From an early period, as indicated in their sacred texts, the Indo-Āryans and their descendants propounded the idea that human society ideally should be stratified, with each social class having clearly defined functions and duties. At the top of the hierarchy were the brahmins, or priestly class, whose sacred duty was to perform sacrifices to the gods described in the Vedas. Many of these gods were personifications of natural phenomena, such as the sun, moon, wind, and so forth. Many gods were believed to have dominion over a particular natural force or phenomenon, and the rituals of the Vedas were commonly directed either to one god or to a small group of gods who were considered to have the ability to affect a particular sphere of divine provenance.

---

[1] The term *Āraṇyaka* literally means "Forest Text" because they were attributed to sages who removed themselves from society and lived in remote areas in order to devote themselves to a solitary pursuit of truth. The term *Upaniṣad* derives from the root word *ṣad*, "to sit," with prefixes meaning "around," implying that they were spoken by sages to an audience of students sitting around them in a semicircle.

The role of the priests was central in this system: They were expected to remain ritually pure and to preserve the sacred texts, along with the lore of priestcraft. Their social function prevented them from engaging in manual labor, trade, agriculture, or other nonpriestly occupations that were considered polluting. In exceptional circumstances occasioned by special need, they were allowed to earn a living by other means, but ideally their lives should be devoted to study of the sacred Vedas and performance of Vedic rituals. This was crucial to the maintenance of the system of "upholding the world" *(loka-saṃgraha)*, a core concern of Vedic religion.

In this system, the brahmins performed a pivotal function in offering sacrifices to the gods. The sacrifices generally were transmuted into smoke through the agency of Agni, god of fire (who is manifested in the ritual fire, as well as in other forms of combustion). Smoke converted the material of the sacrifice into a subtle essence suitable for the gods' consumption, and the process required that the brahmins remain ritually pure because any pollution they acquired was passed on to their sacrifices. The gods would naturally be insulted if offered unclean food and would respond by denying requests the brahmins made on behalf of the sponsors of the sacrifices.

The Vedic system was based on a symbiosis of gods and humans: The gods required sacrificial offerings, and humans needed the gods to use their supernatural powers to maintain cosmic order *(ṛta)*. The system assumed that humans only prosper in a stable and ordered cosmos, an idea reflected in the story of the slaying of the demon Vṛtra ("Obstructer") by Indra, the king of the gods in the Vedas. Demons thrive in chaos, and at the beginning of time Vṛtra rules over a chaotic cosmos until Indra, after a mighty battle, slays him and thereby makes it possible for the gods to establish order.

This primordial battle reflects the crucial role played by the gods in establishing and maintaining cosmic law. The concerns of Vedic literature are primarily practical and this-worldly. They focus on particular pragmatic goals, such as bountiful crops, fertility, peace, stability, wealth, and so forth. The results of the sacrifices are believed to accrue in the present life, and although a world of the dead is mentioned, it does not play a major role in the early Vedic tradition.

THE UPANIṢADS AND YOGA

The focus shifts in the later Vedic period, in which texts of speculative philosophy and mysticism begin to appear. Referred to as Āraṇyakas and Upaniṣads, they were written by sages who often expressed dissatisfaction with the ritualism and this-worldly focus of the early Vedic texts. Their authors sought the ultimate power behind the sacrifices, the force that gives rise to gods, humans, and all the other phenomena of the universe. They found this by a process of inward-looking meditation that sought an unchanging essence beyond the transient phenomena of existence. The present life was no longer viewed as the beginning and end of one's existence; rather, living beings were said to be reborn in successive lives in accordance with their actions (karma). The actions of the present result in opposite and equal reactions in the future, and one's present life is a result of the karma accrued in the past. The cycle of existence *(saṃsāra)* was said by the sages of the Upaniṣads to be beginningless, but it may be ended. It is perpetuated by a basic misunderstanding of the true nature of reality (*avidyā*, or "ignorance"), but one may escape it by attaining correct understanding of truth, which is found only by people who shift their attention from external things to find the truly real.

By following the path of wisdom that correctly discriminates the real from the unreal, the truly important from the merely pleasant, and the changeless from the transitory, the sage eventually discovers that within everyone is an eternal, unchanging essence, an immortal soul referred to as the "self" *(ātman)*. The Upaniṣads declare that this essence alone survives death and that it has been reborn countless times in an infinite variety of different bodies, while itself remaining unchanged by the multiple identities developed in successive lifetimes. It is characterized by three qualities: being, consciousness, and bliss *(sat cit ānanda)*, meaning that it is pure, unchanging being and its nature is never altered, despite the changing external circumstances of our lives; it is pure consciousness that takes no notice of the vicissitudes of our lives; and it remains unaffected by our joys, sorrows, hopes, disappointments, pleasures, or pains and thus is in a continuous state of equanimity. Moreover, the Upaniṣadic sages identified the self with the cosmic ultimate, something supremely mysterious, hidden from ordinary perception but all-pervasive, supremely subtle, the essence of all that is. This ultimate was said to be beyond words or conceptual thought and was referred to as "Brahman," because it is the purest and most sublime principle of existence, just as in human society brahmins are the purest and holiest class.

According to this system, the perceptions of ordinary beings are profoundly distorted by ignorance, and the only way to attain correct knowledge is through a process of discipline (yoga) in which one's thoughts and body are gradually brought under control and one's attention is turned away from sense objects and directed within.

These premises are shared with the system outlined in the *Yoga Aphorisms (Yoga-sūtra)* of Patañjali, who is credited with gathering the principal practices and premises of the yoga system. Patañjali's system, however, differs in significant ways from that of the Upaniṣads, although both use the term *yoga* to describe their respective training programs. The Upaniṣads outline a monistic system in which the sole reality is said to be Brahman, and everything else is based on mistaken perceptions.

Patañjali, in contrast, contends that both matter *(prakṛti)* and spirit *(puruṣa)* are real entities, and the goal of his system is separation *(kaivalya)* of spirit from matter; the Upaniṣads aim at a final apotheosis in which all dualities are transcended and one realizes the fundamental identity of the self and Brahman. The final goal of the Upaniṣads is expressed in the greatest of the "great statements" *(mahāvākya)* that sum up the central insights of the Upaniṣadic sages: "That is you" *(tat tvam asi)*. This expresses the identity of the individual soul and Brahman. Patañjali's goal is separation that liberates one's spiritual essence from matter.

The aim of both systems is liberation *(mokṣa)* from the cycle of existence, but each conceives of this release differently. Both consider yoga to be the primary practice for attaining the final goal, and for both yoga is a program of introspective meditation that begins with physical discipline; control of random, ignorant thoughts; and development of insight into unchanging truth. But the ontological presuppositions and ultimate goals of the two systems differ in significant details.

SOCIAL STRUCTURE

The Upaniṣads and Patañjali's yoga system represent a shift from the primacy of sacrifices to the gods in the early Vedic period to a general acceptance of the idea that the final aim of the religious path is liberation. As release from cyclic existence came to be viewed as the supreme goal, sacrifices aimed at maintaining the order of the world and the acquisition of mundane benefits became devalued as inferior to the pursuit of knowledge of truth.

In an apparent reaction to this trend, orthodox elements began to stress the importance of performing one's social duties (dharma). Texts like the *Traditions of Manu (Manu-smṛti)* and the *Song of God (Bhagavad-gītā)* emphasized the importance of selfless, devout adherence to the duties of one's social class *(varṇa)*: the brahmins, the warriors and rulers *(kṣatriya)*, the merchants and tradespeople *(vaiśya)*, and the servants *(śūdra)*. Both texts asserted that if people ignore their sacred duty the world will fall into chaos, society will crumble, and essential social functions will not be performed. The *Traditions of Manu* delineate a system in which people eventually should renounce the world and pursue final liberation, but only after first fulfilling the duties assigned to their social class. In its system of "duties of social classes and stages of life" *(varṇāśrama-dharma)*, specific duties for each class are outlined that should be performed diligently in order to maintain the world. The system assumes that only in an ordered universe will some people have the leisure and resources to pursue liberation.

The ideal life begins with the student stage, in which a man finds a spiritual preceptor (guru) who teaches him the lore appropriate to his class. The three highest classes (brahmins, *kṣatriyas*, and *vaiśyas*) are said to be "twice-born" *(dvija)* because they undergo a ceremony (the *upanayana*) that initiates them into adulthood and is considered a "second birth." Only these three classes are permitted to study the Vedas or to participate in Vedic rituals (but officiating in Vedic ceremonies is the special duty of brahmins). After a period of study (which varies in length and content among the four classes), a man should marry, produce male heirs to continue the lineage and perform sacrifices for him and his ancestors after his death, and support the brahmins whose rituals maintain the whole cosmos.

According to Manu, after a man has successfully performed his duty and when he sees his grandson born (assuring that the lineage will continue) and gray hairs on his head, he may withdraw from society (often with his wife) and begin to sever the ties that he cultivated during his life in the world. As a "forest dweller" *(vana-prastha)*, he should be celibate and detached from worldly enjoyments, cultivate meditation on ultimate truth, and pursue liberation. When he knows that his attachment to mundane things has ceased, he may take the final step of becoming a "world renouncer" *(saṃnyāsin)*, completely devoted to the ultimate goal, wandering from place to place and subsisting on alms, intent on final liberation from cyclic existence.

In this system, everything has its time and place. Although liberation is recognized as the ultimate goal of the religious life, it should not be pursued in a way that might destabilize society. When the demands of dharma have been met, one may seek one's own ends, but Manu declares that renouncing the world too soon would lead to a degeneration of the whole society, and the resulting chaos would make the attainment of liberation difficult, if not impossible, for anyone.

THE PATH OF DEVOTION

Another important path to liberation lies in the "yoga of devotion" *(bhakti-yoga)*, in which one finds salvation through completely identifying oneself with God. The yoga of devotion requires that one focus one's attention so completely on God that all thoughts of ego are transcended in a pure experience of union.

There are a variety of ways of conceiving devotion: Sometimes it takes the form of a love affair in which the devotee experiences an ecstatic union surpassing any human love; for others, devotion is characterized by selfless service to an omnipotent master. Often, Hindu devotionalism exhibits elements of both, along with a feeling of an intensely personal relationship between a human being and God.

The selections presented here are arranged in roughly chronological order and are taken from a wide range of Hindu scriptures. Of necessity many important scriptures have been omitted from this survey. Those that have been included were chosen because they exemplify central themes of contemporary and traditional Hindu religious thought.

HOLIDAYS

Festival of Lights (Divālī or Dīpāvalī) Celebrated in the second half of the lunar month of Aśvina, which generally occurs in October/November. It celebrates the homecoming of Rāma and Sītā to Ayodhya after their years in exile as recounted in the *Adventures of Rāma (Rāmāyaṇa)*. Lights adorn houses, temples, and streets; gifts are exchanged; and food and jewels are offered to Lakṣmī, the goddess of fortune. The holiday is also associated with the slaying of a demon by Kṛṣṇa.

Festival of Colors (Holī) Celebrates the immolation of Holikā, a demoness who possessed a magical shawl that made her immune to fire. Her father, the demon Hiraṇyakaśipu, ordered that his son Prahlāda be burned alive because of his devotion to the god Viṣṇu, but Holikā's shawl flew to him and protected him, while she was burned by the fire. On the first day of the festival, huge bonfires are lit all over India, and on the second day people throw colored powders on each other. Holī generally falls in late February or early March.

(Continued)

HOLIDAYS *(Continued)*

Birth of Krishna (Kṛṣṇa-janmāṣṭamī) Celebrates the birth of Kṛṣṇa, the eighth incarnation *(avatāra)* of Viṣṇu. It falls on the eighth day of the dark half of the month of Bhadrapada in the Hindu calendar (generally August or September). Devotees often begin with a fast the day prior to the festival and a night-long vigil commemorating Kṛṣṇa's birth. At midnight an image of Kṛṣṇa is bathed, and in the morning women draw tiny footprints outside the house, symbolizing his entry into his home.

Kumbh Festival (Kumbh Mela) Often referred to as the largest religious gathering in the world, occurring when the sun stands at Aquarius *(kumbh)*. It is celebrated every three years and rotates among Hardwar, Prayaga, Ujjaini, and Nasik. Millions of Hindus come from all over the country to bathe in the sacred waters, and large numbers of world-renouncers from various religious orders congregate, many performing feats of asceticism.

Great Night of Śiva (Mahā-Śivarātri) Celebrated in the month of Māgha in the Hindu calendar, during a night divided into four quarters. Devotees keep a vigil through the night, chanting the divine names of Śiva and making offerings.

TIMELINE

4000 BCE	Composition of earliest Vedic hymns
2700–1500 BCE	Flourishing of Indus civilization
1900 BCE	Age of the *Rāmāyaṇa*
1500–1200 BCE	Composition of the *Ṛg Veda*
1400 BCE	Great Bhārata War; early version of *Mahābhārata*
500 BCE–500 CE	Composition of Epics and early Purāṇas
322–298 BCE	Reign of Candragupta Maurya
100–500 CE	Expansion of Hinduism into Southeast Asia

TIMELINE *(Continued)*

400–500	Vyāsa's Commentary on the *Yoga Aphorisms*; origins of Tantrism
999–1026	Raids by Mahmud of Ghazni; destruction of temples
1336–1565	Kingdom of Vijayanagara, last Hindu empire in India
1526	Battle of Panipat; Mughals become rulers of Delhi and Agra
1526–1757	Mughals rule in north India; destruction of most Hindu temples
1542	Jesuit missionary Francis Xavier arrives in Goa
1651	British East India Company opens first factory in Bengal
1828	Ram Mohan Roy founds Brahmo Samāj
1857	Indian Mutiny; British expelled from India for almost two years
1920	Mahātma Gandhi begins his first All-India Civil Disobedience Movement
1947	India's independence; Partition into India and Pakistan
1948	Mahātma Gandhi assassinated; Pandit Nehru elected first Prime Minister of independent India
1992	Hindu extremists demolish Babri mosque in Ayodhyā
1998–2004	Hindu nationalist party, Bharatiya Janata Party, forms minority government

GLOSSARY

Agni God of fire in the Vedas, who transmutes sacrificial offerings into food for the gods.

Āryan The people who composed the Vedas and whose religion became predominant on the subcontinent.

Ātman "Soul," the divine essence of every individual.

Avidyā "Ignorance," the primary factor that enmeshes living beings in the cycle of birth, death, and rebirth.

Bhagavad-gītā "Song of God," a section of the epic *Mahābhārata* that describes the ethical dilemma of Arjuna, who is torn between the demands of karma and dharma.

Bhakti Selfless devotion to God.

Brahman The ultimate reality described in the Upaniṣads.

Brahmin The priestly caste of traditional Hinduism.

Deva The gods of Hinduism.

Devī The Goddess, who manifests in various female forms.

Dharma "Duty" or "Law," the occupational, social, and religious roles required of individuals as a result of their place in society.

Dravidian Term coined by Western scholars for the inhabitants of India who developed the Indus Valley civilization, portrayed as the enemies of the Āryans in the Vedas.

Hindu An adherent of Hinduism.

Indra King of the gods in the Vedic stories, and the paradigmatic warrior.

Karma "Actions," which bring about concordant results.

Kṣatriya The social class whose members traditionally were warriors and rulers.

Loka-saṃgraha "Upholding the World," the goal of the sacrifices enjoined by the Vedas.

Māyā "Magic" or "illusion," the creative power of Brahman that manifests as the phenomena of the world.

Mokṣa "Release" from the cycle of birth, death, and rebirth.

Rāmāyaṇa *"Adventures of Rāma,"* the epic story of the heroic deeds of Rāma, believed by tradition to be an incarnation of the god Viṣṇu.

Ṛṣi "Seers" who revealed the Vedas.

Ṛta Cosmic order, which is maintained by the gods.

Saṃnyāsin One who renounces the world in order to seek liberation from cyclic existence.

Saṃsāra "Cyclic Existence," the beginningless cycle of birth, death, and rebirth in which ignorant beings are trapped.

Sanātana-dharma "Universal Truth," a term for Hinduism, implying that it is able to embrace the limited "truths" of other religions and philosophies.

Saṃkara Most influential of traditional commentators on the Upaniṣads.

Śiva God who exemplifies yogic practice, who will destroy the world at the end of the present cosmic cycle.

Śūdra The social class whose traditional duty was to serve those above them.

Upaniṣads Mystical texts that speculate on the nature of human existence and the ultimate reality.

Vaiśya The social class whose members traditionally were merchants and skilled artisans.

Varṇa The four main social groupings of traditional Indian society (brahmins, *kṣatriyas*, *vaiśyas*, and *śūdras*).

Veda The four early sacred texts of Hinduism, which describe the gods and rituals connected with them.

Vedānta Tradition of commentary on the Upaniṣads.

Viṣṇu God whose traditional role is to protect dharma.

Yoga System of meditative cultivation involving physical and mental discipline.

VEDAS

CREATION OF THE UNIVERSE

The following selections are taken from the Ṛg Veda *and are hymns and ritual texts devoted to the worship of the Vedic gods. These verses describe the attributes of the gods, recounting the mythos of each deity and his or her particular sacrificial functions and associations. The first hymn depicts the creation of the universe as beginning with the sacrifice of Puruṣa ("Man"), a giant god whose body formed the raw material for the formation of the stars, the planets, and living things. According to the story, the four social classes (*varṇa*) of Hinduism were also created through this sacrifice, thus providing a scriptural justification for the stratification of Indian society.*

1. The Man (Puruṣa) has a thousand heads, a thousand eyes, and a thousand feet. Covering all sides of the earth, he extended a width of ten fingers beyond it.
2. The Man is everything: what is and what will be. He is also the master of immortality when he moves beyond the world through food.
3. So mighty is his greatness, but the Man is still more than this: all living beings are a quarter of him, and three quarters are immortal in heaven.
4. With the three quarters, the Man went upward, but one quarter of him came here again. From there he moved out in different directions, toward what eats and what does not eat. . . .
6. When the gods laid out the sacrifice with the Man as their offering, spring was its clarified butter, summer was its firewood, and autumn was the oblation.
7. They consecrated their sacrifice, the Man, who was born in the earliest time. The gods, the Sādhyas, and the seers sacrificed with him.

8. The dripping fat was collected from that sacrifice in which everything was offered. The sacrifice formed the animals, those who live in the air, those of the wilderness, and domestic animals.

9. The verses and chants arose from that sacrifice in which everything was offered. The meters arose from it, as did sacrificial formulas.

10. Horses arose from it, along with animals with teeth in both jaws. Cows arose from it, as did goats and sheep.

11. When they cut up the Man, how many portions did they make? How do they refer to his mouth, or his arms? How do they refer to his two thighs and his two feet?

12. The priest *(brahmin)* was his mouth, and his arms became the warrior *(kṣatriya)*, his thighs the tradesperson *(vaiśya)*, and the servant *(śūdra)* arose from his two feet.

13. The moon arose from his mind, and the sun from his eye. Indra and Agni arose from his mouth, and Vāyu from his breath.

14. The middle realm of space was born from his navel, and the heavens developed from his ear. In this way, they ordered the worlds.

15. There were seven fencing sticks, and three times seven layers of kindling were prepared when the gods, offering the sacrifice, bound the Man, their sacrificial victim.

16. The gods performed the sacrifice for themselves with the sacrificial victim; these were the first ritual duties. These mighty beings went with it to the crown of heaven, where the ancient Sādhyas live.

Source: *Ṛg Veda* 10.90: Puruṣa-Sukta, from *The Rig Veda*, tr. Wendy Doniger O'Flaherty (New York: Penguin, 1981), pp. 30–31.

ORIGIN OF THE GODS

This passage offers another view of creation. It indicates that originally existence arose from nonexistence. It also suggests an anthropomorphic element in the image of existence and the earth being born from "one whose feet were spread apart," which may be a parallel to the way humans and animals deliver infants. The image is ambiguous, however, and it could also be linking creation is with the practice of yoga, which is believed to produce energy that may be used in the generation of life.

1. Now let us speak eloquently of the births of the gods, so that people of later generations will see them when hymns are recited.

2. The lord of sacred utterances (Bṛhaspati) smelted them like a smith. In an earlier generation of the gods, existence arose from nonexistence.

3. In the first generation of the gods, existence arose from nonexistence. The regions of space arose after that; existence arose from the one whose feet were spread apart.

4. The earth arose from the one whose feet were spread apart, and the regions of space arose from the earth. From Aditi, Dakṣa arose; and from Dakṣa, Aditi.

5. Because Aditi—she who is your daughter, Dakṣa—arose, after her came the glorious gods who share in eternal life.

6. Then you gods, closely merged together, stood there on the waters, and the bitter spray was dispersed by their dancing.

7. O gods, then like he Yatis you caused the living worlds to grow, then you brought the sun here, which had been hidden in the ocean.

8. Aditi had eight sons, who were born from her body. She went to meet the gods with seven of them; she cast away the one that had come from a dead egg (Mārtaṇḍa).

9. Aditi went to the earliest generation with seven sons. And she also brought Mārtaṇḍa there for both procreation and death.

Source: *Ṛg Veda* 10.72; tr. JP, from *The Rig Veda*, pp. 38–39.

INDRA, THE PARADIGMATIC WARRIOR

In Vedic mythology, Indra is the king of the gods, and he embodies the warrior virtues valued by the Indo-Āryans. He is fearless in battle, always victorious over his enemies, and although he is sometimes portrayed as proud and boastful, these qualities do not detract from his prowess as a warrior. This hymn recounts the greatest of his mighty deeds, the slaying of the demon Vṛtra ("Obstructor"), a powerful serpent-like creature that was wreaking havoc throughout the universe, holding back the rainwaters that are essential to the prosperity of living things and obstructing the establishment of cosmic order, which is required for a stable and harmonious world. Wielding his mighty vajra,[2] Indra

---

[2] The *vajra* is Indra's distinctive weapon, described as hand-held and used to smite opponents. It was probably shaped like a mace or a club, although in later literature the *vajra* is Indra's thunderbolt. It was fashioned by Tvaṣṭṛ from the bones of the seer Dadhīchi.

slays the demon, splits open his body, cuts off his limbs, and thus eliminates the threat he poses.

1. I will now proclaim Indra's heroic deeds, the greatest of those performed by the *vajra* wielder. He smashed the serpent and made an opening for the waters; he split open the bellies of the mountains.

2. He smashed the serpent who lay on the mountain; Tvaṣṭṛ made the resounding *vajra* for him. Like lowing cows, the flowing waters flowed down to the sea.

3. Impetuous as a bull, he chose for himself the *soma* and drank the pressed *soma* among the Tikadrukas. Generous Indra grasped his weapon, the *vajra*, and he smashed the first-born of serpents.

4. Indra, when you smashed the first-born of serpents and bested the magicians with your own magic, then you gave birth to the sun, the sky, and the dawn. Since then you have not found anyone who could defeat you.

5. With his great weapon, the *vajra*, he smashed Vṛtra, the greatest obstructer, whose shoulders were spread. Like a tree trunk cut up by an axe, the serpent lay flat on the ground.

6. So Vṛtra, like a drunk who is not a soldier, challenged Indra, the great hero who had bested the mighty and who has the *soma*. Vṛtra could not counter the attack of Indra's weapons; his nose was crushed by a devastating blow, and he who fought with Indra was completely defeated.

7. Footless and handless, he challenged Indra, who smashed his neck with the *vajra*. Vṛtra, the steer who had tried to be the equal of the bull, lay there, scattered into many pieces.

8. The waters, flowing to Manu, flowed over him as he lay there like a broken reed. The waters had been restrained by Vṛtra's power, but now the serpent lay at their feet.

9. Vṛtra's mother's life force faded away; Indra cast his weapon down at her. The mother was above, and the son lay below; and beside her Dānu lies like a cow with her calf.

10. In the midst of the churning channels of the waters that never stopped flowing or rested, his body sank. The waters circulated over Vṛtra's private parts. He who contended with Indra sank into long darkness.

11. The waters, whose husband was the Dāsa and had the serpent for their guardian, were imprisoned like the

cows captured by the Paṇis.[3] After smashing Vṛtra, Indra opened up the hidden waters.

12. Indra, you became like a horse's tail when he lashed at you with his fangs.[4] You, the one god, the victor, won the *soma* and released the seven rivers so that they could flow.

13. Neither the lightning, the thunder, the mist, nor the hail that he spread around him were of any help to him in warding off Indra. When Indra fought the serpent, the generous one gained victory for all time to come.

14. Indra, who did you perceive as the avenger of the serpent when fear entered your heart after you had smashed him? Then you crossed the ninety-nine streams like a frightened hawk through the realms of the air.[5]

15. Indra, who holds the *vajra* in his hand, is the lord of those who wander and those who are settled, of the horned and the hornless. He alone rules the various people as their king, as a rim encompasses the spokes of a wheel.

Source: *Ṛg Veda* 1.32; tr. JP, from *The Rig Veda*, pp. 149–151.

PRAYER TO AGNI, THE GOD OF FIRE

Agni is one of the most important gods of the Vedas. As the god of fire, he transmutes sacrificial offerings into smoke, which is consumed by the gods. Thus he serves as the intermediary between the divine and human realms and is a paradigm for the brahmin priests.

1. I call on Agni, the foremost, the god and priest of sacrifice, the chanter who distributes great wealth.

2. Agni is worthy of the praise of the ancient sages and by those of the present; he will bring the gods to this place.

3. One will earn wealth and prosperity every day through Agni, the glorious one who is richest in heroes.

---

[3] The term *Dāsa*, literally meaning "slave," was used by the Āryans to refer to their rivals. Here it refers to Vṛtra, who is being equated with them, and whose defeat parallels that of the Dāsas. The Paṇis were enemies of the gods, who had captured and penned up the cows needed by humans. Indra defeated the Paṇis and freed the cows.

[4] Through his magic, Indra was able to reduce the width of his body to that of a horse's hair, making it impossible for the demon to strike him.

[5] This refers to the story that after the slaying of Vṛtra, Indra fled the scene, fearful of the consequences of the crime of murder.

4. O Agni, the sacrificial ritual that you encompass on all sides—only that goes to the gods.
5. O Agni, chanter with the insight of a poet, truthful, endowed with the most radiant flame, come to us as a god among the gods.
6. O Agni, when you decide to confer benefits on your worshippers, that, Aṅgiras, certainly comes to pass.
7. O Agni, who lights up the darkness, we come to you every day with prayer; we bring you our devotion.
8. Lord of sacrifices, radiant guardian of the eternal truth, you grow powerful in your own abode.
9. May you be easy for us to approach, like a father with his son. Agni, be with us for our well-being.

Source: *Ṛg Veda* 1.1; tr. JP, from *The Rig Veda*, p. 99.

BURNING DEAD BODIES

This hymn invokes Agni in his role as transporter of the dead. He is asked to burn the corpse of a dead man and to ensure that he is brought to the land of the dead. The concept of afterlife is rather vague in the early Vedas. There are references to a world of the dead, ruled by Yama, who was the first human to die. He found the way to the land of the dead, and now he brings others there. At the end of the ritual the pyre is soaked so thoroughly with water that a small pool is formed, and plants, frogs, and other living things will grow there, symbolizing the renewal of life from the ashes of death.

1. [To Agni:] O Agni, do not completely burn him; do not consume him with your fire. Do not scorch his skin or flesh. Jātavedas, when he is optimally cooked, then deliver him to the forefathers.
2. When he travels the path to the next life, then he will be led at the gods' will.
3. [To the deceased:] May your eye go to the sun and your vital breath to the wind. May you go to the sky or earth, as appropriate. If it is your destiny, may you go to the waters. May you stand among plants with your limbs.
4. [To Agni:] The goat is your portion. Burn it with your heat. May your burn it with your heat, with your flames.
5. Jātavedas, lead him to the world of performers of rituals with the bodies of your accomplished ones. O Agni, release him so that he may rejoin the forefathers; he has been offered to you and proceeds by the power of his own deeds. He has clothed himself in life; let him find a new body, Jātavedas.

6. [To the deceased:] Whatever the black bird has pecked from you, or the ant, snake, or beast of prey, may omnivorous Agni release it from all curses, along with Soma, who has entered the brahmins.
7. Make a protective coat of armor for yourself from the limbs of cows to protect against fire. Cover yourself completely with grease and fat so that bold [Agni,] bursting with flame all around you, cannot completely burn you.
8. [To Agni:] O Agni, do not overturn this vessel, which is dear to the gods and those who deserve *soma*. This is the drinking vessel of the gods, and immortal gods delight in this.
9. I send the flesh-consuming Agni far from here. Let him go to those whose king is Yama, carrying away all defilements. But let only the other Jātavedas bring the offering to the gods, since he knows what is to come.
10. [To the deceased:] The flesh-consuming Agni who entered your house saw this one there, the other Jātavedas, but this god will take the sacrifice to the forefathers. May he bring the drink to the highest place. . . .
12. [To Agni:] We will joyfully install you; we will joyfully kindle you. We will joyfully bring the eager forefathers here to eat the oblation.
13. Agni, you should now extinguish the one you have burned. Let *kiyāmbu* plants grow here, along with *pākadūrvā* and *vyalkuśā* plants.
14. O cool one, bringer of coolness, join together with the female frog and stimulate this Agni here.

Source: *Ṛg Veda* 10.16; tr. JP, from Wendy Doniger O'Flaherty, *Textual Sources for the Study of Hinduism* (Chicago, IL: University of Chicago Press, 1988), p. 7.

THE BENEFICIAL EFFECTS OF DRINKING SOMA

Soma is an intoxicating drink that plays a major role in Vedic literature. It was made from a creeping plant that was crushed and strained to make a whitish beverage that apparently produced visions and ecstatic states of mind. The plant used is a matter of current debate, and a number of theories have been proposed, none of which is considered definitive by contemporary scholars. As this passage indicates, those who drank it experienced a feeling of exaltation and expansion of consciousness. The writer of this hymn claims that drinking it has also made him immortal.

1. I have wisely imbibed the vitality of the sweet drink, which inspires positive thoughts and leads one to find

great expansion, that all the gods and mortals come together to seek, calling it honey.[6]

2. When you have gone inside, you will become Aditi ("Limitless"), who appeases the gods' anger. O drop, enjoying Indra's friendship, may you bring riches like an obedient mare follows the chariot-pole.

3. We have drunk Soma and have become immortal. We have gone to the light, and we have found the gods. O immortal one, what can hostility or the malice of a mortal do to us now?

4. O drop, may you be beneficial to our hearts when we have drunk you, and very kind, like a father to his son, like a friend to a friend, you who are widely famous for your insight. Soma, please extend our lifespans so that we may live.

5. These wondrous drops I have drunk set me free. You bind my joints together like leather strips bind a chariot. May the drops prevent my foot from slipping and keep me free from lameness.

6. May you inflame me like a fire produced by friction. Make us visible, make us prosperous, because when I experience your exhilaration, Soma, I regard myself as wealthy. I will increase in prosperity.

7. May we enjoy you with inspired minds, imbibing some of you after you have been pressed, like ancestral riches. Extend our lifespans, King Soma, as the sun makes shining days grow longer.

8. King Soma, have mercy on us so that we may flourish. You should know that we are commanded by your laws. O drop, our enthusiasm and power increase; do not hand us over to the whims of our enemies.

9. O Soma, because you are the protector of our bodies and watch over humanity, you abide in every limb. O god, if we break your laws, please be merciful to us, as a good friend is, and make us better.

10. May I closely bond with my compassionate friend, who will do no harm to me even after he has been imbibed. Lord of fallow bay horses (Indra), I go to Indra to extend our lifespans due to the Soma that has been installed in us.

11. Famines and diseases have vanished. The allies of darkness have fled in fear. Soma has risen in us with his greatest might. We have gone to the place where lifespans are extended.

---

[6] The implication here is not that *soma* is to be equated with honey produced by bees, but that it is ambrosial.

12. O ancestors, once we drunk the drop, it entered our hearts, the immortal in mortals. We should venerate Soma with ritual offerings and share in his mercy and kindness.

13. O Soma, may you be in agreement with the ancestors, extending throughout heaven and earth. May we venerate him with ritual oblations; may we be lords of wealth.

14. O protector gods, speak out on our behalf. Do not let sleep or harmful speech take hold of us. May we always be loved by Soma, with great heroes in the sacrificial congregation.

15. O Soma, may you confer vital energy on us from all sides. Enter us, finder of sunlight, watching over humanity. O drop, may you and your aides protect us from behind and in front.

Source: Ṛg Veda 8.48; tr. JP, from *The Rig Veda*, pp. 134–136.

SEX AND THE YOGI

This hymn depicts a struggle between a husband and wife named Agastya and Lopāmudrā. Lopāmudrā has just successfully seduced Agastya, who was trying to avoid sexual intercourse in order to store up the vital energy he acquired as a product of yogic exertions. It captures a common theme in classical Indian literature: woman as temptress, whose unrestrained sexual desire and physical charms distract male yogis from their ascetic practice and cause them to dissipate the power they have painstakingly gained through meditation and self-restraint.

1. [Lopāmudrā:] "For many autumns I have worked night and day through dawns that bring aging. Old age diminishes the beauty of bodies; bull-like men should come to their wives now.

2. "For even the ancients—who acted in accordance with truth and spoke truth with the gods—even they withdrew from their discipline if they did not reach the final goal.[7] Women should now unite with their bull-like husbands."

3. [Agastya:] "This striving, which is aided by the gods, is not pointless. The two of us should always contend against all adversaries, and let us win this contest of a hundred maneuvers when we unite together as a couple.

---

[7] The end may refer to final liberation from cyclic existence. The implication is that they did not attain salvation and brought future harm on themselves because they died childless, and so had no progeny to perform sacrifices to assure their well-being after death.

4. "The lust of a mounting bull is aroused in me; this lust arises from this side, that side, all sides." Lopāmudrā causes the bull-like man to flow out. The foolish woman sucks dry the snorting wise man.

5. [Agastya:] "I implore the *soma* in my heart, which I have just drunk: May he forgive any offence we have committed, because mortals have many desires."

6. So Agastya, digging with spades, desiring offspring, descendants, and power, prospered in both ways, this mighty sage. He achieved his wishes, which came to pass among the gods.

Source: *Ṛg Veda* 1.179; tr. JP, from *The Rig Veda*, pp. 250–251.

A CUNNING WOMAN

This hymn is spoken by a woman who has managed to eliminate her rivals and emerge victorious over her husband, who now submits to her will.

1. The sun has risen over there, and my good fortune has risen too. I am a cunning woman who has defeated my husband.

2. I am the beacon; I am the head; I am the mighty discussant. My husband only does what I will; I am utterly victorious.

3. My sons kill their rivals, and my daughter is a ruling queen. And I am the supreme conqueror; for my husband, my voice is supreme.

4. The oblation that Indra performed by which he became the most glorious one has now been performed by me, O gods. I am now rid of all my rival wives. Rid of rival wives, smashing other wives, victorious, triumphant: I have taken for myself the attractiveness of those other women, like the gifts of fools.

6. I have completely subdued these rivals, my fellow wives, so that I will now hold royal sway over this hero and his people.

Source: *Ṛg Veda* 10.159; tr. JP, from *The Rig Veda*, p. 291.

THE HORSE SACRIFICE

The horse sacrifice (aśva-medha) served to establish the dominion of a king by demonstrating how large an area he controlled. For a year prior to the sacrifice, a horse would be set free to wander wherever it wished, indicating the hegemony of the king. To the

*extent that other rulers were unable to turn the horse away, it
served notice of the areas a particular ruler effectively controlled.
At the end of the year the horse was offered as a sacrifice to the
gods, but although it was killed it is stated in the ritual that it
would enjoy a future in heaven. Contemporary Hindus often claim
that Vedic sacrifices never involved killing of animals, and plant
offerings are now commonly substituted, but the gory details of
this passage—including descriptions of cutting up flesh, blood, fat,
and grease oozing into the ground, and flies buzzing around the
corpse—make it clear that real horses were killed, and not effigies.*

5. [To the priests:] With this well-prepared, well-offered
sacrifice, you should fill your stomachs, O invoker, offici-
ant, atoner, fire-kindler, handler of the pressing stones,
and well-versed reciter.

6. Those who hew the sacrificial post and those who carry
it, those who carve the knob of the horse's sacrificial
post, those who bring together the equipment for cooking the horse: may their approval inspire our work.

7. The smooth-backed horse went to the regions of the
gods as I made my aspiration. The inspired seers praise
him. We have made him our good companion to the
god's feast.

8. [To the horse:] May all these things remain with you
among the gods: the steed's rope and harness, the reigns
and bridle on his head, and the grass put into his mouth.

9. May all of these things also remain with you among the
gods: whatever of the horse's flesh has been eaten by
flies, or whatever is smeared on the sacrificial stake or
the axe, or on the hands and nails of the slaughtering
priest.

10. May the slaughtering priest properly prepare and
perfectly cook the ritual offering—the contents of his
bloated stomach, the smell of his raw flesh.

11. Whatever spills from your body while it's being cooked
on the fire after you have been impaled on the spit—may
it not remain in the ground or the grass; may it be given
to the gods who crave it.

12. May the encouragement of those who observe the offering when cooked and say, "It smells good! Take if off (the
fire)!" and those who come wishing to share its flesh help
promote our work. . . .

20. May your dear vital force not burn as you go forward.
May the axe not do lasting harm to your body. May no
greedy or clumsy slaughterer damage your limbs with an
errant cut.

21. In truth, you do not really die, and you are not injured; you will go to the gods on easy paths. The two fallow bays (of Indra) and the two roan mares (of the Maruts) are now your chariot mates. The racehorse has taken his place at the yoke of the (Aśvins') donkey.

22. May this racehorse bring us many cattle and many horses, male children, and all-sustaining riches. May Aditi make us free from wrongdoing. May the horse with our offerings bring us sovereign power.

Source: *Ṛg Veda* 1.162; tr. JP, from *Textual Sources for the Study of Hinduism*, pp. 9–10.

TO THE FIRE ALTAR

This hymn is used to help the officiating priest mentally prepare prior to performance of the sacrifice. He visualizes the fire altar as the entire universe and views the sacrifice as a way to attain spiritual knowledge. It is notable in that it shows the increasingly cosmic significance given to the rituals: They are no longer merely localized sacrifices performed for particular ends, but instead are microcosmic expressions of macrocosmic forces and processes. The sacrificer meditates on the greater ramifications of the ritual about to be performed, its cosmic repercussions, and its transformative effects on the person who performs it. The hymn also shows an expanding view of the cosmos and a corresponding expansion in the religious vision of brahmin priests, who are no longer content simply to perform sacrifices for limited goals but increasingly are interested in the effects they will have beyond this world and in the mind of the sacrificer.

1. The fire altar built here is this world. The stones surrounding it are the waters. Its Yajuṣmati bricks are humans. Its Sūdadohas [a drink of immortality] are cows. Plants and trees are its cement, offerings, and fuel. Agni is its connecting bricks. Thus this constitutes all of Agni. Agni pervades space. Whoever knows this becomes all of Agni, the pervader of space.

2. Moreover, the fire altar is also the air. The horizon is its surrounding circle of bricks.... The birds are its Yajuṣmati bricks....

3. Moreover, the fire altar is also the sky....

4. Moreover, the fire altar is also the sun....

5. Moreover, the fire altar is also the stars....

7. Moreover, the fire altar is also the meters [of verses]....

10. Moreover, the fire altar is also the year....

12. Moreover, the fire altar is also the body....

14. Moreover, the fire altar is also all beings and all gods. All the gods and all beings are the waters, and the constructed fire altar is the same as the waters. . . .

16. Referring to this, the verse states: By way of wisdom they ascend to the place where desires disappear. Neither sacrificial gifts nor the devoted performers of sacrifices who lack wisdom go there. One who is ignorant of this does not go to that world either by sacrificial offerings or devout actions. It belongs to those with wisdom.

Source: *Śatapatha Brāhmaṇa* 10.5.4.1–16. Tr. JP.

WHAT IS THE ORIGIN OF THE WORLD?

This poem represents an early speculative tendency from the Vedic period. The writer of the poem is considering what, if anything, existed before the world as we know it, before creation, and even before the birth of the gods. It posits an unnamed creative force and indicates that this primordial being initiated the process of creation. At the end, it speculates about what preceded creation, but it concludes that even the first being may not know the answers.

1. At that time, neither nonexistence nor existence existed. Neither space nor the heaven beyond it existed.
2. What moved about? Where, and under whose protection? Did water exist, to a vast depth?
3. Death did not exist then, nor did immortality. There were no characteristics of night or day. That One breathed without wind, in accordance with its own volition. There was nothing beyond that.
4. Darkness existed then, cloaked by darkness. Everything was featureless ocean. Due to the power of heat, that One was what arose, hidden by emptiness.
5. Then, in the beginning, that One gave rise to desire, which became the original semen. Poets searched their hearts with wisdom and found what linked existence and nonexistence.
6. Their cord spanned this. Was there anything below? Was there anything above? There were depositors of semen, and there was power. Below it was independent volition; above it were offerings.
7. Who knows for sure? Who might describe it here? From where did it arise, from where did this creation come? The gods came after this creation. So who knows from where it arose?

8. From where this creation arose—whether it was produced or not—only the one who observes it from above in
the furthest heaven truly knows; but what if even he does
not know?

Source: *Ṛg Veda* 10.129; tr. JP, from *Textual Sources for the
Study of Hinduism*, p. 33.

VEDĀNTA: THE UPANIṢADS AND THEIR COMMENTARIES

YAMA'S INSTRUCTIONS TO NACIKETAS

*The Kaṭha Upaniṣad presents the story of a brahmin boy named
Naciketas. His father, Āruṇi, is performing a sacrifice in which
he is required to give away all his possessions, but Naciketas
notices that he is not complying with the spirit of the sacrifice.
Naciketas asks his father, "To whom will you give me?" To
which his father angrily replies, "I give you to Yama [the god
of death]." Unfortunately for both Naciketas and his father,
words spoken in the context of a sacrifice have great power, so
Naciketas is immediately sent to the palace of Yama.*

*Yama, however, is not present when Naciketas arrives and
does not return for three days. When Yama arrives and sees that
Naciketas has been waiting for a long while and has not been
given the courtesy due to a brahmin, he apologizes and offers
to make restitution by granting three wishes. Being a dutiful
son, Naciketas first asks that he be able to return to his father
and that his father receive him with happiness and love instead
of anger. His next wish is noteworthy: He asks Yama to teach
him about the Naciketas fire for which he is named. This is significant because it shows that in this text the traditional values
and practices of brahmins are not being questioned. Naciketas
does not doubt the efficacy of the sacrifices; instead, he wishes
to learn more about them, and only after this does he make his
third request, asking Yama to tell him what happens to a human
being after death.*

*Yama responds by testing Naciketas in order to determine
his sincerity in asking about this. He offers Naciketas worldly
goods instead—things like wealth, land, power, long-lived sons
and grandsons, fame, and so on—but none of these things interest Naciketas. He understands that they are transitory and
fleeting, and he wishes instead for knowledge of the ātman (the
self), which is truly valuable. Having tested his resolve, Yama
praises him for choosing the good (śreyas) over the pleasant
(preyas). Yama then teaches Naciketas about the ātman, the*

essence of each individual, the eternal, unchanging reality that exists forever, unaffected by the circumstances and events of a person's countless rebirths. The ātman, he declares, cannot be known through the senses or the intellect: it must be grasped through direct, intuitive realization. The culmination of the teaching is Yama's revelation that the ātman is not only a personal essence; it is also said to be identical with the cosmic Ultimate, called Brahman.

2.1.1. Yama said: "The good is one thing, and the pleasant another. Both of these different goals blind a person. From among the two, it is better for one who chooses the good. A person who chooses the pleasant does not fulfill his goals.

2. "A person receives both the good and the pleasant. Thoroughly examining the two, a wise person distinguishes them. The wise person chooses the good rather than the pleasant. The stupid person, due to grasping, chooses the pleasant. . . ."

14. Naciketas asked Yama: "Tell me what you see beyond righteousness and unrighteousness, beyond what is done and not done, and what is beyond what was and what will be."

15. Yama said: "I will briefly explain to you all that is taught in the Vedas, all that asceticism declares, and that which sages seek through religious practice: It is *Oṃ*.

16. "This syllable truly is Brahman, it is the supreme syllable. Whoever knows it obtains all wishes.

17. "This is the best support, this is the supreme support. Knowing this support, a person attains happiness in the world of Brahmā.

18. "The wise one is not born, does not die; it does not come from anywhere, does not become anything. It is unborn, enduring, permanent; this one is not destroyed when the body is destroyed.

19. "If someone thinks to destroy and if the destroyed thinks of being destroyed, then neither understands. This [ā*tman*] neither destroys nor is it destroyed.

20. "The ā*tman* hidden in the heart of all living beings is smaller than the smallest and greater than the greatest. A person who does not act with desire and is free from sadness sees it and its greatness through the purity of mind and senses. . . .

23. "The self is not gained through study, nor by the intellect, nor by much learning; it is gained only by whomever it chooses: to such a person the self reveals itself.

24. "Not to one who has not renounced wrongdoing, nor to one who is not tranquil, nor to one who is not calm, nor to one whose mind is not at peace: they cannot gain it through intelligence *(prajñā)*.

2.3.1. "You should know that the ātman is like the rider of a chariot, and the body is like the chariot. You should know that the intellect *(buddhi)* is like the chariot driver, and the mind is like the reins. . . .

4. "The senses are said to be the horses, and sense-objects are the area in which they travel. The self, together with senses and mind, are termed 'enjoyer' by the wise.

5. "If one lacks understanding and does not constantly control the mind, then one's senses become uncontrolled like the bad horses of a charioteer.

6. "If one is wise and constantly controls the mind, then one's senses remain controlled like the good horses of a charioteer.

7. "If one lacks understanding, lacks mental control, and is impure, then one can never reach the goal, but continues in cyclic existence.

8. "If one is wise, however, with a fully disciplined mind, then one reaches the goal and will not be reborn again. . . .

13. "The wise should restrain speech and mind, mind should be restrained in the understanding self, understanding should be restrained in the great self, and that should be restrained in the tranquil ātman.

14. "Arise, awaken, go and attain your wishes; understand them! The poets say that the path is like the sharp edge of a razor, difficult to travel, difficult to obtain.

15. "It is soundless, intangible, formless, inexhaustible. In the same way, it is tasteless, eternal, and odorless, beginningless, endless, beyond the great, unchanging. By understanding it, one escapes the jaws of death."

4.1. Yama said: "The Self-Existent opened the senses outward; thus humans look outward, not toward the inner ātman. But a wise person, seeking immortality, turns in the reverse direction and sees the inner ātman.

2. "Childish people go after outward pleasures. They walk into the net of death that is spread everywhere. But the wise, knowing immortality, do not seek the permanent among the impermanent.

3. "One knows color, taste, smell, sounds, touches, and sexual pleasures only through this *[ātman]*. What else remains? This indeed is That.

4. "By recognizing the great, all-pervading ā*tman*, by which one perceives both sleeping and dream states, the wise overcome sorrow. This indeed is That.

5. "One who knows this experiencer, the living ā*tman* that is nearest to one, which is lord of the past and the future, is never afraid of it. This indeed is That. . . .

9. "The sun arises from it and sets into it. All gods are based in it, and none ever move beyond it. This indeed is That. . . .

11. "Through it the mind attains [realization]. There is absolutely no difference here. If one perceives difference here, one goes from death to death."

6.1. Yama said: "Its root is above, its branches below, this eternal tree. That [root] is the Pure. That is Brahman. That is called the Immortal. All worlds rest on it, and none go beyond it. This, indeed, is That.

2. "The whole world, whatever exists, was created from and moves in life. The great fear, the raised thunderbolt: those who know That become immortal.

3. "From fear of It fire burns, from fear of It the sun gives off heat. From fear of It Indra and Vāyu, and Yama the fifth, speed along. . . .

9. "One cannot see its form, and no one ever sees it with the eye. It is framed by the heart, by thought, by the mind: those who know That become immortal.

10. "When one stops the five knowledges [derived from the senses], together with the mind, and the intellect is still, that is said to be the highest path.

11. "This is said to be yoga, the firm restraint of the senses. Then one becomes undistracted. Yoga, truly, is the beginning and the end.

12. "It is not perceived through speech, through mind, nor by sight. How can it be understood other than by saying, 'It is'?"

Source: *Kaṭha Upaniṣad* selections. Tr. JP.

TRUTH AND TRANSCENDENCE

Dharma is one of the most important concepts in Hinduism, but it is difficult to define because of the multitude of ways in which it is construed and its many associations. It is a universal principle that determines how things ought to be and is linked with the natural order of the universe. It also refers to duty: the actions, attitudes, and ritual performances expected of people according to their respective social class (varṇa), gender, stage of life, and role in society. Although dharma is unalterable and universal, the way in which one actualizes it in one's life may vary over time, as when a person decides to renounce the world and pursue liberation from cyclic existence. In the following passage, we are informed that Brahman, the creator of the universe and the sum total of all that is, originated dharma and that its universality places it above even its creator. Brahman cannot alter dharma or change it. Kings who follow dharma must obey its rules. This makes it possible for society to function; the weak have recourse to the truth and can appeal to it. If one's case is just, one can triumph even over those who stand above one in the social hierarchy. This section links dharma with the ultimate goal of liberation. After dharma was created, Brahman projected the four social classes, each of which had a specific dharma to perform, which, being unalterable and universal, provides a fixed standard of behavior. Similarly, one aspect of the makeup of the universe is the apparent multitude of selves (ātman), which are all ultimately one with Brahman. Those who understand dharma perform their prescribed duties. Spiritually advanced beings recognize the underlying universal reality of Brahman, and through this they are able to pass beyond rebirth after they die.

[Brahman] was still not fully actualized, and so it created dharma, which was a form that was superior to it and surpassed it. Dharma is the kingly power that restrains the kingly power [of Brahman]. Thus there is nothing that transcends dharma. A weaker man can make demands on a stronger one through an appeal to dharma, in the way one makes an appeal to a king. Dharma is nothing other than truth, and so when a man speaks the truth, people say that he speaks dharma; when he expresses dharma, he speaks the truth. They are truly the same thing.... If a person leaves this world without realizing his own world [i.e., *ātman*], because he does not know it, it cannot protect him, just as if the Vedas are not recited or a deed is not performed they do not [produce a positive result.] If one who does not know it [*ātman*] performs many virtuous acts, they will surely perish with him. So one should meditate on the world called the *ātman*. One who meditates on this world called the *ātman* will not see his works perish with him because by this very *ātman* he projects whatever he wishes.

Source: *Bṛhadāraṇyaka Upaniṣad*, 1.4.14–15; tr. JP.

SACRIFICES CANNOT LEAD TO THE ULTIMATE GOAL

This passage expresses a somewhat different opinion of the value of sacrifices: It calls them "unsteady boats" that should not be relied on by a person wishing to leave cyclic existence. It does not, however, urge brahmins to stop performing sacrifices but instead warns them not to rely on them exclusively and advises them also to remove themselves from the world and practice asceticism and devotion in the forest in order to work at achieving a tranquil mind that knows truth.

1.2.1. This is the truth: The sacrificial rites that the sages saw in the hymns are variously elaborated in the three [Vedas]. Perform them constantly, O lovers of truth. This is the path to the world of good deeds.

2. When the flame flickers after the offering fire has been kindled, then between the offerings of the two portions of clarified butter one should give one's main oblations—an offering made with faith. . . .

7. These sacrificial rituals, eighteen in number, are, however, unsteady boats, in which only the lesser work is expressed. The fools who delight in this as supreme go again and again to old age and death.

8. Abiding in the midst of ignorance, wise only according to their own estimate, thinking themselves to be learned, but really dense, these deluded men are like blind men led by one who is himself blind.

9. Abiding variously in ignorance, childishly they think, "We have accomplished our aim." Since the performers of actions do not understand because of desire, therefore, they, the wretched ones, sink down [from heaven] when their worlds are exhausted.

10. Regarding sacrifice and merit as most important, the deluded ones do not know of anything better. Having enjoyed themselves only for a time on top of the heaven won by good deeds, they re-enter this world or a lower one.

11. Those who practice austerities *(tapas)* and devotion in the forest, the tranquil ones, the knowers of truth, living the life of wandering beggars: they depart, freed from desire, through the door of the sun, to where the immortal Man *(Puruṣa)* lives, the imperishable ātman.

12. Having examined the worlds won by actions, a brahmin should arrive at nothing but indifference. The world that was not made is not won by what is done

[i.e., by sacrifice]. For the sake of that knowledge, one should go with sacrificial fuel in hand to a spiritual teacher (guru) who is well-versed in the scriptures and also firm in the realization of Brahman.

13. Approaching the wise [teacher] properly, one with tranquil thoughts, who has attained peace, is taught this very truth, the knowledge of Brahman by means of which one knows the imperishable Man, the only Reality.

Source: *Muṇḍaka Upaniṣad*, ch. 1; tr. JP.

INSTRUCTIONS ON RENOUNCING THE WORLD

This passage instructs the aspiring world renouncer (saṃnyāsin) on the proper motivation for leaving society. It indicates that one should give up performance of the Vedic rituals and leave family, friends, and occupation behind, focusing one's attention on the final goal of realization of the ātman. During a ritual that marks this transition, one takes into oneself the sacred fire that one had maintained as a householder, which now becomes identified with the fire of the digestive processes. One discards the sacred thread that one has worn since the initiation ceremony (upanayana), which designates one as a member of one of the three "twice-born" classes. After this one has no caste identity and can wander anywhere—and take food from anyone—without fear of ritual pollution.

Āruṇi went to the realm of Prajāpati and, approaching him, said: "Lord, by what means does one completely renounce religious activities?"

Prajāpati said: "One should forsake sons, brothers, relatives, and so forth; one should give up the topknot, the sacred string, sacrifices, ritual codes, and Vedic recitation.... One should have a staff and a garment; and renounce everything else.

"A householder or a student *(brahmacāri)* or a forest hermit should discard his sacred string on the ground or in water. He should place the external fires in the fire of his stomach and the *gāyatrī*[8] in the fire of his speech....

"From that point on, he should live without mantras.[9] He should bathe at the start of the three periods of the day[10]

---

[8] The *gāyatrī* is a mantra (ritual invocation) directed toward the god Savitṛ. It is recited by orthodox twice-born males as part of their ritual duties.

[9] In other words, he no longer recites the mantras used in rituals. His only mantra now is the sacred syllable *Oṃ*.

[10] These are the junctures of dawn (between night and day), noon (between morning and afternoon), and dusk (between afternoon and evening).

and, deeply immersed in meditation, he should realize his union with the *ātman*."

Source: *Āruṇi Upaniṣad* 1–2; tr. JP.

SELF-EFFORT AND LIBERATION

The following passage comes from the Crest-Jewel of Discrimination, attributed by Hindu tradition to Śaṃkara, one of the greatest expositors of the thought of the Upaniṣads and the primary exponent of the nondualist (advaita) school of commentary. The author contends that the path to liberation is a solitary one. He states that every person must win salvation alone and that no one else can help. Even the scriptures are only guideposts, and one who becomes attached to them will remain enmeshed in cyclic existence. They point the way, but the goal is reached only by those who transcend all mundane supports and actualize direct, nonconceptual understanding of the ātman.

Children may free their father from his debts, but no other person can free a man from his bondage: he must do it himself. Others may relieve the suffering caused by a burden that weighs upon the head; but the suffering which comes from hunger and the like can only be relieved by one's self. The sick man who takes medicine and follows the rules of diet is seen to be restored to health—but not through the efforts of another. A clear vision of the Reality may be obtained only through our own eyes, when they have been opened by spiritual insight—never through the eyes of some other seer. Through our own eyes we learn what the moon looks like: how could we learn this through the eyes of others? Those cords that bind us, because of our ignorance, our lustful desires and the fruits of our karma—how could anybody but ourselves untie them, even in the course of innumerable ages? Neither by the practice of Yoga or of Sāṃkhya philosophy, nor by good works, nor by learning, does liberation come; but only through a realization that Ātman and Brahman are one—in no other way. . . .

Erudition, well-articulated speech, a wealth of words, and skill in expounding the scriptures—these things give pleasure to the learned, but they do not bring liberation. Study of the scriptures is fruitless as long as Brahman has not been experienced. And when Brahman has been experienced, it is useless to read the scriptures. A network of words is like a dense forest which causes the mind to wander hither and thither. Therefore, those who know this truth should struggle hard to experience Brahman. When a man has been bitten by the snake of ignorance he can only be cured by the realization of Brahman. What use are Vedas or scriptures, charms or herbs? A sickness is not cured by saying the word "medicine." You must take the medicine. Liberation does not come by merely saying the word "Brahman." Brahman must be actually experienced.

Until you allow this apparent universe to dissolve from your consciousness—until you have experienced Brahman—how can you find liberation just by saying the word "Brahman"? The result is merely a noise.

Source: *Viveka-cūḍāmaṇi,* from *Shankara's Crest-Jewel of Discrimination,* tr. Swami Prabhavananda and Christopher Isherwood (Hollywood, CA: Vedanta Press, 1975), pp. 40–41.

MĀYĀ

Māyā plays a central role in Śaṃkara's interpretation of the Upaniṣads. The term literally means "magic" or "illusion," and he claims that it is the power by which Brahman hides the truth from ordinary beings. It is a creative power that causes the apparent phenomena of cyclic existence to be superimposed on the unitary Brahman.

Māyā, in her potential aspect, is the divine power of the Lord. She has no beginning. She is composed of the three qualities *(guṇa),* subtle, beyond perception. It is from the effects she produces that her existence is inferred by the wise. It is she who gives birth to the whole universe. She is neither being nor nonbeing, nor a mixture of both. She is neither divided nor undivided, nor a mixture of both. She is neither an indivisible whole, nor composed of parts, nor a mixture of both. She is most strange. Her nature is inexplicable. Just as knowing a rope to be a rope destroys the illusion that it is a snake, so Māyā is destroyed by direct experience of Brahman—the pure, the free, the one without a second.

Source: *Viveka-cūḍāmaṇi,* from *Shankara's Crest-Jewel of Discrimination,* p. 49.

THAT IS YOU

The Upaniṣadic statement "That is you" (tat tvam asi) is viewed by exponents of nondualist Vedānta as a statement of the nondifference of ātman and Brahman. The following excerpt discusses this statement from the nondualist perspective.

The scriptures establish the absolute identity of Ātman and Brahman by declaring repeatedly: "That is you." The terms "Brahman" and "Ātman," in their true meaning, refer to "That" and "you" respectively. In their literal, superficial meaning, "Brahman" and "Ātman" have opposite attributes, like the sun and the glow-worm, the king and his servant, the ocean and the well, or Mount Meru [a huge mountain that stands at the center of the world according to Indian mythology] and the atom. Their identity is established only when they are understood in their true significance, and not in a superficial sense.

"Brahman" may refer to God, the ruler of Māyā and creator of the universe. The "Ātman" may refer to the individual soul, associated with the five coverings which are effects of Māyā. Thus regarded, they possess opposite attributes. But this apparent opposition is caused by Māyā and her effects. It is not real, therefore, but superimposed. These attributes caused by Māyā and her effects are superimposed upon God and upon the individual soul. When they have been completely eliminated, neither soul nor God remains. If you take the kingdom from a king and the weapons from a soldier, there is neither soldier nor king. The scriptures repudiate any idea of a duality in Brahman. Let a man seek illumination in the knowledge of Brahman, as the scriptures direct. Then those attributes, which our ignorance has superimposed upon Brahman, will disappear. . . .

Then let him meditate upon the identity of Brahman and Ātman, and so realize the truth. Through spiritual discrimination, let him understand the true inner meaning of the terms "Brahman" and "Ātman," thus realizing their absolute identity. See the reality in both, and you will find that there is but one. . . .

Just as a clay jar or vessel is understood to be nothing but clay, so this whole universe, born of Brahman, essentially Brahman, is Brahman only—for there is nothing else but Brahman, nothing beyond That. That is the reality. That is our Ātman. Therefore, "That is you"—pure, blissful, supreme Brahman, the one without a second.

Source: *Viveka-cūḍāmaṇi*, from *Shankara's Crest-Jewel of Discrimination*, pp. 72–74.

QUALIFIED NONDUALISM: RĀMĀNUJA'S INTERPRETATION

Rāmānuja disagrees with the nondualist system of Upaniṣadic interpretation. In this passage, he contends that it is absurd to completely equate the absolute Brahman with the individual ātman. *As an exponent of devotionalism, Rāmānuja rejects the nondualist system because it would make devotion incoherent. If* ātman *and Brahman were one, there would be no real basis for worship. Rāmānuja contends that the Upaniṣadic statement "That is you" does not mean what nondualists think it does; rather, it indicates that there are two separate entities,* ātman *and Brahman, and that the former is wholly dependent upon the latter, like a wave in relation to the ocean. The wave appears to stand apart from the ocean, but its substance and being derive from the ocean, although it has at least a qualifiedly separate identity. Similarly,* ātman *derives from Brahman, but because the history of each* ātman *is distinctly its own, it contradicts reason and actual experience to claim that* ātman *is completely identical with Brahman.*

1.1.1. The word "Brahman" refers to the highest Person, in whom all faults are naturally eliminated, who possesses all the most auspicious qualities, is unlimited, unsurpassed, and incalculable. Everywhere the word Brahman is associated with the quality of magnitude.... [Brahman] is the "Lord of All.". . .

Our [nondualist] opponents say: "Brahman is only consciousness, is completely opposed to all particularity, and is the highest reality; all difference—such as different types of knowers, objects of knowledge, different knowledge produced by them, and anything beyond that—is false when posited of [Brahman]."

[We reply:] Brahman, which is to be understood by means of its distinctive characteristics, has a nature distinguished from all objects other than itself, and those contradictions are eliminated by these three words: The word "truth" excludes anything that is "non-truth," that which is amenable to modification. The word "knowledge" indicates what is excluded from non-sentient things whose illumination depends upon others. And the word "limitless" indicates what is excluded from anything that is circumscribed by space, time, or matter. This exclusion is not a positive or negative quality, but [indicates] Brahman itself as distinguished from everything that is other than itself.... The ramification of this is that Brahman is self-luminous, with all contradictions excluded....

Those who propound the doctrine of a substance devoid of all difference cannot legitimately assert that there is a proof for such a substance, because all means of epistemic warrant have for their objects things that are affected by difference.... All consciousness implies difference. All states of consciousness have for their objects things that are marked by some difference, as we see in the case of judgments like, "I saw this.".... It therefore must be admitted that reality is affected with difference, which is well established by valid proofs....

Instead, what all these scriptures deny is only plurality in the sense of contradicting the unity of the world that is utterly dependent on Brahman as an effect and that has Brahman as the inner controlling principle that is its true Self. They do not deny plurality on the part of Brahman in the sense of deciding to become manifold....

Moreover, in texts like the one that states, "That is you," the connection between the constituent parts does not indicate an absolute unity of undifferentiated substance. Instead, the words "that" and "you" indicate that Brahman is distinguished by difference. The word "that" refers to Brahman, which is omniscient and so forth.... Moreover, it is impossible that ignorance could belong to Brahman, whose essential nature is knowledge, who is free from all imperfections, omniscient, and contains within itself all auspicious qualities; nor [is it possible that Brahman] could be the basis of the faults and afflictions that arise from ignorance.

Source: *Rāmānuja, Śrībhāṣya,* ch. 1; tr. JP.

YOGA

THE MEANING OF YOGA

The following excerpts are taken from the Yoga Aphorisms, *attributed to Patañjali, and an explanatory text titled the* Yoga Commentary, *attributed to Vyāsa. The verses of the* Aphorisms *are given in boldface, and the Commentary is given in plain text.*

As two authors indicate, the term yoga may be used to refer to a range of practices for disciplining mind and body. In Patañjali's system the focus is on developing progressively greater control over the agitations and fluctuations of mind and body in order to arrive at a state of perfect equanimity. One accomplishes this by turning the attention inward, away from sense objects, which leads to detachment and wisdom. A person who becomes detached from external things has no basis for continued existence and thus becomes liberated from the cycle of birth and death. Unlike the system of the Upaniṣads, however,

*Patañjali does not understand liberation as a union of the indi-
vidual* ātman *with the cosmic ultimate Brahman, but rather as
separation of one's spiritual essence* (puruṣa) *from insentient
matter* (prakṛti). *In the yoga system, both are considered to be
real, and the association of the two is beginningless. Because
matter's tendency is to procreate and acquire, and because it is
transitory and prone to decay, beings whose spirits are associated with matter necessarily experience suffering. This suffering
can, however, be transcended by following the path of the "eight
limbs" of physical and mental discipline, which culminate in a
state of perfect mental equipoise.*

1. **Here is an instruction on yoga.**

    Yoga is meditative concentration *(samādhi)*, and it is a
    characteristic of the mind pervading all its states. . . . The
    five states of the mind are (1) wandering; (2) deluded;
    (3) distracted; (4) one-pointed; and (5) cut off.

2. **Yoga is the cessation of states of mind.**

    The mind has the three functions of perception,
    movement, and rest, it is constituted by the three quali-
    ties of purity *(sattva)*, activity *(rajas)*, and darkness
    (tamas). . . .

3. **Then the seer abides in his own nature.**

5. **The states are of five types, and are afflicted and
    non-afflicted.**

    The afflicted are those that are based on afflictions
    like ignorance and so forth and serve as the basis of
    latencies. The nonafflicted are those that have conceptu-
    ality for their object and that oppose the operation of the
    qualities. . . .

12. **The [states of mind] are restrained by practice and
    detachment.**

    The stream of mind flows both ways: it flows toward
    good and it flows toward evil. That which flows on to
    separation down the plane of discriminative knowledge
    moves toward happiness. That which leads to rebirth
    flows down the plane of nondiscrimination and moves
    toward wrongdoing.

17. **Meditative concentration is attained with the help
    of conceptual understanding, analytical thought,
    bliss, and self-awareness.**

    Understanding is the mind's coarse direct experience
    when it is directed toward an object. Analytical thought
    is subtle [cognition]. Joy is happiness. Self-awareness is
    consciousness pertaining to the self. . . . All these states
    have an object of observation *(ālambana)*.

30. Sickness, laxity, doubt, carelessness, laziness, worldliness, wrong views, failure to attain any level [of concentration], instability: these distractions of mind are the obstacles.
31. Pain, despair, unsteadiness of the body, inspiration, and expiration are the companions of these distractions.
32. In order to prevent them, one should become familiar with one entity.
33. By cultivating friendliness, compassion regarding suffering, joy regarding merit, and indifference toward demerit, one attains a calm, undisturbed mind.

Source: *Yoga-sūtras* and *Yoga-bhāṣya,* ch. 1; tr. JP.

YOGIC TECHNIQUES

In section 2, Patañjali describes the process by which one develops one's powers of concentration through disciplining thoughts, bringing mind and body under control, and weaning oneself from attachment to external objects.

2.1. Asceticism *(tapas)*, study, and devotion to God constitute the yoga of action.
3. The afflictions are: ignorance, self-cherishing, desire, aversion, and love of life.

   Ignorance is simply misconception. Self-cherishing and the others are also based on ignorance and, since they cannot exist without it, they are ignorant. Thus when ignorance is destroyed, their destruction also follows.

5. Ignorance is taking the impermanent, the impure, the painful, and the not-self to be permanent, pure, pleasurable, and the self.
6. When one views the appearances of a unitary self through the power of perception, this is self-cherishing.
7. Attachment is abiding in pleasure.
8. Aversion is abiding in revulsion toward pain.
9. Love of life, moving along by its own potency, exists even in the wise.
11. Their mental states are destroyed by meditation.

   The gross dirt of clothes is at first shaken off, and then the fine dirt is washed off by effort and work, so the coarse essential mental states need only slight counteracting efforts, whereas the subtle mental states need very powerful counteragents.[11]

17. **The conjunction of the knower and the knowable is the cause of what is to be escaped.**

18. **The knowable has the nature of purity, activity, and darkness; it consists of the elements and the powers of sensation; its purposes are experience and liberation.**

It is the ascertainment of the nature of the enjoyer, the self. Beyond the knowledge of these two there is no wisdom.

20. **The perceiver is only perception; even though pure, it perceives by way of conditions.**

"Only perception": This means that it is nothing other than the power of becoming conscious; that is to say, it is not touched by the qualities. This self cognizes the intellect by reflection. It is neither quite similar nor quite dissimilar to the intellect.

"It is not quite similar." Why? The intellect, having for its sphere of action objects known and not yet known, is of course changeable.... "It is not quite dissimilar." Why?... Since the self cognizes ideas as the intellect, grasped by consciousness, it is transformed into them; it appears by the act of cognition to be the very self of the intellect, although in reality it is not so....

28. **With the diminution of impurity by the sustained practice of the limbs *(aṅga)* of yoga, the light of wisdom reaches up to discriminating knowledge.**

29. **Restraint, observance, posture, breath control, withdrawal [of the senses], mental stability, meditation, and meditative concentration are the eight limbs of yoga.**

30. **Of these, the restraints *(yama)* are: noninjury *(ahiṃsā)*, truthfulness, not stealing, celibacy, and having few possessions.**

32. **The observances *(niyama)* are: cleanliness, contentment, asceticism, study, and devotion to God.**

---

[11] This is a popular analogy in yoga texts. When clothes are very soiled, one can get rid of most of the dirt by just shaking them, but a stain remains. The first washing removes most of the remaining stain, but the light stain that remains requires a great deal of effort and repeated washings to eliminate. In the same way, the grossest levels of mental afflictions are counteracted fairly easily by meditation, but the subtle residues of these stains are very hard to eradicate, a process that requires prodigious amounts of asceticism and mental training. Although they are subtle, it is necessary to eliminate them because it is impossible to attain liberation while they remain, even in a diminished state.

Regarding these, cleanliness is brought about by such things as earth and water and by eating clean things. This is external. It is internal when it involves washing away impurities of the mind. Contentment is absence of desire to get more of the necessities of life than one already possesses. Asceticism involves bearing extreme conditions, hunger, thirst, cold, and heat, standing or sitting ... or severe penances. Study is reading texts that are concerned with liberation, or the repetition of the sacred syllable *Oṃ*. Devotion to God involves offering one's actions to the supreme Teacher.

33. **When thoughts of wrongdoing bother you, familiarize yourself with their antidotes.**
40. **By cleanliness is meant disgust with one's body and cessation of contact with others.**
46. **Posture is steadily relaxed.**
47. **By relaxation of effort and by limitless absorption.**

It is perfected when effort ceases, so that there may be no more agitation of the body. Or, when the mind achieves balance with regard to the infinite, it brings about the perfection of posture.

49. **Breath control *(prāṇāyāma)* involves restraining the inhalation and exhalation movements [of breath], which follows when that [control of posture] has been achieved.**
54. **Withdrawal [of the senses] *(pratyāhāra)* is that by which the senses do not come into contact with their objects and follow the nature of the mind.**

Source: *Yoga-sūtras* and *Yoga-bhāṣya*, ch. 2; tr. JP.

YOGIC ATTAINMENTS

In this section, Patañjali discusses the results of yogic practice, which include unshakable mental stability, equanimity, dispassion, and eventually liberation from the cycle of birth and death.

3.1. **Mental stability *(dhāraṇā)* is mental steadiness.**

Mental stability involves the mind becoming focused on such places as the sphere of the navel, the lotus of the heart, the light in the brain, the tip of the nose, the tip of the tongue, and similar parts of the body; or on any other external object. . . .

49. **Only one who fully understands the distinction between purity and the self attains supremacy over all states of being and becomes omniscient.**

Omniscience refers to simultaneously discriminating knowledge of the "qualities"—which are of the nature of all phenomena—and showing forth as they do separately the quiescent, the disturbed, and the unpredictable characteristics. This attainment is known as the "sorrowless" *(viśoka)*. Reaching this, the yogi moves omniscient and powerful, with all his afflictions ended.

50. **When the seed of bondage has been destroyed by desirelessness even for those [attainments], absolute separation *(kaivalya)* results.**

Then all the seeds of afflictions pass, together with the mind, into latency. When they have become latent, the self does not then suffer. . . . This state—in which the qualities manifest in the mind as afflictions, actions, and fruitions without having fulfilled their object and come back to action—is the final separation of consciousness from the qualities. This is the state of absolute separation, when the self remains consciousness alone, as in its own nature.

Source: *Yoga-sūtras* and *Yoga-bhāṣya,* ch. 3; tr. JP.

PURĀṆAS AND EPICS

THE FOUR AGES

In contemporary India, the Purāṇas and Epics are among the most widely known of Hindu scriptures. The Purāṇas recount the mythologies of popular gods such as Śiva, Viṣṇu, and Devī (the Goddess). Rich in symbolism and containing a wide variety of divergent traditions, they describe the attributes of the gods and indicate how they should be worshipped.

The two great epics of Hinduism, the Rāmāyaṇa *and the* Mahābhārata, *are monumental stories that weave history, myth, and religion into complex, multifaceted tales that recount important historical and mythical events and indicate the lessons that should be drawn from them. The* Rāmāyaṇa *tells the story of Rāma—considered by tradition to be an incarnation (avatāra) of Viṣṇu—who takes birth among humans in order to fight against evil forces and establish dharma in the world. Forced to leave his kingdom with his dutiful wife Sītā, he wanders in the wilderness, spreading righteousness wherever he goes. In a climactic battle he faces the demon Rāvaṇa, who has captured Sītā. Rāma slays Rāvaṇa, thus enabling dharma to be established in the demon's realm.*

The Mahābhārata—*which contains the* Bhagavad-gītā, *one of the most important religious texts in contemporary*

Hinduism—tells the story of a conflict between related clans for supremacy in northern India. Unlike the heroes of the Rāmāyaṇa, *the protagonists of the* Mahābhārata *(the Pāṇḍavas) often make mistakes, question what is the right course of action, and regret wrong decisions.*

In this passage from the Liṅga Purāṇa, *Indra teaches a human sage about the cyclical nature of time. According to this system, when the universe is first created, a golden age begins. During this period, beings have long lifespans, beautiful bodies, and great happiness. As time goes on, however, things begin imperceptibly to worsen, and eventually it becomes necessary to divide people according to their predispositions.*

[Chapter 39] Indra said: O sage, you should know that the Kṛta Age comes first, and next the Tretā, followed by the Dvāpara and the Tiṣya (Kali) Age. These, in brief, are the four ages. The character of the Kṛta Age is purity *(sattva)*. Activity *(rajas)* is the character of the Tretā. A mixture of activity and darkness *(tamas)* is the character of the Dvāpara. Darkness is the character of the Kali Age. You should know that these are the distinctive qualities of each of the different ages.

Meditation is the main activity of the Kṛta Age, sacrifice *(yajñā)* of the Tretā; worship is the main activity of the Dvāpara, and pure charity of the Kali Age. Four thousand divine years constitute the Kṛta Age, followed by the Twilight (Sandhyā) interregnum, which lasts for four thousand of these years, followed by a Partial Twilight interregnum of the same duration. O Śilāsana, you should know that in the Kṛta beings live for four thousand human years. Following the end of the Kṛta Age and its interregnum, the dharmas of the ages are reduced by one fourth.

The wondrous Tretā Yuga has a duration of one quarter less than the Kṛta. You should know that the Dvāpara continues for half the duration of the Kṛta, and the Kali Age is half again of this. O sage, the Twilight interregnum periods are respectively 300, 200, and 100 divine years, and the Partial Twilights are the same. This is true of all eons *(kalpa)* and ages.

In the Kṛta, the eternal dharma stands on all four feet; in the Tretā, it has three feet. In the Dvāpara it stands on two feet; in the Kali, it is missing three feet and lacks the element of goodness. In the Kṛta, beings are born in pairs; their activity is full of taste and enjoyment. They are always satisfied; they revel in all pleasures and happiness, and there are no distinctions of inferiority or superiority. There are no special characteristics among them, and all are good.

In the Kṛta, all beings have the same lifespans, enjoyments, and features. They have no individual preferences, and there are no contrasting qualities [e.g., cold and heat] and no anger, and they do not get tired. Those who have no dwellings live on mountains or in the oceans. They have no suffering. They mainly have the quality of purity and are generally isolated. They move about as they wish, with no specific desires, and their minds are always happy. They do not engage in either virtuous or nonvirtuous activities.

At that time, the arrangement of social classes and stages of life was not well-defined, but there was no intermingling of social classes. O brahmin, over time, in the Tretā their tastes and happiness fade away. When those potencies vanished, another arose. When water reaches a subtle state, it is transformed into clouds. From those thundering clouds, rain falls. When the surface of the earth comes into contact with rain, trees grow. These trees then became their houses. Those beings found their sustenance and enjoyments in those trees.

In the beginning of the Tretā, beings sustained themselves through those trees. But after the passage of a long period of time, beings began to change, and feelings of craving and greed suddenly arose. The trees that were their homes began to die, and when they died these beings born as twins became bewildered. Then they began to think about what was happening, and because their thoughts were truthful, the trees reappeared. They used them to make clothes, fruits, and ornaments. On these same trees, very potent honey not made by bees was produced in every bud. This was wonderfully fragrant and had a good color and sweet taste. These beings always sustained themselves with it and lived comfortably their whole lives. They were happy and well-fed, and through this achievement they were free from illness.

But after some time had passed, they became greedy. They cut off the trees' branches and forcibly took the honey that no bees had made. Because of their misdeeds and their greed, the trees of that age and their honey disappeared in certain places, and as time passed little of this perfection survived. As the Tretā progressed, in every cycle contrasting qualities arose, and then these beings became very miserable because of cold rain and scorching sun.

Tormented by the contrasting qualities, they began to make clothes and garments to cover themselves. They built houses on the mountains in order to protect themselves from the contrasting qualities. In the past, they wandered as they pleased and had no fixed abodes. Now they began to live in houses in accordance with their availability and their wishes....

Then those who wished to sustain themselves took up agriculture. The word "sustenance" means livelihood, and in this context it refers to work and desire for agriculture. Other than this, by the end of the Tretā the beings had no means of livelihood and water mostly had to be raised by hand. In the Tretā, those beings in their rage seized one another and took their sons, wives, and wealth by force. This was the character of that age.

Aware of this, the Lotus-Born (Brahmā) created *kṣatriyas* to protect people from injuries and to establish firm rules of conduct. Through his own splendor, the Lord established the social classes and the stages of life. The lord of the universe then created the livelihoods and proper lifestyle for each of the social classes. The livelihood of sacrifices gradually evolved during the Tretā. But even then some people of good and holy rituals did not engage in animal sacrifices. Then the seer Viṣṇu performed sacrifices by force, and that is why brahmins praise nonviolent sacrifices.

In the Dvāpara, people also developed differing inclinations of mind, speech, and action; and agriculture requires great effort during that age. Then all beings exert themselves and become physically exhausted, and so they become subject to greed, working for pay, business, fighting, indecision regarding basic principles, lack of interest in the divisions of the Vedas, confusing regarding their dharmas, destruction of the discipline among the four social classes and the stages of life, and finally lust and hatred; these are the specific characteristics of this age.

During the Dvāpara, passion, covetousness, and arrogance begin to affect people. In the early part of the Dvāpara, Vyāsa [an ancient sage] divides the Vedas into four parts. It is declared that during the Tretā the Vedas were a single unity with four sections; as the lifespan progressively diminishes, the Vedas are divided in the Dvāpara. In accordance with their divergent opinions, the sons of sages further differentiated them according to their whims. They changed the order of the mantras (of the *Ṛg Veda*) and the Brāhmaṇas, and they also changed the accents and syllables. Scholars compiled the collections of the *Ṛg Veda, Yajur Veda*, and *Sāma Veda*. Although the texts were composed in common, they were later differentiated in accordance with various viewpoints. The different sections of the Vedas evolved—the Brāhmaṇas, Kalpasūtras, and Mantrapravacanas. Some adhered to them, while others deviated from them. . . .

Drought, death, and pestilence occur. Various sufferings of mind, speech, and body lead one to become indifferent to worldly affairs. As a result of this indifference, people begin to think about attaining liberation from pain and misery. This process of thought gives rise to detachment, and as a result of detachment they begin to realize the problems and defects of the world. Due to this realization, perfect knowledge becomes possible in the Dvāpara. This is a result of the behavior that is a mixture of activity and darkness. Dharma has its origins in the first age, the Kṛta. It begins to function during the Tretā. It becomes disturbed during the Dvāpara, and during the Kali it gradually becomes confused and then completely perishes.

[Chapter 40] Indra said: During the Kali Age, people's senses are disturbed by the quality of darkness and so fall into illusion and jealousy. They even kill ascetics, and they are always plagued with jealousy. In the Kali Age, there is always carelessness, sickness, hunger, fear, and terrible suffering as a result of drought. There is also division between different parts of a country. Sacred scripture is not regarded as authoritative, and people engage in sinful actions. People are wicked, irritable, and narrow-minded. They misbehave. Greedy and wicked beings who are born during the Kali Age speak falsehoods and indulge in evil desires, evil studies, wrongdoing, and misleading scriptures. Because of the defects of the actions of brahmins, fear arises among beings. The twice-born social classes (brahmins, *kṣatriyas*, and *vaiśyas*) neglect study of the Vedas and do not perform the sacrifices as prescribed.

People die, and the *kṣatriyas* and *vaiśyas* gradually decline. During the Kali Age, *śūdras* claim kinship with brahmins due to their learning and through eating with them and sharing seats and beds. Most kings are *śūdras*, and they harass brahmins. Abortion is widespread, along with murder of heroes. *Śūdras* adopt the lifestyle prescribed for brahmins, and brahmins follow the ways of *śūdras*. Thieves serve as kings, and kings serve as thieves. Virtuous women cease to exist, and the number of wanton sluts increases. The durability and discipline of the four social classes and stages of life disappear everywhere. At that time the earth produces little fruit in one place and great amounts of fruit in others. . . .

You should know that toward the end of this age predators will become very violent, cows will decline in number, and good people will withdraw from public life. Their dharma—which is subtle, contributes to good outcomes and is difficult to grasp and has its roots in charitable giving—becomes tenuous because of the instability of the four stages of life. . . . Men will steal money from others and violate the chastity of other men's wives. They will be lustful, evil in their hearts, degenerate, and foolish. They will lose the proper perspective. They will have upset stomachs and disheveled hair.

Toward the end of the age, people will be born with a lifespan of only sixteen years. Some will sell Vedas, and others holy water. When the Kali Age begins, heretics will be born who oppose the system of four social classes and stages of life. *Śūdras* will learn the Vedas and will become experts in the meaning of dharma. Kings born in *śūdra* wombs will perform horse sacrifices, and people will harass each other by killing women, children, cows, and one another. Because people are inclined toward evil, their actions will be motivated by the quality of darkness. Then crimes like brahmin-slaughter will begin to appear. Thus during the Kali Age, lifespan, strength, and features progressively diminish, and people attain maturity quickly.

Outstanding brahmins of holy nature will still practice dharma without animosity even at the end of this age, as enjoined in the sacred scriptures. The merit from practice of dharma during the course of a year during the Tretā will be gained during practice of it for a month in the Dvāpara. During the Kali Age, an intelligent devotee gains the same amount in a day through diligent practice. . . .

In this miserable condition, they will sustain themselves by liquor, meat, roots, and fruit. They will wear tree bark, leaves, or deer skin. They will not perform the sacred rituals or accept donations. They will fall away from strict observance of four social classes and stages of life. They will be caught up in terrible catastrophes. In these ways, the remaining beings at the end of the Kali Age will live in misery. They will be afflicted by old age, illness, and hunger. Due to suffering, their minds will become depressed. But from this depression, reflection *(vicāraṇā)* will begin, and reflection leads to mental balance. This attitude leads to knowledge, and from true knowledge a pious disposition arises. The beings who survive the last years of the Kali Age will lack physical features and mental peace.

Then, at that time the age will be transformed in the course of a day and a night, confusing their minds as with someone who is sleeping or insane. Then, through the impetus of inevitable future developments, the Kṛta Age will begin. When the Kṛta Age has dawned, those beings who survived the Kali Age will become the beings born into that new age.

Source: *Liṅga Purāṇa* chs. 39 and 40; tr. JP.

THE LIṄGAM OF ŚIVA

In this passage, Viṣṇu tells a human sage about the origin of the
liṅgam, the phallus of Śiva. The liṅgam symbolizes both his procre-
ative force and the energy he stores through asceticism. The story
begins with a conversation between Brahmā, the creator of the uni-
verse in Hindu mythology, and Viṣṇu, who is the creator of Brahmā.
Brahmā believes himself to be supreme, self-created, and omnipo-
tent, but Viṣṇu informs him that he is in fact his creature. Both gods
are then amazed to see a huge flaming liṅgam that stretches out
of sight. They agree to try to find its top and bottom, but after one
thousand years flying respectively up and down they are unable
to fathom its dimensions. At this point they realize that there is a
greater power than themselves, which turns out to be Śiva.

In the distant past, when the three worlds had been swallowed up and had not yet rearisen, enshrouded in darkness
by me, I lay there alone, with all beings in my abdomen. I had
a thousand heads, eyes, and feet, and in my hands I held the
conch, discus, and club. I lay on an expanse of pure water.
Then in the distance I saw the great yogi Brahmā, the Lord of
limitless light. He was like a hundred suns, shining with his
own splendor. This four-headed Lord wore a black antelope
skin and carried a water pot. In an instant this excellent Person
came to me. Then Brahmā, to whom all the worlds give praise,
said to me: "Who are you? From where have you come? Why
do you stand here? Tell me, O Lord. I am the creator of all the
worlds, and I am self-created. I have faces in all directions."

When Brahmā had said this, I responded to him: "I am the
creator of all the worlds, and I also destroy them again and
again." As we were speaking together in this way, each seeking to outdo the other, we saw a fire blazing in the northern
quarter. We were surprised to see it, and we were inspired
to join our hands in reverence due to its splendor and power;
we bowed to the light of Śiva. We saw its mass and splendor increasing in size; it was astoundingly miraculous, and
Brahmā and I quickly rushed toward that massive flame. The
circle of flame penetrated heaven and earth. In the middle
of its great splendor, we saw a resplendent *liṅgam* a hands-
breadth in width. It was unmanifest, and yet it was endowed
with surpassing brightness.

In the middle, it was neither gold, nor rock, nor silver. It
could not be described nor contemplated; it was alternately
visible and invisible. It was richly endowed with thousands of
garlands of flames; it was astounding and mysterious. It was
endowed with great luminescence and continued to increase
in size. Clusters of flame spread everywhere. It was terrifying

to living beings, awe-inspiring in its features, penetrating heaven and earth.

Then Brahmā said to me: "Fly down quickly, and we will discover the bottom of this noble *liṅgam*. I will fly upwards to find its top." After we agreed to this plan, we flew upwards and downwards. I flew downwards for one thousand years, but I could not discover its bottom. Then I became very afraid. Similarly, Brahmā flew upwards, but he also failed to reach its highest point. Then he returned with me to that expanse of water. We were astounded and frightened by that noble being, deluded by his magical power. We lost consciousness and became disoriented.

At that point, we meditated on the Lord with faces on all sides, the imperishable Lord who is the source, the beginning of all worlds and the cause of their dissolution. We paid homage to him, with hands joined in reverence to Śiva the trident-bearer, the Lord with an extremely terrifying voice, with frightening features and curved fangs, to the great, unmanifest Lord: "We pay homage to you, O Lord of humans and gods! Obeisance to you, great Lord of all beings, mighty noble soul! We pay homage to you, the eternally accomplished yogi, the Lord who is the foundation of the universe, the highest god, the supreme Brahman, imperishable, the highest place, the primordial one!...

You are the sacrifice, the consecration, and the obeisances, the consecration of all sacred rituals... the Vedas, the worlds, and the gods—the Lord who alone is the true god everywhere. You are the quality of sound in space, and you are the origin and the cause of dissolution of all living beings. You are the quality of smell in the earth, the quality of taste in the waters, and the quality of brightness in fire, the greatest Lord. O God of the gods, you are the quality of touch in wind and the form of the moon's body. Lord of the gods, you are the knowledge of the intellect and the seed of primordial matter *(prakṛti)*. You are the destroyer of all worlds; you are Time (Kāla), the god of Death, the cause of destruction. O Lord, you alone sustain the three worlds; you alone create them.

"O Lord endowed with the potential power of a million million suns, we pay homage to you. We pay homage to you, O Lord, as white as a thousand moons. We pay homage to you who wield the thunderbolt *(vajra)* and the bow Pināka. We pay homage to you, O Lord, with arrows and bow in your hands. We pay homage to you, O Lord, whose body is adorned with sacred ash, the destroyer of Kāma's (the god of erotic love) body. We pay homage to you, O Lord of the golden womb *(hiraṇya-garbha)*, the golden robes, the golden navel, the golden semen. We pay homage to you,

O mysterious Lord with a thousand eyes. We pay homage to you, O Lord of golden color, with golden hair, the Lord of golden heroism, the Lord who dispenses gold. We pay homage to you, O Lord, the master of gold, with the sound of gold, with the bow Pināka in your hand, blue-necked Śaṃkara."

After he had been praised in that way, the Lord of great intellect, the God of gods, the source of the origin of the universe, appeared before us, shining with the light of ten million suns. The great god of supreme brilliance became filled with pity and spoke to us as if he were about to swallow the sky with his billions of mouths. His neck was shaped like a conch shell, and his stomach was beautifully formed. He was adorned with various ornaments, and his body shone with many colors because of a multitude of jewels. He wore many different kinds of garlands and had applied various unguents. The Lord held the Pināka bow in one hand, and in another the trident. He was worthy to be worshipped by the gods. He wore a great serpent for the sacred thread, and he caused the gods to be free from fear.

Then he burst into laughter with the sound of the *dundubhi* drum, like the rumbling of thunder. The sound filled the entire universe. The two of us were terrified by that great sound. Then the Great Lord said: "O best among the gods, I am pleased. May both of you see my great yogic power and overcome all fear. You are both eternal and in the past were born from my limbs. This Brahmā, the grandfather of humans, is my right arm; and Viṣṇu, who is never defeated in battle, is my right arm. I am pleased with both of you, and so I will grant you whatever boon you wish."

Both of us were delighted and bowed down at the Lord's feet. We implored the Great God, standing in front of us and offering his favor: "O God of gods, we are delighted; if you are truly pleased with us and will grant a boon, may we be devoted to you forever!" The God of gods said: "Let it be so, greatly fortunate ones. Produce progeny prolifically!" After speaking thus, the Lord disappeared.

Source: The *Manu-smṛti*, The Laws of Manu, chs. 4, 12, 10; tr. JP.

THE BUDDHA: A FALSE TEACHER

As we saw in the previous selection, a common polemical trope in Puranic literature involves portraying other gods as subordinate to one's own. In the Viṣṇu Purāṇa, *the Buddha, founder of Buddhism, is depicted as a false incarnation of Viṣṇu who is sent to earth to delude the Daityas, a race of superhuman beings who are the enemies of the gods. Viṣṇu grants the gods' request and then creates an apparently wise and benevolent ascetic, dressed in the robes associated with Buddhist monasticism, who teaches them a plausible doctrine but one that deviates from the true path to liberation. Because they foolishly follow his teachings, they abandon their previous practice of Vedic rituals and austerities, which weakens them and leads to their defeat by the gods.*

When mighty Viṣṇu heard their plea, he emitted an illusory form from his body and gave it to the gods, saying, "This deceptive vision will completely fool the Daityas, and because they are led astray from the Vedas they will all be put to death, because all gods, demons, or others who oppose the authority of the Vedas will perish through my power, which is exercised in order to preserve the world. . . ."

[Buddha approached the Daityas and said,] "The dharma I will teach you is the secret path to liberation. There is nothing beyond this or superior to it; by following it you will attain either heaven or liberation from future existence. Mighty Daityas, you deserve such a doctrine." Using such insinuations, and with many specious arguments, this delusive being misled the Daityas from the tenets of the Vedas . . . and so the Daityas were seduced from their proper duties by the repeated lessons of this illusory preacher, who maintained that contradictory tenets are equally true. . . .

When the Daityas had thus deviated from the path of the sacred scriptures, the gods gained courage and assembled for battle. Then fighting ensued and the demons were defeated and killed by the gods, who had adhered to the path of dharma. The armor of religious practice that had formerly protected the Daityas had been discarded by them, and their utter destruction followed this abandonment.

Source: *Viṣṇu Purāṇa*, Book III, chs. 17, 18; tr. JP.

THE POWER OF THE GODDESS

The following reading is from the Ancient Text of the Goddess *(Devī Purāṇa), which generally is classed as a "secondary ancient text" (upapurāṇa) but is regarded as an authoritative scripture by several sects of Śāktas (devotees of the Goddess). The text emphasizes the Goddess in her fierce and terrible aspects—as Kālī, who is worshiped by blood sacrifices, as Durgā, a mighty warrior who rides a tiger and slays demons, or in a variety of other forms. The text describes a number of her manifestations and her essential nature, along with her activities in the world on behalf of devotees. It also describes her relation with Śiva, who, like the*

Goddess, is associated with the magical powers gained through asceticism and yoga. The section below lists a number of magical abilities that accrue to adepts who recite mantras contained in a collection of spells and magical techniques. The acquisition of magical powers is an essential aspect of the path of the tantric adept (siddha), who employs various techniques—including recitation of mantras, visualizations, and rituals—to acquire supernatural abilities, which then can be used in pursuit of liberation.

1. By taking the vow of a hero while speaking the first mantra 100,000 times, an adept becomes respected and popular.
2. By proclaiming the second mantra, an adept is able to separate the subtle body [a form within the physical body composed of subtle matter] from the physical body in order to visit a cremation ground [a power place for tantric practitioners]. . . .
4. The fourth mantra gives an adept the power to repel all weapons hurled by others.
5. By acquiring the power of the fifth mantra, one can stop rain at will.
6. By becoming skillful in reciting the sixth mantra, an adept acquires the power to vanish and reappear at will. . . .
9. The ninth mantra allows one to cut through all obstacles.
10. By performing rituals in accordance with the tenth mantra, a devotee is able to spread epidemic diseases among enemies.
11. By constant chanting of the eleventh mantra during conflict, the enemy's weapons become paralyzed. . . .
13. By chanting the thirteenth mantra, one is able to attract women.
14. By repeatedly chanting the fourteenth mantra, one can kill someone from a distance. . . .
18. If one successfully chants the eighteenth mantra, a female tantric consort will become available.
19. Through successful repetition of the nineteenth mantra, the Goddess becomes pleased and grants whatever the devotee desires. . . .

Source: *Devī Purāṇa*, "Padamalā Mantra Vidyā"; tr. JP.

RĀMA, A GOD AMONG HUMANS

The opening section of the Rāmāyaṇa *contains a synopsis of the main events of the story. The following verses tell of how prince Rāma was banished from his kingdom through the machinations of his stepmother Kaikeyī, who had been told by his father*

*Daśaratha that she could ask him for anything she wished.
Kaikeyī requested that Rāma, the rightful ruler, not assume
the throne and that her son Bharata instead become king. As
a righteous king, Daśaratha could not refuse, so he reluctantly
acceded. Kaikeyī knew that the people of the kingdom wanted
Rāma to rule, so to ensure that Bharata would remain king she
asked that Rāma be banished in order that popular opinion
would not undermine her son's authority. The king agreed but as
a result died of a broken heart soon after.*

*Accompanied by his brother Lakṣmaṇa and by Sītā, the
model of a devout Hindu wife, Rāma went off to the forest.
During his travels he was beset by a horde of demons (rākṣasa),
but he defeated them all. This angered the demon lord Rāvaṇa,
who captured Sītā and imprisoned her in his city of Laṅkā.
Rāvaṇa then fell in love with Sītā and tried to convince her to
renounce Rāma and become his queen, but Sītā spurned his
advances. With the help of Hanumān, lord of monkeys, Rāma
eventually located Sītā, slew Rāvaṇa, and rescued her. He then
returned in triumph to his kingdom, and Bharata abdicated in
Rāma's favor because he had never wished to usurp Rāma.*

*Following Rāma's return, however, his subjects began to
gossip about Sītā, insinuating that while she was in Rāvaṇa's
castle she may have succumbed to his advances. Rāma knew that
Sītā was innocent but reluctantly realized that the gossip could
undermine his moral authority, which was closely connected to
his wife's conduct. Following the dictates of dharma, Rāma was
forced to banish Sītā from the kingdom. Rāma was heartbroken,
knowing that her love for him kept her chaste in the castle of
Rāvaṇa, but his royal duty required him to maintain his reputation
for righteousness. The following verses describe how he left the
kingdom, joined forces with Hanumān, and then defeated Rāvaṇa.*

8. There is a famous king named Rāma ... who is self-controlled, very powerful, radiant, resolute, and illustrious.

9. Wise and established in good conduct, he is eloquent and regal. He vanquishes his enemies. He has wide shoulders and powerful arms. . . .

12. He understands dharma and always keeps his promises. He always thinks of his subjects' welfare. He is famous, pure, disciplined, and contemplative.

13. Protector of all living beings, guardian of dharma, he knows the essence of the Vedas and their subsidiary lore and is equally skilled in the science of combat. . . .

18–19. His generosity is equal to that of Kubera, the provider of wealth, and his devotion to truth is like that of Dharma [the god of righteousness]. Daśaratha, the lord of the

earth, loved him and wanted to name Rāma, his eldest
son, as his successor....

20. As Queen Kaikeyī, the king's wife, watched the corona-
tion preparations, she [decided] to ask for a wish that
had been promised long ago. She demanded that Bharata
[her son] be crowned instead and that Rāma be exiled.

21. Daśaratha was a man who kept his promises, and so,
caught in the trap of his own righteousness, he had to
exile his beloved son Rāma.

22. To please Kaikeyī, the hero Rāma honored the promise
made by his father and went into the forest....

37–38. Then in battle Rāma killed all the demons.... About fourteen thousand demons were killed while he resided in
Daṇḍaka.

39–42. Then Rāvaṇa, king of *demons*, heard of the massacre
of his relatives; he flew into a rage and... he lured the
king's sons far away. Then he kidnapped Rāma's wife....

47. Then [Rāma] met the monkey Hanumān on the shores of
Lake Pampā....

56. This bull among monkeys wished to find Janaka's daughter [Sītā] and sent all the monkeys searching in all directions....

58. When he reached the city of Laṅkā, which was ruled by
Rāvaṇa, he saw Sītā pensive and sad in a grove of *aśoka*
trees....

62. The great monkey burned the city of Laṅkā, but spared
Sītā, and then returned to tell Rāma the good news....

65. Then the god of the ocean appeared before Rāma, and
Rāma followed his advice by having Nala build a bridge
[to Laṅkā].

66. Using this [bridge], he went to the city of Laṅkā, and
after killing Rāvaṇa in battle he crowned Vibhīṣaṇa as
lord of the demons in Laṅkā.

67. One who reads the story of Rāma, which brings merit and
purity, will be freed from all sin. One who reads it with
devotion and faith will ultimately be worshipped, together
with his sons, grandsons, and servants after death.

Source: *Rāmāyaṇa,* ch. 1; tr. JP.

THE *BHAGAVAD-GĪTĀ*: ARJUNA'S REFUSAL TO FIGHT

The following passages are taken from the Bhagavad-gītā, *one of
the most influential of Hindu religious texts. A part of the monumental epic* Mahābhārata, *it tells the story of a climactic battle*

*between the Pāṇḍavas and the Kauravas, two rival clans con-
tending for supremacy in northern India. As the story opens, the
Pāṇḍava Arjuna, perhaps the greatest warrior of his generation,
decides to scout the opposition. He asks his charioteer Kṛṣṇa
[Krishna] (who, unbeknownst to him, is really an incarnation of
the god Viṣṇu) to drive the chariot in front of the enemy lines. As
he rides past the Kauravas, however, he experiences a crisis of
conscience: he recognizes that many of his opponents are relatives, friends, and teachers and he fears that that killing them
would result in a great deal of negative karma.*

*It is important to note that Arjuna is not concerned with kill-
ing per se; as a warrior he has killed in the past, but these particular people are linked to him by close karmic bonds, and so he
perceives a contradiction between the demands of his warrior
duty (dharma) and the dictates of the law of karma. He decides
that the only solution is to opt out of the conflict altogether and
become a world renouncer. In response, Kṛṣṇa lectures him on
the necessity of correctly performing dharma and indicates that
Arjuna will receive more negative karma by dereliction of duty
than by killing. Furthermore, Kṛṣṇa asserts, his opponents have
already assured their own destruction by their evil deeds, and
Arjuna is merely the instrument through which God will exact
punishment.*

*Then Kṛṣṇa gives Arjuna a solution to the problem he faces,
which involves a mental reorientation. Arjuna's problem, as
explained by Kṛṣṇa, is that he sees himself as an agent and is
attached to the results of his actions. If, however, he learns the
technique of "disciplined action" (karma-yoga), he can develop
the ability to act without involving the false sense of ego. Arjuna
is told to act selflessly, perceiving himself as an impersonal
agent of dharma who is simply following God's will. If he offers
all of his actions to God as an act of devotion and cultivates
complete detachment, then Arjuna may act without acquiring
any negative karma. Moreover, Kṛṣṇa tells him, such a mental
perspective is the mindset of the true world renouncer, and this
alone leads to liberation from cyclic existence.*

[Chapter 1] Then Arjuna, whose banner is a monkey,
saw Dhṛtarāṣṭra's men marshaled as weapons were about
to clash and raised his bow. Then, O King, standing between
the two armies he said to Kṛṣṇa: "Unconquered one, stop the
chariot so that I can see those who wish to fight and know
with whom I must do battle. . . ." As they stood there, Arjuna
saw fathers and grandfathers, teachers, uncles, brothers,
sons, grandsons, and comrades, fathers-in-law, and friends in
both armies.

When he saw all his kinsmen assembled, Arjuna was filled with profound compassion and sadly said: "Kṛṣṇa, when I see my kinsmen standing here, eager to fight, my limbs sink down, my mouth is dry, my body shakes, and my hair stands up in fear. The bow Gāṇḍīva slips from my hand, my skin is on fire; I am unable to stand, and my mind reels. Kṛṣṇa, I see evil omens, and I cannot see any positive outcome in striking down my own kinsmen in battle.

"Kṛṣṇa, I have no desire for victory, nor for the kingdom or pleasures. What would I do with a kingdom? What would I do with enjoyments, or even life?... Kṛṣṇa, even if they were to kill me, still I have no wish to slay them, not even for dominion over the three worlds; how much less for the earth! Kṛṣṇa, if we were to kill Dhṛtarāṣṭra's sons, what reward would we gain? Nothing but evil will come to stay with us if we were to kill them, even though they hate us. Therefore, we should not kill the sons of Dhṛtarāṣṭra and their clansmen.

"Kṛṣṇa, if we were to slaughter our own family, how could we be happy? Even though they have become insane with greed and cannot see the wickedness of ruining one's family and that lying is a crime, why shouldn't we be wise enough to avoid this awful thing? When the family is ruined, the primordial dharmas of that family disappear. Once dharma disappears, then disorder *(adharma)* overwhelms the family.

"Kṛṣṇa, when disorder triumphs, the women of the family become corrupted; once the women are corrupted, there will be a mixing of social classes. Mixing of social classes leads to hell—the hell for those who destroy the family and for the family itself. In the same way, their ancestors also sink to hell because their ritual offerings of rice balls and water are discontinued. . . .

"I should let Dhṛtarāṣṭra's sons, with weapons in their hands, kill me in battle while I am unarmed and offer no defense. This would lead to greater happiness for me." After saying this in the midst of the conflict, Arjuna slumped down onto the seat of the chariot and loosened his grip on his bow and arrows, his mind agitated by grief."

[Chapter 2; Kṛṣṇa:] "Why do you show such weakness in this time of difficulty? Arjuna, this is unworthy, does not lead to heaven, and is disgraceful; do not give in to unmanliness, Arjuna! It is unnatural to you. Give up this faint-heartedness and rise up, O tormenter of your enemies!. . .

"You grieve for those who do not deserve grief, but still you speak words of wisdom. The learned do not grieve for either the dead or the living. There has never been a time when I did not exist, nor you, nor these rulers; nor will any of us cease to exist in the future. Just as in this body the essence of embodiment passes from childhood to youth and then old age, so does it appropriate another body after death. The wise are not confused by this. . . .

"You should know that this which pervades the entire world is indestructible. No one can cause the destruction of this immutable reality. The bodies of this eternal embodied Self *(ātman)*, the indestructible, the incommensurable, are said to be finite; so you should fight, descendant of Bhārata! Whoever thinks of this Self as the slayer or slain—both of them do not understand. This Self does not slay, nor can it be slain. It is not born, nor does it die; nor having come to be will it again cease to be. This unborn, eternal, everlasting, primordial Self is not slain when the body is slain. . . .

"Just as a man, after discarding worn-out clothes, puts on other new ones, so the embodied Self, after discarding worn-out bodies, appropriates other new ones. . . . This embodied Self in everyone's body can never be killed, descendant of Bhārata; so you should not grieve for any creature.

"Moreover, you should be aware of your own dharma, and so you should not waver. For a *kṣatriya*, there is nothing better than a just war. Arjuna, happy is the *kṣatriya* who by good fortune finds a battle like this, an open door to heaven. Now if you do not fight this dharma-ordained conflict then, having abandoned your own dharma and reputation, you will only gain evil. Also, people will forever recount your disgrace. For a person who has been revered, such ignominy is worse than death. The great chariot warriors will think you avoided battle due to fear; and although you have been revered by them, you will now earn their contempt.

"In addition, your enemies too will say many derogatory things about your abilities; could there be any greater suffering than that? If you are killed, you will go to heaven; if you are victorious, you will enjoy the earth. Therefore, Arjuna, get up and resolve to fight! Then, indifferent to pleasure or pain, victory or defeat, prepare yourself for battle; in this way you will not incur any sin. . . .

"Be focused only on karma, not on its results. The results of karma should not be your concern, nor your attachment to inaction. Be steadfast in devotion to your karma, Arjuna, casting off attachment, indifferent to success or failure: yoga is defined as indifference. Karma is surely inferior to the yoga of wisdom, Arjuna. You should seek shelter in wisdom. Those whose motivation is the result are wretched. One who has disciplined wisdom casts off both good and bad karma. So you should discipline yourself in yoga. The yoga of action is auspicious. This is because those of disciplined action abandon the results of karma. These intelligent people, released from the bondage of rebirth, go to the place that is free from evil. . . .

"Arjuna, when one abandons desires in one's mind and finds contentment by oneself in that Self alone, then one is said to have a stabilized mind. When one's mind is unperturbed by sufferings, when desire for pleasures has ceased, when attachment, fear, and anger have vanished, one is called a sage, a person of stabilized mind. . . . Controlling all one's senses, one should remain disciplined, focused on Me. One whose senses are controlled has mental stability. . . . Abandoning all desires, one who moves about free from attachment, selfishness, or egotism attains peace. This is the divine state, Arjuna. One who attains it is free from delusion. Remaining in this state even at the time of death, one goes to the nirvana of Brahman."

[Chapter 4] "Arjuna, many births have passed for me, and also for you. I know all of them, but you do not know them, harasser of enemies. Although I am unborn and my Self is eternal, and although I am the Lord of all beings, still, ruling over my essential nature, I come into being through my own magical power. Whenever dharma degenerates, Arjuna, and chaos reigns, then I manifest myself. . . .

"I created the four social class system, each with different qualities and karmas. Although I am the maker of this, you should know me as one who eternally does not act. Karmas do not defile me, nor do I have any desire for the results of karma. One who comprehends me in this way is not bound by karma."

[Chapter 6] "Arjuna, you should know that yoga is what is called renunciation. No one becomes a yogi without renouncing intention. Karma is said to be a means for a sage who wants to attain yoga. For that same sage who has attained yoga, quiescence is said to be the means. For when one is not attached to sense objects nor to karma, renouncing all purpose, one is said to have attained yoga. . . .

"When thought comes to rest, restrained by the practice of yoga; and when, contemplating the Self by the Self, one is satisfied in one's own Self; when one knows the infinite joy that, transcending the senses, is apprehended by consciousness—when one knows this and does not deviate from the truth in the slightest and steadily abides in it; and, having attained it, thinks that no other attainment is superior to this; when, established in this one is not moved by any pain, however terrible—know that this state of separation from any connection with suffering is called 'yoga.' That yoga must be practiced with determination and with an undepressed heart."

[Chapter 9] "Whatever you do, whatever you eat, whatever oblations you offer or give, whatever austerities you perform: you should do them as offerings to Me, Arjuna! In this way you will be liberated from the bonds of both good and evil karmic results. Mentally equipped with the yoga of renunciation, liberated, you will come to Me."

Source: *Bhagavad-gītā* selections; tr. JP, from *The Bhagavad-gītā: Kṛṣṇa's Counsel in Time of War*, tr. Barbara Stoler Miller (New York: Columbia University Press, 1986), pp. 23–27, 29, 31–34, 36, 37, 39, 50, 52, 86.

THE LIFE OF A SAGE

Although the Bhagavad-gītā *counsels against running away from one's dharma when conflicts arise, the larger work within which it appears, the* Mahābhārata, *contains a number of passages that recognize the validity of the renunciant path and extol the actions of the sages who pursue it. They leave behind society and subsist on alms, and through their austerities and meditation engage in practices that can lead to liberation. The following passage is spoken by the god Śiva to his wife Umā following an incident in which she playfully covers his eyes, which plunges the world into darkness. In answer to a series of questions about his role in the universe, he describes how sages should live. They inhabit the fringes of society, sleep on the ground and subsist on leftovers, practice meditation and subdue their senses, and thus develop patience and insight.*

[Śiva:] In all the dharmas of seers, selves should be conquered; sense faculties should be conquered.... Renouncing food prepared with cows' milk and delighting in lying on the bare ground, practicing yoga, enjoying vegetables and leaves, eating fruits and roots, ingesting wind, water, and duck-weed: these are some of the observances of the seers through which they master the way of those who are disciplined. When the smoke has gone, when the pestle has been set down, when there are no more coals, when the people have eaten their meals, when the [cooking and eating] vessels are no longer passed around, after the time for begging alms has passed, then, while they are still eager to have guests, [the renunciant] eats the food that is left over. Delighting in the dharma of truth, patient, he is yoked to the dharma of sages. He is not arrogant or conceited, is not confused or surprised, is friendly to friends and enemies, and is the foremost knower of dharma.

Source: *Mahābhārata,* ch. 13, "Umā-Maheśvara-saṃvāda"; tr. JP.

DEVOTIONAL LITERATURE

PRAISE OF THE GODDESS

This passage declares that the Goddess is the real source of all creation. All the male deities of Hinduism—as well as all that exists—have their origin in her. It also indicates how she should be worshiped: with all one's heart, as the Divine Mother who protects her devotees as a mother protects her children.

> This blessed goddess Mahāmāyā, having forcibly seized the minds even of men of knowledge, leads them to delusion.
> Through her is created the entire three-tiered universe, that which both does and does not move.
> Just she is the gracious giver of boons to men, for the sake of (their) release. From bondage to mundane life; she is indeed the queen (governing) all who have power. . . .
> Brahmā said: By you is everything supported, by you the world created; By you is it protected, O Goddess, and you always consume (it) at the end (of time). . . .
> Terrible with your sword and spear, likewise with cudgel and discus, With conch and bow, having arrows, sling, and iron mace as your weapons,
> Gentle, more gentle than other gentle ones, exceedingly beautiful, You are superior to the high and low, the supreme queen.
> Whatever and whenever anything exists, whether it be real or unreal, O you have everything as your very soul,
> Of all that, you are the power; how then can you be adequately praised?

Source: *Devī-Māhātmya* I.42–I.63, from *Encountering the Goddess,* tr. Thomas B. Coburn (Albany, NY: State University of New York Press, 1991), pp. 35–37.

PRAYER FOR IDENTITY WITH THE GODDESS

The Goddess is described as both fearful and benevolent, indicating that she is connected with both the pleasant and the unpleasant aspects of existence. This poem, traditionally attributed to Śaṃkara, asks for her help in attaining perfect identification with her in a state of perfect devotion in which notions of separateness and personality are transcended.

> If Śiva is united with Śakti, he is able to exert his powers as lord; if not, the god is not able to stir.
> Hence to you, who must be propitiated by Hari [Viṣṇu], Hara [Śiva], Virarñca [Brahmā], and the other [gods],
> How can one who has not acquired merit be fit to offer reverence and praise? . . .
> For the ignorant you are the island city of the sun, for the mentally stagnant you are a waterfall of streams of nectar [flowing] from a bouquet of intelligence,
> For the poor you are a rosary of wishing-jewels; for those who in the ocean of birth are submerged, you are the tusk of that boar who was the enemy of Mura [a demon killed by Viṣṇu], O Lady.
> Banded with a tinkling girdle, heavy with breasts like the frontal lobes of young elephants,
> Slender of waist, with face like the full moon of autumn, bearing on the palms of her hands bow, arrows, noose, and goad,
> Let there be seated before us the pride of him who shook the cities [Śiva]. . . .
> May you, O Blessed Lady, extend to me, your slave, a compassionate glance!
> When one desiring to praise you utters the words "you, O Lady" [which also mean, "May I be you"],
> At that moment you grant him a state of identity with you.
> With your feet illuminated by the crests of Mukunda, Brahmā, and Indra.

Source: *Saundaryalaharī*, attributed to Śaṃkara, tr. W. N. Brown (Cambridge, MA: Harvard University Press, 1958), pp. 48, 50, 56.

MĪRĀBĀĪ'S MYSTICAL MARRIAGE TO KṚṢṆA

Mīrābāī remains one of the most popular devotional poets of medieval India. She was probably born around 1550 and is said to have been the wife of a Rājput prince who was the son of the ruler (Rana) of Mewar. According to legend, before her marriage she had fallen in love with Kṛṣṇa [Krishna] and refused to consummate her marriage to the prince because her relationship with the Lord took precedence. One story that is told of her relates that one time she was exchanging words of love to a visitor on the other side of a locked door. Her father-in-law, the ruler, overheard her and, outraged by the shame she had brought on his family, threatened to kill her. She told him that the person to whom she was speaking was the Lord Kṛṣṇa, not a human lover, and her life was spared. In this poem she alludes

*to an incident in which the Rana tried to poison her, but she
believes that she was saved by Kṛṣṇa. She indicates that her
devotion to the Lord has caused her to leave behind her family
and friends and the privileged life she led in the palace and to
seek the company of fellow devotees.*

My love is reserved for Gopāl, the Mountain Lifter
And for no one else.
O saints and ascetics,
I have seen the world and its ways.
I left my brothers and relatives
And all my possessions.
Abandoning worldly shame,
I came to sit with ascetics.
Together with devotees [of Kṛṣṇa,] I was happy.
[But] when I looked at the world, I wept.
I planted the vine of love
And watered it with my tears.
I churned curds
And extracted the ghee;
I threw out the buttermilk.
The King sent me a cup of poison,
And I gladly drank it all.
Mira's love is deeply rooted;
She accepts whatever comes to her.

Source: Poem from *Mīrābāī ki Padāvalī;* tr. JP.

CHEATING ON HER HUSBAND

*Akka ("Elder Sister") Mahādēvi (ca. late twelfth century) was
an important poet of the iconoclastic Vīraśaiva tradition, which
began in Karnataka in the twelfth century. In her poetry, her
devotion to Śiva was often expressed in sexual terms. Her verses
contrast the intense love she feels for him with her loveless
marriage and tense relations with his family. She characterizes her husband as a worthless philanderer who is unworthy
of the devotion prescribed in Hindu literature, in which a wife
is enjoined to venerate her husband as a god. In the following
verses, she describes her affair with Śiva and dismisses the traditional bonds of human marriage.*

Mother, I am united with the beautiful one
Who has no death, no faults, and no form.
I am united with the handsome one
Who has no end, no parts, and no distinguishing marks,
No birth, and no fear.

The beautiful one I have married is brave,
Without country and without equal.

Channamallikārjuna the beautiful is my husband;
Mother, throw into the fire all these husbands
Who are subject to death and decay!

Source: Jagadguru Śrī Annadānīśvara Mahāsvāmigaḷu, *Mahādēviyakkana vacana-cintana* (Mysore, India: Jagadguru Śrī Śivarātrīśvara Granthamāle, 2001); tr. JP.

TREATISES ON DHARMA

ACTIONS AND THEIR RESULTS

The Traditions of Manu *codify the hierarchy of medieval Indian society and outline the duties of the four primary social groups: (1) brahmins, the priests; (2) kṣatriyas, the warriors and rulers; (3) vaiśyas, tradespeople and merchants, and (4) śūdras, or servants. Each of them is said to have a role to play in creating a stable, ordered society. Manu also outlines the duties for four stages of life: the student, the householder, the forest-dweller, and the world renouncer. According to this scheme, liberation is recognized as the supreme goal of the religious life, but its pursuit should be postponed until the proper time: when one has seen a grandson born (indicating that one's lineage will continue) and gray hairs have appeared on one's head (indicating that one has lived long enough to fulfill the requirements of dharma).*

4.97. It is better [to discharge] one's own dharma incompletely than to perform completely that of another; for he who lives according to the law of another [social class] is instantly excluded from his own....

12.3. Action, which springs from the mind, from speech, and from the body, produces either good or bad results; by actions are caused the conditions of humans: the highest, middling, and lowest.

4. You should know that the mind is the instigator here below, even for actions that are connected with the body....

40. Those endowed with purity *(sattva)* reach the state of gods, those endowed with activity *(rajas)* the state of humans, and those endowed with darkness *(tamas)* always sink to the condition of animals; that is the three-fold course of transmigrations....

95. All those traditions *(smṛti)* and all those despicable systems of philosophy, which are not based on the Veda, produce no reward after death; for they are declared to be founded on darkness....

104. Austerity and sacred learning are the best means by which brahmins gain supreme happiness; by austerity they destroy guilt, by sacred learning they obtain the cessation of death....

173. If [retribution falls] not on [the offender], it falls on his sons, and if not on the sons, on his grandsons; but an iniquity once committed never fails to produce consequences for one who incurs it.

174. One prospers for a while through unrighteousness, then one gains great good fortune; next one conquers one's enemies, but [in the end] one perishes to the root....

240. Every being is born alone, and alone it dies; it enjoys its virtue alone, and suffers from its sins....

1.31. For the sake of the prosperity of the worlds, He [Brahmā] caused the brahmin, the *kṣatriya*, the *vaiśya*, and the *śūdra* to proceed from His mouth, his arms, His thighs, and His feet....

87. But in order to protect this universe He, the most glorious one, assigned separate occupations to those who came from his mouth, arms, thighs, and feet....

10.1. The three twice-born social classes, performing their dharma, study [the Vedas]; but among them the brahmin will teach it, and not the other two; this is an established rule....

3. On account of his pre-eminence, on account of the superiority of his origin, on account of his observance of restrictive rules, and on account of his particular sanctification, the brahmin is the lord of the social orders.

4. The brahmin, the *kṣatriya*, and the *vaiśya* classes are the twice-born ones, but the fourth, the *śūdra*, has only one birth; there is no fifth (class).

5. In all social classes only children are conceived in the direct order with wedded wives, equal [in social class] and virgins, are regarded as belonging to the same social class [as their fathers]....

45. All this world's clans, those not included among people born from the mouth, the arms, the thighs, and the feet [of Brahmā] are called Dasyus ["slaves"], whether they speak the language of the barbarians *(mleccha)* or that of the Āryans....

Source: The Manu-smṛti, The Laws of Manu, chs. 4, 12, 10; tr. JP.

The Four Stages of Life

6.87. The four respective stages of life—student, householder, forest-dweller, and world renouncer—all depend on the householder.

88. When pursued in the proper order as described in the scriptures, they bring a brahmin who acts in the prescribed manner to the supreme goal.

89. But among all of them, the Vedas and traditional texts declare that the householder is preeminent because he supports the other three....

2.36. In the eighth year after conception, one should perform the initiation *(upanayana)* of a brahmin, in the eleventh year after conception that of a *kṣatriya*, and in the twelfth that of a *vaiśya*....

69. Having performed the initiation, the teacher must first instruct the pupil in personal purification, conduct, the fire sacrifice, and the dawn and dusk rituals....

176. Every day, having bathed and purified himself, the student must make offerings of water to the gods and ancestors, worship the gods, and place firewood [on the sacred fire].

177. He should abstain from honey, meat, perfumes, garlands, spicy food, women, food that has soured, and injuring living creatures,...

179. From gambling, gossip, backbiting, lying, looking at and touching women, and hurting others.

180. He should always sleep alone and never ejaculate his semen, because one who voluntarily ejaculates his semen violates his vows. If a brahmin student voluntarily ejaculates his semen while asleep, he should bathe, worship the sun, and softly chant three times: "May my vital energy return to me."...

199. Even if he is out of the teacher's sight, he should not just refer to him by his name [without an honorific] or make fun of how he walks, his speech, or his mannerisms.

200. When one's teacher is slandered or insulted, one should cover one's ears or go somewhere else.

201. By slandering one's teacher, even justifiably, one will become a donkey; by denigrating him, a dog; by living off him, a worm; and by envying him, an insect....

3.1. One must maintain the observance of Vedic study for thirty-six years in the teacher's house, or for half of that time, or one-quarter, or until one has learned them.

3.2. After one has learned the three Vedas in the proper order—or two, or even only one—without breaking the rules of celibate studentship, one should pursue the householder's way of life....

4. After performing the concluding bath and receiving one's teacher's permission, having performed the ceremony of returning to the home life in accordance with the rules, a twice-born man should marry a woman of the same social class who has the correct physical characteristics....

75. He should assiduously apply himself to his daily vedic recitations and to making offerings to the gods, because by making offerings to the gods, he upholds this world, both the movable and immovable parts. . . .

78. Because it is the householders who support people in the other stages of life every day through donating knowledge and food, the householder is the preeminent stage. . . .

4.2. Except during times of adversity, a brahmin should sustain himself by pursuing a livelihood that causes little or no harm to others.

3. He should accumulate wealth that is barely sufficient for subsistence by means of blameless occupations that are appropriate to his [social class and stage of life], without fatiguing his body. . . .

11. He should never follow a worldly occupation for the sake of mere subsistence; rather, he should pursue the pure, upright, and honest livelihood of a brahmin.

Source: The *Manu-smṛti,* The Laws of Manu, chs. 6, 7, 3, 4; tr. JP.

Leaving Home Life

6.1. A twice-born *snātaka* [a brahmin who has finished his studentship and taken a ceremonial bath], who has thus lived according to the rules in the order of householders, may go into the forest after adopting a firm resolution and controlling his organs.

2. When a householder sees his skin wrinkled and his hair turned grey, and the sons of his sons, then he should go into the forest.

3. Renouncing cultivated food and all of his belongings, he should go into the forest after entrusting his wife to his sons or accompanied by her. . . .

8. He should always be diligent in his vedic recitations, remain patient during times of difficulty, be friendly and mentally collected, always a giver rather than receiver of gifts, and compassionate toward all living creatures. . . .

25. After depositing his sacred fires in his body according to the rules, he should become a sage without a fire or a house, subsisting on roots and fruit,

26. Making no effort to obtain pleasurable things, celibate, sleeping on the ground, not caring about any shelter, living at the foot of a tree. . . .

33. After passing the third part of his life in the forest, he should abandon all attachment and wander as an ascetic during the fourth part.

34. A man who passes from life stage to life stage goes forth as an ascetic, who has offered sacrifices, controlled his senses, and become weary of giving alms and offerings of food, will attain benefit after death. . . .

36. Only after he has studied the Vedas in accordance with the rules, fathered sons in accordance with dharma, and offered sacrifices according to his ability should a man direct his mind toward renunciation.

37. If a twice-born man seeks renunciation without first studying the Vedas, without fathering sons, and without offering sacrifices, he will sink downward.

38. Only after he has performed the Iṣṭi ceremony,[12] which is sacred to Prajāpati, in which he gives away all of his possessions as a sacrificial gift, after depositing the sacred fires within himself,[13] may a brahmin go forth from his home as an ascetic. . . .

41. After leaving his home with a cloth for straining water, the silent sage should wander about, indifferent to sensual pleasures that are offered to him. . . .

45. He should not seek death or life, but simply wait for his time, as a servant waits for his wages. . . .

49. Delighting in what pertains to the Self, he should remain seated [in meditation] without belongings or sensual attachments; with himself as his only companion, he should walk about in this world, seeking bliss. . . .

65. By means of yogic meditation, he should reflect on the subtle nature of the supreme Self and how it is present in the highest and lowest organisms. . . .

85. If he follows this sequence of practices, a twice-born man becomes freed from his sins in his world and attains the highest Brahman.

Source: The *Manu-smṛti,* The Laws of Manu, ch. 6; tr. JP.

---

[12] A sacrifice in which one gives up all one's possessions.

[13] Taking the sacred fires into oneself is a ritual indicating that one has cut one's ties to the world. One of the core duties of householders is keeping a fire burning in the house as a constant offering to Agni. This serves to preserve cosmic order through sustaining the gods. This is one of the reasons why householders were seen as the foundation of traditional Hindu society. When their duties have been fulfilled, they symbolically sever their connections to the world in a ceremony in which the fire is taken inside. From this point on, their digestive processes are associated with the fire. This ceremony also frees them from all caste restrictions. The renunciant becomes a wandering mendicant, and due to renunciation of caste status, can no longer be polluted by any offering, even if he was formerly a brahmin and he now receives food from a *śūdra*.

Duties of the Four Social Classes

i. The Brahmin

10.74. Brahmins who are established in the brahmin work specific to them should live by these six occupations in order:

75. Teaching, studying, sacrificing and officiating at sacrifices, making gifts and receiving them are the six acts of a highest-born person. . . .

79. The prescribed livelihood of *kṣatriyas* is use of weapons; for *vaiśyas*, it is trading, animal husbandry, and agriculture. But their dharma is giving gifts, vedic study, and performance of sacrifices.

80. Among the specific occupations of each of them, the most recommended are: studying the Vedas for a brahmin; protecting the people for a *kṣatriya*; and only trade for a *vaiśya*.

81. But if a brahmin is unable to support himself by his specific occupations, he may live by means of the *kṣatriya* dharma, because the latter is just below him in rank.

82. One might ask: "What if he cannot earn a living by either of these two means?" He should earn a living by taking up the occupations of a *vaiśya*: agriculture or raising cattle.

83. But a brahmin or a *kṣatriya* who earns a living by a *vaiśya* occupation should avoid agriculture if at all possible, because it injures many beings and involves dependence on others. . . .

92. By selling meat, lac, or salt, a brahmin immediately loses his caste status; by selling milk, he become equal to a *śūdra* in three days.

93. But by intentionally selling other goods, a brahmin is reduced to the rank of a *vaiśya* in seven days. . . .

95. A *kṣatriya* who has fallen on hard times may subsist by all of the above occupations; but under no circumstances should he even consider adopting the lifestyle of his betters . . .

102. A brahmin who has fallen on hard times may accept gifts from anyone; according to the dharma, it is not possible for something pure to be polluted.

ii. The Kṣatriya

7.18. Only punishment disciplines all the people; punishment protects them and watches over them as they sleep; the wise proclaim that punishment is dharma.

19. When it is applied carefully after careful deliberation, it makes all people happy; but when it is inflicted without careful deliberation, it causes utter chaos.
20. If the king does not tirelessly inflict punishment on those who deserve to be punished, the stronger will roast the weaker like fish on a spit . . . .
22. The whole world is maintained by punishment, because an honest man is hard to find; through fear of punishment, the whole world provides enjoyments. . . .
87. When a king protects his people when challenged by enemies—whether they are stronger, weaker, or equal in strength—he must never back down from a battle, mindful of the dharma of *kṣatriyas*.
88. The surest way for kings to gain happiness is by never turning back in battle, protecting the people, and serving brahmins.
89. When kings fight each other in battles, seeking to kill each other with all their might and refusing to turn back, they go to heaven. . . .
144. For a *kṣatriya*, protecting the people is the supreme dharma; the king who enjoys such rewards is required to perform that dharma . . . .
198. He should first try to conquer his enemies through negotiation, gifts, and fomenting dissention, using these either conjointly or separately, but never through war [if possible].
199. For victory and defeat in battle are uncertain for the two combatants; therefore, he should avoid war.

iii. The Vaiśya

9.326. After a *vaiśya* has undergone a consecrating initiation and married, he should always apply himself to trade and looking after domestic animals.
327. For after Prajāpati created them, he gave them to the *vaiśyas*; and to the brahmins and kings he entrusted all creatures.
328. A *vaiśya* should never wish: "I don't want to keep domestic animals." And if here is a *vaiśya* who is willing to keep them, they must never be kept by anyone else.
329. He should be familiar with the relative values of gems, pearls, coral, metals, threads, perfumes, and spices.
330. He should have expertise regarding seeds and the good and bad qualities of fields, as well as all weights and measures. . . .
333. He should exert himself to the utmost so as to increase his property in accordance with dharma and diligently give food to all creatures.

iv. The Śūdra

9.334. The supreme dharma for a *śūdra* is obediently serving distinguished brahmins who are learned in the Vedas and are householders; this leads to heaven.

   335. If he keeps himself pure and obediently serves his betters, is soft-spoken and humble, and if he always seeks refuge in brahmins, he will attain a higher rebirth....

8.413. Whether or not he has been bought, a brahmin may compel a *śūdra* to perform slave labor; for he was created by the Self-Existent only to be a slave to brahmins.

   414. Even if he has been freed by his master, a *śūdra* is not released from his slave status; since it is innate in him, who can release him from it?...

10.128. A *śūdra* prospers in this world and the next and deserves no disdain to the extent to which he imitates the behavior of the virtuous without envy.

Source: The *Manu-smṛti,* The Laws of Manu, chs. 4, 7, 9, 8, 10; tr. JP.

How Women Should Live

3.55. Fathers, brothers, husbands, and brothers-in-law who wish good fortune should honor and adorn their women.

  56. Where women are honored, there the gods rejoice; but where they are not, no ritual brings rewards.

  57. Where female relatives live in distress, that family soon comes to ruin; but where they are not unhappy, that family always prospers.

  58. When female relatives who do not receive their proper respect pronounce a curse on a house, it will be completely ruined, as if destroyed by magic.

  59. So if men wish to prosper, they should always honor women on festive occasions with gifts of jewelry, clothes, and food.

  60. Lasting happiness will surely come to a family when the husband is pleased with his wife and the wife with her husband....

  67. The marriage ceremony is declared to be the initiation ceremony for women; serving her husband is her residence with a teacher; and household duties are her worship of the sacred fires....

5.147. Even in her own home, a female—whether she is a girl, a young woman, or an old woman—should never do anything independently.

  148. While she is a child, she must remain subject to her father, under her husband's control as a young woman,

and when her lord is dead, under her sons'; a woman must never try to live independently....

150. She must always be cheerful, skillful in housework, careful in cleaning the utensils, and frugal in expenditures.

151. For as long as he lives, she should obey the man to whom her father gives her—or her brother with her father's permission—and she should not be unfaithful to him after he dies...

154. Even if he is devoid of virtue or cheats on her, or is totally lacking in good qualities, a good woman always worships her husband as a god.

155. There is no independent sacrifice, vow, or fast for women; she will be exalted in heaven just for obediently serving her husband.

156. A good woman who wishes to go to the same world as her [deceased] husband should never do anything that might displease the one who took her hand, whether he is alive or dead.

157. After her husband's death, she may voluntarily emaciate her body by eating pure flowers, roots, and fruit; but she must never even mention the name of another man....

160. Just like celibate men, a virtuous woman, even if she has no sons, will go to heaven if she constantly maintains chastity after her husband's death....

164. A woman is disgraced in this world by cheating on her husband; she will be reborn in a jackal's womb and will be afflicted by nasty diseases.

165. A woman who controls her thoughts, words, and body and never cheats on her husband will live with her husband [after death], and virtuous people refer to her as "a good woman."...

167. When a wife who has conducted herself in this way and is of the same social class as her husband dies before him, a twice-born man who knows dharma should cremate her with the sacred fires and the ritual implements.

168. After he has given the sacred fires to his wife who died before him at her funeral, he should marry again and rekindle his sacred fires.

Source: The *Manu-smṛti,* The Laws of Manu, chs. 3, 5; tr. JP.

MANU'S INSTRUCTIONS ON FINDING THE RIGHT MATE

Marriage is a matter of great concern in classical Hindu texts because stable marriages are thought to be essential to the proper ordering of society. According to Manu, marriage should

occur only within one's caste, and he provides a number of other
criteria for men to consider when looking for a wife.

4. After he has taken the final bath and performed the ritual of return to home life with his teacher's permission
   in accordance with the rules, a twice-born man should
   marry a wife of the same social class who has the proper
   bodily characteristics.
5. A woman of different ancestry from his mother's and a
   lineage different from his father's and is related to him
   by marriage is regarded as appropriate for marriage for
   a twice-born man.
6. When contracting a marriage, he should avoid the following ten types of families, even if they are prominent and
   wealthy with many cows, goats, sheep, money, and grain:
7. Families that neglect rituals, those with few males, who
   lack Vedic learning, who have hairy bodies, or families
   with a tendency toward hemorrhoids, tuberculosis, dys-
   pepsia, epilepsy, white leprosy, or black leprosy.
8. He must not marry a girl who has red hair or an extra
   limb, who has poor health, who is bald or has too much
   bodily hair, who chatters too much or is jaundiced;
9. Nor one who is named after a constellation, a tree, or a
   river, who has a low caste name, or who is named after a
   mountain, a bird, a snake, or a slave, or who has a frightening name.
10. He should marry a woman whose limbs have no defects,
    who has a pleasant name, who walks like a swan or an
    elephant, who has a good body, a good head of hair,
    small teeth, and delicate limbs.
11. A wise man should not marry a woman who has no
    brother or whose father is unknown, out of concern for
    the dharma of daughters' sons.
12. For his first marriage, a woman of equal social class is
    recommended for twice-born men; but for those who
    due to desire move on [to another woman], these are, in
    order, the preferable women:
13. A *śūdra* man may only take a *śūdra* woman as is wife;
    the latter and a woman of his own social class can be the
    wife of a *vaiśya*; the latter two and a woman of his own
    social class can be the wife of a *kṣatriya*; and for a brah-
    min, the latter three and a woman of his social class.
14. A *śūdra* woman is not mentioned in a single scriptural
    account as a [first] wife for a brahmin, a *kṣatriya*, or a
    vaiśya, even in a time of distress.

15. When twice-born men are deluded enough to marry low-caste wives, they soon reduce their families, even their children, to the level of *śūdras*. . . .

17. A brahmin who sleeps with a *śūdra* woman goes to hell; if he produces a son by her, he loses his brahmin status.

18. The ancestors and gods will not eat the offering rituals for the gods, ancestors, or guests performed with her primary assistance, and he will not go to heaven.

19. No expiation is provided for a man who drinks the saliva from a *śūdra* woman's lips, who is polluted by her breath, or who fathers a son by her.

20. Now listen to a brief account of these eight marriage rituals for the four social classes; some are beneficial now and after death, while others are not.

21. They are: the Brāhma, the divine, the seers', the Prājāpatyas', the *asuras'*, the *gandharvas'*, the *rakṣasas'*, and the *piśācas'*, the eighth and worst.[14]

22. I will now explain to you which of them is the dharma for each social class and the merits and demerits of each with regard to offspring.

23. You should know that the first six in the order listed are lawful for a brahmin, the last four for a *kṣatriya*, and except for the *rākṣasa* marriage those four are lawful for a *vaiśya* and a *śūdra*. . . .

27. When a man dresses his daughter in fine clothes, adorns her, and gives her to a man who is learned in the Vedas and of good conduct, who is invited by her father, that marriage is known as following the dharma of a Brāhma marriage.

28. When a man adorns his daughter and gives her to the officiating priest during the course of a properly performed sacrifice, this is said to be the dharma of the gods.

29. When he gives away his daughter according to rule after receiving from the bridegroom a bull and a cow, or two pairs of them, this is said to be the dharma of the seers. . . .

---

[14] These all refer to classes of mythological beings. Brahmā is the creator god and custodian of the sacred Vedas. The second type of marriage, the divine (*daiva*), refers to the *devas*, the gods described in the Vedas. The seers (*ṛṣi*) are the ancient revealers of the Vedas. Prajāpati ("Lord of Beings") refers to a group of deities who preside over procreation and protection of life. *Asuras* are the enemies of the *devas*; some are benevolent, while others have evil intentions. *Gandharvas* are the musicians of the gods and guardians of the *soma*. *Rakṣasas* are demons who feast on human flesh; they were created from Brahmā's breath. *Piśācas* are flesh-eating ghouls. They have dark skin, bulging veins, and red eyes, and they haunt cremation grounds.

31. When (the bridegroom) receives a woman after giving as much wealth as he can afford and of his own free will, this is called the *asura* ritual.
32. When a woman and a man have consensual sex as a result of their desire, that ritual is called a *gandharva* marriage.
33. When a man forcibly abducts a woman from her house as she is screaming and crying, after he has killed or wounded [her family] after breaking into their house, this is called the *rākṣasa* ritual.
34. The eighth, the most evil, is the ritual of the *piśakas*, when a man secretly rapes a woman who is asleep, drunk, or mentally deranged. . . .
45. A man should have sex with his wife during her fertile period and should be constantly satisfied by her [alone]. He may also approach her when he desires sexual pleasure, except on the days of the changing moon. According to tradition, the natural season of women is sixteen days and four nights [in each month]. . . .
48. On the even nights, sons are conceived, and daughters on the uneven ones. Therefore, a man who wants sons should have sex with his wife on even nights during her fertile season.[15]
49. When the man's seed is stronger, a male child is born, and when the woman's is stronger, a female child; if both are equal, a hermaphrodite or a twin boy and girl. If both are weak and of low quantity, there will be a failure of conception.
50. Regardless of his order of life, if a man avoids women during the forbidden nights and during the other eight nights, he will be a true celibate.

Source: *Manu-smṛti,* The Laws of Manu, ch. 3; tr. JP, from *Textual Sources for the Study of Hinduism,* pp. 101–103.

---

[15] According to Indian medical literature, a woman is most fertile immediately after her menstrual period.

Jainism

INTRODUCTION

The contemporary Jaina tradition can be traced back to Vardhamāna Jñatṛputra, an ascetic who was born in the northern part of modern-day Bihar in northern India in the sixth century BCE. This was also the area in which the Buddha lived, and the two religious leaders were said to have been familiar with each other's reputations and teachings. Both traditions rejected key elements of the dominant brahmanical system, including the sacrifices enjoined by the Vedas and the caste system, and both emphasized the goal of final liberation from cyclic existence, although they differed significantly in the paths they prescribed.

Jainism's founder, referred to by his followers as Mahāvīra ("Great Hero"), advocated a path of strict asceticism and non-injury (ahiṃsā) to all living things as the keys to liberation (mokṣa). By controlling desires, restraining the wandering of the senses, and limiting consumption to the minimum needed to sustain life, Mahāvīra eliminated all attachments to material enjoyments, wandered naked from place to place (symbolizing his dispassion toward mundane norms and possessions) and, through rigorous spiritual discipline, eventually overcame any possibility of return to cyclic existence. In recognition of his hard-won victory over the temptations of the world, his followers commonly refer to him as Jina, meaning "Victor." The term Jaina means "Followers of the Victor."

Mahāvīra did not claim to be a religious innovator or to have discovered a new path to salvation; rather, he asserted that he was one of a small elite who had discovered the way. According to Jaina tradition, he was the twenty-fourth Tīrthaṅkara, or "Ford-Maker," a name given by Jainas to the great ascetics who not only find the path to liberation but also show it to others.

The most distinctive features of Jainism are its extreme asceticism together with its emphasis on personal effort and its strict adherence to the doctrine of noninjury. The Jaina path to liberation involves renunciation of material things coupled with ascetic practices aimed at purifying the soul (jīva) by cleansing it of the karmic accretions that have colored it and bound it to matter (ajīva). In this process, one can depend only on oneself and one's own effort. In Jainism there is no creator

God and no higher power that can aid one in reaching salvation, which in Jainism is attained by first ridding oneself of all karma, both good and bad, and by then attaining "liberating wisdom" *(kevala-jñāna)*, which allows one to separate oneself from matter.

Jain metaphysics divides the universe into two main categories: *jīva* and *ajīva*. *Jīva* refers to the life principle that is found in all things, while *ajīva* is insentient matter, along with the categories of time and space. It is the main impediment to the release of individual *jīva*s. According to Jainism, all things, even material entities, have a life force. *Jīva* is an eternal substance that adjusts in size and shape to the physical body it inhabits. Matter is nonsentient, and because of its connection to the life force, living beings inevitably suffer because matter is prone to change and decay.

The *jīva*'s natural purview is universal—it is omniscient, but the senses place restrictions on it. To bring the soul to its natural omniscience, one needs to overcome the limitations imposed on it by matter, to let the soul perceive without the constraints caused by the senses, which serve as blinders for the naturally omniscient *jīva*. This leads to full and direct knowledge of all things in all aspects.

God is unnecessary in Jainism because the soul by itself is capable of knowing everything and accomplishing the highest goal of liberation. Furthermore, karma operates according to its own laws and does not require or permit the intervention of a higher power that can alleviate or erase its effects. Each being must suffer the results of his or her actions, and no god can change this. It is up to the individual to work out his or her own salvation. Lay Jains often worship gods, but they provide only mundane benefits; in the final analysis, they also are caught up in the cycle of existence.

In Jain metaphysics, the universe is filled with life. Everything possesses a soul, even plants and such apparently unliving things as stones, which are at such a low level of sentience and so oppressed by matter that they appear to be devoid of life. The soul is considered to be permeable, and all of one's actions lead to influxes of karma, which is seen as subtle matter that pervades the soul (as opposed to merely covering or obscuring it). Karmic matter varies in color in accordance with the relative goodness or evil of the act committed. For instance, killing a living being, even inadvertently, leads to an influx of very dark karma (this is why many Jaina monks wear masks over their noses and mouths and carry brooms to sweep in front of themselves—to avoid inadvertently killing living beings). Humans who engage in occupations that involve a great deal of killing, such as butchers, have jet black *jīva*s, which can be cleansed only through prodigious amounts of asceticism and physical mortification. Because of this, Jainas are strictly prohibited from engaging in occupations that involve the taking of life, which has kept them from being, for instance, hunters and fishermen.

Jainas also hold that each *jīva* has eternally been associated with *ajīva*, and there has never been a time when they were separated or a "fall" through which *jīva* became associated with *ajīva*. *Jīva*'s association with *ajīva* is beginningless, but it is possible to terminate it. In addition, there is no creator deity that made the world as it is. It has always been as it is and always will be, although it does go through cycles of relative degeneration and regeneration.

All actions lead to karmic influx, but evil actions color the *jīva* with very dark karma that is difficult to eliminate, while good or meritorious actions color the *jīva* with light karma that is easily cleansed. Elimination of karma occurs naturally, and in every moment beings are working off the effects of past actions. Most beings, however, are simultaneously creating new karma, so the process is self-perpetuating.

The only way to burn off more karma than one creates is to dedicate oneself to a program of asceticism and meditation. The karma accumulated in the *jīva* will burn off naturally, but this is a slow process. It can be aided through fasting, celibacy, and various types of ascetic practices aimed at developing *tapas* (literally, "heat," the energy one acquires through self-restraint and asceticism). *Tapas* may be used to burn off karma.

The first step of the Jaina path to liberation involves halting the influx of new karma *(saṃvara)*, followed by a program of cleansing the karma one has already acquired *(nirjarā)*. When this process is completed, one attains liberation *(mokṣa)*. Because of karma that has not yet been eradicated, one may still have a physical body, but this too will pass away when its past karma is exhausted. At this point, the soul is released from its bondage to matter and is luminous, omniscient, and completely free. It then rises toward the top of the universe (which in traditional Jaina cosmology is pictured as a giant human) and comes to rest at the base of the cranium of the universe in a realm called "World of Saints" *(siddha-loka)*, where it dwells forever with the other perfected beings, completely beyond any future suffering and eternally removed from the world. No outside force or power can aid the individual in this process. Only one's own effort can cleanse one's *jīva* of the effects of accumulated karma. Gods and other human beings are unable to help the individual because they are similarly enmeshed in the process. Even the Tīrthaṅkaras cannot help (beyond providing instruction and guidance during their lifetimes) because their liberation has removed them from any concern with the world and they are thus beyond the reach of prayers and supplications.

Liberation is possible only in the realm in which humans live, which is said to be a small disk in the middle of the universe. Below this realm are various painful destinies, such as hells, and above it are the realms of demigods and gods. Humans are in a position superior to that of the gods, who live a long and blissful existence and thus are unaware that when their good karma is exhausted they will inevitably sink back to the lower levels of rebirth.

Jaina Scriptures

Jainism today has two main sects: the Digambaras ("Sky Clad") and the Śvetāmbaras ("White Clad"). The former group believes that liberation requires renunciation of all possessions, including clothes. Digambara monks, following Mahāvīra's example, are expected to be completely naked; their only permitted possession is a small broom used to whisk away insects before they sit or lie down.

The Śvetāmbaras agree that Mahāvīra wore no clothes but assert that the present time is one of degeneration, so nudity is inappropriate today. Their monks and nuns wear simple white robes, a practice denounced by Digambaras as indicating that they have attachments to worldly things. Digambaras hold that, as a result, Śvetāmbara monastics actually are no more advanced spiritually than laypeople who follow the Jaina precepts.

These differences in monastic discipline parallel the divergences in their respective scriptural traditions. Each school has its own canon and for the most part does not accept the authority of the other's scriptures (although the doctrinal contents of their texts generally are in accord). One reason for the disagreement is the fact that the first Jaina synod was held about two centuries after Mahāvīra's death. The canon that resulted from this forms the core of the Digambara canon, but because it was held well after the death of the founder many texts had become lost or forgotten, and there were differing recensions of many works. In the fifth century, the Śvetāmbaras held a council that resulted in their authoritative texts being written down and distributed to the Jaina community.

The oldest texts of the Jaina canon were written in Prakrits, languages that were related to Sanskrit but that contained numerous grammatical forms and vocabulary from local dialects. In later times Jaina writers began composing texts in local vernaculars, and sometimes in Sanskrit. The most widely accepted scriptures are named "Early Texts" (*Pūrva*), but these are no longer extant. Jaina scholars contend that elements of these texts are incorporated into the present canons. The Digambaras, for example, contend that one of the branches of their canon, the twelfth "Limb" (Aṅga), contains portions of the Early Texts.

The Śvetāmbara canon is referred to as "Tradition" (*Āgama*), or "Doctrine" (Siddhānta), and contains forty-five texts arranged into six divisions: (1) the Limbs; (2) Sub-Limbs (Upāṅga); (3) Miscellaneous Texts (Prakīrṇaka); (4) Treatises on Cutting (Chedasūtra), which mostly focus on matters of discipline; (5) Appendices (Cūlikāsūtras); and (6) Basic Texts (Mūlasūtras). This canon contains a variety of texts of different ages and in different languages, and some texts contain material in different dialects.

The primary texts for Digambaras are scholastic works written by authors who lived around the first century CE. The most important of these are Vaṭṭakera, author of the *Basic Conduct (Mūlācāra)*; Kundakunda, author of the *Essence of Doctrine (Samayasāra)*; and Śivārya, who wrote the *Accomplishment (Ārādhanā)*. Both Digambaras and Śvetāmbaras accept the authority of the *Treatise on Attaining the Meaning of the Principles (Tattvārthādhigama Sūtra)*, a text that summarizes the key points of Jaina doctrine in 350 stanzas. In addition, both schools have extensive collections of didactic and expository works called Supplements (Anuyoga), which cover a wide range of subjects, including rules for right living and dialectical debate, poetry, uplifting stories, and hymns.

The following passages are drawn from texts of the two main sects of Jainism and touch on most of the important themes of Jaina religious practice and the path to liberation. They stress on the total responsibility of the individual for his or her own actions and indicate that salvation is won or lost by oneself alone. The Jaina path begins with renunciation of worldly things, conjoined with avoidance of any action that injures another living being. These practices are also linked to yogic meditation, which allows one to discipline the senses and emotions and to eliminate desire. They also allow one to generate *tapas*, a spiritual energy that can burn up karma and thereby cleanse the *jīva*.

HOLIDAYS

Festival of Lights (Dīvālī) Celebrated during the lunar month of Aso (September–October), two weeks after the autumn Fasting Ceremony. As in Hinduism, offerings are made to the goddess Lakṣmī, who is associated with good fortune. Some Jains believe that Mahāvīra attained final liberation on this day.

Birth of Mahāvīra (Mahāvīr Jayantī) A national holiday in India that is celebrated during the lunar month of Caitra (March–April).

Fasting Ceremony (Olī) Celebrated by Śvetāmbaras during the lunar months of Caitra (March–April) and Aso (September–October). A nine-day festival devoted to worship and meditation.

Abiding Festival (Paryuṣaṇ) Celebrated during the lunar month of Śrāvan (July–August). A religious festival in which monastics remain in one place for the duration and deliver sermons. Many laypeople fast, often for several days.

TIMELINE

599–527 BCE	Life of Mahāvīra
78 BCE	Schism of Digambara and Śvetāmbara Jains
200–400 CE	Life of Kundakunda, Digambara philosopher
454	Council of Valabhī: writing of Jain canon
800	Massacre of Jains at Madurai
12th century	Hemacandra, a Śvetāmbara monk, becomes tutor of king Siddharāja
1451	Loṅka Śāh initiates Jain schism, creating Loṅkā Gacch
1760	Terāpanthī Gacch splits off from Sthānakvāsīs
21st century	Revival of ascetic paradigm and development of mystical sects; Jain immigration to East Africa, Britain, North America

GLOSSARY

Ajīva Lifeless, insentient matter.

Digambara "Sky-Clad," one of the two sects of contemporary Jainism, whose monks abjure the wearing of clothes.

Jaina "Follower of the Conqueror (Mahāvīra)."

Jina "Victor," an epithet of Mahāvīra, symbolizing his victory over ignorance.

Jīva "Soul," the life force that inheres in all beings.

Karma "Actions," which bring about concordant results.

Kevala-jñāna "Liberating Wisdom," which breaks the bonds of ignorance and leads to release from the cycle of birth, death, and rebirth.

Mahāvīra "Great Hero," title of the founder of Jainism.

Mokṣa "Release" from the cycle of birth, death, and rebirth.

Saṃsāra "Cyclic Existence," the beginningless cycle of birth, death, and rebirth in which ignorant beings are trapped.

Siddha-loka Supramundane realm in which liberated souls reside.

Śvetāmbara "White-Clad," one of the two sects of contemporary Jainism, whose monks and nuns wear simple white robes.

Tapas "Heat," the energy generated by ascetic practices, which burns up accumulated karma.

Tīrthaṅkara "Ford Maker," an epithet of Mahāvīra and his legendary predecessors, who are said to have found the path to liberation and taught it to others.

JAINA SCRIPTURES

MAHĀVĪRA, THE ASCETIC PARADIGM

Jaina scriptures contain a number of descriptions of the life and liberation of Mahāvīra. These emphasize his extreme asceticism, his self-control, his unshakable patience and equanimity, and his final victory. Due to his years of fighting the desires of the flesh, he gradually weaned himself of all physical desires and separated his spiritual essence from the bonds of material existence.

Even in places crowded with ordinary people, Mahāvīra remained in profound concentration. When people spoke to him, he would not answer, but would quietly move away. In all situations he remained undisturbed.... He did not pay any attention to harsh words or vicious insults, but remained immersed in religious pursuits. He had no interest in stories, plays, songs, fights, or other entertainments.... He did not do any harm to any living beings, nor did he cause others to do so. . . .

He did not own any clothes, nor did he accept any from anyone else. . . . He knew exactly how much food and drink was needed [to sustain life], and he had no interest in delicious food. He did not even care what sort of food [he ate]. He did not even wipe his eyes, nor did he scratch his body when it itched. When he walked, he moved in silence, not looking to the side, nor backwards. He only spoke when spoken to, and even then only very little. Always fully aware of the dangers of harming living beings, his gaze was fixed on the path ahead of him.

He had forsworn the use of clothing, and in winter would walk with his hands outspread, rather than [warming himself by] folding his arms under his shoulders. . . . He endured many terrible hardships when he stopped. He might be bitten by a snake, a mongoose, or a dog; he was sometimes attacked by ants who made his flesh bleed, and he was often tormented by flies, mosquitoes, bees, and wasps. . . . Mahāvīra endured all of the many hardships and difficulties caused by humans and other beings. . . .

Even in times of bitter cold, he did not even consider [finding shelter], but would stand near a shed and bear the cold with equanimity. When the night grew cold, he would go outside for a while, and in this way he endured the torments of cold with perfect calm and correct conduct. . . . Indifferent to all sensual delights, he cheerfully wandered from place to place, speaking very little. In the winter he would meditate in the shade, and in summer he would expose himself to the blazing heat of the sun. . . . Thoroughly purifying himself, disciplining his mind, body, and speech, Mahāvīra became completely calm and equanimous. During the time [he practiced meditation], he remained in perfect equipoise and peace.

Source: *Ācārāṅga-sūtra* and *Kalpa-sūtra* selections. Tr. JP.

WOMEN CANNOT ATTAIN LIBERATION

Digambara and Śvetāmbara texts disagree on the spiritual aptitude of women. The Digambaras contend that women should not be permitted to go without clothing and that, since nudity is a precondition for liberation, women are unable to attain the supreme religious goal. A woman's best hope is to follow the precepts and work toward a future rebirth as a man.

The Śvetāmbaras reject this idea and assert that women are able to attain liberation. Nudity, while commendable during

Mahāvīra's time, is inappropriate today, and the wearing of simple clothes is no hindrance to liberation. Interestingly, both sects agree on the point that women should not be permitted to renounce clothing because a woman's body is inherently sexual, and a naked woman would attract unwanted sexual desire.

The following passage is perhaps the earliest example of the Digambara doctrine that women are unable to attain liberation because of their gender. They cannot renounce clothing, they are fickle and emotional, their bodies are breeding grounds for small organisms, and their bodily processes lead to the destruction of these creatures—a violation of the dictates of noninjury.

10. [Going] without clothes and [using] the hands as a bowl for receiving alms[1] have been taught by the supreme lords of the Jinas [as] the sole path to liberation *(mokṣa)*; all other [ways of mendicant behavior] are not [valid] paths....

19. [Worldly behavior,] the outward sign of which is the accepting of possessions—be they small or great—is condemned in the teaching of the Jinas; [only] one without possessions is free from household life.

20. One endowed with the five great vows *(mahāvrata)*[2] and the three protections *(gupti)*[3] is restrained [i.e., is a mendicant]. He [alone] is on the path to liberation free from bonds and is worthy of praise.

21. The second outward sign is said to be that of the higher and lower "listeners" [i.e., lay people: the lower, holding] the bowl, wanders for alms silently, with well-controlled movement and speech.

22. The [third] outward sign is that of women: a nun eats food only once per day and wears one piece of cloth [while a female novice who wears two pieces of clothing] eats wearing [only] one.

23. In the teaching of the Jina no person who wears clothes attains [liberation], even if he is a Tīrthaṅkara. The path to liberation is that of nakedness, and all other [paths] are wrong paths.

24. It is taught [in the scriptures] that in the genital organs of women, in the area between their breasts, and in their

---

[1] This means that, like Mahāvīra, monks are not to own bowls for begging food, as other mendicant orders do, but should simply use their cupped hands.

[2] These are vows to observe noninjury, to avoid lying, stealing, sexual intercourse, and owning possessions.

[3] These are practices involved in guarding the three doors of action: body, speech, and mind.

navels and armpits are extremely small living beings, so
how can women be ordained [since their bodies make
them unable to keep the first vow of nonviolence]?

25. If there is purity because of right-view, then she too is
said to be associated with the path. [However, even if]
she has practiced severe [ascetic] practices, it is said in
the teaching that there is no ordination for women.

26. Women do not have purity of mind, and by nature their
minds are slack, women get their period each month,
[and therefore] they have no meditation free from
anxiety.

Source: Kundakunda, *Sūtraprabhṛta;* Tr. Royce Wiles.

WOMEN CAN ATTAIN LIBERATION

2. There is liberation for women, because women possess
all the causes [necessary for liberation]. The cause of
liberation is fulfillment of the three jewels *(ratna-traya),*
and this is not incompatible [with womanhood].

[Commentary:] The cause of liberation from the sickness of cyclic existence is the non-deficiency of the [three
jewels:] correct view, knowledge, and conduct. There is
liberation from cyclic existence for those who perfect
them. Furthermore, because women do not lack the
causes of nirvana, it is not reasonable [to assert] that any
of the three jewels are incompatible with womanhood,
and so it is not the case that there is no liberation for
women....

4. Nuns are able to understand the Jina's words, have faith
in them, and practice them faultlessly.

[Commentary:] Correct knowledge is the proper
understanding of the Jina's words. Correct view is faith
in [the Jina's words].... Correct conduct involves applying them appropriately. And this is just what the three
jewels are said to be. Release [from cyclic existence]
is characterized by complete freedom from all karmas,
[which occurs when the three jewels] are perfected....
All of these are found in women.

[A Digambara opponent] might assert that women
cannot attain release because they have clothes. People
like householders, who are bound by possessions, cannot
attain release. If it were not the case [that people who
own clothes have possessions], then even male [monks]
could wear clothes, and renouncing them would be irrelevant [to the attainment of release]....

If [as the opponent claims] liberation cannot be attained by those who [wear] clothes, and if one could attain liberation by renouncing them, then certainly it would be acceptable for [women] to renounce [clothing]. Clothes are not necessary for life, and since even life itself may be abandoned [in order to attain liberation], then it goes without saying that [one may renounce] mere clothes! If release were attained simply due to the absence of those [clothes], then what fool seeking release would lose it just through wearing clothes?

The Lord Arhats, the guides for the path to release, taught that women must wear clothes and prohibited them from renouncing clothes, and so it follows that clothes are necessary for release, like a whisk broom [that is used to sweep away small creatures].... If women were to give up clothing, this would result in their abandoning the whole corpus of monastic rules. As is well known, women are overpowered by [men who] are excited due to seeing their naked bodies and limbs, in the same way that mares—who naturally have clothing—are overpowered by stallions.... Furthermore, women from good families are naturally very shy, and if they [were required to] abandon clothing [in order to become nuns], then they would refuse to do so.

Clothes are a possession, and so there is some demerit in wearing them, but still by this all of the monastic rules are maintained. Therefore, having ascertained that there is greater benefit and lesser demerit in wearing clothes, rather than renouncing them, the holy Arhats declared that nuns must wear clothes and prohibited them from abandoning them.

Source: *Strīnirvāṇa-pariccheda*; tr. Royce Wiles.

BONDAGE AND LIBERATION

This passage states some of the most important themes of Jaina philosophy and religious practice: the importance of overcoming desire for worldly things, the importance of noninjury, and the way negative actions result in negative consequences.

One should understand the causes of the soul's bondage [to cyclic existence], and through knowing them, one should overcome them....

A person who owns even a little property—of either living or nonliving things—or who acquiesces to others' owning it will not be released from suffering.

Those who kill living beings, or who cause others to kill them, or who consent to their being killed, will have increasing demerit.

A person who is emotionally attached to relatives or friends is a fool who will suffer greatly, because the numbers of those to whom one is attached always increase. Wealth and relatives cannot protect one [from suffering]. Only by understanding this and [the nature of] life will a person overcome karma.

Source: *Sūtrakṛtāṅga* 1.1.1. Tr. JP.

THE WORTHLESSNESS OF POSSESSIONS, FRIENDS, AND RELATIVES

This passage looks at what most people value—possessions, friends, family, and so on—and dismisses them as transitory things that ultimately lead to suffering. In addition, it warns people not to put off religious practice: The best time to begin is right now, because one's faculties will diminish as one grows older. Thus a wise person will recognize the tenuousness of the things of the world and renounce them in order to pursue a life of religious practice and asceticism, which alone can lead to salvation.

Oppressed by great suffering and deluded, worldly people think, "My mother, father, sister, wife, sons, daughters, daughters-in-law, friends, relatives, and associates, my things, transactions, food, and clothes [are all important]." Infatuated by strong attachments to these things, they are immersed in them.

They live constantly tormented by greed. In season and out of season, they strive [to amass wealth]; desiring money and fortune, they become thieves who rob and steal. Their minds are always engrossed [in accumulating wealth], and they repeatedly become killers.

In this world, some lives are short, and their hearing, sight, sense of smell, sense of touch, and tactile sense degenerate [and so they die young and unfulfilled]. Realizing that life is moving [toward its end, they become depressed]. Then eventually they are overcome by senility.

Then, at a certain time, the members of their families begin to grumble at them, and then they begin to grumble at their families. They will be unable to protect or give refuge [to their aging relative], and [the old person] will be unable to protect them or give them refuge. An old person is not fit for laughter, nor play, nor sexual intercourse, nor adornment. Thus, one should make effort to practice asceticism.

Having considered the opportunity [that the present life presents for those intent on liberation], the wise will not relax in their efforts, even for a short while. The years are passing by, and youth is fading away.

Source: *Ācārāṅgasūtra* 1.2.1–12. Tr. JP.

THE IMPORTANCE OF EQUANIMITY

In Jaina practice, asceticism serves to discipline body and mind and also is used to burn off one's karma. In Jainism, karma has a physical manifestation, so it is not enough simply to gain knowledge. A person must also perform physical austerities to eradicate the physical effects of karma. In practicing monastic discipline, self-control is important, and a monk should gain firm control over his emotions and never lose his temper. No matter what others do to him—whether they speak harshly to him, injure him, or disturb him—he should never become angry at them and should always maintain equanimity, because a moment of anger can destroy hard-won self-discipline and can lead to negative mental states and harmful actions.

If someone abuses a monk, he should not become angry. Losing one's temper is foolish, and so a monk does not become heated [with anger]. When a monk hears cruel and harsh words that prick his senses like thorns, he remains perfectly silent and does not take them to heart.

When he is beaten, he does not become angry, nor does he have malicious thoughts. Understanding that patience is the supreme good, a monk should meditate on dharma. If someone hurts a restrained and equanimous monk, he should think, "The soul (*jīva*) is eternal," and bear his torment with a smile. . . .

A monk should seek a bit of food after a householder has finished cooking but, whether or not he receives food, he does not care in either case, [thinking], "I received no food today, but tomorrow I may get some."

For a monk who thinks thus, success and failure are equal. Realizing that he has encountered suffering, if he is oppressed by pain, he should steady his mind cheerfully and bear all the ills that afflict him. . . . Though the monk is physically oppressed by sweat or dust, or the rays of the summer sun, he does not yearn for comfort. A monk who desires liberation bears [all this, practicing] the unsurpassed, noble dharma, bearing untold filth on his body until the body expires.

Source: *Uttarādhyayanasūtra* 2.24–37. Tr. JP.

THE WORLD IS FULL OF SUFFERING

This passage is spoken by a prince named Mṛgaputra to his parents. He wishes to convince them to allow him to renounce household life and become a monk. He tells them that because according to the Jaina doctrine of transmigration he has been reborn an infinite number of times, he has suffered excruciating torments in many lives. He recounts various painful types of physical suffering and death and concludes that he no longer wishes to be a part of the cycle of birth and death.

44. O mother and father... nothing in this world is difficult for one who is free from desire.
45. I have suffered horrible agonies of body and mind innumerable times, great pains and great fears.
46. In cyclic existence, a mine of dangers and a wilderness of old age and death, I have passed through horrible births and deaths.
47. Even though fire is hot here, it is infinitely worse there [in hell]; I have suffered from heat in hell. . . .
61. I have suffered helplessly an infinite number of times from mallets and knives, javelins and maces, which shattered my limbs.
62. With razors, sharp knives, and shears I have been cut, mangled, and skinned alive an infinite number of times.
63. As a deer, helpless, I have been caught in deep snares and traps, bound, held, and killed an infinite number of times.
64. As a fish, helpless, I have been caught with hooks and nets, and scraped, slit, and gutted an infinite number of times.
65. As a bird, I have been caught by hawks, trapped in nets, held in bird-lime, and killed an infinite number of times.
66. As a tree, I have been cut down, split, sawn into planks, and stripped of bark by carpenters with axes and hatchets an infinite number of times.
67. As iron, I have been malleated, cut, ripped apart, and filed by blacksmiths an infinite number of times.
68. I have been forced to drink hissing molten copper, iron, tin, and lead while screaming horribly an infinite number of times.
69. "I love meat!": speaking like this, they cut pieces of my own meat, roasted them on a stick, and made me eat it. . . .
71. Constantly frightened, trembling, anxious, and suffering, I have endured enormous pain and excruciating misery. . . .

74. In every type of existence I have endured suffering with-
    out reprieve, without any pleasant experiences. . . .
85. [His parents responded:] "Dear son, do as you wish."
86. After he had made his parents repeat their consent
    three times, like a snake that casts of its skin he forever
    renounced his claims to any property.
87. He went forth [from the home life] as if shaking off the
    dust from his feet, renouncing his power, wealth, friends,
    wives, sons, and relations.

Source: *Uttarādhyayanasūtra* chapter 19; tr. JP.

FASTING UNTO DEATH

*This passage speaks of the Jaina practice of itvara or sallekhanā,
in which an advanced practitioner may voluntarily starve to
death. This practice is said to eliminate large amounts of negative karma and may even lead to final liberation. According to
legend, Mahāvīra himself did this because he knew he would be
released at the end of his life, and the fast unto death would be
an effective means of eradicating the last subtle vestiges of his
karma. Generally, a monk will prepare for this practice through
a graduated program of fasting that may last for twelve years,
but if he is sick, he can begin the fast without this previous
training. In this passage, fasting to death is described as a difficult discipline, but the end reward is presented as a glorious
culmination of one's spiritual training.*

 If a monk thinks, "Illness is causing my body to wither,
and I am not able to perform my religious duties," he should
gradually reduce his diet, and through this reduction should
pare away his desires. . . . He should enter a village . . . and
beg for straw. After receiving it, he should retire into seclusion somewhere outside the village. After thoroughly examining and clearing the ground—where there are no eggs [of
insects], nor insects, nor seeds, nor sprouts, nor dew, nor
water, nor ants, nor mildew, nor marsh, nor cobwebs—he
should spread the straw on it. Then he should observe [the
religious fast until death] called *itvara*. . . .
 The *itvara* is proper. The monk, remaining true [to his
vows], devoid of desires, successfully crosses over the ocean
of cyclic existence, never doubting his ability to fulfill the
fast, happily accomplishing [his goal], unaffected by circumstances, understanding that the body is mortal, overcoming
various hardships and troubles, understanding that body and
soul are separate, accomplishing the formidable *(bhairava)*
task [of *itvara*]. This is not a miserable or untimely death.

It may even lead to attainment of final liberation. Such a death is a peaceful haven for all monks who are completely free from craving for life. It is beneficial and leads to happiness; it is proper, salutary, and meritorious.

Source: *Ācārāṅgasūtra* 1.7.105. Tr. JP.

THERE IS NO CREATOR GOD

This passage considers various arguments for the existence of a creator of the universe and rejects them all. This reflects a fundamental Jaina emphasis on the individual. There is no other power that is able to help one escape from cyclic existence—we are on our own, and every person's present position is the result of his or her own past actions. No outside power can change the results of one's karma, nor can anyone other than oneself affect one's salvation. The law of karma is absolute and operates according to its own precepts, and no deity can abrogate the workings of karma.

16. *Stupid people say there is some Creator of the universe; "creation-ism" (sṛṣṭi-vāda) will be examined in order to refute that wrong thinking.*
17. If the Creator is outside the creation, then when creating the universe where did he stand?; and if he had no support and is transcendent, after he had created the world, where did he put it?
18. No single, universal being would be able to put together this world; a being with no body giving rise to bodily forms etc., doesn't make sense.
19. How would he have created the world without other material means?; if the response is that he created those and then he created the world, that is an endless regression.
20. If those other material means arose in the world by themselves, this begs the question: why can't the universe successfully arise on its own, without a creator?
21. If an all-powerful creator created without material means, by willing it, who is going to believe that this is just "will?" That is nonsense.
22. If he is perfected, how would the desire to create ever be appropriate for him?; if he is not perfected, then he has no more power to create the universe than a potter.
23. Without form, not acting, pervading, how does such a one create the universe?; a being devoid of changes cannot even have a thought to create.

24. Moreover, what purpose is served by creating the world for one who has no aims and is not seeking the ends that humans seek, namely, things like religion, wealth, and desires?

25. If the creation is out of his own nature, completely without purpose, that doesn't make sense; if this is some game of his, it has a bad end and is linked to delusional thinking.

26. If he creates things like beings in accordance with their karma, then he is no "Lord"; like a weaver, dependent on others [for raw materials].

27. If the Lord is merely a "background" with regard to the action, caused by things like karma, then indeed it is established that you put forward a rather useless [creator].

28. One who cares about beings would create with a desire to show kindness and instead set up a creation filled with happiness, not one completely overwhelmed with affliction.

29. With regard to creation, if the world exists already, then the effort of creation is pointless; when something does not exist, like sky, flowers for example, creating that is not really appropriate.

30. One who is free and separate would not create; one who is involved in the creation wouldn't either. They are not a Lord [because they are part of a creation already]; so there is absolutely no way that this creationism could be plausible.

31. He would have great irreligiosity, creating beings and then destroying them; if the reason is to get rid of the evil ones, wouldn't it be better not to create them in the first place?

32. [If you say] things like the bodies [of living beings] have arisen because of some intelligent design, just as urban areas from a known specific founder, that is not a method that establishes the existence of a Lord; [they can] arise in other ways than because of specific founders.

33. In this world based on volition, linked to the karma of agents, the various types of happiness and unhappiness accord with the various sorts [of beings].

34. We declare that the diversity of things like the major and minor forms of living beings has arisen based on the skill of the [various] agents and their diverse karma.

35. So, due to that diversity of karma the universe is a multitude of kinds of beings; this establishes the driver of karma for the beings who create the universe.

36. Disposer *(vidhi)*, Creator *(sraṣṭr)*, Organizer *(vidhātr)*, Divinity *(daiva)*, First Cause *(karma purākrta)*, and Lord *(īśvara)* are regarded as synonyms [used by] worshippers of gods.
37. The educated need to correct the wrong-thinking and brain-addled creationists, because of their acceptance of things like space in the absence of any [perceivable] Creator.
38. Therefore, this world, like time itself, is uncreated, has no beginning or cessation, is manifest with a nature based on the constituents: things like the soul.
39. Not created, indestructible, continuing solely through dependence on itself; consisting of three parts, the lower [hell world], the middle, and the upper [heaven world].
40. They say that the three worlds are shaped respectively like a seat of tied rushes *(vetra-viṣṭa)*, a *jhallarya* drum or a *mṛdaṅga* drum.

Source: Jinasena, *Ādipurāṇa* 4.16-41; tr. Royce Wiles.

EXCERPTS FROM THE *SŪTRA* ON UNDERSTANDING THE MEANING OF THE CATEGORIES

This text is accepted as canonical by both Śvetāmbaras and Digambaras. It contains a concise overview of the primary categories of the Jaina philosophical system and a summary of the path to liberation.

1.1. Right belief, right knowledge, right conduct: these [together constitute] the path to liberation.
2. Belief or conviction in things ascertained as they are is right belief.
3. This is attained by insight or understanding.
4. The categories *(tattva)* are: (1) soul *(jīva)*; (2) non-soul *(ajīva)*; (3) inflow [of karmic matter into the soul: *āsrava*]; (4) bondage *(bandha)*; (5) stopping [inflow of karmic matter: *samvara*]; (6) elimination [of karmic matter: *nirjarā*]; and (7) liberation *(mokṣa)*. . . .
2.7. The soul's [essence] is life, the capacity to be liberated, and the incapacity to be liberated.
8. The distinctive characteristic of the soul is attention. . . .
10. Souls are of two kinds: worldly and liberated.[4]
11. [Worldly souls] are of two kinds: with mind and without mind.

---

[4] According to Jainism, some souls are able to become liberated and some are not.

12. Worldly souls are again of two kinds: moving and unmoving....
14. Moving souls have two senses, etc.[5]
15. There are five senses....
23. Worms, ants, bumblebees, and humans each have one more than the one preceding....
5.16. Due to expansion or contraction of its enclosure, [the soul occupies space] in the same way that light from a lamp does....[6]
18. [The function] of space is to give place [to all the other substances].
19. [The function] of matter is [to form the basis of] bodies, speech, mind, and breath.
20. [The function] of matter is also to make possible worldly enjoyment, pain, life, and death.
21. [The function] of souls is to support each other.
22. And [the function] of time is [to explain] continued existence, change, movement, and long or short duration....
6.1. Yoga is activity of body, speech, and mind.
2. It [is concerned with] inflow [of karmic matter].
3. [Inflow is of two kinds]: good, which is inflow of meritorious
[karmas]; and bad, which is inflow of negative [karmas]....
12. Compassion for living beings, compassion for those who have taken vows, charity, self-control with some attachment, etc., yoga, patience, and contentment: these are [the causes of inflow] of pleasant karmic matter....
7.1. The vows involve avoidance of harming *(hiṃsā)*, lying, stealing, non-celibacy, and attachment....
3. In order to establish these [in the mind], there are five meditations for each.
4. The five meditations for the vow against harming are carefulness of speech, carefulness of mind, care in walking, care in lifting and laying down things, and thoroughly scrutinizing one's food and drink.[7]
5. And the five meditations for the vow against lying are avoiding anger, greed, cowardice and frivolity, and speaking in accordance with scriptural injunctions.

---

[5] This means that they have two, three, four, or five senses.

[6] This means that in a small room light occupies a smaller place than in a large room, but without any diminution of the light itself. In the same way, the soul expands or contracts in accordance with the size of the body it occupies.

[7] This means that one should examine all food before eating it to make sure that no living beings are hidden in the food. The reason for doing this is to ensure that one does not inadvertently eat a living being.

6. The five meditations for the vow against stealing are living in a solitary place, living in a deserted place, living in a place where one is not likely to be interfered with by others and where one is not likely to interfere with others, purity of alms, and not disputing with followers of the true doctrine.

7. The five meditations for the vow against non-celibacy are renunciation of hearing stories inciting desire for women, renunciation of seeing their beautiful bodies, renunciation of remembrance of past enjoyments, renunciation of aphrodisiacs, and renunciation of beautifying one's own body.

8. The five meditations for the vow against worldly desire are giving up love and hatred for the pleasing and displeasing objects of the senses. . . .

12. In order to develop detachment toward the tribulations [of the world, one should consider] the nature of the world and the body. . . .

8.1. The causes of bondage are wrong belief, non-renunciation, carelessness, passions, and union [of the soul with the mind, body, and speech].

2. The soul, due to its having passion, assimilates matter that is fit to form karmas. This is bondage. . . .

9.1. Stopping [of karmic inflows] is destruction of inflows.

2. It is brought about by discipline, carefulness, observances, meditation, overcoming suffering, and good conduct.

3. Due to asceticism, one eliminates [karmic matter].

4. Discipline is proper control [over mind, speech, and body].

5. Carefulness is [taking proper care] when walking, speaking, eating, lifting and laying down, and in excreting.

6. Observances are: forgiveness, humility, honesty, contentment, truth, restraint, asceticism, renunciation, non-attachment and celibacy, all to the highest degree.

7. The meditations are: impermanence, vulnerability, cyclic existence, aloneness, separateness, inflow, stopping of inflows, elimination of inflows, [the nature of] the world, the difficulty of attaining liberation, and the nature of the true doctrine. . . .

19. External austerities are: fasting, eating less than one's fill, taking a vow to accept food from a householder, renunciation of delicacies,[8] sleeping in a lonely place, and mortification of the body.

---

[8] These include clarified butter (ghee), milk, curd, sugar, salt, and oil.

20. The others, that is, internal austerities, are: expiation, discipline, service, study, giving up attachment, and concentration. . . .

10.1. Separation results from destruction of delusion and by simultaneous destruction of what obscures wisdom and perception.

2. Liberation is complete freedom from all karma due to the nonexistence of the causes of bondage and to the eradication [of karmic matter]. . . .

4. After attainment of separation, there remain perfect correct wisdom, perfect correct perception, and the state of ultimate accomplishment *(siddhatva)*.

Source: *Tattvārthādhigama-sūtra* selections. Tr. JP.

Buddhism

INTRODUCTION

Nearly 2,500 years ago, according to Buddhist tradition, a young man sat under a tree in northern India, determined to find a way to transcend the sufferings that he recognized as being endemic to the world. Born a prince named Siddhārtha Gautama in a small kingdom in what is today southern Nepal, he had renounced his royal heritage in order to escape the cycle of birth, death, and rebirth that inevitably leads to suffering, loss, and pain. As he sat under the tree, he recognized that all the world's problems begin with a fundamental ignorance *(avidyā)* that causes beings to misunderstand the true nature of reality. This causes them to engage in actions that lead to their own suffering and to fail to recognize what leads to happiness.

Siddhārtha remained in meditation throughout the night, and during this time the veils of ignorance lifted from his perception. He came to understand how the lives of all beings in the world are constantly influenced by the effects of their own actions (karma) and that seeking happiness within the changing phenomena of the mundane world is a fundamental mistake. He saw everything in the world as impermanent *(anitya)* and understood that because of the fact of constant change even things that seem to provide happiness—such as wealth, fame, power, sex, relationships—are in fact sources of suffering *(duḥkha)*.

In addition, he perceived that everything comes into being in dependence on causes and conditions—a doctrine referred to in Buddhism as "dependent arising" *(pratītya-samutpāda)*—and he understood that because phenomena are in a constant state of flux and there is no enduring essence underlying them. Nor is there a supreme being who oversees the process of change and decides the fates of beings. Rather, every being is responsible for its own destiny, and the entire system of universal interdependent causation is driven by its own internal forces. Individual beings are what they are because of the actions they performed in the past.

Moreover, beings lack an enduring self or soul. This doctrine is referred to in Buddhist literature as "no-self" *(anātman)* and is a denial of the sort of permanent, partless, and immortal entity called *ātman* (literally, "I" or "self") in Hinduism and soul in Christianity. This doctrine is connected with the idea that all phenomena lack substantial entities and are characterized by an "emptiness" *(śūnyatā)* of inherent existence *(svabhāva*; literally, "own-being").

At dawn of the following morning, full awareness arose in him, and all traces of ignorance disappeared. He had become a buddha, a term derived from the Sanskrit root word *budh*, meaning "to wake up" or "to regain consciousness." Thus he was now fully awakened from the sleep of ignorance in which most beings spend life after life. At first he thought to remain under the tree and pass away without revealing what he had understood because he knew the teachings of an awakened being are subtle and difficult for ordinary beings to comprehend. As he sat there in blissful contemplation, however, the Indian god Brahmā came to him, bowed down before him, and begged him to teach others. Brahmā pointed out that there would be some intelligent people who would derive benefit from his teachings and that such people would find true happiness by following the path he had discovered.

Feeling a sense of profound compassion for suffering beings, Buddha agreed to share his wisdom with them and so embarked on a teaching career that would last for about forty years. He traveled around India, instructing all who wished to listen. Many people recognized the truth of his words and became his disciples. According to Buddhist tradition, he was an accomplished teacher who was able to perceive the proclivities and mind-sets of his listeners and who could skillfully adapt his teachings for each person and group while still retaining the essential message. He had many lay disciples, but he emphasized the centrality of a monastic lifestyle for those who were intent on liberation. According to his biography, he died in a grove of trees near the town of Vaiśālī at the age of 80.

Shortly after his death, his followers convened a council to codify the teachings of the Buddha. According to tradition, the council met in Rājagṛha, a place where the Buddha had delivered many discourses. The participants were 500 of his closest disciples who had become *arhat*s (meaning that they had eradicated mental afflictions and transcended all attachment to mundane things). Such people, it was believed, would not be afflicted by faulty memories or biased by sectarian considerations. The members of the assembly recounted what they had heard the Buddha say on specific occasions, and they prefaced their remarks with the phrase "Thus have I heard: At one time the Exalted One was residing in . . . ." This formula indicated that the speaker had been a member of the audience and provided the context and background of the discourse. Other members would certify the veracity of the account or correct minor details. At the end of the council, all present were satisfied that the Buddha's words had been definitively recorded. The canon of Buddhism was declared closed, and the council issued a pronouncement that henceforth no new teachings would be admitted as the "word of the Buddha" *(buddha-vacana)*.

Despite the intentions of the council, however, new teachings and doctrines continued to appear in the following centuries, and the Buddhist community underwent numerous divisions.[1] The most significant of these was the split into two schools termed "Hīnayāna," or "Lesser Vehicle," and "Mahāyāna," or "Greater Vehicle." These names obviously were coined by the latter group, which considered itself superior to its rivals because it propounded a goal of universal salvation, while the Hīnayāna emphasized the importance of working primarily for one's own emancipation. The Hīnayāna ideal is the *arhat*, a being who overcomes all ties to the phenomenal world and so attains nirvana, which is said to be a state beyond birth and death and also is described as perfect bliss.

Their Mahāyāna rivals condemned this as a selfish and limited goal. The Mahāyāna ideal is the *bodhisattva* (a being— *sattva*—whose goal is awakening—*bodhi*), who seeks to attain the state of buddhahood in order to help others find the path to final happiness. This form of Buddhism later predominated in Central and East Asia—in countries such as Tibet, Mongolia, Korea, Japan, Vietnam, and China—while Hīnayāna schools took hold in Southeast Asia—in countries such as Sri Lanka, Thailand, Burma, Cambodia, and Laos.

Buddhists in these latter countries do not accept the designation of their tradition as a "Lesser Vehicle." Rather, they contend that the dominant Theravāda tradition (the only one of the numerous schools collectively designated "Hīnayāna" that survives today) is in fact the true teaching of Buddha. They further believe that the Mahāyāna *sūtra*s (discourses believed by Mahāyānists to have been spoken by the historical Buddha) are in fact forgeries that proclaim practices and doctrines that the Buddha never taught but that actually were falsely propounded by others long after his death.

---

[1] Traditionally, one becomes a Buddhist by "taking refuge" in the "three refuges" (or "three jewels"): the Buddha, the Buddhist doctrine (dharma), and the community of Buddhist monks and nuns *(saṃgha)*. Taking refuge implies that one has made a conscious decision to rely on these three things as guides for religious practice, believing that they are able to lead one out of suffering and toward salvation.

The oldest distinctively Mahāyāna literature is a group of texts that discuss the "perfection of wisdom" *(prajñā-pāramitā)*. The earliest of these is probably *Perfection of Wisdom in 8,000 Lines*,[2] the oldest version of which may have been composed as early as the first century BCE. The Perfection of Wisdom texts do not make their appearance until several centuries after the death of the Buddha, but they claim to have been spoken by him during his lifetime. Mahāyāna tradition explains the chronological discrepancy by contending that they were indeed taught by the Buddha to advanced disciples but that he ordered that they be hidden in the underwater realm of *nāga*s (beings with snake-like bodies and human heads) until the time was right for their propagation. The legend further reports that the second-century philosopher Nāgārjuna (fl. ca. 150 CE.) was the person preordained by Buddha to recover and explicate the Perfection of Wisdom texts. After one of his lectures, some *nāga*s approached him and told him of the texts hidden in their kingdom, and Nāgārjuna traveled there and returned with the *sūtra*s to India. He is credited with founding the Madhyamaka (Middle Way) school of Buddhist philosophy, which emphasizes the centrality of the doctrine of emptiness.

Nāgārjuna and his commentators (the most influential of whom was Candrakīrti, ca. 550–600) developed the philosophical ramifications of this doctrine, which is closely connected to the notion of dependent arising. Because all phenomena come into being as a result of causes and conditions, abide due to causes and conditions, and pass away due to causes and conditions, everything in the universe is empty of a substantial entity. Ordinary beings, however, perceive them as existing in the way they appear—that is, as real, substantial things that inherently possess certain qualities. Nāgārjuna declared that a failure to understand emptiness correctly leads to mistaken perceptions of things and that erroneous philosophical views are the reifications of such notions.

The Madhyamaka philosophers applied this insight not only to mistaken perceptions but also to the doctrines of rival schools, which they contended were founded on self-contradictory assumptions. Through a process of dialectical reasoning, Madhyamaka thinkers exposed both Buddhist and non-Buddhist systems of thought to a rigorous critique, the goal of which was to lead people to recognize the ultimate futility of attempting to encapsulate truth in philosophical propositions.

---

[2] Sanskrit: *Aṣṭasāhasrikā-prajñāpāramitā-sūtra*; the oldest extant version of this text is a Chinese translation by Lokakṣema in the second century CE.

Approximately two centuries after Nāgārjuna, a new Mahāyāna school arose in India, commonly known as the Yogic Practice School (Yogācāra). The main scriptural source for this school is the *Discourse Explaining the Thought (Saṃdhinirmocana-sūtra)*, which consists of a series of questions put to the Buddha by a group of bodhisattvas. The name "Yogic Practice School" may have been derived from an important treatise by Asaṅga (ca. 310–390) titled *Levels of Yogic Practice (Yogācāra-bhūmi)*. Along with his brother Vasubandhu (ca. 320–400), Asaṅga is credited with founding this school and developing its central doctrines.

Yogācāra emphasizes the importance of meditative practice, and several passages in Yogācāra texts indicate that the founders of the school perceived other Mahāyāna Buddhists as being overly concerned with dialectical debate while neglecting meditation. The Yogācāra school is commonly referred to in Tibet as "Mind Only" (*sems tsam*; Sanskrit: *citta-mātra*) because of an idea found in some Yogācāra texts that all the phenomena of the world are "cognition-only" *(vijñapti-mātra)*, implying that everything we perceive is conditioned by consciousness. In the following centuries, a number of syncretic schools developed. They tended to mingle Madhyamaka and Yogācāra doctrines. The greatest examples of this syncretic period are the philosophers Śāntarakṣita (ca. 680–740) and Kamalaśīla (ca. 740–790), who are among the last significant Buddhist philosophers in India.

In addition to these developments in philosophy, sometime around the sixth or seventh century a new trend in practice developed in India, which was written down in texts called tantras. These texts were purported to have been spoken by the historical Buddha (or sometimes by other buddhas). They incorporated the traditional Mahāyāna ideal of the bodhisattva who seeks buddhahood for the benefit of all beings, but they also proposed some radically new practices and paradigms. The central practices of tantra include visualizations intended to foster cognitive reorientation, prayers (mantra) to buddhas that are intended to facilitate the transformation of the meditator into a fully awakened buddha, and often elaborate rituals.

In the tantric practice of deity yoga *(devatā-yoga)*, meditators first visualize buddhas in front of themselves (this is referred to as the "generation stage," *utpatti-krama*) and then invite the buddhas to merge with them, a process that symbolically transforms them into buddhas (this is referred to as the "completion stage," *niṣpanna-krama*). The practice of deity yoga is intended to help meditators become familiar with having the body, speech, and mind of buddhas and with performing the compassionate activities of buddhas. Because meditators train in the desired effect of buddhahood, adherents of tantra claim that their path is much shorter than that of traditional Mahāyāna, which was said to require a minimum of three "countless eons" *(asaṃkhyeya-kalpa)*[3] to complete. With the special practices of tantra, one may become a buddha in as little as one human lifetime.

Following this last flowering of Buddhist thought in India, Buddhism began to decline. It increasingly became a tradition of elite scholar-monks who studied in great monastic universities like Nālandā and Vikramaśīla in northern India. Buddhism failed to adapt to changing social and political circumstances and apparently lacked a wide base of support. Thus, when a series of invasions by Turkish Muslims descended on India in the ninth through twelfth centuries, with the invaders sacking the great north Indian monastic universities and killing many prominent monks, Buddhism was dealt a death blow from which it never recovered.

THE SPREAD OF BUDDHISM OUTSIDE OF INDIA

During the third century BCE the spread of Buddhism was furthered by Aśoka (r. 272–236), the third of the Mauryan kings, who created the first pan-Indian empire. Aśoka was converted to Buddhism by a Theravāda monk, and after a bloody war of conquest against the neighboring state of Kaliṅga, he recognized that such aggression violated the principles of Buddhism. From this point on, he renounced war as an instrument of foreign policy and began to implement Buddhist principles in the administration of the kingdom. In order to inform the populace of his political and ruling philosophy, he had edicts inscribed on stone pillars and placed throughout his realm. A number of them still survive today. His reign is considered by Buddhists to have been a model of good government, one informed by Buddhist principles of righteousness and respect for life.

Aśoka's advocacy of Buddhism was one of the primary reasons for the spread of the tradition into Southeast Asia. He sent teams of missionaries all over the Indian subcontinent and to Sri Lanka, Burma, and other neighboring areas. Due to Aśoka's influence and personal power, the missionaries generally were well received in the countries they visited and often were successful in convincing people to convert to Buddhism. One of the most successful missions he sponsored was led by his son Mahinda,

---

[3] A "countless eon" is the amount of time that elapses between the creation and destruction of the universe.

who traveled to Sri Lanka along with four other monks and a novice.[4] According to Buddhist tradition, the mission was so successful that the king of Sri Lanka became a Buddhist, and Mahinda then supervised the translation of the Theravāda canon (written in the Pāli language) into Sinhala. He also helped found a monastery, named the Mahāvihāra, which became the main bastion of Theravāda orthodoxy in Sri Lanka for over a thousand years.

It is unclear exactly when Buddhism first arrived in East Asia. China was the first country in the region to record contact with Buddhism. A royal edict issued in 65 CE states that a prince in what is now northern Kiangsu Province performed Buddhist sacrifices and entertained Buddhist monks and laypeople. The earliest Buddhists in China were probably from Central Asia, and for centuries Buddhism was widely perceived as a religion of foreigners. In 148 CE, a monk named An Shigao, from the Central Asian kingdom of Kusha, began translating Indian Buddhist texts into Chinese in Luoyang, which was to become the capital of the later Han dynasty. An Shigao and a number of other monks (mostly from Central Asia) translated about thirty Buddhist texts over the next three decades.

The early translators used a translation system termed "matching concepts" *(keyi)*, which was to have important ramifications for the development of Chinese Buddhism. Realizing that China had a highly developed culture and that the Chinese tended to view people from other countries as uncouth barbarians, the early translators used indigenous terminology—particularly Daoist terminology—to translate Sanskrit technical terms. One result of this practice was that it made many foreign ideas more palatable to Chinese readers, but it also inevitably colored the translations to such an extent that for the first few centuries after Buddhism's arrival in China, many Chinese believed it to be merely another version of Daoism.

In later centuries, Chinese Buddhism developed its own identity, and from China Buddhism was passed on to Korea and Japan.[5] In 552, according to the *Chronicles of Japan*

---

[4] This is the number needed for ordination of monks. Because this was a mission of conversion, and because Buddhism generally places a high value on monasticism, this number was required for the mission to achieve its primary goal of convincing people to enter the Buddhist community of monks and nuns.

[5] According to the *Historical Record of the Three Kingdoms (Samguk sagi)*, the *Biographies of Eminent Korean Monks (Haedong Goseungjeon)*, and the *Memorabilia of the Three Kingdoms (Samguk Yusa)*, Buddhism was first introduced to Korea from China during the Three Kingdoms period. In 372 CE, King Fujian (r. 357–384) sent a monk named Shundao (Kor. Sundo) as an envoy to the Goguryeo court. He brought Buddhist texts and images, and although this visit had little effect, later missionaries succeeded in bringing Buddhism to Korea.

(Nihonshōki), the Korean state of Paekche sent Buddhist texts and images to Japan, hoping to persuade the Japanese emperor to become an ally in its war against the neighboring state of Silla. Some members of the Soga clan wanted to worship the Buddha as a powerful foreign god *(kami)*,[6] hoping to gain influence by associating themselves with what they believed to be a deity of the powerful Chinese empire. The early Japanese interest in Buddhism was connected mostly with purported magical powers of buddhas and Buddhist monks, but after the emperor Yōmei (r. 585–587) converted to Buddhism, Japanese began to travel to China in order to study with Buddhist teachers there, and indigenous Buddhist schools developed in Japan.

Yōmei's son Prince Shōtoku (574–622) enthusiastically propagated Buddhism. He is credited with building numerous Buddhist temples and with sponsoring Japanese monks to travel to China for study. He is also the author of commentaries on three Buddhist texts.[7] In later times he was viewed in Japan as an incarnation of the bodhisattva Avalokiteśvara.[8]

During the reign of the Tibetan king Tri Songdetsen (740–798), the Indian scholar Śāntarakṣita traveled to Tibet, but opposition from some of the king's ministers forced him to leave. Before departing, he urged the king to invite the tantric adept Padmasambhava to Tibet. Upon his arrival, Padmasambhava claimed that Śāntarakṣita's efforts had been frustrated by the country's demons. Padmasambhava then challenged the demons to personal combat, and none were able to defeat him. This so impressed the king and his court that Śāntarakṣita was invited back at Padmasambhava's urging, and the first Buddhist monastery in Tibet was built at Samye. This marked the beginning of the "early propagation" of Buddhism to Tibet, which ended when the devout Buddhist king Relbachen (815–836) was assassinated.

Relbachen's death in 836 marked the beginning of an interregnum period for Tibetan Buddhism, which ended in 1042 when Atiśa (982–1054), one of the directors of the monastic university of Nālandā, traveled to Tibet. This is considered by Tibetan historians to mark the beginning of the "later propagation" of Buddhism to Tibet. Atiśa was so successful in bringing the dharma to Tibet that Buddhism quickly became the dominant religious tradition in the country.

---

[6] For an overview of the veneration of *kami* in Japan, see the "Shintō" chapter.

[7] These are the *Vimalakīrti-nirdeśa-sūtra*; the *Lotus Sūtra*; and the *Śrīmālā Sūtra*.

[8] In Mahāyāna mythology, Avalokiteśvara is said to be the embodiment of the compassion of all buddhas.

Today Buddhism continues to flourish in Asia, despite setbacks such as the suppression of religion in China since the inauguration of the People's Republic of China. The current government follows Karl Marx's notion that religion is "the opiate of the masses" and an impediment to social development. In recent years government persecution of Buddhism has eased somewhat, and currently Buddhism is enjoying increased support from the Chinese populace. The government is also allowing young people to become ordained as Buddhist monks and nuns.

Buddhism is becoming increasingly popular in Western countries, and a number of prominent Buddhist teachers have established successful centers in Europe and North America. The Dalai Lama, Thich Nhat Hanh, Sogyal Rinpoche, a number of Zen masters *(rōshi)*, and Theravāda meditation teachers have attracted substantial followings outside Asia, and books and articles about Buddhism are appearing with increasing frequency in Western countries.

BUDDHIST SCRIPTURES

The early Buddhist canon is traditionally referred to as the "Three Baskets" (*tripiṭaka*; Pāli: *tipiṭaka*), consisting of (1) *vinaya*: rules of conduct mainly concerned with the regulation of the monastic order; (2) *sūtras*: discourses purportedly spoken by the Buddha, and sometimes by his immediate disciples; and (3) *abhidharma*, including scholastic treatises that codify and interpret the teachings attributed to the Buddha. According to Buddhist tradition, this division was instituted at the first council. This canon was written in a language called Pāli, which is believed to have been derived from a dialect used in the region of Magadha. A second council introduced some modifications to the rules of monastic discipline, and later councils added other texts to the canon. At first the canon was transmitted orally, but after a time of political and social turmoil, King Vaṭṭagāmaṇi of Sri Lanka ordered that it be committed to writing. This was accomplished between 35 and 32 BCE. The *sūtras* and *vinaya* were written in Pāli, but some of the commentaries were in Sinhala. The Sinhala texts were translated into Pāli in the fifth century CE.

The *Vinaya* section of the Pāli canon consists of rules of conduct, most of which are aimed at monks and nuns. Many of these are derived from specific cases in which the Buddha was asked for a ruling on the conduct of particular members of the order, and the general rules he promulgated still serve as the basis for monastic conduct.

The *Sūtra* (Pāli: *Sutta*) section of the Pāli canon traditionally is divided into five "groupings" *(nikāya)*: (1) the "long" *(dīgha)* discourses; (2) the "medium length" *(majjhima)* discourses; (3) the "grouped" *(saṃyutta)* discourses; (4) the "enumerated" *(aṅguttara)* discourses, which are arranged according to the enumerations of their topics; and (5) the "minor" *(khuddaka)* discourses, which constitute the largest section of the canon and the one that contains the widest variety of materials. It includes stories of the Buddha's former births *(Jātaka)*, which report how he gradually perfected the exalted qualities of a buddha; accounts of the lives of the great disciples *(apadāna)*; didactic verses *(gāthā)*; an influential work titled *Path of Truth (Dhammapada)*; and a number of other important texts.

The *Abhidharma* (Pāli: *abhidhamma*) section includes seven treatises that organize the doctrines of particular classes of the Buddha's discourses. The Abhidharma writers attempted to systematize the profusion of teachings attributed to the Buddha into a coherent philosophy. Their texts classify experience in terms of impermanent groupings of factors referred to as dharmas (Pāli: *dhamma*), which in aggregations are the focus of the doctrine (dharma) taught by Buddha. They are simple real things, indivisible into something more basic. Collections of dharmas are the phenomena of experience. Everything in the world—people, animals, plants, inanimate objects—consists of impermanent groupings of dharmas. Thus nothing possesses an underlying soul or essence. The collections of dharmas change in every moment, and so all of reality is viewed as a vast interconnected network of causation.

Other early schools developed their own distinctive canons, many of which have very different collections of texts—although the doctrines and practices they contain are similar. Some schools, such as the Sarvāstivādins ("Everything Exists School"), used Sanskrit for their canons, but today only fragments of these collections exist, mostly in Chinese translations. Although Mahāyāna schools developed an impressive literature, there does not seem to have been an attempt to create a Mahāyāna canon in India. The surviving Mahāyāna canons were all compiled in other countries.

Canons compiled in Mahāyāna countries contain much of the material of the Pāli canon but also include Mahāyāna *sūtras* and other texts not found in the Pāli canon. The Tibetan canon, for example, contains a wealth of Mahāyāna *sūtras* translated from Sanskrit, treatises *(śāstra)* by important Indian Buddhist thinkers, tantras and tantric commentaries, and miscellaneous writings deemed important enough to include in the canon. The Chinese canon also contains Mahāyāna *sūtras*, Indian philosophical treatises, and a variety of other texts, but its compilation was much less systematic than that of the Tibetan canon. The Tibetan translators had access to a much wider range of literature, due to the fact that the canon was collected in Tibet centuries after the Chinese one. In addition, Buddhist literature came to China in a rather haphazard way. The transmission of Buddhist texts to China occurred over the course of several centuries, and during this time the tradition in India was developing, creating new schools and doctrines.

The Chinese canon was transmitted to Korea and Japan. Tibet and Mongolia both follow the Tibetan canon, which according to tradition was redacted and codified by Pudön (1290–1364). The Theravāda countries of Southeast Asia follow the Pāli canon and generally consider the texts of Mahāyāna to be heterodox. In addition to this canonical literature, each school of Buddhism has created literature that it considers to be authoritative. We provide examples of such texts from a wide range of schools and periods of Buddhist literature, but the vast scope of canonical and extracanonical literature prevents us from including many important works. The selections are intended to present a representative sampling of early texts that contain central doctrines or that recount important events in the history of Buddhism, along with statements by Buddhist thinkers of later times that illustrate influential developments in Buddhist thought and practice.

HOLIDAYS

Āsāḷha Offering (Āsāḷha Pūjā; Sri Lanka: Esala Perahera) A festival held in Theravāda countries to commemorate the Buddha's first sermon in the Deer Park. It is held in Āsāḷha, the eighth lunar month, generally around July.

Buddhist New Year In Theravāda countries, the New Year is celebrated for three days beginning with the first new moon in April. In Mahāyāna countries, the celebration generally begins on the first new moon in January.

Robe Offering (Kaṭhina) An annual event in Theravāda countries in which laypeople mark the end of the rains' retreat by giving new robes to monks.

(Continued)

HOLIDAYS *(Continued)*

Great Prayer Festival (Mönlam Chenmo) Annual New Year celebration instituted by Tsong Khapa in 1409. It combines religious activities with sporting contests and parties.

Festival of the Hungry Ghosts (Ullambana; China: Yulan; Japan: Obon) A festival celebrated in East Asian Mahāyāna countries commemorating Maudgalyāyana's efforts to help his mother, who had been reborn as a hungry ghost *(preta)*. Traditionally celebrated on the fifteenth day of the seventh lunar month, it involves making offerings of food, money, clothing, and prayers for hungry ghosts and hell beings.

Vesak (Thai: Visākhā Pūjā) A major celebration in Theravāda countries, commemorating the day on which, according to tradition, the Buddha was born, attained awakening, and entered final nirvana. It is celebrated on the full moon day of the month of Visākhā (April–May). In Tibet it is known as Saga Dawa and celebrated in June–July.

TIMELINE

485–405 BCE	Life of Śākyamuni Buddha
405 BCE	First Buddhist Council at Rājagṛha
305 BCE	Second Buddhist Council at Vaiśālī
272–236 BCE	Reign of Aśoka
200 BCE	Beginnings of Mahāyāna Buddhism in India
101–77 BCE	Reign of Duṭṭagāmaṇi in Sri Lanka; establishment of Buddhism as state religion
1st century CE	Buddhism enters Central Asia and China
148	An Shigao arrives in China and establishes first translation bureau
3rd century	Buddhism transmitted to Burma, Cambodia, Laos, Indonesia

TIMELINE *(Continued)*

350–650	Gupta Dynasty in India; flourishing of Buddhist philosophy and art
552	Buddhism enters Japan from Korea
618–650	Life of Songtsen Gampo, first of Tibet's "religious kings"
618–906	Chinese Tang Dynasty; apogee of Buddhism in China
720–1200	Tantric Buddhism arises and develops in India
845	Persecution of Buddhism in China
1042	Atiśa arrives in Tibet; beginning of "later propagation" of Buddhism
1173–1262	Life of Shinran; founding of Jōdo-shinshū in Japan
1200	Destruction of Nālandā Monastic University by Mahmud Ghorī
1603–1867	Buddhism becomes state religion in Japan during Tokugawa period
18th century	Colonial occupation of Sri Lanka, Burma, Laos, Cambodia, and Vietnam by European powers
1851	First Buddhist temple founded in San Francisco for Chinese immigrants
1891–1956	Life of B. R. Ambedkar; mass conversion of former Untouchables in India

GLOSSARY

Anātman "No-self," the doctrine that there is no permanent, partless, substantial essence or soul.

Arhat The ideal of "Hīnayāna" Buddhism, who strives to attain a personal nirvana.

Avidyā "Ignorance," the primary factor that enmeshes living beings in the cycle of birth, death, and rebirth.

Bodhisattva A compassionate being who resolves to bring others to liberation.

Buddha "Awakened One," epithet of those who successfully break the hold of ignorance, liberate themselves from cyclic existence, and teach others the path to liberation.

Chan/Zen A school that developed in East Asia, emphasizing meditation aimed at a nonconceptual, direct understanding of reality.

Completion Stage *(niṣpanna-krama)* Tantric practice in which one visualizes oneself as being transformed into a buddha.

Deity Yoga *(devatā-yoga)* The tantric practice of visualizing oneself as a buddha.

Dependent Arising *(pratītya-samutpāda)* Doctrine that phenomena arise and pass away in dependence on causes and conditions.

Dharma Buddhist doctrine and practice.

Duḥkha "Suffering," the first "noble truth" of Buddhism, which holds that cyclic existence is characterized by suffering.

Eightfold Noble Path Fourth of the "four noble truths," which involves cultivation of correct views, actions, and meditative practices in order to bring an end to suffering.

Five Aggregates The components of the psycho-physical personality and the factors on the basis of which unawakened beings impute the false notion of a "self": (1) form, (2) feelings, (3) discriminations, (4) consciousness, (5) compositional factors.

Four Noble Truths Basic propositions attributed to the Buddha: (1) suffering, (2) the cause of suffering, (3) the cessation of suffering, (4) the eightfold noble path.

Generation Stage *(utpatti-krama)* Tantric practice of visualizing a vivid image of a buddha in front of oneself.

Hīnayāna "Lesser Vehicle," a term coined by Mahāyānists to describe their opponents, whose path they characterized as selfish and inferior to their own.

Karma "Actions," which bring about concordant results.

Keyi "Matching Concepts," a translation style adopted for early Chinese versions of Buddhist texts, which involved using indigenous Chinese terms for Sanskrit words.

Madhyamaka "Middle Way School," one of the most influential systems of Indian Buddhism.

Mahāyāna "Greater Vehicle," the school of Buddhism that emphasizes the ideal of the bodhisattva.

Nirvana Liberation from cyclic existence.

Pure Land A school of Buddhism popular in East Asia whose adherents strive for rebirth in the realm of the Buddha Amitābha.

Śākyamuni "Sage of the Śākyas," an epithet of the historical Buddha, whose name at birth was Siddhārtha Gautama.

Saṃsāra "Cyclic Existence," the beginningless cycle of birth, death, and rebirth in which ignorant beings are trapped.

Skill in Means *(upāya-kauśalya)* The ability to adapt Buddhist teachings and practices to the level of understanding of one's audience.

Śūnyatā "Emptiness," the lack of inherent existence that characterizes all persons and phenomena.

Sūtra Discourses attributed to the historical Buddha.

Tantra Discourses attributed to the historical Buddha that appeared sometime around the seventh century and that advocate practices involving visualizing oneself as a buddha.

Yogācāra "Yogic Practice School," a system of Indian Buddhism whose main early exponents were the brothers Asaṅga and Vasubandhu.

Zen See Chan.

THE LIFE OF THE BUDDHA

According to traditional accounts, the Buddha was born a prince named Siddhārtha Gautama in a small kingdom in what is today southern Nepal. His final incarnation was a culmination of a training program that spanned countless lifetimes, during which he gradually perfected the exalted qualities that would mark him as a buddha. Shortly after his birth, his father consulted a number of astrologers, all of whom declared that the newborn prince would become a great king who would rule with truth and righteousness. One astrologer, however, declared that if the prince were to see a sick person, an old person, a corpse, and a world-renouncing ascetic, he would become dissatisfied with his life and pursue the path of a wandering mendicant in order to seek final peace. These four things became known in Buddhism as the "four sights." The first three epitomize the problems inherent in the world, and the fourth points to the way out of the endless cycle of birth, death, and rebirth, which is characterized by suffering and loss.

According to the Extensive Sport Discourse *(Lalitavistara-sūtra), Siddhārtha's father, king Śuddhodana, decided to prevent his son from encountering any of the four sights and surrounded him with pleasant diversions during his early years. The prince, however, eventually convinced his father to let him visit a part of the city that lay outside the palace gates.*

Before allowing the prince to ride out in his chariot, Śuddhodana first ordered that the streets be cleared of all sick and old people and that the prince not be allowed to see any corpses or world renouncers. Despite the king's efforts, however, at one point the path of the royal chariot was blocked by a sick man. Siddhārtha had never before encountered serious illness, and he turned to Channa, his charioteer, and asked,

> O charioteer, who is this man, weak and powerless?
> His flesh, blood, and skin withered, his veins protruding,
> With whitened hair, few teeth, his body emaciated,
> Walking painfully and leaning on a staff?

Channa informed the prince that the man had grown old and that such afflictions were the inevitable result of age. He added,

> O prince, this man is oppressed by age
> His organs are weak; he is in pain, and his strength and vigor
> are gone.
> Abandoned by his friends, he is helpless and unable to work,
> Like wood abandoned in a forest. . . .
> Lord, this is not unique to his race or his country.
> Age exhausts youth and the entire world.
> Even you will be separated from the company
> Of your mother and father, friends and relatives.
> There is no other fate for living beings.

Siddhārtha was amazed to find that most people see such sights every day but persist in shortsighted pursuits and mundane affairs, apparently unconcerned that they will inevitably become sick, grow old, and die. In three subsequent journeys outside the palace, Siddhārtha saw an old man and a corpse, and when he learned that eventually his young, healthy body would become weak and decrepit, he fell into a profound depression.

On a fourth trip, Siddhārtha saw a world renouncer, a man who stood apart from the crowd, who owned nothing and was unaffected by the petty concerns of the masses, and who radiated calm, serenity, and a profound inner peace. This sight lifted Siddhārtha's spirits because it revealed to him that there is a way to transcend the vicissitudes of mundane existence and find true happiness. Intrigued by the ascetic, Siddhārtha asked Channa what sort of man he was, and the charioteer replied,

> Lord, this man is one of the order of *bhikṣus* [mendicants].
> Having abandoned sensual desires,
> He has disciplined conduct.
> He has become a wandering mendicant.
> Who views himself and the external world with the same regard.
> Devoid of attachment or enmity, he lives by begging.

Realizing the folly of remaining in the palace, Siddhārtha resolved to renounce the world and find inner peace.

> Channa, for countless ages I have enjoyed sensual objects
> Of sight, sound, color, flavor, and touch, in all their varieties;
> But they have not made me happy. . . .
> Realizing this, I will embark on the raft of dharma, which is
> steadfast,
> Endowed with the range of austerities, good conduct,
> Equanimity, effort, strength, and generosity,
> Which is sturdy, made of the firmness of effort, and strongly
> held together.

Siddhārtha then declared his desire to become awakened in order to show other suffering beings a way to end suffering:

> I desire and wish that,
> After attaining the level of awakening,
> Which is beyond decay and death,
> I will save the world.
> The time for that has arrived.

Siddhārtha left the palace and subsequently practiced meditation with several teachers, but none could show him a path leading to the cessation of suffering. At one point he fell in with five spiritual seekers who told him that the way to salvation lies in severe asceticism. He followed their practices and eventually was eating only a single grain of rice per day. After swooning due to weakness, however, Siddhārtha realized that extreme asceticism is just as much a trap as the hedonistic indulgence of his early years. Thus he left his ascetic companions behind and resolved to find a path leading to the cessation of suffering. He recognized that he would have to discover the truth for himself. Before embarking on his final quest for truth, Siddhārtha made a solemn vow:

> As I sit here, my body may wither away,
> My skin, bones, and flesh may decay,
> But until I have attained awakening—
> Which is difficult to gain even during many ages—
> I will not move from this place.

Siddhārtha stood in a spot that is now known as "the Place of Awakening," located in modern-day Bodhgayā. Sitting under a tree, during the night Siddhārtha entered into progressively deeper meditative states in which the patterns of the world fell into place for him, and thus he came to understand the causes and effects of actions, why beings suffer, and how to transcend all the pains and sorrows of the world. By the dawn of the next morning, he had completely transcended the misconceptions of ordinary people. At this point Buddhist texts refer to him as "buddha," indicating that he was now fully awake and aware of the true nature of all things. Scanning the world with his heightened perception, the Buddha recognized that his realization was too profound to be understood by the vast majority of beings in the world, so initially he decided to remain under the tree in equanimity and to pass away without teaching what he had learned.

> Profound, peaceful, perfectly pure,
> Luminous, uncompounded, ambrosial
> Is the dharma I have attained.
> Even if I were to teach it,
> Others could not understand
> Thus, I should remain silent in the forest.

After the Buddha had made this statement, however, the Indian god Brahmā appeared before him and begged him to teach what he had learned for the benefit of those few beings who could understand and profit from his wisdom. Moved by compassion for the sufferings of creatures caught up in the round of cyclic existence, the Buddha agreed, and for the next forty years he traveled around India, teaching all who cared to listen.

Source: *Lalita-vistara* selections. Tr. JP.

PĀLI CANON

THE FIRST SERMON

Shortly after making the decision to teach, Buddha surveyed the world in order to choose a place to begin his teaching career. He decided to travel to Sārnāth, where his five former companions were still practicing pointless austerities, hoping in this way to find happiness. The following excerpt purports to be Buddha's first public teaching. It is referred to as the "Discourse Turning the Wheel of Doctrine" because it set in motion the Buddha's teaching career. In this passage, he lays out some of the themes that would be central to his later teachings, such as the importance of following a "middle way" that avoids the extremes of sensual indulgence and extreme asceticism, as well as the "four noble truths": (1) that all mundane existence involves suffering, (2) that suffering is caused by desire, (3) that there can be a cessation of suffering, and (4) that the eightfold noble path leads to this cessation.

Thus have I heard: At one time, the Exalted One was living near Vārāṇasī, at Isipatana near the Deer Park. Then the Exalted One spoke to the group of five monks: These two extremes, O monks, should not be practiced by one who has gone forth [from the household life]. What are the two? That which is linked with sensual desires, which is low, vulgar, common, unworthy, and useless, and that which is linked with self-torture, which is painful, unworthy, and useless. By avoiding these two extremes the Tathāgata [Buddha] has gained the knowledge of the middle path which gives vision and knowledge, and leads to calm, to clairvoyances, to awakening, to nirvana.

O monks, what is the middle path, which gives vision . . . ? It is the noble eightfold path: right views, right intention, right speech, right action, right livelihood, right effort, right mindfulness, right concentration. This, O monks, is the middle path, which gives vision. . . .

1. Now this, O monks, is the noble truth of suffering: birth is suffering, old age is suffering, death is suffering, sorrow, grieving, dejection, and despair are suffering. Contact with unpleasant things is suffering, not getting what you want is also suffering. In short, the five aggregates of grasping[9] are suffering.
2. Now this, O monks, is the noble truth of the arising of suffering: that craving which leads to rebirth, combined with longing and lust for this and that—craving for sensual pleasure, craving for rebirth, craving for cessation of birth. . . .
3. Now this, O monks, is the noble truth of the cessation of suffering: It is the complete cessation without remainder of that craving, the abandonment, release from, and non-attachment to it.
4. Now this, O monks, is the noble truth of the path that leads to the cessation of suffering: This is the noble eightfold path. . . .

Now monks, as long as my threefold knowledge and insight regarding these noble truths . . . were not well purified, so long, O monks, I was not sure that in this world . . . I had attained the highest complete awakening.

But when my threefold knowledge and insight in these noble truths with their twelve divisions were well purified, then, O monks, I was sure that in this world . . . I had attained the highest complete awakening.

Now knowledge and insight have arisen in me, so that I know: My mind's liberation is assured; this is my last existence; for me there is no rebirth.

Source: *Saṃyutta-nikāya* 5.420–423. Tr. JP.

THE BUDDHA'S GOOD QUALITIES

From a Buddhist perspective, the Buddha is not only important as a person who taught a corpus of texts. The events of his life also serve as an inspiration to devout Buddhists, who see him as the supreme example of how meditative realization should be put into practice in daily life. The following passage describes how he lived and related to the people and things around him.

---

[9] These are the components of the psycho-physical personality: (1) form, (2) feelings, (3) discriminations, (4) consciousness, and (5) compositional factors.

Renouncing the killing of living beings, the ascetic Gotama abstains from killing. He has put down the club and the sword, and he lives modestly, full of mercy, desiring in his compassion the welfare of all living beings.

Having renounced the taking of what is not given, the ascetic Gotama abstains from grasping after what does not belong to him. He accepts what is given to him and waits for it to be given; and he lives in honesty and purity of heart. . . .

Having renounced unchastity, the ascetic Gotama is celibate and aloof and has lost all desire for sexual intercourse, which is vulgar.

Having renounced false speech, the ascetic Gotama abstains from lying, he speaks the truth, holds to the truth, is trustworthy, and does not break his word in the world. . . .

Having renounced slander, the ascetic Gotama abstains from libel. When he hears something in one place he will not repeat it in another in order to cause strife . . . but he unites those who are divided by strife and encourages those who are friends. His pleasure is in peace, he loves peace and delights in it, and when he speaks he speaks words that make for peace. . . .

Having renounced harsh speech, the ascetic Gotama avoids abusive speech. He speaks only words that are blameless, pleasing to the ear, touching the heart, cultured, pleasing to people, loved by people. . . .

Having renounced frivolous talk, the ascetic Gotama avoids gossip. He speaks at the right time, in accordance with the facts, with meaningful words, speaking of the truth *(dhamma)*, of the discipline *(vinaya)*. His speech is memorable, timely, well illustrated, measured, and to the point.

The ascetic Gotama has renounced doing harm to seeds or plants. He takes only one meal per day, not eating at night, nor at the wrong time.

He abstains from watching shows or attending fairs with song, dance, and music. He has renounced the wearing of ornaments and does not adorn himself with garlands, scents, or cosmetics. He abstains from using a large or high bed. He abstains from accepting silver or gold, raw grain or raw meat. He abstains from accepting women or girls, male or female slaves, sheep or goats, birds or pigs, elephants or cows, horses or mares, fields or property. He abstains from acting as a go-between or messenger, from buying and selling, from falsifying with scales, weights, or measures. He abstains from crookedness and bribery, from cheating and fraud. He abstains from injury, murder, binding with bonds, stealing, and acts of violence.

Source: *Dīgha-nikāya* 1.4–10. Tr. JP.

CRITERIA FOR ASSESSING VALID TEACHINGS AND TEACHERS

Although there are many passages in Buddhist literature in which faith is extolled as an important virtue, this faith ideally should be based on evidence and valid reasoning. In addition, there are several places in Buddhist literature in which the Buddha exhorts his listeners to examine teachers and teachings closely before putting trust in them. In the following passage, the Buddha addresses a group of people collectively referred to as Kālāmas, who are confused by the conflicting claims of the religious systems of their day. The Buddha advises them to verify all claims themselves by examining which doctrines lead to positive results and which lead to negative ones. The former should be adopted, and the latter rejected.

> Do not be [convinced] by reports, tradition, or hearsay; nor by skill in the scriptural collections, argumentation, or reasoning; nor after examining conditions or considering theories; nor because [a theory] fits appearances, nor because of respect for an ascetic [who holds a particular view]. Rather, Kālāmas, when you know for yourselves: These doctrines are non-virtuous; these doctrines are erroneous; these doctrines are rejected by the wise; these doctrines, when performed and undertaken, lead to loss and suffering—then you should reject them, Kālāmas.

Source: *Aṅguttara-nikāya* 1.189. Tr. JP.

NIRVANA

Nirvana is said to be the final cessation of suffering, a state beyond the cycle of birth and death. As such, it could be said to be the ultimate goal of the path taught by the Buddha, whose quest was motivated by a concern with the unsatisfactoriness of cyclic existence and a wish to find a way out of the round of suffering that characterizes the mundane world. Despite its importance, there are few descriptions of nirvana in Buddhist literature. This selection provides one of the most detailed analyses of what nirvana is and how one attains it.

> Monks, there exists something in which there is neither earth nor water, fire nor air. It is not the sphere of infinite

space, nor the sphere of infinite consciousness, nor the sphere of nothingness, nor the sphere of neither perception nor non-perception [these are advanced meditative states]. It is neither this world nor another world, nor both, neither sun nor moon.

Monks, I do not state that it comes nor that it goes. It neither abides nor passes away. It is not caused, established, arisen, supported. It is the end of suffering....

What I call the selfless is difficult to perceive, for it is not easy to perceive the truth. But one who knows it cuts through craving, and for one who knows it, there is nothing to hold onto....

Monks, there exists something that is unborn, unmade, uncreated, unconditioned. Monks, if there were not an unborn, unmade, uncreated, unconditioned, then there would be no way to indicate how to escape from the born, made, created, and conditioned. However, monks, since there exists something that is unborn, unmade, uncreated, and uncondi-tioned, it is known that there is an escape from that which is born, made, created, and conditioned....

There is wandering for those who are attached, but there is no wandering for those who are unattached. There is serenity when there is no wandering, and when there is serenity, there is no desire. When there is no desire, there is neither coming nor going, and when there is no coming nor going, there is neither death nor rebirth. When there is nei-ther death nor rebirth, there is neither this life nor the next life, nor anything in between. It is the end of suffering.

Source: *Udāna,* ch. 8.80. Tr. JP.

DEPENDENT ARISING

After attaining awakening, the Buddha indicated that he had come to realize that all the phenomena of the universe are interconnected by relationships of mutual causality. Things come into being in dependence on causes and conditions, abide due to causes and conditions, and eventually pass away due to causes and conditions. Thus the world is viewed by Buddhists as a dynamic and ever-changing system. The following passage describes the process of causation in relation to human exis-tence, which is said to proceed in a cyclical fashion. Because of a basic misunderstanding of the workings of reality (referred to as "ignorance"), people falsely imagine that some worldly things can bring them happiness, and thus they generate desire and try to acquire these things. Such attitudes provide the basis for the aris-ing of negative mental states, and these states in turn provide a basis for beings to return to the world in a future birth. This next life will begin with the conditioning of the last, and thus the entire cycle will repeat itself unless a person recognizes the folly of conventional wisdom and chooses to follow the Buddhist path, which is designed to provide a way out of the trap of cyclic existence.

[Ānanda, quoting Buddha, said:] "Kaccāna, on two things the world generally bases its view: existence and non-existence. Kaccāna, one who perceives with correct insight the arising of the world as it really is does not think of the non-existence of the world. Kaccāna, one who perceives with correct insight the cessation of the world as it really is does not think of the existence of the world. Kaccāna, the world in general seizes on systems and is imprisoned by dogmas. One who does not seek after, seize on, or fixate on this seizing on systems, this dogma, this mental bias does not say, 'This is my self.' One who thinks, 'Whatever arises is only suffering; whatever ceases is suffering' has no doubts or qualms. In this sense, knowledge not borrowed from others comes to one. This, Kaccāna, is right view.

"Kaccāna, 'Everything exists' is one extreme; Kaccāna, 'Nothing exists' is the other extreme. Not approaching either extreme, Kaccāna, the Tathāgata teaches you a doctrine in terms of a middle path: ignorance depends on action; action depends on consciousness; consciousness depends on name and form; name and form depend on the six sense spheres; the six sense spheres[10] depend on contact; contact depends on feeling; feeling depends on attachment; attachment depends on grasping; grasping depends on existence; existence depends on birth; birth depends on aging and death. Suffering, despair, misery, grief, and sorrow depend on aging and death. In this way, the whole mass of suffering arises. But due to the complete eradication and cessation of ignorance comes a cessation of karmas and so forth. This is the cessation of this whole mass of suffering."

Source: *Saṃyutta-nikāya* 3.90. Tr. JP.

QUESTIONS THAT SHOULD BE AVOIDED

The following passage contains a series of questions about metaphysical topics posed to the Buddha by a wandering ascetic named Vacchagotta. The Buddha's response is interesting: He does not even try to provide answers, nor does he indicate that

---

[10] These are the six senses and their objects of contact.

he does not answer because of ignorance on his part. Rather, he tells Vacchagotta that there is no point in answering the questions because they are irrelevant to the goal of salvation. He indicates that people who spend their time pondering such questions and arguing about philosophical conundrums are unlikely to find release from suffering, so the wisest course of action is to avoid such questions as a waste of time.

Thus have I heard: At one time the Exalted One was staying near Sāvatthi in the Jeta Grove in Anāthapiṇḍika's hermitage.... Then the wanderer Vacchagotta approached the Exalted One ... and said, "Gotama, does the reverend Gotama have this view: 'The world is eternal; this is the truth, and all else is falsehood'?"

"Vaccha, I do not have this view...."

"Then, Gotama, does the reverend Gotama have this view: 'The world is not eternal; this is the truth, and all else is falsehood'?"

"Vaccha, I do not have this view...."

"Now, Gotama, does the reverend Gotama have this view: 'The world is finite; this is the truth, and all else is falsehood'?"

"Vaccha, I do not have this view...."

"Then, Gotama, does the reverend Gotama have this view: 'The world is not finite; this is the truth, and all else is falsehood'?"

"Vaccha, I do not have this view...."

"Now, Gotama, does the reverend Gotama have this view: 'The soul (*jīva*) and the body are the same; this is the truth, and all else is falsehood'?"

"Vaccha, I do not have this view...."

"Then, Gotama, does the reverend Gotama have this view: 'The soul is one thing and the body is another; this is the truth, and all else is falsehood'?"

"Vaccha, I do not have this view...."

"Now, Gotama, does the reverend Gotama have this view: 'After death, the Tathāgata exists; this is the truth, and all else is falsehood'?"

"Vaccha, I do not have this view...."

"Then, Gotama, does the reverend Gotama have this view: 'After death, the Tathāgata does not exist; this is the truth, and all else is falsehood'?"

"Vaccha, I do not have this view...."

"Now, Gotama, does the reverend Gotama have this view: 'After death, the Tathāgata both exists and does not exist; this is the truth, and all else is falsehood'?"

"Vaccha, I do not have this view. . . ."

"Then, Gotama, does the reverend Gotama have this view: 'After death, the Tathāgata neither exists nor does not exist; this is the truth, and all else is falsehood'?"

"Vaccha, I do not have this view. . . ."

"Gotama, what is the danger that the reverend Gotama sees that he does not hold any of these views?"

"Vaccha, thinking that 'the world is eternal' is going to a [wrong] view, holding a view, the wilderness of views, the writhing of views, the scuffling of views, the bonds of views; it is accompanied by anguish, distress, misery, fever; it does not lead to turning away from [the world], to dispassion, cessation, calm, clairvoyances, awakening, nor to nirvana. . . . Vaccha, contending that this is dangerous, I do not approach any of these views."

"But does Gotama have any views?"

"Vaccha, holding to any view has been eliminated by the Tathāgata . . . so I say that through destruction, dispassion, cessation, abandoning, getting rid of all imaginings, all supposings, all latent pride that 'I am the doer, mine is the deed,' a Tathāgata is released without desire."

"But Gotama, where is a monk whose mind is thus released reborn?"

"Vaccha, the term 'reborn' does not apply."

"Then, Gotama, is he not reborn?"

"Vaccha, the term 'not reborn' does not apply."

"Then, Gotama, is he both reborn and not reborn?"

"Vaccha, 'both reborn and not reborn' does not apply."

"Then, Gotama, is he neither reborn nor not reborn?"

"Vaccha, 'neither reborn nor not reborn' does not apply." . . .

"I am confused at this point, Gotama; I am bewildered, and I have lost all the satisfaction from the earlier conversation I had with Gotama."

"You should be confused, Vaccha, you should be bewildered. Vaccha, this doctrine *(dhamma)* is profound, difficult to see, difficult to understand, peaceful, wonderful, beyond argumentation, subtle, understood by the wise; but it is difficult for you, who hold another view, another allegiance, another goal, having different practices and a different teacher. Well, then, Vaccha, I will now question you in return. . . . If a fire were burning in front of you, would you know, 'This fire is burning in front of me'?"

"Gotama . . . I would know." . . .

"Vaccha, if the fire in front of you were put out, would you know, 'This fire that was in front of me has been put out'?"

"Gotama... I would know."

"But, Vaccha, if someone were to ask you—'Regarding that fire that was in front of you and that has been put out, in which direction has the fire gone from here: to the east, west, north, or south'—what would you reply to this question, Vaccha?"

"Gotama, it does not apply. Gotama, the fire burned because of a supply of grass and sticks, but due to having totally consumed this and due to a lack of other fuel, it is said to be put out since it is without fuel."

"Vaccha, in the same way, the form by which one recognizing the Tathāgata would recognize him has been eliminated by the Tathāgata, uprooted, made like a stump of a palm tree that has become non-existent and will not arise again in the future. Vaccha, the Tathāgata is released from designation by form, he is profound, immeasurable, unfathomable like the great ocean. 'Reborn' does not apply; 'not reborn' does not apply. The feelings... discriminations . . . compositional factors... consciousness by which one recognizing the Tathāgata might recognize him have been eliminated by the Tathāgata, uprooted... and will not arise again in the future. Vaccha, the Tathāgata is released from all designation by consciousness; he is profound, immeasurable, unfathomable as the great ocean. 'Reborn' does not apply; 'not reborn' does not apply; 'both reborn and not reborn' does not apply; 'neither reborn nor not reborn' does not apply."

Source: *Majjhima-nikāya* 3.72. Tr. JP.

SELFLESSNESS

Buddhism denies that there is anything corresponding to the common idea of a soul or self. Instead, the Buddha taught that the soul is a false notion imputed to a collection of constantly changing parts. These are the five "aggregates" (skandha): form, feelings, discriminations, consciousness, and compositional factors. Form refers to one's physical form, and feelings are our emotional responses to the things we experience. Discriminations are classifications of these experiences into pleasant, unpleasant, and neutral. Consciousness refers to the functioning of the mind, and compositional factors are other aspects connected with the false sense of self, such as one's karmas.

[Buddha:] "Monks, form is selflessness. Monks, if form were the self, then form would not be involved with sickness, and one could say of the body: 'Let my form be thus; let my form not be thus.' Monks, because form is selfless, it is involved with sickness, and one cannot say of form: 'Let my form be thus; let my form not be thus.'

"Feeling is selfless . . . discrimination is selfless . . . the aggregates are selfless . . . compositional factors are self-less . . . consciousness is selfless. Monks, if consciousness were the self, then consciousness would not be involved with sickness, and one could say of consciousness: 'Let my con-sciousness be thus; let my consciousness not be thus. . . .'

"What do you think, monks: Is form permanent or imper-manent?"

"Impermanent, sir."

"And is the impermanent suffering or happiness?"

"Suffering, sir."

"And with respect to what is impermanent, suffering, nat-urally unstable, is it proper to perceive it in this way: 'This is mine; I am this; this is my self?'"

"Definitely not, sir."

"It is the same way with feelings, discriminations, compo-sitional factors, and consciousness. Therefore, monks, every single form—past, future, or present; internal or external; gross or subtle; low or high; near or far—should be viewed in this way, as it really is, with correct insight: 'This is not mine; this is not I; this is not my self.'

"Every single feeling, every single discrimination, every single compositional factor . . . every single consciousness [should be viewed in this way].

"Perceiving [these] in this way, monks, the well-taught, wise disciple feels disgust for form, feels disgust for feeling, feels disgust for discrimination, feels disgust for composi-tional factors, and feels disgust for consciousness. Feeling disgust in this way, one becomes averse; becoming averse, one is liberated. Awareness that the liberated person is liber-ated arises, so that one knows: 'Birth is destroyed; the virtu-ous life has been lived; my work is done; for such a life there is nothing beyond [this world].' "

Source: *Saṃyutta-nikāya* 3.59. Tr. JP.

INSTRUCTIONS ON MEDITATION

Following the example of the Buddha, Buddhism emphasizes the importance of meditation as a means of attaining clarity of perception, eliminating mental afflictions, and escaping from cyclic existence. The following passage, attributed to Aśvaghoṣa (c. second century CE), is believed to contain instructions given by Buddha to his half-brother Nanda.

Now after having closed the windows of the senses with the shutters of mindfulness, you should know the proper measure of food in order to meditate properly and maintain good health. For too much food impedes the intake of breath, makes one lethargic and sleepy, and saps one's strength. Furthermore, just as too much food leads to distraction, eating too little makes one weak.... Thus as a practitioner of yoga you should feed your body simply in order to overcome hunger, and not out of desire for food or love of it.

After spending the day in self-controlled mental concentration, you should shake off sleepiness and spend the night engaged in the discipline of yoga. And do not think that your awareness is properly aware when drowsiness manifests itself in your heart. When you are overcome by sleepiness, you should apply your attention to exertion and steadfastness, strength and courage. You should clearly recite the texts you have been taught, and you should teach them to others and ponder them yourself. In order to remain awake, splash water on your face, look around in all directions, and look at the stars....

During the first three watches of the night, you should practice [meditation], but after that you should lie down and rest on your right side, remaining awake in your heart, your mind at peace, keeping your attention on the idea of light. In the third watch, you should get up and, either walking or sitting, continue to practice yoga, with a pure mind and controlled senses....

Sit cross-legged in a solitary place, keep your back straight, and direct your mindfulness in front of you, [focusing] on the tip of the nose, the forehead, or the space between the eyebrows. Keep the wandering mind focused completely on one thing. If a mental affliction—a desirous thought—arises, you should not hold to it, but should brush it off like dust on your clothes. Even if you have eliminated desires from your mind, there is still an innate tendency toward them, like a fire smoldering in ashes. My friend, this should be extinguished by meditation, in the way that fire is extinguished by water. Unless you do this, desire will arise again from the innate tendency, as plants arise from a seed. Only by destroying [the tendencies] will they finally be eradicated, like plants whose roots have been destroyed....

When one washes dirt from gold, one first gets rid of the largest pieces of dirt, and then the smaller ones, and having cleaned it one is left with pieces of pure gold. In the

same way, in order to attain liberation, one should discipline the mind, first washing away the coarser faults, and
then the smaller ones, until one is left with pure pieces of
dharma.

Source: *Saundarananda* chs. 14, 15. Tr. JP.

ORDINATION OF WOMEN

*When Buddha began his teaching career, his first disciples
were monks, but eventually some women became followers and
began to desire ordination as nuns. The woman who put the
request to Buddha was Mahāpajapatī Gotamī, who had raised
him after his mother died. Buddha first refused her request,
but after she obtained the support of Ānanda, Buddha's personal assistant, he eventually agreed, but he added that the
decision to admit nuns into the order would shorten the period
of "true dharma" by 500 years. It seems clear from the passage, however, that this is not due to any inherent inferiority
on the part of women because Buddha asserts that women are
capable of following the spiritual path and attaining the fruits of
meditative training.*

*Some commentators speculate that the reason for his refusal
may have been that his early followers were homeless wander-
ers, so there were no adequate facilities for separating men and
women. Because of the pervasiveness and strength of sexual
desire, groups of men and women in close proximity inevitably develop attractions and tensions, which lead to conflict.
Whatever the reasons for his initial reluctance, Buddha did eventually ordain women, but he added the condition that nuns must
observe eight additional rules.*

> Then Mahāpajapatī Gotamī approached the Lord and,
> having paid obeisance to him, stood to one side. And
> Mahāpajapatī Gotamī said this to the Lord: "Lord, it would be
> good if women could be initiated into the order, in the doc-
> trine and discipline taught by the Tathāgata."
> [Buddha replied:] "Gotamī, do not request the initiation of
> women into the order. . . ."
> *She made her request two more times, but after being
> refused she despondently concluded that Buddha would not
> allow the ordination of women.*
> Then Mahāpajapatī Gotamī, having cut off her hair,
> putting on saffron robes, went to Vesālī . . . and when she
> arrived, her feet were swollen, her body covered with dust,
> tears covered her face, as she stood outside the grove [where
> the Buddha was staying].

When the venerable Ānanda saw Mahāpajapatī Gotamī standing there . . . he asked, "Gotamī, why are you standing there, your feet swollen, your body covered with dust, and crying?"

"Venerable Ānanda, it is because the Lord does not allow women to be initiated into the order, in the doctrine and discipline taught by the Tathāgata."

On hearing this, Ānanda offered to intercede on her behalf and approached the Buddha, asking why he had refused her.

Then the venerable Ānanda approached the Lord and, having paid obeisance to him, stood to one side. . . . And he said this to the Lord: "Lord, Mahāpajapatī Gotamī is standing outside the grove, her feet swollen, her body covered with dust, tears on her face, and crying, and she says that the Lord will not allow women to be initiated into the order, in the doctrine and discipline taught by the Tathāgata. Lord, it would be good if women were to be initiated into the order. . . ."

"Ānanda, do not request the initiation of women into the order, in the doctrine and discipline taught by the Tathāgata."

Then the venerable Ānanda thought, "The Lord does not allow the initiation of women into the order . . . but perhaps I can ask in another way. . . ." Then the venerable Ānanda said to the Lord: "Lord, are women who have been initiated into the order, in the doctrine and discipline taught by the Tathāgata, able to attain the fruit of a stream-enterer, or the fruit of a once-returner, or the fruit of a non-returner, or *arhat*hood?"

"Ānanda, women who have been initiated into the order . . . are able to attain the fruit of a stream-enterer, or the fruit of a once-returner, or the fruit of a non-returner, or *arhat*hood."[11]

"So, Lord, women who have been initiated into the order are able to attain [these fruits], and Mahāpajapatī Gotamī was very helpful to the Lord: she was the Lord's aunt, foster mother, and nurse, she suckled him when his mother died [and he should repay her kindness]."

---

[11] These are terms indicating levels of spiritual attainment. A stream-winner has entered the path leading to liberation. A once-returner is a person who in one more life will become an *arhat* and attain nirvana. A non-returner will attain nirvana in the present life.

[Hearing this, Buddha said:] "Ānanda, if Mahāpajapatī Gotamī accepts eight cardinal rules she may receive initiation into the order...."

Then Ānanda...went to Mahāpajapatī Gotamī and said, "Gotamī, if you will accept eight cardinal rules,[12] you may receive initiation into the order...."

[She replied:] "Honored Ānanda, I accept these eight cardinal rules and will never transgress them during my entire life."

Ānanda then informed Buddha that Mahāpajapatī had accepted these rules, to which he replied:

"Ānanda, if women had not been given the opportunity to receive initiation into the order, in the doctrine and discipline taught by the Tathāgata, then, Ānanda, the monastic system would have lasted longer, and the true doctrine would have endured for one thousand years. But, Ānanda, since women may now receive ordination...the monastic system will only endure for five hundred years."

Source: *Vinaya-piṭaka, Cullavagga*, ch. 10, from *Rules of Discipline for Nuns (Bhikṣuṇī Vinaya)*. Tr. JP.

THE CESSATION OF SUFFERING

After the Buddha agreed to create an order of nuns, a number of women took monastic vows, and some eventually were recognized as advanced meditators. These verses were written by the nun Paṭācārā after she became an arhatī *(a female* arhat*). Her early biography, recounted in* Songs of the Nuns (Therīgāthā), *graphically illustrates the problems of cyclic existence. Her entire family is killed one by one under tragic circumstances, and she is driven to the brink of madness. In a state of utter despair, she meets the Buddha, who counsels her and allows her to become a nun. After years of meditative practice, she severs all attachments to worldly things, recognizing them as a source of suffering.*

---

[12] The eight rules require that (1) any nun, no matter how senior, must respectfully salute a monk, no matter how junior; (2) aspiring nuns must undergo a two-year training period, and then be ordained by both the communities of monks and nuns; (3) nuns must not criticize monks; (4) nuns may not receive alms before monks; (5) nuns who violate rules of conduct are subject to disciplinary action for a fortnight and must then seek restitution from the communities of monks and nuns; (6) every fortnight the nuns should ask the monks for instruction; (7) nuns may not spend the rainy season retreat in the company of monks; and (8) after finishing the rainy season retreat, nuns should request the ceremony marking the end of the retreat from the communities of monks and nuns.

Plowing their fields, sowing seeds in the ground,
Men care for their wives and children and prosper.
Why is it that I, endowed with morality and adhering to the teachings,
Do not attain nirvana? I am neither lazy nor conceited.
After washing my feet, I observed the water; watching the water flow downwards,
I focused my mind as one [trains] a noble thoroughbred horse.
Then I took a lamp and entered my cell. After observing the bed, I sat on the couch.
Holding a pin, I pulled out the wick.
The lamp goes out: nirvana. My mind is free!

Source: *Therīgāthā,* psalm 47. Tr. JP.

MY TEACHER

The Songs of the Nuns *collection contains a wealth of information on the religious lives of the early Buddhist nuns. Their biographies describe their struggles and tribulations, and many indicate that they saw monastic ordination as a way to escape the drudgery of household work and loveless marriages. The following passage was written by an anonymous nun who celebrates her liberation from sorrow. It praises her teacher, a fellow nun who showed her the path.*

Four or five times I went from my cell
Without having attained peace of mind or control over my mind.
I approached a nun whom I could trust, and she taught me about the doctrine,
The aggregates, the sense spheres, and the elements.
Having listened to her doctrinal instructions, I sat cross legged for seven days,
Possessed of joy and bliss.
On the eighth day I stretched out my feet,
Having eliminated the mass of darkness (of ignorance).

Source: *Therīgāthā,* psalm 38. Tr. JP.

THE JOY OF RELEASE

The following poem was written by the mother of Sumaṅgala (a monk who became an arhat*). She was the wife of a poor umbrella maker who left her home and became a nun. Later she attained the level of* arhathood, *which she celebrates in these verses.*

Free, I am free!
I am completely free from my kitchen pestle!
[I am free from] my worthless husband and even his sun umbrella!

And my pot that smells like a water snake!
I have eliminated all desire and hatred,
Going to the base of a tree, [I think,] "What happiness!"
And contemplate this happiness.

Source: *Therīgāthā,* psalm 22. Tr. JP.

THE BUDDHA'S LAST DAYS
AND FINAL INSTRUCTIONS

After a long and successful teaching career, the Buddha's body had become old and wracked with constant pain. Realizing that his mission had been accomplished, the Buddha decided to enter final nirvana (parinirvāṇa). He first asked his disciples if they had any final questions and then told them that they should rely on the teachings they had already received. Buddha further informed them that he had told them everything of the path and the true doctrine that could be put into words, holding nothing back, and so it was now up to them to put these teachings into practice.

[Buddha:] "Ānanda, I have taught the doctrine without distinguishing 'inner' and 'outer.' As to this, the Tathāgata is not a 'closed-fisted teacher' with reference to the doctrine [i.e., he does not hold anything back]. If anyone thinks, 'I should watch over the order,' or 'The order should refer to me,' then let him promulgate something about the order. The Tathāgata does not think in such terms. Thus the Tathāgata does not promulgate something about the order. . . .

"Ānanda, I am now aged, old, an elder, my time has gone, I have arrived at the age of eighty years. Just as an old cart is made to go by tying it together with straps, so the Tathāgata's body is made to go by strapping it together. Ānanda, during periods when the Tathāgata, by withdrawing his attention from all signs, by the cessation of some emotions, enters into the signless concentration of thought and stays in it, on such occasions the Tathāgata's body is made comfortable.

"Therefore, Ānanda . . . you should live with yourselves as islands, with yourselves as refuges, with no one else as refuge; with the doctrine as an island, with the doctrine as a refuge, with no one else as refuge. . . .

"It might be that you will think, Ānanda, 'The Teacher's word has ceased, now we have no teacher!' You should not perceive things in this way. The doctrine and discipline that I have taught and described will be the teacher after I pass away."

He then told Ānanda that after his death it would be permissible for monks to abolish the minor rules of monastic discipline, but Ānanda neglected to ask him which these were. Buddha again exhorted his followers to rely on the teachings he had already taught them, and Ānanda informed him that none of the monks present had any doubts about the doctrine, the path, or monastic discipline. Buddha then delivered his final teaching to his disciples:

"Monks, all compounded things are subject to decay and disintegration. Work out your own salvations with diligence." These were the Tathāgata's last words.

Source: *Dīgha-nikāya, Mahāparinibbāna-sutta*. Tr. JP.

THE QUESTIONS OF KING MILINDA

According to Buddhist tradition, the Bactrian king Menander (Pāli: Milinda) engaged the Buddhist sage Nāgasena in a series of philosophical discussions in which Nāgasena convinced him of the truth of the Buddha's teachings. The following dialogue concerns the Buddhist doctrine of selflessness, which holds that there is no enduring self, no soul, no truly existent personal identity. The king at first expresses disbelief, pointing out that he is clearly speaking to Nāgasena, who seems to be a concretely existing person.

Nāgasena convinces the king by using the analogy of a chariot, which is composed of parts that separately are incapable of performing the functions of a chariot but which when assembled are given the conventional designation "chariot." Similarly, human beings (and all other phenomena) are merely collections of parts that are given conventional designations, but they lack any enduring entity.

Then King Milinda said to the venerable Nāgasena: "What is your reverence called? What is your name, reverend sir?"

"Sire, I am known as Nāgasena; my fellow religious practitioners, sir, address me as Nāgasena. But although [my] parents gave [me] the name of Nāgasena...still it is only a designation, a name, a denotation, a conventional expression, since Nāgasena is only a name because there is no person here to be found...."

"If, reverend Nāgasena, there is no person to be found, who is it that gives you necessities like robe material, food, lodging, and medicines for the sick, who is it that uses them, who is it that keeps the precepts, practices meditation, actualizes the paths, the fruits, nirvana; who kills living beings, takes what is not given, commits immoral acts, tells lies, drinks intoxicants, and commits the five types of immediate karmas? In that case, there is no virtue; there is no non-virtue; there is no one who does or who makes another do things that are virtuous or non-virtuous; there is no fruit or ripening of good or bad karma. Reverend Nāgasena, if someone kills you, there will be no demerit. Also, reverend Nāgasena, you have no teacher, no preceptor, no ordination....

"Is form Nāgasena?"

"No, sire."

"Is feeling Nāgasena?"

"No, sire."

"Is discrimination Nāgasena?"

"No, sire."

"Are compositional factors Nāgasena?"

"No, sire."

"Is consciousness Nāgasena?"

"No, sire."

"Then, reverend sir, are form, feelings, discriminations, compositional factors, and consciousness together Nāgasena?"

"No, sire."

"Then, reverend sir, is there something other than form, feelings, discriminations, compositional factors, and consciousness that is Nāgasena?"

"No, sire."

"Reverend sir, although I question you closely, I fail to find any Nāgasena. Nāgasena is only a sound, sir. Who is Nāgasena? Reverend sir, you are speaking a lie, a falsehood: there is no Nāgasena."

Then the venerable Nāgasena said to king Milinda: ". . . Your majesty, did you come here on foot, or riding?"

"Reverend sir, I did not come on foot; I came in a chariot."

"Sire, if you came in a chariot, show me the chariot. Is the pole the chariot, sire?"

"No, reverend sir."

"Is the axle the chariot?"

"No, reverend sir."

"Are the wheels . . . the frame . . . the banner-staff . . . the yoke . . . the reins . . . the goad the chariot?"

"No, reverend sir."

"Then, sire, are pole, axle, wheels, frame, banner-staff, yoke, reins, goad together the chariot?"

"No, reverend sir."

"Then, sire, is something other than the pole, axle, wheels, frame, banner-staff, yoke, reins, goad together the chariot?"

"No, reverend sir."

"Sire, although I question you closely, I fail to find any chariot. Chariot is only a sound, sire. What is the chariot? . . ."

"Reverend Nāgasena . . . it is because of the pole, axle, wheels, frame, banner-staff, yoke, reins, and goad that 'chariot' exists as a designation, appellation, denotation, as a conventional usage, as a name."

"Good: sire, you understand the chariot. It is just like this for me, sire: because of the hair of the head and because of the hair of the body . . . and because of the brain of the head, form, feelings, discriminations, compositional factors, and consciousness that 'Nāgasena' exists as designation, appellation, denotation, as a conventional usage, as a name. But ultimately there is no person to be found here. . . ."

"Wonderful, reverend Nāgasena! Marvelous, reverend Nāgasena! The replies to the questions that were asked are truly brilliant. If the Buddha were still here, he would applaud. Well done, well done, Nāgasena!"

Source: *Milinda-pañha,* 2.25–28. Tr. JP.

HOW TO AVOID EXTREME VIEWS

Buddhaghosa, the greatest commentator of the Theravāda tradition, expands on the analogy of the chariot and indicates how this analysis relates to meditative practice and the pursuit of liberation.

Thus, just as when the parts—the axle, wheels, frame, pole—are put together in a certain way, the mere word "chariot" is used, but ultimately there is no such thing as "chariot" when any of the parts are examined; so when the parts of a house, such as the exterior, are put together in a certain way enclosing a space, the mere word "house" is used, but ultimately there is no such thing as a house; or when fingers and so forth are placed together in a certain way, the mere word "fist" is used; or the mere words "lute," "army," "town," "tree" are used when their respective parts—such as the body of the lute and the strings, elephants and horses, walls and houses and gates, trunk and branches and leaves—are arranged in certain positions, but there is ultimately no such thing as a tree when one examines each part. So when the five aggregates of grasping exist, the mere word "being," "person" is used, but when one examines each of the states, ultimately there is no such thing as a being: it is the object of a misconception that makes one say, "I am" or "I"; ultimately there is just name and form. The perception of one who perceives in this way is called perception of reality.

And one who abandons perception of reality and holds to the view that a being exists must admit that it will perish or that it will not perish. If one asserts that it will not perish, then one falls to the [extreme view of] permanence; if one asserts that it will perish, then one falls to the [extreme view of] nihilism. There is no other state which is a product of that being, as curd is a product of milk. One who holds that a being is eternal falls [into the pleasures of the senses]; one who holds that it is annihilated is carried away by an extreme [view]. Therefore, the Exalted One has said:

> Monks, there are two [wrong] views through which some gods and humans fall into the pleasures of existence and are carried away by existence; only those who have the eye [of truth] see the truth. Monks, how do some fall into the pleasures of existence? Monks, there are gods and humans who delight in existence, who are thrilled with existence, who are enraptured by existence. When they are taught the dharma that leads to cessation of existence, their minds do not respond, do not have faith, are not steady and focused. Monks, in this way some fall into existence.
>
> And how, monks, are some extremists? Some are oppressed by, ashamed of, disgusted by existence, some delight in non-existence, saying, "Since it is said that when the body dissolves this self is cut off, dies, and does not exist after death, that is peace, that is wisdom, that is the truth." Monks, in this way some are extremists.
>
> Monks, how do those who have the eye [of truth] see these things? Monks, in this a monk sees the five aggregates as they are. Seeing the five aggregates as they are, he practices in order that he will become disgusted with them, have no desire for them, so that they might cease. Monks, this is how one who has the eye [of truth] sees.

Source: *Visuddhimagga* by Buddhaghosa. Tr. JP.

MAHĀYĀNA SCRIPTURES

THE HEART OF PERFECT WISDOM DISCOURSE

The following passage is the entire text of the Heart of Perfect Wisdom Discourse, *one of the shortest texts of the Perfection of Wisdom corpus. It is said by Mahāyānists to contain the essence of the teachings of this voluminous literature.*

Thus have I heard: At one time the Exalted One was dwelling on the Vulture Peak in Rājagṛha together with a great assembly of monks and a great assembly of bodhisattvas.

At that time, the Exalted One was immersed in a meditative absorption *(samādhi)* on the enumerations of phenomena called "perception of the profound." Also at that time, the bodhisattva, the great being, the superior Avalokiteśvara was considering the meaning of the profound perfection of wisdom, and he saw that the five aggregates *(skandha)* are empty of inherent existence. Then, due to the inspiration of the Buddha, the venerable Śāriputra spoke thus to the bodhisattva, the great being, the superior Avalokiteśvara: "How should a son of good lineage train if he wants to practice the profound perfection of wisdom?"

The bodhisattva, the great being, the superior Avalokiteśvara spoke thus to the venerable Śāriputra: "Śāriputra, sons of good lineage or daughters of good lineage who want to practice the profound perfection of wisdom should perceive [reality] in this way: They should correctly perceive the five aggregates also as empty of inherent existence. Form is emptiness; emptiness is form. Emptiness is not other than form; form is not other than emptiness. In the same way, feelings, discriminations, compositional factors, and consciousness are empty. Śāriputra, in that way, all phenomena are empty, without characteristics, unproduced, unceasing, undefiled, not undefiled, not decreasing, not increasing.

"Therefore, Śāriputra, in emptiness there is no form, no feelings, no discriminations, no compositional factors, no consciousness, no eye, no ear, no nose, no tongue, no body, no mind, no form, no sound, no odor, no taste, no object of touch, no phenomenon. There is no eye constituent, no mental constituent, up to and including no mental consciousness constituent. There is no ignorance, no extinction of ignorance, up to and including no aging and death and no extinction of aging and death. In the same way, there is no suffering, no source [of suffering], no cessation [of suffering], no path, no exalted wisdom, no attainment, and also no non-attainment.

"Therefore, Śāriputra, because bodhisattvas have no attainment, they depend on and abide in the perfection of wisdom. Because their minds are unobstructed, they are without fear. Having completely passed beyond all error, they go to the fulfillment of nirvana. All the buddhas who live in the three times [past, present, and future] have been completely awakened into unsurpassable, complete, perfect awakening through relying on the perfection of wisdom.

"Therefore, the mantra of the perfection of wisdom is the mantra of great knowledge, the unsurpassable mantra, the mantra that is equal to the unequaled, the mantra that thoroughly pacifies all suffering. Because it is not false, it should be known to be true. The mantra of the perfection wisdom is as follows:

> Oṃ *gate gate paragate parasaṃgate bodhir svāha* [*Oṃ* gone, gone, gone beyond, gone completely beyond; praise to awakening.]

"Śāriputra, bodhisattvas, great beings, should train in the profound perfection of wisdom in that way."

Then the Exalted One arose from that meditative absorption and said to the bodhisattva, the great being, the superior Avalokiteśvara: "Well done! Well done, well done, son of good lineage, it is just so. Son of good lineage, it is like that; the profound perfection of wisdom should be practiced just as you have indicated. Even the Tathāgatas admire this."

When the Exalted One had spoken thus, the venerable Śāriputra, the bodhisattva, the great being, the superior Avalokiteśvara, and all those around them, and those of the world, the gods, humans, demigods, and *gandharvas* were filled with admiration and praised the words of the Exalted One.

Source: *Prajñāpāramitā-hṛdaya-sūtra.* Tr. JP.

EXCERPTS FROM THE *DIAMOND SŪTRA*

Perfection of Wisdom texts contain many warnings against holding too rigidly to doctrines, even Buddhist doctrines. In the following passage, Buddha warns his disciple Subhūti against conceiving sentient beings as truly existing, and then applies the reasoning of emptiness to other Buddhist categories.

[Buddha:] "Subhūti,[13] due to being established in the bodhisattva vehicle, one should give rise to the thought, 'As many sentient beings there are that are included among the realms of sentient beings . . . whatever realms of sentient beings can be conceived, all these should be brought by me to nirvana, to a final nirvana that is a realm of nirvana without remainder; but, although countless sentient beings have reached final nirvana, no sentient being whatsoever has reached final nirvana.' Why is this? Subhūti, if a discrimination of a sentient being arises in a bodhisattva [literally, 'awakening-being'], he should not be called an awakening-being. Why is this? Subhūti, one who gives rise to the

---

[13] Subhūti is one of Buddha's great Hīnayāna disciples. He often appears as an interlocutor in Mahāyāna *sūtras*, however. The reason for this is probably that in several Pāli texts he is declared by Buddha to be the foremost of his disciples in understanding of emptiness, which is a central concept in Mahāyāna literature.

discrimination of such a self, the discrimination of a sentient being, the discrimination of a soul, or the discrimination of a person should not be called a bodhisattva. . . .

"Subhūti, all of them produce and acquire an immeasurable and incalculable store of merit. Why is this? Subhūti, it is because these bodhisattvas, great beings, do not give rise to the discrimination of a self, the discrimination of a sentient being, the discrimination of a soul, or the discrimination of a person. Also, Subhūti, these bodhisattvas, great beings, do not give rise to discriminations of phenomena, nor do they give rise to discriminations of non-phenomena, nor do they give rise to discrimination or to non-discrimination.

"Why is this? Subhūti, if these bodhisattvas, great beings, gave rise to discriminations of phenomena, this would be grasping a self, grasping a sentient being, grasping a soul, grasping a person. If they gave rise to discriminations of non-phenomena, this also would be grasping a self, grasping a sentient being, grasping a soul, grasping a person. Why is this? Subhūti, in no way should a bodhisattva, a great being, grasp either phenomena nor non-phenomena. Therefore, this has been said by the Tathāgata with hidden intent: 'For those who understand the teaching of dharma that is like a raft, dharma should be abandoned, and still more non-dharma.'"

Source: *Vajracchedika-prajñāpāramitā-sūtra* selections. Tr. JP.

WHY BODHISATTVAS ARE SUPERIOR TO HEARERS

Some early Mahāyāna texts have a distinctly sectarian tone, particularly when they compare the ideals of the arhat *and the* bodhisattva. *In the following passage from the 8,000 Line Perfection of Wisdom Discourse, Buddha describes to Subhūti the differences between the attitudes of Hīnayānists and those of Mahāyānists.*

[Buddha:] "Subhūti, bodhisattvas, great beings, should not train in the way that persons of the hearer vehicle and solitary realizer vehicle train.[14] Subhūti, in what way do

---

[14] Hearers (*śrāvaka*) and solitary realizers (*pratyeka-buddha*) are the two main classes of Hīnayāna practitioners. The former are so called because they hear the words of Buddha, take them literally, and put them into practice. Their main goal is the attainment of the nirvana of an *arhat*. Solitary realizers are practitioners who travel a more difficult path than that of hearers, but who likewise attain nirvana for themselves. Both of these paths are portrayed as selfish in Mahāyāna literature because those who follow them are primarily concerned with personal salvation, and not with the salvation of others.

persons of the hearer vehicle and the solitary realizer vehicle train? Subhūti, they think thus, '[I] should discipline only myself; [I] should pacify only myself; [I] should attain nirvana by myself.' In order to discipline only themselves and pacify themselves and attain nirvana, they begin to apply themselves to establishing all the virtuous roots. Also, Subhūti, bodhisattvas, great beings, should not train in this way. On the contrary, Subhūti, bodhisattvas, great beings, should train thus, 'In order to benefit all the world, I will dwell in suchness; and, establishing all sentient beings in suchness,[15] I will lead the immeasurable realms of sentient beings to nirvana.' Bodhisattvas, great beings, should begin applying themselves in that way to establishing all virtuous roots,[16] but should not be conceited because of this. . . .

"Those who say, 'In this very life, having thoroughly freed the mind from contamination, without attachment, [I] will pass beyond sorrow' are 'at the level of hearers and solitary realizers.' With respect to this, bodhisattvas, great beings, should not give rise to such thoughts. Why is this? Subhūti, bodhisattvas, great beings, abide in the great vehicle and put on the great armor; they should not give rise to thoughts of even a little elaboration.[17] Why is this? These supreme beings thoroughly lead the world and are a great benefit to the world. Therefore, they should always and uninterruptedly train well in the six perfections."[18]

Source: *Aṣṭasāhasrikā-prajñāpāramitā-sūtra ('Phags pa shes rab kyi pha rol tu phyin pa brgyad stong pa'i mdo)*, ch. 11. Tr. JP.

WHY THE BODHISATTVA WORKS ALONE

In Mahāyāna texts, the bodhisattva is portrayed as a heroic figure, valiantly following the path to buddhahood for the benefit of others. The following passage indicates that this is a long and difficult path that each individual must traverse alone.

---

[15] Suchness *(tathatā)* refers to the true nature of phenomena and is equated in Buddhist texts with emptiness.

[16] Virtuous roots *(kuśala-mūla)* are the result of cultivating good qualities. When a person engages in meritorious conduct and cultivates corresponding attitudes, this creates positive predispositions that motivate that person to continue acting in similar ways in the future.

[17] Elaboration *(prapañca)* refers to proliferation of conceptual thought.

[18] The six perfections *(pāramitā)* are the qualities in which bodhisattvas train on the path to buddhahood, and which form the core of the exalted qualities of buddhas: generosity, ethics, patience, effort, concentration, and wisdom.

The bodhisattva is alone, with no . . . companion, and puts on the armor of supreme wisdom. He acts alone and leaves nothing to others, working with a will that is firm with courage and strength. He is strong in his own strength . . . and he thinks thus: "I will help all sentient beings to obtain whatever they should obtain. . . .

"The virtue of generosity is not my helper—I am the helper of generosity. Nor do the virtues of ethics, patience, effort, concentration, and wisdom help me—it is I who help them. The perfections of the bodhisattva do not support me— it is I who support them. . . . I alone, standing in this round and hard world, must subdue Māra,[19] with all his hosts and chariots, and develop supreme awakening with the wisdom of instantaneous insight."

Just as the rising sun, the child of the gods, is not stopped . . . by all the dust rising from the four continents of the earth . . . or by wreaths of smoke . . . or by rugged mountains, so bodhisattvas, great beings . . . are not deterred from bringing virtuous roots to fruition, whether by the malice of others . . . or by their wrong-doing or error, or by their mental agitation. . . . They will not lay down their limbs of awakening because of the corrupt generations of humanity, nor do they waver in their resolution to save the world because of their wretched quarrels. . . . They do not lose heart on account of their faults. . . .

They think, "All creatures are in pain; all suffer from bad and hindering karma . . . so that they cannot see the buddhas or hear the true doctrine or know the monastic community. . . . All that mass of pain and evil karma I take in my own body . . . I take upon myself the burden of sorrow; I resolve to do so; I endure it all. I do not turn back or run away, I do not tremble . . . I am not afraid . . . nor do I despair. I must definitely bear the burdens of all sentient beings . . . for I have resolved to save them all, I must set them all free, I must save the whole world from the forest of birth, aging, sickness, and rebirth, from misfortune and wrong-doing, from the round of birth and death, from the dangers of error. . . . For all sentient beings are caught in the net of desire, enmeshed in ignorance, held by the desire for existence; they are doomed to destruction, shut in a cage of pain . . . they are ignorant, untrustworthy, full of doubts, always fighting one

---

[19] Māra is a demonic figure in Buddhist literature who attempted to thwart the Buddha's pursuit of nirvana and is commonly blamed when monks or nuns violate monastic rules or return to lay life. His main tool is to use desire to turn their attention from religious activities.

with another, always prone to see evil; they cannot find a refuge in the ocean of existence; they are all on the edge of the gulf of destruction.

"I work to establish the kingdom of perfect wisdom for all sentient beings. I care not at all for my own liberation. I must save all sentient beings from the river of rebirth with the raft of my omniscient mind. I must pull them back from the great precipice. I must free them from all misfortune, ferry them over the stream of rebirth.

"For I have taken upon myself, by my own will, the whole of the pain of all living things. Thus I dare try every place of pain, in ... every part of the universe, for I must not keep virtuous roots from the world. I resolve to live in each bad state for countless eons ... for the salvation of all sentient beings ... for it is better that I alone suffer than that all sentient beings sink to the bad transmigrations [animals, hungry ghosts, hell beings]. There I shall give myself into bondage, to redeem all the world from the forest of suffering, from births as animals, from the realm of death. I shall bear all grief and pain in my own body for the good of all living things. I vow to work for all sentient beings, speaking the truth, trustworthy, not breaking my word. I will not abandon them. . . . I must be their charioteer, I must be their leader, I must be their torchbearer, I must be their guide to safety. . . . I must not wait for the help of another, nor must I lose my resolution and leave my tasks to another. I must not turn back in my efforts to save all sentient beings nor cease to use my merit for the destruction of all pain. And I must not be satisfied with small successes."

Source: *Śikṣāsamuccaya,* pp. 278–283. Tr. JP.

ON THE DIFFERENCES BETWEEN MEN AND WOMEN

The following dialogue applies the doctrine of emptiness to the commonly accepted differences between men and women. When these are closely examined, they are found to be merely the results of misguided conceptuality because there is no inherently existent difference between the sexes.

The dialogue occurs in the house of Vimalakīrti, a lay bodhisattva who is pretending to be sick in order to initiate a discourse on the dharma. The Buddha's disciples follow Mañjuśrī—an advanced bodhisattva who is said to embody wisdom—to Vimalakīrti's house in order to hear the two discuss the perfection of wisdom. The interchange is so profound that a young goddess who lives in Vimalakīrti's house rains down flowers on the assembly. The Hīnayāna monks who are present try frantically to brush them off because monks are forbidden in the Vinaya *to wear flowers or adornments. The bodhisattvas in the audience, however, are unaffected by such rigid adherence to rules, and so the flowers fall from their robes.*

This causes Śāriputra—described in Pāli texts as the most advanced of the Buddha's Hīnayāna disciples in the development of wisdom—to marvel at the attainments of the goddess and the bodhisattvas. She chides him for viewing the fruits of meditative training as things to be acquired, and in response Śāriputra asks her why she does not change from a woman into a man. The question appears to be based on traditional Indian perceptions of authority, according to which wisdom is associated with elder males. The goddess violates these principles because she is young and female. But it is clear from the dialogue that she is very advanced in understanding the perfection of wisdom.

The goddess responds to Śāriputra's challenge by turning him into a woman and herself into a man. This leads to one of the most poignant scenes in the sūtra, in which Śāriputra experiences discomfort in his new body, apparently because of the Vinaya *injunctions preventing monks from physical contact with women. Śāriputra, now in a woman's body, is unable to avoid such contact and tells the goddess that he is a woman without being a woman. The goddess replies that all women are women without being women, because "woman" is merely a conventional designation with no ultimate referent.*

A goddess who lived in the house of Vimalakīrti, having heard the doctrinal teaching of the bodhisattvas, the great beings, was very pleased, delighted, and moved. She took on a material form and scattered heavenly flowers over the great bodhisattvas and great hearers. When she had thrown them, the flowers that landed on the bodies of the bodhisattvas fell to the ground, while those that fell on the bodies of the great hearers remained stuck to them and did not fall to the ground. Then the great hearers tried to use their supernatural powers to shake off the flowers, but the flowers did not fall off.

Then the goddess asked the venerable Śāriputra: "Venerable Śāriputra, why do you try to shake off the flowers?"

"Goddess, flowers are not fitting for monks; that is why we reject them."

"Venerable Śāriputra, do not speak thus. Why? These flowers are perfectly fitting. Why? The flowers are flowers and are free from conceptuality; it is only yourselves, the elders, who conceptualize them and create conceptuality toward them. Venerable Śāriputra, among those who have renounced the world to take up monastic discipline, such conceptualizations and conceptuality are not fitting; it is those who do not conceive either conceptualizations or conceptuality who are fit.

"Venerable Śāriputra, take a good look at these bodhisattvas, great beings: the flowers do not stick to them because they have abandoned conceptuality.... Flowers stick to those who have not yet abandoned the defilements; they do not stick to those who have abandoned them...."

"Well done! Well done, Goddess! What have you attained, what have you gained that enables you to have such eloquence?"

"It is because I have not attained anything nor gained anything that I have such eloquence. Those who think that they have attained or gained something are deluded with respect to the well-taught disciplinary doctrine...."

"Goddess, why do you not change your womanhood?"

"During the twelve years [that I have lived in this house], I have looked for womanhood, but have never found it. Venerable Śāriputra, if a skillful magician created an illusory woman through transformation, could you ask her why she does not change her womanhood?"

"Every illusory creation is unreal."

"In the same way, venerable Śāriputra, all phenomena are unreal and have an illusory nature; why would you think of asking them to change their womanhood?"

Then the goddess performed a supernatural feat that caused the elder Śāriputra to appear in every way like the goddess and she herself to appear in every way like the elder Śāriputra. Then the goddess who had changed into Śāriputra asked Śāriputra who had been changed into a goddess: "Why do you not change your womanhood, venerable sir?"

[Śāriputra:] "I do not know either how I lost my male form or how I acquired a female body."

[Goddess:] "Elder, if you were able to change your female form, then all women could change their womanhood. Elder, just as you appear to be a woman, so also all women appear in the form of women, but they appear in the form of women without being women. It was with this hidden thought that the Exalted One said: 'Phenomena are neither male nor female.'"

Then the goddess cut off her supernatural power and the venerable Śāriputra regained his previous form. Then the goddess said to Śāriputra: "Venerable Śāriputra, where is your female form now?"

[Śāriputra:] "My female form is neither made nor changed."

[Goddess:] "Well done! Well done, venerable sir! In the same way, all phenomena, just as they are, are neither made nor changed. Saying that they are neither made nor changed is the word of the Buddha. . . ."

[Śāriputra:] "Goddess, how long will it be before you reach awakening?"

[Goddess:] "Elder, when you yourself return to being a worldly person, with all the qualities of a worldly person, then I myself will reach unsurpassed, perfect awakening."

[Śāriputra:] "Goddess, it is impossible that I could return to being a worldly person, with all the qualities of a worldly person; it cannot occur."

[Goddess:] "Venerable Śāriputra, in the same way, it is impossible that I will ever attain unsurpassed, perfect awakening; it cannot occur. Why? Because unsurpassed, perfect awakening is founded on a non-foundation. Thus, since there is no foundation, who could reach unsurpassed, perfect awakening?"

[Śāriputra:] "But the Tathāgata has said: '*tathāgata*s as innumerable as the sands of the Ganges river attain, have attained, and will attain unsurpassed, perfect awakening.'"

[Goddess:] "Venerable Śāriputra, the words, 'buddhas past, future, and present' are conventional expressions made up of syllables and numbers. Buddhas are neither past, nor future, nor present, and their awakening transcends the three divisions of time. Tell me, elder, have you already attained the level of *arhat*?"

[Śāriputra:] "I have attained it because there is nothing to attain."

[Goddess:] "It is the same with awakening: it is attained because there is nothing to attain."

Source: *Vimalakīrti-nirdeśa-sūtra* ('*Phags pa dri ma med par grags pas bstan pa'i mdo*), ch. 6. Tr. JP.

THE *LOTUS SŪTRA*: PARABLE OF THE BURNING HOUSE

The parable of the burning house is a famous allegory for the practice of "skillful means" (upāya-kauśalya), one of the important abilities of bodhisattvas and buddhas. It involves adapting the dharma to the interests and proclivities of individual listeners, telling them things that will attract them to the practice of Buddhism. The question posed in this dialogue concerns whether such tactics should be considered under-handed or dishonest.

The answer, not surprisingly, is no: The means used are for the good of the beings and benefit them greatly in the long run. Moreover, with beings who are thoroughly enmeshed in the concerns of the world, it is necessary to draw their attention away from mundane pleasures toward the dharma, which can lead to lasting happiness.

[Buddha:] "Śāriputra, let us suppose that in a village somewhere . . . there was a householder who was . . . very wealthy. Suppose that he owned a great mansion, lofty, spacious, built long ago, inhabited by hundreds of living beings. The house had one door and was covered with thatch, its terraces were collapsing, the bases of its pillars were rotting, and the plaster and coverings of the walls were falling apart. Now suppose that all of a sudden the whole house burst into flames and that the householder managed to get himself out, but that his little boys [were still inside]. . . .

"[He thought:] 'I was able to get out of the burning house through the door safely, without being touched by the flames, but my children remain in the house, playing with their toys, enjoying themselves. They do not realize . . . that the house is on fire, and so are not afraid. Even though they are caught up in the fire and are being scorched by flames, though they are actually suffering, they are unaware of it, and so they do not think to come out. . . .'

"So he called to the boys: 'Come, my children, the house is burning with a mass of flames! Come out, so that you will not be burned in the inferno and come to disaster!'

"But the ignorant boys paid no attention to the man's words, even though he only wished for their well-being. . . . They did not care, and did not run from the house, did not understand, and did not comprehend even the meaning of the word 'inferno.' Instead, they continued to run and play here and there, occasionally looking at their father. Why? Because they were ignorant children.

"So then, Śāriputra, the man thought: . . . 'I should use a skillful method to cause the children to come out of the house.' The man knew the mental dispositions of his children and clearly understood their interests. He knew of the kinds of toys they liked. . . . So he said to them: 'Children, all the toys that you like . . . such as little ox carts, goat carts, and deer carts, which are pleasing and captivating to you, have all been put outside by me, so that you can play with them. Come, run out of the house! I will give each of you what you want! Come quickly! Come and get these toys!'

"Then the boys, hearing him mentioning the names of the toys they liked . . . quickly ran from the burning house, not waiting for each other, and calling, 'Who will be first? Who will be foremost?'

"Then the man, seeing that his children had come out of the house safely, knowing that they were out of danger . . . gave his children . . . ox carts only. They were made of seven precious metals, and had railings, were hung with strings of bells, were high and lofty, adorned with wonderful and precious jewels, illuminated by garlands of gems, decorated with wreaths of flowers. . . .

"Now what do you think, Śāriputra, did that man lie to his children by first promising them three vehicles and then later giving them only great vehicles, the best vehicles?"

Śāriputra said: "No indeed, Lord! Not at all! There is no reason to think that in this case the man was a liar, because he was using skillful means in order to cause his children to come out of the burning house, and because of this he gave them the gift of life. Moreover, Lord, in addition to keeping their lives, they also received those toys. But, Lord, even if the man had not given them a single cart, he would still not have been a liar. Why is this? Because, Lord, that man first thought, 'By using skillful means, I will liberate those children from a great mass of suffering. . . . '"

"Well said, Śāriputra, well said! You have spoken well! In the same way, the Tathāgata also . . . is the father of the world, who has attained the supreme perfection of understanding of great skillful means, who is greatly compassionate, who has a mind that is unwearied, who is concerned for the well-being of others. He appears in this triple world, which is like a burning house blazing with the whole mass of suffering and despair . . . in order to liberate from desire, aversion, and obscuration those beings who remain trapped in the mists of ignorance, in order to liberate them from the blindness of ignorance, birth, old age, death, sorrow, grief, suffering, sadness, and dissatisfaction, in order to awaken them to supreme, perfect awakening. . . . In this triple world, which is like a burning house, they enjoy themselves and run here and there. Even though they are afflicted by a great deal of suffering, they do not even think that they are suffering. . . .

"Therefore, Śāriputra, the Tathāgata, who is just like that strong-armed man who . . . employed skillful means to coax his children from the burning house . . . speaks of three vehicles: the hearers' vehicle, the solitary realizers' vehicle, and the bodhisattvas' vehicle.... So the Tathāgata is not a liar when he uses skillful means, first holding out the prospect of three vehicles and then leading beings to final nirvana by means of a single great vehicle."

Source: *Saddharma-puṇḍarīka-sūtra*, ch. 3. Tr. JP.

JUST WAR PRINCIPLES

Buddhism is commonly associated with pacifism and nonviolence, but the Buddhist canon contains a number of works that characterize conflict as an inevitable aspect of worldly affairs and that provide advice to rulers regarding how best to manage it. The following passage from the Discourse on the Realm of the Bodhisattva *contains a response by the ascetic (nirgrantha) Satyaka (who is later revealed to be Śākyamuni Buddha in disguise) to King Caṇḍapradyota. The sage urges the king to attempt mediation and to make friendly overtures toward aggressive rivals, but in some cases this approach will not work, and war is the only option. Satyaka informs the king that if he acts only in order to save his people from harm and has no thoughts of benefiting himself, and if he uses the minimum amount of force necessary to achieve his objectives, he may avoid any negative karma; and if his intention is pure, he may even benefit from fighting.*

[219] Initially, skillful means should be employed by a ruler or minister, using friendship to avoid war. If they can benefit their opponents and resolve a conflict, they should do so in order to avoid war. If they can frighten an enemy by forming an alliance with a large force and if this can prevent war, then they should form an alliance in order to avoid war initially. If he cannot avoid war by friendship or benefitting enemies, or by frightening them, then a ruler should wage war, keeping three thoughts in mind.... First, he must think of fully protecting his subjects. Second, he must think of conquering the enemy. Third, he must think of protecting all life. Keeping these three thoughts in mind, a ruler should arrange the four divisions of his army. In this way, in the midst [of conflict], he should employ skillful means. In the final stage, he should set up the four divisions in groups that are inferior, mediocre, and best. The inferior fighters should be on the front line, and the mediocre fighters should be behind them. The cavalry should be placed behind these two. The ruler should be at the rear, along with the best fighters. [220] This formation will produce the best results and will bring success

to the ruler. The brave and faint-hearted fighters can demonstrate their loyalty and use their skills to fight for the ruler, and to overcome their fear. Thus they will not retreat. Thus a ruler employs skillful means during the final period. Thus a ruler who uses skillful means and prepares for battle will destroy the enemy army but, even though he wounds and kills, through these [three thoughts] the ruler will commit fewer atrocities and fewer negative acts, and he may not necessarily experience retribution for these actions. Why not? Because his intention is compassionate and free from greed, and he engages in these actions without producing karma.

Source: *Bodhisattva-caritopāya-viṣayarddhivikṛyā-sūtra (Byang sems spyod yul thabs kyi yul la rnam 'phrul bstan pa'i mdo).* sDe dge *bKa' 'gyur* vol. 57.

EVERYTHING IS CONTROLLED BY THE MIND

The following passage comes from the Cloud of Jewels Discourse. *It indicates that all phenomena are productions of mind and that everything is created by mind. Ordinary beings allow the mind to wander at will, thereby enmeshing them in confused and harmful thoughts, but bodhisattvas are advised to train the mind in order to bring it under control.*

All phenomena originate in the mind, and when the mind is fully known all phenomena are fully known. For by the mind the world is led ... and through the mind karma is piled up,[20] whether good or bad. The mind swings like a firebrand, the mind rears up like a wave, the mind burns like a forest fire, like a great flood the mind carries all things away. Bodhisattvas, thoroughly examining the nature of things, remain in ever-present mindfulness of the activity of the mind, and so do not fall into the mindpower, but the mind comes under their control. And with the mind under their control, all phenomena are under their control.

Source: *Ratnamegha-sūtra,* from the *Śikṣā-samuccaya,* ch. 6. Tr. JP.

THE BASE CONSCIOUSNESS

This passage from the Discourse Explaining the Thought *is one of the earliest descriptions of the "base consciousness"* (ālaya-vijñāna), *a doctrine that was central to the Indian*

---

[20] The reference to mind is based on a traditional etymology that associates the Sanskrit word *citta* (mind) with the verbal root *ci,* meaning to accumulate or pile up.

Yogācāra school and also was influential in other Mahāyāna countries, particularly Tibet and China. The base conscious-ness is the most fundamental level of mind and is said to be comprised of the "seeds" of past actions and mental states. The seeds become part of the continuum of the base consciousness, which is moved along by their force. If one cultivates positive actions and thoughts, for example, one's mind will become habit-uated to positive actions and thoughts. The converse is true for those who engage in negative actions and thoughts.

Under appropriate conditions, the seeds give rise to cor-responding thoughts and emotions, which are the phenomena of ordinary experience. Mind and its objects arise together, so there is no substantial difference between subject and object. Because of this, phenomena are said to be "cognition-only" (vijñapti-mātra), meaning that all we ever perceive are mental impressions, and not things in themselves.

> [Buddha:] "Initially in dependence upon two types of appropriation—the appropriation of the physical sense pow-ers associated with a support and the appropriation of pre-dispositions that proliferate conventional designations with respect to signs, names, and concepts—the mind which has all seeds ripens; it develops, increases, and expands in its operations. . . .
>
> "Consciousness is also called the 'appropriating con-sciousness' because it holds and appropriates the body in that way. It is called the 'base consciousness' because there is the same establishment and abiding within those bodies. . . . It is called 'mind' because it collects and accumu-lates forms, sounds, smells, tastes, and tangible objects."

Source: *Saṃdhinirmocana-sūtra,* ch. 5. Tr. JP.

NĀGĀRJUNA ON EMPTINESS

Nāgārjuna, founder of the Madhyamaka school of Indian Mahāyāna, emphasized the centrality of the doctrine of empti-ness in his philosophy. In the following verses he indicates that concepts are empty because language is simply an intercon-nected system of terms that do not capture actual things but instead simply relate to other words. One who fully recognizes this fact becomes freed from the snares of language and attains correct realization, an important part of the path to liberation.

1. Through the force of worldly conventions, buddhas
   Have spoken of duration, arising, disintegration, existence, non-existence, inferior, middling, and superior,

> But they have not spoken [of these] in an ultimate sense.
> 2. Self, non-self, and self-non-self do not exist,
> And so conventional expressions do not [really] signify.
> Like nirvana, all expressible things are empty of inherent existence.
> 3. Since all things completely lack inherent existence—either in causes or conditions, [in their] totality, or separately—they are empty.
> 4. Because it exists, being does not arise;
> Because it does not exist, non-being does not arise.
> 5. Because they are discordant phenomena, being and non-being [together] do not arise.
> Thus they neither endure nor cease....
> 7. Without one, many does not exist; without many, one is not possible.
> Thus dependently arisen things are indeterminable....
> 56. In dependence upon the internal and external sense spheres *(āyatana)* consciousness arises.
> Thus just like mirages and illusions, consciousness is empty.
> 57. In dependence upon an apprehendable object, consciousness arises.
> Thus the observable does not exist [in itself].
> [The subject of consciousness] does not exist without the apprehendable and consciousness.
> Thus the subject of consciousness does not exist [by itself]....
> 65. Due to correctly perceiving that things are empty, one becomes non-deluded.
> Ignorance ceases, and thus the twelve limbs [of dependent arising][21] cease....
> 67. Nothing exists inherently, nor is there non-being there.
> Arising from causes and conditions, being and non-being are empty.
> 68. All things are empty of inherent existence,
> And so the incomparable Tathāgata teaches dependent arising with respect to things....
> 72. One with faith who seeks the truth, who considers this principle with reason,
> Relying on the dharma that is free of supports, is liberated from existence and non-existence [and abides in] peace.

---

[21] This refers to the twelve stages of dependent arising, which are described in an earlier excerpt titled "Dependent Arising."

73. When one understands that "this is a result of that," the net of wrong views is eradicated.
Due to abandoning attachment, obscuration, and hatred, undefiled, one attains nirvana.

Source: Nāgārjuna, *Śūnyatā-saptati*. Tr. JP.

THE BODHISATTVA'S VOWS OF UNIVERSAL LOVE

The following verses, written by Śāntideva, are among the most eloquent expressions in Mahāyāna literature of the ideal mind-set of bodhisattvas, who should dedicate all of their energies to helping other beings in every possible way.

16. May those who malign me, or harm me, or accuse me falsely, and others all be recipients of awakening.
17. May I be a protector of the helpless, a guide for those on the path, a boat, a bridge, a way for those who wish to crossover.
18. May I be a lamp for those who need a lamp, a bed for those who seek a bed, and a slave for those who desire a slave.
19. May I become a wish-fulfilling jewel, an inexhaustible jar, a powerful mantra, a cure for all sickness, a wish-fulfilling tree, and a cow of plenty for all creatures.[22]
20. As earth and the other elements are enjoyed in various ways by innumerable beings living throughout space,
So may I be the sustenance for various kinds of beings in all the realms of space for as long as all are not satisfied.

Source: Śāntideva, *Bodhicaryāvatāra*, "Bodhicitta-parigraha." Tr. JP.

TANTRIC SKILL IN MEANS

Tantric texts claim that the system of tantra skillfully uses aspects of reality that cause bondage for people who are enmeshed in mundane conceptuality—things like desire and other negative emotions. The following excerpt from the Hevajra Tantra *indicates that these may serve as aids to the path of liberation if the proper means are used.*

---

[22] These are all drawn from Indian mythology. A magical jewel is a gem that gives its owner whatever he or she desires. An inexhaustible jar never runs dry. Spells (mantra) are often used as magical incantations in order to bring about desired results. A universal remedy is able to cure all illness, and a cow of plenty gives vast riches to those who capture it.

Those things by which evil men are bound, others turn into means and gain thereby release from the bonds of existence. By passion the world is bound, by passion too it is released, but by heretical Buddhists this practice of reversals is not known.

Source: *Hevajra-tantra* I.ix.2–3, tr. David Snellgrove, *Indo-Tibetan Buddhism* (Boston: Shambhala, 1987), vol. I, pp. 125–126.

THE STAGE OF COMPLETION

The tantric practice of deity yoga involves first creating a vivid image of a buddha in front of one and then visualizing the buddha as merging with oneself. One views oneself as a buddha—with the body, speech, and mind of a buddha—and as performing the activities of an awakened being. The first procedure is called the "generation stage," and the second, which is described in the following passage from the Guhyasamāja Tantra, *is termed the "completion stage." In order to avoid becoming attached to the visualization, one should be aware that both the buddha and oneself are empty of inherent existence. Thus, at the end of the session, one dissolves both oneself and the buddha into emptiness.*

Everything from the crown of the head to the feet dissolves into the heart; you engage in the perfect yoga (meditation on emptiness).... All sentient beings and all other phenomena dissolve into clear light and then dissolve into you; then you yourself, as the deity, dissolve into your heart.... Just as mist on a mirror fades toward the center and disappears, so does everything—the net of illusory manifestation—dissolve into the clear light of emptiness. Just as fish are easily seen in clear water, so does everything—the net of illusory manifestation—emerge from the clear light of emptiness.

Source: *Guhyasamāja-tantra;* quoted in Khenpo Könchog Gyaltsen, *The Garland of Mahamudra Practices* (Ithaca: Snow Lion, 1986), pp. 56–57.

UNBOUNDED ACTION

The ideal practitioner of tantra is referred to as an "adept" (siddha), who becomes a mighty sorcerer through cultivation of the rituals, visualizations, and manipulations of subtle energies that are the focus of tantric practice. Adepthood is a state of utter transcendence, in which all mundane concerns and limitations are overcome. Adepts wander freely, spontaneously engaging in whatever activities they wish, unconcerned with social norms or the expectations of others. The following passage from the Arising of Supreme Pleasure Tantra *describes this freedom.*

> He should give away his wealth, his wife, and even his own life as offerings; abandoning those ties, he should always be a trainee of the practice. He has great strength attained by reciting magical spells, and he is intent on speaking the truth . . . he should not make a distinction between purity, impurity, or purification, nor between what may or may not be drunk. Being without anger and free from conceit, he should not care about praise or condemnation. Adhering to the idea that everything is equal, he is always without attachment and without desire. He neither practices the fire offering *(homa)* nor worships. He neither recites [mantras] nor uses prayer beads. . . . Having a tiger skin as a garment and adorned with five seals, the yogi should imagine himself to be [the buddha] Heruka, who combines wisdom and method.

Source: *Saṃvarodaya-tantra*. Tr. JP.

WOMEN SHOULD BE HONORED

One notable feature of the tantric movement is an emphasis on the spiritual capacities of women. Classical Indian literature indicates that misogyny was prevalent in the society, which makes this aspect of tantra even more significant. An example of the emphasis on the equality of women is the fact that one of the basic vows required of all tantric practitioners is a pledge not to denigrate women, "who are the bearers of wisdom." The following passage from the Caṇḍamahāroṣaṇa Tantra *expresses a similar sentiment in its praises of women.*

> When women are honored,
> They provide instant accomplishments *(siddhi)*
> To those who wish for the welfare of all beings.
> Thus one should honor women.
> Women are heaven, women are dharma,
> Women are also the supreme asceticism *(tapas).*
> Women are Buddha, women are the monastic community *(saṃgha);*
> Women are the perfection of wisdom.

Source: *Caṇḍamahāroṣaṇa-tantra, 8.27–30.* Tr. JP.

SAMSĀRA AND NIRVANA ARE ONE

The following excerpts from the Hevajra Tantra *discuss the tantric idea that there is no fundamental difference between cyclic existence and nirvana. Buddhas perceive them as undifferentiable, but ordinary beings, because of their delusions, think in terms of dichotomies and so imagine that the path and the goal are separate.*

> Then the essence is declared, pure and consisting in knowledge,
> where there is not the slightest difference between cyclic existence
> and nirvana.
> Nothing is mentally produced in the highest bliss, and no one
> produces it,
> There is no bodily form, neither object nor subject,
> Neither flesh nor blood, neither dung nor urine,
> No sickness, no delusion, no purification,
> No passion, no wrath, no delusion, no envy,
> No malignity, no conceit of self, no visible object,
> Nothing mentally produced and no producer,
> No friend is there, no enemy,
> Calm is the Innate and undifferentiated. . . .
> The Awakened One is neither existence nor non-existence; he has a
> form with arms and faces and yet in highest bliss is formless.
> So the whole world is the Innate, for the Innate is its essence.
> Its essence too is nirvana when the mind is in a purified state.

Source: *Hevajra-tantra,* ch. I.x.32–34, II.ii.43–44, tr. David Snellgrove, *The Hevajra Tantra: A Critical Study* (London: Oxford University Press, 1959), vol. I, p. 92.

USING DESIRE TO ERADICATE DESIRE

Tantric adepts claim that the fact that tantra uses emotions like desire as means in the path is an example of the skillful practices of the system. The following passage from Vīryavajra's Commentary on the Sampuṭa Tantra *contends that there are four levels of the use of desire: visualizing a man and woman looking at each other, laughing with each other, holding hands, and sexual union. Each of these represents a progressively higher level of desire. One should engage in these practices, however, in order to utilize the energy of desire as a force that can eradicate mental afflictions. The skillful use of desire is said in some texts to be like rubbing two sticks together to make a fire, which then consumes the sticks themselves. In this case, the process is compared to the way insects are born in wood and then later consume the wood.*

> Within the sound of laughter non-conceptual bliss is generated; or it is generated from looking at the body, the touch

of holding hands and the embrace of the two; or from the touch [of union]...just as an insect is generated from the wood and then eats the wood itself, so meditative stabilization is generated from bliss [in dependence on desire] and is cultivated as emptiness [whereupon desire is consumed].

Source: *Vīryavajra's Commentary on the Sampuṭa Tantra*; quoted in *sNgags rim chen mo*, II.7. Tr. JP.

THE STATE OF PURE AWARENESS

The following passage from the Hevajra Tantra *describes the state of mind of one who has transcended all discursive and dichotomizing thought through direct, intuitive awareness of the boundless clarity of mind.*

From self-experiencing comes this knowledge, which is free from ideas of self and other; like the sky it is pure and void, the essence supreme of non-existence and existence, a mingling of wisdom and method, a mingling of passion and absence of passion. It is the life of living things, it is the Unchanging One Supreme; it is all-pervading, abiding in all embodied things. It is the stuff the world is made of, and in it existence and non-existence have their origin. It is all other things that there are.... It is the essential nature of all existing things and illusory in its forms.

Source: *Hevajra-tantra* I.x.8–12, tr. David L. Snellgrove, *The Hevajra Tantra*, p. 81.

THE IMPORTANCE OF THE GURU

The special techniques of tantra are said to be very powerful, but they can also be dangerous. Thus tantric texts warn meditators to find qualified spiritual guides (guru) who can help them avoid possible pitfalls. One of the central practices of tantra is "guru yoga," in which one visualizes one's guru as a fully awakened buddha. One who does this successfully moves quickly toward actualization of buddhahood. In the following passage, the tantric master Tilopa teaches that finding a qualified guru is a prerequisite for successful tantric practice.

The ignorant may know that sesame oil—the essence— exists in the sesame seed, but because they do not know how, they cannot extract the oil. So also does the innate fundamental wisdom abide in the heart of all migrators; but unless it is pointed out by the guru, it cannot be realized. By pounding the seeds and clearing away the husks, one can extract the essence—the sesame oil. Similarly, when it is shown by the guru, the meaning of suchness is so illuminated that one can enter into it.

Source: Tilopa; quoted in *The Garland of Mahamudra Practices*, p. 58.

TIBETAN BUDDHIST SCRIPTURES

ULTIMATE REALITY

The "great completion" (dzogchen) tradition of Tibetan Buddhism is practiced by all four main orders—Nyingma, Kagyu, Sakya, and Geluk—but is most closely associated with the Nyingma. In this system all phenomena are said to be creations of mind that, like mind, are a union of luminosity and emptiness. In the following passage, meditators are instructed on the nature of ultimate reality, in which phenomena spontaneously appear to the mind although they have no real substance.

Since [things exist] only in the manner of mirages, dreams, and delusions, you should abandon [false appearances] and adopt [virtuous practices], work for the sake [of others], avoid [non-virtue] and practice [virtue]. Wash away the afflictions of desire, anger, and obscuration with the waters of their antidotes: [meditation on] repulsiveness, love, and dependent arising. Because ultimate reality is non-arisen and pure, it is free from elaborations such as the duality of cyclic existence and nirvana.... All phenomena merely appear naturally to your own mind on the *mandala*[23] that is the sphere of the foundation, the buddha nature. They are falsities, not really things, empty, and only appear as forms, as the aggregates, realms, spheres, and so forth.... The unsurpassed, supreme, secret great completion directly actualizes the sphere of the spontaneously existent. This foundational sphere is unchanging, like space. [All good] qualities [reside] in it spontaneously, as the sun, moon, planets, and stars [reside] in the sky. There is no need to seek it, since it has existed since beginningless time. No work or effort [is necessary,] as this path is naturally manifest.

Source: Longchen Rapjampa, *Chos bzhi rin po che'i phreng ba (Four Themed Precious Garland)*. Tr. JP.

---

[23] Mandalas are circular diagrams used as aids for visualizations in tantric practice.

BARDO, THE STATE BETWEEN LIVES

The following excerpts are drawn from a Tibetan classic on death and dying titled Liberation through Hearing in the Intermediate State, *attributed to Padmasambhava. According to the tradition, it was hidden by Padmasambhava and rediscovered by the "treasure finder" Karma Lingpa in the fourteenth century. The book describes the "intermediate state" (*bardo; *translated here as "the between") that all beings enter after death.*

During the process of dying, the physiological changes that occur are accompanied by mental changes in which the coarser levels of mind drop away, revealing progressively subtler aspects of consciousness. At the moment of death, the subtlest level of mind dawns. This is called the "mind of clear light," and compared to it all other minds are adventitious.

At this point one enters the intermediate state and experiences strange and terrifying sights. These are aspects of one's own mind, and they include visions of mild and terrifying beings, deafening sounds, and other intense sense experiences. The intermediate state is a time of great opportunity, however, and if one is able to maintain awareness and focus on the clear light nature of mind and perceive all experiences as merely aspects of mind, one may become a buddha, or at least attain rebirth in the pure land of a buddha. In such places the conditions are optimal for beings who seek buddhahood. If one is unable to maintain mindfulness, one will be reborn in accordance with one's accumulated karma.

> Hey! Now when the life between dawns upon me,
> I will abandon laziness, as life has no more time,
> Unwavering, enter the path of learning, thinking, and meditating,
> And taking perceptions and mind as a path,
> I will realize the Three Bodies[24] of enlightenment! . . .
> Conscious of dreaming, I will enjoy the changes as clear light.
> Not sleeping mindlessly like an animal,
> I will cherish the practice merging sleep and realization! . . .
> Now when the death-point between dawns upon me,
> I will give up the preoccupations of the all-desiring mind,
> Enter unwavering the experience of the clarity of the precepts,
> And transmigrate into the birthless space of inner awareness;
> About to lose this created body of flesh and blood,
> I will realize it to be impermanent illusion! . . .
> I will . . . enter into the recognition of all objects as my mind's own visions,
> And understand this as the pattern of perception in the between;

---

[24] This refers to the three bodies of buddhas according to Mahāyāna: the truth body (*dharma-kāya*), which is the buddha's mind and its emptiness of inherent existence; the complete enjoyment body (*saṃbhoga-kāya*), a subtle form that resides in pure buddha lands; and emanation bodies (*nirmāṇa-kāya*), which are physical emanations created by buddhas in order to benefit sentient beings.

Come to this moment, arrived at this most critical cessation,
I will not fear my own visions of deities mild and fierce! . . .
Now courage and positive perception are essential.

Source: *Bar do thos grol, from Bar do thos grol: The Tibetan Book of the Dead: Liberation through Understanding in the Between*, tr. Robert A. F. Thurman (New York: Bantam, 1994), pp. 115–116.

MILAREPA ON MEDITATION

Milarepa, one of the most influential figures in Tibetan Buddhism, was born into a fairly well-to-do family, but his greedy aunt and uncle took everything away from him, his mother, and sister. Overcome by rage, his mother coerced Milarepa into learning black magic and sending a curse on the aunt and uncle, with the result that a number of people died, but not the primary objects of his revenge. Milarepa, terrified of the consequences of his evil deeds, searched for a spiritual guide (lama) who could help him escape the consequences of his actions. He eventually found Marpa, who gave Milarepa a series of difficult and dispiriting tasks that cleansed his negative karma. After this Milarepa spent many years living in a cave and practicing solitary meditation, which culminated in his attainment of awakening. He is considered in Tibet to be the supreme example of the attainment of buddhahood in one lifetime through tantric practice.

Look up into the sky, and practice meditation free from the fringe and center.
Look up at the sun and moon, and practice meditation free from bright and dim.
Look over the mountains, and practice meditation free from departing and changing.
Look down at the lake, and practice meditation free from waves.
Look here at your mind, and practice meditation free from discursive thought.

Source: *rJe btsun mi la ras pa'i rnam thar (Religious Biography of the Master Milarepa)*, pp. 49bff. Tr. JP.

NIGUMA ON MAHĀMUDRĀ

Niguma is said by Tibetan tradition to have been the founder of the Shangpa lineage of the Kagyu tradition. In the following passage, she describes the view of mahāmudrā *(literally, "great seal"), which is said by the Kagyu school to be the supreme form of Buddhist practice. In* mahāmudrā, *one dispenses with the visualizations and rituals of tantra and focuses on the natural state of mind, which is a union of clear light and emptiness. All phenomena are viewed as the spontaneous play of mind, and by cultivating this awareness, the meditator moves quickly toward the attainment of buddhahood.*

> Do nothing at all with the mind;
> Abide in a non-artificial and natural state.
> Your own unwavering mind is the truth body *(dharma-kāya).*
> The important thing for meditation is an unwavering mind.
> You should realize the great [reality] that is free from extremes.
> The afflictions, desires, aversions, and conceptualizations
> That arise like bubbles on the ocean of cyclic existence
> Should be cut off with the sharp sword of non-production
> That is not different from the nature of things.
> When you cut off the trunk and roots,
> The branches will not grow.
> Just as in the clear ocean
> Waves pop up and sink into the water,
> So conceptualizations are not really different from reality.
> So don't look for faults, remain at ease.
> Whatever arises, whatever materializes,
> Don't hold on to it, but immediately let it go.
> Appearances, sounds, and phenomena are one's own mind;
> There are no other phenomena apart from mind.
> Mind is free from the elaborations of arising and cessation.
> The nature of mind, awareness,
> Enjoys the five qualities of the Desire Realm, but
> Does not wander from reality. . . .
> In the great realm of reality *(dharma-dhātu)*
> There is nothing to abandon or adopt,
> No meditative equipoise or post-meditation period.

Source: Niguma, *Rang grol phyag rgya chen po (Individual Liberation of the Great Seal).* Tr. JP.

INSTRUCTIONS FROM MAÑJUŚRĪ

The following verses, according to the Sakya tradition of Tibetan Buddhism, were spoken to Günga Nyingpo (1092–1158). They are a summary of the entire Buddhist path, including the renunciation of the world, the development of compassion, and the importance of avoiding extreme views.

> If you cling to this life, then you are not a dharma practitioner.
> If you cling to existence, then you do not have renunciation.
> If you are attached to your own interests, then you do not have the mind of awakening.
> If you hold to [a position], then you do not have the correct view.

Source: Drakpa Gyeltsen, *Zhen pa bzhi bral (Parting from the Four Attachments).* Tr. JP.

THE TRIPLE APPEARANCE

The Sakya order teaches that there are three main levels of awareness, which are summarized in the following stanzas from Virūpa's Vajra Verses. The first verse refers to the perceptions of ordinary beings, which are colored by ignorance and mental affliction. The second verse describes the perceptions of people on the path, who have some experience with meditation and thus have overcome some of their mental afflictions. The final verse indicates that buddhas perceive the world unafflicted by ignorance, hatred, desire, and so on, and so are at the level of the "pure appearance." The Sakya tradition stresses that although they appear to be incompatible, the three appearances are fundamentally non-different.

> For sentient beings with the afflictions is the impure appearance.
> For the meditator with transic absorption is the appearance of experience.
> For the ornamental wheel of the Sugata's [Buddha's] inexhaustible awakened body, voice and mind is the pure appearance.

Source: *rDo rje tshigs rkang (Vajra Verses),* ch. 1. Tr. JP.

DEVELOPING THE MIND OF AWAKENING

Ordinary beings are consumed by self-centered desires and think primarily of their own narrow interests. Bodhisattvas spend countless eons working toward buddhahood for the benefit of all beings, cheerfully accepting all the tribulations that occur along the path. Given the vast gulf between the attitudes of bodhisattvas and those of ordinary beings, it is difficult for people enmeshed in mundane concerns to imagine making the transition to true altruism.

The following passage by Tsong Khapa (the founder of the Gelukpa order of Tibetan Buddhism) outlines a seven-step program for developing the "mind of awakening," which marks the beginning of the bodhisattva path. It begins by recognizing that because one has been reborn into an infinite variety of situations since beginningless time, one has been in every possible relationship with every other sentient being. Thus every sentient being has been one's mother and has been a nurturing and caring friend. One should reflect on the kindness of one's own mother and then think that every other being has been equally kind. One then resolves to repay this kindness and generates a feeling of love toward others, wishing that they have happiness and the causes of happiness. One then develops compassion for sentient beings because they are experiencing suffering as a result of contaminated actions and afflictions.

In the next stage one attains the "unusual attitude," which involves vowing to work to free all beings from suffering and establish them in buddhahood. The final step is attainment of the mind of awakening, which is a resolve to do whatever is necessary to attain buddhahood in order to help all sentient beings.

From one's own viewpoint, since one has cycled beginninglessly, there are no sentient beings who have not been one's friends hundreds of times. Therefore, one should think, "Whom should I value?" "Whom should I hate?" . . .

Imagine your mother very clearly in front of you. Consider several times how she has been your mother numberless times, not only now, but from beginningless cyclic existence. When she was your mother, she protected you from all danger and brought about your benefit and happiness. In particular, in this life she held you for a long time in her womb. Once you were born, while you still had new hair, she held you to the warmth of her flesh and rocked you on the tips of her ten fingers. She nursed you at her breast . . . and wiped away your filth with her hand. In various ways she nourished you tirelessly. When you were hungry and thirsty, she gave you drink, and when you were cold, clothes, and when poor, money. She gave you those things that were precious to her. Moreover, she did not find these easily. . . . When you suffered with a fever she would rather have died herself than have her child die; and if her child became sick, from the depths of her heart she would rather have suffered herself than have her child suffer. . . .

Source: *Lam rim chen mo (Great Exposition of the Stages of the Path),* pp. 572.5, 575.1. Tr. JP.

CHINESE AND JAPANESE BUDDHIST SCRIPTURES

THE ONE MIND

The following passage is taken from the Awakening of Mahāyāna Faith (Dasheng qishin lun 大乘起信論序), *one of the most influential works of East Asian Buddhism. Traditionally attributed to the Indian master Aśvaghoṣa (c. first–second century CE), modern scholarship has generally concurred that it is most likely a Chinese apocryphon. One of its most influential aspects is its presentation of the "buddha matrix" (rulai zang 如來藏; Sanskrit: tathāgatha-garbha), according to which all beings have an innate potential for buddhahood. Another important notion in this text is the "One Mind" (yixin 一心): there is a universal intelligence, and the minds of all sentient beings participate in this.*

All phenomena (*fa* 法; Sanskrit *dharma*) from the very beginning transcend characteristics of speech, transcend characteristics of naming, and transcend mental cognition of them as objects. They are absolutely undifferentiated, changeless, and indestructible. There is only this One Mind; for this reason it is called "suchness." Because all distinctions are nominal and devoid of reality and only follow in consequence of deluded thoughts, it refers to the limit of language. This word is used in order to do away with words. In this suchness itself there is nothing that can be discarded, because all phenomena are suchness. There is also nothing to be established because all phenomena are equal as "such." It must be understood that since all phenomena are verbally inexpressible and mentally inconceivable, this is termed "suchness...."

With respect to mind's arising and cessation: in dependence on the buddha matrix there is mind that arises and ceases. This means that non-arising and non-cessation are harmoniously integrated with arising and cessation. They are neither the same nor different. It is called "base consciousness." This consciousness has a twofold sense: it contains all qualities *(dharma)* and generates all qualities. What are the two? The first is the sense of awakening; the second is the sense of non-awakening. The sense of awakening is that mind itself transcends thought. That which transcends the characteristics of thought is equal to the realm of space; there is nowhere that it does not pervade. It has the single characteristic of the realm of reality, that is to say, it is the buddha matrix and equal to the truth body (*fashen* 法身; Sanskrit: *dharma-kāya*). For this reason, the truth body is described as inherently awakened.

Source: CBETA (Chinese Buddhist Electronic Text Association) *Chinese Electronic Tripiṭaka* V1.15: 576a.13-20, 576b.8-14 (*Taishō Tripiṭaka* vol. 32, No. 1666).

THE *PLATFORM SŪTRA* OF THE SIXTH PATRIARCH

The Chan (Japanese: Zen) school developed in China. Asserting that the teachings of the school were a "special transmission outside of the scriptures," Zen masters claimed that their tradition represents the authentic teaching of the Buddha, who passed on the essence of his awakened mind to his disciple Mahākāśyapa. He in turn taught it to his main disciple, and so it continued in India through an unbroken chain of transmission until Bodhidharma, the last Indian "patriarch," traveled to China.

Bodhidharma, a semilegendary figure, is said to have arrived at the Shaolin monastery in China, where he sat in silent meditation in front of a wall for several years. At the end of this period, he began teaching the tradition to Chinese disciples, one of whom became the first Chinese patriarch.

The following passage was spoken by Hui Neng, the sixth patriarch, to a group of disciples. It contains many of the important doctrines of the developed Chan tradition, including the doctrine of "sudden awakening," which holds that buddhas become awakened in a flash of insight, and not gradually as traditional Indian Buddhism taught. According to Indian Buddhist meditation texts, meditators should enter into concentrated meditative states called samādhi, and these states lead to the awakening of wisdom (prajñā).

Hui Neng declared that such ideas impose a false dualism on the path to buddhahood. He contended that both concentration and wisdom are present in every moment of thought and that they cannot legitimately be separated. He also opposed the goal-oriented practices of traditional Mahāyāna and said that one becomes awakened by eliminating discursive thought. When all conceptual thoughts drop away and one attains the state of "no-thought" (wu nian), the mind flows freely and unimpededly, in harmony with the rhythms of the world. This is the state of mind characteristic of buddhahood, and any notions of "path" and "goal," or "cultivation" and "attainment," are products of dualistic thinking that will impede one's progress toward awakening.

"The Fourth Sermon on Meditation and Wisdom"
The Master said to the assembly: "Good friends! My Dharma is rooted in meditation and wisdom. Monks, do not be confused and say that meditation and wisdom are two different things. Meditation and wisdom form one whole; they are not two separate things. Meditation is the form of wisdom, and wisdom is the function of meditation. When there is wisdom, meditation exists in that wisdom. When there is meditation, wisdom exists in that meditation. Understanding this means attaining balance in learning meditation and wisdom. Students of the path should not say that meditation

comes first and is what gives rise to wisdom, or that wisdom comes first and is what gives rise to meditation, and that the two are different from each other. Those who hold this view have a dualistic Dharma."

The Master said to the assembly: "Good friends! There was originally no sudden or gradual [awakening] in the True Dharma. However, among people there are those who are naturally bright and those who are naturally dull. Deluded people have cultivated gradual [awakening]; awakened people have cultivated sudden [awakening]. When you know your original mind, you will see your original nature. Then, you will see that there is no difference and that sudden and gradual are only nominal.

"Good friends! My Dharma has always taken non-thought as its main doctrine, non-form as its substance, and non-abiding as its root. Non-form means being separated from form even when participating in form. Non-thought means having no thoughts even when thinking. Non-abiding is the original nature of humans.

"In this world, good and evil, beauty and ugliness, all lead to injustices befalling those who are close to us. When [other people's] words assault you and try to deceive you, you should treat them as empty and do not think of taking revenge. Nor should your thoughts dwell on the past. If you are always thinking of past, present, and future, then successive thoughts will go on ceaselessly. This is called becoming fettered. If you think of non-abiding being in all phenomena, then you will be unfettered. It is by this means that you can take non-abiding as the root."

Source: Hui Neng, *Liuzu dashi fabaotan jing,* Taishō Tripitaka, vol. 48, #2008; tr. Thomas McConochie.

KŪKAI: EXOTERIC AND ESOTERIC BUDDHISM

Kūkai (774–835), posthumously known as Kōbō daishi, was one of the most influential thinkers of the Heian period (794–1185). He traveled to China in 804 to study Buddhism and learned the doctrines and practices of Esoteric Buddhism (Chinese: Zhenyan; Japanese: Shingon) under the Chinese master Hui Guo. This school is a branch of Vajrayāna ("Vajra Vehicle"), which is based on the tantras of Indian Buddhism. Like its counterparts in South Asia, East Asian Esoteric Buddhism emphasizes the importance of visualizations, mantras, and rituals for bringing about a cognitive transformation of one's mind into the mind of a buddha.

In the following passage, Kūkai compares the path of Esoteric Buddhism to that of Exoteric Buddhism. He contends that Esoteric Buddhism is far superior to the Exoteric teachings and practices and is more effective in bringing about mundane benefits as well as final awakening. Kūkai believed that human beings have the capacity to become "awakened in this very body" (sokushin jōbutsu) and that the rituals and symbols of Esoteric Buddhism appeal directly to humans' basic nature of buddha-potential and enable them to quickly attain the state of buddhahood. These practices bring the body, speech, and mind of the meditator into concordance with those of the truth body and thus allow the primordial buddha Mahāvairocana to communicate directly with advanced practitioners.

I have heard that there are two kinds of preaching of the Buddha. One is shallow and incomplete while the other is esoteric. The shallow teaching is comprised of the scriptures with long passages and verses, whereas the esoteric teaching is the *dhāraṇī* [esoteric prayers thought to have magical properties] found in the scriptures.

The shallow teaching is, as one text says, like the diagnosis of an illness and the prescription of a medicine. The esoteric method of reciting *dhāraṇī* is like prescribing appropriate medicine, ingesting it, and curing the ailment. If a person is ill, opening a medical text and reciting its contents will be of no avail in treating the illness. It is necessary to adapt the medicine to the disease and to ingest it in accordance with proper methods. Only then will the illness be eliminated and life preserved.

However, the present custom of chanting the *Sūtra of Golden Light*[25] at the Imperial Palace is simply the reading of sentences and the empty recital of doctrine. There is no drawing of buddha images in accordance with proper technique nor the practice of setting up an altar for offerings and for the ceremonies of empowerment. Although the reading of the *Sūtra* may appear to be an opportunity to listen to the preaching of the nectar-like teachings of the Buddha, in actuality it lacks the precious taste of the finest essence of Buddhist truth.

I humbly request that from this year on, fourteen monks skilled in esoteric ritual and fourteen novices be selected

---

[25] The most important text of the Shingon school is the *Mahāvairocana-sūtra* (Japanese: *Dainichi-kyō*), which is said to have been taught by the truth body (*dharma-kāya*) to advanced students.

who, while properly reading the *Sūtra*, will for seven days arrange the sacred images, perform the requisite offerings, and recite mantra in a specially adorned room. If this is done, both the exoteric and esoteric teachings, which express the Buddha's true intent, will cause great happiness in the world and thereby fulfill the compassionate vows of the holy ones.

Source: Kūkai, *Petition to Supplement the Annual Reading of Sūtra in the Imperial Palace;*[26] tr. David Gardiner.

DŌGEN'S MEDITATION INSTRUCTIONS

Dōgen (1200–1253), founder of the Sōtō (Chinese: Zaodong) school of Zen, traveled to China in 1223 and studied with Rujing, a Chinese Chan master. One day during meditation practice, another monk fell asleep, and Rujing woke him up, admonishing him to practice meditation diligently in order to "drop off body and mind" (Japanese: shinjin datsuraku*). This idea became a cornerstone of Dōgen's system of meditative practice. The following passage contains instructions on meditation practice* (zazen)*, which in Dōgen's system is based on the experience of "not thinking"* (hishiryō)*.*

In the state of not thinking, a meditator moves beyond discursive and dichotomizing thought (shiryō)*, transcends the tendency to stop ordinary thought by suppressing it* (fushiryō)*, and thus enters into a spontaneous awareness of reality in which thoughts flow along of their own accord. In this state of spontaneous mindfulness, the meditator experiences his or her own "buddha nature," an inherent propensity toward awakening that is shared by all beings.*

    1. When you are physically stable and your breathing is under control, then as a thought arises, just be aware of it. If you are aware of it, it will disappear. Upon forgetting such experiential objects, you will naturally attain a concentrated oneness. This is the essential technique of sitting in meditation (*zazen*). This *zazen* is the gate to great peace.

Source: "Fukan Zazen-gi," in *Dainihon Zoku Zōkyō,* p. 4; tr. Paul Swanson.

---

[26] This was submitted to the court in 834, one year before Kūkai's death. The emperor Nimmyō ordered that the ceremonies be performed in the manner requested in perpetuity. They are still performed annually at New Years' time in Kyoto, the former capital, and the emperor regularly sends a representative from Tokyo.

2. When the body and mind are under control as explained above, take a deep breath and then exhale. Sit in a concentrated and stable manner, thinking yet not thinking. How can you think yet not think? By not thinking. This is the technique of sitting in meditation (*zazen*). *Zazen* is not merely the graded practice of [various levels of] *dhyāna* meditation. This is the gate to great peace and the undefiled cultivation of enlightenment.

Source: "Zazengi" chapter of the *Shōbōgenzō*, Iwanami edition p. 126; tr. Paul Swanson.

THE MU KŌAN

The Rinzai (Chinese: Linji) school of Zen is renowned for its use of kōan, *riddles that cannot be answered by rational or discursive modes of thought. The following passage contains the* kōan *that is generally given to beginning students, referred to as the "Mu* kōan." *It reports that a monk asked the Zen master Jōshū if a dog has the buddha nature, to which Jōshū answered, "Mu!" Mu may be translated as "not," but in the* kōan *Jōshū's answer is not a denial, but rather an indication that the question makes no sense from the point of view of awakening.*

The dilemma behind the question is based on traditional Japanese Buddhist ideas about the path. It is widely accepted in Japanese Buddhism that all beings—including dogs—have the buddha nature, that is, an inherent potential for buddhahood. Thus, from the point of view of tradition, Jōshū's answer should be "Yes." But because Zen claims to transcend blind adherence to tradition, this would be an unacceptable answer. On the other hand, if Jōshū were to state that dogs do not have the buddha nature, he could be accused of contravening Buddhist doctrine and setting himself above the buddhas.

Thus Jōshū's answer is an invitation to move beyond tradition and conceptualization to a direct perception of truth. The Zen tradition refers to this kōan *as the "closed opening," or the "gateless barrier," because once a meditator perceives the meaning behind Jōshū's statement, it marks the first dawning of realization that will eventually culminate in full awakening, referred to in Zen as* satori. *It is intended to cause a cognitive crisis as the meditator attempts to solve the riddle by means of conceptual thought but finds all such attempts utterly frustrated. This leads to the development of the "great doubt" (daigi), which is said to burn inside of one like a red-hot ball of iron. When the* kōan *is solved, however, the pain and frustration disappear and are replaced by a serene, nonconceptual awareness.*

A monk once asked Master Jōshū, "Has a dog the Buddha Nature or not?" Jōshū said, "Mu!"

Mumon's commentary: In studying Zen, one must pass the barriers set up by ancient Zen Masters. For the attainment of incomparable *satori*, one has to cast away his discriminating mind. Those who have not passed the barrier and have not cast away the discriminating mind are all phantoms haunting trees and plants.

Now Tell me, what is the barrier of the Zen Masters? Just this "Mu"—it is the barrier of Zen. It is thus called "the gateless barrier of Zen." Those who have passed the barrier will not only see Jōshū clearly, but will go hand in hand with all the Masters of the past, see them face to face. . . .

Wouldn't it be wonderful? Don't you want to pass the barrier? Then concentrate yourself into this "Mu," with your 360 bones and 84,000 pores, making your whole body one great inquiry. Day and night work intently at it. Do not attempt nihilistic or dualistic interpretations. It is like having swallowed a red hot iron ball. You try to vomit it but cannot. . . .

You kill the Buddha if you meet him; you kill the ancient Masters if you meet them. On the brink of life and death you are utterly free, and in the six realms and the four modes of life you live, with great joy, a genuine life in complete freedom.

Source: From *Zen Comments on the Mumonkan,* tr. Zenkei Shibayama (New York: Mentor, 1974), pp. 19–20.

PURE LAND: SHINRAN ON AMIDA'S VOW

The Pure Land (Chinese: Jingtu; Japanese: Jōdo) tradition focuses on a buddha named Amitābha ("Limitless Light"), or Amitāyus ("Limitless Life"), who as a merchant named Dharmākara made a series of vows concerning the sort of "buddha-land" he would create after his attainment of buddhahood.[27] *In the* Discourse on the Array of the Joyous Land (Sukhāvatīvyūha-sūtra)*, Dharmākara indicates that his land will be especially wonderful, a place in which the conditions for buddhahood are optimal. Beings fortunate enough to be born into*

---

[27] A buddha-land *(buddha-kṣetra)* is created by a buddha after the attainment of awakening and is designed to be an environment for a certain type of sentient being. The land of each buddha is a reflection of his or her awakened mind and is a result of the meritorious actions performed by that buddha during innumerable lifetimes.

this land will receive teachings from buddhas and bodhisattvas, and they will progress quickly toward awakening.

Amitābha also teaches that beings may be reborn in his land if they have sincere faith in him. The Japanese Pure Land teacher Shinran (1173–1262) states that anyone may be reborn in Amitābha's paradise, regardless of past actions. Previous teachers had contended that birth in Sukhāvatī required good moral character and constant repetition of the formula "Praise to Amida Buddha" (Namu Amida Butsu),[28] *but Shinran declares that all that is necessary is one moment of sincere belief (shinjin, literally, "believing mind").*

Shinran makes a distinction between "self-power," which characterizes the practices of early Buddhism, and "other-power," in which one relies completely on the saving power of Amitābha. Shinran contends that the former practice was appropriate in the Buddha's day, but that the present age is one of degeneration and human beings have become so depraved that their only hope is to rely on Amitābha. The Tannishō *was written by a direct disciple of Shinran, probably Yuien (d. 1290), in the decades after Shinran's death, and it remains a respected record of Shinran's teachings.*

"When from faith that you will be saved by the wondrous vow of Amida, and attain rebirth in the Pure Land, in the heart there spontaneously arises the urge to speak the *nembutsu* phrase, at that moment Amida will bestow upon you blessing that once grasped is never relinquished. Amida's vow makes no distinction between old and young, good and bad—you must know that sole importance lies in the believing heart. This is because that vow is to save all sentient beings caught in the throes of deep karmic evil and raging passion. Thus, it is enough simply to have faith in the vow; no other virtue is necessary. For there is no higher virtue than that of the *nembutsu*. Nor should you fear evil, for there is no evil great enough to obstruct the vow of Amida." These were the teacher's words.

Even a virtuous person can gain rebirth in the Pure Land, to say nothing of an evil person. Yet consider the common saying, that "even an evil person can gain rebirth in the Pure Land, to say nothing of a virtuous person." This statement may seem reasonable at first glance, but in fact it goes against the meaning of the Primal Vow's "power from without." The reason for this is that as long as you perform good deeds through "power from within," you are lacking

---

[28] This formula is referred to in Japanese Pure Land Buddhism as the *"nembutsu."*

the spirit of depending on the "power from without," and hence you are not in accord with Amida's vow. However, if you overturn this reliance on power from within, and instead place your faith in the power from without, you will achieve rebirth in the true land. Amida's vow arose from an impulse of pity toward those of us who are in the grip of passions, and who cannot transcend the cycle of life and death no matter what practice we embrace; the essence of that vow is that it is precisely the evil person who has faith in power from without who possesses the true basis for rebirth in the Pure Land. This is why the teacher said, "Even a virtuous person can gain rebirth in the Pure Land, to say nothing of an evil person."

Source: Shinran, *Tannishō* selection; tr. Meredith McKinney.

TRUTH DECAY: NICHIREN ON THE TITLE OF THE *LOTUS SŪTRA*

Nichiren (1222–1282) was one of the most charismatic figures of Japanese Buddhism. Initially trained in the Tendai school, he became disenchanted with its doctrines and practices, considering them inappropriate to the current age, which he believed to be the "age of degenerate dharma" (Japanese: mappō*) that the Buddha had predicted would begin 1,500 years after his death. Many Japanese Buddhists of the Kamakura period (1185–1333) believed that the turmoils of the time indicated the arrival of the final age of dharma, and a number of teachers believed that in such a time new models and practices were required.*

Because in the final age people become progressively more degenerate, Nichiren contended that the practices of the past—including intensive meditation practice and adherence to monastic vows—were no longer possible for most people, and thus simpler and more effective practices, appropriate to mappō*, were required. Nichiren focused on the* Lotus Sūtra *(Saddharma-puṇḍarīka-sūtra) as the only viable teaching for* mappō*, and he counseled his followers to place all of their faith in it. Its teachings, however, were deemed too profound for most people to understand, so Nichiren developed the practice of chanting the title of the sūtra (Namu Myōhōrengekyō in Japanese) and trusting to the saving power of the sūtra to bring worldly benefits and final salvation.*

Question: If a person does not understand the real meaning of the *Lotus Sūtra*, or grasp its import, but simply recites the words "*Namu Myōhō Rengekyō*," perhaps once a day, or once a month, or once a year or once every ten years, or even once in a lifetime, without yielding to the temptation of any evil action, great or small, will such a person not only be able to avoid the four evil realms, but manage thereby to attain that place from which there is no backsliding?

Answer: He will.... All the beings of the nine worlds and the buddha world are contained within the syllables "*Myōhō Rengekyō*." And since these words contain the ten worlds, they naturally include all the states of rebirth possible in those worlds. Given that all doctrines are contained within the five syllables of the name of this *sūtra*, one single word from it is lord of all *sūtra*s. The whole body of *sūtra*s is contained therein.

Source: Nichiren, *Hokke Damokushū* selections; tr. Meredith McKinney.

Sikhism

INTRODUCTION

Early one morning in 1499, Nānak (1469–1539), the founder of the Sikh tradition, went to a river to perform his daily religious ablutions. When he failed to return, search parties were sent out, but all they found were his clothes on the bank of the river. Assuming that the current had carried Nānak away, they returned to town and reported the news. Several days later Nānak reappeared, and after first refusing to speak for three days he told his friends and family that he had been taken to the presence of God and given a mission: to teach Hindus and Muslims that both groups in fact worship the same God. God, he said, was distressed by the sectarian violence perpetrated in His name in India and wanted Nānak to call his followers from rigid adherence to dogmas and the performance of empty rituals to the true essence of religion, which is known only by those who move beyond external observances like ceremonies, prayers, pilgrimages, and study to the rich inner life of true spirituality. This spirituality is characterized by selfless devotion *(bhakti)* to God.

Nānak summarized God's message with this statement: "There is neither Hindu nor Muslim, so whose path should I follow? I will follow God's path, and God is neither Hindu nor Muslim." These words were the cornerstone of his later speeches and writings, in which he stressed the unity of God and the idea that the differences in how religions characterize Him are due merely to human failure to grasp the divine essence. Nānak further contended that there is no reason for religious groups to fight each other because any system necessarily is limited and all theological ideas are inadequate.

After his meeting with God, Sikh texts refer to Nānak as "Gurū," a teacher and devotee of God. Throughout his life he worked to reconcile Hindus and Muslims, to teach them that God is everywhere and continually calls His creatures to experience Him directly and intuitively. This cannot be accomplished by those who rely on external religious observances. Rather, God is found only by practitioners of pure devotion who open themselves to the divine call and experience mystical union. Nānak taught that devotion is the highest form of religious practice, but also the most difficult. The ego is a powerful force in human beings, and it causes us to recoil from the experience of union in which all sense of individuality is swept away by a transcendent vision of the divine presence.

Nānak belonged to a widespread but unorganized group of mystics known as Sants, whose members stressed the unity of God and criticized both Hindus and Muslims for being overly concerned with the external aspects of their traditions while failing to recognize that all theistic religions worship the same ultimate source of all being. The greatest early exponent of this tradition was Kabīr (1440–1518), a weaver from Vārāṇasī. He was born into a Muslim family that converted from Hinduism, but his writings indicate that he saw himself as having transcended any sectarian affiliation. In his poetry he accuses both Muslim and Hindu religious leaders of hypocrisy and of failing to grasp the true essence of religion. Hindu *paṇḍit*s (religious scholars) are portrayed as being concerned mainly with profit and position, with empty ceremonies and external observances. Muslim clerics, he contends, tend to be caught up in systems and words and so do not understand that God is one and that all religious traditions have their source in the same ultimate reality. This reality is beyond the reach of human thought; it cannot be grasped by words or doctrines and is truly understood only by those who abandon external religious observances and devote themselves wholeheartedly to meditation and worship.

The poetry of Nānak stresses similar themes. He denounces idol worship and indicates that practices such as pilgrimages, ritual bathing, and ceremonies tend to keep the individual far from God. Nānak, like Kabīr, views God as having two aspects: God is both immanent (*saguṇa*, literally, "having qualities") and transcendent (*nirguṇa*, "without qualities"). In essence God is completely transcendent, and any qualities imputed to God are merely human attempts to grasp the ultimate reality in terms that we are able to understand. God is completely other, unknowable, and ineffable, but He may still be experienced by those who empty themselves of ego and open themselves to the divine presence.

Nānak died in 1539 after founding and guiding a small group of followers he referred to as "Sikhs," or students. His students were both Hindus and Muslims, who saw Nānak as a great religious leader whose mystical experiences transcended their sectarian divisions. According to Sikh legends, he continually worked to help them overcome the limitations of their religious vision.

Nānak's final teaching was given on his deathbed. When it became clear that death was near, a dispute arose between Hindu and Muslim Sikhs. The former group wanted to cremate him in accordance with their traditions, while the latter argued for burying his body. Nānak settled the dispute by telling them that each group should place a garland of flowers on one side of his body, and that the group whose garland remained unwilted after three days would be able to dispose of his corpse in accordance with its traditions. The next morning the shroud was removed, but his body was gone. All that remained were two garlands of unwilted flowers. Thus, even in death Nānak taught his followers the importance of overcoming sectarian differences. Before Nānak died, he designated his disciple Gurū Aṅgad (1504–1552) as his successor. According to Sikh tradition, this event marks the inauguration of the Sikh path *(panth)*. The office of Gurū was in turn passed on to Amar Dās (1479–1574) and then to Rām Dās (1534–1581). The fifth Gurū, Arjan (1563–1606), worked to mold the Sikhs into a cohesive religious, social, and economic community. He initiated construction of the Golden Temple (Dārbar Sāhib) at Amritsar, which today is the holiest shrine of the Sikhs, and he directed the compilation of the *Ādi Granth*, the holiest scripture of the Sikh tradition. This text contains writings by Nānak and the early Gurūs, as well as works by Kabīr and other devotional poets. Today the *Ādi Granth* is the center of the religious life of the community. Ornate copies of the text are placed on special pedestals in the center of each Sikh temple (*gurdvārā*, literally, "door to the Gurū"), and portions of it are chanted almost constantly while the temple is open.

Arjan's tenure marks a change of direction for the Sikh community. During the reigns of the first four Gurūs, the Panth had enjoyed generally amicable relations with the Muslim Mughal rulers who controlled northern India. With the ascension of the emperor Jehangir, however, the situation changed. Hearkening back to the militancy of the early Muslim conquerors, Jehangir actively persecuted other religious groups, including the Sikhs. He had Arjan captured and tortured with the intention of forcing the Gurū to renounce his faith. Arjan refused to submit to the emperor's demands, and he eventually died in prison. Shortly before his death, he advised his son Hargobind (1595–1664) to "sit fully armed upon the throne," because Arjan recognized the threat the new Mughal ruler posed for his community.

Gurū Hargobind followed the wishes of his father, Gurū Arjan, and began wearing two swords at all times—one symbolizing his religious authority, and the other his temporal authority. His tenure marks the beginning of the transition of the Panth from a group of devotional mystics concerned with reconciling the differences between Hindus and Muslims to a tradition stressing the importance of combat readiness and willingness to fight—and die if necessary—in order to defend the faith.

The seventh Gurū, Hari Rāi (1630–1661), ruled during a time of increasing tensions between the Sikhs and the Mughal emperor. The eighth, Hari Krishan (1656–1664), died as a child and was succeeded by Tegh Bahādur (1621–1675), who became another Sikh martyr as a result of his opposition to the emperor's imposition of a tax on all non-Muslims in his empire. Intending to make an example of the Gurū, the emperor had him imprisoned and tortured. He was ordered to renounce his faith and his opposition to the tax. When he refused, Tegh Bahādur was executed.

His son Gobind Siṅgh (1666–1708) became the tenth and last Gurū. Realizing that the position made its holder a target, as the Gurū lay dying from wounds inflicted by a Muslim assassin, he declared that henceforth the *Ādi Granth* would be the Gurū. He told the community to view the text as the condensation of the inspired words of the Gurūs, the mouthpieces of God, which should guide them in their religious lives. Gobind Siṅgh's other major contribution to the development of Sikhism was his institution of the Khālsā, the community of Sikh believers. Recognizing that survival of the faith required that Sikhs become fully committed to preparing themselves to defend the community against attacks by its enemies, in a special ceremony he called on the faithful to step forward if they were truly prepared to die for their religion. Five stepped forward, and they became the first members of the new community. The Gurū then instructed his followers to adopt five distinctive marks symbolic of their new commitment, referred to as the "Five Ks" because their names in the Punjabi language all begin with the letter K. These are: (1) *kes*, hair, which refers to the Sikh practice of not cutting the hair; (2) *kanghā*, a comb used to keep the hair neat; (3) *kirpān*, a short sword symbolizing the warrior ethos of the Khālsā; (4) *kara*, a steel wristband; and (5) *kachch*, short pants. Many male members of the community also began wearing turbans as a way of managing their hair, and most males also changed their family name to Siṅgh, meaning lion, as a symbol of their devotion to the Gurū. Women changed their names to Kaur, meaning princess, and all Sikhs were declared by the Gurū to be members of the warrior caste *(kṣatriya)*, symbolizing both their emphasis on combat readiness and the equality of all believers.

Nānak had established the Panth as a community dedicated to reconciling Hindus and Muslims, but Gobind Siṅgh realized that peaceful relations with the Mughal emperor were no longer possible. In order to maintain its survival, the community would have to defend itself against attacks and would need to develop into a cohesive and well-trained military force in order to protect itself from its neighbors. It is ironic that Sikhism, which began as a movement dedicated to reconciling different faiths, was pushed by historical circumstances to become a tradition that stressed the differences of its members from other religious groups and that was determined to defend itself against hostile opponents.

SIKH DOCTRINES AND PRACTICES

Sikh theology contends that God is one without a second, the transcendent ultimate that cannot be grasped by human intelligence or described by language. God is commonly referred to by such negative terms as Timeless *(akāl)* and Unproduced *(ajuni)* but also is described positively as Truth or Being *(sat)*. God is both utterly transcendent and accessible to His creatures through grace. God chooses some beings to draw near to Him through devotion, and He speaks to all beings through the words of the Gurūs.

Sikhs commonly refer to God as Akal Purukh, "Timeless Being." He creates and sustains the universe and is known only by those who approach Him with devotion. God reveals Himself through the Divine Name *(nām)*, which expresses aspects of the divine Reality as understood by the limited intellects of His creatures. All of creation reflects the glory and activity of God, so in this sense everything is an expression of the Name. People are able to approach God through meditation on the Name, through which they may transcend ordinary understanding and approach the Divine Presence. The Name is said in Sikh texts to be "the total expression of all that God is," and those who open themselves to the Name through selfless devotion may come to know God in a way that transcends ordinary knowing.

One of the most important of Sikh meditative practices is "remembering the Name" *(nām simraṇ)*, in which the devotee contemplates various epithets of God, along with the adumbrations of the divine essence that are found throughout creation. In this practice, the meditator generally repeats a particular word or mantra, or chants the songs of the Gurūs, in order to bring about intuitive understanding of God.

Sikhism teaches that there is only one God, although He is known in various guises by different religions. In essence, however, God transcends all creeds and systems. Sikhism rejects the idea that God takes physical incarnations *(avtāra)*. God is utterly transcendent and cannot be contained within the limited form of a created being. Like Hinduism, however, Sikhism contends that living creatures are reborn in a beginningless cycle *(sansār; Skt: saṃsāra)* and that each being's situation is a result of past actions *(karam; Skt: karma)*. The ultimate goal of Sikhism is liberation *(mukti)* from cyclic existence, but this can be attained only through God's grace and not by personal effort.

The primary factor preventing the attainment of liberation is self-reliance *(haumai)*, which causes beings falsely to imagine that they are independent and autonomous, that their fates are within their own control, and that salvation may be attained through actions. In order to combat self-reliance, one must cultivate proper attitude *(hukam)*, which involves recognizing one's utter dependence on God. Humble and devoted repetition of the Name helps one develop humility and leads one to recognize the transcendent glory of God.

God is within everyone, so rituals are unnecessary, according to Sikhism, nor is there any point in making pilgrimages because God is everywhere. One may worship God anywhere and at any time, and Sikhism urges its followers to strive toward realization of the Divine Presence all around them. Sikhism contends that ignorance is the primary factor preventing one from knowing God and that ignorance is eliminated only when followers humbly submit themselves to the divine will and listen to God's message as revealed by the words of the Gurūs and other inspired devotional mystics.

Because God is the ultimate source of everything, all is really God, although ignorant beings fail to realize this. God's presence is hidden from us by the power of illusion *(māyā)*, a process of projection that causes beings mistakenly to imagine that they have an existence apart from Him. In reality, everything is a part of Him, and nothing can exist apart from Him. When one is awakened to the reality behind this illusion (which can occur only through God's grace), one realizes the unity of God and gradually comes to perceive God in everything. Sikhism's formulation of the doctrine of *māyā* differs from that of Advaita Vedānta, in that in Sikh philosophy *māyā* is not an objective reality projected by God, but a subjective error resulting from a wrong point of view, a belief in duality rather than unity. This belief causes the mirage of the world to be seen as an end in itself. It is eliminated by devotion and meditation on the divine Name. One who is wholeheartedly immersed in this practice may, through the grace of God, escape the cycle of birth and death and attain final liberation, which Sikhism contends is an eternally blissful state of union with the Ultimate.

SIKH SCRIPTURES

The first attempt to create a collection of authoritative Sikh texts was made during the tenure of the third Gurū, Amar Dās (r. 1552–1574), who supervised a compilation of works by his predecessors. The fifth Gurū, Arjan, began the collection of texts that became the *Ādi Granth*, the most revered scripture of the tradition. Sikhs consider it to be the Gurū because it contains the collected wisdom of the early Gurūs and their Sant predecessors. There are three known recensions of the *Ādi Granth*: (1) one believed to be the original text written by Bhāī Gurdās and owned by a Sikh family in Kartārpur; (2) the "Damdama Recension," which was compiled during the seventeenth century and includes works by Gurū Tegh Bahādur; and (3) the "Banno Recension," which is widely regarded by Sikhs as noncanonical. The Damdama Recension is the standard text for all copies of the *Ādi Granth* published in modern times. Modern published texts of the *Ādi Granth* follow this version even to the extent of adopting its pagination. Thus, all copies of the *Ādi Granth* have 1,430 pages, and every individual page mirrors the contents of the original Damdama text.

The *Ādi Granth* is divided into three main portions: (1) *Introductory Material* (pp. 1–13), (2) *Rāg*s (pp. 14–1353), and (3) *Miscellaneous Works* (pp. 1353–1430). The introductory section begins with the *Mūl Mantra*, the basic statement of Sikh faith. The next portions are the works of the *Japjī* of Guru Nānak, which is regarded as containing his quintessential teachings. The introductory material ends with works by Guru Aṅgad, Nānak's immediate successor. The second portion of the introductory section is referred to as the *Sodār* because the first word of the first hymn is *sodār*. This section contains four poems by Guru Nānak, three by Guru Rām Dās, and two by Guru Arjan. The third section of the introduction is named *Sohilā* or *Kirtan Sohilā*. It contains three works by Guru Nānak, one by Guru Rām Dās, and one by Guru Arjan.

The term *Rāg* refers to various meters used in the works of the second section of the *Ādi Granth*. This is the largest portion of the text and is divided into thirty-one sections, each of which contains hymns of a particular type. Within each *Rāg*, works are arranged according to length and content. Hymns in four stanzas are placed at the beginning, followed by hymns in eight stanzas. The last part of the *Rāg*s contains poems by predecessors of Sikhism whose religious visions are considered to be consonant with the vision of Guru Nānak and his successors. Works by Kabīr and the devotional poets Nāmdev and Ravidās are found in this section.

Miscellaneous Works has more writings by Kabīr and some compositions by the Sufi teacher Sheikh Farīd. The final portion of the *Ādi Granth* consists of fifty-seven verses by Guru Tegh Bahādur, two works by Guru Arjan, and the *Rāg-mālā*, which summarizes the contents of the *Rāg*s. The language of the *Ādi Granth* is referred to as "Sant Bhāṣā," the language of the Sants. Linguistically similar to modern Punjabi, it was the language adopted by the devotional Sant poets of the fifteenth and sixteenth centuries in northern India. The words of the *Ādi Granth* are recorded in the Gurmukhī script, which also is used for modern Punjabi.

Another important scriptural source for Sikhism is the *Dasam Granth*, the compilation of which is associated with the tenth Guru, Gobind Siṅgh. Like the *Ādi Granth*, it is referred to as "Guru" and is widely regarded as an authoritative text, but it is less important for the tradition than the *Ādi Granth*. It contains a range of literature, including extensive portions of stories from Hindu literature, many of which are written in different dialects.

The compositions of the mystic poets Bhāī Gurdās and Bhāī Nand Lāl are also highly regarded by Sikhs and have the status of scriptures. The former writer lived during the tenure of the third through sixth Gurūs, and the latter was a follower of Gurū Gobind Siṅgh. Along with the *Ādi Granth* and the *Dasam Granth*, their writings are the only works approved for recitation in Sikh temples.

Mention also should be made of the *janam-sākhīs*, hagiographical stories of Gurū Nānak's life. They stress the themes of the unity of God, the pointlessness of sectarianism, and the worthlessness of external religious observances. They were probably composed during the sixteenth century, and although these stories have not been granted the status of scriptures, they are widely popular.

HOLIDAYS

New Year Celebration (Saṅgrāṅd) First day of the Indian lunar calendar, when Sikhs visit *gurdwārā*s for prayers.

Commemoration of the Gurū (Gurpurb) Festivals celebrating the birth of a Gurū or other special occasions, such as the installation of the *Ādi Granth* as the Gurū in 1704:

1. Gurū Nānak's birthday (generally celebrated in November).
2. Gurū Gobind Siṅgh's birthday (generally celebrated in December–January).
3. Inauguration of the Khālsā (Vaisākh Baisākhī; mid-April).
4. Martyrdom of Gurū Arjan (generally June).
5. Gurū Tegh Bahādur's martyrdom (generally November).

Festival of Lights (Divālī or Dīpāvalī) Celebrated in the second half of the lunar month of Aśvina, which generally occurs in October–November. This holy day, shared with Hinduism, is associated by Sikhs with the construction of the Dārbar Sāhib and the return of the sixth Gurū from imprisonment.

TIMELINE

1440–1518	Life of Kabīr
1469	Birth of Gurū Nānak
1479–1574	Life of Gurū Amar Dās
1504–1552	Life of Gurū Aṅgad
1534–1581	Life of Gurū Rām Dās
1563–1606	Life of fifth Sikh Gurū, Arjan; construction of Dārbar Sāhib; compilation of *Ādi Granth*
1595–1664	Life of sixth Sikh Gurū, Hargobind
1621–1675	Life of ninth Sikh Gurū, Tegh Bahādur
1666–1708	Life of Gobind Siṅgh, last human Gurū of Sikhism; formation of Sikh Khālsā
1780–1839	Life of Rañjit Siṅgh; Sikh rule of the Punjab
1849	British conquer Duleep Siṅgh and end Sikh control of Punjab
1897	Publication of *We Are Not Hindus* by Kahn Singh Nabha
1925	Gurdwārās Act of 1925 gives control of all *gurdvārā*s in the Punjab to Shiromaṇī Gurdwārā Parbandhak Committee
1984	Operation Bluestar; Indira Gandhi assassinated

GLOSSARY

Ādi Granth "First Book," the holiest book of the Sikhs, which contains writings of Gurū Nānak and his successors along with poems of Sants.

Akāl Purukh "Timeless Being," one of the Sikh names of God.

Avidyā "Ignorance," the basic factor that enmeshes beings in the cycle of birth, death, and rebirth.

Bhakti Selfless devotion to God.

Five Ks Distinctive marks of Sikh believers, instituted by Gurū Gobind Siṅgh: (1) *kes*, unshorn hair; (2) *kaṅghā*, comb; (3) *kirpān*, short sword; (4) *kara*, steel wristband; (5) *kachch*, short pants.

Gobind Siṅgh The tenth Gurū, founder of the Khālsā (1666–1708).

Gurū "Teacher," a designation for Nānak and his successors, and later for the *Ādi Granth*.

Haumai Self-reliance, the false notion that one is independent of God.

Hukam An attitude of humility, brought about by the realization of one's utter dependence on God.

Karma Actions that lead to concordant results.

Khālsā The Sikh community, founded by Gurū Gobind Siṅgh.

Māyā "Illusion," a falsehood caused by ignorance, which causes beings to perceive multiplicity instead of the unitary truth of God.

Mukti "Release" from the cycle of birth, death, and rebirth, which is brought about by God's grace.

Mūl Mantra "Root Prayer," the fundamental statement of Sikh doctrine.

Nām "Divine Name," which refers both to the various epithets of God and to His manifestations in the world.

Nām Simraṇ "Remembering the Name," the practice of contemplating God's attributes and actions.

Nānak The founder of the Sikh tradition (1469–1539).

Nirguṇa "Without Qualities," a designation of God's essential nature.

Saṃsāra "Cyclic Existence," the beginningless cycle of birth, death, and rebirth in which ordinary beings are trapped.

Sants Indian mystics who advocated pure devotion to God and who denounced religious sectarianism.

Sikh "Disciple," a term coined by Gurū Nānak to designate his followers.

SIKH SCRIPTURES

NĀNAK, THE FIRST GURŪ

According to the Sikh tradition, Gurū Nānak was born in the northern Punjab in an area that today is part of Pakistan. In this region Muslims and Hindus frequently came into conflict, which deeply troubled Nānak. As a member of the Sant tradition, he believed that both groups worship the same God and so should not fight. Even as a child Nānak was drawn to religious contemplation, and as he grew up his interest in the divine Reality became so intense that he cared little for mundane things.

One day he went to a nearby river to perform his ritual ablutions, but he disappeared. A search was conducted, but all that was found of Nānak were his clothes. After three days he reappeared, but he refused to discuss where he had been. After three days he told his friends and relatives that he had been taken to the presence of God and given a special mission. God had informed him that Hindus and Muslims both worship Him and that He wished them to join together in faith and not fight against each other. Gurū Nānak was to be the prophet of the message of reconciliation, and he spent the remainder of his life working to bring the two groups together.

Bābā Nānak was born in Talvandi, the son of Kalu, who was a Bedī Khatrī by caste. In this Age of Darkness he proclaimed the divine Name and founded his community of followers, the Panth. Bābā Nānak was born in the year S. 1526 on the third day of the month of Vaisakh [April 15, 1469].... Celestial music resounded in heaven. A mighty host of gods hailed his birth, and with them all manner of spirit and divinity. "God has come to save the world!" they cried....

As he grew older he began to play with other children, but his attitude differed from theirs, in that he paid heed to the spiritual things of God. When he turned five he began to give utterance to deep and mysterious thoughts. Whatever he uttered was spoken with profound understanding, with the result that everyone's doubts and questions were resolved. The Hindus vowed that a god had taken birth in human form. The Muslims declared that a follower of divine truth had been born....

After returning home in the evening Bābā Nānak would devote his nights to singing hymns, and when it came to the last watch of the night he would go to the river and bathe. One morning, having gone to bathe, he entered the waters of the Vein stream but failed to emerge. His servant looked for him until mid-morning and then taking his clothes returned home to tell Jai Rām what had happened.... [A] thorough search was made, but to no avail.

Eventually, however, Bābā Nānak did return. After three days and three nights had passed he emerged from the stream, and having done so he declared: "There is neither Hindu nor Muslim...."

Source: *Janam-Sākhī* selections, tr. W. H. McLeod, *Textual Sources for the Study of Sikhism* (Chicago: University of Chicago Press, 1984), pp. 18–21.

GURŪ NĀNAK'S DEATH

Although Hindus and Muslims became Nānak's followers, members of each group often retained strong ties to their original religion, despite Nānak's efforts to wean them of sectarianism. As he was preparing to die, members of each group proposed to dispose of his physical remains in accordance with their respective burial customs. Nānak's final lesson to his followers gently chided them for this behavior.

Gurū Bābā Nānak then went and sat under a withered acacia which immediately produced leaves and flowers, becoming verdant again. . . . Bābā Nānak's wife began to weep and the various members of his family joined her in her grief. . . . The assembled congregation sang hymns of praise and Bābā Nānak passed into an ecstatic trance. While thus transported, and in obedience to the divine will, he sang the hymn entitled The Twelve Months. It was early morning and the time had come for his final departure. . . .

"Even the Gurū's dogs lack nothing, my sons," he said. "You shall be abundantly supplied with food and clothing, and if you repeat the Gurū's name you will be liberated from the bondage of human life." Hindus and Muslims who had put their faith in the divine Name began to debate what should be done with the Gurū's corpse. "We shall bury him," said the Muslims. "No, let us cremate his body," said the Hindus. "Place flowers on both sides of my body," said Bābā Nānak, "flowers from the Hindus on the right side and flowers from the Muslims on the left. If tomorrow the Hindus' flowers are still fresh let my body be burned, and if the Muslims' flowers are still fresh let it be buried."

Bābā Nānak then commanded the congregation to sing. . . . Bābā Nānak then covered himself with a sheet and passed away. Those who had gathered around him prostrated themselves, and when the sheet was removed they found that there was nothing under it. The flowers on both sides remained fresh, and both Hindus and Muslims took their respective shares. All who were gathered there prostrated themselves again.

Source: *Purātan Janam-Sākhī*, pp. 111–115, from *Textual Sources for the Study of Sikhism*, p. 25.

THE *MŪL MANTRA:* THE BASIC STATEMENT

Gurū Arjan placed the Mūl Mantra, *the basic Sikh statement of faith, at the beginning of the holiest book of the Sikhs, the Ādi* Granth. *It expresses the primary attributes of the Sikh conception of God: His absolute unity and absolute transcendence. The following passages contain the mantra and a discussion of its significance by Gurū Rām Dās.*

> There is one supreme God, known by grace by the true Gurū.
> The True Name, the Creator, fearless and formless;
> Timeless, never incarnated, self-existent.

Source: *Ādi Granth* 1.1. Tr. JP.

DISCUSSION OF THE MŪL MANTRA

Contemplate the Fearless One, who is true, and always remains true. Devoid of enmity, the Timeless One, never incarnated and is self-existent. Meditate day and night on the Formless One, my man, who transcends any need of sustenance.

Source: Gurū Rām Dās, *Ādi Granth*, Sārang 2, p. 1201. Tr. JP.

THE DIVINE NAME

The Divine Name (nām) *is an important motif in the* Ādi Granth. *The nature of God is intimated through the various epithets used to call and describe Him, and although none of these is able adequately to convey God's essence, each provides some insight into what God is.*

> Even if I were an adept *(siddha)*, master of spiritual attainments, performing miracles,
> Manifesting or concealing any form at will, focus of the world's devotion,
> If I were to become engrossed in these wonders and forget You,
> Your name erased from my mind,
> If I were a king with vast armies,
> Setting my foot on a great throne,
> My will spreading far and wide,
> Nānak! All would be empty! . . .
> If I were to live for millions upon millions of years;
> If I could subsist on nothing but air through austerities;
> If I lived in seclusion never seeing the sun or moon
> And never slept even in thought—
> Even in this Your greatness would forever transcend my striving;
> What inkling could I give of your Name?
> The Lord, holy, formless, forever remaining in His immutable essence:
> I express His greatness as I hear it through His grace.
> Only through grace can we know.
> If through austerities I were beaten like grass,
> Killed and my body dismembered, ground up in a mill;
> If I were burned in a great fire and mingled with ashes and dust,
> Still Your glory would forever transcend my striving.

Source: *Ādi Granth*, "Siri Rāg," pp. 35–36. Tr. JP.

THE ONE PATH TO GOD

In this passage, Nānak catalogs various religious practices current in India in his day and dismisses them all as basically useless. Those who engage in austerities, who chant texts, and who travel to holy places, all fail to grasp the omnipresence of

God. Nānak enjoins us to cast aside all such endeavors and open ourselves to God's grace.

> I do not know how to win His favor.
> My self! Seek the path to Him.
> Meditators engage in contemplation;
> Scholars adopt the way of learning;
> But realization of the Lord only comes to a small few.
> The devotees of Viṣṇu (Vaiṣṇava) engage in ritual;
> Yogis claim to attain liberation through training;
> Ascetics engage in austerities.
> Those with vows of silence do not speak;
> Monastics maintain celibacy;
> Those who practice dispassion remain dispassionate;
> They practice nine forms of devotion [including listening to texts, worshipping idols, prayer, supplication, meditation, serving the deity, etc.];
> Brahmin scholars of the Vedas chant;
> Householders cling to the householder's dharma.
> Some speak slogans, others put on disguises;
> Some discard all clothing,
> While others wear strange robes.
> Some speak in rhymes,
> While others keep night-long vigils,
> And others swim in bathing places.
> Some go without food, others avoid touching;
> Some hide themselves and remain invisible.
> Some sit in silent contemplation.
> None considers himself inferior to any of the others—
> All claim God-realization.
> But the true devotee is the one to whom He grants union.
> I have renounced all disputation and all ritual;
> I only seek shelter at His feet.
> Nānak falls at the Master's feet.

Source: *Ādi Granth*, "Siri Rāg," p. 71. Tr. JP.

NUDITY DOES NOT MAKE ONE A SAINT

In this poem, Kabīr stresses the need for true devotion to God, referred to here as Rām (an incarnation of Viṣṇu). Kabīr indicates that asceticism is useless because one reaches liberation only through ecstatic love of God, in which all sense of self is eliminated and one is consumed by pure love.

> Whether you are naked or clothed, what does it matter
> If you have not recognized the inward Rām?
> If one could achieve yoga by wandering naked,
> Then would not deer in the forest achieve liberation?
> If by shaving one's head one could have spiritual mastery *(siddhi)*
> Then would sheep also not go to heaven?

My brother, if by holding back your seed you could be saved,
Then surely eunuchs would attain the highest place in heaven.
Kabīr says: Listen brother, without the name of Rām
Who has ever achieved liberation?

Source: *Kabīr Granthāvalī*, pad 174. Tr. JP.

BOOKS AND LEARNING ARE OF NO USE

A central theme of Kabīr's poems is a rejection of the value of study and prayer as performed by the religious leaders of his day, who are characterized as holding to the letter of the scriptures without grasping the true meaning.

Pundit, why are you so foolish?
You don't speak of Rām, you fool!
Carrying your Vedas and Purāṇas, moving like a donkey loaded with sandalwood,
Unless you learn about the name of Rām,
You will come to grief.
You slaughter living beings and call it dharma;
What then, brother, would non-dharma be?
You refer to each other as "Great Saint"; whom, then, should I call "Butcher"?
Your mind is blind, your understanding dull.
Brother, how can you preach to others?
You sell your knowledge for money, and spend your human life in vain.

Source: *Kabīr Granthāvalī*, pad 191. Tr. JP.

EXTERNAL OBSERVANCES ARE OF NO USE

Like their Sant predecessors, Sikhs denounced the practice of external religious observances. Far from bringing people closer to God, Sikhs believe that such practices tend to obscure the divine presence, which is all around us, in all things, and directly accessible to human intuition.

He cannot be made into an image,
Nor can humans make a likeness.
He is self-created and self-existent,
Maintained forever on high.
Those who meditate on Him are honored in His shrine.
O Nānak! Sing the hymns of God, the repository of the highest qualities.
If one sings of God and listens to [songs about] Him,
And lets love of God arise within,
All suffering will disappear, and God will create enduring peace in the soul.

The word of God is the inner music;
The word of God is the highest scripture;
The word of God is all-pervading.
The Gurū is Śiva, the Gurū is Viṣṇu and Brahmā, the Gurū is the
Goddess.
If I could know Him as He truly is,
What words could express this knowledge? . . .
May I never forget Him!

Source: *Ādi Granth*, "Japjī" 5. Tr. JP.

ON *HUKAM*

Hukam *is central to Sikh meditative practice. It literally means "propriety," putting things where they belong. It involves understanding one's relation to God and God's place in the universe. Cultivating* hukam *is necessary to overcoming self-reliance* (haumai), *the false notion that one is an autonomous individual independent of God's grace.*

All forms are created by *hukam*, but it cannot be described. Living beings were created by *hukam*, and greatness is obtained through it. Through *hukam* the high and the low are established, and it determines who suffers and who is happy. Due to *hukam* some are saved while others are caused to transmigrate. Everyone is subject to *hukam*; no one is exempt from it. Nānak, if a person understands *hukam*, he will eliminate selfish conceit.

Source: *Ādi Granth*, "Japjī" 2; tr. JP.

ON *HAUMAI*

Haumai *is born of ignorance, which is the root cause of continued transmigration. It is a perceptual error in which one mistakenly believes that one is independent and autonomous, although in fact everything in the universe is created and sustained by God. Those who hold to mistaken views of separateness and individuality fail to recognize the omnipresence of God and their utter dependence on his grace.*

Innumerable are the blind fools, sunk in folly;
Innumerable those living on thievery and dishonesty.
Innumerable the tyrants ruling by brute force;
Innumerable the violent cutthroats and murderers;
Innumerable those revolving in their own falsehood;
Innumerable the polluted living on filth;
Innumerable the slanderers bearing on their heads their loads of sin.
The sinner Nānak thus enumerates the evil-doers,

I who am unworthy even once to be made a sacrifice to You.
All that You will is good, Formless One, abiding in Your peace.

Source: *Ādi Granth*, "Japjī" 18. Tr. JP.

THE ECSTASY OF MYSTICAL UNION

Kabīr's poetry contains a wealth of striking metaphors and images intended to convey nuances of the experience of mystical union that cannot be expressed through ordinary language. In this poem, he describes the bliss of devotional union experienced by one who abandons ego and ritual and is granted the transcendent experience of union with God.

2. The radiance of the Supreme Brahman cannot be imagined;
   Its beauty is ineffable, and seeing it is the only real evidence.
3. The fortunate hail fell to earth, and so lost its selfhood;
   When it melted, it became water and flowed into the lake.
4. I found the one I sought just where I was,
   And it has now become me, though I previously spoke of it as "Other."
5. Light shines in the Unapproachable, the Inaccessible.
   Kabīr has brought his worship there, beyond the realm of "merit" and "sin.". . .
7. Love illuminated the cage [of physical existence], an eternal flame arose, My doubts disappeared, and happiness dawned when I encountered my Beloved. . . .
9. Water turned into ice, and then the ice melted;
   Everything that was has become It, and so what more can be said? . . .
12. Kabīr has found the One, the Unapproachable, whose radiance is indescribable,
    The Luminous wife who is a *paras* [a stone that brings immortality]
    The god whom I now see. . . .
19. Sun and moon have become merged, and both dwell in one house.
    My mind has attained the goal of its search due to my past actions.
20. Transcending all limitations, I entered into the Boundless,
    Dwelling in Emptiness *(sunni)*.
    I now reside in the palace that the sages cannot find.

Source: Kabīr, *Sākhī* 9. Tr. JP.

GUIDELINES FOR A HAPPY MARRIAGE

Gurū Gobind Siṅgh advises married couples to view themselves as one entity and to avoid deceit in their relationship. Wives are urged to remain faithful and to be subservient to their husbands, and husbands are warned of the negative consequences of mistreating their wives.

When husband and wife sit side by side why should we treat them as two?
Outwardly separate, their bodies distinct, yet inwardly joined as one.
Comply with whatever your Spouse may desire, never resisting,
spurning deceit. . . .
Obey his commands in total surrender, this is the fragrance to bring. . . .
Abandon self-will, the Beloved draws near; no cunning will ever avail.
Be humble in manner and practice restraint, let sweetness of speech be
your prayer.
If these are the garments adorning a bride, the husband she seeks will
be found.
Sweet is her speech, approved by the Loved One; grant that the joy
may endure evermore.
Filled with the spirit of truth and contentment, the family's pride and joy.
The one who is constant in goodness and virtue is cherished and loved
by the Spouse.
Behind closed doors and a forest of curtains he lies with another's wife.
When the angels of Death shall demand your account, how then can the
truth be concealed?
This is the message the Gurū has brought; let this be your vow while
your body has breath.
Bestow your affection on none save your wife; spurning temptation,
avoid other beds.
Watchful, untainted, even in dreams.

Source: *Sukhamani 4.5: Textual Sources for the Study of Sikhism*, pp. 117–118.

FORMATION OF THE *KHĀLSĀ*

This passage tells the story of how the tenth Gurū, Gobind Siṅgh, inaugurated the institution of the Sikh Khālsā (community). Besieged by Muslim rulers who wanted to eliminate the Sikhs, the Gurū realized that in order to survive his followers would have to develop into a military force. In a move that permanently changed the character of the Sikh community, he gathered the faithful together and asked if any were willing to die for their faith. Five men stepped forward, and the Gurū led them one by one to a tent, emerging each time with his sword dripping blood. Many of the people in attendance believed that the Gurū had gone mad, but Gobind Siṅgh later showed them that the five men were unharmed. He had killed five goats, and the blood they had witnessed had been that of the animals. The following day the Gurū completed the process of transforming the community into a warrior group by declaring that henceforth the Sikhs would adopt external signs differentiating them from other communities. They would consider themselves members of the Khālsā, and membership henceforth would be exclusive.

On the day before . . . the Gurū [Gobind Siṅgh] arranged for a large tent made of fine woolen fabric to be pitched on the area known as Keshgaṛh. Earlier he had given instructions for a large dais to be erected at the edge of the area. At that place he held a magnificent reception attended by five thousand Sikhs, all with eyes for none save the Gurū. While they were gazing with rapture, the Gurū rose from his throne and in order to test them addressed the mighty assembly as follows. "I want the heads of five Sikhs to offer as a sacrifice to God," he proclaimed. "Those Sikhs, beloved of the Gurū, who cheerfully give their heads will enjoy in the eternal hereafter all the happiness that their hearts desire."

Terror gripped the hearts of all who heard him. All fell silent, the blood draining from their faces. The Gurū drew his sacred sword and called them again. "Why are you silent?" he cried. "Who amongst you sincerely believes his body to be of no account? Let him stand up."

Hearing this Daya Siṅgh, a pious Khatrī from Lahore, stood with hands respectfully joined. The Gurū conducted him into the tent where five goats were secretly tethered. He felled one of them, letting its blood gush out. When he returned to the assembly, the people were stunned by the sight of his bloodstained sword. When he proceeded to demand the head of another Sikh, they stood petrified. "He must have been bewitched by the goddess," they said. "Why else should he demand the heads of Sikhs?" Some said one thing, some another. . . . [The Gurū repeated the procedure with four other Sikhs.]

All were faithful disciples, pious men wholly given to worship and meditation who valued true wisdom and principle more than their own lives. When the Gurū called for heads to be sacrificed, these five Sikhs offered theirs. Faint-hearted Sikhs . . . tricked by the goat ruse into believing that men were really being killed, whispered anxiously to each other, desperately wanting to flee. This they were unable to do. Overpowered by the radiant presence of the Gurū, each was firmly rooted to the spot.

Although many more Sikhs, faithful and brave, were by this time clamoring to give their heads the Gurū demanded only five. . . . To those who responded, the Cherished Five, he gave new garments and fine weapons so that their appearance should resemble his own. Then he led them from the tent, back to his assembled Sikhs. All were thunderstruck, believing that the Gurū had restored to life those whom he had previously slain. . . .

[The Gurū said:] "Now it is clear for all to see that the Panth will win renown, that it will strike down the enemies of this land while it spreads abroad the message of the Sikh faith. All this will happen because God has made himself manifest in these five.... We give thanks to God that he has destroyed the religion of Muhammad and his successors, replacing it with the supremacy of the Gurū's chosen five...."

On the morning following this momentous event... after pouring water from the Satluj river into a large iron vessel, the Gurū gave instructions for the Cherished Five to be clad in white garments together with a sword and other symbolic forms. He then had them stand before him and commanded them to repeat the divine name "Vāhigurū," fixing their minds on God as they did so. This they were to continue doing while he stirred the sanctified water *(amrit)* in the iron vessel with a double-edged sword held vertically....

The Gurū then used the tip of his sword to take a small quantity of *amrit* from the iron vessel. This he did five times, letting each portion run from his sword on to his face. Then he applied *amrit* to each of the Cherished Five.... Finally, he promulgated the code of conduct which they were to observe.... Thus did the Gurū lay the foundations of the Khālsā, determine its form, and define the obligations of its members.

Sources: *Tavārīkh Gurū Khālsā* selections, from *Textual Sources for the Study of Sikhism*, pp. 34–37.

JUSTIFICATION FOR USE OF FORCE

This poem, written by Gurū Gobind Siṅgh to the Mughal emperor Aurangzeb, accuses him of treachery and argues that Sikhs should fight to defend themselves against the unjust attacks of India's Muslim rulers. These verses stand in obvious contrast to the vision of religious harmony articulated by Nānak, who looked for ways to bring Hindus and Muslims together in a religious community that transcended their differences and emphasized the essential unity of religions.

What could forty starving men do when they were suddenly attacked by ten thousand?
The violators of solemn oaths came suddenly and began attacking.
Then I was forced to do battle, using arrows and gunfire in self-defence.
When all attempts at negotiation have failed, one is justified in unsheathing the sword.
You tell me that I can rely on your oaths on the Qur'an,
But if I had not done so earlier, this would not have come to pass....

One should know that it is evil to deviate from the truth. . . .
You should not wield the sword carelessly in order to draw blood from anyone.
God will shed your blood in the same way.
You should not be indifferent, but should know that God cares nothing for human praise.
He is the Lord of the earth and the sky, the Fearless,
Creator of the universe and of all that is in it. . . .
If you are strong, do not harm the poor,
And do not renege on your promises with axes and clubs.
When God is on one's side, what can an enemy do, even if he uses many tricks?
Even if the enemy attacks thousands of times,
He cannot harm one who has God on his side
And who is protected by His benevolence.

Source: Gurū Gobind Siṅgh, *Zafar-nāmā*. Tr. JP.

GOD, THE SWORD SUPREME

Gobind Siṅgh realized that the continued existence of his religion required that Sikhs learn to defend themselves. In this poem, he indicates that military preparedness is a sacred duty and that God requires his followers to become warriors in order to fight for the truth.

O Sword that strikes in a flash, that scatters the armies of the wicked in the great battlefield; you symbol of the brave.
Your arm is irresistible, your brightness shines forth, the blaze of your splendor dazzling like the sun.
O Sword, you are the protector of the saints, you are the scourge of the wicked; scatterer of sinners, I take refuge in You.
Victory to you, O Sword;
Savior and Sustainer, hail to You: Sword supreme.

Source: Gurū Gobind Siṅgh, *Bachitar Nāṭak*, 1. Tr. JP.

Confucianism

INTRODUCTION

Of all the traditions discussed in this book, Confucianism probably has the least in common with what most contemporary Westerners associate with "religion." Confucius (c. 551–479 BCE), the founder of Confucianisvm, did not assert the existence of a creator god, although he did mention an impersonal force called "Heaven" *(tian)* that watches over human affairs and confers a mandate on rulers that legitimates their power. Confucianism has no churches and no ecclesiastical hierarchy, and Confucius never clearly articulated any vision of the afterlife or a path to salvation. The focus of Confucius was squarely on human beings and their social relations with others. Confucius's philosophy articulated his vision of the Way *(dao)* of the "noble man" *(junzi),*[1] who embodies the qualities of a truly good human being. When asked about "religious" topics such as the nature of Heaven, the existence and propitiation of spirits, and so forth, Confucius generally cautioned his audiences to focus on the present life and on their personal conduct, and not to waste time on idle speculation.

Confucius is the Latinate form of Kong Fuzi, or "Master Kong." According to Chinese tradition, he lived during the fifth century BCE. He was born in the small state of Lu, in modern-day Shandong Province. Some accounts claim that he was a descendant of the royal house of the Shang Dynasty (1751–1122 BCE, the earliest authenticated dynasty of China), but his family had become impoverished by Confucius's time. His father is said to have been a soldier, and his mother was not the first wife. According to later tradition, when Confucius was born, dragons appeared in his house and a unicorn was sighted in his village.

His father died when Confucius was young, and his mother died while he was still a child. According to Sima Qian, when Confucius was a boy, he had little interest in the games of other children and instead preferred to arrange sacrificial implements and pretend to be performing rituals. Apparently Confucius did not have a formal education, but through independent study he became renowned for his learning.

In his twenties he began to attract students. He held a minor government position that required him to keep records of stores

---

[1] This term is often translated as "gentleman," which is how it appears in the selections that follow from Confucius's writings.

of grains and animals used for official sacrifices. According to some accounts, his interest in rituals led him to visit Laozi to seek advice on the performance of sacrifices, but Confucius was admonished for being excessively concerned with external observances and thus neglecting the Dao.[2]

Confucius was married around the age of 19 to a woman from Bin Guan in the state of Song. They had a son and a daughter. Fearing the onset of social disruption in Lu, he traveled to the state of Qi, hoping to gain a position of influence. He was well received but, failing to achieve his primary objective, returned to Lu at the age of 51. There he was appointed minister of justice. According to Confucian accounts, he instituted a period of good government. Records of his tenure claim that articles left on the road were returned to their owners, and people could travel freely without fear of crime. He became an advisor to the duke of Lu but reportedly resigned in disgust after the duke received a present of eighty dancing girls from the rival duke of Qi, after which he no longer attended to his duties in the morning.

Confucius lived during a time of social and political turmoil, and this had a powerful effect on his thinking. The Zhou dynasty (1122–221 BCE), which had unified China and fostered the development of Chinese culture, was losing control, and China was in the process of breaking up into fiefdoms that were vying with each other for territory and power. Confucius lamented this social disintegration and hoped to guide his country back to the norms and practices of the early days of the Zhou dynasty as reported in the *Book of Poetry* and the *Book of History*, both of which extolled the superior qualities of sage-emperors of the Shang and Zhou dynasties. Confucius hoped to find a position of political power that would allow him to help the rulers of his time rediscover the traditions of the past, which he believed would help China correct its problems and reestablish good government.

Unable to find a suitable position in Lu, at the age of 53 Confucius began a trek through China in search of a ruler who would allow him to put his ideas into practice. During the course of thirteen years he journeyed to nine states. Some received him warmly and asked for his advice, but in one state he was surrounded and threatened, in another he was a target of assassination, and in a third state he was detained by government authorities.

He promised that any state that allowed him significant control of domestic matters and foreign affairs would soon enjoy prosperity and enhanced prestige and would have a contented

---

[2] An account of this meeting is excerpted in the "Daoism" chapter under the heading "Laozi Instructs Confucius."

populace that fully supported the policies of the rulers. But his ideas of government by wise and humane rulers were considered dangerous at a time when most rulers controlled their domains by force. After realizing that no one would give him an opportunity to implement his political philosophy, he returned to Lu at the age of 68 and devoted himself to teaching, convinced that his life's mission had been a failure.

His fame as a teacher grew, however, and traditional sources report that young men came from far and wide to study with Confucius and that he never turned away a student who was unable to pay him. As a result, young men of humble origins had access to education, which was an important factor in securing employment in government.

Confucius taught his students to cultivate themselves and urged them to aspire to become "noble men." The noble man, according to Confucius, possesses an unwavering moral compass and thus knows what is correct in all situations. He has the virtue of "human-heartedness" (ren), the coalescence of moral qualities that characterize those who are truly good. A noble man is honest, is courageous, stands in awe of Heaven and constantly seeks to perfect himself, is learned but does not boast of his learning, does not set his mind "for" or "against" anything, holds to no particular political philosophy, but rather seeks to follow what is right in every situation. He has no needs of his own and so is able to work selflessly for others. His unassuming manifestation of good qualities inspires others to become better. Society, according to Confucius, is perfected by such people, who set a moral standard that subtly motivates others to correct themselves in order to emulate them.

Although Confucius was unable to acquire the political power he desired during his lifetime, his students passed on his teachings, becoming teachers themselves. Some of them became influential educators and helped install his notion of the superior person as a standard for conduct among the educated elite of China. In addition, Confucius introduced to China the idea that the primary criteria for holding public office should be intelligence, learning, and highly developed moral character rather than hereditary status. He believed that universal standards of ethical behavior are outlined in the classics, and he urged his students to study these texts in order to develop their moral awareness.

THE CONFUCIAN REVIVAL

In the centuries following Confucius's death, many of his disciples became educators, and as a result Confucian philosophy became a part of the standard curriculum of educated Chinese. Despite its widespread influence, however, the vitality of the tradition languished from the fourth through tenth centuries. Most of the best minds of China were either Daoists or Buddhists, and although Confucianism was widely studied, there were few notable interpreters of the tradition.

This situation changed dramatically in the eleventh century, when several prominent Confucian philosophers began to revive the tradition. Many of them were influenced by Buddhism and Daoism, and several had been Buddhists in their early years but ultimately rejected Buddhism because they considered its doctrine of "emptiness" *(śūnyatā)* to be nihilistic. They also saw the Buddhist emphasis on monasticism as unnatural but found that the Confucian tradition valued the family and the norms of traditional Chinese society. A growing number of Confucian thinkers characterized Buddhism as a religion of "barbarians," unsuited to refined Chinese sensibilities, and found in Confucianism a tradition that accorded with the norms and values of cultured Chinese. Among the early figures of this revival—referred to in China as "Study of Nature and Propriety" *(xing li xue)*[3] and by Western scholars as "Neo-Confucianism"—were prominent philosophers such as Zhou Dunyi (1017–1073), Shao Yong (1011–1077), Zhang Zai (1020–1077), and the two brothers Cheng Hao (1032–1085) and Cheng Yi (1033–1107).

The Neo-Confucian revival is divided by contemporary scholars into two streams, one rationalistic and one idealistic. The major figure of the rationalist tradition was Zhu Xi (1130–1200); Wang Yangming (1472–1529) was the main exponent of the idealists. Confucians in the first group focused on the foundational principles *(li)* of the natural world, human behavior, and society, whereas the idealists were concerned primarily with how to develop a moral consciousness through training the mind *(xin)*.

CONFUCIAN SCRIPTURES

According to Confucian tradition, Confucius edited the texts that came to be regarded as the Confucian classics: the *Book of Poetry (Shijing)*, the *Book of Change (Yijing)*, the *Book of History (Shujing)*, the *Book of Rites (Liji)*, and the *Spring and Autumn Annals (Qunqiu)*. These are regarded as the primary canonical texts of the tradition, along with the "Four Books":

---

[3] It is also referred to as "Study of Propriety from the Song and Ming Dynasties" *(song ming lixue)*, or sometimes as "Study of Propriety" *(lixue)*.

the *Analects (Lunyu)*, *Centeredness (Zhongyong)*, the *Great Learning (Daxue)*, and the *Mencius (Mengzi)*.[4]

The *Book of Poetry* is the earliest anthology of Chinese poetry. It contains 305 poems dating from early times until the later part of the Zhou dynasty. Confucian tradition holds that Confucius selected these poems from an earlier collection of three thousand poems, choosing those written in the finest style and with a high level of moral consciousness. The poems in the collection are written mostly in a style using rhymed quatrains with four characters per line, which became the standard for Chinese poetic writing after the time of Confucius.

The *Book of Change* discusses how natural systems change and has long been regarded as a manual for divination. It contains sixty-four hexagrams, along with explanations of the significance of each one, and "ten wings" of commentary that indicate how they should be interpreted. According to Confucian tradition, the ten wings were composed by Confucius, but this attribution has been rejected by most contemporary scholars (although it is admitted that he may have had a hand in composing one of the wings).

The hexagrams are composed of two trigrams each, and the trigrams are composed of broken and unbroken lines. The lines signify interactions of *yin* and *yang*, the two opposing polarities whose movements govern the developments of natural systems. *Yin* is passive, wet, yielding, and feminine and is represented by broken lines, whereas *yang* is aggressive, dry, forceful, and masculine and is represented by unbroken lines. The pattern of the lines of a hexagram is believed to provide indications of the directions of natural elements and forces.

The *Book of History* is a collection of historical records and speeches purportedly dating from the early dynasties of China. It is the earliest Chinese historical work, containing documents from seventeen centuries, back to the time of the legendary sage-emperors (third millennium BCE). According to tradition, it was compiled and edited by Confucius, who chose selections for their historical and moral import. Each selection reports an event in Chinese history and contains a colophon that indicates the moral judgments of the author.

The *Book of Rites* describes the implements used in state rituals and the rules of the royal court and contains ethical exhortations for women and children, discussions of education, descriptions of proper performance of funerals and sacrifices to ancestors, and instruction in how a scholar should behave.

---

[4] Mencius is the Latinate form of the name of the philosopher Mengzi (372–289 BCE), some of whose work is excerpted in the readings.

The *Spring and Autumn Annals* are historical records from the state of Lu from the period between 722 and 481 BCE. It describes the behavior of rulers and is composed in a way that indicates the moral judgment of the compiler, believed by tradition to be Confucius.

Confucian tradition also holds that Confucius edited the *Book of Music (Yuejing)*, which is now lost. It was replaced in the twelfth century by a ritual text titled *Rites of Zhou (Zhouli)*. During the Han period these six texts came to be referred to as the "six disciplines" *(liu shu)*, and later as the "six classics" *(liujing)*. Modern scholarship questions whether Confucius actually had a hand in editing these texts because no evidence exists for this except for relatively late traditions. It is clear from accounts of his life that he was thoroughly familiar with these texts and taught them to his students, but contemporary scholars see little reason to accept the tradition that he edited them.

The *Analects*, 492 chapters collected into twenty books, contains pithy instructions on the core concepts of Confucius's philosophy. The primary focus is the training and character of the noble man, who is morally upright, learned, and restrained in his appetites.

Centeredness was originally chapter 42 of the *Book of Rites*. According to Confucian tradition, it was authored by Zeng Can (c. 505–436 BCE), but Zhu Xi contended that the opening paragraph was written by Confucius and that the rest of the work was an explanation composed by Zeng Can. It outlines three goals for the noble man: "making luminous virtue shine" *(ming ming de)*, "having sympathy for the people" *(qin min)*, and "abiding in attainment of perfect goodness" *(zhiyu zhishan)*. These are the first steps toward ordering society and establishing good government.

The *Great Learning* was originally chapter 31 of the *Book of Rites* but came to be regarded as a separate text by the Confucian tradition. Zisi, a grandson of Confucius, is traditionally held to be its author, but this attribution is rejected by most contemporary scholars. It discusses the Dao of Heaven, which is a principle that transcends the world but is manifest in its workings.

The *Mencius* contains teachings of the Confucian scholar Mengzi. These teachings were written down by his students. The writings of Mencius represented an influential commentary on the thought of Confucius concerning the conduct of the sage and the nature of good government. The text consists of seven chapters, each divided into two parts.

Qin Shihuangdi, the founder of the Qin dynasty (221–206 BCE), ordered Confucian texts to be burned, and as a result some works were lost. Most of the important texts survived, however, hidden by scholars until the political climate changed. The emperor also ordered the execution of a number of Confucian scholars, because he viewed the Confucian ideals of benevolent government as being at odds with his own authoritarian style.

When the Qin dynasty was overthrown by the Han dynasty, Confucianism again became the state ideology, largely due to the efforts of the Confucian scholar Dong Zhongshu, an advisor to emperor Wudi (r. 140–87 BCE). In 125 BCE he created a university whose educational program was based on the study of the Five Classics (the *Book of Music* had been lost during the persecution of Confucianism) and the Four Books.

In the twelfth century CE, Zhu Xi published an edition of the Four Books that became the primary text for Confucian studies, eclipsing the Five Classics. In his system, students were advised to read the *Great Learning* first in order to learn the basic patterns of Confucianism and then move on to the *Analects*, which developed the ideas contained in the *Great Learning*. After that they should study the *Mencius* for its ability to inspire thought, and finally they should study *Centeredness*, which he described as profound and subtle. Due to Zhu Xi's influence, these texts formed the basis for topics of the imperial examination system until it was abolished in 1905.

Although Confucius himself seldom mentioned topics such as spiritual beings, the nature of Heaven, life after death, or spirituality in general, his teachings became the basis for the most influential tradition of philosophy in China, one that eventually developed religious characteristics. Later Confucians propounded elaborate cosmological theories, doctrines concerning death and afterlife, and cultic practices. The tradition spread into other parts of Asia and has been an important influence in Korea, Japan, and Vietnam. Although no longer part of the ruling philosophy of the current leadership of the People's Republic of China, the ideas and values of Confucianism continue to exert a powerful influence on the Chinese people today.

HOLIDAYS

Chinese New Year (Xin Nian) Celebrated on the first day of the first lunar month (generally February).

Clear Brightness Festival (or Tomb Sweeping Day; Qingming) Falls on the 105th day after the winter solstice (generally April). Families visit the graves of their ancestors, pay their respects, and clean the site.

(Continued)

HOLIDAYS *(Continued)*

Confucius's Birthday Celebrated on the twenty-seventh day of the eighth lunar month (generally the end of September).

Ghost Month (Yulan) On the first day of the seventh lunar month, the gates of hell open and the spirits of the dead emerge for a month of feasting among the living. Paper "ghost money" is provided, along with food and entertainment.

Jade Emperor's Birthday (Bai tian gong) Celebrated on the ninth day of the first lunar month, this festival commemorates the legendary Jade Emperor (Yu Huang) with incense and other offerings.

Lantern Festival (Yuan xiao jie) Celebrated on the fifteenth day of the first lunar month. Families gather and make lanterns with candles inside them, which then are placed along roads and floated in water.

TIMELINE

2357 BCE	Time of the sage emperors Yao and Shun
1122–221 BCE	Zhou dynasty in China
551–479 BCE	Life of Confucius (Kong Fuzi)
372–289 BCE	Life of Mencius (Mengzi)
221–206 BCE	Qin dynasty in China; Legalism adopted as state ideology, and Confucianism persecuted
136 BCE	Han emperor Wu decrees that Confucian classics be adopted as the basis for state examinations
372 CE	King Sosurim of Koguryŏ establishes a national academy for the study of Confucianism on the Korean peninsula
404	Official introduction of Confucianism to Japan

TIMELINE *(Continued)*

918–1392	Koryŏ dynasty in Korea; civil examination following Chinese model established
932	First printing of Confucian classics in China
1127–1279	Southern Song dynasty in China; neo-Confucian revival
1130–1200	Zhu Xi, greatest exponent of neo-Confucianism
1313	Mongol Yuan government adopts civil service examination system based on Confucian classics; Zhu Xi's system declared orthodox
1392–1910	Yi dynasty in Korea; Confucianism declared state ideology
1472–1529	Wang Yangming, exponent of neo-Confucian Idealist school
1917	May Fourth Movement begins in China; some try to eradicate Confucianism's influence, "smash Confucius's shop"
1947	Communist revolution in China led by Mao Zedong; beginning of religious persecution in mainland China
1966–1976	Cultural Revolution in China; widespread religious persecution, destruction of religious sites
1973–1974	Anti-Confucius campaign in China
1986	Chinese government allows annual sacrifice to Confucius to be performed in Qufu

GLOSSARY

Confucius (c. 551–479 BCE; Chinese: Kong Fuzi) Founder of Confucianism and one of the great sages of China.

Dao "Way," a pattern of action that applies to all human societies and to natural forces.

Junzi "Noble Man," one who embodies the ideal qualities of a Confucian gentleman.

Li "Propriety," one of the primary Confucian virtues, involving proper social conduct and rituals.

Lunyu (Analects) A collection of aphorisms attributed to Confucius.

Mencius (c. fourth century BCE; Chinese: Mengzi) One of the most influential Confucian thinkers.

Neo-Confucianism A movement to revive Confucianism that began in the eleventh century.

Rectification of Names (zhengming) The principle of using words nondeceptively, of saying what one actually means.

Ren "Human-heartedness," one of the primary Confucian virtues, evidenced by proper attitudes and actions toward others.

Tian "Heaven," an impersonal force that watches over human affairs.

CONFUCIAN SCRIPTURES

SIMA QIAN'S ACCOUNT OF CONFUCIUS'S LIFE

Sima Qian's account of Confucius's life, compiled in the second century BCE, is very influential in China, though considered rather unreliable by modern scholars. Written on the basis of legends that had arisen around the figure of Confucius, it purports to describe his early life and to provide a biography of his adult years. The admiration of the writer is evident throughout the account, especially in the concluding remarks.

Confucius was born in Zou, a village in the region of Zhangbing in the state of Lu.... As a child, Confucius liked to play with sacrificial implements, arranging them as if for a ceremony.... Confucius was poor and humble. Growing up and working as keeper of the granaries for the Ji clan he measured the grains fairly; when he was keeper of the livestock the animals flourished, and so he was made minister of works. Subsequently he left Lu, was dismissed from Ji, driven out of Song and Wei and ran into trouble between Zhen and Zai. Finally he returned to Lu.

Well over six feet, Confucius was called the Tall Man, and everybody marveled at his height. He returned to the state of Lu as it had treated him well....

All the men of Lu from the ministers down overstepped their rightful bounds and did not act correctly. This is why Confucius did not take an official position, and instead edited the *Book of Songs*, *Book of History*, *Book of Rites*, and the *Book of Music* in his retirement, and more and more pupils came even from distant places to study with him....

When Confucius had spent three years in Zai, Wu attacked Zhen, and Zhu sent its army. . . . Hearing that Confucius was living between Zhen and Zai, the people of Zhu sent an invitation to him. Before he was able to accept it, however, the ministers of Zhen and Zai discussed the situation and said, "Confucius is a worthy man who has correctly pointed out the failings of every state. He has spent a great deal of time between Zhen and Zai, and he disapproves of all our actions and policies. Now the powerful state of Zhu has invited him. If he serves Zhu, it will be bad for us." They sent men to surround Confucius in the countryside, keeping him from leaving. His supplies ran out, his followers were too weak to move, but Confucius went on teaching and singing, accompanying himself on the lute.

Zi Lu came up to him and said with indignation, "Must a noble man endure privation?"

Confucius answered, "A noble man can withstand privation, but a small man who faces privation tends to go wrong."

Zi Kong looked unhappy, and Confucius said to him, "Do you consider me to be a learned and educated man?"

Zi Kong replied, "Of course; aren't you?"

Confucius said, "Not at all; I have merely grasped the thread that links the rest. . . ."

Confucius taught his students the old songs, records, rituals, and music. In all he had 3,000 pupils, and seventy-two of them were proficient in all of the six arts.[5] Many other people, such as Yan Zhuozou, were taught by him. In his teachings, Confucius stressed on four things: culture, good conduct, loyalty, and honesty. He avoided four things: rash judgments, arbitrary opinions, hardheadedness, and vanity. He advocated caution during sacrifices, war, and illness, and he only helped those who were sincere. If he provided one corner of a square and a student could not infer the other three corners, he would not repeat himself. . . .

He said to Zi Kong, "The world has strayed from the true Dao, and no one is able to follow me." . . . He died seven days later at the age of seventy-three, on the *ji zhou* day of the fourth month of the sixteenth year of the reign of Duke Ye of Lu (479 BCE). . . .

[Sima Qian comments:] Although I cannot reach him, my heart goes out to him. When I read the words of Confucius, I try to see the man himself, and when in Lu I visited his temple and saw his carriage, clothes, and sacrificial implements. . . . The world has seen countless princes and powerful

---

[5] These are ceremonies, music, archery, chariot riding, writing, and mathematics.

people who found fame and praise during their lives but were forgotten after death, while Confucius, though a commoner, has been revered by scholars for more than ten generations. From the emperor, princes, and nobles on down, all regard him as the highest authority. He is appropriately called the Supreme Sage.

Source: Sima Qian, *Shiji (Records of the Historian)*; tr. JP.

EMPEROR YAO'S GOOD QUALITIES

The Book of History *purports to record events from early Chinese history. It was an important source for Confucius in his understanding of the exalted qualities of the sage emperors Yao and Shun, who are described as exemplars of righteousness, wisdom, and benevolent government.*

It is said that if we investigate antiquity, Emperor Yao was called Fangxun. He was reverent, clear-sighted, cultivated and thoughtful, contented and at ease; truly he was respectful, and he was capable of deference; his light shone to the four frontiers, reaching heaven above and earth below. He was able to manifest eminent character, and with this he brought affection to the nine lineages. Having reconciled the nine lineages, he distinguished and honored the one hundred clans. When the one hundred clans had become illustrious, he brought the myriad states into accord. And the multitude of commonfolk were transformed and became harmonious.

Source: *Shujing*, "Canon of Yao"; tr. Kurt Vall.

CONFUCIUS: SELECTIONS FROM THE *ANALECTS*

The following selections are excerpted from the Analects (Lunyu), *which record instructions given by Confucius to his students and events in his life. The title of the text literally means "conversations," and it received this name because it mainly contains conversations between Confucius and his students. They emphasize an interrelated set of themes, including the character and training of the "noble man," the idea that rulers should govern by moral persuasion and should treat their subjects as a loving father treats his children, the importance of following tradition, the role of rituals and sacrifices in establishing a harmonious state, and the importance of providing for the basic needs of the populace.*

Confucius believed that the righteousness of leaders is the key to social stability and told rulers that it is important to practice scrupulously the social rituals that help a society function harmoniously. The noble man, he taught, has a strong sense of propriety (li), a general term for the day-to-day norms of social interaction as well as for the rules for state ceremonies.

In addition, the noble man speaks the truth as he understands it and so is concerned with the "rectification of names" (zheng ming), which involves calling things what they are and using terms in a nondeceptive manner. Rulers who equivocate and who use euphemisms that attempt to cloak the truth of things lose the confidence of the people as surely as those who are morally degenerate or who blunder in their decisions.

According to his student Zeng Zi, there is "one thread" running through all of Confucius's teachings: an emphasis on the centrality of morality and cultivation of an ethical foundation, which leads the noble man to treat others like himself (shu). Human beings are said to have a basically moral nature (zhong), which needs to be developed by education and by contact with superior persons. Such people cultivate their own moral consciousness and seek to establish others in virtue.

Confucius taught that a person with the virtue of human-heartedness (ren) knows how to treat others and acts appropriately in all situations. A central virtue of such a person is filial piety (xiao), which is evidenced by respect for elders and persons in authority, as well as by proper performance of rituals for the ancestors. Such behavior accords with the dictates of Heaven.

Confucius believed that Heaven watches over human affairs and confers a mandate to rule (tianming). This concept was first developed by the founders of the Zhou dynasty to justify their conquest of the Shang rulers. According to this theory, the emperor is the "son of Heaven" (tianzi), appointed to oversee human affairs, but rulers who become lazy, corrupt, or despotic cause Heaven to withdraw the mandate and thereby lose their legitimacy. Heaven first sends warnings in the form of natural disasters, internal turmoil, or personal crises, and those who reform themselves may again earn Heaven's favor. Those who persist in their immoral actions, however, are eventually deposed by Heaven, which appoints other rulers of better moral character.

1.1 The Master said: "To learn something and practice it when applicable, is this not pleasing? To have friends come from afar, is this not joyous? To go unrecognized and yet not be resentful, is this not what it is to be a noble man?'

1.4   Zengzi said: "I reflect daily on three things in myself: Am I undutiful in my undertakings for others? Am I untrustworthy in my relations with friends and acquaintances? Do I fail to put into practice what I transmit?"

1.6 The Master said: "At home, younger brothers and sons should be filial; when they go out, they should act as younger brothers; they should be prudent and faithful; they should have generalized love for the masses; and they should have affection for the humane. If they do these things and still they have energy, they should cultivate themselves through learning."

1.9 Zengzi said: "Be attentive in seeing off the deceased, persevere with sacrifices to remote ancestors, and the character of the common people will return to fullness."

1.10 Ziqin asked Zigong: "Whenever our Master arrives in a state, he always hears about its government. Does he seek this out? Or is it given to him?"

Zigong said: "The Master is mild, courteous, respectful, restrained and deferential, and thus he obtains it. Our Master's way of seeking it is perhaps different from the ways in which others seek it?"

1.11 The Master said: "When his father is alive, observe his intent. When his father is gone, observe his conduct. If for three years he makes no adjustments to his father's way, he can be called filial."

1.14 The Master said: "The noble man eats without seeking his fill. He resides without seeking to settle. He is diligent in his affairs and prudent in his speech. He turns to those who possess the way to be put right by them. Of such a man it can be said that he is fond of learning."

2.2 The Master said: "The *Poems* number three hundred; yet they can be summarized in one sentence: 'Go forth without swerving'."

2.3 The Master said: "Guide them with laws and bring them into line with punishments, and the common people will avoid these but will be without a sense of shame. Guide them with character and bring them into line with ritual, and they will have a sense of shame and, what is more, they will conform."

2.4 The Master said: "When I was fifteen, I was set on learning. At thirty, I was established. At forty, I was no longer perplexed. At fifty, I understood the decrees of Heaven. At sixty, my ears were receptive. At seventy, I followed what my heart desired and I did not step over the line."

2.6 Meng Wubo asked about being filial. The Master said: "It is one's parents only worrying about illness."

2.13 Zigong asked about the noble man. The Master said: "He puts actions before speech, and afterwards his speech follows his actions."

2.20 Ji Kangzi asked: "How does one get the common people to be reverent and dutiful, and to be encouraged?"

The Master said: "Preside over them with gravity, and they will be reverent; be filial and kind, and they will be dutiful; raise up those who excel and instruct those who are lacking capability, and they will be encouraged."

3.5 The Master said: "The eastern Yi and northern Di barbarians with their rulers are inferior to any of the Chinese states without theirs."

4.4 The Master said: "If one were only intent toward humaneness, then one would be free from ill will."

4.10 The Master said: "As for the noble man in relation to the world, there is nothing that he is either predisposed towards or against; he aligns himself with what is right."

4.14 The Master said: "Do not be concerned by your lack of an official position; concern yourself with the means by which you can establish yourself. Do not be concerned about being unrecognized; seek to become someone who is worthy of being recognized."

4.16 The Master said: "The noble man is conversant with rightness; the petty man is conversant with profit."

4.17 The Master said: "When you see someone who is worthy, think of equaling them. When you see someone who is unworthy, look within and examine yourself."

4.25 The Master said: "Character is not solitary, it always has neighbors."

5.16 The Master said of Zichan: "He possesses four attributes of the noble man's way (*dao*). In conducting himself, he is respectful. In serving his superiors, he is reverent. In providing for the people, he is generous. In commanding the people, he is righteous."

7.1 The Master said: "I transmit and I do not innovate. I trust in antiquity and I am fond of it. I may be so bold as to compare myself to Old Peng."[6]

7.2 The Master said: "Silently comprehending. Learning without tiring of it. Teaching without becoming weary. What difficulties do these present for me?"

7.4 When the Master was at leisure, he was composed and he was at ease.

---

[6] Peng Wan was an official of the Shang Dynasty (ca. 1600–1046 BCE). According to legend, he was fond of reciting old stories, and so it is notable that Confucius mentions him in this passage, in which he denies that his teachings are innovative; rather, they simply transmit the wisdom of the past.

7.6 The Master said: "Be intent on the way *(dao)*. Rely upon character. Lean on humaneness *(ren)*. Explore the arts."

7.7 The Master said: "Whenever someone has only had the means to offer up a bundle of dried meat, there has not been an occasion where I did not provide instruction to them."

7.21 The Master did not talk about the prodigious, feats of strength, disorder, or spiritual beings.

7.22 The Master said: "If I am walking in a group of three, there will always be a teacher for me among them. I discern that which is excellent and follow it; and that which is deficient, and I reform myself."

7.37 The Master said: "The noble man *(junzi)* is even and relaxed, while the petty man is constantly distressed."

7.38 The Master is mild yet stern, imposing yet not forceful, respectful yet relaxed.

8.2 The Master said: "Without ritual, being respectful is toilsome; without ritual, being cautious is cowering. Without ritual, being courageous is being disorderly. Without ritual, being straight is being wound up tight.

"The noble man is earnest toward his family, and so the common people are lifted up toward humaneness. Old relationships are not left behind, and so the common people will not be callous toward one another."

8.7 Zengzi said: "The gentleman cannot but be expansive and resolute, as the burden is weighty and the way is long. He takes humaneness as his burden; is this not weighty? It only comes to an end when he dies; is this not long?"

8.13 The Master said: "Be earnest and faithful and fond of learning; unto death be vigilant with regard to the excellent way. Do not enter a state that is imperiled; do not reside in a state that is disorderly. If in the world there is the way, be seen; if the way is not there, keep out of sight. In a state with the way, being poor and lowly is shameful; in a state without the way, being wealthy and exalted is shameful."

9.14 The Master wanted to live among the nine groups of the eastern Yi barbarians. Someone said: "But they are uncouth; what could be done about that?"

The Master responded: "If a noble man lived there, what uncouthness could there be?"

9.18 The Master said: "I have not yet met a man who was as fond of character as he was of feminine beauty."

11.12 Jilu asked about serving spirits and gods. The Master said: "You are as yet unable to serve people; how could you serve spirits?" He persisted and also asked about death.

[The Master] said: "You do not as yet understand life, how could you understand death?"

12.1 Yan Yuan asked about humaneness. The Master said: "Mastering oneself and returning to the rituals is being humane. Master the self and return to the rituals for one day, and from this the world would return to humaneness. Being humane comes from oneself; how could it come from other people?"

Yan Yuan then said: "May I ask about the specifics of this?"

The Master said: "If it is contrary to the rituals, do not look upon it; if it is contrary to the rituals, do not listen to it; if it is contrary to the rituals, do not speak it; if it is contrary to the rituals, do not do it."

Yan Yuan responded: "Though Hui [Yan Yuan] is unintelligent, he requests that he apply himself to what you have said."

12.4 Sima Niu asked about the noble man. The Master said: "The noble man does not worry and is not fainthearted."

Sima Niu then said: "Not worrying and not being fainthearted: is that all there is to being called a noble man?"

The Master responded: "If looking within and examining yourself you find nothing that ails you, how could you be either worried or fainthearted?"

12.7 Zigong asked about governing. The Master said: "Enough food; enough armaments; and the common people having trust in their rulers."

Zigong said: "What if you cannot provide all of these and have to forgo one; which of these three should be foregone first?"

The Master said: "Forego armaments."

Zigong then said: "What if you cannot provide both of the other two and have to forego another one; which of these two should be foregone next?"

The Master said: "Forego food. Ever since antiquity there has been death; but if they have no trust, the common people will not remain standing."

12.11 Duke Jing of Qi asked Confucius about governing. Confucius replied: "A ruler should be a ruler, a minister should be minister; a father should be father; and a son should be a son."

The Duke said: "Excellent! Truly, if a ruler is not being a ruler, a minister is not being a minister, a father is being not a father, and a son is not being a son, then even if there is grain, would I get to eat it?"

12.16 The Master said: "The noble man perfects what is excellent in other people; he does not perfect what is odious in other people. The petty man does the opposite of this."

12.22 Fan Chi asked about humaneness. The Master said: "It is loving other people." He then asked about understanding. The Master said: "It is understanding other people." Fan Chi did not comprehend. The Master said: "Raise up the straight and arrange them over the crooked, and you can make the crooked straight."

13.1 Zilu asked about governing. The Master said: "Lead them by precedent and they will be moved to work hard." Zilu asked for this to be further expounded. The Master said: "Be indefatigable."

13.3 Zilu said: "If the Lord of Wei were to rely upon you to govern *(zheng)*, what would you put first?"

The Master said: "If this was necessary, it would be the rectifying *(zheng)* of names!"

Zilu responded: "Is that so? What an indirect course the Master takes! Why this rectifying?"

The Master said: "How boorish you are! The noble man in regard to what he does not understand is surely silent. If names are not correct, words will not be congruent. If words are not congruent, affairs will not culminate in success. If affairs do not culminate in success, then ritual and music will not flourish. If ritual and music do not flourish, then punishments will not be appropriate. If punishments are not appropriate, the common people will not have anywhere to put their hands and feet. Thus the noble man in naming something ensures that it can be spoken of; and in speaking of something ensures that it can be acted upon. As for the noble man in regard to his speech, for him nothing is trivial, and that is it."

13.13 The Master said: "If you can rectify yourself, how would there be any difficulty in taking part in government? If you cannot rectify yourself, how would you go about rectifying other people?"

13.18 The Duke of She spoke with Confucius, saying: "In my district there is one who is a 'straight arrow' [lit. "straight-body"]. His father stole a sheep and the son testified against him."

Confucius said: "The upright men of my district are different from this. Fathers cover up for sons, and sons cover up for fathers. Uprightness lies in this."

13.20 Zigong asked: "What would someone be like such that they could be called a gentleman?"

The Master said: "He conducts himself with a sense of shame; and when deployed to the four quarters, he does not dishonor his ruler's mandate; thus he can be called a gentleman."

15.37 The Master said: "The noble man is steadfast but not rigidly trustworthy."

16.8 Confucius said: "There are three things the noble man is in awe of: he is in awe of Heaven's decree; he is in awe of eminent people; he is in awe of the words of sages. The petty man does not understand heaven's decree and thus is not in awe of it; he is overly familiar with eminent people; and he ridicules the words of sages."

Source: *Lunyu* selections; tr. Kurt Vall.

THE *GREAT LEARNING*

According to Confucian tradition, the Great Learning *was composed by Zeng Can, a student of Confucius. It is a short work that contains a condensed blueprint for personal cultivation and the ordering of the state. It has been the focus of a debate between the Neo-Confucian schools of Zhu Xi and Wang Yangming. Zhu Xi contended that the text is concerned with propriety, while Wang Yangming believed that it accords with his theory of the unity of humanity and Heaven.*

The way of the Great Learning consists of making luminous virtue shine; this entails having sympathy for the people and abiding in attainment of perfect goodness. After knowing [where to] abide, one is settled; once one is settled, one is able to be calm; once one is calm, one is able to be tranquil; once one is tranquil, one is able to have foresight; once one has foresight, one is able to begin consideration. Only after beginning consideration will the goal be attained. Things have roots and branches. Affairs have beginnings and ends. Knowing what is first and later, one will thus be near the Dao.

The ancients who wished to make their luminous virtue shine in the world first ordered their own states. Wishing to order their states, they first put their families in order. Wishing to put their families in order, they first cultivated their persons. Wishing to cultivate their persons, they first rectified their hearts. Wishing to rectify their hearts, they first made their intentions sincere. Wishing to make their intentions sincere, they first perfected their knowledge to the highest level.

Perfecting one's knowledge to the highest level consists in examination of things. Once things are examined, knowledge is perfected. When knowledge is perfected, intentions are sincere. When intentions are sincere, the heart is rectified. When the heart is rectified, one's person is cultivated. When one's person is cultivated, families are put in order. When families are put in order, states are ordered. When states are ordered, the whole world is tranquil.

Source: *Daxue (The Great Learning)*; tr. JP.

CENTEREDNESS

The following text, the title of which is often translated as the Doctrine of the Mean, *consists of 3,567 characters and contains teachings attributed to Confucius. It describes the workings of Heaven and how they affect human life. According to the text, the Dao is a transcendent principle that pervades the entire universe, setting a standard and paradigm that sages seek to understand and emulate in their thoughts and behavior.*

1. That which is Heaven's decree is called innate, following nature is called the Way (Dao), and cultivating the Way is called education. One cannot deviate from the Way for a moment; if one could, it would not be the Way. Because of this, the noble man is wary of what he does not see and apprehensive of what he does not hear. Nothing is better seen than what is hidden, and nothing is more apparent than what is obscure. Hence the noble man guards over his private realm. When happiness, anger, sorrow and pleasure have not yet arisen, this refers to centeredness; when these arise and are all balanced, this refers to harmony. The great foundation of the world is centeredness, and its great Way is harmony. When centered harmony is realized, heaven and earth will thereby be correctly aligned and all things will be fully developed.
2. Zhongni [Confucius] said: "The noble man, in the round of his life, is centered, but the inferior man's life is contrary to centeredness. The centered life of the noble man comes from his persisting in that centeredness; the life of the inferior man's being contrary to centeredness comes from his lack of scruples."
3. The Master said: "Centeredness is of itself consummate, but few people have been adept in it for a long time now."
4. The Master said: "I know why the Way is not followed: Those who are wise exceed it, and those who are foolish do not reach it. And I know why the Way is not clear: Those

who are worthy exceed it, and those who do not emulate it do not reach it. There is no one who does not eat and drink, yet few are able really to perceive flavors." . . .

6. The Master said: "Shun was indeed a man of great wisdom.[7] Shun liked to query people, liked to examine their most trivial words, putting aside the evil, exalting the good. He grasped the two extremes and employed centeredness in regard to the people. This is why he was Shun [the sage-emperor]." . . .

12. The noble man's Way is extensive yet hidden. The most foolish of men and women may share in some knowledge of it, but when it reaches its utmost even sages are ignorant of it. The most worthless of men and women may be able to practice it, but when it reaches its utmost even sages are not adept in it. In all the greatness of heaven and earth, there are still things that people complain about. Nothing in the world has adequate capacity to bear what is large in the Way of the noble man; nothing in the world can split what is small in it. The noble man's Way originates in ordinary men and women; yet at its utmost reach it reveals all heaven and earth.

Source: *Zhongyong (Centeredness)*; tr. Kurt Vall.

THE LIFE OF *MENCIUS*

According to Sima Qian's account of Mencius's life, he was born in the small state of Zou and followed the example of Confucius in seeking public office in order to put his ideas into practice. Like his predecessor, however, he was unable to realize his ambitions and had his greatest impact as a teacher.

Mencius (Mengzi) was born in Zou and was taught by a student of Master Si. After mastering the Dao, he traveled abroad and served King Xuan of Qi (r. 342–324 BCE). King Xuan was unable to use him, so he went to Liang. King Hui of Liang did not find his counsel helpful. He was considered impractical and removed from the reality of affairs. . . . Wherever he went, he did not fit in. He retired, and together with students such as Wan Zhang he discussed the *Songs* and *Documents* and elucidated the ideas of Confucius, composing [his text entitled] *Mencius* in seven sections.

Source: Sima Qian, *Shiji*; tr. JP.

---

[7] Shun was one of the legendary sage-emperors of China, reported to have lived during the third millennium BCE.

SELECTIONS FROM THE *MENCIUS*

The Mencius *contains teachings attributed to the Confucian scholar Mengzi, the most influential early disciple of Confucius. Mencius believed that the first rule of "humane government" (ren zheng) is to provide for the basic needs of the people, and he agreed with Confucius that rulers should rectify their own behavior and cultivate moral awareness.*

He taught his students that human nature (xing) is basically good but that people become corrupted through exposure to negative influences. No matter how depraved a particular person might become, however, the basic nature remains good, and through proper education one's fundamental goodness may be reawakened.

In one passage he compares human nature to the shoots of plants growing on a hill called Ox Mountain, on which cattle graze. Plants constantly send up shoots, but the cattle eat them, so the plants are not able to grow. If the cattle leave, however, the plants will be able to grow, just as human nature will find its innate goodness if the conditions inhibiting its growth are removed. In order for this to happen, people must train their minds (xin), which provide guidance in the process of moral development. The mind possesses a faculty of discernment that, when attuned to human nature, develops into an unwavering sense of right and wrong.

Like Confucius, Mencius believed that Heaven confers a mandate on rulers and acts to remove corrupt rulers, but Mencius also contended that the people may become instruments of Heaven's will. When rulers become cruel and oppressive, they lose all legitimacy, and thus it becomes permissible for their subjects to remove them from office. Such doctrines were viewed by the rulers of his day as dangerous, and not surprisingly he was unable to find anyone to offer him a position of real power. The following selections are drawn from his collected teachings, titled the Mencius.

1A1. Mencius met with King Hui of Liang. The king said: "Venerable sir, you do not consider it a long journey to have come a thousand *li*.[8] Surely you will have some way of bringing profit to my state?"

Mencius replied: "Why must your majesty speak of profit? There is just humaneness and rightness, and that is all. If your majesty says, 'How will you bring profit to my state?,' then the grandees will say, 'How will you bring profit to my

---

[8] A *li* is an ancient Chinese measure, equivalent to about 400 meters.

house?,' and the gentry and commoners will say, 'How will you bring profit to me?' And those above and those below will quarrel with each other for profit and the state will be imperiled.... But if rightness is put last and profit put first, unless they seize it they are not sated. There has never been anyone who was humane and abandoned their parents; and there has never been anyone who was righteous and put their ruler last. A king just speaks of humaneness and rightness, and that is all. What need has he to speak of profit?"

1A3. King Hui of Liang said: "With regard to my state, I put all my heart into it and that is all there is to it. When there is famine in Henei, I relocate its people to Hedong and transport its grain to Henei. I do likewise when there is famine in Hedong. Examining the governments of neighboring states, there is no one who employs their heart as I do. Yet the populations of neighboring states do not decrease, and the population of my state does not increase. Why is this so?"

Mencius replied: "Your majesty is fond of warfare; permit me to use warfare to illustrate. Amid the throbbing of the drums, when soldiers' blades have just been engaged, discarding their armor and dragging their weapons, some flee. Some of them go one hundred paces and then stop, while some others stop after fifty paces. If those who went fifty paces laughed at those who went one hundred paces, what would you think?"

The king responded: "That wouldn't be right. It is just that they did not go one hundred paces and that's all. But this is still fleeing."

Mencius said: "If your majesty understands this, he shouldn't expect his populace to be more numerous than those of neighboring states. If the farming seasons are not disregarded, there will be more crops than can be eaten. If fine nets are not used in the pools and ponds, there will be more fish and turtles than can be eaten. If axes and hatchets only enter the forests and hills in the proper season, there will be more wood and timber than can be used. When the crops, the fish, and the turtles are more than can be eaten, and the wood and the timber are more than can be used, this will ensure that the commonfolk can nourish the living and bury their dead, and they will be without regrets. Nourishing the living, burying the dead, and being without regrets: this is the beginning of the kingly way....

"Dogs and pigs eat food meant for people, and you don't know how to restrain this. On the roads, there are people starving and dead from hunger, and you don't know to send out food. People die and you say, 'It was not me, it was the harvest.' How is this different from stabbing someone and killing them and then saying, 'It was not me, it was the weapon?' Were your majesty not to blame the harvest, then all the people in the world would come to you."

1B6. Mencius spoke to King Xuan of Qi, saying: "Suppose that among your majesty's subjects there was a man who entrusted his wife and children to his friend and travelled to Chu. If at the time of his return his wife and children were famished and freezing, then what could he do about it?"

The king said: "Cast the friend aside."

Mencius said: "If the chief official cannot maintain order among his officers, what could he do about it?"

The king said: "Dismiss him."

Mencius said: "If all within the four frontiers is misruled, then what could be done about that?" The king turned to look at those around him and spoke of other things.

1B8. King Xuan of Qi asked: "Is it true that Tang ousted Jie, and that King Wu struck down Zhou?"

Mencius replied: "According to what has been transmitted, that is so."

The king said: "Is it permissible for vassals to regicide against their sovereign?"

Mencius responded: "Those who injure humaneness are deemed cripplers; those who injure rightness are deemed mutilators; cripplers and mutilators are deemed mere commoners. I have heard of executing this commoner Zhou, but I am yet to hear of regicide against a sovereign."

1B2. Zou and Lu clashed on the border. Duke Mu asked: "Thirty-three of my officers have died, but not one of the commonfolk sacrificed themselves. If I execute them, there will be more than I could execute. If I don't execute them, then it remains that they looked spitefully on the deaths of leaders and superiors and didn't save them. What can I do about this?"

Mencius replied: "In years of famine when the crops fail, the old and feeble of my lord's people who tumble into ditches and gullies and the vigorous who disperse and go in the four directions are in their thousands. And yet my lord's granaries and storehouses are full, and the treasuries and armories are well-stocked. But not one of your officials reported on it. This is a case of those above being contemptuous and cruel to those below. Zengzi said, 'Beware this, beware this! That which goes out from you is what will return to you.' In any case, the people have now finally been able to return the injury. My lord should not find them at fault. If my lord practices humaneness in governing, then the people will treat their superiors like parents and will die for their leaders." . . .

2A2. "Intent is the commander of *qi* (vital energy); *qi* is what fills up the body. Wherever it is that intent arrives, that is where *qi* will encamp. Thus it is said, 'Hold fast your intent and do not inflame your *qi*'."

"May I be so bold as to ask what the Master excels at?"

Mencius said: "I understand discourse, and I excel in nourishing my flood-like *qi*."[9]

"May I be so bold as to ask what it is you mean by flood-like *qi*?"

Mencius said: "It is difficult to speak of. It is a *qi* that is utterly great and utterly strong. Nourish it with straightness and do it no harm, and it will fill the space between Heaven and earth. It is a *qi* that brings together rightness and the way *(dao)*; without these, it starves. It is something that is born from the aggregation of rightness; it is not that rightness is feigned and it is seized. If any of your actions disquiet the heart, it will starve. . . .

"You have to work at it and not disregard it. Don't disregard it, and don't help it to grow. Don't be like the man from Song. There was a man from Song who, concerned about the shoots of his grain not growing, pulled on them. Weary and worn out, he returned home. He called to his family, saying, 'Today I am exhausted; I have been helping the shoots of grain grow.' His son hurried and went to look, and the shoots were all withered. In all the world those who don't help shoots of grain grow are surely few. Those who consider it to be without benefit and ignore it are the ones who don't weed amongst the shoots of grain. Those who help it grow are the ones who pull on shoots of grain. It's not that it is simply unbeneficial, but more than that, it is harmful."

2A6. Mencius said: "Everybody possesses a heart sympathetic to others. The former Kings possessed a heart sympathetic to others, and so there was government that was sympathetic to the people. With this heart that was sympathetic to others, they practiced government that was sympathetic to the people; and they ruled the world as if turning it in the palm of the hand.

---

[9] This is an important concept for Mencius. As the superior person develops exemplary moral qualities, this naturally affects others. The truly moral person acquires "flood-like qi," so called because it moves others inexorably toward virtue, just as a flood sweeps objects along with it.

"The reason I say everybody has a heart sympathetic to others is this. If a person were to suddenly see a child about to fall into a well, each one of us would have a concerned and empathetic heart. It is not that we would try to ingratiate ourselves to the child's parents; and it is not that we would try to gain fame in village and district, or among friends and acquaintances; nor is it dislike of the child's cry.

"From this it can be seen: if there is a heart that feels no empathy, this is not a person; if there is a heart that feels no shame, this is not a person; if there is a heart that feels no deference, this is not a person; if there is a heart that does not feel right and wrong, this is not a person. An empathetic heart is the sprout of humaneness; a heart that feels shame is the sprout of rightness; a heart that feels deference is the sprout of ritual; a heart that feels right and wrong is the sprout of understanding.

"With regard to people possessing these four sprouts: this is similar to them having four limbs. To possess these four sprouts and deem yourself incapable is to be someone who robs himself; to deem one's ruler incapable is to be someone who robs his ruler. Since we possess these sprouts within ourselves, if each of us were to understand how to develop them to fullness, it would be like a flame igniting or a spring spouting out. If we could bring them to fullness, it would be sufficient for us to sustain all within the four seas; if we cannot bring them to fullness, it will not be enough for us to serve our parents."

6A2. Gaozi said: "Nature is similar to swirling water. Cut a channel to the east, and it flows to the east. Cut a channel to the west, and it flows to the west. Human nature is indiscriminate with regard to excellence and deficiency: this is similar to water being indiscriminate with regard to east and west."

Mencius said: "Water is certainly indiscriminate with regard to east and west. But is it indiscriminate with regard to up and down? The excellence of human nature is similar to the tendency of water to go downwards. There are no people who are truly deficient [i.e., bereft of innate moral inclinations], and there is no water that does not go downwards. Now in the case of water, if you strike it and launch it up, it can be made to go above the forehead. And if you dam it and guide it, it can be put on top of a mountain. How could this be the nature of water? Rather, it is circumstances that make it like that. With regard to the ability to make people deficient: this is their nature also being similar to this."

Source: *Mengzi* selections; tr. Kurt Vall.

XUNZI: THE NATURE OF HUMAN BEINGS IS EVIL

The most influential interpreter of Confucius prior to the Han dynasty was Xunzi (Xun Qing, d. 215 BCE), a younger contemporary of Mencius who lived in the state of Zhao and who is best known today for his treatises on government and warfare. Unlike Mencius, Xunzi believed that human nature is basically evil and that rulers must employ strict controls in order to keep their subjects in line. He advocated strong centralized rule and the use of punishment to restrain the population, but he also believed that human beings can be taught to be good through discipline and education. He reportedly was a teacher of Han Fei, the exponent of the philosophy of Legalism that became the dominant ideology of the Qin dynasty.

Xunzi rejected Mencius's ideas about human nature, contending that humans have innate desires that can never be fully satisfied. People naturally desire to possess things and envy others who have things that they do not, and these basic tendencies oppose the cultivation of virtue. Goodness is attained only through training that teaches people to restrain their urges and to recognize higher goods. This training requires study of the classics and education in the proper performance of rites. He also rejected Mencius's idea of Heaven as a moral force that oversees human affairs. For Xunzi, Heaven is simply nature, which is impersonal and has no ethical dimension but instead operates in accordance with its own laws, without regard to individual virtue or human desires.

Human nature is evil. Goodness in people is something that we have to make ourselves. People are born with a nature that loves profit. Acting in accordance with this nature leads to competition and taking things by force and diminishes deference and courtesy. People already have jealousy and hatred within them when they are born. Acting in accordance with this nature causes cruelty and treachery to come about and diminishes loyalty and trustworthiness. When people are born, they already have the desires of the ears and eyes, so they are born with fondness for music and sex already within them. Acting in accordance with this nature gives rise to debauchery and diminishes rites *(li)* and moral conduct *(yi)*, civilization *(wen)*, and reason *(li)*.

Thus, when people follow their nature, their feelings, competition, and taking things by force are sure to develop. This combines with violations of division [of duties and class] and reason and leads to tyranny. Thus, people need the transformations of a master's teachings: they need the ways of rites and moral conduct. These ways bring about deference and courtesy. They combine with civilization and reason and bring about orderly governance. When you look at it from this perspective, you can see that human nature is clearly evil and that goodness is something we have to make for ourselves.

Source: D.C. Lau, Che Wah Ho, and Fong Ching Cheng, eds. *A Concordance to the Xunzi (Xunzi zhuzi suoyin)* (Hong Kong: Commercial Press, 1996): 23/113/1–7; tr. Thomas McConochie.

YANG XIONG: HUMAN NATURE IS A MIXTURE OF GOOD AND EVIL

The question of whether human nature is basically good or evil was an important one for the Confucian tradition after Confucius. Mencius declared that human nature is basically good, while Xunzi believed it to be basically evil. Confucius himself did not make a definitive statement on the matter and said only that people are born alike but become different through training and practice. He did contend, however, that all men have the potential to become noble men, so it seems clear that his view of human nature was probably closer to that of Mencius than to Xunzi's negative assessment.

In the following passage, Yang Xiong (53 BCE–18 CE) stakes out a middle position, contending that human nature is a mixture of good and evil. He asserts that people become either good or evil as a result of their training: The good cultivate good, and the evil cultivate evil. His treatise helped focus the attention of Confucian thinkers on this issue, but it was criticized by later Confucians for its contention that human nature is partially evil.

> Human nature is a mixture of good and evil. If we cultivate goodness, we will be good people; if we cultivate evil, we will be evil people; vital energy *(qi)* is the horse on which we ride to good or evil. Because of this, the noble man strives hard in learning and exerts himself in practice. The consummate Way is for him to make his goods precious before selling them, to perfect his person before forming relations with other people, to complete his plans before acting.

Source: *Fuyan* 3.1a–b; tr. Kurt Vall.

HAN YU: ATTACK ON BUDDHISM AND DAOISM

Han Yu (768–824) was a public official who led a Confucian attack on Buddhism and Daoism and called on the emperor to suppress them. He described Buddhism as a religion of barbarians at odds with cultured Chinese sensibilities, and he denounced Daoism as a religion that panders to primitive superstition.

The following excerpt is from a letter he wrote to the emperor regarding the veneration of a relic of the Buddha. He advised the emperor to reconsider his decision to publicly view a fragment of bone believed to have been left over after the Buddha was cremated, on the grounds that this may seem to the common people to be lending imperial support to the Buddhist practice of relic veneration, which Han Yu considered barbaric.

Your servant begs leave to say that Buddhism is nothing more than a barbarian creed. It only entered China during the Later Han dynasty. It did not exist here in ancient times. . . .

When Emperor Gaozu succeeded the Sui, he considered getting rid of Buddhism. However, at that time, his ministers were not capable in knowledge and forethought. Nor did they understand the way of former kings, or what should have been done in the past and the present. Hence, they could not implement the emperor's will and save the age from this corruption. There, the matter stopped. Your servant has constantly regretted this situation. . . .

The Buddha was a barbarian man. He did not speak the language of China, and his clothing was of a different fashion. He did not speak of the laws of our former kings. He did not obey the laws of our former kings. He did not understand the duties of lord and vassal nor the feelings between father and son. If he were to come to pay tribute in our capital now, on the orders of his kingdom, Your Majesty might grant him an audience . . . but then you would place him under guard, expel him from your realm, and not allow him to confuse the masses. Moreover, his body has been dead for a long time now. How could you allow his rotten bones and remains into your palace?

Confucius said: 'Respect ghosts and spirits, but keep them at a distance.' . . . Now, without reason, You Majesty has taken this dirty thing and personally viewed it. . . . Your vassal is truly ashamed of this. I beg that we give this bone to the relevant authorities so that they may cast it into fire and water, thereby extinguishing it forever and wiping out this mistake in the world, and sparing future generations its confusion. . . . If the Buddha does have miraculous power and can bring down calamity and punishment, then let it be only on the person of your vassal. With Heaven on high as my witness, I would not regret it.

Source: Han Yu, Changli *Xiansheng Wenji,* in *Si Bu Cong Kang,* 39:2b–4b; tr. Thomas McConochie.

ZHOU DUNYI: THE GREAT ULTIMATE

Zhou Dunyi (1017–1073) was one of the important early fig-
ures in the Neo-Confucian revival that took place during the
Song dynasty (960–1279). His most significant text was The
Diagram of the Great Ultimate Explained (Taiji tu shuo), *a*
short work that equates the "great ultimate" (taiji) with the
"non-ultimate" (wuji), which he describes as a reality tran-
scending space and time. Its movement generates yin, *the*
active force in nature, and its rest gives rise to yin, *the pas-*
sive element of natural systems. Through the interaction of
these two, the "five agents" or "five elements" (wuxing) are
produced, and the combinations of these elements give rise to
the phenomena of the world. Zhou conceives of the universe
as a dynamic and holistic system in which natural forces and
human conduct are interrelated.

1. [It is] the non-ultimate, yet also the great ultimate.
2. The great ultimate moves and produces *yang*. Moving to
   the limit, it rests. Resting, it produces *yin*. Resting completely, it moves again. Movement and rest alternate:
   each is the other's root. It distinguishes *yin* and *yang*: the
   two modes are established by it.
3. *Yang* diversifies and *yin* harmonizes, producing water,
   fire, wood, metal, and earth. The five substances *(qi)*
   propagate accordingly, and the four seasons are brought
   about by it.
4. The five phases *(xing)* are the one *yin* and *yang*. *Yin* and
   yang are the one great ultimate. The great ultimate is
   based in the non-ultimate. As for the production of the
   five phases, each has its own nature.
5. The non-ultimate reality and the essence of the Two *(yin*
   and *yang)* and the Five Agents marvelously harmonize
   and integrate. The Way of *tian* [Heaven] becomes masculine, and the Way of *kun* [earth] becomes feminine. The
   two affect each other, the changes producing all things:
   producing and reproducing and changing endlessly.
6. Humans alone get the finest endowment, and are the
   most spiritually potent. It is thus that their physical form
   is produced, and their spirit obtains understanding. The
   five principles of their natures respond, good and evil
   are distinguished, and affairs thus proceed along their
   courses.
7. The sage settles these matters with centeredness and
   rectitude, humanity and righteousness (the Way of the
   sage is nothing but centeredness and rectitude, humanity and righteousness), makes tranquility dominant (he

is without desire and thus tranquil). In this way he sets up a standard for human perfection. Thus the sage harmonizes his power with heaven and earth, his brilliance with the sun and the moon, his time with the four seasons, and his good and bad fortunes with the spirits.

8. The noble man cultivates these qualities and earns good fortune; the inferior man goes against them and suffers misfortune.

9. Thus it is said that *yin* and *yang* establish the Way of heaven, yielding and firmness establish the Way of earth, and humanity and righteousness establish the Way of humans. It is also said that by looking into the cycle of things the explanation of life and death will become known.

10. How great is the *Book of Change*! This is where its utmost value lies!

Source: Zhou Dunyi, *Taiji tu shuo*, ch. 1, tr. Kurt Vall.

ZHU XI: NATURE AND HUMANITY

Zhu Xi's philosophy is sometimes referred to as "study of principle" (li xue), because he was concerned with developing an understanding of the principles underlying human behavior and social interaction. He believed that society can be rectified through diligent study of the patterns of organization and development that underlie both human civilization and nature. In 1313, Zhu Xi's interpretations of Confucius were officially recognized as the orthodox system of Confucianism and became the basis for civil examinations administered by the government. As a result, they exerted tremendous influence in Chinese education until the abolition of the system by the Nationalist government in 1905.

His philosophy was influenced by Zhou Dunyi's The Diagram of the Great Ultimate Explained. *Zhu Xi interpreted the "ultimate" (ji) as the furthest point that can be reached, and he defined the "great ultimate" (taiji) as the sum total of the principles of all the phenomena of the universe and the highest principle of each individual thing. According to Zhu Xi, the entire universe is one principle, and he interpreted the notion of "investigation of phenomena" as described in the* Great Learning *as a procedure of examining things in order to become aware of how each phenomenon manifests principle.*

He also contended that principle and material force, though inseparable, are separate factualities in phenomena. Principle is immaterial, unitary, eternal, changeless, and indestructible.

He viewed it as constituting the essence of things and as being always good. Material force is the energy that sustains physical things and provides the impetus for their production and transformation. It is corporeal, manifold, changeable, differentiated, and impermanent. It can become either good or evil in accordance with the choices made by human beings.

Nature corresponds with the great ultimate, and mind corresponds with *yin* and *yang*. The great ultimate is just within *yin* and *yang*; it cannot be separated from them. Yet on fully considering the great ultimate, it is of itself the great ultimate, as *yin* and *yang* are of themselves *yin* and *yang*. Nature and mind are also this Way. It is what is meant by the [notion that] they are one and yet two, and yet one.

Though nature is insubstantial, it is a concrete principle; and though the mind is an actual thing, it is yet insubstantial; thus it can embrace all principle. This is something that comes to be grasped only when people examine their own being. Nature is thus the principles that the mind has, and the mind is where principles come together.

Nature is principle *(li)*, and the mind is what embraces everything and applies it to things.

Nature is before movement, and feelings are when it has already moved. Mind embraces the already moving and the not yet moving. So, the mind before it moves is nature, and when it has already moved it is feelings. Desire is what comes out of feelings. Mind is like water: nature resembles the water's stillness; feelings, the water's flow; desire, its great waves. But great waves have both what is good and what is not good. The good desires are the kind that resemble the idea, "I desire humaneness." The ones that are not good persistently race forth as if they were billowing waves. When such desires are preponderate, then heavenly principle is excluded. It is like water rising to burst the levee: there is nothing that is not damaged.

Mind designates what is in command, the ruler. It rules over both movement and stillness. It is incorrect to say that it is not doing anything during stillness, so that only when we get to movement is there a ruler. To call it "the ruler" is to say that it is an all-pervasive presence in both movement and stillness. The mind brings together nature and feelings. Yet it is incorrect to say that it is one thing that is all of a piece with them, not something separate on its own.

Source: Zhu Xi, *Xing qing xin yi deng mingyi* selections, tr. Kurt Vall.

WANG YANGMING: QUESTIONS ON THE *GREAT LEARNING*

Wang Yangming (1472–1529) was an important opponent of Zhu Xi who lived during the Ming dynasty (1368–1644). He was a government official and scholar, as well as an eminent military strategist whose real name was Wang Shouren. He became known as Wang Yangming because he maintained a retreat in Yangming Valley in Chekiang Province. His Inquiry on the Great Learning *was his most important work and was widely debated by other Chinese thinkers. In this text he rejects Zhu Xi's explanation of the* Great Learning, *which places the investigation of things* (kewu) *before making thoughts sincere. Wang primarily emphasized the study of mind* (xin xue), *which focuses on developing moral awareness through education and ethical instruction.*

Understanding, Wang contended, comes from within and not through external actions. He believed that knowledge of the good is innate and that principle (li) *is a universal factor found in human beings as well as natural phenomena. He followed Mencius's idea that human beings are naturally good and that those who fully cultivate their nature are able to overcome selfish tendencies and embrace the truth of the* Great Learning.

Wang also rejected Zhu Xi's notion that the investigation of things is an examination of external phenomena. Wang contended that goodness is an innate quality of the mind and believed that it involves "eliminating what is incorrect in the mind in order to preserve the correctness of its original nature." For Wang, the investigation of things entails an ethical imperative to put moral standards into practice and to cultivate one's character.

A previous scholar considered the *Great Learning* to be the learning of great men. I venture to ask why the *Great Learning* should consist in manifesting lucid character? Master Yangming said: The great man takes heaven and earth and all the things as one entity; he sees that the world is but one family, and that the Middle Country [China] is an individual in it. Now, those who make entities separate and self and other distinct are petty people. The great man's ability to take heaven and earth and all things as one entity is not a result of his attention to it; but because the humanity of his mind is fundamentally thus: he becomes one with heaven and earth and all things. This is surely not confined to the great man: even in an inferior man's mind this is so. It is he himself who nevertheless makes it inferior, and that's all. Thus if he sees a child falling into a well, he cannot fail to have a concerned and compassionate mind towards it.[10] This comes from his humanity and the child forming one entity. A child is still one of his own kind. Yet even if he sees a bird or animal shivering fearfully and calling pitifully, his mind cannot abide it. This comes from his humanity and the birds and animals forming one entity. This then is the mind that is capable of forming one entity with other things, and even though someone's mind may be that of an inferior man, it cannot but possess this capacity. And this has its root in heaven-decreed nature, which is inherently clear and unobscured. That is why it is called "lucid character."

So when unobscured by selfish desires, even an inferior man with an inferior man's mind—because of his humaneness which is capable of forming one entity with other things—is yet a noble man. But when obscured by selfish desire, even a noble man, because he cuts himself off from other beings, is nevertheless an inferior man. So, engaging in the learning of the noble man just means getting rid of the obscuration of selfish desires, thereby spontaneously manifesting lucid character and resuming essential oneness with heaven and earth and all things. It is not that there is something separate, something that can be added onto his basic being.

The utmost good is the ultimate principle of manifesting character and loving people. Heavenly decreed nature is purely of the utmost good. It is clear and unobscured, thus evincing its perfection. It is the substance of lucid character: it is what is called innate understanding. As the highest good is manifested, right and wrong are known by it, and it is affected and responds commensurately with the situation. There is nothing that does not inherently possess Heaven's centeredness: this is the unchanging principle of people and things.

The Teacher said: The endeavor of great learning is manifesting lucid character; manifesting lucid character is just making thought sincere; the endeavor of making thought sincere is just plumbing things and gaining understanding. So making dominant the task of making thought sincere and then going on to practice the endeavor of examining things and gaining understanding means that that endeavor will have results from the beginning. This is to say that being good and getting rid of evil are nothing but the task of making thought sincere. With [Zhu Xi's] new edition [of the *Great Learning*,] exhaustively examining the principle *(li)* of things and affairs comes first; but this approach makes the task vast

---

[10] This idea comes from Mencius and is mentioned in the selections from his writings excerpted previously.

and hazy, so that there will be no result at all. In the main, the endeavor of centeredness is just making the self sincere. When making the self sincere reaches its furthest point, then it is consummate sincerity. When making thought sincere is at the utmost, then it is consummate good. All these endeavors are the same.

Source: Wang Yangming, *Daxue wen,* ch. 1, tr. Kurt Vall.

Daoism

INTRODUCTION

For many modern Chinese, religion is primarily a matter of participation in community activities and rituals connected with important transitions rather than adherence to doctrines and codes of conduct. Chinese rituals mark and celebrate the important rites of passage of human existence—birth, marriage, and death—as well as events in the agricultural calendar, such as planting and harvest. These rituals developed in a culture that was overwhelmingly agrarian and rural, in which the majority of people were (and still are) engaged in agricultural work. Underlying many Chinese religious practices is a deeply felt sense of the importance of promoting community solidarity and an emphasis on the rootedness of the individual and the collective in the natural world.

Another important feature of Chinese religious traditions is their eclecticism. The indigenous Chinese religious systems borrowed elements from each other and from traditions like Buddhism that were imported to China, and the foreign systems in turn adopted Chinese motifs and ideas in order to accommodate themselves to Chinese sensibilities. Among contemporary Chinese, sharp distinctions are seldom drawn between the major religious traditions of China: Daoism, Confucianism, and Buddhism. Rather, they are viewed as harmoniously intersecting to form a comprehensive system able to adapt itself to a wide spectrum of religious needs. The three traditions are collectively referred to as the "lineage of teachings" *(zongjiao)* or "the three teachings" *(sanjiao)*, indicating that they are perceived not as separate systems of doctrine and practice but as mutually complementary emphases.

Confucianism is viewed as being concerned primarily with the interactions of people in a social context. It outlines the norms and values that ensure social harmony, along with the rituals and duties that enable people to act appropriately when in the company of others. Daoism focuses on the connections between human beings and their natural environment: how natural processes and forces affect human existence, and how to predict the movements of these forces and manipulate them for the benefit of individuals and society. The purview of Buddhism is mainly life after death. Buddhism brought to China a highly developed eschatology and a pantheon of compassionate buddhas and bodhisattvas willing and able to give aid both in the present life and after death.

The origins of Daoism lie in popular religious practices and ideas of ancient China. According to popular Daoist belief, the earliest codification of the central concepts of the tradition was set forth by Laozi, a sage who lived in the sixth century BCE and who worked as an archivist in the state of Lu. Laozi became concerned with the degeneration of his society and decided to leave China and travel beyond the Western Gate that marked the border between Chinese civilization and the regions inhabited by non-Chinese peoples. As Laozi was leaving, the gatekeeper Yin Xi asked him to write a short outline of his philosophy for the benefit of posterity. Initially reluctant to commit his ideas to writing because words inevitably distort the truth, Laozi eventually agreed and summarized the essentials of what later came to be Daoist philosophy in the classic work *Treatise on the Way and Power (Daodejing)*.

It should be noted that the text makes no claim to originality. Rather, Laozi stresses that his thoughts accord with those of the sages of the past and merely recapitulate the wisdom found by all who understand the subtle and profound workings of the universe. His text has two primary concerns: the Way *(dao)* and Virtue or Power *(de)*, which is connected with its manifest operations. The Dao is described as a universal force, subtle and omnipresent, that gives rise to all things and provides their sustenance. It is the vital energy that makes all life possible, and it pervades the entire universe, providing a pattern for the growth and development of living things.

Transcending and embracing all dichotomies, the Dao is comprised of two opposite but complementary polarities, *yin* and *yang*. Originally these terms seem to have referred to the shady and sunny sides of mountains, respectively. *Yin* is described as yielding, wet, passive, dark, and feminine, and *yang* is aggressive, dry, active, light, and masculine. These distinctions reflect distinctive tendencies within natural systems, but they are not diametrically opposed. Rather, each contains elements of the other, and their interaction provides the creative and dynamic force behind the changes that occur in the natural world.

The Dao is ineffable. It transcends all sense experience and all thought. It may, however, be understood by the sage who is open to it and thus "becomes one with the Great Thoroughfare." The primary obstacle to this attainment is the senses, in combination with the intellect, which trick people into thinking that ordinary perceptions and cognitions provide a true picture of reality. Those who seek to become sages are counseled to empty themselves, to cast off learning, reasoning, words, and intellection. In this way they become open to direct experience of Dao, through which they can find true harmony with their environment and enjoy a long and tranquil life.

The workings of Dao tend toward harmony and balance, and whenever any part of a natural system develops extreme qualities, the imbalance triggers a corresponding backlash. This is true of both natural phenomena and human beings. Imbalances in nature are corrected by automatic reactions, and the more extreme the imbalance, the more powerful will be the reaction. Similar principles operate in individual human lives and in the actions of collectives. Any person or group that develops extreme qualities or disturbs the natural harmony of the world will reap corresponding consequences, which inevitably will right the balance of nature. Thus the Daoist sage goes along with the operations of the Dao, not forcing things, and so is able to live long and peacefully. Those who do not understand this principle are doomed to waste their vital energies in fruitless aggression and activity, like a strong swimmer who pushes against a current but eventually becomes exhausted and is carried downstream.

Laozi compares human beings at birth to uncarved blocks of wood *(pu)*, with rough edges and an unsymmetrical shape, like natural phenomena that have not been tampered with. Confucians shared this idea but proposed to carve the block in order to properly socialize it, whereas Laozi sees this notion as profoundly misguided. Humans at birth are supple and yielding, full of life energy, but through the process of acculturation they are placed into artificial molds and unnatural situations, which dissipate their energies in useless activities. Those who allow themselves to become caught up in the rat race inevitably wear themselves down and become like withered, dead branches—hard, stiff, and unyielding—and so shorten their life spans.

According to Laozi, the operations of Dao may be compared to the movement of water. When water encounters a hard obstacle like a rock, it simply flows around it rather than battering against it. Water, which is soft and yielding, does not contend against obstacles placed in its way but instead moves around them, finding the path of least resistance. As it does this, however, it also slowly and inexorably wears down the resistance of even the hardest rock, and over the course of time it overcomes all obstacles and may even create deep chasms in solid rock. Similarly, the sage avoids direct confrontation and goes along with the natural flow of Dao, practicing the Daoist virtue of "non-action" *(wuwei)*. A person who perfects this technique appears to do nothing, but in reality moves with the natural rhythms of the world, thus working in accordance with the Dao to promote harmony and prosperity.

Zhuangzi, the other major figure of the early Daoist mystical tradition, shares similar views of the workings of Dao and the way of the sage. Where Laozi's text uses terse aphorisms to make its points, however, Zhuangzi tells stories that describe the way of the sage. Many of these stories have bizarre characters and strange situations, and they are pervaded by a subtle humor that gently mocks the ordinary ways of the world and the concerns of human society.

Zhuangzi also differs from Laozi in that he has little interest in applying Daoist principles to the political arena. The second half of Laozi's text is concerned with how rulers should act and the principles of good governance, while Zhuangzi repeatedly emphasizes his utter disinterest in becoming involved in such matters. Rather, Zhuangzi counsels his readers to cultivate uselessness because things that are truly useless cannot be used by others and thus are left alone. The sage, according to Zhuangzi, moves unobtrusively among the hustle and bustle of the world, living at the margins of society, and generally is not even recognized as a sage by his or her contemporaries.

The establishment of Daoism as a distinctive religious tradition dates back to 142 CE, when Zhang Daoling received the first of a series of revelations from Taishang Laojun, Lord Lao the Most High. This deity is the personification of the Dao and is believed by Daoist tradition to be Laozi, who in reality was a human form taken by the Dao in order to teach the truth to human beings. Zhang Daoling began to spread the teachings he had received and established the first organized Daoist system, named True Unity of Celestial Masters. Because of his connection with the first revelation, he was recognized as the first of the Celestial Masters, the patriarchs of the school.

The tradition continues today. The 64th Celestial Master currently resides in Taiwan and is considered to be the direct descendant of Zhang Daoling. The Celestial Masters tradition traces its philosophical roots to the works of Laozi and Zhuangzi. It has also developed into a communal religion that emphasizes rituals for purification and exorcism, along with teachings on morality.

Contemporary scholars commonly distinguish two main streams of Daoist thought. The system of the philosophers of the fourth and third centuries BCE is termed "philosophical Daoism," and the later tradition that was concerned with techniques leading to immortality is termed "religious Daoism." Although this division does capture an important distinction of emphases within the tradition, it is also overly simplistic. Daoism has a long and complex history that has produced numerous strands of thought and practice, and recent research has shown that elements of the "religious" strand may be found in the works of the early "philosophical" Daoists, and texts of "religious" Daoism are strongly influenced by the thought of "philosophical" Daoists.

Zhuangzi's stories contain several mentions of the "immortals" *(xian)*, who are said to live on a remote mountain (or, according to other accounts, on a hidden island).[1] They avoid eating cereals, guard their vital energies, and are able to fly through the air. While most people dissipate their vital energies through involvement in mundane affairs, worry, and eating unhealthy foods, the immortals practice physical regimens that safeguard the life force *(qi)*, while avoiding activities and environments that weaken it. The search for immortality was an important concern of the developed Daoist tradition, which created elaborate systems of practice designed to promote long life. Among these were physical exercises that emulated the movements of long-lived animals (who were considered to be naturally adept at guarding vital energies), sexual techniques *(fang zhong)* that were believed to increase one's store of energy, special diets to promote the cultivation of energy, and chemical elixirs designed to replenish lost energy. Many of these elixirs contained cinnabar (mercuric sulfide), a red-colored liquid metal that was widely believed to contain a high concentration of vital energy.

Daoist masters also developed systems of meditative practices designed to promote longevity, such as "meditation on the One" *(shouyi)*, in which one guards the vital energies, concentrating on the universal life force emanated by the Dao. This practice culminates in an ecstatic vision of multicolored light. Other techniques described five primary energy centers in the body, each of which was inhabited by a particular god. Meditators were advised to increase the energy levels in these centers by safeguarding the energy drawn into the body through breathing, by avoiding grains, by ingesting specific medicinal plants, and by medical techniques such as acupuncture and control of the pulse.

DAOIST SCRIPTURES

Given the long and varied history of Daoism and the range of concerns of Daoist authors, it is not surprising that the Daoist canon *(daozang)* contains a great variety of texts. All traditions of Daoism trace their origins back to the works of Laozi, Zhuangzi, and other early masters such as Liezi. Later developments incorporate their ideas and symbols, although they

---

[1] The connection between immortals and mountains is evidenced by the fact that the character *xian* (仙) is comprised of graphs for "person" and "mountain."

often diverge from their systems in significant ways. Moreover, despite the importance of these early masters for the later tradition, the development of the religion of Daoism took place many centuries after their deaths. An organized religion of Daoism first arose in the second century CE and can be traced to the movements of the Great Peace (Taiping) and the Celestial Masters, which formed around charismatic leaders and spread throughout China, among both common people and the cultural and political elite.

During the fourth and fifth centuries, Daoism became a widely popular tradition that appealed to all classes of Chinese society, and it is during this time that it began to develop a distinctive collection of scriptures. The earliest listing of Daoist texts was attempted by Ban Gu (32–92), in his *History of the Han (Han shu)*, but not until the latter part of the fifth century was the first comprehensive catalog of Daoist scriptures prepared. Lu Xiujing (406–477), sponsored by Song Mingdi (r. 465–477), compiled the *Index to the Scriptures of the Three Caverns (Sandong Jingshu Mulu)*, which he presented to the emperor in 471. Now lost, this massive compilation was said to have listed more than 1,200 fascicles *(juan)*, including philosophical texts, alchemical works, and descriptions of talismans.

The next important listing of Daoist literature was prepared by order of Emperor Tang Xuanzong (r. 713–756), who believed himself to be a direct descendant of Laozi (who by this time was widely regarded as a celestial deity). The emperor ordered a search throughout his empire for all existing Daoist literature, which was eventually brought together in a collection called *Sublime Compendium of the Three Caverns (Sandong Qiong Gang)*, said to have comprised 3,700 texts. He had a number of copies made of the collection, which were then stored in Daoist temples. Shortly after this, however, the imperial libraries of the capitals of Chang'an and Luoyang were destroyed during the An Lushan and Shi Siming rebellions, and much of this huge collection was also lost.

Another compilation was ordered during the Song dynasty (960–1279). Song Zhenzong (r. 998–1022) ordered his advisor Wang Qinruo (962–1025) to compile a catalog of existing Daoist literature, and later Zhang Junfang (c. 1008–1029) headed a team of Daoist priests who compiled a collection of Daoist scriptures called *Precious Canon of the Celestial Palace of the Great Song (Song Tiangong Daozang)*, which had 4,565 titles. This is regarded by the tradition as the first definitive edition of the Daoist canon.

During subsequent dynasties, other compilations of the Daoist canon were prepared. The latest version of the canon was printed in 1926, under the sponsorship of the Nationalist government. Consisting of 1,120 fascicles, it is the largest collection of Daoist literature ever compiled. Fu Zengxiang (1872–1950), a former minister of education, convinced President Xu Shichang (1855–1939) to allocate government funds to preserve this literature. Based on the collection of the White Cloud Abbey (Baiyun Guan) of Beijing, it is believed to be descended from an edition of the canon prepared in 1445 and emended in 1845.

Since the compilation of the canon by Lu Xiujing in 471, editions of the *Daozang* have traditionally followed his division of Daoist texts into the "Three Caverns": (1) *Cavern of Perfection (dongzhen)*, which derives from the Supreme Clarity *(shangqing)* texts; (2) *Cavern of Mystery (dongxuan)*, which derives from the Numinous Treasure *(lingbao)* literature; and (3) *Cavern of Spirit (dongshen)*, which is based on the texts collectively called "Three Kings" *(sanhuang)*. This format appears to be patterned on the division of Buddhist teachings into the Three Baskets.

In addition to the works in this central division, the Daoist canon also contains other texts, such as the "Four Supplements" *(sifu)*, which follow the Three Caverns, named respectively *Great Mystery (taixuan)*, *Great Peace (taiping)*, *Great Purity (taiqing)*, and *True Unity (zhengyi)*. The first three of these have traditionally been regarded as supplements to the Three Caverns, although in fact they are thought by contemporary scholars to have been composed originally in reference to other texts. The *Great Mystery* supplement is based on the *Daodejing*; the *Great Peace*, *Great Purity*, and *True Unity* collections appear to be based on the *Scripture on the Great Peace (Taipingjing)*; the *Great Purity (taiqing)* texts are based on alchemy; and the *True Unity* on the Celestial Masters tradition.

As Daoist literature developed, other texts found their way into the canon that did not fit neatly into the early divisions. As a result, the canon was further subdivided. In the modern canon, each of the Three Caverns is divided into twelve sections: (1) original revelations; (2) celestial talismans; (3) commentaries; (4) sacred diagrams; (5) histories and genealogies; (6) codes of conduct; (7) rules for ceremonies; (8) outlines of rituals; (9) techniques for alchemy, geomancy, and numerology; (10) hagiographical works; (11) hymns and prayers; and (12) memorial addresses. Despite the apparently detailed nature of this division, individual sections contain a range of literature, and texts within a given division may not correspond to the general category.

In addition to the *Daozang*, another important compilation of Daoist scriptures should be mentioned: the *Edition of Essentials from the Daoist Canon (Daozang Jiyao)*, a smaller collection of texts compiled during the Qing dynasty (1644–1912). The 1906 edition of this corpus contains 287 titles, including works attributed to Sun Buer, a sample of whose writings is provided in the readings. These two collections of scriptures contain hundreds of rituals for renewal *(jiao)*, funeral liturgies *(zhai)*, philosophical texts, cosmological treatises, rituals for festivals and healing, discussions of external and internal alchemy, medical literature, meditation texts, descriptions for the identification and preparation of healing herbs and roots, mythological stories and hagiographies of great Daoist masters and immortals, and a variety of other types of literature.

Due to the diffuse nature of the Daoist canon, it is possible to provide only a small cross section of this literature. The following selections are but a representative sampling of some of the most important texts and genres of literature in the canon and focus on topics that have had a significant impact on the development of Daoism.

HOLIDAYS

Chinese New Year (Xin Nian) Celebrated on the first day of the first lunar month (generally February).

Clear Brightness Festival (or Tomb Sweeping Day; Qingming) This falls on the 105th day after the winter solstice (generally in April). Families visit the graves of their ancestors, pay their respects, and clean the site.

First Feast Celebrated on the second day of the second lunar month, this festival honors the Earth God (Tudigong), who is treated to fireworks and other offerings, including a banquet.

Ghost Month (Yulan) On the first day of the seventh lunar month, the gates of hell open and the spirits of the dead emerge for a month of feasting among the living. Paper "ghost money" is provided, along with food and entertainment.

Jade Emperor's Birthday (Bai tian gong) Celebrated on the ninth day of the first lunar month, this festival commemorate the legendary Jade Emperor (Yu Huang) with incense and other offerings.

Lantern Festival (Yuan xiao jie) Celebrated on the fifteenth day of the first lunar month. Families gather and

HOLIDAYS *(Continued)*

make lanterns with candles inside them, which then are placed along roads and floated in water.

Laozi's Birthday Celebrated on the fifteenth day of the second lunar month.

TIMELINE

2357 BCE	Time of the sage emperors Yao and Shun
145–90 BCE	Life of the great historian Sima Qian
24–220 CE	Eastern Han dynasty in China; beginnings of religious Daoism
142	First revelation by Taishang Laojun to Zhang Daoling, the first Celestial Master
215	Dispersion of adherents of Celestial Masters (Tianshi)
330–386	Life of Yang Xi, founder of Highest Clarity (Shangqing)
406–477	Life of Lu Xuijing, systematizer of Lingbao Daoist revelation
440	State patronage of Daoism
456–536	Tao Hongjing, systematizer of Shangqing Daoist revelation
1019	State-sponsored printing of Daoist canon *(daozang)*
1113–1170	Life of Wang Zhe, founder of Complete Perfection (Quangzhen) tradition of Daoism
1403–1425	Reign of Emperor Chengzu; Daoism receives imperial support; compilation of a new Daoist canon
1947	Communist revolution in China led by Mao Zedong; Nationalists defeated, with remnants of government moving to Taiwan; beginning of religious persecution in mainland China
1966–1976	Cultural Revolution in China; widespread religious persecution and destruction of religious sites

GLOSSARY

Cinnabar Mercuric sulfide, believed by Daoist alchemists to be the key to an elixir of immortality.

Dao "Way," the impersonal force that sustains all life and dictates patterns of growth and development.

Daodejing *Treatise on the Way and Power*, a classic work of Daoism attributed to Laozi.

De The power or virtue of Dao, which enables it to influence the movements of natural systems.

Immortals (*xian*) Daoist sages and alchemists who have discovered the secrets of physical immortality.

Laozi The legendary founder of Daoism, said to have lived during the sixth century BCE.

Philosophical Daoism A term coined by Western scholars to designate the strand of Daoism represented by Laozi and Zhuangzi, which is concerned with the nature and activities of Dao.

Pu "The Uncarved Block," a metaphor for human beings in their natural state before society distorts their true nature through training and education.

Qi Vital energy or life force that sustains living beings.

Religious Daoism A term coined by Western scholars to designate the strand of Daoism that was concerned primarily with the quest for immortality.

Wuwei "Not Acting," the attitude of the Daoist sage, which involves allowing events to happen naturally, in accordance with the movements of Dao.

Yang The active and aggressive aspect of Dao.

Yin The passive aspect of Dao.

Zhuangzi One of the most influential figures of early philosophical Daoism.

Zuowang "Sitting and forgetting," a method of Daoist meditation involving dropping off the accumulated training that interferes with understanding of Dao.

DAOIST SCRIPTURES

A BRIEF ACCOUNT OF LAOZI'S LIFE

A number of contemporary scholars believe that Laozi (whose name means "Old Master") may not have been a historical figure. In addition, there is significant textual evidence that the work attributed to him comprises materials from different authors and was compiled centuries after he supposedly lived.

His historicity is doubted because there is little solid evidence that he ever lived and considerable confusion among the sources that mention him. According to the record composed by the historian Sima Qian (154–80 BCE), Laozi was reportedly born in a small village in southern China in the later period of the Zhou dynasty. His surname was Li, and his personal name was Er. He worked as an archivist for most of his life, but after becoming concerned with what he perceived as a degeneration of his society, Laozi decided to leave through the Western Gate, which marked the boundary of China. According to Sima Qian, he was not heard from again. In later times, however, numerous sightings of Laozi were reported, and a wealth of legends concerning this mysterious figure circulated throughout China.

Laozi cultivated the Dao and the Virtue. His teaching focused on remaining apart [from society] and avoiding fame. After living under the Zhou for a long time, he saw that the Zhou was in decline, and he decided to leave. When he reached the pass [on the western frontier of China], Yin Xi, the Guardian of the Pass, said, "Since you are about to completely withdraw, I ask you to write a text for me." Laozi thus composed a book in two sections which described the meaning of the Dao and the Virtue in more than five thousand characters. He then left. No one knows what became of him.

Source: Sima Qian, *Shiji*, p. 63.2142; tr. JP.

LAOZI INSTRUCTS CONFUCIUS

According to traditional sources, Laozi was an older contemporary of Confucius, and the two supposedly met on several occasions. When Daoist texts report their meetings, Laozi is portrayed as utterly surpassing Confucius in his understanding of Dao and as admonishing him to give up his attachment to rituals, propriety, and learning and embrace simplicity. Not surprisingly, Confucian sources portray Confucius as the victor. In the following selection, drawn from Sima Qian's history, Confucius comes to Laozi for instruction on the proper performance of rituals but is advised instead to give up his rigidity and affectations and embrace Dao.

Confucius traveled to Zhou with the intention of questioning Laozi about rites. Laozi said, "The people you mention have decomposed, both the people and their bones. Only their words remain here. Also, when the noble person attains his season, he will harness his horses. If he does not attain it, he will be pushed along like a tumbleweed moving with the wind. . . . Get rid of your arrogant manners and many desires, get rid of your artificial mannerisms and your grand ambitions. These all are of no benefit to you. This is all I have to tell you."

Confucius left and told his disciples, "I know that birds can fly, I know that fish can swim, and I know that animals can run. One may make traps for things that run, one may put out lines for that which swims, and one may make arrows with attached twine for that which flies. But regarding the dragon, I may never know how it flies in the wind and clouds and ascends into the sky. Today I have met Laozi. Is he like the dragon?"

Source: Sima Qian, *Shiji*, p. 63.2139; tr. JP.

LAOZI CONVERTS THE BARBARIANS

When Buddhism first arrived in China, many Daoists welcomed it as a kindred system, but over time rivalries between the two traditions developed, although they continued to borrow from each other. In the following passage, a Daoist author claims that the Buddha was really Laozi, who traveled to India after passing through the Western Gate. He intended to teach the barbarians the essence of Daoism but soon realized that they were only capable of understanding the "Lesser Way," an inferior version of his teaching suitable for them. The passage reflects traditional Chinese attitudes toward non-Chinese peoples, who are seen as savages.

Using his divine powers, [Laozi] then summoned all the barbarian kings. Without question they appeared from far and near. There were numerous kings and nobles. . . . They all came with their wives and concubines, families and other dependents. They crowded around the Venerable Lord, coming ever closer in order to hear the law.

At this time the Venerable Lord addressed the assembled barbarian kings:

"Your hearts are full of evil! You engage in killing and harm other beings! Since you feed only on blood and meat, you cut short manifold lives!

"Today I will . . . prohibit meat-eating among you and leave you with a diet of wheat and gruel. This will take care of all that slaughter and killing! Those among you who cannot desist shall themselves become dead meat!

"You barbarians are greedy and cruel! You make no difference between kin and stranger. You are intent only to satisfy your greed and debauchery! Not a trace of mercy or sense of social duty is within you!

"Look at you! Your hair and beards are unkempt and too long! How can you comb and wash them? Even from a distance you are full of rank smell! How awfully dirty your bodies must be!

"Now that you are made to cultivate the Dao all these things will be great annoyances to your practice. I therefore order all of you to shave off your beards and hair.... By teaching you the Lesser Way, I will, by and by, lead you to more cultivated manners. In addition, I will give you a number of precepts and prohibitions, so that you gradually get to exercise mercy and compassion. Each month on the fifteenth day, you shall repent your sins."

Source: Huahujing, p. 1266b: *The Taoist Experience: An Anthology*, tr. Livia Kohn (Albany: State University of New York Press, 1993), pp. 76–77.

LAOZI BECOMES AN IMMORTAL

The following excerpt is taken from the Scripture of the Western Ascension, *which portrays Laozi as an immortal after his departure from China. The text reports that he traveled to India, where he became known as the Buddha. He taught the essentials of Daoism to his Indian audiences, and shortly before leaving human society forever he returned to China to impart a final instruction to Yin Xi.*

Suddenly Laozi was nowhere to be seen. The office building was illuminated by a brilliance of five colors, simultaneously dark and yellow. Yin Xi went into the courtyard, bowed down and said: "Please, dear spirit man, let me see you once again. Give me one more rule, and I can guard the primordial source of all."

He looked up and saw Laozi suspended in midair several feet above the ground. He looked like a statue. The image appeared and disappeared; it was vague and indistinct and seemed to waver between young and old.

Laozi said: "I will give you one more admonition; make sure you get it right: Get rid of all impurity and stop all thoughts; calm your mind and guard the One. When all impurities are gone, the myriad affairs are done. These are the essentials of my Dao."

Then the vision vanished. Yin Xi did not know where it had gone. He cried bitterly and worshipped it in remembrance. Then he retired from office on grounds of illness.

He gave up all thinking and guarded the One, and the myriad affairs were done.

Source: Xishengjing selections, from Livia Kohn, Early Chinese Mysticism: Philosophy and Soteriology in the Taoist Tradition (Princeton: Princeton University Press, 1992), p. 131.

LAOZI: THE *DAODEJING*

Regarded by Daoist tradition as the oldest text of the canon, the Treatise on the Way and Power (Daodejing) *is attributed to Laozi. Containing about 5,000 characters, it is also popularly known as the* Five Thousand Character Classic. *Modern versions of the text are divided into two sections: The first describes the Dao, and the second is concerned with how rulers should follow the way of Dao in order to rule wisely and well. Some contemporary scholars believe that the text we have today is not in fact a unitary work but instead contains materials from various periods. It is widely believed to have been compiled during the Warring States Period, around 250 BCE, and the earliest known version of the text dates to the beginning of the Han dynasty (202–220). It has been the subject of numerous commentaries, many of which may still be found today in the Daoist canon.*

1. The Dao that can be described
    Is not the eternal Dao.
    The name that can be spoken
    Is not the eternal name.
    The nameless is the origin of Heaven and Earth;
    The named is the mother of all things.
    Remain always free from desire,
    And you will see its subtlety.
    Always hold onto desires,
    And you will only see its results.
    The two develop together
    But have different names.
    They are deep and mysterious.
    Deeper and more mysterious, the gate of all wonders.
2. When beauty is recognized, ugliness is born.
    When good is recognized, evil is born.
    Is and is not give rise to each other;
    Difficult requires easy;
    Long is measured by short;
    High is determined by low;
    Sound is harmonized by voice;
    Back follows front.
    Therefore, the sage applies himself to non-action (*wuwei*),
    Moves without speaking,

    Creates the ten thousand things[2] without hindrance,
    Lives, but does not possess,
    Acts, but does not presume,
    Accomplishes, but takes no credit.
    Since no credit is taken, his accomplishments endure.

3. Do not exalt heroes,
    And people will not quarrel.
    Do not value rare objects,
    And people will not steal.
    Don't display things of desire,
    And their hearts will not be troubled.
    Therefore, the sage governs by emptying their hearts and filling their stomachs,
    Discouraging their ambitions and strengthening their bones;
    Leads people away from knowledge and desire;
    Keeps the learned from imposing on others;
    Practices non-action, and the natural order is not disturbed.

4. Dao is empty.
    Use it, and it will never overflow;
    It is bottomless, the origin of all things.
    It blunts sharp edges,
    Unties knots, softens light,
    Merges with the dust.
    I do not know from where it comes,
    Its appearance precedes the Ancestor.

6. The spirit of the valley never dies.
    It is called the mysterious female.
    The gate of the mysterious female
    Is called the root of heaven and earth.
    It is continuous and exists forever;
    Use it and you will never wear it out.

8. It is best to be like water;
    Which benefits the ten thousand things and does not compete.
    It collects in the places in which humans disdain to live,
    Near the Dao.
    Live in goodness;
    Keep your mind deep;
    Treat others with kindness;
    Keep your word;
    Do what is right;
    Work at the proper time;
    If you do not contend, you cannot be blamed.

10. Can you balance your life force
    And embrace the One without differentiation?
    Can you gently control your breath like an infant?
    Can you purify your profound insight so it will become stainless?

---

[2] In classical Chinese literature, the expression "ten thousand things" refers to everything in the world.

Can you love people and govern the state without [clinging to] knowledge?
Can you open and shut the Gate of Heaven
Without clinging to the earth? . . .
Produce and cultivate
Produce but not possess,
Act without depending,
Excel but do not try to master [others]:
This is called profound virtue *(de)*.

14. We look at it and do not see it;
    It is called the Invisible.
    We listen to it and do not hear it;
    It is called the Inaudible.
    We touch it and do not feel it;
    It is called the subtle. . . .
    Infinite and boundless, it cannot be named;
    It subsists in nothingness.
    It is shape without shape, form *(xiang)* without form.
    It is the vague and elusive. . . .

17. With the best rulers
    The people know that they exist.
    The next best they see and praise.
    The next they fear.
    And the next they revile.
    If you do not have basic trust
    There will be no trust at all,
    Be circumspect in the use of words.
    When your work is done,
    The people will say, "We have done it ourselves."

18. With the decline of the great Dao,
    The [doctrines of] humanity and righteousness appeared.
    When learning and cleverness are recognized,
    Great hypocrisy arises.
    When family relations are forgotten,
    Filial piety and affection arise.
    When a country falls into chaos,
    Loyal citizens come forth.

22. The crippled becomes whole.
    The crooked becomes straight.
    The hollow becomes filled.
    The worn becomes renewed.
    The meager becomes increased.
    The full becomes deluded.
    Therefore, sages embrace the One
    And maintain the world.
    Do not display themselves
    And are therefore luminous.
    Do not assert themselves
    And are therefore exalted.
    Do not boast
    And therefore succeed.

Are not complacent
And thus endure.
Do not contend
And so no one in the world
Can contend against them.

28. One who knows the male and maintains the female
Becomes the valley of the world.
Being the valley of the world,
Virtue will endure.
Return to the state of infancy.
Know the white, maintain the black,
Become the model for the world.
Being the model for the world,
One will never deviate from virtue.
Return to the state of the uncarved block *(pu)*.

37. The Dao does nothing
Yet through it everything is done.
If kings and princes could hold to it,
The world would be transformed of its own accord.
When transformed, beings wish to engage in action.
Still them through wordless simplicity.
Then there will be no desire.
Absence of desire is tranquility,
And the world becomes peaceful of its own accord.

41. When superior people hear of Dao
They endeavor to live in accordance with it.
When the mediocre hear of Dao
Sometimes they are aware of it, and sometimes they are not.
When the lowest type hear of Dao
They break into loud laughter.
If it were not laughed at, it would not be Dao.

43. The softest thing in the world overcomes the hardest.
Non-being penetrates that which has no space.
This indicates the benefit of non-action.
Few in the world can understand wordless teaching and the
benefit of non-action.

48. In pursuing knowledge, one gains daily;
Pursuing Dao, one loses daily.
Through losing and losing again,
One arrives at non-action.
By doing nothing everything is done.
View the whole world as nothing.
When one makes the slightest effort,
The world is beyond one's grasp.

49. The sage has no fixed opinions,
The opinions of ordinary people become his own.
I am good to people who are good;
I am also good to those who are not good:
That is the goodness of virtue.
I believe honest people;

I also believe the dishonest:
This is the trust of virtue.
Sages create harmony in the world.
They mingle their hearts with the world.
Ordinary people fix their eyes and ears on them,
But sages become the children of the world.

63. Act without acting.
Serve without serving.
Taste without tasting.
Whether it is great or small, many or few,
Repay hatred with virtue.
Deal with the difficult through what is easy;
Deal with the big through the small.
The difficulties of the world
Should be dealt with through the easiest;
The great things of the world
Should be accomplished through the smallest.

65. The rulers of old did not enlighten the people,
But kept them ignorant.
Therefore, ruling through cleverness
Leads to rebellion.
Not ruling through cleverness
Leads to good fortune.

76. When people are born, they are soft and weak;
At death, they are stiff and strong.
The ten thousand plants and trees are born soft and supple,
And at death are brittle and dry.
Hardness and strength are the companions of death,
And softness and weakness are the companions of life.
Therefore, the strongest armies do not seek to conquer.
The mightiest trees are cut down.
The strong and great sink down;
The soft and weak rise.

78. Nothing in the world is softer and weaker than water
But nothing is superior to it in overcoming the hard and strong;
Weakness overcomes strength
And softness overcomes hardness.
Everyone knows this, and no one practices it.

81. True words are not fine-sounding;
Fine-sounding words are not true.
Good people do not argue;
Argumentative people are not good.
Wise people are not learned;
The learned are not wise.
The sage does not accumulate things;
Has enough by working for others;
Gives to others and has even more.
The Dao of Heaven benefits and does not harm.
The Dao of the sage accomplishes, but does not contend.

Source: *Daodejing,* selections; tr. JP.

WANG BI: COMMENTARY ON THE *DAODEJING*

Wang Bi (226–249), author of the most influential commentary on the Treatise on the Way and Power, *is renowned in China as one of the foremost representatives of the Dark Learning* (xuanxue) *school of Chinese philosophy. This school is based on the "Three Dark Texts": the* Yijing, *the* Daodejing, *and the* Zhuangzi. *The philosophers of the Dark Learning school proposed a return to the ancient classics, whose ideas they mingled with Confucian notions about the ideal society and Daoist metaphysics. One of Wang Bi's original contributions to Chinese thought was the notion of "original non-being"* (benwu), *according to which prior to the creation of the universe there was only undifferentiated non-being. From this arose the One, another way of conceiving of the Dao. From the One arose the Two, and from this came the myriad things of the universe.*

All being originates from nonbeing. Therefore, the time before there were physical shapes and names is the beginning of the myriad beings. When shapes and names are there, [the Dao] raises them, educates them, adjusts them, and causes their end. It serves as their mother. The text [the *Daodejing*] means that the Dao produces and completes beings on the basis of the formless and the nameless. They are produced and completed but do not know how or why.

Source: *Laozi* 1.1.1a; tr. JP.

VISUALIZING THE DAO

The following passage is an example of how Laozi's ideas became mingled with long-life practices in later Daoist literature. It indicates techniques for visualization that will enable the meditator to harmonize vital energies and acquire esoteric wisdom.

These are the secret instructions of the Highest Lord.
First burn incense and straighten your robes, greet the ten directions with three bows each. Concentrate your mind inside and visualize Master Yin and the Master on the River, as well as Laozi, the Great Teacher of the Law. Then recite the following in your mind:
Mysterious, again mysterious, the origin of Dao,
Above, virtue incorporates chaos and the prime. . . .
In my room, the seven jewels come together,
Doors and windows open of themselves.
Utter in my purity, I strive for deeper truth,
Riding on bright light, I ascend the purple sky.
Sun and moon to my right and left,
I go to the immortals, and eternal life.

All seven ancestors arise, are reborn in heaven,
The world, how true, the gate to virtue and to Dao.

Finish this mental recitation, then clap your teeth and swallow the saliva thirty-six times each. Visualize the green dragon to your left, the white tiger to your right, the red bird in front of you, and the dark warrior at your back. . . .

On three sides you are joined by an attendant, each having a retinue of a thousand carriages and ten thousand horsemen. Eight thousand jade maidens and jade lads of heaven and earth stand guard for you.

Then repeat the formula, this time aloud, and begin to recite the five thousand words of the Scripture [the *Daodejing*]. Conclude by three times clapping your teeth and swallowing the saliva.

Source: *Laozi Daodejing Xuzhui: The Taoist Experience:* An Anthology, tr. Livia Kohn (Albany: State University of New York Press, 1993), pp. 173–174.

THE DAO OF IMMORTALITY

According to legend, Heshang Gong, the Master on the River, lived during the reign of the Han emperor Wen (179–156 BCE), but the earliest dated stories of his life come from the third century CE. He is said to have lived near the Yellow River, where he studied the Treatise on the Way and Power *in solitude. Eventually he came to the attention of the emperor, who asked him to teach the essentials of Laozi's text. In the passage that follows, he indicates how the ideas of the* Daodejing *became mingled with immortality practices such as breathing exercises and gymnastics. In the system of Heshang Gong, people receive vital energy (qi) from Heaven, but they ordinarily dissipate it unless they practice special techniques to keep it stored in the vital organs.*

[The *Daodejing* says]: The valley spirit does not die.

[Heshang Gong comments]: Valley means nurture. People can nurture their spirit and thus not die. Here, spirit refers to the spirits of the five internal organs. The liver contains the spiritual soul *(hun)*. The lungs contain the material soul *(po)*. The heart contains the vital spirit *(shen)*. The kidneys contain the vital essence *(jing)*. The spleen contains the will *(zhi)*. When the five internal organs come to harm, the five spirits depart.

[The *Daodejing* says]: It is called the Mysterious Female.

[Heshang Gong comments]: This is saying that the existence of longevity resides with the Mysterious Female.

Mystery refers to Heaven. It is within the nose of each person. Female refers to Earth. It is within the mouth of each person.

Heaven feeds people with the five energies *(qi)*. The five energies enter through the nose and are contained in the heart. The five energies are subtle and minute. They are the five characteristics of vital essence, vital spirit, the clear hearing, clear sight, and voice. Their vital spirit is the spiritual soul. The spiritual soul is male. It mainly comes and goes through a person's nose. It pervades Heaven. Thus, the nose is mysterious.

Earth feeds people with the five flavors. The five flavors enter through the mouth and are contained in the stomach. The five flavors are coarse. They form the body, skeleton, bones, flesh, blood, veins, and the six emotions. Their spirit is the material soul. The material soul is female. It mainly comes and goes through a person's mouth. It pervades Earth. Thus, the mouth is female.

[The *Daodejing* says]: The gate of the Mysterious Female is called the root of Heaven and Earth.

[Heshang Gong comments]: Root refers to the origins. This is talking about the gates of the nose and mouth, which are the means by which the vital energy that pervades Heaven and Earth comes and goes.

[The *Daodejing* says]: Dimly visible, as if it were right here.

[Heshang Gong comments]: The nose and mouth inhale and exhale, they work and rest. When breathing becomes dim and subtle, it seems like it can go on like that, but then it returns to a state that is not like that at all.

[The *Daodejing* says]: Use will never drain it.

[Heshang Gong comments]: When your breathing becomes comfortable and relaxed, you should not hurry it or force it.

Source: *Laozi Daodejing Xuzhui* 6.1; http://ctext.org/heshanggong/6; tr. Thomas McConochie.

PURITY AND TRANQUILLITY

As the Daoist tradition developed, Laozi's successors developed techniques for incorporating his doctrines into religious practice. The following excerpt, which became popular during the Song dynasty (960–1260), was used as a guide to meditation practice by the Complete Perfection (Quanzhen) school of Daoism and is still in use today in its religious services.

The Great Dao has no form;
It brings forth and raises heaven and earth.
The Great Dao has no feelings;
It regulates the course of the sun and the moon.
The Great Dao has no name;
It raises and nourishes the myriad beings.
I do not know its name—
So I call it Dao.
The Dao can be pure or turbid, moving or tranquil.
Heaven is pure, earth is turbid;
Heaven is moving, earth is tranquil.
The male is moving, the female is tranquil. . . .
Always be pure and tranquil;
Heaven and earth
Return to the primordial.
The human spirit is fond of purity,
But the mind disturbs it.
The human mind is full of tranquility,
But desires meddle with it.
Get rid of desires for good,
And the mind will be calm.
Cleanse your mind,
And the spirit will be pure.

Source: *Qingjing jing: The Taoist Experience:* An Anthology, tr. Livia Kohn (Albany: State University of New York Press, 1993), pp. 25–26.

ZHUANGZI'S LIFE AND WORK

Zhuangzi, one of the two main figures of "philosophical Daoism," is believed to have lived during the fourth century BCE. Little is known about his life except for the enigmatic descriptions found in his own works. Sima Qian reports that he lived in the southern country of Mang, in modern-day Henan, and that he died around 290 BCE. He is said to have held a minor government post but refused any offers of higher office, preferring to retain his autonomy and personal freedom. According to his own account, he sought to live apart from his society, refusing honors and political involvement, and cultivated the virtue of "uselessness," which enabled him to move unmolested in the world and to attain a state of harmony with the Dao.

Zhuangzi lived in Mang. His given name was Zhou. Zhou once worked as a functionary at Qiyuan in Mang. He was a contemporary of King Hui of Liang (r. 370–335 BCE) and King Xuan of Qi (r. 342–324 BCE). There was nothing his teachings did not consider, and their essence hearkened back to the words of Laozi. His texts, comprising more than

100,000 characters, all used allegories. . . . He mocked people like Confucius and elucidated the meanings of Laozi . . . and he was adept at creating texts with hidden allusions and analogies. He used them to attack the Confucians and followers of Mozi. Even the greatest scholars of his day could not defend themselves against him. His words flowed and swirled freely, at his whim, and powerful people could not use him, including kings, dukes, and others.

Source: Sima Qian, *Shiji*, 63.2144; tr. JP.

THE DAO IS IN EVERYTHING

In the following selection, Zhuangzi indicates that Dao is everywhere and in everything and that those who truly know it understand that it pervades even the lowest and most despised parts of the world.

> Dong Guo asked Zhuangzi, "The thing called Dao: where does it exist?"
> Zhuangzi said, "There's no place it doesn't exist."
> "Come," said Dong Guo, "you must be more specific!"
> "It is in ants."
> "How can it be in something so low?"
> "It is in grass."
> "But that's even lower!"
> "It is in bricks and shards."
> "But that's even lower!"
> "It is in excrement."

Source: *Zhuangzi*, ch. 22; tr. JP.

DAO IS BEGINNINGLESS

According to Zhuangzi, most people waste their energies striving and planning for the future and so fail to live in the moment. Sages, however, learn to move with the flow of Dao, so they lead long and peaceful lives.

> [Ruo of the North Sea said to the Lord of the River]: "Dao has no beginning or end. Things live and die; you cannot rely on their completion. They are sometimes empty and sometimes full; they do not sit in any one form. The years cannot be moved. Time cannot be stopped. Melting and coming together; filling and emptying; their ending is also a beginning. It is thus that we can talk about the method of great rightness (*dayi*) and discourse about patterns (*li*) in the ten thousand things. The life of things is like a wild gallop: there is no movement that does not change, and there is no time

that does not alter. What should you do? What should you not do? In any case, you will be transforming yourself."

The Lord of the River said: "Well then, what is so valuable about *dao*?" Ruo of the North Sea said: "The mind of one who understands *dao* attains the patterns. The mind of one who attains the patterns understands how to weigh things up. One who understands how to weigh things up will not get harmed by things. One of attained power *(zhide)* cannot be burned and cannot be drowned. Neither cold nor heat can damage him. Birds and animals cannot harm him."

Source: *Zhuangzi Yinde* (Cambridge: Harvard University Press, 1956; Harvard-Yenching Institute Sinological Series no.20), 44/17/45–49; tr. Thomas McConochie.

DOES WHAT I SAY MEAN ANYTHING?

A central theme of Zhuangzi's philosophy is the limitations of language. Those who become caught up in expressions and concepts inevitably fail to recognize truth, which cannot be captured in words.

Now, I will say some words about "this." However, I do not know if they belong to the same category as "this" or not. Belonging to a category and not belonging to a category both belong to a category anyway, so there is no difference between them. Even so, I am still going to try to say something about it.

There is a beginning. There is a not-yet-beginning to be a beginning. There is not not-yet-beginning to be not-yet-beginning to be a beginning. There is existence. There is nonexistence. There is not-yet-beginning to be nonexistence. There is not-yet-beginning to be not-yet-beginning to be nonexistence. Suddenly, there is nonexistence! However, I do not know if nonexistence really exists or not. Now, I have just said something, but I do not know if what I have said really says anything. Have I just not really said anything after all?

Nothing in the world is larger than an Autumn hair. Mount Tai is small. No one lives longer than a dead infant. Pengzu died young. Heaven and Earth live within me. The ten thousand things and I are one.

Since we are already one, can there be words? Since I have already said that we are one, can there be no words? The one and the saying [that it is one] makes two. Two and one make three. If we go on like this, even a skilled chronicler could not get to the end, much less an ordinary person! In going from nonexistence to existence, we get three. How much more if going from existence to existence! Let us not go that way then. Let us go along with the "this" that is already here. . . .

Dao that is illuminated is no longer a *dao*. Disputing things in words does not get to the point. Humaneness *(ren)* that is constant is not mature. Uprightness that is pure is not trustworthy. Courage that is harmful is not successful. These five things seem as if they are round, but they tend toward squareness.

Source: *Zhuangzi Yinde* 5/2/47–55, 5/2/59–60; tr. Thomas McConochie.

SITTING AND FORGETTING

Zhuangzi teaches that most problems come from entanglement with words and concepts. As an antidote, he advises that we "unlearn" the lessons others have taught us "for our own good." Ideas of morality, justice, truth, and so on merely confuse people and make them think of doing the opposite. To counteract this, an important meditative practice is "sitting and forgetting" (zuowang), in which one simply lets thoughts flow freely, in harmony with Dao, and thus artificial concepts disperse of their own accord. A person who perfects this is able to attain the state of "free and easy wandering," in which one acts spontaneously, in accordance with the impulses of the moment. The following passage contains a section from Zhuangzi and a commentary by Guo Xiang, who compiled the edition that is the only extant version of the Zhuangzi.

Confucius was taken aback. He asked: "What does it mean to sit and forget?" Yanhui said: "I drop off my limbs and body. I dispel keen hearing and clear-sightedness. I separate [myself from] form and get rid of understanding. Thus, I go along with Great Pervader. This is called sitting and forgetting."

Source: *Zhuangzi Yinde,* 17/6/92–93; tr. Thomas McConochie.

[Guo Xiang explains] With regard to sitting and forgetting, what is it that is not forgotten? One forgets the traces [of things] and also forgets the means by which those traces are made. Internally, one is not aware of one's own body. Externally, one does not recognize that the world is there. Afterwards, one becomes vast with his body acting with the transformations, and there is nowhere that he does not pervade.

Source: Guo Qingfan, *Zhuangzi Ji Shi,* vol. 1; *Soshi Kaku Sho Chu Sakuin* (Kita Kyushu Shi: Kita Kyushu Chugoku Shoten Shi, 1990), 6/551/162/5–6; (Beijing: Zhonghua Shuju: Xinhua Shudian Beijing Faxingsuo Faxing, 1961): 285; tr. Thomas McConochie.

THE PERFECTED MAN IS MIRACULOUS

A person who is in harmony with Dao is able to move freely in the world, unharmed by things that injure ordinary people. The following passage was cited by the later Daoist tradition as evidence that Zhuangzi was interested in immortality practices because his description of the sage indicates that understanding of Dao makes a person godlike, able to fly and to transcend death.

> Wang Ni said: "The perfected man is miraculous! Swamps might burn, but he will not feel hot. Rivers may freeze, but he will not feel cold. Violent thunder might shatter mountains, and winds might quake the seas, but he will not be afraid. Such a person chariots on clouds and wind, straddles the sun and moon, and wanders beyond the four seas. Death and life do not change him, much less the differences between benefit and harm!"

Source: *Zhuangzi Yinde*, 6/2/71–73; tr. Thomas McConochie.

ZHUANG ZHOU DREAMED HE WAS A BUTTERFLY

In the following passage, Zhuangzi falls asleep and dreams that he is a butterfly, but when he awakes he is unsure whether he is Zhuangzi or a butterfly dreaming of being Zhuangzi. The passage exemplifies the way Zhuangzi merges dreams and waking "reality" while indicating that the boundaries between the two are not as rigid as ordinary people assume.

> Once Zhuang Zhou dreamed he was a butterfly. He fluttered about just as a butterfly would! In this state, he did not know that he was Zhou. He suddenly awoke and found that he was Zhou. He did not know if he was Zhou dreaming of being a butterfly, or a butterfly dreaming of being Zhou. However, there must be a distinction between Zhou and the butterfly. Such is called the transformation of things.

Source: *Zhuangzi Yinde* 7/2/94–96; tr. Thomas McConochie.

ZHUANGZI VISITS HUIZI, PRIME MINISTER OF LIANG

Throughout his life, Zhuangzi avoided all attempts to make himself useful to his society. When offered important positions, he turned them down, preferring instead to live in the moment, unharried by the concerns of busy and important people.

> Zhuangzi went to see Huzi, who was the prime minister of Liang. Someone said to Huizi, "Zhuangzi is coming; he

must want to replace you as prime minister." Thereupon, Huizi was afraid. He searched the kingdom for three days and nights [for Zhuangzi]. Zhuangzi went to see him and said, "There is a bird in the south called the Yuanchu. Have you heard of it? The Yuanchu sets out from the South Ocean and flies to the North Ocean. It perches on nothing but the parasol tree. It eats nothing but good fruit. It drinks nothing but pure spring water. Along its journey, it comes across an owl that has caught a putrid rat. The Yuanchu just goes past, but the owl looks up and says: 'Shoo!' Now, are you trying to shoo me away from the Kingdom of Liang?"

Source: *Zhuangzi Yinde* 45/17/84–87; tr. Thomas McConochie.

THE SAGE RIDES THE SUN AND MOON

According to Zhuangzi, the sage completely transcends the limitations felt by ordinary beings and cares nothing for their judgments.

The sage stands by the sun and moon. He tucks the universe under his arm and melds it all into a harmonious whole. He treats servants as exalted. While ordinary people go about menial tasks, the sage seems foolish and stupid. He takes part in the ten thousand harvests and turns them into a pure unity. For him, the ten thousand things are complete as they are, and they contain each other just as they are.

Source: *Zhuangzi Yinde* 6/2/77–78; tr. Thomas McConochie.

THE TRUE MEN OF OLD

The sage moves in the world without becoming attached to anything. Living in the moment, he simply takes things as they come and so is at peace. Ordinary people, in contrast, are full of desires, cares, and worries and so fail to realize their potential.

One who understands what it is that Heaven does and what it is that humans do is perfected. One who understands what Heaven does lives naturally. One who understands what humans do uses his knowledge of what humans do to cultivate understanding of what he knows he does not know. He lives out his natural years and does not die before his time. This is the flourishing of knowledge.

Nevertheless, there is some danger here. Knowledge is only deemed appropriate after it has something on which it depends, but what knowledge depends on is not fixed.

How do I know that what I call heavenly is not actually human? How do I know that what I call human is not actually heavenly? So, there must first be a genuine person *(zhenren)* in order for genuine knowledge *(zhenzhi)* to be possible.

What is a genuine person? The genuine people of old did not go against the few, did not seek to be heroes, and did not scheme to achieve their ends. People like that did not regret making mistakes. Nor were they smug when they got things right. People like that climbed mountains without trembling, entered water without getting wet, and entered fire without being burned. The abilities of their knowledge were such that they could ascend to the Dao in this manner.

The genuine people of old slept without dreaming and woke without worries. Their food was plain, and their breaths were deep. Genuine people breathe from the heels, whereas ordinary people breathe from the throat. When [ordinary] people lose out, they spew forth their words as if crying. Their desires run deep. Their heavenly mechanisms are shallow.

The genuine people of old did not know of loving life and hating death. They emerged, but it did not make them glad. They submerged, but they did not resist. They were composed when they came and went, and that was it. They did not forget where they came from. They did not go and search for where they were going: they just accepted it and were happy. Then they gave it back and forgot about it. This is called not using the mind to renounce Dao and not using the human to assist the natural. This is what I call a genuine person.

Such people have forgetting minds. They have a quiet appearance. Their cheeks seem cold like Autumn, and warm like Spring. Their happiness and anger merge with the four seasons. They find something right in all things, and no one knows their limits.

So when the sage uses weapons, he can destroy a state without losing the hearts of the people. He benefits and blesses the ten thousand things, but because he loves people [preferentially]. Thus, one who delights in things is not a sage. One who has preferential relationships is not humane. One who just takes advantage of natural timing is not a worthy. One who does not encompass both profit and loss is not a noble person *(junzi)*. One who enacts what his title requires at the expense of his own interests is not a noble person. One who loses his life in what is not genuine is not serving others. Men such as Hu Buxie, Wu Guang, Bo Yi, Shu Qi, Qi Zi Xuyu, Ji Ta, and Shen Tudi all performed services for others and accorded with what suited others. But they did not accord with what suited themselves.

The genuine people of old upheld righteousness but were not partisan. They appeared to be in want but did not accept charity. They were solitary but not rigid. They spread their emptiness everywhere but were not inglorious. They had the appearance of being happy! They just moved along with whatever they were doing. ... Therefore, their likes formed a oneness, and their dislikes formed a oneness. Their oneness was a unity. Their non-oneness was a unity. Their oneness moved along with Heaven. Their non-oneness moved along with humanity. Neither Heaven nor humanity won out with them: these are what I call genuine people.

Source: *Zhuangzi Yinde* 15/6/1–16/6/20; *Zhuangzi Jishi*, 1:224–235; tr. Thomas McConochie.

ZHUANGZI AND HUIZI OVER THE RIVER HAO

Zhuangzi's friend, the logician Huizi, is a favorite target of the subtle humor for which Zhuangzi is famous. Portrayed as a philosopher who is fond of hair-splitting distinctions, Huizi is chided by his friend for becoming overly attached to logic and words and thus failing to embrace the myriad mysteries of the natural world.

Zhuangzi and Huizi were wandering over the River Hao. Zhuangzi said: "See how the minnows swim around with ease: that is what makes fish happy."

Huizi said: "You're not a fish, so how could you know what makes fish happy?"

Zhuangzi said: "You're not me, so how could you know that I don't know what makes fish happy?"

Huizi said: "I'm not you, so I don't know what you know. Similarly, you're not a fish, so it should be clear that you cannot know what makes fish happy."

Zhuangzi said: "Let's go back to the beginning; you said: 'How do you know what makes fish happy?' That means that you already knew that I knew it when you asked me. I knew it standing here over the River Hao."

Source: *Zhuangzi Yinde* 45/17/87–91; tr. Thomas McConochie.

HUIZI AND ZHUANGZI ON EMOTIONS

In this passage, Huizi attempts to turn the tables on Zhuangzi, suggesting that despite his friend's emphasis on naturalness, what he advocates is really contrary to nature. Human beings naturally have feelings of attachment toward certain things and aversion toward others, and it is absurd to suggest that anyone can truly view all things as equal.

> Huizi said to Zhuangzi: "Can a person be without emotion?"
>
> Zhuangzi said: "Of course."
>
> Huizi said: "If a person has no emotion, how can we call him human?"
>
> Zhuangzi said: "Dao gave him a face. Heaven gave him a human form. Why would we not call him human?"
>
> Huizi said: "So, if we call him human, how could he have no emotion?"
>
> Zhuangzi said: "This is not what I call emotion. What I call having no emotion is when a person does not allow likes and dislikes to enter and harm his body. He constantly goes along with spontaneity *(ziran)*, but does not add to life."
>
> Huizi said: "If he does not add to life, how could he have a body?"
>
> Zhuangzi said: "Dao gave him a face, and Heaven gave him a form. He does not allow likes and dislikes to enter his body and cause harm. Now, you are just putting your spirit outside yourself and exhausting your essence. You prop up against a tree and repeat yourself. You lean on your desk and doze. Heaven chose your form for you, but you chirp on about hardness and whiteness!"

Source: *Zhuangzi Yinde* 14/5/55–15/5/60; *Zhuangzi Jishi*, 1:220–223; tr. Thomas McConochie.

CARPENTER SHI GOES TO QI

In his writings, Zhuangzi frequently extols the value of becoming useless. Those who make themselves useful are used by others and so dissipate their vital energies and die young. The sage, however, appears to be stupid and blockish, so others believe that he is useless and thus leave him alone.

> Carpenter Shi was travelling to Qi when he reached Quyuan. There he saw an oak tree by the village shrine. This tree was so large that it could shade a thousand oxen. It measured hundreds of hands around. It was as tall as the surrounding hills; its branches only started after a height of eighty feet. Dozens of its branches were wide enough to make into boats. People gathered around it as if in a market place, but the carpenter did not even glance twice at it and just walked on by without stopping.

However, one of his apprentices marveled while looking at the tree. He ran along and caught up to Carpenter Shi and said: "I have never seen timber as beautiful as this since I took up my axe and hatchet as your apprentice. But Master, you won't even look at it. You just walk on by without stopping. Why?"

Carpenter Shi said: "That's enough! Don't talk any more about it! It's a worthless tree! If you made it into a boat, it would sink. If you made it into a coffin, it would soon rot. If you made it into tools, they would soon break. If you made it into doors, its sap would leak out. If you made it into posts, they would get infested with grubs. This is a worthless tree; it can't be used for anything. That is why it has lived for so long."

After Carpenter Shi had gone home, the tree appeared to him in a dream and said: "What are you comparing me with? Are you comparing me with those elegant trees? Fruit-bearing trees like the hawthorn, the pear, the orange, and the pumelo get cut down as soon as they bear fruit. Getting cut down like that is so humiliating. Their large branches get broken off, and their small branches get drained. Their abilities are what makes their lives so bitter. Hence, they die before their time and do not get to live out their natural lifespan. They injure themselves with the vulgar customs of the world; everything does. I, on the other hand, have been trying to be of no use at all for a long time. I have come close to death along the way, but now, I have finally gotten it. This is of great use to me. Do you think I could have grown so large if I were of any use? Moreover, you and I are both things, so how can one go about treating another as though it is the only thing? What can you, a useless man about to die, understand of this useless tree?!"

Carpenter Shi woke up and told his apprentice about his dream. The apprentice asked: "If it wants to be useless, then what's it doing being a shrine?"

Carpenter Shi said: "Keep that a secret! Don't talk about it! It's just happened to be there. It considers those who don't understand it to just be annoying it. If it were not a shrine, wouldn't it just get clipped to bits? Besides, what it's protecting is different from what ordinary people protect. If we were to praise it according to righteousness, wouldn't we just be getting it wrong?!"

Source: *Zhuangzi Yinde*, 11/4/64–75; *Zhuangzi Jishi*, 1:170–175; tr. Thomas McConochie.

ZHUANGZI FISHING ON THE RIVER PU

In ancient China, rulers often asked renowned sages to be their advisors in order to receive wise counsel. In the following story, Zhuangzi is approached with such an offer.

Zhuangzi was fishing on the River Pu. The King of Chu sent two high-ranking officials to him. They said: "Our king wishes to employ you in the governance of his realm."

Zhuangzi kept hold of his rod, and without even turning his head to them said: "I have heard that there is a sacred turtle in Chu which has been dead for around 3,000 years. The king keeps it wrapped in cloth inside a basket that is stored in his ancestral temple. Do you think this turtle would rather be dead with its bones venerated, or would it rather be alive, dragging its tail in the mud?"

The two officials said: "It would rather be alive, dragging its tail in the mud."

Zhuangzi then said: "Well then, go away! I too, would rather drag my tail in the mud!"

Source: *Zhuangzi Yinde* 5/17/81–84; tr. Thomas McConochie.

ZHUANGZI'S WIFE DIED

Because death is an inevitable part of life, the sage embraces it along with other aspects of the natural world. For most people death is fearful and oppressive, but for the sage death is part of the cosmic mystery constantly unfolding around us.

When Zhuangzi's wife died, Huizi went to console him. Huizi found Zhuangzi squatting and singing while drumming on a pot.

Huizi said: "After living with someone for so long and raising children together, it isn't right for you to be drumming on a pot and singing instead of crying now that she is dead."

Zhuangzi said: "Not at all! When she first died, I couldn't help but cry like that. Then I looked back to when she had not been alive. Not only was she not alive, but when she had no form. Not only did she have no form, but she had no *qi* (life force). In the mingling chaos, she changed into *qi*, and the *qi* changed into form, and the form changed into life. Now, she has changed into death. This is being a companion with Spring and Autumn, Winter and Summer, in the motion of the four seasons. Now, she is going to lie down in a great chamber, but if I were to follow after her crying, I would not think that I understood fate. So, I stopped crying."

Source: *Zhuangzi Yinde* 46/18/15–19; tr. Thomas McConochie.

THE LADY OF GREAT MYSTERY

Although the position of women was well below that of men in classical China, there are many stories of female sages in the Daoist canon. These women managed to transcend the boundaries imposed on them by their society. Applying esoteric lore in secret, they became recognized as teachers and sometimes even as immortals. The following selection, from a collection of stories of immortals from the Han dynasty, reports on the life of the "Lady of Great Mystery," who successfully practiced the secret arts of immortality and ascended to heaven in broad daylight, a sign of exceptional accomplishment.

The Lady of Great Mystery had the family name Zhuan and was personally called He. When she was a little girl she lost first her father and after a little while, also her mother.

Understanding that living beings often did not fulfill their destined lifespans, she felt sympathy and sadness. She used to say: "Once people have lost their existence in this world, they cannot recover it. Whatever has died cannot come back to life. Life is so limited! It is over so fast! Without cultivating the Dao, how can one extend one's life?"

She duly left to find enlightened teachers, wishing to purify her mind and pursue the Dao. She obtained the arts of the Jade Master and practiced them diligently for several years.

As a result she was able to enter the water and not get wet. Even in the severest cold of winter she would walk over frozen rivers wearing only a single garment. All the time her expression would not change, and her body would remain comfortably warm for a succession of days.

The Lady of Great Mystery could also move government offices, temples, cities, and lodges. They would appear in other places quite without moving from their original location. Whatever she pointed at would vanish into thin air. Doors, windows, boxes, or caskets that were securely locked needed only a short flexing of her finger to break wide open. Mountains would tumble, trees would fall at the pointing of her hand. Another short gesture would resurrect them to their former state. . . .

The Lady of Great Mystery perfectly mastered all thirty-six arts of the immortals. She could resurrect the dead and bring them back to life. She saved innumerable people, but nobody knew what she used for her dresses or her food, nor did anybody ever learn her arts from her. Her complexion was always that of a young girl; her hair stayed always black as a raven. Later she ascended into heaven in broad daylight. She was never seen again.

Source: *Biographies of Spirit Immortals,* "The Lady of Great Mystery": *The Taoist Experience:* An Anthology, tr. Livia Kohn (Albany: State University of New York Press, 1993), pp. 291–292.

SUN BUER: IMMORTALITY PRACTICES FOR WOMEN

Sun Buer, known in Daoist literature as "Clear and Calm Free Human," lived during the twelfth century. Perhaps the best-known of Daoist women immortals, externally she lived an unremarkable life, raising three children and performing the duties expected of a Chinese wife. At the age of 51 she undertook the training of Daoist immortality practices, and it is reported that she quickly mastered difficult esoteric techniques. She composed a number of texts on immortality, most of which focus on distinctive techniques for women. A central concern is harnessing the vital energy and causing it to move up along the spine through subtle energy channels, and thus to the top of the head. It then cascades down the front of the body, bringing indescribable bliss and restoring vitality. The verses are written in a code using the terminology of the Daoist immortalists, so an explanatory commentary by Zhen Yangming, a twentieth-century Daoist master, is included.

> Tie up the tiger and return it to the true lair;
> Bridle the dragon and gradually increase the elixir.
> Nature should be clear as water,
> Mind should be as still as a mountain.
> Tuning the breath, gather it into the gold crucible;
> Stabilizing the spirit, guard the jade pass.
> If you can increase the grain of rice day by day,
> You will be rejuvenated.

Commentary by Zhen Yangming

The tiger is energy, while the dragon is spirit. The "true lair" is the general area between the breasts. To tie up the tiger and return it to the true lair is what was explained by the Master of Higher Light, One Who Has Reached Emptiness, in these terms: "When women cultivate immortality, they must first accumulate energy in their breasts."

This is the distinction between primal and acquired energy. Refinement of acquired energy uses the method of tuning the breath and freezing the spirit; to gather primal energy, you wait until there is living energy stirring in your body to start. To bridle the dragon simply means to freeze the spirit so as to join it to energy. When spirit and energy unite, the earthly soul and the celestial soul link, and the elixir is crystallized. One of the Celestial Teachers of the Zhang clan, the Empty Peaceful One, said, "Once the original spirit emerges, then gather it back in; when the spirit returns, energy in the body spontaneously circulates. Do this every morning and every evening, and eternal youth will naturally form a spiritual embryo." This is the meaning of bridling the dragon and gradually increasing the elixir. . . .

"Nature should be clear as water, mind should be as still as a mountain." Real Human Zhang Sanfeng said, "Freezing the spirit, tune the breath; tuning the breath, freeze the spirit. This should be done all at once, as one operation. Freezing the spirit means gathering the clarified mind within. When the mind is clear and cool, peaceful and light, then you can practice gathering it into the lair of energy. This is called freezing the spirit. After you do this, you feel as though you are sitting on a high mountain, gazing at the myriad mountains and rivers, or as though you have lit a heavenly lamp that lights up all dark realms. This is what is called freezing the spirit in the void. And tuning the breath is not hard; once mind and spirit are quiet, following the breath spontaneously, I keep this spontaneity. . . ."

The Real Human Zhang said, "When you sit, you should embrace energy with spirit, and keep your mind on breath, in the elixir field, with clear serenity, concentrating undistracted. The energy stored within combines with energy coming from outside to crystallize in the elixir field, filling it and growing stronger day by day and month by month, reaching the four limbs, flowing through the hundred channels, striking open the double pass at the middle of the spine, floating up to the nirvana chamber in the center of the brain. Then it turns and goes down to the heart and enters the field of elixir below in the abdomen. Spirit and energy keep to one another, resting on one another with each breath, and the course of the Waterwheel (the cycle of energy circulation) is opened. When the work reaches this point, the effective construction of the foundation is already half done. . . .

"If you can increase the grain of rice day by day, you will be rejuvenated." In response to questions about what this "grain of rice" is, I can bring up an alchemical classic by Zhang Boduan. This classic . . . says, "The Undifferentiated encloses Space, Space encloses the worlds of desire, form, and formlessness. When you look for the root source of it all, it is a particle big as a grain." It also says, "A grain, and grain again; at first scarcely perceptible, it eventually becomes clearly evident."

This is the meaning of the statement "If you can increase the grain of rice day by day. . . ." Put simply, it is a matter of gradual culling and refinement of spirit and energy, gradually solidifying and combining them. It does not mean that this little ball of spirit and energy combined has a definite shape like a grain of rice that you can find.

Source: *Cultivating the Elixir;* from *Immortal Sisters,* tr. Thomas Cleary (Boston: Shambhala, 1989), pp. 34–37.

SEXUAL TECHNIQUES FOR MEN

The Daoist canon contains a wealth of information on long-life practices developed over the centuries by Daoists intent on extending their life spans. Among these are various sexual techniques that enable people to increase their energy level. Sexual practices for men often include ways to increase yang *energy, whereas females are taught how to increase* yin *energy. Many of these techniques describe a sort of sexual vampirism in which the energy of the partner is transferred to the practitioner. In other texts, it appears that the sexual practices awaken and augment one's natural energy. The following passage is written for men, who are advised to take as many sexual partners as possible, and ideally women in their early teens because young women have a greater store of energy. They are also counseled to avoid partners who are familiar with these techniques because female adepts may turn the tables on them and take their energy.*

The Master of Pure Harmony says: "Those who would cultivate their *yang* energy must not allow women to steal glimpses of this art. Not only is this of no benefit to one's *yang* energy, but it may even lead to injury or illness. . . ."

According to Pengsu the Long-Lived, if a man wishes to derive the greatest benefit [from sexual techniques], it is best to find a woman who has no knowledge of them. He also had better choose young maidens for mounting, because then his complexion will become like a maiden's. When it comes to women, one should be vexed only by their not being young. It is best to obtain those between fourteen or fifteen and eighteen or nineteen. In any event, they should never be older than thirty. Even those under thirty are of no benefit if they have given birth. My late master handed down these methods and himself used them to live for three thousand years. If combined with drugs, they will even lead to immortality.

In practicing the union of *yin* and *yang* to increase your energy and cultivate long life, do not limit yourself to just one woman. Much better to get three, nine, or eleven: the more the better! Absorb her secreted essence by mounting the "vast spring" and reverting the essence upward. Your skin will become glossy, your body light, your eyes bright, and your energy so strong that you will be able to overcome all your enemies. Old men will feel like twenty and young men will feel their strength increase a hundredfold.

When having intercourse with women, as soon as you feel yourself aroused, change partners. By changing partners, you can lengthen your life. If you return habitually to the same woman, her *yin* energy will become progressively weaker and this will be of little benefit to you.

Source: Yufang Bizhui, "Sexual Instructions of the Master of Pure Harmony," 636: The *Taoist Experience: An Anthology,* tr. Livia Kohn (Albany: State University of New York Press, 1993), pp. 155–156.

SEXUAL TECHNIQUES FOR WOMEN

The procedure for women is similar to that for men: They are advised to have as many partners as possible, and ideally young partners because the young have a greater store of energy. Women should avoid becoming aroused because orgasm dissipates the energies cultivated by sexual activity. Those who succeed in restraining themselves will acquire the energy dissipated by their partners through seminal emission.

The Master of Pure Harmony says: "It is not only that *yang* can be cultivated, but *yin* too." The Queen Mother of the West, for example, attained the Dao by cultivating her *yin* energy. As soon as she had intercourse with a man he would immediately take sick, while her complexion would be ever more radiant without the use of rouge or powder. She always ate curds and plucked the five-stringed lute in order to harmonize her heart and concentrate her mind. She was quite without any other desire.

The Queen Mother had no husband but was fond of intercourse with young boys. If this is not fit to be taught to the world, how is it that such an elevated personage as the Queen Mother herself practiced it?

When having intercourse with a man, first calm your heart and still your mind. If the man is not yet fully aroused, wait for his energy to arrive and slightly restrain your emotion to attune yourself to him. Do not move or become agitated, lest your *yin* essence become exhausted first. If this happens, you will be left in a deficient state and susceptible to cold wind illnesses....

If a woman is able to master this Dao and has frequent intercourse with men, she can avoid all grain for nine days without getting hungry. Even those who are sick and have sexual relations with ghosts attain this ability to fast. But they become emaciated after a while. So, how much more beneficial must it be to have intercourse with men?

Source: Yufang Bizhui 635: *The Taoist Experience: An Anthology,* tr. Livia Kohn (Albany: State University of New York Press, 1993), p. 156.

THE GREAT MAN

The Great Man (daren) *is an important motif in Daoist literature. Described as a perfected sage, the Great Man is said to wander to the farthest reaches of the cosmos, visiting strange and mysterious realms and acquiring esoteric knowledge, along with substances that promote immortality. The following excerpt is from Ruanji's (210–263) poem "Biography of Master Great Man," which describes the Great Man as a natural ruler with sovereignty over the whole universe.*

> Heaven and Earth dissipate;
> The six harmonies open up.
> The stars and constellations drift along;
> The sun and moon tumble.
> I leap up, but which should I embrace?
> My garments have no seams, yet my clothes are exquisite;
> My belt is unadorned, yet it has its own gracefulness.
> I wander about, back and forth;
> Who could understand my enduring constancy?

Source: Ruan Ji, *Daren Xiansheng Zhuang,* ch. 1; tr. Thomas McConochie.

ODE TO THE VIRTUE OF WINE

The following poem was written by Liu Ling (221–300 ce), one of the "Seven Sages of the Bamboo Grove," a group of poet-philosophers who came together to discuss ultimate reality and engage in "pure conversation" (shingtan). In this poem he appears to refer to his own way of life. He was renowned for his fondness for wine and is said to have traveled throughout the Chinese countryside accompanied by a servant who carried a shovel and a jug of wine. The wine enabled him to maintain a constant state of inebriation (which he believed helped him harmonize with the Dao). The purpose of the shovel was to allow the servant to bury him on the spot when he died.

There goes Master Great Man. He takes Heaven and earth as one morning, and all of time as one moment. He takes the Sun and Moon as his window, and the eight wildernesses as his walkway. He walks without leaving tracks, and he lodges without a bedroom or stove. He takes Heaven as his curtain and earth as his mat. He indulges in whatever pleases him.

He stops and takes out his wine cup and goblet. He goes and takes out his wine flask. His only duty is to wine; how could he know any other?

Here come a respectable prince and an eminent scholar. They listen to my song and then comment on my behavior. They flap their sleeves and rustle their robes. They flash their eyes and chatter their teeth. They blather on about ritual propriety and raise their speartips of right and wrong.

Thereupon, Master Great Man just raises his drinking vessels. He sloshes unfiltered wine from his cup. His beard waves about as he sits with legs spread. He rests his head against yeast, and he reclines on dregs. He is without a care in the world; he is completely happy and at ease.

He goes from being in a drunken stupor to sobering up right away. He listens quietly, but does not hear the sound of thunder. He peers intently, but does not see the shape of Mount Tai. He does not feel cold and heat on his skin. Nor does he feel any covetousness. He leans over and views the ten thousand things floating about haphazardly like duckweed on the Jiang and Han Rivers. The two noblemen by his side seem like wasps and caterpillars to him.

Source: Liu Ling, *Jinshu liezhuan,* #19; tr. Thomas McConochie.

TRANSCENDING THE WORLD

The texts of Laozi and Zhuangzi contain suggestions that sages transcend the world and that its cares no longer burden them. This theme was developed in other Daoist texts that extol the prowess of the "Great Man," who is portrayed as a mighty figure traveling in the remote corners of the world—and the highest reaches of heaven—without obstruction, complete master of all things.

Heat and cold don't harm me; nothing stirs me up.
Sadness and worry have no hold on me; pure energy at rest.
I float on mist, leap into heaven, pass through all with no restraint.
To and fro, subtle and wondrous, the way never slants.
My delights and happinesses are not of this world, how could I ever fight with it?

Source: *Yuan You: Early Chinese Mysticism,* p. 103.

THE MUSIC OF DAO

This excerpt is taken from the Scripture of the Western Ascension (Xishengjing), *a fifth-century text that brings together the "three traditions" of Daoism, Confucianism, and Buddhism in a harmonious religious vision. Most of the text reports oral teachings given by Laozi to Yin Xi, the guardian of the Western Gate and recipient of the* Daodejing. *In this text Laozi reveals that he is really a divinity, the manifestation of Dao, and he further describes its workings so that Yin Xi might merge with it and thus attain immortality. The text is notable for its description of Laozi's ascension into Heaven as an immortal and for its use of the Buddhist concepts of karma, rebirth, and selflessness. It also incorporates Buddhist meditation techniques, integrating them into the Daoist quest for immortality.*

The Dao is nature.
Who practices can attain [it]. Who hears can speak [about it].
Who knows does not speak; who speaks does not know.
Language is formed when sounds are exchanged.
Thus in conversation, words make sense.
When one does not know the Dao, words create confusion.
Therefore I don't hear, don't speak; I don't know why things are.
It can be compared to the knowledge of musical sound.
One becomes conscious of it by plucking a string.
Though the mind may know the appropriate sounds, yet the mouth is unable to formulate them.
Similarly the Dao is deep, subtle, wondrous; who knows it does not speak.
On the other hand, one may be conscious of musical sounds and melodies. One then dampens the sounds to consider them within.
Then when the mind makes the mouth speak, one speaks but does not know.
Laozi said: The Dao is deep and very profound, an abyss of emptiness and non-being.
Though you may hear its doctrine, in your mind you don't grasp its subtlety.
Why is this so? The written word does not exhaust speech, and by relying on scriptures and sticking to texts your learning remains on the same [intellectual] level.
Rather, you must measure it: recollect it within, meditate on it and consider it carefully. . . .
Laozi said: Heaven, earth, people, and all beings originally contain the primordial source of the Dao.
They emerge together from the Grand Immaculate, from the first beginning of emptiness and non-being; they come from the radiance of essence, flickering softly, from supreme mystery, subtle and wondrous.
It can be compared to a dam ten thousand miles in height. It has gushing, gurgling streams beneath. Looking down they seem all turbid and confused; looking closer there are countless sand grains on the bottom.

Obscure in the extreme, utterly undifferentiated, we don't know where they come from: as in a person recently deceased one cannot see the numinous spirit soul:
It has merged with the engulfing power of *yin*, and *yang* can no longer shine forth to make it distinct.
Look at the past and the future as you look at the present.
If you can't even understand that, how will you know about not existing or being alive? . . .
Talented and analytical, you have a certain wisdom, receiving the teaching by word of mouth. But while you claim to have penetrated the innermost part of the Dao, you cannot intuit its true inner essence.
Therefore if you have lost the foundation of life, how could you know the primordial source of the Dao?

Source: *Xishengjing* selections: *Taoist Mystical Philosophy: The Scripture of the Western Ascension*, tr. Livia Kohn (Albany: State University of New York Press, 1991), pp. 235, 240.

Shintō

INTRODUCTION

In ancient Japan there was no term for indigenous religious practices, but when Buddhism was introduced to the country in the sixth century, the term Shintō, or "way of the *kami*," was coined to differentiate Japanese traditions from the foreign faith (which was labeled *butsudō*, or "way of the Buddha"). The *kami* are the indigenous gods of Japan, and Shintō is a general term that refers to religious practices relating to them. Shintō has no founder, no organization based on believers' adherence to particular doctrines, and no beliefs or practices that are required of all. In contemporary Japan, Shintō is most visibly practiced at the many shrines found throughout the country, in popular festivals and pilgrimages, and in the continuing manifestations of reverence for the forces inhabiting the natural world that are celebrated in prayers and offerings to the *kami*.

The Japanese have traditionally believed that their country is the residence of many powerful beings and that these beings directly influence the lives of humans, as well as natural phenomena. *Kami* are commonly associated with natural forces such as wind and storms; with awe-inspiring places such as mountains, waterfalls, and rivers; and with spirits of deceased humans.

Most *kami* have a delineated sphere of influence, and their worship generally centers on a particular shrine or area. Other *kami* have a national significance and are venerated throughout Japan. The most prominent *kami* is the sun goddess, Amaterasu Ōmikami (Great Heavenly Illuminating Goddess), who in ancient myths is said to be the progenitor of the Japanese race. Amaterasu is also closely associated with the ruling house of Japan, which claims descent from her. This claim is a part of the official legitimation for the rule of the emperor, who was traditionally believed to be semidivine. This belief was expressed in the title "Living Kami" (Akitsumi Kami), which was given to the emperor and implied that he was a direct descendant of Amaterasu.

Shintō is not a unified system of beliefs and practices but rather a general term that encompasses many different traditions dating from the earliest periods of Japanese history. Some of the elements and practices of Shintō may be derived from the religious lives of Japanese who lived thousands of years ago in prehistoric times; others have been influenced by the imported

271

traditions of Daoism, Buddhism, and Confucianism, along with various indigenous practices and beliefs.

For the average contemporary Japanese, Shintō is not concerned primarily with doctrines. Rather, practicing Shintō involves performing actions expected of Japanese people who recognize the existence and power of the *kami* and engage in actions traditionally associated with them. In the broadest sense, Shintō includes all the actions—festivals, rituals, prayers, offerings, pilgrimages, and so on—that pertain to the *kami*.

Because *kami* are believed to reside throughout the Japanese archipelago, shrines to local and national *kami* are scattered throughout the islands and are an important focus of Shintō practice. There are between 78,000 and 79,000 Shintō shrines in Japan today, and traditional households generally have an altar to the clan deity *(ujigami)* at which regular offerings are presented.[1]

In the modern period, Shintō can be classified into three broad categories, which although distinguishable are interrelated: Shrine Shintō (Jinja Shintō), Sectarian Shintō (Kyōha Shintō), and Folk Shintō (Minzoku Shintō). The first type includes rituals and other activities performed at Shintō shrines. It centers on the prayers and offerings addressed to the *kami*, which generally are expected to lead to specific concrete results, such as material success, health, academic accomplishments, or protection. It is believed that prayers and offerings make the *kami* positively predisposed toward the people who present them and that the *kami* in return may grant their requests. The most important deity of Shrine Shintō is Amaterasu, whose main shrine is at Ise. The deities worshipped in Shintō shrines are collectively referred to as "the gods of heaven and earth" *(tenshin chigi)*. Rituals and prayers are also offered for the well-being of deceased ancestors and to ensure the peace, stability, and prosperity of the country.

Contemporary Shintō commonly contends that ritual actions must be combined with a pure mind because the *kami* will respond positively only to people whose thoughts are sincere. To gain the blessing and aid of the *kami*, one must have the "heart of truth" *(makoto no kokoro)* or "true heart" *(magokoro)*, which is characterized by reverence for the natural world, concordance between one's thoughts and actions, and, most important, an attitude of truthfulness that is the result of cultivating purity of heart.

Sectarian Shintō includes a number of Shintō groups that have developed into cohesive religious movements. Primarily composed of thirteen sects officially recognized by the government during the Meiji era (1868–1912), Sectarian Shintō

---

[1] Shintō practice is generally not seen as being exclusive, and so it is common for Japanese households to also have a Buddhist altar *(butsudan)*.

groups generally have a historical founder and tend to emphasize group solidarity. In addition, their religious centers are often churches rather than shrines.

Folk Shintō is a general term applied to the practices and beliefs of the mass of Japanese people who visit shrines and engage in activities relating to the *kami* but do not feel a strong affiliation with any particular sect. Such practices emphasize reverence for natural forces, purification, and the idea that by performing certain actions one may gain access to the power of the *kami* in order to influence particular aspects of one's life.

Although many Japanese believe that Shintō is an enduring tradition of indigenous religious practices, contemporary Shintō practice is in fact an amalgamation of numerous influences, including Buddhism, Confucianism, Daoism, and Chinese philosophy. The focus of Shintō practice is the natural world, and Shintō emphasizes the connection of individuals to their environment. In modern times, the development of Shintō has been strongly influenced by revivalist movements that seek to link it with Japan's past. One particularly important movement has been the school of Revival Shintō (Fukko Shintō), which was linked to the National Learning (Kokugaku) movement of the early Edo period (late seventeenth century). This movement was an attempt to purge Shintō of the influence of Buddhism and other foreign traditions and return to a "pure" and "original" form of Shintō. The most important exponent of Revival Shintō was Motoori Norinaga, whose study of Japanese classics such as the *Tale of Genji* convinced him that there is a discernible Japanese character, which is based on awareness of and reverence for the natural environment. Norinaga stressed the polytheistic character of Shintō and contended that mundane affairs are shaped by the will of the *kami*.

During the Meiji period, the nationalistic tendencies of Revival Shintō were highlighted and Shintō became the official state cult. The government stressed the divine origin of Japan and pointed out that no foreign invasion of the nation had ever succeeded. This was attributed to the actions of the *kami*, who protected Japan and worked to ensure its well-being. The government also emphasized the traditional connection between the emperor and Amaterasu Ōmikami, which was believed to confer on the emperor a divine right to rule.

Because these nationalistic notions were a part of the militaristic policies of Japan prior to and during World War II, State Shintō was outlawed during the Allied occupation, and the emperor publicly repudiated his divine status. With the removal of government patronage, Shintō again became the popular religion of the Japanese people, a position that it holds today. Throughout the Japanese archipelago, people worship at the numerous Shintō shrines; participate in Shintō festivals; purchase amulets empowered by *kami* and believed to bring success, protection, or good health; and pay reverence to their clan deities and the spirits of their ancestors. Shintō remains a diffuse tradition that incorporates elements of other systems but is distinctively Japanese.

SHINTŌ SCRIPTURES

Shintō is a practice-oriented tradition that focuses on rituals, prayers, and attitudes associated with worship and veneration of the *kami* and so has no distinct canon and few traditional texts. The earliest literary use of the term Shintō is found in the *Nihonshōki (Chronicles of Japan*, written in 720), which purports to be a record of the early history of Japan and is an important source of information on ancient Japanese religious ideas and practices. The *Nihonshōki* (also referred to as the *Nihongi*) and the *Kojiki (Records of Ancient Matters)* are among the oldest sources available for pre-Buddhist Japanese religious practices and myths and are the oldest known sacred literature of Shintō.

According to the accounts of these texts, before the arrival of humans on the Japanese islands, two *kami* named Izanami and Izanagi stood on the "floating bridge of heaven" and stirred the primordial waters with a jeweled spear. When the water began to coagulate, they gathered up the sediment and let drops fall to form the islands of Japan.

Izanami died after giving birth to Kagutsuchi, the fire god, and Izanami followed her to the netherworld hoping to ask her to return to the land of the living. She replied that she had already eaten the food of the dead and so could not return without special permission. She then instructed him not to follow her when she made the request, but after waiting for a long time he became impatient and went after her. When he found her, however, her flesh was putrefying and decomposed, which revolted him, so he fled the netherworld, returned to the land of the living, and bathed in order to purify himself. When he washed his eyes, the dripping water gave rise to Amaterasu, the sun goddess, and her brother, Tsukiyomi the moon god.

Both the *Kojiki* and the *Nihonshōki* indicate that Amaterasu is the divine ancestor of the emperor, an idea that played an important role in the legitimation of the royal line. In addition, their descriptions of Japan as a special place created and guarded by the *kami* have been influential in shaping Japanese ideas about themselves and their country. The legends of these two works link the origin of the Japanese people with the *kami* and indicate that humans and *kami* are intimately interrelated. Humans need the power of *kami* in order to achieve their goals, and the *kami* on their part require reverence and offerings from humans.

Other important Shintō texts include the *Fudoki (Records of Wind and Earth)*, a collection of myths and legends written in the eighth century; the *Man'yōshū (Collection of Ten Thousand Poems)*, compiled in the late eighth century and containing poems expressing the beliefs and practices of the common people; and the *Sendai Kujihongi (Narrative of Ancient Matters)*, compiled in the ninth century and containing accounts of the practices of the Mononobe clan.

HOLIDAYS

Shōgatsu Matsuri The New Year celebration, which emphasizes renewal and fresh beginnings.

Hina Matsuri A festival of dolls that celebrates the daughters in the family; dolls are often dressed in Heian-era costumes.

Obon The festival of the dead, which is shared with Buddhism. During Obon, people make offerings to the spirits of the deceased, particularly those who have become "hungry ghosts."

Shubun-sai An equinox day on which people visit graves and remember ancestors.

Hatsumōde The first shrine visit of the New Year. Many people go to the better-known shrines for the first visit and commonly exchange the amulets they purchased the year before for new ones. An estimated 80 million Japanese make this visit every year.

TIMELINE

661 BCE	Kami Ninigi-no-mikoto, grandfather of the first emperor, Jimmu Tennō, descends from the High Plain of Heaven
300 BCE–300 CE	Yayoi (Bronze-Iron) period; artifacts include mirrors; beginning of concept of *kami*

(Continued)

TIMELINE *(Continued)*

672	Emperor Temmu (r. 673–686) institutes the practice of rebuilding the Grand Shrine of Ise every twenty years
712	*Kojiki (Records of Ancient Matters)* presented to Empress Gemmei (r. 707–715)
720	Publication of *Nihon-shōki (Chronicles of Japan)*
1561–1619	Fujiwara Seika, influential Shintō theorist; rejects *honji-suijaku* and tries to purge Shintō of Buddhist influences
1615–1691	Waratai Nobuyoshi, priest of Outer Shrine of Ise, rejects Buddhist and Confucian elements in Shintō and works to purify tradition
1730–1801	Motoori Norinaga, most influential figure of Native Studies movement
1868–1912	Meiji period; Shintō linked with imperial cult and used to justify Japanese military expansion
1870	System of national Shintō shrines established; Yasukuni Shrine established to honor those who died during Commander Perry's invasion
1872	State Shintō (Kokka Shintō) proclaimed national ideology
1945	Unconditional surrender by Japan; General Douglas MacArthur assumes command of Allied occupation forces; Shintō Directive issued in December, mandating that Shrine Shintō will no longer receive government support
1985	Prime minister Nakasone Yasuhiro visits Yasukuni Shrine, leading to condemnation of Japan by China and Korea
1991	Japanese Supreme Court rules that official visits to Yasukuni Shrine by the emperor or prime minister violate separation of religion and government
1998	First Cyber-Jinja, Sakura Jinja, goes online, allowing virtual pilgrimages

GLOSSARY

Amaterasu Ōmikami The Sun Goddess, believed to be the divine progenitor of the imperial line.

Folk Shintō (Minzoku Shintō) A term for popular practices connected with the *kami*.

Ise The most prominent shrine of Shintō, dedicated to the Sun Goddess Amaterasu Ōmikami.

Kami The indigenous gods of Japan, often associated with particular places.

Makoto no kokoro "Heart of Truth," an attitude of reverence toward the natural world and pure moral character.

Sectarian Shintō (Kyōha Shintō) Distinctive schools of Shintō thought and practice.

Shintō "Way of the Gods," believed by many traditional Japanese to be the native religious tradition of Japan.

Shrine Shintō (Jinja Shintō) A form of Shintō that centers on ritual activities connected with shrines.

Ujigami Clan deity.

SHINTŌ SCRIPTURES

BIRTH OF THE KAMI OF SUN AND MOON

The following passage describes the birth of Amaterasu Ōmikami, the sun goddess, and her brother Tsukiyomi, the moon god. It also indicates that Izanami and Izanagi produced various other kami *of various temperaments, some of which were good while others were malevolent.*

Izanagi no Mikoto and Izanami no Mikoto consulted together, saying: "We have now produced the Great-Eight-Island Country [Japan], with the mountains, rivers, herbs, and trees. Why should we not produce someone who shall be lord of the universe?" They then together produced the Sun Goddess, who was called O-hiru-me no muchi.[2]

The resplendent luster of this child shone throughout all the six quarters.[3] Therefore the two Deities rejoiced, saying: "We have had many children, but none of them have been equal to this wondrous infant. She ought not to be kept long in this land, but we ought of our own accord to send her at

---

[2] Great-moon-female-of-possessor. In another version of the text she is called Amaterasu O-kami, Heaven-illumine-of-Great-Deity.

[3] North, south, east, west, above, below.

once to Heaven, and entrust to her the affairs of Heaven."
At this time Heaven and Earth were still not far separated,
and therefore they sent her up to Heaven by the ladder of
Heaven.

They next produced the Moon-god. His radiance was next
to that of the Sun in splendor. This god was to be the consort
of the Sun-goddess, and to share in her government. They
therefore sent him also to Heaven.

Next they produced the leech-child, which even at the age
of three years could not stand upright. They therefore placed
it in the rock-camphor wood boat of Heaven, and abandoned
it to the winds.

Their next child was Susa no o no Mikoto. This god had a
fierce temper and was given to cruel acts. Moreover he made
a practice of continually weeping and wailing. So he brought
many of the people of the land to an untimely end. Again he
caused green mountains to become withered. Therefore the
two gods, his parents, addressed Susa no o no Mikoto, saying: "You are exceedingly wicked, and it is not fitting that
you should reign over the world. Certainly you must depart
far away to the Nether-land." So at length they expelled him.

Source: *Nihongi*, ch. 1: W. G. Aston, *Nihongi* (London: George
Allen & Unwin, 1956) I, pp. 18–20; pp. 16–17.

THE BIRTH OF GREAT KAMI

*According to the following account, the first beings to arise
in the world were three* kami. *They were followed by two
more* kami, *and the five together became the progenitors of
all the other* kami. *It then describes a confrontation between
Amaterasu and her brother Susa no o, who has a wicked and
deceitful disposition. When he decided to ascend into Heaven,
she stopped him and demanded to know what his intentions
were. He assured her that he meant no harm, but she did not
believe him. In order to ensure that he would remain true to his
word, he proposed that both should swear and produce children,
which apparently made Susa no o keep his promise.*

At the beginning of heaven and earth, there came into
existence in the Plain of High Heaven the Heavenly Center
Lord Kami, next, the Kami of High Generative Force, and
then the Kami of Divine Generative Force.

Next, when the earth was young, not yet solid, there
developed something like reed-shoots from which the Male
Kami of Excellent Reed Shoots and then Heavenly Eternal
Standing Kami emerged.

The five *kami* mentioned earlier are the heavenly *kami* of special standing. . . .

Then, there came into existence Earth Eternal Standing Kami, Kami of Abundant Clouds Field, male and female Kami of Clay, male and female Kami of Post, male and female Kami of Great Door, Kami of Complete Surface and his spouse, Kami of Awesomeness, Izanagi (Kami-Who-Invites) and his spouse, Izanami (Kami-Who-Is-Invited). . . .

So thereupon His-Swift-Impetuous-Male-Augustness (Susa no o) said: "If that be so, I will take leave of the Heaven-Shining-Great-August Deity (Amaterasu), and depart." [With these words] he forthwith went up to Heaven, whereupon all the mountains and rivers shook, and every land and country quaked. So the Heaven-Shining-Deity, alarmed at the noise, said: "The reason of the ascent hither of His Augustness my elder brother is surely no good intent. It is only that he wishes to wrest my land from me." And she forthwith, unbinding her august hair, twisted it into august bunches; and both into the left and into the right august bunch, as likewise into her august head-dress and likewise on to her left and her right august arm, she twisted an augustly complete [string] of curved jewels eight feet [long] of five hundred jewels; and, slinging on her back a quiver holding a thousand [arrows], and adding a quiver holding five hundred [arrows], she likewise took and slung at her side a mighty and high [sounding] elbow-pad, and brandished and stuck her bow upright so that the top shook; and she stamped her feet into the hard ground up to her opposing thighs, kicking away [the earth] like rotten snow, and stood valiantly like a mighty man, and waiting, asked: "Why do you ascend here?" Then Susa no o replied, saying: "I have no evil intent. It is only that when the Great-August-Deity [our father] spoke, deigning to enquire the cause of my wailing and weeping, I said: 'I wail because I wish to go to my deceased mother's land'; whereupon the Great-August-Deity said: 'You will not dwell in this land,' and deigned to expel me with a divine expulsion. It is therefore, solely with the thought of taking leave of you and departing, that I have ascended here. I have no strange intentions."

Then the Heaven-Shining-Deity said: "If that is so, how shall I know the sincerity of your intentions?" Thereupon Susa no o replied, saying: "Let each of us swear, and produce children." So as they then swore to each other from the opposite banks of the Tranquil River of Heaven, the august names of the Deities that were born from the mist [of their breath] when, having first begged Susa no o to hand her the ten-grasp saber which was girded on him and broken into three fragments, and with the jewels making a jingling sound and having brandished and washed them in the True-Pool-Well of Heaven, and having crunchingly crunched them, the Heaven-Shining-Deity blew them away, were Her Augustness Torrent-Mist-Princess . . . next Her Augustness Lovely-Island-Princess . . . next Her Augustness Princess-of-the-Torrent.

Source: *Kojiki*, ch. 1: *Kojiki, Records of Ancient Matters, ch. 1: The Great Asian Religions: An Anthology* (New York: MacMillan, 1969), pp. 231–232.

THE CREATION OF JAPAN

When the earth was newly formed, the islands of Japan were still below the waters, and Izanami and Izanagi decided to create a special land. They thrust a spear into the waters, and the brine that dripped from it formed the islands of the Japanese archipelago. After this they united, and their union resulted in the birth of more kami.

Izanagi and Izanami stood on the floating bridge of Heaven, and held counsel together, saying: "Is there not a country beneath?" Thereupon they thrust down the jewel-spear of Heaven, and groping about with it found the ocean. The brine which dripped from the point of the spear coagulated and became an island which received the name of Ono-goro-jima.

The two deities then descended and lived on this island. Accordingly they wished to become husband and wife together, and to produce countries. So they made Ono-goro-jima the pillar of the center of the land.

Now the male deity turning by the left, and the female deity by the right, they went round the pillar of the land separately. When they met together on the side, the female deity spoke first and said: "How delightful! I have met with a lovely youth." The male deity was displeased, and said: "I am a man, and by right should have spoken first. How is it that on the contrary you, a woman, should have been the first to speak? This was unlucky. Let us go round again." Upon this the two deities went back, and having met again, this time the male deity spoke first and said: "How delightful! I have met a lovely maiden."

Then he inquired of the female deity, saying: "In your body is anything formed?" She answered, and said: "In my body there is a place which is the source of femininity." The male deity said: "In my body again there is a place which is the source of masculinity. I wish to unite this source-place of my body to the source-place of your body." Then the male and female first became united as husband and wife.

Now when the time of birth arrived, first of all the island of Ahaji was reckoned as the placenta, and their minds took no pleasure in it. Therefore it received the name Ahaji no Shima. Next was produced the island of O-yamato no Toyo-aki-tsu-sha (Rich-harvest Island of Yamato). Next they produced the island of Iyo no futa-na, and next the island of Tsukushi. Next the islands of Oki and Sado were born as twins. . . . Next was born the island of Koshi, then the island of Ō-shima, then the island of Kibi no Ko. Thus first arose the designation of the Great Eight-Island Country.

Source: *Nihongi*, ch. 1: *Nihongi*, pp. 10–17. W. G. Aston, Nihongi (London: George Allen & Unwin, 1956)

IZANAGI VISITS IZANAMI IN THE NETHERWORLD

This passage describes how Izanagi, longing for his deceased love, decided to visit her in the land of the dead and plead with her to return with him. When he saw her body putrefying and covered with maggots, however, he ran away in horror and purified himself by bathing. The drops of water from his eyes and nose produced three kami: *Amaterasu, Tsukiyomi (the moon god), and Susa no o.*

After giving birth to the land, they [Izanami and Izanagi] proceeded to bear *kami* [such as the *kami* of the wind, of the tree, of the mountain, and of the plains]. But Izanami died after giving birth to the *kami* of fire. . . .

Izanagi, hoping to meet again with his spouse, went after her to the land of Hades. When Izanami came out to greet him, Izanagi said, "Oh my beloved, the land which you and I have been making has not yet been completed. Therefore, you must return with me." To which Izanami replied, "I greatly regret that you did not come here sooner, for I have already partaken of the hearth of the land of Hades. But let me discuss with the *kami* of Hades about my desire to return. You must, however, not look at me." As she was gone so long, Izanagi, being impatient, entered the hall to look for her and found maggots squirming around the body of Izanami.

Izanagi, seeing this, was afraid and ran away, saying, "Since I have been to an extremely horrible and unclean land, I must purify myself." Thus, arriving at [a river], he purified and exorcised himself. When he washed his left eye, there came into existence the Sun Goddess, or Heavenly Illuminating Great Kami [Amaterasu], and when he washed his right eye, there emerged the Moon Kami [Tsukiyomi].

Finally, as he washed his nose there came into existence Valiant Male Kami [Susa no o].

Source: *Kojiki,* chs. 7, 9, 10, 11: *The Great Asian Religions, An Anthology* (New York: MacMillan, 1969) pp. 232–233.

AMATERASU HIDES IN A CAVE

The following passage recounts a well-known Shintō myth in which Amaterasu decides to hide herself in a cave as a result of the misdeeds of Susa no o. When she enters the cave, the world is plunged into darkness, so the other kami work together to draw her out again. When she leaves the cave, a sacred rope is placed across the entrance to ensure that she will never again conceal her radiance from the world.

[At one time] the Sun Goddess [shocked by the misdeeds of her brother, Valiant Male Kami], opened the heavenly rock-cave door and concealed herself inside. Then the Plain of High Heaven became completely dark, and all manner of calamities arose.

Then the 800 myriads of *kami* gathered in a divine assembly, and summoned Kami of the Little Roof of Heaven and Kami of Grand Bead to perform a divination. They hung long strings of myriad curved beads on the upper branches of a sacred tree, and hung a large-dimensioned mirror on its middle branches. They also suspended in the lower branches white and blue cloth. These objects were held by Kami of Grand Bead as solemn offerings, while Kami of the Little Roof in Heaven intoned liturgical prayers *(norito)*. Meanwhile, Kami of Heavenly Strength hid himself behind the entrance of the rock-cave, and Kami of Heavenly Headgear bound her sleeves with a cord of vine, and stamped on an overturned bucket which was placed before the rock-cave. Then she became *kami*-possessed, exposed her breasts and genitals. Thereupon, the 800 myriads of *kami* laughed so hard that the Plain of High Heaven shook with their laughter.

The Sun Goddess, intrigued by all this, opened the rock-cave door slightly, wondering why it was that the 800 myriads of *kami* were laughing. Then Kami of Heavenly Headgear said, "There is a *kami* nobler than you, and that is why we are happy and dancing." While she was speaking thus, Kami of the Little Roof and Kami of Grand Bead showed the mirror to the Sun Goddess. Thereupon, the Sun Goddess, thinking this ever more strange, gradually came out of the cave, and the hidden Kami of Grand Bead took her hand and pulled her out. Then as the Sun Goddess reappeared, the Plain of High Heaven was naturally illuminated.

Source: *Kojiki,* chs. 17: *The Great Asian Religions, An Anthology* (New York: MacMillan, 1969) pp. 232–233.

THE SHRINE AT ISE

The Grand Shrine at Ise, dedicated to Amaterasu, is the most important Shintō shrine in Japan today. The following passage describes the events surrounding its inauguration and refers to the link between the emperor and Amaterasu.

Twenty-fifth year, Spring, and month, eighth day. The Emperor commanded the four officers, Takenu Kaha-wake, ancestor of the Abe no Omi; Hiko-kuni-fuku, ancestor of the Imperial Chieftains; Ō-kashima, ancestor of the Nakatome Deity Chieftains; and Tochine, ancestor of the Mononobe Deity chieftains . . . saying: "The sagacity of Our predecessor on the throne, the Emperor Mimaki-iri-hiko-inie, was displayed in wisdom; he was reverential, intelligent, and capable. He was profoundly unassuming, and his disposition was to cherish self-abnegation. He adjusted the machinery of government, and did solemn worship to the Gods of Heaven and Earth. He practiced self-restraint and was watchful of his personal conduct. Every day he was heedful for that day. Thus the welfare of the people was sufficient, and the Empire was at peace. And now, under Our reign, will there be any remissness in the worship of the Gods of Heaven and Earth?"

3rd month, 10th day. The Great Goddess Amaterasu was taken from [the princess] Toyo-suki-iri-hime, and entrusted to [the princess] Yamato-hime no Mikoto. Now Yamato-hime sought for a place where she might enshrine the Great Goddess. So she proceeded to Sasahata in Uda. Then turning back from there, she entered the land of Omi, and went round eastwards to Mino, and so she arrived in the province of Ise.

Now the Great Goddess Amaterasu instructed Yamato-hime, saying: "The province of Ise, of the divine wind, is the land in which the waves from the eternal world reside, the successive waves. It is a secluded and pleasant land. In this land I wish to reside." In compliance, therefore, with the instruction of the Great Goddess, a shrine was erected to her in the province of Ise. Accordingly an Abstinence Palace was built at Kawakami in Isuzu.[4] This was called the palace

---

[4] An unmarried princess of the imperial house was appointed to be caretaker of the shrine, which was referred to as the Abstinence Palace.

of Ise. It was there that the Great Goddess Amaterasu first descended from Heaven.

Source: *Nihongi,* ch. 5: *Nihongi,* p. 175. G. Aston, Nihongi (London: George Allen & Unwin, 1956)

WHY JAPAN IS SPECIAL

According to ancient legends, Japan was created by the kami, *who continue to take an active interest in the Japanese islands and the people who inhabit them. In the opening passage of* Chronicle of the Lineage of Divine Kings, *Kitabatake Chikafusa presents a vision of Japanese exceptionalism based on the connection between the gods and the country's rulers.*

Great Japan is the divine land. The heavenly ancestor created it, and the Sun Goddess designated her descendants as its eternal rulers. This is only the case in our land, and no other countries are like this. This is why our country is referred to as the divine land.

Source: *Jinnō Shōtōki* by Kitabatake Chikafusa, p. 1; tr. JP.

PROTECTING THE STABILITY OF THE COUNTRY

The following passage reflects an idea that is common in East Asia—that natural calamities reflect on the personality and moral character of the ruler and serve as a sign of the displeasure of Heaven. It reports that when the ancient emperor Sujin experienced difficulties he asked the kami *to explain the cause, and he was informed that he had failed properly to venerate the Kami Omononushi. The problems the emperor was experiencing were a manifestation of the* kami's *displeasure, and he was told that they would end when he provided the appropriate offerings.*

During the reign of the tenth legendary emperor Sujin, there were many people who wandered away from their homes, and there were also some rebellions. The situation was such that the imperial virtue alone could not control the nation. Therefore, the emperor was penitent from morning till night, asking for divine punishment of the *kami* of heaven and earth upon himself. Prior to that time the two *kami*, the Sun Goddess and the Kami of Yamato, were worshipped together within the imperial palace. The emperor, however, was afraid of their potencies and did not feel at ease living with them. Therefore, he entrusted Princess Toyosukiri to worship the Sun Goddess at the village of Kasanui in Yamato, where a sacred shrine was established. Also he commissioned Princess Nunakiri to worship the Kami of Yamato.

[Then] the emperor stated, "I did not realize that numerous calamities would take place during our reign. It may be that the lack of good rule might have incurred the wrath of the *kami* of heaven and earth. It might be well to inquire the cause of the calamities by means of divination." The emperor therefore assembled the eighty myriads of *kami* and inquired about this matter by means of divination. At that time the *kami* spoke through the *kami*-possession of Princess Yamatotohimomoso, "Why is the emperor worried over the disorder of the nation? Doesn't he know that the order of the nation would be restored if he properly venerated me?" The emperor asked which *kami* was thus giving such an instruction, and the answer was: "I am the *kami* who resides within the province of Yamato, and my name is Omononushi-no-kami." Following the divine instruction, the emperor worshipped the *kami*, but the expected result did not follow. Thus the emperor cleansed himself and fasted as well as purifying the palace, and addressed himself to the *kami* in prayer, asking, "Is not our worship sufficient? Why is our worship not accepted? May we be further instructed in a dream as to the fulfillment of your divine favor toward us."

That night a noble man who called himself Omononushi-no-kami appeared and spoke to the emperor in his dream, "The emperor has no more cause to worry over the unsettled state of the nation. It is my divine wish to be worshipped by my child, Otataneko, and then the nation will be pacified immediately." Upon learning the meaning of the dream, the emperor was greatly delighted and issued a proclamation throughout the country to look for Otataneko, who was subsequently found in the district of Chinu and was presented to the court. Whereupon the emperor asked Otataneko as to whose child he was, and the answer was: "My father's name is the Great Kami Omononushi. My mother's name is Princess Ikutamayori." The emperor then said, "Now prosperity will come to us." Thus, Otataneko was made the chief priest in charge of the worship of the Great Kami Omononushi. After that the emperor consulted divination as to the desirability of worshipping other *kami*, and found it desirable to do so. Accordingly he paid homage to the eighty myriads of *kami*. Thereupon the pestilence ceased and peace was restored in the nation, and good crops of the five kinds of grain made the peasantry prosperous.

Source: *Nihongi*, ch. 5, 6th and 7th years: *Nihongi*, pp. 239–240. G. Aston, Nihongi (London: George Allen & Unwin, 1956)

PRINCE SHŌTOKU'S PROCLAMATION ON VENERATION OF KAMI

Prince Shōtoku is a pivotal figure in Japanese history. He embraced Buddhism and propagated it throughout the country. But as the following passage indicates, he continued the ancient practices of venerating the indigenous kami.

[In 607 during the reign of Empress Suiko, r. 592–628] the following edict was issued [by the Prince Regent Shōtoku, 573–621]: "We are told that our imperial ancestors, in governing the nation, bent humbly under heaven and walked softly on earth. They venerated the *kami* of heaven and earth, and established shrines on the mountains and by the rivers, whereby they were in constant touch with the power of nature. Hence the winter (*yin*, negative cosmic force) and summer (*yang*, positive cosmic force) elements were kept in harmony, and their creative powers blended together. And now during our reign, it would be unthinkable to neglect the veneration of the *kami* of heaven and earth. May all the ministers from the bottom of their hearts pay homage to the *kami* of heaven and earth."

Source: *Nihongi,* ch. 12: *Nihongi,* p. 241. G. Aston, *Nihongi* (London: George Allen & Unwin, 1956)

FESTIVAL OF THE GATES

This is a ritual prayer (norito) *recited to ask the* kami *to protect the imperial palace. It requests that they guard against evil spirits and safeguard the gates.*

We do most humbly invoke your hallowed names: Kushi-iha-mato, Toyo-iha-mato. For you dwell in all the inner and outer august gates of the four quarters, defending them like massive sacred rocks. For if from the four sides and the four quarters the hateful and unruly god Ame-no-maga-tsu-hi should appear, you are not enchanted by his wicked words, nor deceived into consenting to them. For if this evil should come from above you defend from above, and if it should come from below you defend from below, lying in wait to drive off and protect, and to exorcize with words. For you open the gates in the morning, and close the gates in the evening, and inquire and know the names of all who come in and of all who go out. For if there be any error or misdeed, you rectify it to the eye and to the ear as do the deities Kamu-naho-bi and Oho-naho-bi, and cause those in the service of the divine descendant to serve him in tranquility and peace.

Thus do we most humbly praise your hallowed names, Toyo-iha-mato, Kushi-iha-mato. Thus humbly we speak.

Source: *Mikado Matsuri (Festival for the Imperial Palace Gates)*, tr. Meredith McKinney.

PRAYER TO AMATERASU DURING THE FESTIVAL OF THE SIXTH MONTH

This is a prayer spoken by the head priest of the Grand Shrine of Ise during a regular festival performed every six months. It asks Amaterasu to ensure that the emperor has a long life, to protect the country, and to promote the prosperity of the people.

> This prayer I make
> by the Emperor's solemn command.
> Make his life long,
> and may his reign prosper in abundance,
> unshakeable and eternal as the mighty sacred rock.
> Look with favor also upon the princes,
> protect the numerous officials,
> keep their lives long and tranquil,
> and likewise the common people of the empire's four quarters.
> I offer herewith the tribute threads that the Kamube people[5] by tradition present,
> from the three counties, the many lands and their many places.
> I likewise place in offering, piled high and long as lofty mountains,
> the abundant First Fruits and Wine prepared in ritual purity.
> Thus the great Nakatomi,[6] who dwells concealed behind the sacred *tama-gushi*,[7]
> on this seventeenth day of the sixth month of the year,
> most humbly praises you, as the morning sun comes rising up in splendor and might.

Source: *Norito*; tr. Meredith McKinney.

PRAYER FOR MOVING THE SHRINE OF ISE

Every twenty years, the grand shrine of Ise is rebuilt. There are two sites on which the shrines are constructed, and builders alternate between them. When the time comes to construct a new shrine, the following prayer is spoken to the goddess to inform her that the time has come for her to move again.

---

[5] Kanube are peasants who farm plots of land, the profits of which support shrines.

[6] Nakatomi is the name of a family that claims descent from the deity Ame-no-ko-yane-no-mikoto. The Great Nakatomi is presumably the family member who presided at official ceremonies.

[7] This is a ritual implement made from the branch of a sacred tree to which strips of cloth are attached.

Humbly I speak these words in the presence of the Great Sovereign
Deity
by the Sovereign Grandchild's[8] solemn command.
From ancient custom, this great shrine
is built afresh once every twenty years.
The various items of clothing of the fifty-four ages are thus set forth,
as also are the sacred treasures of the twenty-one types,
and exorcism, purification, and cleansing rituals are performed
herewith.

Source: *Norito*; tr. Meredith McKinney.

MOUNT FUJI

Mount Fuji is widely viewed in Japan as a particularly sacred place and as the abode of powerful kami. *The following poem, contained in the* Man'yōshū *collection, describes the grandeur of the mountain and the power of its* kami.

Between the provinces of Kai and Suruga
Stands the lofty peak of Fuji.
Heavenly clouds would not dare cross it;
Even birds dare not fly above it.
The fire of volcano is extinguished by snow,
And yet snow is consumed by fire.
It is hard to describe;
It is impossible to name it.
One only senses the presence of a mysterious *kami*. . . .
In the land of Yamato,
The land of the rising sun,
The lofty Mount Fuji is its treasure and its tutelary *kami*. . . .
One is never tired of gazing at its peak in the province of Suraga.

Source: *Man'yōshū, The Great Asian Religions, An Anthology* (New York: MacMillan, 1969) p. 239.

LIFE IS TRANSITORY

A common theme in Shintō literature is the notion that things in the natural world are transitory. The following poem describes how the changes of the seasons are similar to the changes experienced by human beings.

It has been told from the beginning of the world
That life on earth is transitory. . . .
Indeed we see even in the sky the moon waxes and wanes. . . .
In the spring flowers decorate mountain-trees,

---

[8] This refers to the emperor, who is sometimes called "Sovereign Grandchild" because he is descended from *kami*.

But in the autumn with dew and frost
Leaves turn colors and fall on the ground. . . .
So it is with human life:
Rosy cheek and black hair turn their color;
The morning smile disappears in the evening
Like the wind which blows away.
Changes continue in life like the water passing away,
And my tears do not stop over the uncertainty of life.

Source: *Man'yōshū, The Great Asian Religions, An Anthology*
(New York: MacMillan, 1969) p. 239.

Zoroastrianism

INTRODUCTION

With approximately 150,000 followers today, Zoroastrianism is a shadow of its former self as a dominant religion of the Near East. Zoroastrianism developed in what is now Iran and southern Russia around 1200 BCE., and at its height was the state religion of Persia's empires from the third century CE until the expansion of Islam in the seventh century. Although the face of Zoroastrianism changed over its long history, several doctrines have remained consistent: (1) Ahura Mazda is worshiped as the one supreme God; (2) Zarathushtra (or "Zoroaster" in Greek) is Ahura Mazda's prophet who delivers his unique revelation; (3) the universe is a battleground between opposing good and evil forces, and this cosmological dualism accounts for the presence of good and evil everywhere; Angra Mainyu, the primary evil spirit that embodies evil, is to be opposed; (4) Ahura Mazda created several divine beings, or Beneficent Immortals, who are to be venerated; (5) humans will be judged in the afterlife for their good or evil deeds.

BACKGROUND AND LIFE OF ZARATHUSHTRA

Between 2000 and 1500 BCE, there occurred a mass migration of Aryan people, perhaps from Eastern Europe, to the region of what is now Iran. Over the next few centuries they successfully assimilated with the native people, as indicated by the name "Iran," which means home or land of the Aryans. The Aryan newcomers brought with them an ancient polytheistic religion that involved the worship of daevas, or divine beings. After some centuries, a group of these Aryans migrated farther, to northern India, forming the basis of the early Hindu religion. Aryan culture had three principal social classes (priests, warriors, and cattle breeders), and different deities were associated with each. The gods of the priestly class included Mithra, Anahita, and Varuna (the last perhaps identified as Ahura Mazda). The priestly class also had religious rituals involving sacrificing oxen, imbibing the intoxicating juice of the haoma plant (*soma* in Sanskrit), and fire rituals perhaps derived from Agni, the fire god of early India's religion.

Zarathushtra emerged as a religious reformer, reacting against both the polytheism and the rituals of the Aryan religion. Little historical information is available about the life of Zarathushtra, and scholars have variously placed his appearance between 1500 and 500 BCE. The most plausible tradition places him around 1200 BCE. in the Azerbaijan province of Northwest Iran; some linguistic and archaeological evidence, however, suggests that he was from an oasis tribal setting in Eastern Iran, near what is now the Afghanistan border.

According to later Zoroastrian tradition, Zarathushtra began his mission at age 30 after having a series of visions in which he was escorted to Ahura Mazda's presence, where he received his divine message. The first ten years of his mission were especially unsuccessful, and his only convert was his cousin. His teaching antagonized a group of priests who conspired against him and threw him into prison. At age 42, when he was still in prison, his fortune changed with the conversion of King Vishtaspa (Hystaspes in Greek), an as yet unidentified monarch. Vishtaspa had an ill horse, and Zarathushtra healed it, leg by leg. During the process, the king was required to make certain concessions. The king was impressed, and the whole court accepted Zarathushtra's teachings.

Although Zarathushtra's life events remain hazy, there is greater knowledge about the content of his teachings and his role as a religious reformer. His foremost reform was advocating the supremacy of Ahura Mazda. The name *Ahura Mazda* means "Wise Lord," and Zarathushtra described him as holy, eternal, just, all knowing, and creator of all. Ahura Mazda is also said to be the source of all goodness, including success, glory, honor, physical health, and immortality. Zarathushtra condemned the daevas of the Indo-Iranian pantheon as subordinate devils, and their priests as devil followers. He also attacked many of the traditional Indo-Iranian religious rituals, especially the wasteful slaughter of great numbers of oxen, bulls, and cows in ritual sacrifices. Aspects of the haoma ritual were condemned, but Zarathushtra continued this tradition with some modifications. The traditional fire rituals also were modified so as to reflect worship of Ahura Mazda, who is symbolized by undying fire.

Zarathushtra emphasized the religious conflict between good and evil. This ethical emphasis is best described as dualistic insofar as all key players—both human and divine—choose either good or evil. Ahura Mazda demands ethical and ritual purity and judges the souls of people after death. The principal evil force, called the Lie *(druj)*, wages war against Ahura Mazda. To assist in the war against evil, Ahura Mazda created Beneficent Immortals *(Amesha Spentas)*. Later Zoroastrian tradition sees them as guardians over areas of Creation. They are Asha Vahishta (Best Order or Best Truth), associated with fire; Vohu Manah (Good Thought), associated with the ox; Khshathra Vairya (Desirable Dominion), associated with metals; Spenta Armaiti (Beneficent Devotion), associated with the earth; Haurvatat (Wholeness), associated with water; and Ameretat (Immortality), associated with plants. The theological status of the Beneficent Immortals is not entirely clear, and it is not certain whether they are distinct entities or merely different aspects of Ahura Mazda. Some scholars believe that their names and functions are derived from traditional Indo-Iranian deities, particularly the deities of the lower classes.

According to Zarathushtra, the cosmic ethical drama began when two twin spirits chose between good and evil. The spirit Spenta Mainyu (Beneficent Spirit) allied himself with good, and Angra Mainyu (Destructive Spirit) chose evil. As Zoroastrianism developed over the centuries, Angra Mainyu became the embodiment of all evil, and even the rival of Ahura Mazda. Although his role is more limited in Zarathushtra's teachings, Zoroastrian tradition consistently describes Angra Mainyu as working for evil in the service of the Lie and as the source of misfortune, disaster, war, sickness, and death. To aid him in the assault on good, Angra Mainyu created several devils *(daevas)* that correspond with the Beneficent Immortals. The demon opposing Vohu Manah is Ako Mano (Bad Mind); against Asha Vahishta is Spozgar (Disorder); against Khshathra Vairya is Bushyasp (Sloth); against Spenta Armaiti is Asto Vidhatu (Death, literally, Bone Dissolver); against Haurvatat is Az (Greed); and against Ameretat is Tishn (Thirst). Angra Mainyu also counter-created demons/fiends that correspond to the other spiritual beings *(Yazads)*.

THE RISE AND DECLINE OF ZOROASTRIANISM

Zarathushtra's new religion continued to spread after his death. During the Achaemenian Persian dynasty (550–330 BCE), the first documented period of Zoroastrian influence, the religion was associated with the Magi. Although the identity and role of the Magi is unclear, they were experts in cultic ritual and claimed to be descendants of Zarathushtra's first converts. They may originally have been an early hereditary class of priests who allied themselves with Zarathushtra's teachings. When Mesopotamia was conquered by Alexander the Great in 331 BCE, the impact of Greek culture caused a decline of Zoroastrianism. It was revived during the Parthian period (141 BCE–224 CE), although there is little reliable information to indicate its character at this time.

Zoroastrianism peaked in influence during the Sasanian period (227–651 CE) when it became the state religion of Persia. Zoroastrian expansion throughout the empire was mostly the result of conversion, although at times adherents to rival forms of worship were punished. Sasanid theologians developed Zoroastrianism's great cosmological myths, dividing cosmic history into four 3,000-year periods. During the final period, Zarathushtra and his three descendant prophets appeared at thousand-year intervals to wage war on Angra Mainyu. The world currently awaits the last prophet, Saoshyant, who will bring about final judgment and usher in a new world. The dead will then be resurrected, Ahura Mazda will judge all people according to their conduct as recorded in the book of deeds, and Angra Mainyu will be destroyed. Hell will also be dismantled, and the wicked (with few exceptions), having been purified, will be released.

Zoroastrianism gradually declined after 633 when the Muslims entered Persia and forced most of the population to convert to Islam. Zoroastrianism was still tolerated for about three hundred more years, but persecution in the tenth century prompted many to leave Iran for India. Known as the Parsis, the immigrating Zoroastrians settled near Bombay and today number around 70,000. They are generally financially well off, and many help support the remaining Zoroastrians in Iran, who today number around 30,000. An additional 50,000 Zoroastrians live in other parts of the world.

Parallels between Zoroastrian beliefs and those of Judaism, Christianity, and Islam are striking, for example, the messianic figure of Saoshyant, the Armageddon-like final battle, bodily resurrection, final judgment, and heaven and hell. Many historians of religion believe that Zoroastrianism is the source of these beliefs. However, the complex web of Zoroastrian doctrines themselves developed over time, and precisely when certain doctrines first appeared is unclear.

ZOROASTRIAN SCRIPTURES

The foundational and oldest Zoroastrian scripture is the *Avesta*, a compilation of liturgical texts composed over a 1,000-year period. The original *Avesta* probably comprised 22 books and included historical, medical, and legal information along with liturgical texts. Only a small part of the original *Avesta* has survived. Zoroastrian legend recounts that two official copies were destroyed by Alexander during his campaign in the Persian capital. Priests gathered the remaining orally transmitted fragments, which were regularly recited in liturgies. The *Avesta* was kept alive through recitation until about 400 CE, when an official edition was ordered by the Sasanid rulers. It is written in an archaic language called Avestan, which is related to Sanskrit and uses a modified Pahlavi alphabet. The *Avesta* is the only surviving example of a text in this language.

In its current form, the *Avesta* is about 1,000 pages and is written in different dialects from different periods of time. The most important division is the *Yasna*, a collection of prayers and liturgical formulas in 72 chapters. A 50-page section in the middle of the *Yasna*, called the *Gathas* (Chapters 28–34, 43–54), contains hymns in an older dialect and is believed to have been written by Zarathushtra himself. The other key divisions of the *Avesta* are these:

- *Visparat* (all the leaders): liturgical extension of the Yasna (22 chapters)
- *Vendidad* (law against demons): instructions for ritual purification and moral practice to ward off evil powers, also containing myths and medical texts (22 chapters)
- *Khorde Avesta (Smaller Avesta)*: book of daily prayer used by the laity. Among other texts, it includes
    - *Yashts* (songs of praise): long hymns to various divine beings, some paralleling those found in the Hindu Vedas, plus epic narratives about kings and heroes
    - *Niyayeshs*: litanies to the Sun, Mithra, the Moon, the Waters, and Fire
    - *Gahs*: dedications for each period of the day
    - *Afrinagans*: blessings

The *Avesta* also includes several shorter fragments of lost books.

In addition to the *Avesta*, Zoroastrians have numerous scriptures from the Sasanian period that are written in the middle-Persian dialect called Pahlavi. Thus, the writings are typically called *Pahlavi texts*. Many are exegetical commentaries (called *Zand*) that translate, summarize, and explain the *Avesta*. The Pahlavi texts are more numerous than those of the *Avesta*. The primary ones are these:

- *Bundahishn (Original Creation)*: 36 chapters on cosmogony, mythology, and cosmic history
- *Denkard (Acts of the Religion)*: a collection of doctrines, customs, traditions, history, and literature, originally written in nine books, the first two of which are now lost
- *Datastani Denik*: religious opinions of the high priest Manushkihar in response to 92 questions
- *Zatsparam*: a collection by the high priest Zadsparam, younger brother of Manushkihar, which discusses cosmology and the life of Zarathushtra

In addition to the Pahlavi texts, several later Zoroastrian texts are written in a more modern Persian language. The most important of these is the *Sad Dar (One Hundred Doors)*, the first Zoroastrian text known to the West, having been translated into Latin in 1700.

HOLIDAYS

Proper Season (Gahambars) Six five-day festivals held throughout the year commemorating events of the six days of creation (sky, waters, earth, plants, cattle, and humans).

Feast of All Souls (Farvardigan; ten days before New Year's Day) Commemorates Zoroastrians of the past.

New Year's Day (No Ruz; March 21) Begins on the day of the spring equinox.

Zarathushtra's Birthday (Khordad Sal; March 26)

Zarathushtra's Death Day (Zartusht-No-Diso; December 26)

TIMELINE

1200 BCE	Birth of Zarathushtra
550–330 BCE	Zoroastrianism influence during Achaemenian Persian dynasty
330–141 BCE	Decline of Zoroastrianism during Hellenistic Seleucid rule
141 BCE–224 CE	Reemergence of Zoroastrianism during Parthian Arcasids; *Vendidad* compiled
227–651 CE	Zoroastrianism peaks in influence during Sasanian dynasty; *Avesta* compiled
633	Defeat of Sasanian Empire by Muslims, Zoroastrianism declines
950	Arrival of the Iranian Zoroastrians in India

GLOSSARY

Ahura Mazda (*Ohrmazd in Pahlavi*) Literally, "Wise Lord"; supreme God and originator of all good.

Amesha Spentas, or Beneficent Immortals Servant angels who assist Ahura Mazda in the battle against evil; alternatively, they are sometimes seen as aspects of Ahura Mazda.

Angra Mainyu *(ahriman in pahlavi)* Literally, "Destructive Spirit" (antonym of "Beneficent Spirit"); the evil rival of Ahura Mazda in later Pahlavi texts.

Asha Literally, "The Truth"; the good moral principle in opposition to the *druj* (the lie).

Avesta Literally, "Basic Text"; the oldest and most sacred collection of Zoroastrian scriptures, written in the Avestan language.

Chinvat Bridge Literally, "Separator Bridge"; bridge by which people enter heaven; it spans the abyss of hell below.

Daevas Literally, "Heavenly Beings" in early Aryan religion; evil devils, demons in Zoroastrianism.

Druj Literally, "The Lie"; evil spirit or spirits that wage war against Ahura Mazda and are opposed to Truth *(asha)*.

Magi Zoroastrian priests, or, perhaps, cult leaders who claimed to be descendants of Zarathushtra's first converts.

Pahlavi An early form of the Persian language, in which later Zoroastrian scriptures were written.

Saoshyant Literally, "Savior"; final descendant of Zarathushtra and the spiritual leader who will usher in the final judgment.

Spenta Mainyu Literally, "Beneficent Spirit"; the good son of Ahura Mazda in the *Avesta,* or, perhaps, a synonym for Ahura Mazda.

Zurvan Literally, "Time"; supreme God of the Zurvan sect, who is the father of Ahura Mazda and Angra Mainyu.

THE AVESTA

ZOROASTRIAN CREED

Most of the surviving texts of the Avesta *were used ceremonially. The following creed from Yasna Chapter 12 is among the oldest and most central Zoroastrian statements of faith, perhaps initially required of converts. In both thought and deed, the believer vows to reject all evil as associated with daevas and the Lie* (druj)*, and instead adhere to the good of Ahura Mazda and the Beneficent Immortals* (Amesha Spentas)*.*

1. I curse the Daevas. I declare myself a Mazda-worshipper, a supporter of Zarathushtra, hostile to the Daevas, fond of Ahura's teaching, a praiser of the Amesha Spentas, a worshipper of the Amesha Spentas. I ascribe all good to Ahura Mazda, "and all the best," the Asha-owning one, splendid, xwarena-owning, whose is the cow, whose is Asha, whose is the light, "may whose blissful areas be filled with light."

2. I choose the good Spenta Armaiti for myself; let her be mine. I renounce the theft and robbery of the cow,

and the damaging and plundering of the Mazdayasnian settlements.

3. I want freedom of movement and freedom of dwelling for those with homesteads, to those who dwell upon this earth with their cattle. With reverence for Asha, and (offerings) offered up, I vow this: I shall nevermore damage or plunder the Mazdayasnian settlements, even if I have to risk life and limb.

4. I reject the authority of the Daevas, the wicked, no-good, lawless, evil-knowing, the most druj-like of beings, the foulest of beings, the most damaging of beings. I reject the Daevas and their comrades, I reject the demons (yatu) and their comrades; I reject any who harm beings. I reject them with my thoughts, words, and deeds. I reject them publicly. Even as I reject the head (authorities), so too do I reject the hostile followers of the druj.

5. As Ahura Mazda taught Zarathushtra at all discussions, at all meetings, at which Mazda and Zarathushtra conversed;

6. As Ahura Mazda taught Zarathushtra at all discussions, at all meetings, at which Mazda and Zarathushtra conversed—even as Zarathushtra rejected the authority of the Daevas, so I also reject, as Mazda-worshipper and supporter of Zarathushtra, the authority of the Daevas, even as he, the Asha-owning Zarathushtra, has rejected them.

7. As the belief of the waters, the belief of the plants, the belief of the well-made (Original) Cow; as the belief of Ahura Mazda who created the cow and the Asha-owning Man; as the belief of Zarathushtra, the belief of Kavi Vishtaspa, the belief of both Frashaostra and Jamaspa; as the belief of each of the Saoshyants (saviors)—fulfilling destiny and Asha-owning—so I am a Mazda-worshipper of this belief and teaching.

8. I profess myself a Mazda-worshipper, a Zoroastrian, having vowed it and professed it. I pledge myself to the well-thought thought, I pledge myself to the well-spoken word, I pledge myself to the well-done action.

9. I pledge myself to the Mazdayasnian religion, which causes the attack to be put off and weapons put down; which upholds khvaetvadatha (kin-marriage), which possesses Asha; which of all religions that exist or shall be, is the greatest, the best, and the most beautiful: Ahuric, Zoroastrian. I ascribe all good to Ahura Mazda. This is the creed of the Mazdayasnian religion.

Source: *Yasna,* ch. 12, tr. Joseph H. Peterson. Reprinted by permission.

DUALISM

The dualistic battle between good and evil forces is the most characteristic feature of Zoroastrianism during all phases of its history. The following is from a section of the Yasna known as the Gathas—texts believed to have been written by Zarathushtra. In this Gatha, Zarathushtra describes the foundational moral conflict between Ahura Mazda and the Lie (druj). The conflict is carried on further by Ahura Mazda's twin sons, identified in other passages as the good Spenta Mainyu (Beneficent Spirit) and the evil Angra Mainyu (Destructive Spirit). This passage presents significant interpretive problems. In one interpretation, Spenta Mainyu is regarded as separate from Ahura Mazda; thus, both of these battling spirits—including Angra Mainyu—were created by Ahura Mazda. A second interpretation is that the twin sons are merely ethical concepts, not spiritual beings. Thus, Zarathushtra is retelling a traditional myth that was familiar to his audience and then reinterpreting it in the light of his own revelations. "Spenta Mainyu," then, is a synonym for Ahura Mazda. In either interpretation, the cosmic dualism established between Spenta Mainyu and Angra Mainyu is paralleled by an ethical dualism between druj *(the lie, evil) and* asha *(truth, righteousness).*

There are two primal spirits, twins renowned to be in conflict. In thought, word and action, they are the better and the bad. Between these two the wise ones chose correctly, but the foolish did not. When these two spirits came together in the beginning, they established Life and Not-Life. In the end, the Worst Existence [i.e., hell] will be for the followers of the Lie, while the Good Thought [i.e., heaven] will be for the followers of Truth. Of these two spirits, followers of the Lie chose to do the worst things, whereas the most beneficent Spirit chose Truth, who clothes himself with the massive heavens as a garment. So too with those who willingly please Ahura Mazda through proper actions. Between these two, the daevas also chose wrongly, for delusion infatuation came over them as they planned together, and they chose the Worst Thought. They rushed together towards Violence, so that they might corrupt humanity.

To mankind came Dominion, Good Thought, and Truth. Piety will resurrect our bodies and make us indestructible, so that, by Ahura Mazda's retribution through molten metal [on the last day], we may become superior over those others. When the time comes for the evil ones to be punished, then, at Ahura Mazda's command, Good Thought will establish [as a reward] the Dominion in the Consummation for the people who deliver [followers of] the Lie into the hands of Truth. Accordingly, we should strive to be the ones that regenerate the world. May you—Ahura Mazda, the other Ahuras, and also Truth—gather together the Assembly so that thoughts may meet where Wisdom is at home. Then, the blow of destruction will fall on [followers of] the Lie. But those who that get the good name will have the promised reward in the beautiful home of Good Thought, Ahura Mazda, and Truth.

Source: *Yasna* 30:3–10, tr. Lawrence Heyworth Mills (adapted).

REMOVAL OF HAIR AND NAILS

The moral battle between good and evil touches not only the spiritual realm of thoughts and deeds, but the material realm as well. Things associated with contamination and death, for example, are deemed evil. Although no longer widely practiced today, Zoroastrian rituals concerning the removal of hair and nails vividly illustrate how physical things can be tainted by evil. The following purification rituals are from the Vendidad.

Zarathushtra asked Ahura Mazda: Which is the most deadly deed by which a man increases the strength of the daevas, as he might do by offering them a sacrifice?

Ahura Mazda answered: It is when a man here on earth, by combing or shaving his hair, or cutting off his nails, places them into a hole or in a crack. Then, when failing to perform the required rites, daevas are produced in the earth. When the required rites are not observed, vermin *(khrafstras)* [created by daevas] are produced in the earth, which men call lice, and devour grain in the field and clothes in the closet. Therefore, Zarathushtra, whenever here on earth you comb or shave your hair, or cut off your nails, you must take them away ten paces from the faithful, twenty paces from the fire, thirty paces from the water, and fifty paces from the consecrated bundles of baresma [i.e., grasses used in sacrifice]. Then you must dig a hole in the earth, ten fingers deep if the soil is hard and twelve fingers deep if it is soft. You must place the hair down there and say aloud these fiend-smiting words: In reward for his piety, Mazda made the plants grow up out of him. Then you must draw three lines around the hole with a metal knife (or six or nine channels) and chant the Ahuna-Vairya three, six or nine times. For nails, you must dig a hole outside of the house as deep as the top joint of your little finger. You must place them there and say out loud these fiend-smiting words: "The words that are heard from the pious in holiness and good thought." Then you must draw three lines with a metal knife around the hole (or six or nine channels) and chant the Ahuna-Vairya three, six or nine times. Then say, "Look here, bird-of-truth, here are nails for you, look here at these nails. May they be for you like so many spears, knives, bows, falcon-winged arrows, and sling-stones to use against the daevas from Mazana [i.e., a neighboring region of sorcerers]." If the nails have not been dedicated to the bird-of-truth, they will fall into the hands of the daevas from Mazana. Followers of the Lie are the Lie incarnate. Those who reject one teaching reject all teachings. Those who disobey are entirely disobedient. Those who are not Truth-owning are entirely Truth-disowning, and have forfeited their bodies [i.e., become mortal sinners].

Source: *Vendidad* 17:1–11, tr. James Darmesteter (adapted).

REMOVAL OF THE DEAD

The problem of physical things being contaminated by evil is most pronounced with dead human bodies. When one dies, a Corpse Demon (druj nasu) comes into the body and contaminates it and any items that touch it. Burial is not possible, because this contaminates the sacred earth, and cremation contaminates the fire. As described in the following selection from the Vendidad, the preferred method of corpse disposal is for dead bodies to be devoured by corpse-eating dogs and birds that frighten off the Corpse Demon. To facilitate this, Zoroastrians construct Towers of Silence (dakhmas), cylindrical walled structures that expose corpses to vultures. This practice has been noted frequently in literature and is one of the most distinctive aspects of Zoroastrian ritual.

Disposing of Bodies

[Zarathushtra asked:] "Creator of the material world, where should we take and lay the bodies of the dead?"

Ahura Mazda answered: "On the highest mountain peaks, where corpse-eating dogs and birds can most easily find them. There the worshippers of Mazda will attach the corpse by the feet and hair, with brass, stones, or horn, to prevent the corpse-eating dogs and birds from carrying the bones to the water and trees."

[Zarathushtra asked:] "If they do not fasten the corpse to prevent the corpse-eating dogs and birds from carrying the bones to the water and trees, what is the penalty that they must pay?"

Ahura Mazda answered: "They must be whipped: two hundred lashes with a horse whip and two hundred lashes with another whip."

[Zarathushtra asked:] "Where should we bring and lay the bones of the dead after this?"

Ahura Mazda answered: "The worshippers of Mazda must build an elevated container that is out of the reach of dogs, foxes, and wolves, and wherever rain water cannot collect. If they can afford it, they should build the elevated container with stones, chalk, and clay. If they cannot afford it, they should lay the dead man on the ground, with the earth as his bed, and the sunlight as his clothing." . . .

Things Defiled by Death

Zarathushtra asked Ahura Mazda: "When a man dies, at what moment does the Corpse Demon *(druj nasu)* rush in upon him?"

Ahura Mazda answered: "Directly after his death. As soon as consciousness has left the body, the Corpse Demon comes and rushes in upon him from the northern regions of hell, like the most ghastly vermin, with knees and tail sticking out and all covered with stains, like the most disgusting animal.

It stays in him until a dog has seen the corpse or has eaten it up, or until a flesh-eating bird has flown towards it. When dogs have seen it or eaten it up, or when the flesh-eating birds have flown towards it, then the Corpse Demon rushes back to the northern regions of hell like the most disgusting animal."

[Zarathushtra asked:] "If a man has been killed by dogs, wolves, witchcraft, poison, falling off a cliff, betrayal, murder, or strangulation, how long after death does the Corpse Demon come and rush in upon the dead?"

Ahura Mazda answered: "In a few hours after death, the Corpse Demon comes and rushes in upon the dead."

[Zarathushtra asked:] "If there are a number of men resting in the same place, on adjoining bedding or on adjoining pillows—whether there two men near each other, or five, or fifty, or a hundred next to each other—and one of those people happens to die, how many of them does the Corpse Demon cover with infection, pollution, and uncleanliness?"

Ahura Mazda answered: "If the dead person is a priest, the Corpse Demon rushes in and overtakes the eleventh and defiles the first ten. If the dead person is a warrior, it overtakes the tenth and defiles the first nine. If the dead person is a farmer it overtakes the ninth and defiles the first eight. If it is a shepherd's dog it overtakes the eighth and defiles the first seven. . . ."

[Zarathushtra asked:] "What part of his bedding and pillow does the Corpse Demon defile with infection, uncleanliness, and pollution?"

Ahura Mazda answered: "The Lie *(druj)* defiles with infection, uncleanliness, and pollution the upper sheet and the inner garment."

[Zarathushtra asked:] "Can a garment be made clean if it has been touched by the carcass of a dog or the corpse of a man?"

Ahura Mazda answered: "It can. If the garment has been defiled with semen, blood, feces, or vomit, the worshippers of Mazda must cut it into pieces and bury the defiled part in the ground. But if it has not been defiled with semen, blood, feces, or vomit, then the worshippers of Mazda must wash it with cow urine." . . .

Contamination from Corpses

[Zarathushtra asked:] "Can someone be clean again if he has eaten the carcass of a dog or the carcass of a man?"

Ahura Mazda answered: "He cannot. His vermin hole will be dug out, his life will be torn out, his bright eyes will be put out; the Corpse Demon will fall upon him, takes hold of him even to the end of the nails, and he is unclean, thenceforth, for eternity."

[Zarathushtra asked:] "Can someone be clean again who has brought a filthy corpse to either water or fire, and made either unclean?"

Ahura Mazda answered: "He cannot. It is those wicked ones, those men turned to demons, who most increase spiders and locusts. It is those wicked ones those men turned to demons, that most increase crop-destroying drought. It is those wicked ones, those men turned to demons, who most increase the power of the winter, produced by the demons [daevas], that cattle-killing, heavy-snowing, overflowing, the piercing, fierce, mischievous winter. The Corpse Demon comes and rushes in on them; she takes hold of them right to the end of their nails, and makes them unclean forever."

[Zarathushtra asked:] "Can wood be made clean, which carried dead flesh from a dead dog, or from a dead man?"

Ahura Mazda answered: "It can. If the dead flesh has not yet been smitten by the corpse-eating dogs, or by the corpse-eating birds, they must lay the wood separately on the ground, five fingers in length all around the dead flesh, if the wood is dry; if it is wet, fourteen fingers in length of all around. They must then sprinkle it once over with water, and it will be clean."

Source: *Vendidad* 6:44–51; 7:1–14, 23–29, tr. James Darmesteter (adapted).

THE DAILY PRAYER

The Khorde Avesta (Smaller Avesta) is a book of the Avesta *that contains daily prayer used by the laity. One such text is the Nam Setayashne. An interesting theological point of this devotional is the identification of Spenta Mainyu with Ahura Mazda.*

1. I praise the name of that Spenta Mainyu, the increaser, worthy to be praised, who always was, always is, and always will be; whose one name is Ahura Mazda, the God who is the greatest among all, wise, Creator, supporter, protector, endurer, the Lord of Truth *(asha)*, forgiver, and dispenser of excellent and pure justice.

2. Thanks be to the exalted Lord of the world, who, of his own power and wisdom, created six Bounteous Immortals of high rank, numerous spiritual beings *(yazads)*, the shining paradise of Garothman, the surrounding heavens, the hot sun, the shining moon, the numerous stars, the wind, the atmosphere, the fire, the water, the earth, the trees, the cattle, the metals, and humankind.

3. Adoration and prayers to the righteous Lord who has given us speech and the power to think, thereby making us superior to other creatures of this world. He has done this so that we might rule over people and make people walk together to fight against the Daevas.

4. I bow in the presence of the omniscient and caretaking Lord, who has sent, through Zarathushtra of the adorable farohar [i.e., guardian angel], the wisdom of the religion, for the purpose making people friendly towards Him. This wisdom we gain through natural intelligence and knowledge of science, and is the best guidance for all persons who are, were and will be. Through this wisdom the soul is freed from the pains of hell, and reaches into the shining, fragrant, ever-happy, and highest mansions of the pure.

5. Lord Protector, in obedience to your command, I am firm in the pure religion and I promise to think, speak and do every righteousness. Forgive me of my many sins. May I keep my conduct pure and, in accordance with your

wishes, keep my six powers of the soul uncontaminated: work, speech, thought, reasoning, memory, and intellect.

6. In order to obtain the riches of the next world through good thoughts, good words, and good deeds, I will worship you, so that I may open for myself the path to the shining paradise. Through this, the heavy punishment of hell will not be inflicted upon me and I may, passing over the Chinvat bridge, reach into the fragrant all-adorned and eternally happy mansions of paradise.

7. I praise the Lord of gifts, who gives to those who obey his commandments the reward of righteous wishes and who will at the end liberate transgressors from hell and adorn the world with purity.

Source: *Khorde Avesta,* The Nam Setayashne 1–7, tr., Ratanshah E. Kohiyar (adapted).

PAHLAVI WRITINGS

THE CHINVAT BRIDGE, HEAVEN AND HELL

Zarathushtra taught that heaven awaits good people, and hell evil people. Entrance into heaven requires crossing the Chinvat Bridge, which spans the abyss of hell below (Yasna 46:10, 11; 51:13). The details of this journey of the soul were worked out in later Pahlavi texts, such as the following by ninth-century Zoroastrian high priest Manushkihar from his Datastani Denik. On the fourth day after death, our souls leave our bodies and we cross the Chinvat Bridge. If we sided with good during our lives, then the bridge is as wide as seven spears and we easily pass to heaven, which is filled with beauty, light, pleasant scents, and happiness. If we sided with evil during our lives, however, the bridge turns sideways and becomes as narrow as a razor's edge; we plummet into hell, which is filled with stench, filth, and pain.

Crossing the Chinvat Bridge

20. The nineteenth question that you ask is this: Where do the righteous and wicked go?

The reply is this. It is said that the souls of the dead remain three nights on earth. On the first night satisfaction comes to them from their good words, but discomfort and punishment from their evil words. On the second night comes pleasure from their good words, but discomfort and punishment from their evil words. On the third night comes exaltation from their good deeds, but punishment from their evil deeds. On that third night, at dawn, they go to the place of judgment on Alburz [i.e., the mountain surrounding the world]. Once judgment is rendered, they proceed to the [Chinvat] bridge. He who is righteous passes over the bridge on the ascent, and if belonging to Hamistagan [i.e., Purgatory] he goes there where their place is. If he has an excess of good works and his habits are correct, he goes to heaven. But if, in addition to an excess of good works and correct habits, he has also chanted the sacred hymns, he goes to the supreme heaven. However, the wicked fall from either the lower end or middle of the bridge, head first into hell, and is thrown into that level which is appropriate for his wickedness.

21. The twentieth question that you ask is this: Concerning the Chinvat bridge, the Daitih peak, and the path of the righteous and wicked, how are they when someone is righteous, and when someone is wicked?

The reply is this, as the high priests have said: the Daitih peak is in Eranwej, in the middle of the world. The beam-shaped spirit, the Chinvat bridge, reaches to the vicinity of that peak and is thrown across from the Alburz enclosure back to the Daitih peak. That bridge is like a many-sided beam, whose edges are broad in some places, yet thin and sharp in others. Its broad sides are so large that its width is twenty-seven reeds, but its sharp sides are so slender that they are as thin as the edge of a razor. When the souls of the righteous and wicked arrive, it turns to that side which is appropriate to their outcome, through the great glory of the creator and the command of him who makes the just assessment.

Moreover, the bridge becomes wide for the righteous, as great as the length of nine spears, and the length of those which they carry is each separately three reeds. But, it becomes narrow for the wicked, like the edge of a razor. Those who are righteous pass over the bridge. Their paths are filled with pleasantness, as when they eagerly and unweariedly walk in the golden-colored spring, and with the gallant body and sweet-scented blossom in the pleasant skin of that maiden spirit. This is the reward of goodness.

But for the wicked, as they place their feet on the bridge, the pain from its sharpness causes them to fall from the middle of the bridge, and roll over head first. This path to hell has an unpleasant smell, similar in this world to being surrounded by stinking and dying things. Further, many sharply-pointed darts are planted there, inverted and pointing upwards, which force the person to run, thereby

preventing him from staying behind or delaying. This pleasantness and unpleasantness to these souls is much more
intense than their worldly types, since what is suitable for
the spirit is greater than what is suitable for the world. . . .

Heaven and Hell Compared

26. The twenty-fifth question that you ask is this: what is the
nature of heaven and what are the comforts and pleasures
like in heaven?

The reply is this. It is grand, exalted, and supreme. It
is dazzling, fragrant, and pure. It is supplied with the most
beautiful things, the most desirable, and the best. It is the
place and home of the sacred beings. It contains every comfort, pleasure, joy, happiness, and welfare, more and better
even than the greatest and most supreme happiness and
pleasures in this world. There is no need, pain, distress, or
discomfort in it whatsoever. Its pleasantness and the welfare
of the angels are from that constantly-beneficial place, the
full and undiminishable space, the goodness and boundless
world. The freedom of the heavenly from danger from evil in
heaven is like their freedom from disturbance, and the coming of the good angels is like the heavenly ones' own good
works. This prosperity and welfare of spiritual existence is
greater than that of this world, insofar as that which is unlimited and everlasting is greater than that which is limited and
demoniacal.

27. The twenty-sixth question that you ask is this: what is
the nature of hell, and what are the pains, discomforts, punishments, and stench like in hell?

The reply is this. It is sunken, deep, and descending.
It is dark, stinking, and terrible. It is filled with the most
wretched things, very worst. It is the place and cave of the
demons and fiends. It contains no comfort, pleasantness, or
joy whatever. There is only stench, filth, pain, punishment,
distress, evil, and discomfort. There is nothing whatsoever to
compare it to in this world in terms of stench, filthiness, pain,
and evil. Since there is no resemblance between the various
evils of this world to good things, there is also a deviation of
it from the source and home of evil.

The most grievous evil in hell is much worse than the
most grievous evil on earth, to the degree that spiritual existence is so much greater than worldly existence. The terror
of the soul's punishment is more grievous than the vileness
of the demons on the body. The soul will be punished by the
demons who live in hell and its darkness, in correspondence

to the evil in hell, the head of which is the deadly Angra Mainyu.

The high priests say, "The fear we might have of a thing is greater than that thing itself, but hell is something worse than the fear of it."

Source: *Datastani Denik* 20, 21, 26, 27, tr. Edward William West (adapted).

CREATION AND THE MILLENNIA

In later Pahlavi Zoroastrian writings, Angra Mainyu has a more elevated role in cosmic history. The following selection from the Bundahishn, a Pahlavi text on cosmogony and cosmic history, describes the initial confrontation between Ahura Mazda and Angra Mainyu and their ensuing 12,000-year battle. During the first 3,000 years, Ahura Mazda created the Beneficent Immortals and the world. Angra Mainyu responded by creating helper demons. They then agreed to limit the struggle to an additional 9,000 years.

Ahura Mazda and Angra Mainyu at Creation

As revealed by the religion of the Mazda Worshipers [i.e., the Zoroastrians], it is declared that Ahura Mazda is supreme in omniscience and goodness, and unrivalled in splendor. The region of light is the place of Ahura Mazda, which they call "endless light," and the omniscience and goodness of the unrivalled Ahura Mazda is what they call "revelation."

Revelation is the explanation of both spirits together. One is he who is independent of unlimited time, because Ahura Mazda and the region, religion, and time of Ahura Mazda were and are and ever will be. Meanwhile, Angra Mainyu in darkness, with backward understanding and desire for destruction, was in the abyss, and it is he who will not be. The place of that destruction, and also of that darkness, is what they call the "endlessly dark." Between them was empty space, that is, what they call "air," in which is now their meeting.

Both are limited and unlimited spirits, for the supreme is that which they call endless light, and the abyss that which is endlessly dark, so that between them is a void, and the one is not connected with the other. Again, both spirits are limited as to their own selves. Second, because of the omniscience of Ahura Mazda, both things are in the creation of Ahura Mazda, the finite and the infinite. For, this they know is that which is in the covenant of both spirits. Again, the complete sovereignty of the creatures of Ahura Mazda is in the future existence, and that also is unlimited for eternity. The creatures of Angra Mainyu will perish at the time when the Final Body occurs, and that also is eternity.

Ahura Mazda, through his omniscience, knows that Angra Mainyu exists, and that everything Angra Mainyu schemes he infuses with malice and greediness until the end. Because Ahura Mazda accomplishes the end by many means, he also produced spiritually the creatures which were necessary for those means, and they remained three thousand years in a spiritual state, so that they were unthinking and unmoving, with intangible bodies.

The evil spirit, because of backward knowledge, was not aware of the existence of Ahura Mazda. Later, he arose from the abyss, and came into the light which he saw. Because of his desire for destruction and his malicious nature, he rushed in to destroy that light of Ahura Mazda that was unconquerable by fiends. He saw that its bravery and glory were greater than his own, so he fled back to the gloomy darkness, and formed many demons and fiends. These creatures of the destroyer then emerged and brought about violence.

Conflict erupts between Ahura Mazda and Angra Mainyu

Ahura Mazda observed the creatures of the Destructive Spirit, which were horrible, corrupt, and evil, and he judged them to be reprehensible. Afterwards, the evil spirit saw the creatures of Ahura Mazda. Many of these creatures appeared, and they seemed praiseworthy to him. He praised the creatures and creation of Ahura Mazda. Then Ahura Mazda, with a knowledge of which way the end of the matter would be, went to meet the evil spirit, and proposed peace to him, and spoke: "Evil spirit! Bring assistance to my creatures and give praise, so that, in reward for it, you and your creatures may become immortal and undecaying, without hunger and thirst."

The evil spirit shouted, "I will not leave, or provide assistance for your creatures, or give praise among your creatures, and I do not agree with you regarding good things. I will destroy your creatures for eternity. Further, I will force all your creatures to be hostile towards you, and instead show affection towards me." The reason for this is that the evil spirit understood that Ahura Mazda was helpless regarding him. So, Ahura Mazda offered peace, but Angra Mainyu did not agree and continued to the point of conflict with him.

Ahura Mazda said: "You are not omniscient and almighty, evil spirit, so it is not possible for you to destroy me, and it is not possible for you to prevent my creatures from returning to me." Through omniscience, Ahura Mazda knew that if he did not grant a period of contest, then it would be possible for Angra Mainyu to seduce his creatures. For even now there are many among the variety of human beings who practice wrong more than right. Ahura Mazda spoke to the evil spirit: "Appoint a period so that the intermingling of the conflict may be for nine thousand years." For he knew that by appointing this period the evil spirit would be defeated. Then the evil spirit, unobservant and through ignorance, was content with the agreement, just like two men quarrelling together, who propose a time by saying "Let us appoint such-and-such a day for a fight."

Through his omniscience, Ahura Mazda also knew that, within these nine thousand years, for three thousand years everything would proceed according to the will of Ahura Mazda. In the next three thousand years, there would be an intermingling of the wills of Ahura Mazda and Angra Mainyu. In the last three thousand years the evil spirit would be made powerless, and kept away from Ahura Mazda's creatures.

Afterwards, Ahura Mazda recited the Ahunvar [the Zoroastrians' most sacred prayer]. He also displayed to the evil spirit his own triumph in the end, the powerlessness of the evil spirit, the annihilation of the demons, and the resurrection and undisturbed future existence of the creatures for eternity. The evil spirit, who saw his own powerlessness, and the annihilation of the demons, became confused, and fell back to the gloomy darkness. Just as it is declared in revelation, "When one of the Ahunvar's three parts was uttered, Angra Mainyu became confused and powerless as to the harm he caused the creatures of Ahura Mazda, and he remained three thousand years in that confusion."

Ahura Mazda created his creatures in the confusion of Angra Mainyu. First he produced Vohu Manah (Good Thought), by whom the movement of the creatures of Ahura Mazda was advanced. The evil spirit first created Mitokht (Falsehood), and then Akoman (Evil Thought). The first of Ahura Mazda's creatures of the world was the sky, and his good thought, by good procedure, produced the light of the world, along with which was the good religion of the Mazda Worshipers. This was because the resurrection which happens to the creatures was known to him. Afterwards arose Ardavahist, then Shatvairo, then Spendarmad, then Horvadad, and then Amerodad [the Beneficent Immortals].

From the dark world of Angra Mainyu were Akoman and Andar, then Sovar, then Nakahed, and then Tairev and Zairik. Of Ahura Mazda's creatures of the world, the first was the sky, the second water, the third earth, the fourth plants, the fifth animals, and the sixth mankind.

Source: *Bundahishn* 1, tr. Edward William West (adapted).

LIFE OF ZARATHUSHTRA

During the second 3,000-year period of cosmic history, Angra Mainyu stays in darkness only to wage a full-scale assault on creation during the third 3,000-year period. The fourth and final 3,000-year period begins with the birth of Zarathushtra, who rallies humans to the cause of Ahura Mazda. The following describes the miraculous conception of Zarathushtra, attempts to kill him at an early age, and his encounter with Vohu Manah and call to prophethood at age 30. The selections are from the Pahlavi Denkard, a Pahlavi compendium of Zoroastrian doctrine, and the Zatspram, a collection of doctrines from ninth-century CE Zoroastrian high priest Zatspram.

Consider now the miraculous manifestations that occurred before the birth of that most fortunate child by his mother. As is stated in revelation, one miracle that happened before the birth of Zarathushtra is how the creator passed his divine grace on to Zarathushtra through the material nature of various creatures. When Ahura Mazda gave the command, the glory from the spiritual existence transferred to the worldly, and then to the material substance of Zarathushtra. This great wonder was displayed to the multitude. It is just as revelation describes: "Immediately, when Ahura Mazda had produced the material of Zarathushtra, the glory then, in the presence of Ahura Mazda, flew down towards the material Zarathushtra, on to the germ. From that germ it moved on to the endless light. From the endless light it moved on to that of the sun. From that of the sun it moved on to the moon. From the moon it moved on to those stars. From those stars it moved on to the wife which was in the house of Zoish. From there it moved on to the wife of Frahimrvana-Zoish, when she gave birth to the girl who became the mother of Zarathushtra. . . .

As it is stated, these are the trials that occurred to Zarathushtra, and the signs of revelation that appear in them. When the child had been born, Porushaspo [his father] called one of the five brothers from a family of Priests, and said: "Fully examine the evil marks and specks on my son

Zarathushtra." The priest came and sat down in front of Zarathushtra, then began twisting the child's head attempting to kill him. But Zarathushtra, being fearless, watched the priests whose terror was distressing. Ahura Mazda then sent Spandarmad, Ardvisur, and Arda-frawash [i.e., angels] down to the earth to provide hospitality and care for ten days. Immediately no marks (of evil) were observed on the child. But the hand of that priest withered, and the priest demanded the life of Zarathushtra from Porushaspo for the harm that came to him, which he brought upon himself from his own action.

Porushaspo then took Zarathushtra, and gave him to the priest, so that the priest might do with Zarathushtra as he wished. He grabbed him and threw him in front of the feet of the oxen who were going down a path to the water. The leader of that herd of oxen stood still near Zarathushtra, and the 150 oxen, which walked behind, were thereby kept away from Zarathushtra. Porushaspo took Zarathushtra and carried him back to the house. On the second day, the priest threw him in front of the feet of the horses. The leader of the horses stood still near Zarathushtra, and the 150 horses, which walked behind, were thereby kept away from Zarathushtra. Porushaspo took him, and carried him back to the house. On the third day, the priest gathered firewood, threw Zarathushtra on it, and stirred the fire. Yet, with the same result, the child was not burnt by it. . . .

When Zarathushtra reached the age of thirty, in commemoration of Ahura Mazda, the archangel Vohu Manah came to Zarathushtra as he was bringing his Haoma-water from the river Aevatak. . . . Vohu Manah asked: "Zarathushtra, what is your main distress? What is your main effort? What is the goal of your desire?"

Zarathushtra replied, "My main distress is about truth (*asha*). My main effort is about truth, and truth is the goal of my desire."

Vohu Manah said, "Zarathushtra, that which is true exists, so that whatever is true is thus what is one's own."

Zarathushtra replied, "I fully understand that that which is true exists. But, tell me, where does that radiance come from that appeared when you arrived?"

Vohu Manah said to him, "Zarathushtra, put down the vessel that you are carrying, so that we may discuss who it is that produced you and produced me. For he is the greatest of spirits, the most beneficent of existences, and he is the one about whom I am testifying as a reminder of him."

Zarathushtra then thought, "The creator is great, better even than this reminder." Vohu Manah and Zarathushtra then walked together, Vohu Manah first and Zarathushtra after.

Source: *Denkard* 7.2.1–3; Zadspram 16.1–7; *Denkard* 7.3.51, 56–61; tr. Edward William West (adapted).

COMING OF SAOSHYANT

After Zarathushtra, three additional saviors are to come at 1,000-year intervals. They will be born from virgins who bathe in a lake guarded by 99,999 angels who preserve Zarathushtra's seed. The saviors are Hushedar, Aushedar-Mah, and Saoshyant. Saoshyant's coming marks the end of the 12,000-year cosmic struggle between Ahura Mazda and Angra Mainyu. The following, from the Pahlavi Denkard, describes the birth of Saoshyant and his defeat of Angra Mainyu in the final battle.

Thirty years before the end of the tenth century [in the final millennium], the maiden Eredat-fedhri will walk up to the water. She is the mother of that testifying Saoshyant who is the guide for leading away the opposition of the destroyer. . . . [Just as revelation states,] "That maiden whose title is All-Overpowerer is thus all-overpowering. This is because through giving birth she brings forth him who overpowers all, both the affliction resulting from demons, and that resulting from mankind." When she is fifteen years old, she will sit in that water and it will introduce [Saoshyant] into her, the one whose name is the Triumphant Benefiter, and whose title is the Bodymaker. As benefiter he benefits all physical existence, and as body-maker he similarly possesses both body and life. As such, he inquires about the disturbances of the embodied existences and mankind. Prior to this, the maiden will not have associated with men, nor will she after she becomes pregnant and before the time when she gives birth. When Saoshyant becomes thirty years old, the sun will stand still in the zenith of the sky for a period of thirty days and nights, and it will arrive again at that place where it was appointed by allotment. . . .

In his fifty-seventh year the two-legged race and others will be annihilated, and defeated will be disease, decrepitude, death, persecution, the original evil of tyranny, apostasy, and depravity. There will arise a perpetual lush growth of vegetation and the original gift of joyfulness. For seventeen years everyone will abstain from meat, then thirty more years where people live on water alone, and then ten years where they live on spiritual food alone.

All the splendor, glory, and power which have arisen in possessors of splendor, glory, and power, are in him on whom they arrive together and for those who are his, when many inferior human beings are aroused splendid and powerful. Through their power and glory, all the troops of the fiend are smitten. All mankind remain of one accord in the religion of Ahura Mazda, owing to the will of the creator, the command of that apostle, and the resources of his companions.

At the end of the fifty-seven years, Angra Mainyu and the fiend will be annihilated, the restoration of future existence will occur, and all of wonderful creation will enjoy purity and perfect splendor. Just as revelation states, "When that millennium has fully elapsed, which is the third in the religion of the Mazda-worshippers, that Mazda-worshipper [i.e., Saoshyant] whose name is so triumphant will then march forward from the water Kasava with a thousand companions. With them will be maidens of controlled disposition and blindly striving- behavior. He will attack the wicked people who are tyrannical, and annihilate them."

Then the Mazda-worshippers will attack, and no one will attack them back. Then the Mazda-worshippers will create a longing for restoration among the existences, one ever-living, ever-beneficial, and ever-desiring Lord. [Just as revelation states,] "Then I, who am Ahura Mazda, will bring about the restoration according to the longing among the existences, one ever-living, ever-beneficial, and ever desiring Lord."

Source: *Denkard* 7.10.15-19; 7.11.4-9; tr. Edward William West (adapted).

THE FINAL JUDGMENT AND RESTORATION OF THE UNIVERSE

After the defeat of Angra Mainyu in the final battle, the dead will resurrect on the spot where they died, and Ahura Mazda will judge everyone. The evil of the world will be purged with molten metal, Angra Mainyu will be destroyed, and a new universe will come into being. These events are described in the following passage from the Pahlavi Bundahishn.

The Resurrection of the Dead

Concerning the nature of the resurrection and future existence, it says in revelation that Mashya and Mashyang [i.e, Adam and Eve], who grew up from the earth, first fed upon water, then plants, then milk, and then meat. Similarly, when the time of death comes for people, they first abstain from eating meat, then milk, then bread, until when they will die they only drink water. So, likewise, in the millennium of Hushedar-mah, the strength of one's appetite will thus diminish, when, after one taste of consecrated food, men will remain three days and nights in complete sufficiency. They will then abstain from meat, and eat only vegetables and milk. Afterwards, they will abstain from milk and vegetables, and drink only water. For ten years before Saoshyant comes they will remain without food, yet will not die.

After Saoshyant comes they will prepare the raising of the dead. . . . First, the bones of Gayomard [the primordial human] will be awakened, then those of Mashya and Mashyang, then those of the rest of mankind. Within fifty-seven years Saoshyant will raise all the dead. Every human being, whether righteous or wicked, will awaken from the spot where his life departed. Afterwards, when all material living beings once again assume their bodies and forms, they will give them their protoplasm. Of the light accompanying the sun, one half will be given to Gayomard, and one half will give enlightenment to the rest of men. Through this, the person's soul and body will recognize that this is his father, and this is his mother, and this is his brother, and this is his wife, and these are some other of his nearest relations.

Final Judgment

Then the assembly of Isat-Vastar [Zarathushtra's son] will meet, where all people will stand at this time. In that assembly everyone will see his own good and evil deeds. A wicked man will become as visible as a white sheep among black ones. Suppose that a righteous man was friends with a wicked one while alive, and the wicked man complains about the righteous man saying, "When we were alive, why did you not acquaint me with the good deeds which you practiced yourself?" If he the righteous man did not inform him, then it will be necessary for the righteous man to suffer shame in that assembly.

Afterwards, they will separate the righteous from the wicked. The righteous will be carried to heaven, and they will throw the wicked back into hell. For three days and nights they will inflict punishment on the wicked in hell, and for those three days observe the happiness of the righteous in heaven. As revelation says, on the day when the righteous man is parted from the wicked, the tears of everyone will run down to his legs. When, after they separate sons from their fathers, a brother from his brother, and a friend from his friend, everyone will suffer for his own deeds. They will weep, the righteous for the wicked, and the wicked for himself. For there may be a father who is righteous and a son wicked, and there may be one brother who is righteous and the other wicked. Those for whose deeds uniquely deserve death, such as those committed by Dahak and Frasiyav of Tur, they will undergo a punishment that no other men will experience. They call it "the punishment of the three nights."

Among those who help bring about the restoration of the universe, fifteen righteous men and fifteen damsels among the living will assist Saoshyant, as it is written. A meteor called Go-chihr will fall to earth from heaven on a moonbeam and cause destruction on earth like that of a sheep when a wolf falls upon it. The meteor's fire and halo will then melt the metal of the archangel Shehrevar, which is in the hills and mountains, and the metal will flow on earth like a river. All men will then go into the molten metal and become pure. If the person is righteous, then it will seem to him like he is walking in warm milk. But if wicked, then it will seem to him like he is walking through molten metal as when he was alive.

Paradise

Then, all men will come together with the greatest affection. Father and son, brother and friends will ask each other: "Where have you been these past years, and what was the judgment upon your soul? Have you been righteous or wicked?" These are the words that will be asked of the first soul that the restored body sees. All men will become one voice and give loud praise to Ahura Mazda and the archangels.

Ahura Mazda will complete his work at this time, and the creatures will become such that it will not be necessary [for Ahura Mazda] to make any effort with them. Concerning those who will prepare the dead, it will not be necessary [for Ahura Mazda] to make any effort with them. Saoshyant, with his assistants, will perform the rite for the restoration of the dead (*yazishn*). They will slaughter the ox Hadhayos for this rite. From the fat of that ox and white haoma, they prepare the immortal beverage (*hush*), and give it to all men, which will make all men immortal for eternity. Whoever had been an adult, they will restore him to the age of forty years. Those who died when will be restore to the age of fifteen years. They will give each man his wife, and present him with his children and wife. Thus, they will act as they did when alive, although they will produce no more children.

Then Saoshyant and his assistants, by order of the creator Ahura Mazda, will give each person the reward and recompense according to his deeds. . . . Afterwards, Ahura Mazda will seize the evil spirits . . . and the dragon called Go-chihr will be burnt in molten metal. The stench and pollution that are in hell will also be burned in that metal, and hell will become completely pure. Ahura Mazda will make a hiding place within the metal to which the evil spirits will flee. He will bring the land of hell back for the enlargement of the world. This restoration of the universe will come about by his will, and the world will be immortal for eternity. This earth will become an iceless, slopeless plane. Even the mountain whose summit supports the Chinvat bridge will be flattened and will not exist.

Source: *Bundahishn* 30, tr. Edward William West (adapted).

SIX RITUAL OBLIGATIONS

Zoroastrians have a variety of rituals, such as seven holy days of obligation; rites of passage, including the navjote initiation ceremony for young adolescents; and rituals of cleansing and purification. Six primary ritual obligations are discussed in the following from the Sad Dar *(Hundred Doors), a text on a hundred subjects that is written in Persian.*

Of the many good works, there are some which, when performed, result in great rewards. If someone does not perform them, then he will be gripped with severe punishment at the head of the Chinvat bridge.

First is celebration of the season festivals *(gahambars)*. Second is keeping the days of the guardian spirits *(fravashis)* [during the last ten days of the religious year]. Third is attending to the souls of fathers, mothers, and other relations. Fourth is reciting the Sun Litany *(khwarshed nyaish)* three times every day. Fifth is reciting the Moon Litany *(mah nyayis)* three times every month, once when it becomes new, once when it becomes full, and once when it becomes slender. Sixth is celebrating the Rapithwin ceremony once every year.

If someone is not able to celebrate them, it is necessary for him to arrange for them, so that they may be celebrated every single time. These six good works are obligatory for everyone. On some occasion these might not be performed because it is not possible to do so, and another occasion these might not be performed, but are done twice as often at a different time. In these situations when any one of them is not performed, it should be considered as an advantage, which occurs in retribution for it, or as atonement for the transgression.

6. They call the transgression of each of these six a "bridge-sin". That is, those who commit the transgression are held back at the beginning head of the Chinvat bridge, until he receives punishment. No good work is possible in this place, which is torment and punishment for him. Thus, it is necessary for a person to make an effort to perform them, each one at its own time, so that he may receive a reward, rather than a severe punishment.

Source: *Sad Dar* 6:1–7, tr. Edward William West (adapted).

VIRTUES AND SOCIAL OBLIGATION

In addition to ritual obligations, Zoroastrians have strict codes of moral obligation that encourage virtues and condemn vices. Often these moral instructions are in the form of aphorisms (Andarz), such as the following from the Denkard.

There are five best things in religion. They are truthfulness, generosity, virtue, diligence, and advocacy. This truthfulness is best: one who acts (in such a manner) to the creatures of Ahura Mazda that the recipient of his action has so much more benefit when he acts like that to him. This generosity is best: One who makes a present to a person from whom he has no hope of receiving anything in reward in this world, and he has not even this (hope), namely, that the recipient of his gift should hold him abundantly in gratitude and praise. This possession of virtue is best: One who makes battle against the non-material demons, whatever they may be, and in particular does not let these five demons into his body: Greed, Envy, Lust, Wrath, and Shame. This diligence is best: One who does the work which he is engaged in doing in such a manner that at every moment he has certainty in himself with regard to the following: were he to die at that hour it would not be necessary to do anything whatsoever in a way different from that in which he is doing it. That advocacy is best: One who speaks for a person who is inarticulate, who cannot speak his own misery and complaint; that person speaks out the voice of his own soul and of that of the poor and good person to the people of this world and these six Amesha Spentas.

They held this too: Wisdom is manifest in work, character in rule, friend in hardship.

When food offerings *(myazd)*, seasonal festivals *(gahambar)* and acts of charity to good people diminish, there is increase of evil government for men, pain for grain plants, bad husbandry, diminution of the fertility of the land and rains. When the virtue of consanguine marriage diminishes, darkness increases and light diminishes. When worship of the gods and the protection and advocacy of good people diminish, the evil government of rulers and unlawful action increase, and evil people gain the upper hand over good.

Source: *Denkard* 6:23, 24, C82, from *The Wisdom of the Sasanian Sages* (Denkard VI), tr. Shaul Shaked (Boulder, CO: 1979), pp. 11, 173. Reprinted by permission.

ZURVAN WRITINGS

ZURVAN AND HIS TWIN SONS

The Zurvan sect of Zoroastrianism flourished between the fifth and tenth centuries CE. While Zurvan is only a minor deity mentioned in the Avesta, *this sect sees him as the supreme God. The* Avesta *also alludes to rival twin spirits: "There are two primal Spirits, twins renowned to be in conflict. In thought, word and action, they the better and the bad" (Yasna 30). The Zurvan sect interprets this literally and sees Ahura Mazda and Angra Mainyu as twin sons of Zurvan. The good and evil twins both created the world and wage war on each other, but the evil twin is ultimately defeated. The following is from a lost fourth-century Pahlavi Zurvan text, as paraphrased by Eznik of Kolb, an Armenian Christian apologist from the fifth century.*

They say that before anything existed—neither the heavens, nor the earth, nor any creature in them—there was a being called Zurvan, which may be translated as "fortune" or "fame." He performed sacrifices for one thousand years so that he might have a son, who he would name Ahura Mazda, and who would create the heavens and the earth and everything that is in them.

After a thousand years of sacrificing, Zurvan began to think, "Will these sacrifices that I am doing be of any use to me? Am I going to have my son Ahura Mazda? Are all my efforts in vain?" While he considered this, Ahura Mazda and Angra Mainyu were conceived in their mother's womb—Ahura Mazda because of Zurvan's sacrifices, and Angra

Mainyu because of his doubts. When Zurvan learned about this he said: "Two sons are in the womb, and I will make king the one that comes out first."

When Ahura Mazda learned about his father's plan, he revealed it to Angra Mainyu, saying "Zurvan our father thought that whichever one of us comes out first he will make king." When Angra Mainyu heard this, he broke through the womb, got out and walked up to his father. When Zurvan saw him he did not recognize him, and asked, "Who are you?" Angra Mainyu replied "I am your son." Zurvan said to him: "My son is fragrant and luminous, but you are dark and smelly." While they were talking together about this, Ahura Mazda was born in his turn, bright and fragrant. He went out and stood in front of Zurvan. When Zurvan saw him, he immediately knew it was his son Ahura Mazda, for which he had performed the sacrifices. Zurvan took the sacred poles that he had in his hand, with which he performed the sacrifices, and gave them to Ahura Mazda saying, "So far I have done sacrifices for you, and from now on you will do them for me."

While Zurvan gave the sacred poles to Ahura Mazda and blessed him, Angra Mainyu went up to Zurvan and asked, "Did you not make an oath that whichever of my two sons is born first I will make king?" In order to not break his vow Zurvan said to Angra Mainyu: "You liar and evildoer, I will give you this kingdom for nine thousand years, during which time Ahura Mazda will be placed over you as a ruler. But after that nine thousand years, he will reign and make of it what he wants. Ahura Mazda and Angra Mainyu then began making creatures. Everything Angra Mainyu Mazda made was good and right, but that which Angra Mainyu did was evil and wrong.

Source: Eznik of Kolb, *Against the Sects,* 2.

Judaism

INTRODUCTION

Judaism, with its 3,000-year existence, is one of the world's oldest living religions. Like all faith traditions, Judaism has evolved over time, but several key beliefs pervade its rich history. First and foremost is the belief that YHWH (usually pronounced Yahweh) is the only God and creator of all. Second, humans should obey God's law as found in both written and oral law. Third, God made a series of covenants with the Jews to designate their lineage as chosen. The most significant of these covenants are with Abraham, who received the promise of a nation; with Moses, who received the Law; and with David, who received the kingdom. Fourth is the belief that a coming King-Messiah will free the Jews from foreign domination. Unlike the other major monotheistic religions in the Western tradition—Christianity and Islam—Judaism is distinguished by being *this-worldly*. Although a doctrine of the afterlife can be found in its teachings, greater emphasis is placed on the nation, the land, and traditions.

JUDAISM'S BEGINNINGS

Judaism is inseparably tied to the history of the Jewish people; their scriptures, feasts, and worship practices recall events of the past. The earliest historical archaeological record derived from the period of Israel's settlement in its land is from the twelfth century BCE, during the period of the Judges. At this time the Israelites were occupied with capturing territory from the previous inhabitants of perhaps a thousand years, the Canaanites, and settling into agrarian life. The land, *Israel* to the Jews and *Canaan* to the Canaanites, is an area about the size of New Jersey, located on the southeast shore of the Mediterranean Sea. Some of the Israelite stories defined their identity as a nation and entitled them to the land. In these stories, their lineage is traced back to Abraham, a Mesopotamian nomad from a few hundred years earlier. Abraham made a special pact with God whereby God would make him the father of a nation. Abraham and his clan migrated to Canaan, the land later given to him by God. Two generations later, famine drove his descendants to Egypt. For a while all was fine, until the Pharaoh of Egypt resorted to forced labor for his building projects. Abraham's descendants were enslaved for this purpose.

Eventually, they were led by Moses out of Egypt and into the desert, where they wandered for forty years. During the journey, Moses received detailed codes of law directly from God. The story further recounts that Moses' successors led the Israelites into Canaan to capture the land promised to Abraham.

Politically, Canaan was a decentralized collection of tiny independent kingdoms. Religiously, the Canaanites performed plant and animal sacrificial rites in temples and open-air places, and fertility rites of prostitution. Key deities of the Canaanites were El the creator, Asherah the consort of El, Baal the son of El and god of storm, and Anat daughter of El and goddess of war. The Israelites and Canaanites already shared a common ethnic and language family, which was Semitic. As the Israelites occupied the land and eventually controlled the region, many intermarried with the locals and adopted the Canaanite ways, including worship of their deities. Politically the Israelites were a loose confederation of twelve tribes. A political balance of power was maintained among the chosen tribal leaders, legal and military judges, prophets, and priests from a thirteenth, landless group or tribe, Levi. Geographically there was a more delicate balance of power between two southern tribes—Judah (the largest of the twelve) and Benjamin—and the remaining ten tribes located primarily in the north, who felt threatened by Judah's size and political dominance.

UNITED AND DIVIDED KINGDOMS

An unexpected influx of warring invaders called the Philistines came from the northeast Mediterranean area, and they forced the Israelites to unify politically. The Philistines had a special military advantage in iron weaponry, compared to the less effective bronze weapons used by the Israelite army of drafted civilians. The need for a monarchy arose to facilitate a more concerted effort to block the Philistine power. The first King, Saul, died in battle with the Philistines. The kingdom and military leadership passed to his son-in-law, David, who instituted a standing professional army. Equipped with iron weapons, David's army effectively put an end to the Philistine threat. Through military and diplomatic maneuvers, the Kingdom of Israel took control of territory as far south as Egypt and as far north as Mesopotamia. At David's death, the throne passed to his young son, Solomon. Legendary for his wisdom and multiple diplomatic marriages, Solomon launched monumental building projects, including several fortified cities, a palace, and Israel's first permanent temple. Although Solomon taxed the entire country to fund his projects, benefits were seen primarily in Judah, which further alienated the northern tribes.

Solomon died about 922 BCE, and the throne passed to his son, Rehoboam. When Rehoboam announced that he would continue his father's policy of taxation, the northern tribes split from the south and proclaimed their own kingdom. The southern kingdom was thereafter referred to as *Judah,* and the northern kingdom retained the name *Israel.* During this period, both the northern and southern kingdoms continued to be influenced by Canaanite religious practices, and efforts were made at monotheistic reform in both kingdoms by prophets and kings.

After a 200-year existence, the northern kingdom was conquered by the Assyrian empire. For several decades, the north had tried several strategies of resistance, but in 722 BCE its kingdom was annexed as an Assyrian province. Some Israelites were deported, and others fled to Judah. Colonists from Mesopotamia settled in the region and intermarried with the remaining inhabitants, forming the group known as Samaritans, a remnant of which remains today. The southern kingdom escaped immediate annexation by becoming a vassal of the Assyrians. Two decades later, though, Judah's King Hezekiah broke with the Assyrians, prompting a military confrontation that ended in a loss of territory for Judah and a return to vassal status. He, and later King Josiah, made valiant efforts at monotheistic reform, but each time the people returned to Canaanite practices.

EXILE AND RESTORATION

In Mesopotamia, the power structure shifted and the Babylonians overtook the Assyrians. The new Babylonian Empire invaded surrounding countries to bring them within its control, and in three separate invasions (596, 587, and 583 BCE), two of which were provoked by the Judeans, Judah was crushed. Cities and homes were destroyed, thousands of skilled craftsmen and potential troublemakers were deported to Babylon, and thousands more fled to Egypt, some of whom went to the Island of Elephantine. Most significant, Solomon's temple was destroyed.

Although records of events during the Babylonian captivity are sketchy, the trauma of the exile apparently forced the Israelites to reexamine and solidify their religious beliefs. In the absence of the temple, the *Torah,* or books of Moses, became more important. Their understanding of Yahweh may also have changed so that they now viewed him as sovereign authority over the universe. The term *Jew,* which means someone from Judah, became common at this time.

Yet again the power structure in Mesopotamia shifted. In 539 BCE, the Persian Emperor Cyrus overthrew the Babylonians, returned 40,000 Jews to Judah (now known by its Greek pronunciation, *Judea*), and authorized the rebuilding of the temple. Judea, however, remained a province of the Persian Empire. The Jews who stayed in Babylon continued to prosper and grow in number, and their views may have been influenced by Zoroastrianism, the Persian religion at the time. Angelology and demonology become more prominent themes in post-exilic writings. Greater emphasis was placed on the resurrection of the dead, cataclysms of the end times, and the age of a redeemer or Messiah. In 458 BCE an additional 17,000 people returned to the land under the leadership of the priest Ezra. He left Babylon with a complete *Torah* in the form we have today, which is the five books of Moses. He and governor Nehemiah instituted a theocratic state with power vested in the priests. The Jews were required to take an oath to observe the Torah, tithe, sacrifice, and attend feasts. Marriage with foreigners was condemned in order to ensure cultural and religious survival. He also established a council called *The Great Synagogue* to formulate doctrine and perhaps compile the texts of the *Tanakh*. Ezra's and Nehemiah's reforms set a new direction for the Jewish religion.

MACCABEAN REVOLT AND THE HASMONEAN DYNASTY

The Persian Empire collapsed in 333 BCE during Alexander the Great's campaign for world domination. The next year Judea also fell under his control. After Alexander's death, the empire was divided among four of his generals, whose dynasties were committed to Hellenization, that is, the propagation of Greek culture. Judea was passed back and forth between two dynasties of the divided empire: the Selucid Dynasty of Persia and the Ptolemaic Dynasty of Egypt. From 301 to 198 BCE, life was peaceful under the Ptolemies. Then it changed hands to the Selucids. By 165 BCE, the extreme Hellenizing policies of the Selucid king Antiochus Epiphanes reduced central Jewish religious rites to capital crimes. For many young Jews their heritage became an embarrassment, as evidenced by a frequently practiced surgical reversal of circumcision. The ultimate assault against the Jewish religion was the erection in the temple of an altar to Zeus upon which pigs were sacrificed. Further plans were made to confiscate land from Jews who followed their traditions. In revolt, an old priest named Mattathias killed a commissioner who had ordered him to sacrifice to Zeus. Gathering his five sons and followers, he fled to the desert. From there his son Judas Maccabeus launched a guerrilla attack, recapturing Jerusalem and restoring worship. Although the Selucid army responded to the revolt, the Selucids could not engage in a protracted guerrilla war and ultimately recognized Judea as a semi-independent temple-state. The Maccabean leaders declared themselves a dynasty of Priest Kings, also called the Hasmonean Dynasty, and for the next hundred years engaged in relatively independent, though frequently despotic, rule.

The Hasmoneans expanded Judea's borders and fortified key cities. It is probably during this time that synagogues emerged as centers of local religious education and worship. According to Josephus, a noted Jewish historian of the first century CE, three religious orders also emerged: the Pharisees, the Sadducees, and the Essenes. The Pharisees were priests and laypeople who adopted a priestly life; they were proponents of oral tradition, purity rituals, a messianic kingdom, and the resurrection of the dead. They were also dedicated teachers of these doctrines to the masses. The Sadducees were aristocratic and priestly rivals of the Pharisees and denied many of their doctrines, especially those listed earlier. They also competed with the Pharisees for political influence in the Sanhedrin, the legislative assembly of Judea. The Essenes shared key doctrines with the Pharisees, such as food rituals, a messianic kingdom, and the resurrection of the dead. However, they became disgusted with the tyrannical rule of the Hasmoneans and the quarreling religious leaders and established a monastic community in the desert along the Dead Sea.

ROMAN DOMINATION

Hasmonean rule of Judea ended in 63 BCE when a civil war broke out between Jewish parties. Roman general Pompey was called in to arbitrate, but instead he occupied Judea and declared it a Roman province. The first Roman governors were particularly brutal, enslaving or crucifying those who disobeyed them. A cunning Jewish governor from Galilee, Herod the Great, was appointed King of the Jews in 37 BCE. Herod had non-Jewish ancestry and was never completely accepted by the Jews. Preoccupied with conspiracies against him, Herod built massive fortifications for protection. He also rebuilt Jerusalem and the temple on a grand scale. But taxation for these projects economically crippled the peasant population. After Herod's death in 4 BCE, the Romans appointed a series of governors who were insensitive to the religious practices and economic concerns of the people. Growing anti-Roman sentiment among the peasants led to revolts in which thousands of Jews were massacred. Incited by a prophecy that a Jewish Messiah would rule the world, a territory-wide peasant revolt finally erupted in 66 CE. Although it was initially success-ful, the Romans marched on the rebellious Jewish territories, destroying everything in their path. Most important, the elabo-rate new temple in Jerusalem was destroyed, bringing an end to temple sacrifices in 70 CE. Many Jews were sold as slaves, and the Jewish territories forfeited statehood status within the Roman Empire. With the temple in ruins for three generations, in 132 CE Jewish peasants and leaders were easily seduced by the messianic leader Simeon Bar Kokhba, who promised to restore the temple. His unsuccessful three-year revolt brought more destruction to the country and a massive dispersion, or Diaspora, of the Jews throughout Europe. Jerusalem became officially off limits to all Jews, and the country was ironically renamed *Palestine,* after the ancient Philistines, arch-enemies of the early Israelites.

DIASPORA

With the Diaspora, the center of Judaism shifted from Jerusalem to Babylonia, where a large population of Jews had remained after the 586 BCE exile. At its peak, 1 million Jews lived in Babylon in the years following the exile and restoration. The figure of the Rabbi emerged at this time as an authority in scrip-tural interpretation and Jewish law, culminating in the creation of the Babylonian *Talmud,* the ultimate repository of Jewish oral law and commentary. Babylonian Jews remained the dominant voice of Judaism until the Arab conquest of the region in the sev-enth century CE.

In the centuries following, Jews of the Diaspora attempted to settle in communities throughout Europe, only to be forced out as host countries became intolerant of them. In the reshuffling, two distinct groups emerged, each with its own distinct lan-guage and religious rituals. The Sephardic Jews were expelled from Spain and Portugal and moved to the Ottoman Empire. The Ashkenasic Jews were expelled from other countries and moved to eastern Europe.

Beginning in the eighteenth century, Judaism evolved in several directions. In reaction to impersonal rabbinic legalism and widespread disillusionment in the absence of the expected Messiah, the Hasidic movement was founded by Baal Shem Tov. Hasidism offered a more mystical and joyous approach to Judaism, particularly for the laity. Although Hasidim were at first persecuted by traditional rabbinic schools, eventually half of the traditional Rabbis joined them.

It was not until the eighteenth-century Enlightenment that European countries finally granted civil rights to their Jewish citizens. As an outgrowth of their freedom, Reform Judaism was founded in Germany by Abraham Geiger in the nineteenth century. Geiger believed that Judaism should pertain more to the sphere of religion than to culture and that Jewish worship practices should be modified to parallel those of Protestant Christians. In reaction, the Orthodox denomination reaffirmed the traditional elements of Judaism. Mediating between the reformed and orthodox views, the Conservative denomination emerged as an attempt to "conserve" historical traditions that the Reform denomination had eliminated. Finally, in the twentieth century the Reconstructionist denomination was founded by Mordecai Kaplan as a development from the Conservative denomination. Reconstructionists offer a more pragmatic approach in the modern world, placing more emphasis on the cultural development of Judaism than on its religious elements.

Jewish population was at its peak in 1939 with 17 million people world-wide (.8% of the world's population). The Nazi holocaust in World War II reduced that number to 11 million. Currently Jewish population is approximately 14 million (.2% of the world's population), 85% of whom reside in Israel and the United States, with approximately 6 million in each.

THE TANAKH

The most sacred collection of writings for Judaism is the *Tanakh*. The word *Tanakh* is an acronym coined in the middle ages from the initials of its three divisions: the Torah (Law), the Neviim (Prophets), and the Ketuvim (Writings). The twenty-four books of the *Tanakh* are traditionally categorized as follows:

Torah: Genesis, Exodus, Leviticus, Numbers, Deuteronomy
Neviim:
     Former Prophets: Joshua, Judges, Samuel, Kings
     Latter Prophets: Isaiah, Jeremiah, Ezekiel, The Twelve (Hosea, Joel, Amos, Obadiah, Jonah, Micah, Nahum, Habakkuk, Zephaniah, Haggai, Zechariah, Malachi)
Ketuvim: Psalms, Job, Proverbs, Ruth, Song of Songs, Ecclesiastes, Lamentations, Esther, Daniel, Ezra-Nehemiah, Chronicles

The books of the *Tanakh* were written and compiled over a period of a thousand years, from approximately 1100 to 100 BCE. Each book has a detailed history of authorship, editing, and reediting. The writings appear in a variety of literary genres, including song lyrics, historical chronicles, wisdom literature, laws, prophecies, and apocalypses. The oldest stories and poems, such as the

Song of Deborah, included here, may have been orally transmitted before taking written form. Much of the *Tanakh* bears the mark of post-exilic Judaism, either in composition or in editing. The books and main divisions of the *Tanakh* were in place when in 90 CE a Sanhedrin council in the Palestinian city of Jabneh gave the list its official stamp.

Of all writings within Judaism, the five books of the Torah have always been considered the most sacred. Thus an understanding of its development is important. The term *Torah* means law, in the sense of instruction or teaching, which traces its authority to Moses. More specifically, *Torah* has come to mean the collection of writings consisting of Genesis, Exodus, Leviticus, Numbers, and Deuteronomy. Any account of the origin and authorship of the Torah must take place against the backdrop of a theory in biblical scholarship known as the Documentary Hypothesis, most famously articulated by Julius Wellhausen (1844–1918). According to this theory, the Torah is a fabric sewn from four distinct textual sources identified as J, E, P, and D. The J source acquired its name from its continued use of the word *Yahweh* (often mispronounced *Jehovah*) for God in early parts of the narrative (prior to the revelation of the divine name of God to Moses). The E source is so named for its pervasive use of the term *Elohim* for God. The D source refers to the bulk of the text of Deuteronomy, with its unique style. Finally, the P source derives its name from the priestly content of its text.

Since Wellhausen, biblical scholars have identified more precisely the authors and dates of the four sources. One interpretation is that the J source was written by an author of the southern kingdom and reflects the political interests of Judah. Sometimes this involves besmirching the north. The E source, by contrast, was written by an author of the northern kingdom, possibly a Levitic priest, who endorsed the north's political structure but attacked its religious establishment. Both J and E appear to have been written between 922 and 722 BCE. Shortly after the fall of the north to the Assyrians in 722 and during Hezekiah's reign in the south, J and E were spliced or *redacted* together into a single document as a conciliation to the northern Israelites who had migrated to Judah. In reaction to the influx of northern priests, the P source was created as an alternative to the J and E story. One hundred years later, during the reign of Josiah, the framework of the D source was written around an old law code as a catalyst for religious reform. The D source is the first part of a larger historical sequence encompassing Joshua, Judges, Samuel, and Kings, compiled and edited by a single historian. The complete sequence of texts, called the Deuteronomistic

History, details God's covenant with David for an unbroken royal lineage and rejection of local altars in favor of a single sacrificial site at the temple in Jerusalem. Finally, all four sources (J, E, P, and D) were redacted together into the five books of Moses, the Torah, by a priest (possibly Ezra) during or shortly after the Babylonian exile.

POST-EXILIC WRITINGS

From 300 BCE until about 200 CE, the notion of an official Jewish canon of scriptures was fluid, even after the council of Jabneh in 90 CE. Hundreds of religious texts appeared that were considered authoritative by many at this time. Although the authority of these texts was rejected by later Jewish scholars, even today they continue to have historical importance. These writings are classified into three collections: Apocrypha, Pseudepigrapha, and Dead Sea Scrolls.

The term *Apocrypha* is Greek for "concealed" and refers to thirteen texts that at one time were associated with the Jewish canon but were officially rejected at the council of Jabneh. The original source of the Apocrypha is a Greek translation of the Jewish scriptures called the Septuagint (meaning "Seventy"), so called because seventy-two Jewish scholars were brought to Egypt to create a Greek translation of Jewish scriptures between 285 and 246 BCE. Legend has it that each translated the first five books within seventy-two days, compared the various translations, and found them to be exactly the same. Completed around 100 BCE, the Septuagint contains the thirteen Apocryphal books interspersed among the other books of the *Tanakh,* with no clear distinction in importance. The thirteen books include Esdras 1 and 2, Tobit, Judith, the rest of the book of Esther, the Wisdom of Solomon, Ecclesiasticus (Sirach), Baruch, a Letter of Jeremiah, additions to the Book of Daniel (the Song of the Three Children, Susanna, and Bel and the Dragon), the Prayer of Manasseh, and Maccabees 1 and 2.

The term *Pseudepigrapha* means "writings with false subscriptions" and refers to a collection of fifty-two Jewish religious writings from 200 BCE to 200 CE, attributed to famous figures in Jewish history such as Abraham and Moses. In literary styles paralleling those of the *Tanakh,* its four theological themes are the origins of sin and evil, God's transcendence, a coming Messiah, and the resurrection of the dead. The Pseudepigrapha is important in showing the diversity of Jewish theology at this time and the development of doctrines such as the coming of a Messiah, which are only hinted at in the *Tanakh.*

The Dead Sea Scrolls are a collection of writings and fragments discovered between 1947 and 1960 in the Qumran Valley
area on the northwest shore of the Dead Sea. The religious community of Qumran was established around 200 BCE as a desert
haven against the oppressive political and religious realities of
the time and was destroyed in 70 CE by the Romans during the
Jewish revolt. The messianic community was preparing to be
joined by angels for a final war against evil on earth. Although
the Qumran community is often identified with the Essenes as
described by Josephus, its association with that or any other
sect is uncertain. Scriptures of the Qumran community were
discovered in 1947 and were made fully public in 1991. The
writings include the earliest copies of many texts of the *Tanakh*
as well as an array of previously unknown religious texts. When
first discovered, the new documents were thought to represent
the unique views of the post-exilic monastic community. More
recently, however, some historians believe they originated in
Jerusalem, the center of Jewish religious activity, and thus, like
the Pseudepigrapha, reflect the breadth of Jewish scripture at
the time.

RABBINIC WRITINGS

During the first five centuries CE, Judaism witnessed a dramatic
flourishing of literary activity among Rabbis. One such was the
composition of verse-by-verse commentaries on the *Tanakh,*
known collectively and stylistically as *midrash*. Another and
more important type of activity was the development of oral
law, culminating in the texts of the *Mishnah* and the *Talmud*.
Traditionally, the oral law of Judaism is believed to have been
given to Moses by God at Mount Sinai and orally transmitted for
1,500 years. In view of its divine origin, the oral law is on the
same scriptural plane as the *Tanakh*. Historically, the foundation
of the oral law tradition is thought to have been laid with Ezra's
Great Synagogue, continuing through the Pharisees and then
extensively developed by the *Tannaim,* scholarly Rabbis who
lived during the first two centuries CE. Although the *Tannaim*
resisted committing the oral traditions to writing, in 200 CE
the Palestinian Rabbi Judah Ha-Nasi did just that. The resulting work is the *Mishnah,* a collection of sayings attributed to
specific *Tannaim* and rabbinic schools from the first two centuries CE. The sayings are stylistically rhythmic, which facilitated
their early memorization. Much of its content derives from the
legal codes in the Torah, although it rarely quotes the *Tanakh*
directly. The text contains six key divisions: agricultural rules,
laws governing the Sabbath and holidays, laws on marriage and

divorce, the system of civil and criminal law, rules of temple sacrifices, and rules of purities and impurities.

Early Rabbis developed a tradition of commenting on the
contents of the *Mishnah*. One collection, called the *Tosefta,*
was written by the *Tannaim* themselves. After the *Tannaim,*
two other groups of Rabbis continued commenting on the
Mishnah: the *Amoraim* (200–500 CE) and the *Saboraim* (500–
700 CE). Their comments became the basis of the *Talmud,* the
grandest expression of this rabbinic tradition. A first version
of the *Talmud* appeared in 450 CE in Jerusalem, and a second
and longer version in 600 CE in Babylon. Material was added
to each version in the following century. Both the Jerusalem
and Babylonian Talmuds have two parts: first, the text of the
Mishnah, and second, the *Gemara,* a several-thousand-page
collection of comments on the *Mishnah* written by the *Amoraim*
and *Saboraim.* Both Talmuds are structured according to the
main divisions of the *Mishnah,* although the Babylonian *Talmud*
covers more divisions than its Jerusalem counterpart and thus
is more definitive.

MEDIEVAL AND RECENT WRITINGS

At the close of the Rabbinic period, Jewish writers continued
penning commentaries on the *Tanakh* and *Talmud.* Only two
of these writers will be mentioned here. First is the great philosopher Moses Maimonides (1135–1204), whose family left
Spain for North Africa to avoid persecution. When only 23,
Maimonides began writing an extensive commentary on the
Mishnah, included in which is a statement of thirteen articles
of faith that subsequently became a regular part of Jewish
prayer services. The second influential author of the period
was the thirteenth-century Spaniard Moses de Leon, who, writing in the Jewish mystical tradition of Kabbala, composed the
multivolume *Book of Splendor (Sefer ha-Zohar).* The hero of
the book, Rabbi Shimon, a second-century CE *Tannaim,* presents to his followers a verse-by-verse mystical commentary
on several books of the *Tanakh.* To gain a receptive audience
and lend authenticity to its content, de Leon claimed that his
work was a recently discovered ancient text written by Rabbi
Shimon himself. For almost 600 years, Kabbalists took de
Leon at his word. The various Jewish movements of the past
few centuries—Hasidism, the Jewish Enlightenment, Reform
Judaism, Orthodox Judaism, Conservative Judaism, Zionism,
Reconstructionist Judaism—have each given birth to revered
works in several genres, including commentaries, tales, statements of faith, and polemics.

HOLIDAYS

Sabbath (Shabbat; literally, "seventh," i.e., "Saturday") Weekly day of worship that commemorates God's rest on the seventh day of creation.

New Year's Day (Rosh Hashanah; usually September) Beginning of the Jewish year.

Day of Atonement (Yom Kippur; late September or early October) Commemorates the Jewish people's wanderings in the desert.

Festival of Booths (Sukkot; September or October) Commemorates the Israelites' living in booths after their exodus from Egypt.

Pentecost (Shavu'ot; usually May) Commemorates Moses receiving the Torah at Mount Sinai.

Festival of Lights (Hanukkah; December) Commemorates the re-dedication of the Second Temple in Jerusalem to holy service by the Maccabees.

Festival of Lots (Purim; usually March) Commemorates the rescue of the Jews of ancient Persia.

TIMELINE

922 BCE	Kingdom of Israel divided between north and south
722 BCE	Assyrian invasion of northern kingdom
587 BCE	Babylonian invasion of southern kingdom
200–100 BCE	*Tanakh* canonized
164 BCE	Jews under Judas Maccabeus
63 BCE	Judea becomes a Roman province
66–70 CE	Jewish revolt; destruction of temple and fall of Jerusalem
132–135	Simeon Bar Kokhba revolt and mass dispersion (Diaspora) of Jews

TIMELINE *(Continued)*

200	*Mishnah* compiled
450–600	Jerusalem and Babylonian Talmuds compiled
900–1090	Golden age of Jewish culture in Spain
1135–1204	Maimonides, leading Rabbi of Sephardic Judaism
1250–1300	Moses de Leon, publisher of the *Zohar*
1492	Jews expelled from Spain
1700–1760	Ba'al Shem Tov, founder of Hasidic Judaism
1820–1860	Development of Orthodox Judaism and Reform Judaism
1897	Theodor Herzl advocates creating an independent Jewish state in Israel
1938–1945	Nazi Holocaust
1948	Israel declares itself an independent nation

GLOSSARY

Amoraim Rabbinic sages from 200 to 500 CE whose comments on the *Mishnah* are in the *Talmud*.

Deuteronomistic History The historical sequence of books in the *Tanakh* from Deuteronomy through Chronicles, connected in terms of authorship and theology.

Diaspora Dispersion of the Jews outside of Israel.

Elohim Hebrew for *God*.

Israelite People of Israel until the return from the Babylonian exile.

Jew Descendants of the Israelites from the return from the Babylonian exile to the present. *Jew* is from the Hebrew *jehudi,* meaning a descendant of Jacob's son Judah.

Judea The name for the land of the Jews from the post-exilic period to the early Roman period.

Kabbala Literally, "Tradition"; the largest school of Jewish mysticism, from the twelfth century CE to the present.

Midrash A verse-by-verse style of commentary on the *Tanakh,* especially as used by early Rabbis.

Mishnah The written expression of the oral law, compiled in 200 CE by Rabbi Judah Ha-Nasi.

Saboraim Rabbinic sages from 500 to 700 CE whose comments on the *Mishnah* were added to those of the Amoraim in the *Talmud*.

Sefirot The ten emanations of God, as described in early Kabbalist theology.

Talmud An extensive collection of commentaries on the *Mishnah* compiled from the sayings of Rabbis from 200 to 500 CE.

Tanakh The Hebrew Bible. The term comes from the initials of its three divisions: Torah (Law), Neviim (Prophets), Ketuvim (Writings).

Tannaim Rabbinic sages of the first two centuries CE whose sayings are compiled in the *Mishnah*.

Torah Hebrew for law, teaching, or instruction. In the broad sense, *Torah* refers to the law of Moses, both written and oral. In the narrow sense, it refers to the first five books of the *Tanakh*, traditionally called the Books of Moses.

Yahweh The personal name of God in Judaism.

BOOKS OF MOSES

CREATION

The first eleven books of the Tanakh *present a continuous historical narrative from the creation of the world until the Babylonian exile. Genesis opens with two creation stories, one from the P or Priestly source, and one from the J or Yahwist source. Central to both is the idea that human beings are the pinnacle of God's creative activity. The P source creation story, presented here, emphasizes the cosmic structure of creation, as opposed to the earlier and perhaps agrarian-oriented account of the J source. Also, the writer sees creation as involving three mandates. First, people are to fill the earth and master it. Second, people are to eat plants for food. Finally, the seventh day of the week is declared holy.*

In the beginning God created the heavens and the earth. The earth was formless and empty. Darkness covered the surface of the abyss. A mighty wind hovered over the surface of the waters. God said, "Let there be light," and there was light; he saw that the light was good. God separated light from darkness and called the light Day and the darkness Night. Evening came, then morning, making it the first day.

God said, "Let there be an arch in the middle of the waters to separate water from water." God made the arch, and it divided the water above it from that below it. Thus it happened. God called the arch sky. Evening came, then morning, making it the second day.

God said, "Let the water under the sky be gathered together to one place, and let dry land appear;" and it happened. God called the dry land Earth, and the gathering together of the water he called seas. He saw that it was good. God said, "Let the earth produce vegetation, plants producing seed, and fruit trees bearing fruit with its own seeds. And so it happened on the earth. The earth produced vegetation making its own seeds, and trees bearing fruit with its own seeds. God saw that it was good. Evening came, then morning, making it the third day.

God said, "Let there be lights in the arch of the sky to separate day from the night; and let them designate the seasons, the days and the years. Let the lights in the arch of the sky give light on the earth," and it happened. God made the two great lights: the greater light to rule the day, and the lesser light to rule the night. He also made the stars. God set them in the arch of the sky to illuminate the earth, to rule over the day and the night, and to separate light from darkness. God saw that it was good. Evening came, then morning, making it the fourth day.

God said, "Let the waters swarm with living creatures, and let birds fly above the earth in the open arch of the sky." God created large sea creatures, and every living creature that moves and swarms in the water, after their kinds, and every winged bird after its kind. God saw that it was good. He blessed them, saying, "Be fruitful, multiply, fill the water in the seas, and let birds multiply on the earth." Evening came, then morning, making it the fifth day.

God said, "Let the earth produce living creatures after their kind, livestock, creeping things, and animals of the earth after their kind," and it happened. God made the animals of the earth after their kind, and the livestock after their kind, and everything that creeps on the ground after its kind. God saw that it was good.

God said, "Let us make human beings in our image, after our likeness, and let them rule over the fish of the sea, the birds of the sky, domestic animals, wild animals, and every creature that crawls on the earth."

> God created human beings in his own image.
> In God's image he created them;
> male and female he created them.

God blessed them and said to them, "Be fruitful, multiply, fill the earth, and subdue it. Rule over the fish of the sea, the birds of the sky, and every living thing that moves on the earth." God said, "I have given you every plant-producing seed that is on the surface of all the earth, and every tree that produces fruit with seed. This will be your food. I have given green plants for food to every animal of the earth, every bird of the sky, and everything that creeps on the earth in which there is life." And so it happened. God saw everything that he had made, and it was very good. Evening came, then morning, making it the sixth day.

The heavens and the earth were finished, and all the variety in it. On the seventh day God finished the work that he had made. On the seventh day he rested from all the work that he made. God blessed the seventh day and made it holy, because on that day he rested from all the work that he had created.

Source: Genesis 1:1–2:3. This and the following selections from the *Tanakh* are adapted from the *American Standard Version*.

ADAM AND EVE

The second creation story in Genesis, found in Chapter 2, is from the J or Yahwist source, which some scholars believe predates the P source story in Genesis Chapter 1. Unlike the P source story, which emphasizes cosmological themes, this one is earthier with its description of geography, plants and animals, and the Garden of Eden. In this chapter, God is referred to "Yahweh Elohim" in the original Hebrew, which is traditionally translated as "Lord God." In this context, "Yahweh" is the proper name of God, and "Elohim" a more generic title of God.

This is the story of the heavens and the earth when they were created. When the LORD God made the earth and the heavens, there was no shrub or plant growing in the ground, for the LORD God had not yet made it rain on the earth and there was no one to cultivate the ground. A mist swelled up from the earth and watered the surface of the ground. The LORD God formed a man from the dust of the ground, and breathed into his nostrils the breath of life. The man then became a living soul.

The LORD God planted a garden eastward, in Eden, and placed in it the man he had formed. Out of the ground, the LORD God made every tree grow that is pleasing to the sight, and good for food. In the middle of the garden was the tree of life and the tree of the knowledge of good and evil.

A river flowed out of Eden to water the garden, and from there it split into four branches. The name of the first is Pishon, which is the one that flows through the land of Havilah, where there is gold. The gold of that land is good, and it also has aromatic resin and the onyx stone. The name of the second river is Gihon, which is the one that flows through the land of Cush. The name of the third river is Hiddekel, which is the one which flows east of Assyria. The fourth river is the Euphrates.

The LORD God took the man and put him in the garden of Eden to cultivate and care for it. The LORD God commanded the man, saying, "You may freely eat from every tree in the garden except for the tree of the knowledge of good and evil; the day that you eat from it you will surely die."

The LORD God then said, "It is not good for the man to be alone; I will make a suitable helper for him." Out of the ground the LORD God formed every wild animal and bird of the sky, and brought them to the man to see what he would call them. Whatever the man called each living creature, that became its name. The man gave names to all domestic animals, to the birds of the sky, and to every wild animal. But for the man himself there was not found a suitable helper. The LORD God made the man fall into a deep sleep, and as he slept he took one of his ribs, and closed up his flesh in that place. The LORD God then built up the rib that he had taken from the man into a woman, and brought her to the man. The man said,

"This is now bone of my bones, and flesh of my flesh.
She will be called woman, because she was taken out of man."

For this reason a man will leave his father and his mother to join with his wife, and they will be one flesh. The man and his wife were both naked, but were not ashamed.

Source: Genesis 2:4–25.

THE FALL

Following the second creation story in Genesis, the text continues with one of the most famous stories of world literature; namely, the expulsion of Adam and Eve from the Garden of Eden for eating fruit from a forbidden tree.

The serpent was shrewder than any wild animal that the LORD God had made. He said to the woman, "Did God really forbid you from eating from any tree of the garden?"

The woman said to the serpent, "We may eat the fruit from the trees of the garden, except the fruit from the tree which is in the middle of the garden; God has forbidden us to eat from it or even touch it, otherwise we will die."

The serpent said to the woman, "Surely you will not die, for God knows that when you eat it, your eyes will be opened, and you will be like God, knowing good and evil."

When the woman saw that the tree was good for food, delightful to the eyes, and desirable for making one wise, she took its fruit and ate it. She then gave some to her husband, and he ate it. The eyes of both of them were then opened, and they knew that they were naked. They sewed fig leaves together and made themselves aprons. When the man and his wife heard the voice of the Lord God walking in the garden in the cool of the day, they hid within the trees of the garden from the presence of the Lord God.

The Lord God called to the man, "Where are you?"

The man said, "I heard your voice in the garden, and I was afraid because I was naked, so I hid myself."

God said, "Who told you that you were naked? Have you eaten from the tree that I commanded you not to eat from?"

The man said, "The woman that you placed here with me, she gave me the fruit of the tree, and I ate it."

The Lord God said to the woman, "What is this you have done?"

The woman said, "The serpent tricked me, and I ate it."

The Lord God said to the serpent,

> "Because you have done this, you are cursed,
> more than all domestic animals and wild animals.
> On your belly you will go, and you will eat dust all the days of your life.
> I will put animosity between you and the woman, and between your offspring and her offspring.
> They will strike at your head, and you will strike at their heel."

He said to the woman,

> "I will greatly multiply your pain in childbirth.
> In pain you will bring forth children.
> You will desire your husband, but he will rule over you."

He said to Adam, "Because you have listened to your wife and ate from the tree which was forbidden of you,

> Cursed is the ground because of you. In toil you will eat from it all the days of your life.
> It will produce thorns and thistles for you, and you will eat wild plants.
> Only by the sweat of your brow will you eat your bread, until you return to the ground, for from it you were taken.
> For you are dust, and to dust you will return."

The man called his wife Eve because she was the mother of all the living. The Lord God made coats of skins for Adam and his wife, and clothed them.

The Lord God said, "The man has become like one of us, knowing good and evil. Now, what if he also puts out his

hand and takes from the tree of life, eats it, and lives forever?" The LORD God then banished him from the garden
of Eden, to till the ground from which he was taken. After
he drove out the man, he placed Cherubs at the east of the
garden of Eden, and a flaming sword whirling every way, to
guard the way to the tree of life.

Source: Genesis 3:1–24.

COVENANT WITH NOAH

The first great covenant in the Tanakh *is between God and
Noah. The P text story relates how God finds all the earth's
inhabitants wicked, except for Noah, and destroys the earth in
a flood. When the water subsides, God promises that he will not
again destroy the world by water, and permits humans to eat
animal flesh. The authors of the P text note later (in Exodus 40)
that all slaughter of animals must be done within the context of
a sacrificial rite conducted by a priest.*

God blessed Noah and his sons, and said to them, "Be fruitful and multiply, and replenish the earth. The fear of you
and the dread of you will come upon every animal of the
earth, on every bird of the sky, on everything in the ground
that moves, and on all the fish of the sea. They are delivered
into your hand. Every moving thing that lives will be food
for you. I have given everything to you, as I have the green
plant. But you are forbidden from eating flesh still with its
lifeblood. I will require an accounting of your lifeblood, I will
require it of every animal, and I will require from every man
an accounting of the death of his fellow-man. Whoever sheds
a man's blood, his blood will in turn be shed, for God made
man in his own image. Be fruitful and multiply. Populate the
earth and subdue it."

God said to Noah and his sons with him, "I am establishing
my covenant with you, and with your descendants after you,
and with every living creature that was with you: the birds, the
domestic animals, the wild animals, all that left the ark, all the
animals of the earth. I will establish my covenant with you that
never again will all creatures be destroyed by flood waters, neither will there ever again be a flood to destroy the earth."

God also said, "This is the sign of the covenant which I
make between me and you and every living creature that is
with you, for endless generations:

I place my rainbow in the clouds,
and it will be for a sign of the covenant
between me and the earth.

> When I bring clouds over the earth, the rainbow will be seen in the clouds.

I will then remember my covenant with you and every living creature of all flesh: that flood waters will never again destroy all creatures. When the rainbow is in the clouds, I will look at it and remember the unending covenant between God and every living creature of all kinds that is on the earth." God said to Noah, "This is the sign of the covenant that I have established with all creatures on the earth."

Source: Genesis 9:1–17.

COVENANT WITH ABRAHAM

The second great covenant of the Tanakh, *as it appears in the J text, is between God and Abraham, when Abraham is selected by God to be father of a multitude. God indicates that he will inherit the land of Canaan, and circumcision is to be the sign of that covenant. Circumcision is a rite to be performed by priests. The Hebrew term "Yahweh" when it appears by itself, is traditionally translated as "Lord," as it is in the context below.*

When Abram was ninety-nine years old, the Lord appeared to Abram, and said to him, "I am God Almighty. Walk before me, and be blameless. I will make my covenant with you, and you will have many descendants."

Abram fell on his face, and God said to him, "As for me, this is my covenant with you: You will be the father of many nations. Your name will no longer be Abram, but now will be Abraham; for I have made you the father of many nations. I will make you exceedingly fruitful, and will make nations of you. Kings will descend from you. I will establish my covenant with you and your offspring after you, throughout the ages, for an endless covenant, to be your God and the God of your offspring after you. I will give to you, and your offspring after you, the land in which you are traveling, all the land of Canaan, as a permanent possession. I will be their God."

God said to Abraham, "As for you, you will keep my covenant, you and your offspring after you throughout the ages. This is my covenant with you and your offspring after you, which you will keep: every male among you must be circumcised. You must circumcise the flesh of your foreskin. It will be a sign of the covenant between us. Throughout your generations, every male among you who is eight days old, will be circumcised, including servants who are born in your house, or bought with money from any foreigner who is not of your offspring. Yes, servants who are born in your house, and those bought with your money, must be circumcised. My covenant will be in your flesh as everlasting covenant. The uncircumcised male whose flesh of the foreskin is not circumcised, that soul will be cut off from his people. He has broken my covenant."

God said to Abraham, "As for Sarai your wife, you will no longer call her by the name Sarai, but her new name will be Sarah. I will bless her, and I will give you a son by her. Yes, I will bless her, and she will be a mother of nations. Kings of nations will come from her."

Then Abraham fell on his face laughing and said to himself, "Will a child be born to someone one hundred years old? Will Sarah, who is ninety years old, give birth?" Abraham said to God, "If only Ishmael were acceptable to you."

God said, "No, your wife Sarah will bear you a son, and you will call him by the name Isaac. I will establish my covenant with him for an everlasting covenant for his offspring after him. As for Ishmael, I have heard you. I have blessed him, and will make him fruitful, and will greatly multiply him. He will become the father of twelve princes, and I will make him a great nation. But I will establish my covenant with Isaac, whom Sarah will bear to you at this time next year."

Source: Genesis 17:1–22.

PASSOVER AND EXODUS

Abraham's descendants migrate to Egypt to avoid famine in Canaan, and within a few generations their population dramatically increases. Intimidated by their numbers, the Pharaoh enslaves the Israelites and issues an edict that male infants are to be drowned. To save her child, one woman places her toddler, Moses, in a basket and floats it down the Nile, where it is discovered and he is adopted by the Pharaoh's daughter. When Moses grows up, God appears to him and instructs him to lead his people out of Egypt and into Canaan. To break the Pharaoh's resistance to releasing the Israelites, God kills the firstborn humans and cattle in Egypt. In preparation for the event, the Israelites are instructed to perform a series of activities as described here. Passover, one of Judaism's most sacred feasts, is a celebration of this event.

At midnight the Lord struck down all the firstborn in the land of Egypt, from the firstborn of Pharaoh who sat on his throne, to the firstborn of the prisoner who was in the dungeon. So too with the firstborn of livestock. Pharaoh, his officials and all the Egyptians woke up in the night because of a loud cry in Egypt: there was not a house without someone dead. At night he sent for Moses and Aaron, and said, "Get up, get away from my people, you and the Israelites. Go and serve the LORD, as you requested. Take your flocks and herds, as you requested, and leave; and may you bless me also."

The Egyptians urged the people to quickly leave their land and said, "We are all dead men." The people took their dough before it was leavened in their kneading bowls, which they wrapped in their clothes on their shoulders. As Moses instructed, the Israelites asked the Egyptians for their gold and silver jewelry and for their clothing. The LORD made the people well-favor in the eyes of the Egyptians, so that they let them have what they requested. In this way they plundered the Egyptians.

The Israelites traveled from Rameses to Succoth, about six hundred thousand men on foot, plus women and children. Other ethnic groups went with them, including much livestock, both flocks and herds. They baked unleavened bread from the dough that they brought from Egypt; it had no leavening because they left Egypt in a hurry and could not wait to prepare any food for themselves. The time that the Israelites lived in Egypt was four hundred thirty years. At the end of four hundred thirty years, to the exact day, all the armies of the LORD left the land of Egypt. . . .

When the king of Egypt was told that the people fled, Pharaoh's attitude, and that of his officials, changed toward the people, and they said, "What have we done? We released the Israelites from serving us." Pharaoh prepared his chariot and took his army with him. They had six hundred select chariots, and all the other chariots in Egypt, with captains over them all. As for Pharaoh the king of Egypt, the LORD made his mind persistent, and he pursued the Israelites as they defiantly left. The Egyptians chased after them, all the horses and chariots of Pharaoh, his horsemen, and his army. They overtook them where they camped by the sea, at Pi-hahiroth, near Baal-zephon.

When Pharaoh approached, the Israelites looked up and saw the Egyptians marching toward them. They were very frightened and cried out to the LORD. They then said to Moses, "Were burial sites unavailable in Egypt so that you brought us out here to die in the wilderness? Look at what you have done by taking us out of Egypt like this. Is this not precisely what we meant when we said to you in Egypt, 'Leave us alone so that we may serve the Egyptians?' It would have been much better for us to serve the Egyptians than to die here in the wilderness."

Moses said to the people, "Do not be frightened. Stand firm and watch the LORD save you, which he will do for you today. As for the Egyptians that you see here now, you will never see them again. The LORD will fight for you, and so just stay still."

The LORD said to Moses, "Why are you crying out to me? Tell the Israelites to move forward. Lift up your staff, stretch out your hand over the sea and divide it, so that the Israelites can go through the middle of the sea on dry ground. I will make the minds of the Egyptians persistent, and they will go in after them. I myself will gain honor over Pharaoh, his armies, his chariots, and his horsemen. The Egyptians will know that I am the LORD when I have gained honor over Pharaoh, his chariots, and his horsemen." Then the angel of God, who had been guiding the Israelite army, moved behind them, and the cloud column also moved from in front to behind. The cloud came between the Egyptian camp and the Israelite camp. During the night, the cloud made it dark on one side but light on the other, so neither camp went near the other all night long.

Moses then stretched out his hand over the sea, and the LORD pushed the sea back by a strong east wind throughout the night, which made the sea dry land. The water was thus divided. The Israelites went through the middle of the sea on the dry ground, and the water was a wall for them on their right and left sides. The Egyptians followed in pursuit, and went in after them into the middle of the sea, including all of Pharaoh's horses, chariots, and horsemen. Before dawn, the LORD looked out over the Egyptian army through the column of fire and cloud, and threw them into confusion. He locked their chariot wheels, so they moved slowly. The Egyptians then said, "Let us get away from these Israelites, for the LORD fights for them against Egypt."

The LORD then said to Moses, "Stretch out your hand over the sea, so that the water may fall on the Egyptians, their chariots, and their horsemen." When morning came, Moses stretched out his hand over the sea, and the sea returned to its place. The Egyptians fled directly into it and the LORD threw the Egyptians into the middle of the sea. The waters returned and covered the chariots, the horsemen, and Pharaoh's entire army that followed them into the sea. Not one of them remained. But the Israelites walked on dry land in the middle of the sea, with the waters making a wall for them on their right and left sides.

Source: Exodus 12:29–41, 14:5–29.

MOSAIC COVENANT

The third great covenant in the Tanakh *text consists of God giving the Law to Moses at Mount Sinai, a means by which the Israelites could become a holy people. Mosaic Law is articulated throughout the books of Exodus, Leviticus, Numbers, and Deuteronomy, interspersed with narratives about the Israelites' forty years of wandering. Exodus 19, a JE text, describes the people's preparation for receiving the Law from God. Exodus 20, which is possibly a reworked version of an ancient P text, presents the best-known part of the Mosaic Law, the Ten Commandments.*

Moses at Mount Sinai

On the first day of the third month after the Israelites had left the land of Egypt, they came into the Sinai desert. When they left Rephidim, and arrived at the Sinai desert, they encamped in the desert where the Israelites set up before the mountain. Moses went up to God, and the LORD called to him from the mountain, "This is what you will tell the house of Jacob, and tell the children of Israel: You have seen what I did to the Egyptians, and how I carried you on eagles' wings, and brought you here to me. Now if you obey me and keep my covenant, then you will be my treasured possession from among all nations; for the whole earth is mine. You will be to me a kingdom of priests and a holy nation. These are the words that you must speak to the Israelites."

Moses went back down and called for the elders of the people, and set before them everything that the LORD commanded of him. All the people responded together, "Everything that the LORD has said we will do."

Moses reported the words of the people to the LORD. The LORD said to Moses, "I am coming to you in a thick cloud so that the people may hear when I speak to you, and may always trust you." Moses told the LORD how the people responded. The LORD said to Moses, "Go to the people and purify them today and tomorrow. Have them wash their clothes, and be ready for the third day; for on the third day the LORD will come down on Mount Sinai in the sight of all the people. Set boundaries all around for the people and tell them, Be careful that you do not go up into the mountain, or touch its border. Whoever touches the mountain must be put to death. No hand must touch him, but he must be stoned or shot through with arrows; whether it is animal or man, he must not live. Only when the ram's horn sounds a long blast, may they come to the mountain."

Moses went down from the mountain to the people and purified the people, and they washed their clothes. He said to the people, "Be ready by the third day. Do not be intimate with a woman."

On the morning of the third day there was thunder and lightning. A thick cloud appeared on the mountain, a horn blew very loudly, and everyone in the camp trembled. Moses then led the people out of the camp to meet God, and they stood at the lower part of the mountain. Mount Sinai was covered with smoke, because the LORD descended on it in fire. The smoke rose like that from a furnace, and the whole mountain shook violently. When the sound of the horn grew louder and louder, Moses spoke, and God answered him in a thunderous voice. The LORD came down onto the top of Mount Sinai, and the LORD called Moses to the top of the mountain. Moses went up.

The LORD said to Moses, "Go down and warn the people, otherwise they will break through to gaze at the LORD, and many of them will perish. Even the priests, who come near to the LORD must purify themselves, otherwise the LORD will break out against them."

Moses said to the LORD, "The people cannot come up to Mount Sinai, for you warned us, saying, 'Set boundaries around the mountain, and purify it.'"

The LORD replied, "Go down and bring Aaron up with you, but do not let the priests and the people break through to come up to the LORD, otherwise he will break out against them."

So Moses went down to the people and told them.

The Ten Commandments

God then spoke all these words, saying, "I am the LORD your God, who brought you out of the land of Egypt, out of the place of slavery. Do not have other gods before me.

"Do not make for yourselves an idol, nor any image of anything that is in the heavens above, or that is in the earth beneath, or that is in the water under the earth. You must not bow down to them, nor serve them, for I, the LORD your God, am a jealous God, punishing the sins of the parents on their children, on through the third and fourth generation of those who hate me, but show loving kindness to thousands of those who love me and keep my commandments.

"Do not take the name of the LORD your God in vain, for the LORD will not hold him guiltless who takes his name in vain.

"Remember the Sabbath day, to keep it holy. Labor six days, and do all your work, but the seventh day is a Sabbath to the LORD your God. Do not do any work on it, neither you, your son, your daughter, your male servant, your female servant, your livestock, nor your stranger who is within your gates. For in six days the LORD made heaven and earth, the sea, and all that is in them, and rested on the seventh day; accordingly the LORD blessed the Sabbath day and made it holy.

"Honor your father and your mother, so that your days may be long in the land which the LORD your God gives you.

"Do not murder.

"Do not commit adultery.

"Do not steal.

"Do not give false testimony against your neighbor.

"Do not covet your neighbor's house. Do not covet your neighbor's wife, his male servant, his female servant, his ox, his donkey, nor anything that is your neighbor's."

All the people witnessed the thunder and lightning, the sound of the horn, and the mountain smoking. They trembled when they saw it and stayed at a distance. They said to Moses, "Speak with us yourself, and we will listen; but do not let God speak with us, or we will die."

Source: Exodus 19, 20:1–19.

HOLINESS CODE

The Mosaic Law contains a series of codes on social, ethical, and religious topics, such as the Covenant Code (Exodus 21–23), the Purity Code (Leviticus 11–16), the Holiness Code (Leviticus 17–27), and the Law Code (Deuteronomy 12–26). The literary and legal style of these codes is frequently compared to other codes of the ancient Near East, such as the Code of Hammurabi, king of Ur. For example, on the issue of kidnapping, the Hammurabi code states, "If a man has stolen the young son of a freeman, he shall be put to death." By comparison, the Covenant Code in Exodus 21:16 states, "He who kidnaps a man—whether he has sold him or is still holding him—shall be put to death." The following is from the Holiness Code, a P text in the Book of Leviticus.

The LORD said to Moses, Speak to the entire Israelite community, and tell them, Be holy, for I the LORD your God am holy.

Each of you must respect you mother and his father, and keep my Sabbaths. I am the LORD your God.

Do not turn to idols, or make molten gods for yourselves. I am the LORD your God.

When you make a sacrifice of peace offerings to the LORD, you must offer it so that it may be accepted. It must be eaten the same day you offer it, or on the next day. If anything remains until the third day, it must be burned. If any is eaten on the third day, it is impure and will not be accepted. Anyone who eats it must take responsibility, because he has defiled what his holy to the LORD, and that person must be cut off from his people.

When you reap the harvest of your land, you must not reap it to the corners of the field, or gather what is leftover from your harvest. You must not pick clean your vineyard, or gather the fallen grapes of your vineyard; you must leave them for the poor and for the foreigner. I am the LORD your God.

Do not steal, do not cheat, and do not lie to each other.

Do not swear falsely by my name and profane the name of your God. I am the LORD.

Do not exploit your neighbor or rob him. Do not retain the wages of a hired worker overnight.

Do not insult the deaf, or put an obstacle in front of the blind; you must fear your God. I am the LORD.

Do not be unjust in judgment: do not be biased against the poor or show favoritism to the great; rather, you must judge others fairly.

Do not spread slanderer among your people; do not act against the life of your neighbor. I am the LORD.

Do not hate your brother in your heart. Openly correct your neighbor so you do not incur sin because of him.

Do not take vengeance, or bear any grudge against your own people; but love your neighbor as yourself. I am the LORD.

Keep my statutes. Do not crossbreed different kinds of animals. Do not plant your field with two kinds of seeds. Do not make a garment from two kinds of material.

If a man lies sexually with a woman who is a slave, pledged to be married to another man, and not ransomed or given her freedom, there must be punishment. But they must not be put to death, because she was not free. The man must bring a ram as a trespass offering to the LORD at the door of the Tent of Meeting. The priest must make atonement for him with the ram of the trespass offering before the LORD for the sin which he committed. The sin will be forgiven.

When you come into the land and plant any kind of tree for food, you must consider its fruit as forbidden. For three years it is forbidden from you and must not be eaten. In the fourth year all its fruit will be holy, an offering of praise to the LORD. But in the fifth year you may eat its fruit so that its yield may increase for you. I am the LORD your God.

Do not eat any meat with the blood still in it; do not practice magic spells or soothsaying.

Do not cut the hair on the sides of your heads, or clip off the edge of your beard.

Do not make any cuts on your body for the dead, or tattoo yourselves. I am the LORD.

Do not degrade your daughter by making her a prostitute, or the land will fall into prostitution and become full of wickedness.

Keep my Sabbaths, and have reverence for my sanctuary; I am the LORD.

Do not consult mediums or spirits of the dead, by which you will be defiled. I am the LORD your God.

Stand up in the presence of the aged, respect the elderly, and fear your God. I am the LORD.

If a foreigner lives with you in your land, you must not wrong him. You must treat the foreigner living among you as native-born. You must love him as yourself, for you were once foreigners in Egypt. I am the LORD your God.

Do not be dishonest with measurements of length, weight, or quantity. Have fair balances, fair weights, and fair dry and liquid measurements. I am the LORD your God, who brought you out of Egypt. Observe all my statutes, all my laws, and keep them. I am the LORD.

Source: Leviticus 19:1–37.

CONQUEST AND UNITED KINGDOM

ENTRY INTO CANAAN

After forty years of wandering, the Israelites enter Canaan under the leadership of Joshua, Moses' successor. This account is part of a larger text sequence called the Deuteronomistic History, edited just before the Babylonian exile and encompassing the books of Deuteronomy through second Kings. The story emphasizes Deuteronomist themes, such as the importance of the Ark of the Covenant as the focus of God's presence and the command to annihilate the present occupants of Canaan as a means of ensuring religious purity.

Joshua rallies the Israelites

After the death of Moses the servant of the LORD, the LORD spoke to Joshua the son of Nun, Moses' assistant, and said, "Moses my servant is dead; prepare now to go across the Jordan River, you, and all these people, the Israelites, to the land which I am giving them. I have given you every place on which you put the sole of your foot, as I told Moses. Your borders will be from the desert to Lebanon, and from the great river, the river Euphrates, the land of the Hittites, to the Great Sea where the sun sets. No one will be able to oppose you as long as you live. Just as I was with Moses, so too will I be with you. I will not fail you or abandon you. Be strong and courageous, for you will lead these people to inherit this land which I promised their fathers to give them. Be strong and courageous, and carefully follow the law that Moses my servant gave you. Do not turn from it, either to the right or the left, so that you may have good success wherever you go. This book of the law must always be on your lips; meditate on it day and night, so that you may carefully obey everything written in it. Then you will be prosperous and have much success. As I commanded you, be strong and of good courage. Do not be afraid or discouraged, for the LORD your God is with you wherever you go."

Joshua then commanded the officers of the people, "Go through the camp, and command the people, saying, 'Prepare food, for within three days you will cross the Jordan River to go and take possession of the land which the LORD your God gives you to possess.'"

Joshua spoke to the Reubenites, the Gadites, and the half-tribe of Manasseh, "Remember the word that Moses the servant of the LORD commanded you when he said, 'the LORD your God gives you rest, and will give you this land. Your wives, your little ones, and your livestock, will stay in the land that Moses gave you east of the Jordan River. But your warriors and mighty men of valor must first cross it. You must help them until the LORD has given your brothers rest, as he has given you, and they have also possessed the land that the LORD your God gives them. After that you will return to the land of your possession, which Moses the servant of the LORD gave you beyond the Jordan River toward the east, and occupy it.'"

They replied to Joshua, "Everything that you have commanded us we will do, and wherever you send us we will go. Just as we listened to Moses in all things, so too will we listen to you. May the LORD your God be with you, as he was with Moses. Whoever rebels against your orders, and does not listen to your words in everything that you command him, he will be put to death. Be strong and of good courage." . . .

Early in the morning Joshua and all the Israelites left Shittim, and came to the Jordan River. They camped there before they crossed over. Three days later, the officers went through the camp and commanded the people, "When you see the ark of the covenant of the Lᴏʀᴅ your God, with the Levitical priests carrying it, then you must move from your position, and follow it, so that you may know which way to go since you have not travelled this way before. But there must be a distance of about 200 cubits between you and it. Do not get near it."

The Israelites Cross the Jordan

Joshua said to the people, "Purify yourselves, for tomorrow the Lᴏʀᴅ will do wonders among you." Joshua said to the priests, "Lift up the ark of the covenant, and cross over ahead of the people." They lifted the ark of the covenant, and went in front of the people.

The Lᴏʀᴅ said to Joshua, "Today I will begin to exalt you in the eyes of all Israel, so that they may know that just as I was with Moses, so too will I be with you. Command the priests who carry the ark of the covenant, 'When you come to the edge of the water of the Jordan River, stand still there.'"

Joshua said to the Israelites, "Come here, and listen to the words of the Lᴏʀᴅ your God." Joshua said, "By this you will know that the living God is with you, and that he will without fail drive out ahead of you the Canaanites, the Hittites, the Hivites, the Perizzites, the Girgashites, the Amorites, and the Jebusites. Observe, the ark of the covenant of the Lᴏʀᴅ of all the earth crosses over ahead of you through the Jordan River. Select now twelve men out of the tribes of Israel, one per tribe. When the soles of the feet of the priests who carry the ark of the Lᴏʀᴅ, the Lᴏʀᴅ of all the earth, touch the water of the Jordan River, its water will be cut off, and the upstream water will stand in one heap."

When the people moved from their tents to pass across the Jordan, the priests who carried the ark of the covenant were ahead of them. When the priests who carried the ark arrived at the Jordan, and dipped their feet in the waters' edge, (for the Jordan overflows its banks throughout the time of harvest), the upstream water stood. It rose up in one heap a great way off at the town of Adam, near Zarethan. The water flowing down toward the sea of the Arabah, that is, the Dead Sea, was completely cut off. The people then crossed over opposite to Jericho. The priests who carried the ark of the covenant of the Lᴏʀᴅ stood firm on dry ground in the middle of the Jordan. All Israel passed over on dry ground, until the whole nation had completely passed over the Jordan.

Source: Joshua 1, 3.

SONG OF DEBORAH

After their entry into Canaan, the Israelites fight to dislodge the Canaanites. Israel is then governed by a series of legal and military judges, including Deborah, one of a few female leaders in Jewish history. With the aid of the military leader Barak, Deborah and a small group defeat the army of Jabin, King of Canaan. The Canaanite army, headed by Sisera, has an initial advantage of 900 chariots. Due to a sudden divinely caused cloudburst and flash flood, the Israelites gain the advantage. The Song of Deborah, which commemorates this victory, is one of the oldest passages of the Tanakh. *Composed about 1100 BCE, it is similar in structure to Canaanite poems of the period. Historically it denotes the Israelites' successful habitation of the hillsides, overshadowing Canaanite occupation of the valley regions.*

Because the leaders took the lead in Israel,
    because the people offered themselves willingly,
    bless the LORD
Hear, you kings.
    Give ear, you princes.
    I, even I, will sing to the LORD.
    I will sing praise to the LORD, the God of Israel.
LORD, when you went out of Seir,
    when you marched out of the field of Edom,
    the earth trembled, the sky also dropped.
    Yes, the clouds dropped water.
The mountains quaked at the presence of the LORD,
    even Sinai, at the presence of the LORD, the God of Israel.
In the days of Shamgar the son of Anath,
    in the days of Jael, the highways were unoccupied.
    The travelers walked through byways.
The rulers ceased in Israel.
    They ceased until I, Deborah, arose;
    Until I arose a mother in Israel.
They chose new gods.
    Then war was in the gates.
    Was there a shield or spear seen among forty thousand in Israel?
My heart is toward the governors of Israel,
    who offered themselves willingly among the people.
    Bless the LORD.
Tell of it, you who ride on white donkeys,
    you who sit on rich carpets,
    and you who walk by the way.
To the sound of the musicians, in the places of drawing water,
    there they will repeat the righteous acts of the LORD,
    Even the righteous acts of his rule in Israel.
    Then the people of the LORD went down to the gates.

>Awake, awake, Deborah.
>>Awake, awake, sing a song!
>>Arise, Barak, and lead away your captives, son of Abinoam.

Source: Judges 5:2–12.

DAVIDIC COVENANT

In response to the need for a ruler who could unify the country against Philistine attacks, Saul is appointed the first king. The Deuteronomistic History relates how Saul's disobedience quickly puts him in disfavor with God, after which God selects David as Saul's more obedient successor. This reflects the most consistent theological theme throughout all seven books of the Deuteronomistic History: Obedience to God results in prosperity, while disobedience results in hardship. The fourth and final great covenant in the Tanakh *is with King David, wherein a promise is given that David's house and kingship will be secure and his throne established forever.*

> [God said to the prophet Nathan] "You must now tell my servant David that the LORD of heaven's armies says, I took you from tending the sheep in the pasture and selected you to be ruler over my people Israel. I have been with you wherever you went, and have cut off all your enemies from before you. I will now make your name great, like the names of the great ones on earth. I will make a location for my people Israel, and will put them there so that they may live in their own place, and not be relocated again. Wicked people will not afflict them anymore, as before from the time that I appointed judges to rule over my people Israel, and I will give you rest from all your enemies.
>
> Moreover, the LORD tells you that the LORD will make you a dynasty. When your days are over, and you sleep with your ancestors, I will establish your offspring after you, who will proceed out of your body, and I will establish his kingdom. He will build a house for my name, and I will establish the throne of his kingdom forever. I will be his father, and he will be my son. If he does wrong, I will punish him with the rod of men, and with the lashes of the children of men. But my loving kindness will not be taken away from him, as I took it from Saul, whom I removed before you. Your house and your kingdom will be secure forever before me, and your throne will be established forever."

Source: 2 Samuel 7:8–16.

PSALMS ASCRIBED TO DAVID

The Book of Psalms is a collection of 150 songs and prayers written over a 600-year period, many after the Babylonian exile. The book may have taken its final form under the editorship of Ezra and sometimes is referred to as the hymn book of the second temple. Although the authorship of most of the psalms is uncertain, seventy-three are ascribed in the text to David and are traditionally said to reflect happy or troubled periods of his life. The psalms are classified as they relate to the themes of deliverance, penitence, praise, pilgrimages, historical episodes, and messianic hope. The following is a selection of psalms of David.

Psalm 8

The LORD, our LORD, how majestic is your name in all the earth,
    who has set your glory above the heavens.
From the lips of babes and infants you have established strength,
    because of your adversaries, that you might silence the enemy
    and the avenger.
When I consider your heavens, the work of your fingers,
    the moon and the stars, which you have ordained;
what is man that you think of him?
    What are the children of man that you care for them?
You have made him a little lower than God,
    and crowned him with glory and honor.
You make him ruler over the works of your hands.
    You have put all things under his feet:
All sheep and cattle,
    yes, and the animals of the field,
The birds of the sky, the fish of the sea,
    and whatever passes through the paths of the seas.
The LORD, our LORD,
    how majestic is your name in all the earth.

Psalm 23

The LORD is my shepherd:
    I will lack nothing.
He makes me lie down in green pastures.
    He leads me beside still waters.
He restores my soul.
    He guides me in the paths of righteousness for his name's sake.
Even though I walk through the valley of the shadow of death,
    I will fear no evil, for you are with me.
    Your rod and your staff, they comfort me.
You prepare a table before me in the presence of my enemies.
    You anoint my head with oil.
    My cup runs over.
Surely goodness and loving kindness will follow me all the days of my life,
    and I will dwell in the LORD's house forever.

Psalm 27

The Lord is my light and my salvation.
    Whom will I fear?
    The Lord is the strength of my life.
    Of whom will I be afraid?
When evil-doers came at me to eat up my flesh,
    even my adversaries and my foes, they stumbled and fell.
Though an army should encamp against me,
    my heart will not fear.
    Though war should rise against me,
    even then I will be confident.
One thing I have asked of the Lord, that I will seek after,
    that I may dwell in the house of the Lord all the days of my life,
    to see the Lord's beauty,
    and to inquire in his temple.
For in the day of trouble he will keep me secretly in his pavilion.
    In the concealment of his tent he will hide me.
    He will lift me up on a rock.
Now my head will be lifted up above my enemies around me.
    I will offer sacrifices of joy in his tent.
    I will sing, yes, I will sing praises to the Lord.
Hear, Lord, when I cry with my voice.
    Have mercy also on me, and answer me.
When you said, "Seek my face,"
    my heart said to you, "I will seek your face, Lord."
Do not hide your face from me.
    Do not put your servant away in anger.
    You have been my help.
    Do not abandon me,
    neither forsake me, God of my salvation.
When my father and my mother abandon me,
    then the Lord will take me up.
Teach me your way, Lord.
    Lead me in a straight path, because of my enemies.
Do not deliver me over to the desire of my adversaries,
    for false witnesses have risen up against me,
    such as breathe out cruelty.
I am still confident of this:
    I will see the goodness of the Lord in the land of the living.
Wait for the Lord.
    Be strong, and let your heart take courage.
    Yes, wait for the Lord.

Psalm 32

Blessed is he whose disobedience is forgiven,
    whose sin is covered.
Blessed is the man to whom the Lord does not attribute iniquity,
    in whose spirit there is no deceit.
When I kept silence, my bones wasted away through my groaning all
    day long.

For day and night your hand was heavy on me.
>My strength was sapped in the heat of summer.

I acknowledged my sin to you.
>I did not hide my iniquity.
>I said, I will confess my transgressions to the Lord,
>and you forgave the iniquity of my sin.

For this, let everyone who is godly pray to you in a time when you may be found.
>Surely when the great waters overflow, they will not reach to him.

You are my hiding place.
>You will preserve me from trouble.
>You will surround me with songs of deliverance.

I will instruct you and teach you in the way which you will go.
>I will counsel you with my eye on you.

Do not be like the horse, or like the mule, which have no understanding,
>who are controlled by bit and bridle, or else they will not come near to you.

Many sorrows come to the wicked,
>but loving kindness will surround him who trusts in the Lord.

Be glad in the Lord, and rejoice, you who are righteous.
>Shout for joy, all you who are upright in heart.

Psalm 51

Have mercy on me, God, according to your loving kindness.
>According to the multitude of your tender mercies, blot out my transgressions.

Wash me thoroughly from my iniquity.
>Cleanse me from my sin.

For I know my transgressions.
>My sin is constantly before me.

Against you, and you only, have I sinned,
>and done that which is evil in your sight;
>that you may be proved right when you speak,
>and justified when you judge.

I was brought forth in iniquity.
>In sin my mother conceived me.

You desire truth in the inward parts.
>You teach me wisdom in the inmost place.

Purify me with hyssop, and I will be clean.
>Wash me, and I will be whiter than snow.

Let me hear joy and gladness,
>That the bones which you have broken may rejoice.

Hide your face from my sins,
>and blot out all of my iniquities.

Create in me a clean heart, God.
>Renew a right spirit within me.

Do not throw me from your presence,
>and do not take your holy Spirit from me.

Restore to me the joy of your salvation.
>Uphold me with a willing spirit.

Then I will teach transgressors your ways.
>Sinners will be converted to you.

Deliver me from blood-guiltiness, God, the God of my salvation.
>My tongue will sing aloud of your righteousness.

Lᴏʀᴅ, open my lips.
>My mouth will declare your praise.

For you do not delight in sacrifice, or else I would give it.
>You have no pleasure in burnt offering.

The sacrifices of God are a broken spirit.
>A broken and contrite heart, God, you will not despise.

Do well in your good pleasure to Zion.
>Build the walls of Jerusalem.

Then you will delight in the sacrifices of righteousness,
>in burnt offerings and in whole burnt offerings.
>Then they will offer bulls on your altar.

Source: Psalms 8, 23, 27, 32, 51.

SOLOMON'S TEMPLE

Israel's glory peaked during the reign of King Solomon, David's son. Its borders extended farther than they ever would again (though not as far as under David), and Israel was a key player in ancient Near Eastern politics. The jewel in the crown of Solomon's achievements was his temple, said to have taken thirteen years to complete. According to the Deuteronomistic History, all sacrifices were to be performed only at the temple in Jerusalem; thus, the temple became the focus of all religious activity in Israel. The following describes the extent and wealth of Solomon's kingdom, his wisdom, and his construction of the temple.

Solomon's Wealth and Wisdom

The people of Judah and Israel were as numerous as the sands of the sea in quantity, eating, drinking and being happy. Solomon ruled over all the kingdoms from the Euphrates River to the land of the Philistines, and to the border of Egypt: they brought tribute, and served Solomon throughout his life. Solomon's provision for one day was thirty measures of fine flour, sixty measures of meal, ten head of fat cattle, twenty head of cattle from the pastures, and one hundred sheep, as well as deer, gazelles, roebucks, and fattened fowl. He ruled over all the region east of the Euphrates River, from Tiphsah to Gaza, over all the kings west of the River: and he had peace on all sides around him. Throughout Solomon's life, Judah and Israel lived safely, every man under his own vine and under his own fig tree, from Dan to Beersheba, Solomon had forty thousand stalls of horses for his chariots, and twelve thousand horsemen.

The regional governors provided food for king Solomon, and for all who came to king Solomon's table, each in his assigned month; they left nothing lacking. They also brought barley and straw for the horses and swift steeds, to the place where the governors were, each according to his duty.

God gave Solomon wisdom and understanding beyond measure, and breadth of knowledge as measureless as the sand on the seashore. Solomon's wisdom excelled that of all the people of the east, and the wisdom of Egypt. He was wiser than everyone, than Ethan the Ezrahite, Heman, Calcol, and Darda, and the sons of Mahol. He was famous throughout all surrounding nations. He composed three thousand proverbs and one thousand five songs. He spoke about vegetation from the cedars of Lebanon to the hyssop that grows out of walls. He also spoke about animals, birds, creeping things, and fish. People everywhere came to hear Solomon's wisdom, sent by kings of the earth who had heard about his wisdom.

Building the Temple

Hiram king of Tyre sent ambassadors to Solomon when he heard that Solomon became king succeeding his father: for Hiram was a friend of David. Solomon replied to Hiram, saying, "You know that my father David could not build a temple to honor the name of the LORD his God, since wars surrounded him on every side, until the LORD put his enemies under his feet. But now the LORD my God has given me rest on every side; there is no enemy or threat. So, I intend to build a temple to honor the name of the LORD my God, just as the LORD spoke to David my father, saying, Your son, whom I will set on your throne in your place, he will build the temple in my name. Therefore give the command to cut the cedars of Lebanon for me; my workers will be alongside your workers; and I will pay your workers whatever you establish. As you know, there is no one among us who knows how to cut timber like you Sidonians."

When Hiram received Solomon's message, he was very glad and said, "Blessed be the LORD this day, who has given David a wise son to rule over this great people." Hiram replied to Solomon, saying, "I have heard the message that you have sent to me: I will do everything you desire concerning cedar and cypress timber." . . .

King Solomon conscripted labor out of all Israel, consisting of thirty thousand men. He sent them to Lebanon, ten thousand a month in shifts: One month they were in Lebanon, and two months at home. Adoniram was over the forced laborers. Solomon had seventy thousand transporters, and eighty thousand stone cutters in the mountains, besides Solomon's three thousand and three hundred chief officers who were over the work, and ruled over the people who labored in the work.

At the king's command, they cut out large and high quality stones to serve as the temple's foundation for the finished stone. Solomon's builders, Hiram's builders and the Gebalites cut and prepared the timber and the stones to build the temple. . . .

So Solomon built the temple, and finished it. He lined the inside walls of the temple with cedar boards, from the temple's floor to its ceiling, and he covered the interior with wood. He covered the floor of the temple with cypress boards. He built twenty cubits of the rear part of the house with cedar boards from floor to ceiling to form within the temple an inner sanctuary as the most holy place. The main room of the temple, outside the inner sanctuary, was forty cubits long. There was cedar inside the temple, carved with buds and open flowers. Everything was cedar, and no stone was visible. He prepared an inner sanctuary within the middle of the temple to place the ark of the covenant of the LORD. The inner sanctuary was twenty cubits in length, twenty cubits in width, and twenty cubits in its height. He overlaid it with pure gold and covered the altar with cedar. Thus, Solomon overlaid the inside of the temple with pure gold, he hung chains of gold across the front of the inner sanctuary, which was overlaid with gold. He overlaid the whole temple with gold, until it was finished. The whole altar that belonged to the oracle was also overlaid with gold.

Source: 1 Kings 4:20–43; 5:1–8, 13–18; 6:14–22.

PROVERBS ATTRIBUTED TO SOLOMON

In the preceding passage, Solomon is said to have been the wisest of all men and author of 3,000 proverbs. The Book of Proverbs contains seven distinct collections of sayings, the first four of which are traditionally attributed to Solomon. Compiled during the time of Ezra, Proverbs contains sayings from throughout periods of the united and divided kingdom, in the form of two-line sentences about an aspect of human experience, usually secular. Three literary styles are exhibited in the proverbs: synonymous parallelism, in which the second line repeats the content of the first; antithetic parallelism, in which good behavior in the first line is contrasted with bad behavior in the second line; and ascending parallelism, in which the second line completes the train of thought in the first line. The following is from the second collection within Proverbs—thought to be the oldest part of the book—titled "The Proverbs of Solomon."

A gentle answer turns away wrath,
    but a harsh word stirs up anger.
The tongue of the wise expresses knowledge,
    but the mouth of fools gush out folly.
The Lord's eyes are everywhere,
    keeping watch on the evil and the good.
A gentle tongue is a tree of life,
    but a deceitful one crushes the spirit.
A fool despises his father's correction,
    but he who learns from correction shows good sense.
In the house of the righteous there is much treasure,
    but the income of the wicked brings trouble.
The lips of the wise spread knowledge;
    not so with the heart of fools.
The sacrifice made by the wicked is detestable to the Lord,
    but the prayer of the upright is his delight.
The way of the wicked is detestable to the Lord,
    but he loves him who pursues righteousness.
There is stern discipline for one who abandons the way;
    whoever hates correction will die.
Death and destruction lie open before the Lord:
    how much more, then, do human hearts.
A ridiculer does not love to be corrected;
    he will avoid the wise.
A glad heart makes a cheerful face;
    but an aching heart breaks the spirit.
The heart of one who has understanding seeks knowledge,
    but the mouths of fools feed on folly.
All the days of the afflicted are wretched,
    but one who has a cheerful heart enjoys a continual feast.
Better is little, with the fear of the Lord,
    than great treasure with trouble.
Better is a dinner of vegetables, where love is,
    than a fattened calf with hatred.
A wrathful man stirs up contention,
    but one who is slow to anger eases conflict.
The way of the sluggard is like a thorny hedge,
    but the path of the upright is an open highway.
A wise son makes a father glad,
    but a foolish man despises his mother.
Foolishness brings joy to one who is without wisdom,
    but a man of understanding keeps his way straight.
Plans fail where there is no counsel;
    but plans succeed where there are many counselors.
An appropriate reply comes to a man with joy.
    How good is the right word at the right time!

The path of life leads upward for the wise,
    and keeps them from going downward to the grave.
The LORD will tear down the house of the proud,
    but he will keep the widow's boundaries intact.
The LORD detests the thoughts of the wicked,
    but the thoughts of the pure are pleasing.
He who is greedy for gain troubles his own house,
    but he who hates bribes will live.
The heart of the righteous weighs its answers,
    but the mouth of the wicked gushes out evil.
The LORD is far from the wicked,
    but he hears the prayer of the righteous.
The light of the eyes brings joy to the heart.
    Good news gives health to the bones.
The ear that listens to life-changing correction
    will be at home among the wise.
He who refuses correction despises his own soul,
    but he who listens to correction gains understanding.

Source: Proverbs 15.

DIVIDED KINGDOM AND EXILE

ELIJAH VERSUS THE PRIESTS OF BAAL AND ASHERAH

After Solomon's reign, Israel divided into northern and southern kingdoms. The explanation given for this in the Deuteronomistic History is Solomon's continual worship of regional deities. Writers of the Tanakh *condemn these worship practices and praise the Yahwist prophets and kings who challenge them. Israelite worship of the goddess Asherah is of particular interest. Asherah is the wife of the Canaanite high god, El, and in some popular Israelite religion may have been a consort of Yahweh. Worship rituals of Asherah center on sacred pillars, which in the Deuteronomistic History are strictly forbidden (Deuteronomy 16:21–22). The following story from the Deuteronomistic History dramatically presents a showdown between the prophets of Asherah and Baal on one side, and the prophet Elijah on the other. Elijah is the lone defender of Yahweh in the northern kingdom at this time.*

Israel Punished for Idolatry

In the thirty-eighth year of Asa king of Judah, Ahab the son of Omri began his reign over Israel. He reigned over Israel in Samaria twenty-two years. Ahab the son of Omri committed evil in the sight of the LORD more than all that were prior to him. Considering it a minor thing to follow the sins of Jeroboam the son of Nebat, that he took as wife Jezebel the daughter of Ethbaal king of the Sidonians, and proceeded to served and worship Baal. He set up an altar for Baal in the temple of Baal, which he had built in Samaria. Ahab made an Asherah pole, and so he did more to provoke to anger the LORD, the God of Israel, than all the kings of Israel who were before him. . . .

Then Elijah the Tishbite, who was a foreigner from Gilead, said to Ahab, "As the LORD, the God of Israel, lives, before whom I stand, there will be no dew or rain these coming years, unless I command it so." . . .

Time passed, and in the third year the word of the LORD came to Elijah: "Meet with Ahab; and I will send rain down on the earth." So Elijah went to meet with Ahab. The famine was severe in Samaria. . . .

Elijah challenges the Priests of Baal

When Ahab saw Elijah, Ahab said, "Is this you, you troubler of Israel?" Elijah answered, "I have not created trouble in Israel. But you, and your father's family, have done so because you abandoned the commandments of the LORD, and followed the various Baals. Now summon and gather all Israel to meet me at Mount Carmel, including the four hundred fifty prophets of Baal and the four hundred prophets of the Asherah, who eat at Jezebel's table. So Ahab summoned all the Israelites, and gathered the prophets together at Mount Carmel. Elijah approached the people and said, "How long will you waver between these two sides? If the LORD is God, follow him; but if Baal is, then follow him." The people did not utter a word. Then Elijah said to the people, "I, and I alone, remain a prophet of the LORD, while Baal's prophets number four hundred fifty. Bring us two bulls. Let them choose one bull for themselves, cut it into pieces, lay it on the wood, but not set fire to it. I will prepare the other bull, lay it on the wood, and not set fire to it. You then call on the name of your god, and I will call on the name of the LORD. The God who answers with fire, he is God."

The people answered, "Very well." Elijah said to the prophets of Baal, "Choose one bull for yourselves, and prepare it first since there are many of you. Call on the name of your god, but do not set fire to it."

They took the bull that was given to them, dressed it, and called on the name of Baal from morning until noon, shouting, "Baal, hear us." But there was no voice; no one answered. They danced around the altar that they made. At noon Elijah mocked them, "Shout louder, for surely he is a god. Maybe he is reflecting, or preoccupied, or traveling, or perhaps he is asleep and needs awakening. They shouted louder and cut themselves as they customarily do with knives and swords, until blood gushed out on them. When midday past, they continued prophesying until the time of the evening offering. But there still was neither voice. No one answered or paid any attention. Elijah then said to all the people, "Come here" and all the people approached him. He repaired the altar of the LORD that had been torn down. Elijah took twelve stones, according to the number of the tribes of the sons of Jacob, to whom the word of the LORD came, saying, "Your name will be Israel." With these stones he built an altar in the name of the LORD. He dug a trench around the altar, wide enough to hold two measures of seed. He arranged the wood, cut the bull into pieces, and laid it on the wood. He said, "Fill four containers with water, and pour it on the offering and the wood." He said, "Do it a second time" and they did it the second time. He said, "Do it a third time" and they did it the third time. The water ran around the altar and also filled the trench. At the time of the evening offering, Elijah the prophet approached it and said, "LORD, God of Abraham, of Isaac, and Israel, let it be known today that you are God in Israel, and that I am your servant and have done all these things at your command. Hear me, LORD, hear me, so that these people may know that you, the LORD, are God, and that you have turned their heart back again." Then fire from the LORD came down and consumed the offering, the wood, the stones, the dust, and licked up the water that was in the trench. When all the people saw this, they fell face down and said, "The LORD, he is God; the LORD, he is God." Elijah said to them, "Seize the prophets of Baal and do not let one of them escape." They seized them and Elijah brought them down to the Kishon Valley, and killed them there.

Source: 1 Kings 16:29–33; 17:1; 18:1–2, 17–40.

ISAIAH'S WARNING TO JUDAH

In 722 the northern kingdom fell to Assyria, the Mesopotamian superpower of the time. Although the southern kingdom of Judah survived Assyrian encroachment, it was embroiled in foreign political conflicts. The prophet Isaiah was an advisor to two kings of the southern kingdom at the time: Ahaz and his successor Hezekiah. Under the leadership of King Hezekiah, the Kingdom of Judah survived the Assyrian attack and continued for another 150 years. His advice to both kings was the same: Do not participate in anti-Assyrian conspiracies, but trust in God for deliverance. The Book of Isaiah is an anthology of prophetic writings from Isaiah's time through the Babylonian exile. Of the book's sixty-six chapters, Isaiah's own words are confined to Chapters 1–11 and 28–32. Chapter 1 expresses Isaiah's indictment against the people of Judah: They have forsaken God and risk being purged. Chapter 6 is Isaiah's call to prophethood.

Isaiah's Indictment against Judah

The vision of Isaiah the son of Amoz, which he saw concerning Judah and Jerusalem, in the days of Uzziah, Jotham, Ahaz, and Hezekiah, kings of Judah.

Hear, heavens,
    and listen, earth; for the L has spoken:
    I have nourished and brought up children,
    but they have rebelled against me.
The ox knows his owner,
    and the donkey his master's feeding stall;
    but Israel does not know,
    my people do not consider.
You sinful nation,
    a people filled with iniquity,
    offspring of evil-doers,
    children who deal corruptly.
    They have abandoned the L .
    They have despised the Holy One of Israel.
    They have walked away from him.
Why do you bring on chastisement?
    Why do you revolt more and more?
    Your whole head is sick,
    and your whole heart is injured.
From the sole of the foot even to the head there is no healthiness in it:
    wounds, welts, and open sores.
    They have not been closed or bandaged, or treated with ointment.
Your country is desolate.
    Your cities are burned with fire.
    Strangers devour your land in your presence,
    and it is desolate,
    as overthrown by foreigners.
The daughter of Zion is left like a shelter in a vineyard,
    like a hut in a field of melons,
    like a besieged city.
If he L of heaven's armies had not left a few survivors,
    we would have been like Sodom;
    we would have been like Gomorrah. . . .

"Come now, and let us reason together," says the LORD:
> "Though your sins be as scarlet, they will be as white as snow.
> Though they be red like crimson, they will be as wool.

If you are willing and obedient,
> you will eat the best of the land;
> but if you refuse and rebel, you will be devoured with the sword;
> for the mouth of the LORD has spoken it."

Observe how the faithful city [of Jerusalem] has become a prostitute.
> She was full of justice; righteousness lived within her,
> but now murderers. . . .

Isaiah's Call to Prophethood

In the year that king Uzziah died, I saw the LORD sitting on a throne, high and elevated; the train of his robe filled the temple. Above him stood the seraphim, each with six wings. With two he covered his face. With two he covered his feet. With two he flew. One called to another, and said,

> "Holy, holy, holy, is the LORD of heaven's armies.
> The whole earth is full of his glory!"

The posts of the door shook at the cry of their voices, and the house was filled with smoke. Then I said,

> "Woe is me, for I am doomed, because I am a man of unclean lips. I live among a people of unclean lips. My eyes have seen the King, the LORD of heaven's armies."

Then one of the seraphim flew to me, having a hot coal in his hand, which he had taken with the tongs from off the altar. He touched my mouth with it, and said,

> "Observe, this has touched your lips; and your wickedness
> is taken away, and your sins are forgiven

I heard the LORD's voice, saying, "Whom will I send, and who will go for us?"

> Then I said, "Here I am. Send me."

He said, "Go, and tell these people,

> You hear indeed, but do not understand;
> and you see indeed, but do not perceive.
> Make the heart of these people insensitive.
> Make their ears dull, and shut their eyes.
> Otherwise they might see with their eyes,
> hear with their ears,
> understand with their heart,
> and turn again, and be healed."

Then I said, "LORD, for how long?"

> He answered,
> "Until cities are in ruins without inhabitant,
> houses are without people,
> the land is completely desolate,
> the LORD has moved everyone far away,

and there are many abandoned places throughout the
land.
Even if a tenth are left in it,
that also will again be burned.
Just as the stump of a terebinth or an oak remains after it
is cut down,
so too the holy seed will be a stump."

Source: Isaiah 1:1–9, 18–21; 6.

BABYLONIAN CONQUEST AND EXILE

*Around 610 BCE, a group of Semites in Babylon, the Chaldeans,
overthrew the Assyrians and formed a new Babylonian Empire.
At first Judah's king paid tribute to the Empire, but he later
rebelled, thinking that Egypt would come to his defense if necessary. In retaliation, the Babylonian army marched into Judah,
looted the temple and royal treasury, and exiled the royal
family and upper-class Israelites to Babylon. The Babylonians
appointed Zedekiah as a puppet king, but, when pressured by
the Egyptians, he too rebelled. In 586 BCE, the Babylonian army
again marched into Judah, this time destroying Jerusalem and
the temple. The following recounts the tragedy of the exile.*

Jehoiachin was eighteen years old when he became king,
and he reigned in Jerusalem three months. His mother's
name was Nehushta, the daughter of Elnathan of Jerusalem.
He committed evil in the eyes of the LORD, just as his father
had done. At that time the officers of Nebuchadnezzar king
of Babylon came to Jerusalem, and the city was besieged.
Nebuchadnezzar king of Babylon then came to the city, while
his officers were besieging it. Jehoiachin the king of Judah
surrendered to the king of Babylon, he, and his mother, his
advisers, his princes, and his officers. The king of Babylon
took him prisoner in the eighth year of his reign. Just as the
LORD had said, Nebuchadnezzar removed all the treasures in
the temple of the LORD, and the treasures of the king's palace, and cut into pieces all the vessels of gold that Solomon
king of Israel had made in the temple of the LORD. He carried
away all Jerusalem, all the commanders, all the warriors,
even ten thousand captives, and all the craftsmen and the
artisans. No one remained except the poorest people in the
land. He exiled Jehoiachin to Babylon. The king's mother,
the king's wives, his officers, and the important people of the
land, he carried into captivity from Jerusalem to Babylon. The
king of Babylon also exiled to Babylon seven thousand warriors, one thousand craftsman and artisans, all of which were

strong and capable of fighting. The king of Babylon made Mattaniah, Jehoiachin's uncle, king in his place, and changed his name to Zedekiah.

Zedekiah was twenty-one years old when he began to reign. He reigned eleven years in Jerusalem. His mother's name was Hamutal, the daughter of Jeremiah of Libnah. He committed evil in the eyes of the LORD, just as Jehoiakim had done. All this happened because of the LORD's anger against Jerusalem and Judah, until he cast them out from his presence. Zedekiah rebelled against the king of Babylon.

In the ninth year of his reign, in the tenth day of the tenth month, Nebuchadnezzar king of Babylon marched with his army against Jerusalem and surrounded it. They built siege works all around it. The city was besieged until the eleventh year of king Zedekiah. On the ninth day of the fourth month the famine was so severe in the city that there was no bread for the people of the land.

Then a breach was made in the city walls, and all the soldiers fled at night through a gate between the two walls, which was near the king's garden, even though the Babylonians surrounded the city. The king went toward the Arabah. But the army of the Babylonians pursued the king and overtook him in the plains of Jericho; his entire army was scattered from him. Then they took Zedekiah and carried him up to the king of Babylon at Riblah; and they pronounced judgment on him. They killed Zedekiah's sons before his eyes. They put out Zedekiah's eyes, bound him in fetters, and carried him to Babylon.

In the seventh day of the fifth month, which was the nineteenth year of king Nebuchadnezzar, king of Babylon, Nebuzaradan the captain of the guard, and servant of the king of Babylon, came to Jerusalem. He burned down the temple of the LORD, the king's palace, and all the houses in Jerusalem. Even great houses he burned with fire. The whole army of the Babylonians, who were with the captain of the guard, tore down the walls around Jerusalem. Nebuzaradan, the captain of the guard, carried away the people who were left in the city, those who defected to the king of Babylon, and the remainder of the population. But the captain of the guard left the poorest in the land to work the vineyards and fields.

The Babylonians broke into pieces the pillars and stands of bronze that were in the temple of the LORD, and the bronze pool that was also in the temple of the LORD, and carried the bronze to Babylon. They took away the pots, the shovels, the snuffers, the spoons, and all the vessels of bronze with which they ministered. The captain of the guard took away the fire

pans and basins that were pure gold. The two pillars, the
one pool, and the stand, which Solomon had made for the
house of the LORD, the bronze of all these vessels was beyond
weight. The height of one pillar was eighteen cubits, and a
capital of bronze was on it that measured three cubits, with
a bronze latticework of pomegranates around it. The second
pillar had a similar latticework.

Source: 2 Kings 24:8–20, 25:1–17.

REMEMBERING ZION

*Captive in Babylon, the psalmist in the following passage
reflects nostalgically on the beauty of Zion, referring to the city
of Jerusalem, possibly the Temple Mount.*

> By the rivers of Babylon, we sat down.
> > We wept when we remembered Zion.
> On the poplar trees in its midst,
> > we hung up our harps.
> For there, our captors asked us for songs.
> > Those who tormented us demanded songs of joy:
> > "Sing us one of the songs of Zion."
> How can we sing the LORD's song in a foreign land?
> If I forget you, Jerusalem,
> > let my right hand forget its skill.
> Let my tongue stick to the roof of my mouth if I do not remember you;
> > if I do not prefer Jerusalem above my greatest joy.
> Remember, LORD, the Edomites who,
> > on the day Jerusalem fell,
> > said, "Tear it down,
> > tear it down to its foundation."
> Daughter of Babylon, doomed to be destroyed,
> > he will be happy who repays you,
> > for what you have done to us.
> Happy he will be,
> > who takes your little ones and smashes them against the rocks.

Source: Psalms 137.

RETURN FROM EXILE AND RESTORATION

*When Persian King Cyrus overthrew the Babylonian Empire in
539 BCE, he reversed the policy of exiling foreign captives as
practiced by the Babylonians and, earlier, by the Assyrians. With
his encouragement, 40,000 exiled Jews returned to their homeland. Cyrus promoted the rebuilding of Jerusalem's temple and
returned to the Jews the temple treasures that had been taken
by the Babylonians.*

Cyrus's Proclamation

In the first year of Cyrus, king of Persia, in fulfillment of the words of the LORD spoken through Jeremiah, the LORD moved the spirit of Cyrus, king of Persia, so that he made a proclamation throughout his kingdom, which was also put in writing:

"Thus says Cyrus king of Persia, The LORD and God of heaven has given me all the kingdoms of the earth. He has commanded me to build him a temple in Jerusalem in Judah. Any of his people among you, may his God be with him, may go to Jerusalem in Judah, and build the temple of the LORD, the God of Israel (he is God), which is in Jerusalem. Let every survivor, in any place where he lives, be assisted by men of that place with silver, gold, goods, and animals, in addition to a freewill offering for the temple of God in Jerusalem.

Then the family leaders of Judah and Benjamin, the priests, the Levites, and everyone whose spirit was moved by God, all left to build the house of the LORD in Jerusalem. Their neighbors assisted them with vessels of silver, gold, goods, animals, and precious things, in addition to freewill offerings. Cyrus the king also brought out the vessels from the temple of the LORD, which Nebuchadnezzar brought from Jerusalem and put in the temple of his gods; Cyrus king of Persia had them brought by Mithredath the treasurer, counted them out to Sheshbazzar, the prince of Judah. This is the inventory: thirty platters of gold, one thousand platters of silver, twenty-nine knives, thirty bowls of gold, four hundred and ten silver bowls of a second sort, and one thousand other vessels. All the vessels of gold and silver totaled five thousand and four hundred. Sheshbazzar brought all these when the captives left Babylon for Jerusalem. . . .

Worship Restored in Jerusalem

When the seventh month arrived and the Israelites settled in their towns, the people gathered together as one person in Jerusalem. Then Jeshua the son of Jozadak, with his fellow priests, and Zerubbabel the son of Shealtiel, with his kinsmen, built the altar of the God of Israel, to sacrifice burnt offerings on it, as it is written in the law of Moses, the man of God. Although they were fearful of the people around them, they nevertheless set the altar on its base and sacrificed burnt offerings on it to the LORD, both morning and evening burnt offerings. They observed the Festival of Booths, as it is written, and offered the required number of daily burnt sacrifices by number, in compliance with the ordinance as each day necessitated. Afterwards, they sacrificed regular burnt offering, offerings of the new moons, for all the established feasts of the LORD that were consecrated, and from everyone who willingly gave a freewill offering to the LORD. On the first day of the seventh month they began to sacrifice burnt offerings to the LORD, even though the foundation of the temple of the LORD was not yet laid. They also gave money to the masons and carpenters, and gave food, drink, and oil to the workers of Sidon and Tyre to bring cedar trees by sea from Lebanon to Joppa, according to the authorization they received from Cyrus king of Persia.

Work began in the second month of the second year of arriving at the temple of God in Jerusalem, by Zerubbabel the son of Shealtiel, and Jeshua the son of Jozadak, and the rest of their fellow priests and the Levites, and all those who came out of captivity to Jerusalem. They appointed the Levites, from twenty years old and upward, to oversee the work of the temple of the LORD. Jeshua with his sons and brothers, Kadmiel with his sons, and the sons of Judah, came together to oversee the workmen in the temple of God, along with the sons of Henadad, their sons and their fellow Levites.

When the builders laid the foundation of the temple of the LORD, they set in place the priests in their robes with horns, and the Levites the sons of Asaph with cymbals, to praise the LORD, according to the direction of David king of Israel. They sang together responsively praising and giving thanks to the LORD, saying, "he is good, and his loving kindness toward Israel endures forever." All the people then shouted with a loud voice when they praised the LORD, because the foundation of the house of the LORD was laid. But many of the priests, Levites, and heads of families, the old men who had seen the first house, then wept with a loud voice when seeing the foundation of the temple being set. Many others shouted aloud for joy, so that the people could not distinguish between the noise of the shout of joy from the noise of the weeping of the people. As the people shouted with a loud voice, the noise was heard from far away.

Source: Ezra 1, 3.

ESTHER

The Book of Esther is one of two books of the Tanakh *focusing on the life of a Jewish heroine, the other being the Book of Ruth. Esther is queen to Persian King Ahasuerus (Xerxes I), one of Cyrus's successors who reigned from 486 to 465 BCE. Unknown to the king, Esther is a Jew. When for religious reasons her cousin Mordecai refuses to bow to Haman, a member of the court, Haman is outraged and plots to have Mordecai, along with the rest of the Jews in the region, executed. The king authorizes Haman's plan. When Mordecai pleads with Esther to speak to the king on behalf of the Jews, she arranges a banquet for the king during which she reveals Haman's plot. Haman is hanged on the very gallows he had prepared for Mordecai. The Jews are granted the right to defend themselves against their anti-Jewish enemies. The story of Esther is the basis for the Jewish feast Purim.*

Haman's Plot

King Ahasuerus promoted Haman the son of Hammedatha the Agagite; he advanced him and set his seat above all the princes who were with him. All of the king's officials who were in the king's gate bowed down and paid homage to Haman; for the king had commanded this concerning him. But Mordecai did not bow down or pay him homage. Then the king's officials who were in the king's gate said to Mordecai, "Why do you disobey the king's command?" They spoke daily to him, but he did not listen to them. They then told Haman, to see whether Mordecai's conduct would be tolerated, for he had told them that he was a Jew. When Haman saw that Mordecai did not bow down or pay him homage, Haman was filled with rage. But he rejected the idea of laying hands on Mordecai alone, since he was told about Mordecai's nationality. So Haman sought to destroy all the Jews throughout Ahasuerus's whole kingdom of Ahasuerus, including Mordecai's people.

In the first month, which is the month Nisan, in the twelfth year of King Ahasuerus, they cast Pur, that is, the lot, before Haman from day to day, and from month to month, and they chose the twelfth month, which is the month Adar. Haman said to King Ahasuerus, "There is a certain nationality scattered and dispersed among the nationalities in all the provinces of your kingdom, and their laws are different than other nationalities. They do not keep the king's laws. Therefore it is not in the king's interest to allow them to remain. If it pleases the king, let it be written that they be destroyed; and I will pay ten thousand talents of silver into the hands of those who are in charge of the king's business, to bring it into the king's treasuries." The king took his ring from his hand, and gave it to Haman the son of Hammedatha the Agagite, the Jews' enemy. The king said to Haman, "The silver is yours, and the people also; do with them as you see fit." . . .

Esther's Banquet

So the king and Haman came to banquet with Queen Esther. The king said again to Esther on the second day at the banquet while they were drinking wine, "What is your request, Queen Esther? It will be granted to you. Whatever is your request, even up to half of the kingdom, it will be performed."

Then Queen Esther answered, "If I have found favor in your sight, my king, and if it pleases the king, grant me my life and the life of my people as my request, and that of my people as my request. For I and my people were sold to be destroyed, slain, and to perish. If we had been sold as slaves, men and women, I would have stayed silent, because our distress would not justify troubling the king."

Then King Ahasuerus said to Queen Esther, "Who is he, and where is he who dared to presume in his heart to do this?"

Esther said, "An adversary and an enemy, this wicked Haman."

Then Haman became terrified in front of the king and the queen. The king arose in anger from his wine drinking, and went into the palace garden. Haman stayed behind to beg Queen Esther for his life, since he saw that the king was determined to harm him. The king returned from the palace garden to wine banquet. Haman had fallen on the couch where Esther was. The king said, "Will he even assault the queen in front of me in the palace?" As the words left the king's mouth, they covered Haman's face.

Then Harbonah, one of the eunuchs who was with the king said, "Observe the gallows fifty cubits high is standing at Haman's house. Haman made this for Mordecai, who spoke to protect the king."

The king said, "Hang him on it."

So they hanged Haman on the gallows that he had prepared for Mordecai. Then the king's wrath was pacified.

Source: Esther 3:7–11; 7.

EZRA AND THE LAW

The concluding events of the Tanakh *focus on the activities of Ezra and Nehemiah, found in the books that bear their names. Ezra was a Babylonian-born Jewish priest devoted to the Law of Moses. In 458 BCE, he petitioned Artaxerxes, the reigning king of the Persian Empire, to lead another migration of Jews back to their homeland. Artaxerxes agreed and empowered him to make political and religious reforms as Ezra saw fit. On arrival, Ezra was distressed to see that the returning Jews before him had intermarried, and he proclaimed that 114 priests and laymen should have their marriages annulled. Thirteen years after Ezra's return, Nehemiah, a Jewish cupbearer to the Persian king, was granted permission by the king to rebuild the walls of Jerusalem, still in ruins from the Babylonian invasion. A gifted administrator, Nehemiah completed the project in fifty-two days, even in the face of opposition from neighboring provinces. Shortly after completion of the walls, the Jews celebrated a series of feasts, during which Ezra publicly read and interpreted the scrolls of Moses. The following recounts Ezra's reading of the scrolls.*

All the people gathered together as one person into the square that was before the Water Gate. They asked Ezra the scribe to bring the book of the law of Moses, which the Lord had commanded to Israel. Ezra the priest brought the law before the assembly, both men and women, and all who were able to understand what they heard, on the first day of the seventh month. He read from it in the square that was before the water gate from early morning until midday, in the presence of the men and the women, and of those who could understand. The people's ears were attentive to the book of the law.

Ezra the scribe stood on a wooden platform, which they had made for that purpose. Next to him on his right stood Mattithiah, Shema, Anaiah, Uriah, Hilkiah, and Maaseiah; on his left was Pedaiah, Mishael, Malchijah, Hashum, Hashbaddanah, Zechariah, and Meshullam. Ezra opened the book in sight of all the people (since he stood above them all), and when he opened it, all the people stood up. Ezra blessed the Lord, the great God. All the people answered, Amen, Amen, lifting up of their hands. They bowed their heads, and worshiped the Lord with their faces to the ground. The Levites, including Jeshua, Bani, Sherebiah, Jamin, Akkub, Shabbethai, Hodiah, Maaseiah, Kelita, Azariah, Jozabad, Hanan, and Pelaiah, helped the people understand the law while the people remained in their place. They read from the book of the law of God, making it clear and giving it sense, so that they understood the reading.

Nehemiah the governor, Ezra the priest and scribe, and the Levites who taught the people, said to them all, "This day is holy to the Lord your God; do not mourn or weep." For all the people had wept when they heard the words of the law. Then he said to them, "Go your way, eat the fat, drink sweet wine, and send portions to those who have prepared nothing. This day is holy to our Lord. Do not grieve, for the joy of the

L ORD is your strength." So the Levites calmed all the people, saying, "Be at peace, for the day is holy, and do not grieve." All the people left to eat, drink, send portions, and have a great celebration, because they had understood the words that were declared to them.

On the second day the heads of families of everyone, the priests and the Levites, gathered around Ezra the scribe, to give attention to the words of the law. They found written in the law how the L ORD commanded through Moses that the Israelites should live in booths during the feast of the seventh month. So they proclaimed and disseminate this throughout their towns and Jerusalem, saying, "Go to the mountain, get branches of olive, wild olive, myrtle, palm, and thick trees, to make booths, as it is written." So the people went out to get them, and made themselves booths on the roof of their houses, in their courts, in the courts of the temple of God, in the square in front of the Water Gate, and in the square in front of the Gate of Ephraim. The entire community of those who returned from captivity made booths and lived in them. Since the days of Joshua the son of Nun to that day the Israelites had not done this. There was great gladness. Day after day, from the first day to the last, he read from the book of the law of God. They kept the feast seven days; and on the eighth day was a solemn assembly, according to the ordinance.

Source: Nehemiah 8.

POST-EXILIC WRITINGS

GREEK RULE AND THE COMING OF THE MESSIAH

Although the final events reported in the Tanakh *take place around 430 BCE, the religious drama of the Jewish people continues in post-exilic writings, considered scriptural in many Jewish circles at the time. The extreme Hellenizing policies of the Selucid king Antiochus Epiphanes created a crisis for traditional Jews, further intensified by the advocacy of these policies by Jewish High Priests themselves. Loyal Jewish writers sought a divine explanation for this crisis, which threatened the Jews' very existence. They wrote apocalyptic texts reporting vision-like revelations about a messianic deliverer and a cataclysmic end to the empires of their oppressors, culminating with final divine judgment. The Book of Daniel in the* Tanakh *is thought to be an apocalyptic work from this period. The following is from the First Book of Enoch, one of the best-known apocalyptic texts of the*

Pseudepigrapha. The work, written by several authors between 200 BCE and 100 CE, reflects traditional apocalyptic themes.

The Son of Man

46. There I saw one who was the Ancient of Days, and His head was white like wool. With Him was another being who had the appearance of a man, and his face was full of graciousness, like one of the holy angels. I asked the angel who went with me and showed me all the hidden things, concerning that Son of Man, who he was, from where he came, and why he went with the Ancient of Days. He answered, "This is the Son of Man who has righteousness, with whom lives righteousness, and who reveals all the treasures of that which is hidden because the LORD of Spirits has chosen him, and whose destiny has supremacy before the LORD of Spirits in uprightness forever. This Son of Man whom you have seen will remove the kings and the mighty from their seats, and the powerful from their thrones. He will loosen the reins of the strong, and break the teeth of the sinners. He will remove the kings from their thrones and kingdoms because they do not exalt and praise Him, nor humbly acknowledge from what source their kingdom was given to them. He will remove the pretense of the strong, and will fill them with shame. Darkness will be their home, and worms will be their bed. They will have no hope of rising from their beds, because they do not praise the name of the LORD of Spirits, raise their hands against the Most High, and tread upon the earth and live upon it. All their deeds display unrighteousness and their power rests upon their riches. Their faith is in the gods that they have made with their hands. They deny the name of the LORD of Spirits, and they persecute the houses of His congregations and the faithful who rely upon the name of the LORD of Spirits.". . .

48. In that place I saw the fountain of righteousness which was inexhaustible. Around it were many fountains of wisdom: all the thirsty drank of them and were filled with wisdom. Their homes were with the righteous and holy and elect. At that hour that Son of Man was named in the presence of the LORD of Spirits, and his name before the Ancient of Days. Even before the sun and the signs were created, before the stars of the heavens were made, his name was named before the LORD of Spirits. He will be a staff to the righteous whereon to sturdy themselves and not fall. He will be the light of the Gentiles, and the hope

of those who are troubled of heart. All who live on earth will fall down and worship before him, and will praise and bless and celebrate with song the LORD of Spirits. For this reason he has been chosen and hidden before Him, before the creation of the world and for evermore. And the wisdom of the LORD of Spirits has revealed him to the holy and righteous. For he has preserved the destiny of the righteous, because they have hated and despised this world of unrighteousness, and have hated all its works and ways in the name of the LORD of Spirits. For in his name they are saved, and according to his good pleasure it has been in regard to their life. In these days will the kings of the earth become shamed because of the works of their hands—the strong who possess the land. For on the day of their anguish and affliction they will not be able to save themselves. I will place them into the hands of My elect. As straw in the fire, so will they burn before the face of the holy. As lead in the water, so will they sink before the face of the righteous, and no trace of them will be found again. On the day of their affliction there will be rest on the earth, and before them they will fall and not rise again. There will be no one to take them by the hand and raise them. For they have denied the LORD of Spirits and His Messiah. The name of the LORD of Spirits be blessed. . . .

The Resurrection of the Dead

51. In those days the earth will also give back that which has been entrusted to it. Sheol also will give back that which it has received, and hell will give back that which it owes. In those days the Elect One will arise, and he will choose the righteous and holy from among them [i.e., the risen dead]. The day is approaching that they should be saved. The Elect One will in those days sit on My throne, and his mouth will pour our all the secrets of wisdom and counsel. For the LORD of Spirits has given them to him and has glorified him. In those days the mountains will leap like rams, the hills will also skip like lambs satisfied with milk, and the faces of all the angels in heaven will be lighted up with joy. The earth will rejoice, the righteous will live on it, and the elect will walk on it. . . .

Judgment

54. I looked and turned to another part of the earth, and saw there a deep valley with burning fire. They brought the kings and the mighty, and began to throw them into

this deep valley. There my eyes saw how they made instruments, iron chains of immeasurable weight. I asked the angel of peace who went with me, "For whom are these chains being prepared?" He said to me: "These are being prepared for the hosts of [the demon] Azazel, so that they may take them and throw them into the abyss of total condemnation, and they will cover their jaws with rough stones as the LORD of Spirits commanded. Michael, Gabriel, Raphael, and Phanuel will take hold of them on that great day, and throw them on that day into the burning furnace. The LORD of Spirits may then take vengeance on them for their unrighteousness in becoming subject to Satan and leading astray those who dwell on the earth." In those days punishment will come from the LORD of Spirits. He will open all the chambers of water that are above the heavens, and of the fountains which are beneath the earth. All the waters will be joined with the waters: that which is above the heavens is the masculine, and the water that is beneath the earth is the feminine. They will destroy all who dwell on the earth and those who dwell under the ends of the heaven. When they have recognized their unrighteousness which they have created on the earth, then by these they will die.

Source: *First Enoch*, 46, 48, 51, 54, tr. Robert Henry Charles (adapted).

MACCABEAN REVOLT

The Book of Maccabees chronicles the clash between Hellenistic and Jewish culture, culminating in the Maccabean revolt and rise to power. The Book of Maccabees, written about 100 BCE and included in the Septuagint, is the primary source of information for this period of Jewish history. The following describes the Hellenizing policies of Antiochus Epiphanes and the initial revolt launched by Mattathias.

Antiochus Attacks Jerusalem and Defiles the Temple

1. After Alexander the Macedonian, Philip's son, who came from the land of Kittim, had defeated Darius, king of the Persians and Medes, he became king in his place, having first ruled in Greece. He fought many campaigns, captured fortresses, and put kings to death. He advanced to the ends of the earth, gathering plunder from many nations; the earth fell silent before him, and his heart

became proud and arrogant. He collected a very strong army and conquered provinces, nations, and rulers, and they became his tributaries. But after all this he took to his bed, realizing that he was going to die. He therefore summoned his officers, the nobles, who had been brought up with him from his youth, to divide his kingdom among them while he was still alive. Alexander had reigned twelve years when he died.

So his officers took over his kingdom, each in his own territory, and after his death they all put on royal crowns, and so did their sons after them for many years, causing much distress over the earth.

There sprang from these a sinful offshoot, Antiochus Epiphanes, son of King Antiochus, once a hostage at Rome. He became king in the year one hundred and thirty-seven of the kingdom of the Greeks.

In those days there appeared in Israel men who were breakers of the law, and they seduced many people, saying: "Let us go and make an alliance with the Gentiles all around us; since we separated from them, many evils have come upon us." The proposal was agreeable; some from among the people promptly went to the king, and he authorized them to introduce the way of living of the Gentiles. Thereupon they built a gymnasium in Jerusalem according to the Gentile custom. They covered over the mark of their circumcision and abandoned the holy covenant; they allied themselves with the Gentiles and sold themselves to wrongdoing.

When his kingdom seemed secure, Antiochus proposed to become king of Egypt, so as to rule over both kingdoms. He invaded Egypt with a strong force, with chariots and elephants, and with a large fleet, to make war on Ptolemy, king of Egypt. Ptolemy was frightened at his presence and fled, leaving many casualties. The fortified cities in the land of Egypt were captured, and Antiochus plundered the land of Egypt.

After Antiochus had defeated Egypt in the year one hundred and forty-three, he returned and went up to Israel and to Jerusalem with a strong force. He insolently invaded the sanctuary and took away the golden altar, the lampstand for the light with all its fixtures, the offering table, the cups and the bowls, the golden censers, the curtain, the crowns, and the golden ornament on the facade of the temple. He stripped off everything, and took away the gold and silver and the precious vessels; he also took all the hidden treasures he could find. Taking all this, he went back to his own country, after he had spoken with great arrogance and shed much blood. . . .

Two years later, the king sent the Mysian commander to the cities of Judah, and he came to Jerusalem with a strong force. He spoke to them deceitfully in peaceful terms, and won their trust. Then he attacked the city suddenly, in a great onslaught, and destroyed many of the people in Israel. He plundered the city and set fire to it, demolished its houses and its surrounding walls, took captive the women and children, and seized the cattle. Then they built up the City of David with a high, massive wall and strong towers, and it became their citadel. There they installed a sinful race, perverse men, who fortified themselves inside it, storing up weapons and provisions, and depositing there the plunder they had collected from Jerusalem. And they became a great threat. . . .

Then the king wrote to his whole kingdom that all should be one people, each abandoning his particular customs. All the Gentiles conformed to the command of the king, and many Israelites were in favor of his religion; they sacrificed to idols and profaned the Sabbath.

The king sent messengers with letters to Jerusalem and to the cities of Judah, ordering them to follow customs foreign to their land: to prohibit holocausts, sacrifices, and libations in the sanctuary, to profane the sabbaths and feast days, to desecrate the sanctuary and the sacred ministers, to build pagan altars and temples and shrines, to sacrifice swine and unclean animals, to leave their sons uncircumcised, and to let themselves be defiled with every kind of impurity and abomination, so that they might forget the law and change all their observances. Whoever refused to act according to the command of the king should be put to death.

Such were the orders he published throughout his kingdom. He appointed inspectors over all the people, and he ordered the cities of Judah to offer sacrifices, each city in turn. Many of the people, those who abandoned the law, joined them and committed evil in the land. Israel was driven into hiding, wherever places of refuge could be found.

On the fifteenth day of the month Chislev, in the year one hundred and forty-five, the king erected the horrible abomination upon the altar of holocausts, and in the surrounding cities of Judah they built pagan altars. They also burnt incense at the doors of houses and in the streets. Any scrolls of the law which they found they tore up and burnt. Whoever was found with a scroll of the covenant, and whoever observed the law, was condemned to death by royal decree. So they used their power against Israel, against those who were caught, each month, in the cities. On the twenty-fifth day of each month they sacrificed on the altar erected over the altar of holocausts. Women who had had their children circumcised were put to death, in keeping with the decree, with the babies hung from their necks; their families also and those who had circumcised them were killed. But many in Israel were determined and resolved in their hearts not to eat anything unclean; they preferred to die rather than to be defiled with unclean food or to profane the holy covenant; and they did die.

Terrible affliction was upon Israel.

Mattathias and Sons Rebel

2. In those days Mattathias, son of John, son of Simeon, a priest of the family of Joarib, left Jerusalem and settled in Modein. He had five sons: John, who was called Gaddi; Simon, who was called Thassi; Judas, who was called Maccabeus; Eleazar, who was called Avaran; and Jonathan, who was called Apphus. When he saw the sacrileges that were being committed in Judah and in Jerusalem, he said: "Woe is me! Why was I born to see the ruin of my people and the ruin of the holy city, and to sit idle while it is given into the hands of enemies, and the sanctuary into the hands of strangers? . . ."

Then Mattathias and his sons tore their garments, put on sackcloth, and mourned bitterly.

The officers of the king in charge of enforcing the apostasy came to the city of Modein to organize the sacrifices. Many of Israel joined them, but Mattathias and his sons gathered in a group apart. Then the officers of the king addressed Mattathias: "You are a leader, an honorable and great man in this city, supported by sons and kinsmen. Come now, be the first to obey the king's command, as all the Gentiles and the men of Judah and those who are left in Jerusalem have done. Then you and your sons shall be numbered among the King's Friends, and shall be enriched with silver and gold and many gifts." But Mattathias answered in a loud voice: "Although all the Gentiles in the king's realm obey him, so that each forsakes the religion of his fathers and consents to the king's orders, yet I and my sons and my kinsmen will keep to the covenant of our fathers. God forbid that we should forsake the law and the commandments. We will not obey the words of the king nor depart from our religion in the slightest degree."

As he finished saying these words, a certain Jew came forward in the sight of all to offer sacrifice on the altar in Modein according to the king's order. When Mattathias saw him, he was filled with zeal; his heart was moved and his just fury was aroused; he sprang forward and killed him upon the altar. At the same time, he also killed the messenger of the king who was forcing them to sacrifice, and he tore down the altar. Thus he showed his zeal for the law, just as Phinehas did with Zimri, son of Salu.

Then Mattathias went through the city shouting, "Let everyone who is zealous for the law and who stands by the covenant follow after me!" Thereupon he fled to the mountains with his sons, leaving behind in the city all their possessions.

Source: First Maccabees 1:1–24, 25–36, 41–64; 2:1–7, 12–28, from *The New American Bible* (Washington, DC: Confraternity of Christian Doctrine, 1970). Reprinted by Permission.

QUMRAN COMMUNITY: RIVAL SPIRITS OF TRUTH AND FALSEHOOD

Isolating itself from despotic foreign rulers and politically driven religious leaders, the desert community of Qumran near the Dead Sea believed it was preparing for a final battle between good and evil. This is reflected in the following selection from the Dead Sea Scrolls. It describes how our dual human nature as caught between a conflict between a spirit of truth and a spirit of falsehood—the sources of proper and improper conduct, respectively. Reminiscent of Zoroastrianism, it holds that God has established these two spirits in equal proportion until the end times. Followers of truth (the children of light), will ultimately prevail over the followers of falsehood (children of darkness).

Two Spirits with Two Paths

These instructions are for the teacher who will illuminate the children of light about the nature of men, based on the type of spirit that men follow. This will explain men's actions throughout their lives, why they are sometimes visited with affliction, yet other times experience moments of peace.

Everything that now exists and ever will exist comes from the God of knowledge. Before things came into existence, God planned their complete design. When things come into existence at their designated times, they fulfill their objective, which cannot be changed. The laws controlling everything are in God's hands, and he maintains them in everything they do.

God created man to rule over the world, and, until the designated time of God's judgment, he selected two spirits for man to follow. They are the spirits of truth and falsehood. Truth arises from the fountain of light, and falsehood from the fountain of darkness. The children of righteousness are ruled by the prince of light, and they walk in the path of light. But the children of falsehood are ruled by the angel of darkness, and thus walk in the path of darkness.

The angel of darkness leads astray the children of righteousness, and, consequently, all their sins, iniquities, guilt and wayward deeds result from that angel's rule. This follows God's unknowable plan until the end times. All of the hardships and periods of suffering of the righteous result from this angel's malevolence. The angel's companion spirits are intent on making the children of light stumble. However, the God of Israel and his angel of truth will assist the children of light. It is God who created the spirits of light and darkness and made them the foundation of every action. God loves the spirit of light for eternity, and forever delights in all that it does. But God detests any association with the other spirit, and forever hates its actions.

This is how the two spirits operate in the world. The spirit of truth enlightens man's heart, and provides a straight path of truth and righteousness. It places in man's heart a fear for God's laws. It gives humility, patience, compassion, goodness, insight, knowledge, and an abundant wisdom about God's actions and his great mercy. It fosters an understanding about every plan of action, a zeal for lawful governance, and an unwavering motivation toward a holy objective. It promotes compassion toward the followers of truth, a wonderful purity that abhors unclean idols, and humble conduct that arises from wisdom about everything, while concealing the mysteries of truth. This, then, is the guidance of the spirit of truth for the children of truth. The reward for those who walk in the path of this spirit is health, great peace, long life, and abundant offspring. Additionally, there will be eternal blessings and boundless joys through an everlasting life, as well as a crown of glory and a robe that dazzles forever.

The path of the spirit of falsehood is this: greed, neglect of good deeds, wickedness, falsehood, pride, arrogance, deception, lies, hypocrisy, ill-temper, foolishness, insolence, horrible actions driven by lust, lecherous behavior, a blasphemous tongue, blind eyes, deaf ears, a stiff neck, and a hard heart. This is the path of darkness and treachery. The punishment for all who walk this path will be numerous miseries at the hands of all the angels of destruction, and eternal damnation through the furious anger of a vengeful God. There will be everlasting torment and disgrace, and shameful extinction in the fire of hell's darkness. Throughout the ages, generation after generation, they will experience unspeakable suffering, with bitter sadness in darkness. Ultimately, they will be annihilated without survival or hope of rescue.

Final Judgment and Destruction of the Spirit of Falsehood

Thus, the nature of man is ruled by these two spirits. Throughout their lives, the multitudes of men participate in these two divisions and walk in the path of the two spirits. Throughout eternity, the outcome of all of their deeds, which fall within the two divisions, depends on whether their participation in each is great or small. God has equally separated the two spirits until the end times, and has established an enduring animosity between their two divisions. The deeds of falsehood are an outrage against truth, and the works of truth an outrage against falsehood. There is an intense conflict between their judgments since they do not walk the same path.

But God in his unknowable ways and infinite wisdom has established an end of falsehood, and, when the time of judgment arrives, he will destroy it forever. Then truth will victoriously emerge in the world, even though, prior to the appointed time of judgment, truth had been compromised by wickedness through the domination of falsehood. Through his truth, God will then cleanse every act of man and refine some men for himself by destroying every spirit of falsehood from within those men's bodies. He will purify these men from all wicked acts through the spirit of holiness. Like cleansing waters, he will wash the spirit of truth over them to remove the abomination of falsehood and contamination put there by the spirit of impurity. Thus men will become upright, gain knowledge of the most high, and acquire wisdom of the sons of heaven on the perfect path. God has chosen them for an eternal covenant, and all the glory of Adam will be theirs. Falsehood and false deeds will be put to shame.

Until that time, the spirits of truth and falsehood battle within human hearts, thus making people walk the paths of both wisdom and foolishness. To the degree that a person sides with truth, he will be righteous and hate falsehood. To the degree that a person sides with falsehood, he will be unrighteous and hate truth. God has made these two spirits in equal proportion until the end times of renewal. He knows the outcome of these spirits' actions for all eternity. He has allowed them to rule over men so they may know good and evil. Thus, when judgment comes, the fate of every living being will be determined based on the spirit they have followed.

Source: Dead Sea Scrolls, 1QS III 13—IV 26.

RABBINIC WRITINGS

WISDOM OF THE FATHERS

The best-known section of the Mishnah *is* Abot *(literally, fathers), also called Wisdom of the Fathers. This section was considered so important that medieval copies of the* Talmud *have* Abot *as the conclusion of each of its six key divisions. The typical style of the* Mishnah *is a give-and-take legal debate between the* Tannaim. Abot *is different in that it is a collection of proverbs by the* Tannaim *that are not debated. The first two divisions of* Abot, *presented here, begin by listing the transmitters of the oral law from Moses to the* Tannaim *themselves.*

1. Moses received the Oral Law from Sinai and delivered it to Joshua, and Joshua delivered it to the elders, and the elders to the prophets, and the prophets to the men of the Great Synagogue who said three things: "Do not be hasty in judgment. Raise up many disciples. Build a fence to protect the Torah."
2. Simon the Just was one of the last men of the Great Synagogue. He used to say, "The world rests on three things: the Torah, worship, and kindness."
3. Antigonus of Soco received the oral law from Simon the Just. He used to say, "Do not be like servants who serve their master for the sake of receiving a reward, but be like servants who serve their master without the view of receiving a reward. Let the fear of heaven be upon you."
4. Yosa ben Yoezer of Zeredah, and Yosa ben Yohanan of Jerusalem, received the oral law from him. Yosa ben Yoezer of Zeredah said, "Let your house be meeting place of the wise, sit gladly at their feet, and drink in their words with eagerness."
5. Yosa ben Yohanan of Jerusalem, said, "Let your house be so wide open that the poor may be like your children.

Do not discourse much with women, not even with your wife, much less with your neighbor's wife; hence the wise men warned that whoever converses much with women brings evil on himself, neglects the study of the Torah, and ultimately will inherit hell."

6. Joshua ben Perahya and Natai the Arbelite received the oral law from them. Joshua ben Perahya said, "Get yourself a good teacher. Obtain a companion. Judge everyone by his good qualities."

7. Natai the Arbelite said, "Stay away from an evil neighbor, do not associate with the wicked, and do not grow thoughtless of God's punishment."

8. Judah ben Tabbai, and Simon ben Shatah, received it from them. Judah ben Tabai said, "When people stand before you in judgment, do not consider yourself as a counselor. Rather, judge them as guilty, but consider them as innocent when they leave you and submit to the punishment."

9. Simon ben Shatah said, "Make full examination of witnesses, but be cautious with your words, in case they might learn to lie."

10. Shemaya and Abtalyon received it from them. Shemaiah said, "Love your work, hate to obtain superiority, and be unknown to government."

11. Abtalyon said, "Sages, be guarded in your words, in case you become doomed to exile, and exiled to a place of bad waters, where your disciples who follow you might drink and die, thereby profaning the name of heaven."

12. Hillel and Shammai received it from them. Hillel said, "Be one of the disciples of Aaron who loved and pursued peace. Love your fellow humans and allure them to the study of the Torah."

13. He used to say, "Whoever glorifies his own name, destroys his name. He who does not increase his knowledge, decreases it. He who does not learn from his teachers is not worthy of life. He who serves himself with the crown of knowledge will perish."

14. He also said, "If I perform no good works myself, who will do them for me? If I am concerned only with myself, what am I? If not now, when shall I?"

15. Shammai said, "Set a fixed time to study of the Torah. Promise little and do much. Greet all people with an open and pleasant disposition."

16. Rabban Gamaliel said, "Find an instructor for yourself so that you may not be in doubt. Do not routinely calculate your tithes through mere guesswork."

17. Simon, his son, said, "All my life I have been brought up among wise men. I have never found anything as good for the body as silence. The study of the Torah is not as important as practicing it. Whoever talks a lot causes sin."

18. Rabban Simon ben Gamaliel said, "Three things support the world: justice, truth, and peace. As it is written, 'judge truth, justice, and peace in your gates' (Zechariah 8:16)."

Source: *Babylonian Talmud*, Abot, 1, Mishna, tr., Joseph Barclay (adapted).

RABBINIC AUTHORITY

The chief theological paradox of the Talmud is how collected opinions of early Rabbis can count as divine law. Although Judaism traces its oral law back to Moses, the Mishnah and Talmud are only the collected sayings of the Tannaim and Amoraim. Early Rabbis themselves were aware of this paradox and provide an answer in the following selection, one of the most famous passages of the Talmud. It describes how Rabbis were debating whether oven tiles that had previously been defiled could be reconfigured in a way that would remove their impurity. Rabbi Eliezer said it could, and God spoke from heaven confirming the Rabbi's judgment. Rabbi Joshua then protested that God's voice meant nothing since the law was given at Mount Sinai and its interpretation was determined by the majority. That is, the majority position held by the carriers of oral law in fact becomes the law. At that time, the sages of the Talmud were the carriers.

Mishna 8

As cheating is prohibited in buying or selling, so it is in words. (How so?) One must not ask the price of a thing when he does not intend to buy it. To a person who has repented one must not say, Remember your former acts. To a descendant from proselytes one must not say, Remember the acts of your parents. As it is written [Exodus xxii. 20]: "Do not wrong or oppress a stranger."

Gemara

There is a Mishna (Keilim, V., 10) which discusses of an oven which became exposed to uncleanliness. Rabbi Eliezer said it can be made clean again, while other sages said that it remains unclean. It is called the oven of a snake.

Why is it called the oven of the snake? Rabbi Judah replied in the name of Samuel: It suggests that they encircled it with their arguments for and against uncleanliness, just as a snake winds itself around an object. One tradition states that Rabbi Eliezer gave every possible answer, but they were all rejected. Rabbi Eliezer then said, "Let this carob-tree prove that the law prevails as I state," and the tree miraculously flew off to a distance of 150 feet, and according to others 600 feet. But the sages said: The tree proves nothing. Rabbi Eliezer again said: "Let this spring of water prove that the law prevails," and the water miraculously began to run backwards. Still, the sages said that this proved nothing. Rabbi Eliezer again said: "Let the walls of this school prove that I am right," and the walls leaned and were about to fall. Rabbi Joshua, however, rebuked the walls, saying: "If the scholars of this school are discussing a law, why should you interfere?" In respect for Rabbi Joshua, the walls did not fall, out of respect for Rabbi Eliezer, but they did not become straight again.

Rabbi Eliezer said again, "Let it be announced by the heavens that the law prevails according to my statement," and a heavenly voice was heard, saying, "Why do you argue with Rabbi Eliezer, who is always right in his decisions?" Rabbi Joshua then arose and proclaimed, "The Law is not in the heavens" (Deuteronomy 30:12). What does this mean? Rabbi Jeremiah said, "It means that the Torah was given already to us on Mount Sinai, and we do not care about any heavenly voice, for it is written "Incline after the majority" (Exodus 23:2). Rabbi Nathan then met with the Prophet Elijah and questioned him: "What did the Holy One, blessed be he, do when Rabbi Joshua talked back to the heavenly voice? Elijah replied: "He laughed and said, 'My children have overruled me, my children have overruled me'."

Source: *Babylonian Talmud*, Baba Mezia, 1.4.8, tr. Michael L. Rodkinson (adapted).

WHY GOD IS JEALOUS OF IDOLS

The Rabbis of the Talmud *often used metaphors and parables to make their arguments. A case in point is the selection below which records various colorful parables that aim to show why God would be jealous of idols.*

Mishna 7

The Jewish elders were asked by the philosophers at Rome: If God is displeased with idol-worship, why then does he not destroy the idols? They replied: If the heathens only worshipped things that were not needful to the world, he would surely annihilate them. But the fact is that heathens worship the sun, moon, stars and planets; should then God destroy his world on account of these fools? Then retorted the others: Why cannot God destroy the unnecessary objects but then leave the others that are needed for the preservation of the world? The elders replied: If he did so, the idol-worshippers would then be confirmed in their belief and say: you see here that these are true gods since they are indestructible.

Gemara

The Lord allows the world to take its natural course. As for these fools who spoil it, they will not escape punishment. In other words, when someone steals wheat and sows it, the seed should not bear fruit by reason of its being stolen. But no, God lets nature take her course, while the thief will be given what he deserves. In like manner, with adultery it is appropriate that the woman should not conceive, but nature takes its course while the culprit is not spared. Resh Lakish says something to this effect: The Holy One says, not only do the wicked of this earth misuse my coins, but they force me yet to put my stamp on them.

A philosopher once asked Rabbi Gamaliel: Your law says "For the Lord your God is a consuming fire, a jealous God" (Deuteronomy. 4:24); why is it that he is so jealous regarding the worshipper but not the idol? Rabbi Gamaliel said: I will answer your question by a metaphor. Suppose a king's son named his dog with his father's name and, when occasion arises, swears by the life of this dog. Would the father, once informed about this, get angry at his son or at the dog? Clearly, at the son. The philosopher then said: You compare the idol to a dog, which is not analogous, since the idol has greater abilities. You ask what those abilities are? Why, once a fire consumed our entire city, and the idol temple remained intact. Rabbi Gamaliel answered: I will use a metaphor again: A province once revolted against the king; against whom do you suppose he used his weapons, against the living or against the dead? Clearly, against the living. The philosopher answered: You compare our gods to dogs and the dead; well, then, if they really are so worthless why does God not annihilate them altogether? Rabbi Gamaliel replied: yes, he would surely do it, if they were not objects that are useful to the preservation of the world, such as are the sun, moon, stars, planets, mountains. and valleys. For it is written: "I will utterly sweep away everything from

the face of the earth, says the LORD. I will sweep away man
and beast; I will sweep away the birds of the heavens and
the fish of the sea, and the stumbling blocks of the wicked"
(Zephaniah. 1:2-3). That is to say, The LORD wonders, should
I do this when the heathens worship man, too? I would then
destroy the whole universe.

Agrippus, the general of Rome, said to Rabbi Gamaliel:
Your law says "For the LORD your God is a consuming fire, a
jealous God." In our everyday lives we find it to be the rule
that a ruler is jealous only of his equal, a sage of another
sage, a hero of another hero, a rich person of another rich
person. Now, then, if God is jealous of an idol, then the idol
must be of some power. Rabbi Gamaliel explained it to him
with the following metaphor: If a man who has a wife, takes
a second one, the first will not be jealous unless the new wife
is nothing compared with herself.

Source: *Babylonian Talmud,* Abuda Zara 4.7, tr. Michael L.
Rodkinson.

RESURRECTION OF THE DEAD

*The notion of resurrection of the dead is not a clear theme in
the* Tanakh. *The book of Job, for example, poetically pronounces
against it: "As a cloud breaks up and disperses, so no one who
goes down to Sheol ever comes back." The idea of resurrection
took hold in post-exilic writings and, by the time of the Rabbinic
period, it had become an important tenet of Judaism. In this
selection from the* Talmud, *several Rabbis debate the issues surrounding the resurrected.*

Mishna 1

All Israel has a share in the world to come. As it reads: "All
your people will be righteous. They will possess their land
forever, for I will plant them there with my own hands in
order to bring myself glory" (Isaiah 60:21). He will have no
place in the world to come who says that there is no allusion
in the Torah concerning resurrection, and who says that the
Torah was not given by Heaven. . . .

Gemara

Is he who does not believe that the resurrection is hinted at
in the Torah such a criminal that he loses his place in the
world to come? It was taught: He denies resurrection therefore he will not have a place in it, as punishment corresponds

to the deed; for all punishments of the Holy One are in correspondence with man's doing. . . .

Queen Cleopatra questioned Rabbi Mair: I am aware that
the dead will be restored. As it reads: "And men will blossom
out of the city like herbs of the earth" (Psalms 72:16). My
question, however, is this: When they are restored, will they
be naked or dressed? He answered: This may be showed by
an even stronger conclusion from wheat. A grain of wheat
which is buried naked comes out dressed in so many garments. The upright, then, who are buried in their dress, will
even more so emerge dressed in many garments. . . .

Caesar questioned Rabbon Gamaliel: You say that the
dead will be restored. Does not the corpse become dust?
How, then, can dust be restored? The daughter of Caesar
said to Rabbi Gamaliel: Leave the question to me and I
myself will answer it. She said to her father: If there were
two potters in our city, of whom one would make a pot from
water and the other from clay, to which of them would you
give preference? And he said: Certainly to him who creates from water; for if he is able to create from water, he is
undoubtedly able to create from clay. She said: This is an
answer to your question.

The school of Rabbi Ismael taught: We may learn from
glasswares, which are made by human beings, that if they
break there is a repair for them, and they can be renewed.
Human beings, who are created by the spirit of the LORD, will
be restored even more so. . . .

Antoninus said to the Rabbi: The body and the soul of
a human may free themselves on the day of judgment in
Heaven. How so? The body may say: The soul has sinned;
for since she has departed I lie in the grave like a stone. And
the soul may say: The body has sinned; for since I am separated from it, I fly in the air like a bird. The Rabbi answered:
I will give you a parable to which this is similar: A human
king, who had a great garden which contained excellent figs,
appointed two watchmen for it—one of whom was blind, and
the other had no feet. The one who was without feet said
to the one who was blind: I see some excellent figs in the
garden. Take me on your shoulders, I will get them, and we
will eat them. He did so, and while on his shoulders he took
them off, and both ate them. When the owner of the garden
came and did not find the figs, and questioned them what
became of them, the blind one answered: Have I, then, eyes to
see them, that you should suspect my taking them? And the
lame one answered: Have I, then, feet to go there? The owner
then put the lame one on the shoulders of the one who was

blind, and punished them together. So also the Holy One puts the soul into the body and punishes them together. As it reads: "He will call to the heavens above, and to the earth beneath, to judge his people" (Psalms 1:4). "To the heavens above" means the soul, and, "to the earth beneath" means the body.

Source: *Babylonian Talmud,* Sanhedrin 11.1, tr. Michael L. Rodkinson (adapted).

COMING OF THE MESSIAH

During the Babylonian exile, the Jews lost hope in the ability of any present leader to return Israel to its former glory and so they placed their hopes in a future Messiah, or anointed one. The notion gained momentum and complexity during post-exilic times, and by the time of the Rabbinic period the coming of the Messiah was linked to the culmination of human history and the establishment of God's kingdom on earth. In the following selections from the Talmud, several Rabbis debate about the events leading up to the Messiah's arrival.

The rabbis taught: In this Sabbatic period in which the son of David will appear, in the first year what is written will be fulfilled: "I sent rain on one town, but withheld it from another." (Amos 4:7). In the second year, arrows of famine will be sent. In the third, a great famine, from which men, women, and children, pious men and men of good deeds will die, and the Torah will be forgotten by their scholars. In the fourth there will be abundance, and not abundance. In the fifth there will be great abundance, and the people will eat, drink, and enjoy themselves, and the Torah will return to her scholars. In the sixth, voices will be heard saying that the Messiah is near. In the seventh, war will be, and at the end of the seventh, the son of David will come. Said Rabbi Joseph: Were there not many Sabbatical periods which were like this, but still he did not come? Said Abayi: Were then the above-mentioned voices heard in the sixth? And was there in the seventh war? And secondly, has it then happened in the same order as said above? . . .

Rabbi Jehudah said: In the generation that the son of David will come, the houses of assembly will be converted into houses of prostitution. Galilee will be destroyed. The place called Gablan will be desolate. Men of the borders of Palestine will travel from one city to another, but will not be welcome. The wisdom of the scribes will be corrupted. Men fearing sin will be hated. The leaders of that generation will have the nature of dogs. . . .

Rabbi Nehuraia taught: In the generation that the son of David will come, young men will make pale the faces of the old, old men will stand up before youth, a daughter will rebel against her mother, a daughter-in-law against her mother-in-law, the leaders of the generation will have the nature of dogs, and a son will not be ashamed when his father scolds him.

Rabbi Nehemiah said: In the generation that the son of David will come, insolence will increase, an evil man will be honored, respect will be missed, the vine will give forth its fruit abundantly; wine, however, will be dear, and all the governments will embrace heretics, and no preaching will help. This is similar to Rabbi Itz'hak, who said that the son of David will not come unless all governments are turned over to heretics. Where is to be found a hint to this in the Scripture? (Leviticus 13:13): "It has all turned white, he is clean."

Source: *Babylonian Talmud,* Sanhedrin 11.1, tr. Michael L. Rodkinson (adapted).

UNITY OF THE TEN COMMANDMENTS

In addition to debates on fine points of law and theology, Rabbis and other Jewish writers for hundreds of years had developed legends and embellishments surrounding the historical narrative in the Tanakh*—from creation to the restoration. The stories are scattered throughout the Apocrypha, Pseudepigrapha, Talmud, and Midrash, and are even found in early Christian writings. The following is a collection of legends from these various sources, compiled by Talmudic scholar Louis Ginzberg, which explain how the Ten Commandments are woven into a unified whole.*

The Ten Commandments are so closely interwoven, that the breaking of one leads to the breaking of another. But there is a particularly strong bond of union between the first five commandments, which are written on one table, and the last five, which were on the other table. The first commandment: "I am the LORD, thy God," corresponds to the sixth: "Thou shalt not kill," for the murderer slays the image of God. The second: "Thou shalt have no strange gods before me," corresponds to the seventh: "Thou shalt not commit adultery," for conjugal faithlessness is as grave a sin as idolatry, which is faithlessness to God. The third commandment: "Thou shalt not take the name of the LORD in vain," corresponds to the eighth: "Thou shalt not steal," for theft leads to false oath. The fourth commandment: "Remember the Sabbath day, to keep it holy," corresponds to the ninth: "Thou shalt not bear false witness against thy neighbor," for he who bears false witness against his neighbor commits as grave a sin as if he had borne false witness against God, saying that He had not created the world in six days and rested on the seventh, the Sabbath. The fifth commandment: "Honor thy father and thy mother," corresponds to the tenth: "Covet not thy neighbor's wife," for one who indulges this lust produces children who will not honor their true father, but will consider a stranger their father.

The Ten Commandments, which God first revealed on Mount Sinai, correspond in their character to the ten words of which He had made use at the creation of the world. The first commandment: "I am the LORD, thy God," corresponds to the first word at the creation: "Let there be light," for God is the eternal light. The second commandment: "Thou shalt have no strange gods before me," corresponds to the second word: "Let there be a firmament in the midst of the waters, and let it divide the waters from the waters." For God said: "Choose between Me and the idols; between Me, the fountain of living waters, and the idols, the stagnant waters." The third commandment: "Thou shalt not take the name of thy God in vain," corresponds to the word: "Let the waters be gathered together," for as little as water can be gathered in a cracked vessel, so can a man maintain his possession which he has obtained through false oaths. The fourth commandment: "Remember to keep the Sabbath holy," corresponds to the word: "Let the earth bring forth grass," for he who truly observes the Sabbath will receive good things from God without having to labor for them, just as the earth produces grass that need not be sown. For at the creation of man it was God's intention that he be free from sin, immortal, and capable of supporting himself by the products of the soil without toil. The fifth commandment: "Honor thy father and thy mother," corresponds to the word: "Let there be lights in the firmament of the heaven," for God said to man: "I gave thee two lights, thy father and thy mother, treat them with care." The sixth commandment: "Thou shalt not kill," corresponds to the word: "Let the waters bring forth abundantly the moving creature," for God said: "Be not like the fish, among whom the great swallow the small." The seventh commandment: "Thou shalt not commit adultery," corresponds to the word: "Let the earth bring forth the living creature after his kind," for God said: "I chose for thee a spouse, abide with her." The eighth commandment: "Thou shalt not steal," corresponds to the word: "Behold, I have given you every herb-bearing seed," for none, said God, should touch his neighbor's goods, but only that which grows free as the grass, which is the common property of all. The ninth commandment: "Thou shalt not bear false witness against thy neighbor," corresponds to the word: "Let us make man in our image." Thou, like thy neighbor, art made in My image, hence bear not false witness against thy neighbor. The tenth commandment: "Thou shalt not covet the wife of thy neighbor," corresponds to the tenth word of the creation: "It is not good for man to be alone," for God said: "I created thee a spouse, and let not one among ye covet his neighbor's wife."

Source: Louis Ginzberg, *The Legends of the Jews,* vol. 3, ch. 2 (Philadelphia: The Jewish Publication Society of America, 1909).

MEDIEVAL JUDAISM

MAIMONIDES: THIRTEEN PRINCIPLES OF BELIEF

Judaism has resisted the formulation of creeds or other statements of belief, perhaps in part because of the dialogical nature of the Talmud *and its other principal theological works. Nevertheless, the medieval Jewish philosopher Moses Maimonides (1135–1204) developed a list of thirteen principles of belief, which was embraced by Judaism and, in an abbreviated form, appears in most Jewish prayer books today. The following is from Maimonides' original discussion of the principles.*

I must now mention, and this is the correct place for doing so, that there are thirteen fundamental principles that form the foundation of our religion.

The first fundamental principle is belief in the existence of the Creator. That is, there is an existing Being who possesses the highest perfection of existence. He is the cause of the existence of all existing things. They exist in him and their continued existence emanates from him. We cannot conceive of his non-existence, since then the existence of everything else would completely cease and there would be nothing left to exist whatsoever. But if on the other hand we imagine the non-existence of all existing things but he, then his existence would not cease, nor would he be diminished in any way. For he is self-sufficient, and his existence does not depend on any existence outside of him. Whatever is outside him, whether the angels, celestial bodies or things beneath these, they all depend on him for their existence. This is the first fundamental principle, which is taught in the commandment, "I am the LORD your God" (Exodus 20:2).

The second fundamental principle is belief in the Unity of God. That is, God is one. He is not one of a genus or of a species. He is not like one human being who is a whole that is divisible into many parts. He is not a unity like the ordinary material body which is numerically one, but can take on endless divisions and parts. Instead, he is a unity in the sense that there is no unity like his in any way. This is the fundamental principle, which is taught by the statement, "Hear, Israel, the LORD our God, the LORD is one" (Deuteronomy 6:4).

The third fundamental principle is belief that God is immaterial. This means that God is not a body or the power within a body. He cannot possess the properties of bodies, such as motion and rest, either essentially or accidentally. It was for this reason that our sages denied to him both cohesion and separation of parts, when they remarked "no sitting and no standing, no division, and no cohesion" (Hagigah 15a). . . .

The fourth fundamental principle is belief in the eternal priority of God. This means that God is first in the absolute sense. No existent thing outside him is primary in relation to him. The proofs of this in the Scriptures are numerous. This fourth principle is taught by the phrase "The eternal God is a refuge" (Deuteronomy 33:27).

The fifth fundamental principle is belief that he must be worshipped, glorified, proclaimed, and obeyed. This must not be done to any existing beings lower than him—not the angels, the celestial spheres, the elements or things composed from them. For these are all fashioned for the work they are intended to perform. They have no judgment or free-will, but only a love for him. We must not adopt mediators to help us approach God, but instead let our thoughts be directed to him, and turn away from whatever is below him. This fifth principle is a prohibition against idolatry. The greater part of the Torah is taken up with the prohibition of idol-worship.

The sixth fundamental principle is belief in prophecy. This means that, among this human species, there are people with higher intellects and perfections whose souls are predisposed to receiving the higher intellectual form. Their human intellect then joins with the divine active intellect, and an exalted emanation is shed upon them. These are the prophets. This is prophecy, and this is its meaning. The complete clarification of this fundamental principle would be very long, and it is not our purpose to prove every principle or to offer a way to understand them. Such a task would involve the totality of the sciences. We can give them a passing mention only. Many verses of the Torah bear witness to prophecies of prophets.

The seventh fundamental principle is belief in the prophecy of Moses, our teacher. This means that we must believe that he was the father of all the prophets before him, and that those who came after him were all beneath him in rank. Moses was chosen by God from all of mankind. He understood more about God than any man in the past understood, or any future man will understand. We must believe that he reached an exalted state above the sphere of humanity, so that he attained an angelic rank and became included in the order of the angels. There was no barrier which he did not break. No physical obstacle stood in his way, and no defect whether small or great mixed with him. The imaginative and sensual abilities of his perceptive faculty were stripped from him. His appetites were subdued and he remained pure intellect only. It is in this way that it is said of him that he spoke with God without any angelic intermediary. . . .

The eighth fundamental principle is belief that the Torah has been revealed from heaven. This means that our belief that the entire Torah that rests in our hands was handed down by Moses and that it is all of divine origin. By this I mean that the whole of the Torah came to him from God in a manner that is metaphorically called "speaking." But the real nature of that communication is unknown to everybody except Moses himself to whom it came. In handing down the Torah, Moses was like a scribe writing the entirety of it from dictation—its chronicles, its narratives, and its precepts. It is in this sense that he is termed "lawgiver.". . . The interpretation of traditional law is similarly of divine origin. That which we know today about the nature of [the ceremonial] Succah, Lulab, Shofar, Fringes, and Phylacteries is essentially the same as that which God commanded Moses, and which Moses told us. In the success of his mission Moses achieved the calling of a faithful servant of God (Numbers 12:7). The text in which the eighth fundamental principle is taught is, "This is how you will know that the LORD has sent me to do all these works; for I have not done them on my own" (Numbers 16:28).

The ninth fundamental principle is belief in the irrevocability of the Torah. This means that this Law of Moses will not be changed and that no other law will come from God. Nothing is to be added to it nor taken away from it, neither in the written nor oral law, as it is said, "You will not add to it or diminish from it" (Deuteronomy 13:1). At the outset of this treatise we already discussed the explanation of this fundamental principle.

The tenth fundamental principle is the belief that God knows the actions of men and does not overlook them. It is not as those who said, "The LORD has abandoned the earth" (Ezekiel 8:12; 9:9), but is instead as he who exclaimed, "Great are your purposes and mighty are your deeds; your eyes are open to the ways of all mankind" (Jeremiah 32:19). It is further said, "The LORD saw that the wickedness of man became great on the earth" (Genesis 6:5). And again, "the outcry against Sodom and Gomorrah is great" (Genesis 18:20). This is the meaning of our tenth fundamental principle.

The eleventh fundamental principle is belief that God rewards those who obey the commands of the Torah, and punishes those who violate its prohibitions. God's greatest reward to man is the world to come, and his strongest punishment is being annihilation. We have already said enough on this topic. The scriptural verses in which the principle is pointed out are, "But now, forgive their sin; but if not, then blot me out of the book that you have written" (Exodus 32:32). God then replied to him, "Whoever has sinned against me I will blot out of my book" (Exodus 32:33). This is evidence of what the obedient and the sinner will each obtain. God rewards the one and punishes the other.

The twelfth fundamental principle is belief in the era of the Messiah. This means that we must firmly believe that he is coming, and not think that he is late in arriving. "Though he tarries, wait for him" (Habakkuk 2:3). No date must be fixed for his appearance, neither may the scriptures be interpreted with the aim of deducing the time of his coming. The Sages said. "A plague on those who calculate periods for the Messiah's appearance" (Sanhedrin 97b).

We must have faith in the Messiah, honoring and loving him, and praying for him in proportion to the importance with which he is spoken of by every prophet, from Moses to Malachi. Whoever doubts about him or holds his authority lightly accuses the Torah of falsehood, since it clearly promises his coming in the chapter of Balaam (Numbers 23–24), and in the passage "you are standing" (Deuteronomy 30:1–10). From the general nature of this fundamental principle we infer that there will be no king of Israel but from David and the descendants of Solomon exclusively. Everyone who disputes the authority of this family denies God and the words of his prophets.

The thirteenth fundamental principle is belief in the resurrection of the dead. We have already explained this.

Source: Maimonides, *Commentary on the Mishnah*, Introduction to Sanhedrin, ch. 10, tr. Joshua Abelson (adapted).

KABBALA: CREATION

Since the twelfth century, the most dominant school of Jewish mysticism has been Kabbala, the classic statement of which is the Book of Splendor (Sefer ha-Zohar), *written between 1280 and 1286 by Moses de Leon, a Spanish Jew from Guadalajara. The work emphasizes ten emanations—or Sefirot—of God's personality. These attributes of the divinity permeate all of creation, including our personal lives. De Leon does not systematically discuss the emanations and typically does not refer to them by their formal names. Instead, he relies heavily on metaphors, leaving it to the reader to make the association. The following is part of de Leon's account of creation, presented as a commentary on the first phrase of the Book of Genesis, that is, "In the beginning." He describes how God (Eyn Sof, or the Infinite) created two primary emanations. The first is Hokhmah (wisdom), described below as "point" and "beginning," which is the primal point of God's emanation. The second is Binah (derivative wisdom), described below as "palace," which is the prime mother who receives seed from Hokhmah and gives birth to seven lower emanations.*

Creation through a Primal Point Radiating Outward

"In the beginning" [*Brashith*] (Gen. 1.1) was Ein Sof, the Divine, the self-existent infinite being, without likeness or reflection, the incomprehensible, the unknowable One, the blessed and only Potentate, the King of Kings and LORD of Lords, who alone has immortality, dwelling in Light which no one can approach, whom no man has seen or can see. The great archangel with face beneath his wings bends in lowly reverence and adoration before Him, crying, "Holy! Holy! Holy! who are and was and always will be.

Time had begun. Its great pendulum, whose beats are the ages, began to vibrate. The era of creation or manifestation had at last arrived. The primal point [*nekuda reshima*] or nucleus, appeared. From it emanated and expanded the primary substance, the illimitable phosphorescent ether, of the nature of light, formless, colorless, being neither black nor green nor red. In it, dormant yet potentially as in a mighty womb, lay the countless prototypes and numberless forms of all created things as yet indiscernible, indistinguishable. By the secret and silent action of the divine will, from this primal luminous point radiated forth the vital life-giving spark which, pervading and operating in the great, enteric ocean of forms, became the soul of the universe, the fount and origin of all mundane life and motion and terrestrial existence, and in its nature and essence and secret operation remains ineffable, incomprehensible, and indefinable. It has been conceived of as the divine Logos, the Word, and called "in the beginning" [*Brashith*], for the same was in the beginning with God.

"Those who are wise will shine like the brightness of the heavens, and those who lead many to righteousness, like the stars forever and ever" (Daniel. 12.3). The word zohar (brightness) designates that primal point [*nekuda reshima*], the central ray or point of light which was the primal manifestation of the Divine, Ein Sof. From it proceeded vibrations which made luminous the illimitable ether, from which was formed the universe that became the glorious palace of the great Unknown. It was in a manner the holy seed or germ that gave origin and birth to the world, and is occultly referred to in the words: "The holy seed will be the stump in the land" (Isaiah 6.13). Its analogy in nature is the silkworm which, unseen and in secret, elaborately prepares a product that ultimately makes up the material of the monarch's purple robe of splendor. . . .

We now proceed to investigate and acquaint ourselves with the hidden mysteries and teachings of the secret doctrine regarding creation which have just been outlined in a general manner. So far we have dwelt upon the secret operation of Ein Sof, or the unknown infinite and eternal Being, in preparing the earth and impregnating its substance with a mysterious divine virtue or power. This made the earth capable of becoming the medium for containing and manifesting pre-existing spiritual entities and beings. With these effects achieved, there was needed the all-creating, life-giving Logos, or Word, to originate and utter the symphonal vibration that would impart life and breath and motion to the universe. Then and not until then was it spoken; then and not until then, when the celestial and terrestrial worlds became bound and associated together by a reciprocal influence, a new and a living way was opened for the incarnation and exhibition of life upon the earth. . . .

Worlds enveloping Worlds within the Cosmos

When King Solomon went down into the garden of nuts, as the scripture says (Song 6.11), he took up a nutshell that gave rise to reflections and ideas. These enabled him to understand the reason and cause why anything that is pure and holy becomes surrounded by what is evil, just as the nut is enclosed within a shell. He understood that evil spirits attach themselves to the pure and good, surrounding them similar to shells by exciting and producing certain kinds of pleasing emotions and feelings that tend to defile and corrupt, as it is written: "The pleasures of man produce and bring forth evil spirits" (Ecclesiastes 2.8) which occurs during the hours of sleep. It was necessary that the Holy One would create them in the world in order that it might be complete.

The universe as a whole is a system of worlds, enveloping the other from the lowest to the highest, from the most material to the highly spiritual, from the darkest and most dense to the most luminous and ethereal, all is a scale of graduated worlds of being and existence, and therefore the saying: "as above so below, and as below so above." Each world is a garment or envelope to the next in sequence. From the primal point of light issue forth luminous rays which extend through and pervade all the separate encircling worlds of existence, converting them into palaces of the great king, the splendor, beauty and magnificence of which are beyond description, and, as with these worlds rising in their order one above the other, so is it with regard to the human form, which in its grace and beauty of contour is the highest expression and approximate image of the divine, more than all other physical forms below it in the scale of being. All this is in accordance with the divine plan of creation, man himself being a microcosm or miniature of the universe, and composed of a series of coverings or envelopes, one within the other, as spirit, astral form and physical body. As long as the substance of the moon was conjoined with that of the sun, it shone with its own light, but becoming separated and disjoined from it and independent, it reflected a diminished luminosity and became itself enveloped with zones of decreasing light, so that we may now understand why the scripture says: "Let there be lights," using the defective word meoroth, by which is designated occultly the zones or planes of existence of varying degrees of light which encircle each star and planet in the universe, as also this, our earth, through whose circumambient envelopes of more ethereal substance the primal life-giving light is reflected, and thus differentiated and adapted to become a blessing to man and every animate and inanimate creature.

Source: Moses de Leon, *Zohar,* 1.1-3, tr. Nurho de Manhar (adapted).

RECENT MOVEMENTS

HASIDISM: STORIES OF BAAL SHEM TOV

The Hasidic movement was founded by Ukrainian Rabbi Israel ben Eliezer (1700–1760), better known as Baal Shem Tov, meaning "master of the good name," often abbreviated "Besht." Hasidism was a mystical response to disillusionment with both rabbinic legalism and messianic hope brought on by messianic pretenders of the previous century. Baal Shem Tov and his immediate followers were preachers, rather than scholars, and communicated orally rather than in writing. Baal Shem Tov himself is historically an obscure figure who wrote little or nothing, but had a great impact on ordinary people in his surrounding community as a model of piety. A central doctrine for him is that God is in all things and can be directly accessed through mystical experience. The selections are anecdotes about his life that appeared in Praises of Israel Baal Shem Tov *(1814), the earliest collection of stories about him.*

Birth and Youth of Baal Shem Tov

The father of Baal Shem Tov, Rabbi Eliezer, lived on the frontiers of Wallachia, from where he was carried away by robbers to a distant land, where he was sold as a slave to one of the King's ministers. The King was then engaged in a war that threatened the destruction of the kingdom, when suddenly the means of averting the calamity were revealed to Rabbi Eliezer in a dream. A second dream raised him to a dignity equal to that which Joseph enjoyed in Egypt, and he received the King's daughter in marriage. His piety prevented him from living with this Gentile woman: he, however, revealed to her his history and religion, which was altogether forbidden in that land, and she assisted him in escaping with great riches. On his road home, he was robbed of all he had, but was comforted by the appearance of the prophet Elijah, who said, Because of your great merits you are found worthy to have a son, who will enlighten the eyes of Israel, and in him will be fulfilled the verse, "You are my servant, Israel, and you will bring me glory" (Isaiah 49:3). On his return home, Rabbi Eliezer found his wife, and Israel Baal Shem Tov was born; they were in their old age, for both were one hundred years old. The child grew and was weaned; and when the time of the father's death drew near, he took him in his arms, and said, "You will shine as a great light, so remember throughout your life that God is with you, and as He is with you, do not be afraid of anything."

After his father's death, the townspeople, out of respect for him, took care of the child, and acquired a tutor for him. His talents were great and he made rapid progress. But he was in the habit of studying only a few days at a time, and would then run away into the woods to enjoy private study and prayer. So, the people thought he was a hopeless youth and they withdrew their support. Poor Israel was then obliged to accept a position as helper in a school. His job was to call for the children at their homes, convey them to school, and repeat certain prayers to them. When he sang the words, and concluded with the Amen, his voice pierced the heavens, for it was such a song as the Levites used to sing in the Temple, and in heaven it was a time of great favor and acceptance.

Satan observed this, and fearful of the consequences, determined to stop this devotion. To accomplish this, Satan changed himself into a werewolf, and when Israel was conducting the children to school, he terrified them so much that they were afraid to go any more, and thus the praying and singing were interrupted. Israel then remembered the dying command of his father, to be afraid of nothing. Thus, he begged the parents to entrust the children to him and said he would protect them. He persuaded the parents, and Baal Shem, with one strike of his staff, laid the werewolf lifeless at his feet. After this, Baal Shem became a watcher of the Beth House of Learning (Hamidrash), and, to all appearance, neglected his studies. His custom was to sleep while others studied, and when the others slept he spent that time in diligent study and prayer.

Baal Shem and Rabbi David

I heard from the great Rabbi of the holy congregation of Meseritz, that once, on the Day of Atonement, Baal Shem was late arriving to prayer, and the people waited a long time for him. Eventually he arrived, sat down in his usual seat, and laid his head upon the desk. After lifting up his head several times, he made signs to begin prayer. The famous Rabbi David stepped forward, for he always read prayers on solemn occasions. But no sooner had he reached the reading-desk, than Baal Shem began to pour forth upon him a torrent of abuse, which he continued for half an hour, putting Rabbi David to shame in the presence of all the people. Rabbi David, afraid that Baal Shem saw some sin in him, started to leave, but Baal Shem stopped him with a loud cry, commanding him to stand still and pray. Rabbi David began the prayers with weeping and sobbing, and hardly knew what he was doing, since his heart was nearly broken. When the Day of Atonement was over, Rabbi David went to Baal Shem, and asked him what wickedness he had seen in him which required shaming him before the congregation. Baal Shem replied, "I saw no wickedness, but I saw Satan the Accuser obstructing the path by which the prayers ascend to heaven. Therefore I delayed the prayers until I could find another path for them [through you]. But I was afraid that there might be some vain thoughts in you [where Satan might enter]. Because of that I wounded your heart to keep away any unexpected thoughts."

Baal Shem and the Oral Law

On another occasion, on the eve of the Day of Atonement, Satan the Accuser made a serious allegation against the Jews, the object of which was to take away the oral law. Baal Shem went about the entire day in great agitation. In the evening, when the whole town went to him to receive his benediction, he blessed only one or two, so great was his sorrow. He then went into the synagogue, leaned into the Ark of the Covenant, and spoke words of criticism, crying out, "What will we do if they take the holy law away from us? We will not be able to exist among the nations for half a day." He was particularly critical with the Rabbis who teach false doctrines.

He afterwards went into the House of Learning, and said the prayer beginning, "Kol nidre." But the Accuser grew more violent; and Baal Shem hurried all the men of prayer to finish with their prayers, so that he might be able to begin the prayer called 'N'ilah' in good time. Before this prayer he again urged the people to repent, and wept. He then laid down his head upon the reading-desk, and sobbed and cried aloud, and then began to pray with a loud voice. His custom was not to look into the book. Rabbi Yenkel from Mezbesh, repeated the words first, and he answered. Rabbi Yenkel began as usual. He said the words once: he said them again; but as Baal Shem did not answer, he stood silent. Baal Shem then began to make the most wonderful movements, and bowed down his head to his feet. The congregation feared every moment in case he should fall, and yet they were also afraid to lay hold of him. They therefore made the matter known to Rabbi Wolf Kotzis. He came, and, looking into Baal Shem's face, made signs that no one should touch him, for his eyes were turned, and he uttered sounds like a wounded ox.

This lasted for two hours, after which he stood upright in his place, and soon finished the prayer.

As soon as the Day of Atonement was over, all the people went to Baal Shem to pay their respects, and to ask what was the end of the heavenly accusation. He related to them how, during the N'ilah prayer, he quickly went from world to world, until he arrived at the sanctuary, from which place, he said, "I had only one gate to pass, in order to come to the Name Blessed-be-He. In the sanctuary I found prayers which had been waiting for the last fifty years, and had found no entrance. But today, by means of our great devotion, all these prayers were admitted, and shone as bright as the morning star. I said to the prayers, 'Why have you waited here all this time?' They replied, 'We had orders to wait for you to be our guide'. I said, 'Come along', for the gate was open, in fact the gate was as big as the whole world. But when we approached, an angel came and locked it, and the lock was as large as the whole town of Mezbesh. I tried to open the lock, but failed. I then ran to my Rabbi, the author of the book *Toldoth Jakob Joseph,* and said to him, the Jews are now in great trouble, and I am not permitted to enter. At another time I would not insist on entering, but now it is necessary. My Rabbi said, I will go with you, and if it is possible, they will certainly open the gate. But when he came, he could do nothing with the lock. I began to weep in front of the Rabbi, and said, Will you abandon me in this time of trouble? He said, I cannot do anything more, but come, let us go to the Messiah's sanctuary, and perhaps we can find help there. When the righteous Messiah saw me still at a distance, he said, 'do not cry,' and he gave me two sacred letters of the alphabet. I took these back to the gate, and, with the help of God, it opened. I then led all the prayers; and as soon as the prayers entered, the Accuser stopped talking, the decree was changed, and nothing remained of it but a memorandum."

Source: *The Praises of Israel Baal Shem Tov* (Shivhei Ha-Besht, 1814). Tr. Alexander McCaul (adapted).

JEWISH ENLIGHTENMENT: MENDELSSOHN ON REVEALED LAW

The Jewish Enlightenment (haskalah) *was an intellectual movement in Central and Eastern Europe during the nineteenth century. With the removal of legal discrimination against European Jews in the late eighteenth century, many Jews began integrating into their surrounding communities through secular*

education, the adoption of vernacular language, and participa-
tion in wider economic opportunities. At the same time, they
maintained the religious and cultural identity of Jewish society.
German-Jewish philosopher Moses Mendelssohn (1729–1786)
was an early promoter of the ideals of the Jewish Enlightenment.
He became a successful businessman in the textile industry
and in his private time made important literary contributions,
including philosophical works and a German translation of the
Pentateuch. The selection below is from his work Jerusalem:
Religious Power and Judaism *(1783) in which he argues that*
Judaism does not have a revealed religion like Christianity and
other faiths, but rather has a revealed law. An enlightenment
theme of his discussion is that the primary doctrines of religion,
such as the existence and nature of God, are not supernaturally
revealed, but instead imprinted on nature and accessible to
everyone through reason. This natural religion thus forms the
content of "the universal religion of mankind." At the same time,
however, he holds that the laws of Judaism were indeed super-
naturally revealed to Moses, and these laws are what makes
Judaism unique.

I believe that Judaism knows nothing of a revealed religion,
in the sense in which it is taken by Christians. The Israelites
have a divine legislation: laws, judgments, statutes, rules
of life, information of the will of God, and lessons for how
to conduct themselves in order to attain both temporal and
spiritual happiness. Those laws, commandments, etc., were
revealed to them through Moses, in a miraculous and supernatural manner; but no dogmas, no saving truths, no general
self-evident positions. Those the Lord always reveals to us,
the same as to the rest of mankind, by nature and by events;
but never in words or written characters.

I fear this will appear strange, and again be found new
and difficult by many readers. This distinction has always
been ignored. Supernatural legislation has been taken for
supernatural revelation; and Judaism was considered nothing
but a sort of earlier revelation of religious propositions and
tenets, necessary for the salvation of man. . . .

Judaism boasts of no exclusive revelation of immutable truths indispensable to salvation, and of no revealed
religion in the sense in which that term is usually taken.
Revealed religion is one thing, revealed legislation is
another. The voice which was heard on Sinai, on that memorable day, did not say, "I am the Lord, your God, the eternal, self-existing Being, omnipotent and omniscient, who
rewards men, in a future life, according to their works." All

this is the universal religion of mankind, and not Judaism.
And it was not the universal religion of mankind, without
which they can be neither virtuous nor saved, that was to
be revealed there. On the whole, it could not have been. For
whom were the voice of thunder, and the sound of trumpets
to convince of those eternal tenets of salvation? Surely, not
the animal man, to whom his own reflections had never yet
suggested the existence of an invisible Being that rules and
governs this visible world. Such a marvelous voice would
not have inspired him with ideas, and, therefore, could not
have convinced him. Still less would it have convinced the
sophist, about whose ears so many doubts and quibbles
are buzzing so that he is no longer able to discriminate the
voice of sound common sense. Logical demonstration is
what he demands, not miracles. . . .

I am now able to concentrate my ideas of Judaism of former times, and bring them under one focus. Judaism consisted, or, according to the founder's design, was to consist
of the following:

1. It contains religious dogmas and propositions of immutable truths of God, of his government and providence,
   without which man can neither be enlightened nor
   happy. These were not forced on the belief of the people by threats of eternal or temporal punishment, but
   instead were recommended for rational consideration
   as is suitable to the nature and evidence of immutable
   truths. They needed not be suggested by direct revelation, or declared by words or in writing, which are understood only in this or that place, at this or that time. The
   Supreme Being revealed them to all rational beings, by
   events and by ideas, and inscribed them in their soul, in
   a character legible and intelligible at all times, and in all
   places. So sings the frequently quoted Psalmist:

   The heavens tell the glory of God; and the firmament shows his
       handy work.
   One day streams this unto another, and night therein instructs
   night.
   No lesson or words of which the voice is not heard; their chord rings
       through the entire globe; their discourse penetrates to the
       extremes of the inhabited world, where he set a tabernacle
       to the sun, etc. (Psalms 19:1–3)

   Their effect is as universal as the beneficial influence of
   the sun, which, while revolving round its orbit, diffuses
   light and heat over the whole globe, as the same Psalmist
   still more distinctly declares, in another place:

> From where the sun rises to where it sets, the name of the Lord is praised. (Psalms 113:3)

Or, as the prophet Malachi says, in the name of the Lord:

> From where the sun rises to where it sets, my name is great among the Gentiles; and in all places, incense, sacrifice, and pure meat-offerings are offered unto my name, for my name is great among the heathen. (Malachi 1:11)

2. It contains historical truths, or accounts of the occurrences of the primitive world, especially memoirs of the lives of the first ancestors of the nation; of their knowledge of the true God, even of their failings, and the paternal correction immediately following; of the covenant which God entered into with them, and his frequent promise to make of their descendants a nation dedicated to himself. These historical truths contain the groundwork of the national union, and, as historical truths, they cannot, according to their nature, be received otherwise than on trust. Authority alone gives them the necessary evidence. They were, moreover, confirmed to the nation by miracles, and supported by an authority which was sufficient to place faith beyond all doubt and hesitation.

3. It contains laws, judgments, commandments, rules of life, which were to be unique to that nation. By observing these, that nation was to arrive at national happiness, as well as individual happiness for every single member. The lawgiver was God himself; God, not in his relations as Creator and Preserver of the universe, but God as Lord Protector and ally of their forefathers; as the liberator, founder, and leader, as the king and ruler of that people. And he gave the laws a sanction, than which nothing could be more solemn; he gave them publicly, and in a marvelous manner never before heard of, whereby they were imposed on the nation, and on their descendants forever, as an unalterable duty and obligation.

   Those laws were revealed. That is, they were made known by the Lord, by words, and writing. Still, only the most essential part of them was entrusted to letters; and without the unwritten laws, without explanations, limitations, and more particular definitions, even those written laws are mostly unintelligible, or must become so in course of time; since neither any words or written characters whatever retain their meaning unaltered, for the natural age of man.

   As to directions to general practice, and rules of conduct, both the written and the unwritten laws have public and private happiness for their immediate object. But they must also be mostly considered as a mode of writing; and as ceremonial laws, there is sense and meaning in them. They lead inquiring reason to divine truths; partly to eternal, partly to historical truths, on which the religion of that nation was founded. The ceremonial law was the bond for uniting practice with speculation, and conduct with doctrine. The ceremonial law was to offer inducements to personal interaction and social connection between the school and the professor, the inquirer and the instructor, and to excite and encourage competition and emulation; and that purpose it actually did answer in the first times, before the polity degenerated, and human folly again intermeddled to change, by ignorance and misguidance, good to evil, and the beneficial to the hurtful.

Source: Moses Mendelssohn, *Jerusalem: Religious Power and Judaism* (*Jerusalem oder über religiöse Macht und Judenthum*, 1783), 2.2. Tr. Moses Samuel.

REFORM JUDAISM: DECLARATION OF PRINCIPLES

The European and Jewish Enlightenments of the eighteenth and nineteenth centuries sparked a movement among Jews in Germany to reform their religious practices. Initial efforts focused on revamping the liturgy: modernizing music and integrating some components of Christian practice. This was followed by a more "scientific" approach to Judaism advocated by Abraham Geiger (1810–1875), who was influenced by the critical methodology taught at German universities. Geiger believed that the Jewish Torah was fluid, adaptable to different historical contexts. Reform Judaism was brought to the United States with the immigration of German Jews, and in 1885 a conference of Rabbis was held in Pittsburgh, Pennsylvania, which explored the direction of that denomination. The outcome was the following Declaration of Principles—or the Pittsburgh Platform, as it is often called. Although the statement was modified at later conferences, Reform Judaism today still holds to these basic tenets.

1. We recognize in every religion an attempt to grasp the Infinite, and in every mode, source or book of revelation held sacred in any religious system the consciousness of the indwelling of God in man. We hold that Judaism presents the highest conception of the God-idea as taught in our Holy Scriptures and developed and spiritualized by

the Jewish teachers, in accordance with the moral and philosophical progress of their respective ages. We maintain that Judaism preserved and defended midst continual struggles and trials and under enforced isolation, this God-idea as the central religious truth for the human race.

2. We recognize in the Bible the record of the consecration of the Jewish people to its mission as the priest of the one God, and value it as the most potent instrument of religious and moral instruction. We hold that the modern discoveries of scientific researches in the domain of nature and history are not antagonistic to the doctrines of Judaism, the Bible reflecting the primitive ideas of its own age, and at times clothing its conception of divine Providence and Justice dealing with men in miraculous narratives.

3. We recognize in the Mosaic legislation a system of training the Jewish people for its mission during its national life in Palestine, and today we accept as binding only its moral laws, and maintain only such ceremonies as elevate and sanctify our lives, but reject all such as are not adapted to the views and habits of modern civilization.

4. We hold that all such Mosaic and rabbinical laws as regulate diet, priestly purity, and dress originated in ages and under the influence of ideas entirely foreign to our present mental and spiritual state. They fail to impress the modern Jew with a spirit of priestly holiness; their observance in our days is apt rather to obstruct than to further modern spiritual elevation.

5. We recognize, in the modern era of universal culture of heart and intellect, the approaching of the realization of Israel's great messianic hope for the establishment of the kingdom of truth, justice, and peace among all men. We consider ourselves no longer a nation, but a religious community, and therefore expect neither a return to Palestine, nor a sacrificial worship under the sons of Aaron, nor the restoration of any of the laws concerning the Jewish state.

6. We recognize in Judaism a progressive religion, ever striving to be in accord with the postulates of reason. We are convinced of the utmost necessity of preserving the historical identity with our great past. Christianity and Islam, being daughter religions of Judaism, we appreciate their providential mission, to aid in the spreading of monotheistic and moral truth. We acknowledge that the spirit of broad humanity of our age is our ally in the

fulfillment of our mission, and therefore we extend the hand of fellowship to all who cooperate with us in the establishment of the reign of truth and righteousness among men.

7. We reassert the doctrine of Judaism that the soul is immortal, grounding the belief on the divine nature of human spirit, which forever finds bliss in righteousness and misery in wickedness. We reject as ideas not rooted in Judaism, the beliefs both in bodily resurrection and in Gehenna and Eden (Hell and Paradise) as abodes for everlasting punishment and reward.

8. In full accordance with the spirit of the Mosaic legislation, which strives to regulate the relations between rich and poor, we deem it our duty to participate in the great task of modern times, to solve, on the basis of justice and righteousness, the problems presented by the contrasts and evils of the present organization of society.

Source: *Proceedings of the Pittsburg Rabbinical Conference, November 16, 17, 18, 1885* (Richmond, VA: Old Dominion Press, 1923).

ORTHODOX JUDAISM: SERVICE PRAYER FOR THE DAY OF ATONEMENT

The term Orthodox Judaism *was first used in the late eighteenth century to distinguish traditional Judaism from the Reform Judaism movement that modernized many aspects of Jewish theology and ritual. Today Orthodox Judaism is diverse in its belief and practices, and contains divisions such as between modernists and centrists. A common theme within this diversity, though, is adherence to the traditional view that God is the source of the Torah and that the oral law is authoritative. The selection below is from a Jewish prayer book that gained wide acceptance in English-speaking Orthodox Jewish communities. The prayer is specifically earmarked for one of Judaism's most sacred days, Yom Kippur—that is, the Day of Atonement—during which time Jewish people seek God's forgiveness for the wrongs they have committed. Accordingly, the Yom Kippur service prayer enumerates a range of possible sins, requesting God's forgiveness for the commission of each.*

May it then be thy will, O Lord our God and God of our fathers, to forgive us for all our sins, to pardon us for all our iniquities, and to grant us remission for all our transgressions.

For the sin which we have committed before thee under compulsion, or of our own will;

And for the sin which we have committed before thee in hardening of the heart;

For the sin which we have committed before thee unknowingly;

And for the sin which we have committed before thee with utterance of the lips;

For the sin which we have committed before thee by unchastity;

And for the sin which we have committed before thee openly and secretly;

For the sin which we have committed before thee knowingly and deceitfully;

And for the sin which we have committed before thee in speech;

For the sin which we have committed before thee by wronging our neighbor;

And for the sin which we have committed before thee by the sinful meditating of the heart;

For the sin which we have committed before thee by association with impurity;

And for the sin which we have committed before thee by confession with the mouth alone;

For the sin which we have committed before thee by despising parents and teachers;

And for the sin which we have committed before thee in presumption or in error;

For the sin which we have committed before thee by violence;

And for the sin which we have committed before thee by the profanation of the divine Name;

For the sin which we have committed before thee by unclean lips;

And for the sin which we have committed before thee by folly of the mouth;

For the sin which we have committed before thee by the evil inclination;

And for the sin which we have committed before thee wittingly or unwittingly;

For all these, O God of forgiveness, forgive us, pardon us, grant us remission.

For the sin which we have committed before thee by denying and lying;

And for the sin which we have committed before thee by taking of bribes;

For the sin which we have committed before thee by scoffing;

And for the sin which we have committed before thee by slander;

For the sin which we have committed before thee in business;

And for the sin which we have committed before thee in eating and drinking;

For the sin which we have committed before thee by usury and interest;

And for the sin which we have committed before thee by the stretched forth neck of pride;

For the sin which we have committed before thee by the conversation of our lips;

And for the sin which we have committed before thee with wanton looks;

For the sin which we have committed before thee with haughty eyes;

And for the sin which we have committed before thee by effrontery;

For all these, O God of forgiveness, forgive us, pardon us, grant us remission.

For the sin which we have committed before thee by breaking off the yoke of thy commandments;

And for the sin which we have committed before thee by contentiousness;

For the sin which we have committed before thee by ensnaring our neighbor;

And for the sin which we have committed before thee by envy;

For the sin which we have committed before thee by levity;

And for the sin which we have committed before thee by being stiff-necked;

For the sin which we have committed before thee by running to do evil;

And for the sin which we have committed before thee by talebearing;

For the sin which we have committed before thee by vain oaths;

And for the sin which we have committed before thee by causeless hatred;

For the sin which we have committed before thee by breach of trust;

And for the sin which we have committed before thee with confusion of mind;

For all these, O God of forgiveness, forgive us, pardon us, grant us remission.

And also for the sins for which we owe a burnt offering;

And for the sins for which we owe a sin offering;

And for the sins for which we owe an offering, varying according to our means;

And for the sins for which we owe an offering, whether for certain or for doubtful trespass;

And for the sins for which we are liable to the penalty of chastisement;

And for the sins for which we are liable to the penalty of forty stripes;

And for the sins for which we are liable to the penalty of death by the hand of heaven;

And for the sins for which we are liable to the penalty of excision and childlessness;

For all these, O God of forgiveness, forgive us, pardon us, grant us remission.

Source: *The Standard Prayer Book,* tr. Simeon Singer (New York: Bloch Publishing Company, 1915).

CONSERVATIVE JUDAISM: SCHECHTER ON JEWISH DOGMAS

Conservative Judaism (Masorti) emerged in the United States in the late nineteenth-century, taking a middle ground between the extreme views of Reform and Orthodox Judiasm. It is "conservative" in the sense of attempting to conserve Jewish tradition by acknowledging the relevance of modern culture and secular scholarship, on the one hand, and Jewish Law on the other. Thus, one of its mottos is "tradition and change." The selection below is by Solomon Schechter (1847–1915), a founding father of the movement. He rejects Mendelssohn's claim that Judaism has no dogmas, and credits that misunderstanding to a growing interest within Judaism toward historical studies at the expense of theological speculation. Nevertheless, he argues, there are important dogmas that are central to Judaism, even if they are difficult to articulate.

The object of this essay is to say about the dogmas of Judaism a word which I think ought not to be left unsaid.

In speaking of dogmas it must be understood that Judaism does not ascribe to them any saving power. The belief in a dogma or a doctrine without abiding by its real or supposed consequences (e.g., the belief in creatio ex nihilo without keeping the Sabbath) is of no value. And the question about certain doctrines is not whether they possess or do not possess the desired charm against certain diseases of the soul, but whether they ought to be considered as characteristics of Judaism or not.

It must again be premised that the subject, which occupied the thoughts of the greatest and noblest Jewish minds for so many centuries, has been neglected for a comparatively long time. And this for various reasons. First, there is Mendelssohn's assertion, or supposed assertion, in his [book] *Jerusalem,* that Judaism has no dogmas—an assertion which has been accepted by the majority of modern Jewish theologians as the only dogma Judaism possesses. You can hear it pronounced in scores of Jewish pulpits; you can read it written in scores of Jewish books. To admit the possibility that Mendelssohn was in error was hardly permissible, especially for those with whom he enjoys a certain infallibility. . . .

Another cause of the neglect into which the subject has fallen is that our century is an historical one. It is not only books that have their fate, but also whole sciences and literatures. In past times it was religious speculation that formed the favorite study of scholars, in our time it is history with its critical foundation on a sound philology. Now as these two most important branches of Jewish science were so long neglected—were perhaps never cultivated in the true meaning of the word, and as Jewish literature is so vast and Jewish history so far-reaching and eventful, we cannot wonder that these studies have absorbed the time and the labor of the greatest and best Jewish writers in this century.

There is, besides, a certain tendency in historical studies that is hostile to mere theological speculation. The historian deals with realities, the theologian with abstractions. The latter likes to shape the universe after his system, and tells us how things ought to be, the former teaches us how they are or have been, and the explanation he gives for their being so and not otherwise includes in most cases also a kind of justification for their existence. There is also the odium theologicum, which has been the cause of so much misfortune that it is hated by the historian, whilst the superficial, rationalistic way in which the theologian manages to explain everything which does not suit his system is most repulsive to the critical spirit. . . . [But] Judaism, divested of every higher religious motive, is in danger of falling into gross materialism.

For what else is the meaning of such declarations as "Believe what you like, but conform to this or that mode of life"; what else does it mean but "We cannot expect you to believe that the things you are bidden to do are commanded by a higher authority; there is not such a thing as belief, but you ought to do them for conventionalism or for your own convenience."

But both these motives—the good opinion of our neighbors, as well as our bodily health—have nothing to do with our nobler and higher sentiments, and degrade Judaism to a matter of expediency or diplomacy. Indeed, things have advanced so far that well-meaning, but ill-advised writers even think to render a service to Judaism by declaring it to be a kind of enlightened Hedonism, or rather a moderate Epicureanism.

I have no intention of answering here the question, What is Judaism? This question is not less perplexing than the problem, What is God's world? Judaism is also a great Infinite, composed of as many endless Units, the Jews. And these Unit-Jews have been, and are still, scattered through all the world, and have passed under an immensity of influences, good and bad. If so, how can we give an exact definition of the Infinite, called Judaism?

But if there is anything sure, it is that the highest motives which worked through the history of Judaism are the strong belief in God and the unshaken confidence that at last this God, the God of Israel, will be the God of the whole world; or, in other words, Faith and Hope are the two most prominent characteristics of Judaism. . . .

But it was not my purpose to ventilate here the question whether Maimonides' [thirteen] articles are sufficient for us, or whether we ought not to add new ones to them. Nor do I attempt to decide what system we ought to prefer for recitation in the Synagogue—that of Maimonides or that of Chasdai, or of any other writer. I do not think that such a recital is of much use. My object in this sketch has been rather to make the reader think about Judaism, by proving that it regulates not only our actions, but also our thoughts. We usually urge that in Judaism religion means life; but we forget that a life without guiding principles and thoughts is a Life not worth living. At least it was so considered by the greatest Jewish thinkers, and hence their efforts to formulate the creed of Judaism, so that men should not only be able to do the right thing, but also to think the right thing. Whether they succeeded in their attempts toward formulating the creed of Judaism or not will always remain a question. This concerns the logician more than the theologian.

But surely Maimonides and his successors did succeed in having a religion depending directly on God, with the most ideal and lofty aspirations for the future; whilst the Judaism of a great part of our modern theologians reminds one very much of the words with which the author of Marius the Epicurean characterizes the Roman religion in the days of her decline: a religion which had been always something to be done rather than something to be thought, or believed, or loved.

Political economy, hygiene, statistics are very fine things. But no sane man would for them make those sacrifices which Judaism requires from us. It is only for God's sake, to fulfil His commands and to accomplish His purpose, that religion becomes worth living and dying for. And this can only be possible with a religion which possesses dogmas.

It is true that every great religion is "a concentration of many ideas and ideals," which make this religion able to adapt itself to various modes of thinking and living. But there must always be a point round which all these ideas concentrate themselves. This center is Dogma.

Source: Solomon Schechter, *Studies in Judaism, First Series* (Philadelphia: Jewish Publication Society, 1868).

ZIONISM: HERZL'S VISION OF A JEWISH HOMELAND

Zion in Jewish tradition refers variously to the Temple Mount in Jerusalem, the city of Jerusalem itself, or the larger territory of Judea. Since the days of the Babylonian exile, it has been the focal point in the desires of dispersed Jews to return to their native land. In the 1890s, Hungarian-born Theodor Herzl (1860–1904) founded the modern Zionist movement, which, in response to rampant anti-Semitism throughout Europe, aimed to reunite Jews in a homeland. Herzl's movement continued after his death and, in the aftermath of the Nazi Holocaust, succeeded in creating the modern country of Israel. The following is from Herzl's seminal book, The Jewish State, *in which he argues that Palestine, rather than Argentina, is the most suitable location for Jewish repatriation.*

No one can deny the gravity of the situation of the Jews. Wherever they live in perceptible numbers, they are more or less persecuted. Their equality before the law, granted by statute, has become practically a dead letter. They are debarred from filling even moderately high positions, either in the army, or in any public or private capacity.

And attempts are made to thrust them out of business also: "Don't buy from Jews!"

Attacks in Parliaments, in assemblies, in the press, in the pulpit, in the street, on journeys—for example, their exclusion from certain hotels—even in places of recreation, become daily more numerous. The forms of persecution vary according to the countries and social circles in which they occur. In Russia, imposts are levied on Jewish villages; in Rumania, a few persons are put to death; in Germany, they get a good beating occasionally; in Austria, Anti-Semites exercise terrorism over all public life; in Algeria, there are traveling agitators; in Paris, the Jews are shut out of the so-called best social circles and excluded from clubs. Shades of anti-Jewish feeling are innumerable. But this is not to be an attempt to make out a doleful category of Jewish hardships. . . .

The whole plan is in its essence perfectly simple, as it must necessarily be if it is to come within the comprehension of all.

Let the sovereignty be granted us over a portion of the globe large enough to satisfy the rightful requirements of a nation; the rest we shall manage for ourselves.

The creation of a new State is neither ridiculous nor impossible. We have in our day witnessed the process in connection with nations which were not largely members of the middle class, but poorer, less educated, and consequently weaker than ourselves. The Governments of all countries scourged by Anti-Semitism will be keenly interested in assisting us to obtain the sovereignty we want.

The plan, simple in design, but complicated in execution, will be carried out by two agencies: The Society of Jews and the Jewish Company. . . .

Shall we choose Palestine or Argentine? We shall take what is given us, and what is selected by Jewish public opinion. The Society will determine both these points.

Argentine is one of the most fertile countries in the world, extends over a vast area, has a sparse population and a mild climate. The Argentine Republic would derive considerable profit from the cession of a portion of its territory to us. The present infiltration of Jews has certainly produced some discontent, and it would be necessary to enlighten the Republic on the intrinsic difference of our new movement.

Palestine is our ever-memorable historic home. The very name of Palestine would attract our people with a force of marvelous potency. If his Majesty the Sultan were to give us

Palestine, we could in return undertake to regulate the whole finances of Turkey.

Source: Theodor Herzl, *The Jewish State* (Der Judenstaat, 1896), tr. Sylvie d'Avigdor.

RECONSTRUCTIONIST JUDAISM: KAPLAN'S PRAYER OF THIRTEEN WANTS

An offshoot of Conservative Judaism, Reconstructionist Judaism is a recent American movement founded by Rabbi Mordecai Kaplan (1881–1983). It sees Judaism as an evolving religious civilization, as reflected in its motto "the past has a vote, but not a veto." In 1926, a dedication ceremony took place for the new headquarters of the Society for the Advancement of Judaism, an organization associated with that denomination. On that occasion Kaplan offered the following "Prayer of Thirteen Wants," which subsequently was included in the Reconstructionist Sabbath Prayer Book. The eighth and tenth of these "wants" especially reflect the progressive Reconstructionist ideal of integrating traditional Judaism with contemporary life.

1. We want Judaism to help us overcome temptation, doubt, and discouragement.
2. We want Judaism to imbue us with a sense of responsibility for the righteous use of the blessings wherewith God endows us.
3. We want the Jew so to be trusted that his yea will be taken as yea, and his nay as nay.
4. We want to learn how to utilize our leisure to best advantage, physically, intellectually, and spiritually.
5. We want the Jewish home to live up to its traditional standards of virtue and piety.
6. We want the Jewish upbringing of our children to further their moral and spiritual growth, and to enable them to accept with joy their heritage as Jews.
7. We want the synagogue to enable us to worship God in sincerity and in truth.
8. We want our religious traditions to be interpreted in terms of understandable experience and to be made relevant to our present-day needs.
9. We want to participate in the upbuilding of Eretz Yisrael as a means to the renaissance of the Jewish spirit.
10. We want Judaism to find rich, manifold, and ever new expression in philosophy, letters, and the arts.

11. We want all forms of Jewish organization to make for spiritual purpose and ethical endeavor.
12. We want the unity of Israel throughout the world to be fostered through mutual help in time of need, and through cooperation in the furtherance of Judaism at all times.
13. We want Judaism to function as a potent influence for justice, freedom, and peace in the life of men and nations.

Source: Mordecai Kaplan, "Criteria of Jewish Loyalty," *Sabbath Prayer Book* (New York: Jewish Reconstructionist Foundation, 1945).

Christianity

INTRODUCTION

Christianity is founded on the life and teachings of Jesus, a first century CE Jew who was executed by the Roman authorities for subversion. During its first few decades, Christianity was a sect within Judaism, but it quickly expanded beyond its Palestinian borders and Jewish framework, becoming an independent religion. Two elements of Christian doctrine are essentially Jewish. First, Jesus is the Messiah, or anointed king, who is spoken of in Jewish prophetic writings. The term *christ* is a Greek translation of the Hebrew word *messiah,* so Jesus is referred to as the Christ. Second, the message of Jesus is the kingdom of God. Keeping with Jewish apocalyptic notions of the Messiah, early Christians expected that the kingdom would be established by cataclysmic events. A third element of Christianity departs from its Jewish heritage; namely, the belief that Jesus is God in human form. Building on this, a fourth element is that, by his work, teachings, death, and resurrection, Jesus became the savior of the world.

THE LIFE OF JESUS

Jesus left no writings, and our knowledge of his life and teachings comes almost exclusively from the Gospels of Matthew, Mark, and Luke. These narratives are traditionally ascribed to his disciples, but they probably were written and compiled anonymously between forty and sixty years after his death. They also were written by believers for believers, blending historical memories with early Church teaching. Reconstructing an accurate picture of Jesus, then, is difficult—according to some theologians, impossible.

Jesus was born about 4 BCE and raised in Nazareth, a small agricultural city in the Galilee region. Little is known about Jesus until he began his ministry at about age 30. Jewish territories at that time were under especially oppressive Roman rule, which caused widespread unrest. Since the times of the independent Jewish monarchies hundreds of years earlier, 90 percent of the Jewish population had consisted of agrarian peasants who supported the ruling priestly elite through taxes on their harvest. Additional taxes were imposed by the Romans, and still more were collected to support local building projects, such as those of King Herod. By the time of Jesus,

419

peasant taxes totaled about 40 percent of the harvest, forcing many into debt or sale of family land. Unemployment was also high. As the Romans reduced the size of Jewish territories, Jews from surrounding areas flooded into Judea and Galilee, the two principal territories of Jewish settlement. Occasional famine made economic times worse and intensified the rift between peasants and the ruling class, which supported the Romans.

Desperate peasants rallied around charismatic leaders who offered hope. Some supported social bandits who systematically robbed rich Jewish landowners and shared the wealth with the peasants. Others found comfort in the company of prophets who, in the tradition of the old Jewish prophets, pronounced apocalyptic judgment against the Romans and called the people to repentance. Still others took refuge in the leadership of messiahs, that is, anointed kings. The concept of a Messiah in Jewish literature did not become fixed until rabbinic discussions after the revolt of 66 CE. Prior to that time, written discussions refer to a Davidic king, a prophet-like Moses or a perfect priest; the actual term *Messiah* is rarely used. The notion of Messiah in the minds of the illiterate peasants was somewhat different from that which appeared in the writings of the ruling elite. Although the peasants retained the idea of kingship, they saw the anointing of this king as a revolutionary act of popular election. The Messiah was to be a flesh-and-blood military leader, not simply an apocalyptic figure waging spiritual war.

Jesus began his ministry during his association with John the Baptizer, an apocalyptic prophet who proclaimed impending doom. John baptized Jesus and shortly afterwards was executed by the ruler of Galilee, who feared that John's enthusiastic followers might provoke a rebellion. Jesus attracted his own followers in Galilee, who initially saw him as a popular prophet, rather more like John the Baptizer than a political Messiah. Of his large following of both men and women, later Christian tradition honored twelve as having special authority (although there is disagreement over who exactly the twelve were). With his disciples, Jesus traveled around Galilee teaching, befriending outcasts, healing people, and performing exorcisms. He taught to both small gatherings in synagogues and large peasant crowds in open-air places. His ministry lasted only a couple of years until he was executed on a Roman cross. The precise reasons for his execution may never be known. For John the Baptizer, attracting large crowds in a revolutionary environment was enough to cost him his life. To the extent that Jesus appeared to be another popular prophet, Jewish and Roman leaders had reason for concern.

THE TEACHING OF JESUS

Like the events of his life, Jesus' teachings in the Gospels blend his words with early Church doctrine. Some scholars argue that fewer than 20 percent of the sayings attributed to Jesus in the Gospels were spoken by him. The dominant message that emerges, though, is the kingdom of God. The "kingdom," never actually defined, is the final state of affairs in which the world runs according to God's will. Paradoxically, some teachings proclaim that the kingdom will arrive in the near future, whereas others maintain that the kingdom has already begun. Although the concepts of both a future and a present kingdom of God can be found in Jewish apocalyptic literature, Jesus is unique in making the doctrine of the kingdom the basis of ethical behavior. Moral acts of repentance, love, charity, and nonviolence are God's requirements for acceptance into the kingdom. Because of the urgency in preparing for the kingdom, uncompromising behavior is required. Jesus did not see himself as the messianic ruler of the kingdom he proclaimed, especially in view of the military implications of the popular messiahs.

Along with its content, the style of Jesus' teaching—the parable—is also important. Most broadly, a parable is a statement, story, or dialogue that has a metaphorical or figurative meaning. It can be as short as a single sentence, such as "It is easier for a camel to pass through the eye of a needle than for a rich man to enter the kingdom of God" (Mark 10:25), or paragraphs long. Understood this way, almost everything attributed to Jesus in the Gospels of Matthew, Mark, and Luke is in the form of a parable. More narrowly, parables are extended metaphorical narratives, or figurative stories, about thirty of which appear in these first three Gospels and the Gospel of Thomas (see following). In view of their figurative nature, the parables require interpretation, and sometimes an early Christian explanation is presented within the Gospel text itself. The interpretation of virtually all the parables, though, relates to some challenging aspect of the kingdom. Like much of Old Testament literature, Jesus' parables follow specific literary structures. For example, Luke 11:9–10 follows step parallelism:

    A Ask, and it will be given you
      B Seek, and you will find
        C Knock, and it will be opened to you
    A' For everyone who asks receives
      B' And he who seeks finds
        C' And to him who knocks it will be opened

Even the longest narrative parables use a combination of various parallel structures.

THE EARLY CHURCH

After Jesus' execution, strong leaders and apostles emerged within the Jesus movement, keeping its spirit alive and recruiting even more followers. Jesus was quickly seen as the crucified and risen Messiah who would return from heaven at any moment and begin an apocalyptic (as opposed to military) reign. Old Testament messianic prophecies were applied to him, bolstering the interpretation that Jesus was the Christ. Some followers sold their possessions and awaited his arrival. Others, such as Paul, a former Pharisee, effectively recruited believers from among non-Jews. Early interpretations of Jesus and his message varied greatly among the new followers, and the Christian tradition we inherit was defined in reaction to and in competition with early alternatives. The New Testament canon and early Church hierarchy are products of the winning tradition, whereas the losing traditions were branded as heresies along the way. An early losing interpretation was that of Judaizers who believed that Christianity was the messianic fulfillment of Judaism, and not a different religion. Thus, Christians were still bound by traditional Jewish laws, such as circumcision and food rituals. However, the Judaizers' narrow notion of Christianity did not fit the broader vision of other early Church leaders.

Another unsuccessful early interpretation of Christianity was offered by Gnosticism, a diverse religious movement that flourished throughout the Near East from 100 to 400 CE. The aim of the Gnostic religion in general was to free one's spirit from the illusions of the evil, material world and reascend to heaven. Release was to be accomplished by acquiring special knowledge *(gnosis)*. In Christian Gnosticism, the material world was created by an evil demigod, and Jesus' teachings provide the knowledge that redeems us from worldly illusion. Church leaders reacted vehemently to the Gnostic interpretation, penning many polemics against it.

While theologians battled over doctrine, churches were established throughout the Roman Empire, and bishops—successors of the original Apostles—officiated in key regions. At first, Roman rulers did not distinguish between Christians and Jews. But the rapid advance of Christianity soon made the distinction apparent and, from their perspective, threatened the unity of the Empire. Christianity was outlawed and, throughout the first three centuries CE, several emperors systematically persecuted Christians, some bent on their extinction. A decisive turning point came when Emperor Constantine took the throne. In 313 CE he proclaimed complete religious liberty for Christians. He sponsored a world Church council, at Nicea, which determined that Christ was not subordinate to God but was substantively identical with God. The council also established the bishops of Rome, Antioch, and Alexandria as the primary officiators of the Church; later the bishop of Constantinople was added to the list. In 392 CE Emperor Theodosius declared Christianity the only allowable religion throughout the Empire.

CHRISTIAN DENOMINATIONS

During the fourth century CE, the vast Roman Empire became too difficult to manage from a single location, so it was regionally divided, with the western territory governed by Rome and the eastern territory governed by Constantinople. Now inseparably tied to empire politics, the Church too established parallel jurisdictions. The western jurisdiction, later designated *Catholic,* was led by Rome's bishop, or *Pope,* and the eastern (or *Orthodox*) jurisdiction looked, less formally, to Constantinople's bishop, or *Patriarch.* Differences of worship and authority further divided the regions, such as the east's use of icons, rejection of papal authority, and emphasis on Christ's divinity above his humanity. The rift was complete in 1054 when Rome's Pope Leo IX and Constantinople's Patriarch Michael Cerularius mutually excommunicated each other. Since the great Catholic-Orthodox schism, the three original eastern church jurisdictions (Antioch, Alexandria, and Constantinople) have multiplied to more than twenty, each with its own Patriarch. Although the Orthodox jurisdictions govern independently, they are unified by shared liturgy and doctrine.

After the fall of the western Roman Empire to barbarian invasions in the fifth century, missionary journeys spread Christianity throughout northern Europe. The Pope was on a par with emperors of new and primitive European states, and Christian monasteries were the default centers of learning. By the sixteenth century, growing discontentment with Catholic hierarchy erupted in the Protestant Reformation, led by the German priest Martin Luther. Luther stressed that the Bible, not the Pope and not Church traditions, is Christianity's exclusive authority. Salvation, Luther declared, is achieved through God's grace, not through human achievement, and is available to all who ask. Luther was particularly successful in convincing German nobility of the benefits of breaking ties with Rome. As surrounding European countries soon followed the reformer's lead, Luther believed that the protesters would remain theologically unified because God would guide each person toward the same interpretation of the Bible. This was not to be, and five centuries later hundreds of Protestant denominations have emerged from disputes over doctrine. The largest Protestant denominations are the Lutherans, Baptists, Presbyterians, Methodists, and Episcopalians. The large denominations are often doctrinally divided among themselves; the more conservative emphasize evangelism and biblical inerrancy, whereas the more liberal stress social concerns and metaphorical interpretations of the Bible. Pentecostal churches are part of a movement, rather than a single denomination, and stress spiritual gifts such as prophecy and speaking in tongues.

THE BIBLE

The primary body of scriptures in the Christian tradition is the Bible, which consists of an Old and a New Testament. The Old Testament is the Jewish *Tanakh,* which makes the Christian Bible unique among world scriptures by including the canon of a different religion. The Christian Old Testament initially was based on the Septuagint, the Greek translation of the Jewish canon from 100 BCE. Accordingly, the Old Testament retains the book arrangement of the Septuagint. Catholic and Orthodox Christians also accept the apocryphal books from the Septuagint, although Protestants reject these, opting for what they believe are the older books as they appear in the Jewish *Tanakh*. The term *Old Testament* was coined by Paul, who used it in reference to the writings of the Mosaic covenant (2 Cor. 3:14).

By the fourth century CE, the term *New Testament* was commonly used to refer to a collection of twenty-seven early Christian texts composed in Greek. Traditionally they are thought to have been written by the original Apostles who were Jesus' followers. Historically, though, the texts appear to have been written by second- and third-generation Christians from 50 to 150 CE. For the first few centuries, there was no fixed New Testament canon, and manuscripts of hundreds of individual Christian texts circulated independently among the early churches. Early Church Fathers made recommendations as to which of these were authoritative. The first known list containing the present twenty-seven books appears as a side comment in St. Athanasius's Easter letter of 367 CE.

As Latin became the spoken language of the Roman Empire, Latin translations of the Old Testament and various Christian texts circulated. In 382, the Pope commissioned Jerome, a priest and scholar, to bring order to the chaotic collection of Latin texts. Returning to Hebrew and Greek language texts, Jerome produced a new Latin translation of the Old and New Testaments, referred to as the Vulgate, which after some resistance was accepted as definitive. Even with a more fixed canon, early theologians questioned the authority of several Old and New Testament texts and introduced a distinction between protocanonical and deuterocanonical texts: canonical writings with either primary or secondary status. In the thirteenth century, the traditional chapter divisions were added to each book of the Bible by a cardinal who was preparing a biblical index. The Vulgate continued to be the official text of the Bible until the Protestant Reformation, when several modern-language translations appeared, many of which removed the books of the Old Testament Apocrypha, or at least relegated them to an appendix. Verse divisions also were added at this time. As scholars today discover older manuscript copies of biblical books, passages are revised or deleted to reflect the earliest sources. For example, the well-known story from John 9 of the stoning of the adulterous woman ("Let him who is without sin cast the first stone") is now removed from many modern editions of the Bible.

> The texts of the New Testament fall into five categories:
> Gospels: Matthew, Mark, Luke, John
> Book of Acts
> Letters of Paul: Romans, 1 and 2 Corinthians, Galatians, Ephesians, Philippians,
>   Colossians, 1 and 2 Thessalonians, 1 and 2 Timothy, Titus,
>   Philemon, Hebrews
> General letters: Letter of James; 1 and 2 Letters of Peter; 1, 2, and 3 Letters of John;
>   Letter of Jude
> Book of Revelation

The Gospels, which contain accounts of Jesus, have always been considered the most primary of all Christian texts. Scholars believe that for a few decades after Jesus' execution, the recollections of his immediate followers were transmitted orally. The first written accounts, from perhaps 50 CE, were simply lists of his sayings with no stories. None of these have survived intact. The book of Mark appeared around 70 CE, based on oral traditions of Jesus' life and teachings. Matthew and Luke appeared around 85 CE, both using information from Mark and an earlier lost list of sayings called *Quelle* (German for *source*). Matthew and Luke also contain unique stories and sayings, based on either oral traditions or earlier lost lists of sayings. Mark, Matthew, and Luke are referred to as the *synoptic gospels* because they give very similar accounts of Jesus' life and teachings. Finally, the Gospel of John appeared in 90 CE. Initially considered heretical by some early Church Fathers, it presents an account that is 90 percent different in content from the synoptic Gospels. All four Gospels first circulated anonymously and were not ascribed to the apostles until the middle of the second century.

The Book of Acts is a continuation of Luke, penned by the same author, and discusses the spread of early Christianity immediately after Jesus. Of particular concern is the relationship of Christianity to Judaism in view of the large numbers of non-Jewish converts. More than half of Acts chronicles the conversion and missionary journeys of Paul. Of the fourteen letters ascribed to Paul, only seven are confidently traced to him (Romans, 1 and 2 Corinthians, Galatians, Philippians, 1 Thessalonians, and Philemon). His letters, composed between 50 and 60 CE, contain encouragement and instructions to the churches he helped establish, but they did not gain a wide readership until the end of the first century. The general letters were written at the close of the first century as tracts or sermons addressing problems in early Church communities. Finally, the Book of Revelation, also written at the close of the first century, describes a series of apocalyptic visions that contain instructions for Christians to remain faithful in the face of Roman persecution.

NONBIBLICAL SACRED WRITINGS

Early noncanonical Christian texts are extraordinarily varied and include gospels, creeds, and writings of the Church Fathers. Some collections of early sacred texts have special designations. The term *Apostolic Fathers* was coined in the seventeenth century in reference to a collection of works attributed to followers of the original apostles. The fourteen texts now included under this label were popular in the early Church and were even included in scripture lists by early Church Fathers. Of particular interest in this collection is the *Didache,* or Teaching of the Twelve, which gives instructions on baptism, fasting, prayer, and the Eucharist. The expression *New Testament Apocrypha* is applied loosely to a range of early Christian texts, mostly from the second century, that are not included in the New Testament. Many of these were considered sacred by early churches and are the source of Christian beliefs, such as the assumption of Mary. Frequently they aim to fill gaps in the chronologies of Jesus' life and the early Church. Paralleling the genres of New Testament texts, the writings fall into the categories of gospels, acts, epistles, and apocalypses. They are of particular value as a possible source of stray sayings of Jesus that continued to circulate into the second century.

One collection of early writings that has recently attracted scholarly attention is the Gnostic texts discovered in 1945 in Nag Hammadi, Egypt. The forty-five texts are fourth- and fifth-century Coptic translations of Greek manuscripts, although the originals go back much farther. Representing both Christian and non-Christian Gnostic ideas, they are thought to be the library of an early Gnostic Christian monastery that buried the documents in containers for protection. The texts suggest that early Christianity was more theologically diverse than initially believed. Some texts, for instance, emphasize a divine Mother. Most important among the writings is the Gnostic Gospel of Thomas, a list of 114 sayings of Jesus. Some scholars believe that this list is based on an earlier compilation of sayings, predating the New Testament Gospels, and thus, like Quelle, represents the earliest stratum of sayings attributed to Jesus.

Many early Christian creeds were the outcome of theological disputes and represent official positions arrived at in early Church councils. They are typically short and list the principal propositions of the official Church. The most famous of the early ones are the Apostles' Creed, Nicene Creed, and Chalcedon Creed, which even today are incorporated into worship services in many Christian traditions.

From as early as the first century, another inspirational source of Christian literature was the voluminous writings of early Church Fathers, saints, and mystics. The purposes and genres of these texts are quite varied and include defenses of Christianity against heretics and pagans, stories of martyred Christians, commentaries on books of the Bible, sermons, letters, and theological treatises. Perhaps the most influential of these are the writings of St. Augustine (354–430), Bishop of the North African city of Hippo, and St. Thomas Aquinas (1225–1274), monastic priest and theologian. The Orthodox, Catholic, and later Protestant traditions have a long and continuous history of mystical writings that emphasize the importance of spiritual union with God. One such mystical work from a later period of Catholic thought is *Interior Castle,* by Spanish Carmelite nun Teresa of Avila (1515–1582).

Since the Protestant Reformation, denominations have formed specific statements of faith, and some movements have their own special sacred texts in addition to the Bible. Protestant denominations tend to hold that the Bible is the principal, if not the exclusive, scripture of Christianity. Nevertheless, almost every Protestant group has formed some statement of faith that defines its views and distinguishes it from other denominations. In keeping with the religious freedom and pioneering spirit of nineteenth-century America, some Christian movements gave rise to new sacred texts. The distinct beliefs of the Church of Latter-Day Saints are founded on the *Book of Mormon*, a text produced by founder Joseph Smith (1805–1844). The Christian Science movement reveres *Science and Health* (1875), by founder Mary Baker Eddy (1821–1910), which emphasizes the healing aspect of Christianity. Associated with the New Age movement, American pastor Levi H. Dowling (1844–1911) produced the *Aquarian Gospel* in 1907, which recounts eighteen lost years of Jesus' life as he traveled to India, Tibet, Egypt, Persia, and Greece.

HOLIDAYS

Sunday Weekly day of worship that commemorates God's day of rest and Jesus' resurrection.

Advent (four weeks beginning four Sundays before Christmas) Commemorates the coming of Jesus.

Christmas (December 25) Commemorates the birth of Jesus and begins the Christmas season.

Epiphany (January 6) Commemorates the manifestation of Jesus to the Gentiles and closes the Christmas season.

Lent (forty days prior to Easter) Period of penance.

Holy Week (last seven days of Lent) Commemorates Jesus' final arrival in Jerusalem and his suffering and death; includes Palm Sunday and Good Friday.

Easter (usually April) Commemorates Jesus' rising from the dead and the beginning of the fifty-day Easter season.

Pentecost Commemorates the appearance of the Holy Spirit to the Christian community and concludes the Easter season.

TIMELINE

4 BCE	Jesus born
29 CE	Jesus executed
70	First Gospels written
150	Gnostic controversy and the Apostle's Creed
313	Constantine's Edict of Milan
325	Arian controversy and Council of Nicaea
382	Jerome commissioned to produce the Vulgate
550	Five Patriarchates established
1054	Catholic/Orthodox schism
1204	Roman Crusaders invade Constantinople
1517	Martin Luther posts the Ninety-Five Theses
1545	Catholic Council of Trent
1549	English Book of Common Prayer published
1589	Russian Patriarchate founded
1608	Baptists founded by John Smyth
1784	Methodists founded by John Wesley
1830	Book of Mormon published by Joseph Smith
1914	Assemblies of God founded
1948	World Council of Churches founded
1962	Second Vatican Council

GLOSSARY

Apostles Early followers of Jesus commissioned to lead the Church after his death.

Bible Fundamental Christian scripture consisting of the Old and New Testaments.

Catholic The largest Christian denomination, which follows a Church hierarchy led by the bishop of Rome (i.e., the Pope).

Disciples Jesus' followers.

Eastern Orthodox The church diocese originally of the eastern Roman Empire that rejects the supreme authority of the bishop of Rome.

Gnosticism The Near Eastern religious movement from 100 to 400 CE that aims to free one's spirit from the evil material world by acquiring special knowledge (gnosis).

Holy Spirit Divine presence and agent of guidance for Christians. One person of the Trinity, along with the Father and Son.

Judaizers First-century Jewish Christians who maintained that Christians were still bound by traditional Jewish laws.

Messiah Hebrew term for "anointed one" or "king," indicating that someone is set aside for a divinely appointed office, either in a religious, apocalyptic sense or in a political, revolutionary sense.

New Age Contemporary religious movement based on the astrological view that the present Piscean age is ending and will be succeeded by a new age of Aquarius.

Pentecostal Protestant religious movement emphasizing baptism of the Holy Spirit and speaking in tongues.

Pope Head of the Church and successor to the Apostle Peter according to the Roman Catholic tradition.

Protestant Christian denominations whose lineages derive from the sixteenth-century Protestant Reformation.

Quelle (or Q) A written sayings list, no longer extant, that Matthew and Luke used as a source for Jesus' teachings.

Synoptic Gospels Gospels of Mark, Matthew, and Luke, which are similar in content, in contrast to the Gospel of John, which vastly differs from all three.

Trinity Doctrine that God is a unity of three persons: the Father, Son, and Holy Spirit.

JESUS' BIRTH AND MINISTRY

PRINCE OF PEACE AND SUFFERING SERVANT

The principal value of the Old Testament for Christianity is that Jesus is the ultimate fulfillment of its covenants and messianic prophecies. Nowhere is that seen more clearly than in the following two selections from Isaiah on the birth of the prince of peace and the suffering servant. For Christians, these are allusions to Jesus' birth and his suffering on the cross.

Prince of Peace

For to us a child is born, to us a son is given, and the government will be on his shoulders. And he will be called Wonderful Counselor, Mighty God, Everlasting Father, Prince of Peace. Of the greatness of his government and peace there will be no end. He will reign on David's throne and over his kingdom, establishing and upholding it with justice and righteousness from that time on and forever. The zeal of the Lord Almighty will accomplish this.

Suffering Servant

He grew up before him like a tender shoot, and like a root out of dry ground. He had no beauty or majesty to attract us to him, nothing in his appearance that we should desire him. He was despised and rejected by mankind, a man of suffering, and familiar with pain. Like one from whom people hide their faces he was despised, and we held him in low esteem. Surely he took up our pain and bore our suffering, yet we considered him punished by God, stricken by him, and afflicted. But he was pierced for our transgressions, he was crushed for our iniquities; the punishment that brought us peace was on him, and by his wounds we are healed. We all, like sheep, have gone astray, each of us has turned to our own way; and the Lord has laid on him the iniquity of us all.

He was oppressed and afflicted, yet he did not open his mouth; he was led like a lamb to the slaughter, and as a sheep before its shearers is silent, so he did not open his mouth. By oppression and judgment he was taken away. Yet who of his generation protested? For he was cut off from the land of the living; for the transgression of my people he was punished. He was assigned a grave with the wicked, and with the rich in his death, though he had done no violence, nor was any deceit in his mouth.

Yet it was the Lord's will to crush him and cause him to suffer, and though the Lord makes his life an offering for sin, he will see his offspring and prolong his days, and the will of the Lord will prosper in his hand. After he has suffered, he will see the light of life and be satisfied; by his knowledge my righteous servant will justify many, and he will bear their iniquities.

Source: Isaiah 9:6–7, 53:2–11, from *The Holy Bible, New International Version* (International Bible Society, 1984). Reprinted by permission.

BIRTH OF JESUS

Two of the four canonical Gospels give accounts of the birth of Jesus, each slightly different. The following is Luke's version. The author of Luke was an educated non-Jewish Christian and thus his Gospel reflects the broader non-Jewish implications of both Jesus' life and the Christian Church. Unlike Matthew, Luke begins by placing the birth story in the context of Roman emperor Augustus' reign.

In those days Caesar Augustus issued a decree that a census should be taken of the entire Roman world. (This was the first census that took place while Quirinius was governor of Syria.) And everyone went to their own town to register. So Joseph also went up from the town of Nazareth in Galilee to Judea, to Bethlehem the town of David, because he belonged to the house and line of David. He went there to register with Mary, who was pledged to be married to him and was expecting a child. While they were there, the time came for the baby to be born, and she gave birth to her firstborn, a son. She wrapped him in cloths and placed him in a manger, because there was no guest room available for them.

And there were shepherds living out in the fields nearby, keeping watch over their flocks at night. An angel of the Lord appeared to them, and the glory of the Lord shone around them, and they were terrified. But the angel said to them, "Do not be afraid. I bring you good news that will cause great joy for all the people. Today in the town of David a Savior has been born to you; he is the Messiah, the Lord. This will be a sign to you: You will find a baby wrapped in cloths and lying in a manger."

Suddenly a great company of the heavenly host appeared with the angel, praising God and saying,

> "Glory to God in the highest heaven, and on earth peace to those on whom his favor rests."

When the angels had left them and gone into heaven, the shepherds said to one another, "Let's go to Bethlehem and see this thing that has happened, which the Lord has told us about." So they hurried off and found Mary and Joseph, and the baby, who was lying in the manger. When they had seen him, they spread the word concerning what had been told them about this child, and all who heard it were amazed at what the shepherds said to them. But Mary treasured up all these things and pondered them in her heart. The shepherds returned, glorifying and praising God for all the things they had heard and seen, which were just as they had been told.

On the eighth day, when it was time to circumcise the child, he was named Jesus, the name the angel had given him before he was conceived.

When the time came for the purification rites required by the Law of Moses, Joseph and Mary took him to Jerusalem to present him to the Lord (as it is written in the Law of the Lord, "Every firstborn male is to be consecrated to the Lord"), and to offer a sacrifice in keeping with what is said in the Law of the Lord: "a pair of doves or two young pigeons." . . .

When Joseph and Mary had done everything required by the Law of the Lord, they returned to Galilee to their own town of Nazareth. And the child grew and became strong; he was filled with wisdom, and the grace of God was on him.

Source: Luke, 2:1–24, 39, 40, from the *New International Version.* (International Bible Society, 1984). Reprinted by permission.

JESUS' BAPTISM, TEMPTATION, AND FIRST DISCIPLES

The first canonical Gospel to appear was Mark. Mark focuses more on activities in the life of Jesus than on his teachings. His narrative is concise, matter-of-fact, and probably written for a non-Jewish audience in Rome about 70 CE. Because virtually the entire content of Mark's account is included in the longer Gospels of Matthew and Luke (which use Mark as one of several sources), Mark's Gospel was historically not the most popular. However, as modern scholars try to identify the earliest recorded accounts of Jesus, Mark's narrative now receives greater appreciation. The following selection, from the opening chapter of Mark, describes Jesus' baptism by John the Baptizer. This initiated his ministry, his temptation in the desert where he confronted Satan, and his acquiring of his first followers. Some scholars believe that after Jesus' death early Christians had to explain why the Jewish populace did not recognize Jesus as the Messiah. Mark has an explanation that both Matthew and Luke adopt: Jesus purposefully kept word of his messiahship from circulating in order to minimize conflict with officials. Referred to as the messianic secret, *this explanation appears twice in the following passage.*

Jesus' Baptism and Temptation

The beginning of the good news about Jesus the Messiah, the Son of God, as it is written in Isaiah the prophet:

"I will send my messenger ahead of you,
who will prepare your way"—

> "a voice of one calling in the wilderness,
> 'Prepare the way for the Lord,
> make straight paths for him.'"

And so John the Baptist appeared in the wilderness, preaching a baptism of repentance for the forgiveness of sins. The whole Judean countryside and all the people of Jerusalem went out to him. Confessing their sins, they were baptized by him in the Jordan River. John wore clothing made of camel's hair, with a leather belt around his waist, and he ate locusts and wild honey. And this was his message: "After me comes the one more powerful than I, the straps of whose sandals I am not worthy to stoop down and untie. I baptize you with water, but he will baptize you with the Holy Spirit."

At that time Jesus came from Nazareth in Galilee and was baptized by John in the Jordan. Just as Jesus was coming up out of the water, he saw heaven being torn open and the Spirit descending on him like a dove. And a voice came from heaven: "You are my Son, whom I love; with you I am well pleased."

At once the Spirit sent him out into the wilderness, and he was in the wilderness forty days, being tempted by Satan. He was with the wild animals, and angels attended him. After John was put in prison, Jesus went into Galilee, proclaiming the good news of God. "The time has come," he said. "The kingdom of God has come near. Repent and believe the good news!"

The First Disciples

As Jesus walked beside the Sea of Galilee, he saw Simon and his brother Andrew casting a net into the lake, for they were fishermen. "Come, follow me," Jesus said, "and I will send you out to fish for people." At once they left their nets and followed him.

When he had gone a little farther, he saw James son of Zebedee and his brother John in a boat, preparing their nets. Without delay he called them, and they left their father Zebedee in the boat with the hired men and followed him.

They went to Capernaum, and when the Sabbath came, Jesus went into the synagogue and began to teach. The people were amazed at his teaching, because he taught them as one who had authority, not as the teachers of the law. Just then a man in their synagogue who was possessed by an impure spirit cried out, "What do you want with us, Jesus of Nazareth? Have you come to destroy us? I know who you are—the Holy One of God!"

"Be quiet!" said Jesus sternly. "Come out of him!" The impure spirit shook the man violently and came out of him with a shriek.

The people were all so amazed that they asked each other, "What is this? A new teaching—and with authority! He even gives orders to impure spirits and they obey him." News about him spread quickly over the whole region of Galilee.

As soon as they left the synagogue, they went with James and John to the home of Simon and Andrew. Simon's mother-in-law was in bed with a fever, and they immediately told Jesus about her. So he went to her, took her hand and helped her up. The fever left her and she began to wait on them.

That evening after sunset the people brought to Jesus all the sick and demon-possessed. The whole town gathered at the door, and Jesus healed many who had various diseases. He also drove out many demons, but he would not let the demons speak because they knew who he was.

Very early in the morning, while it was still dark, Jesus got up, left the house and went off to a solitary place, where he prayed. Simon and his companions went to look for him, and when they found him, they exclaimed: "Everyone is looking for you!"

Jesus replied, "Let us go somewhere else—to the nearby villages—so I can preach there also. That is why I have come." So he traveled throughout Galilee, preaching in their synagogues and driving out demons.

A man with leprosy came to him and begged him on his knees, "If you are willing, you can make me clean."

Jesus was indignant. He reached out his hand and touched the man. "I am willing," he said. "Be clean!" Immediately the leprosy left him and he was cleansed.

Jesus sent him away at once with a strong warning: "See that you don't tell this to anyone. But go, show yourself to the priest and offer the sacrifices that Moses commanded for your cleansing, as a testimony to them." Instead he went out and began to talk freely, spreading the news. As a result, Jesus could no longer enter a town openly but stayed outside in lonely places. Yet the people still came to him from everywhere.

Source: Mark 1:1-43, from the *New International Version*. (International Bible Society, 1984). Reprinted by permission.

SERMON ON THE MOUNT

Matthew's Gospel was written for a Jewish audience, and it continually draws parallels from the Old Testament. He

*incorporates Jesus' sayings into five distinct discourses—
possibly representing the five books of Moses, to symbolize a
new Torah. The Sermon on the Mount is the first of these; again,
the mountain motif here parallels the story of Moses receiving the Law at Mount Sinai. Many of the teachings in Matthew
overlap those in Luke, suggesting that they independently drew
their information from a third source (called Q by contemporary scholars). Some sayings in the Sermon on the Mount also
appear in Luke in a section often called the Sermon on the Plain
(6:20–49). Matthew's discourse opens with a description of how
the kingdom of God will involve a dramatic reversal of conditions
for the oppressed and faithful. Citizens of the kingdom must distinguish themselves through obedience to a new law, principally
one of love for others, forgiveness, and trust in God.*

Now when Jesus saw the crowds, he went up on a moun-
tainside and sat down. His disciples came to him, and he
began to teach them. He said:

The Beatitudes and Similes

"Blessed are the poor in spirit,
 for theirs is the kingdom of heaven.
Blessed are those who mourn,
 for they will be comforted.
Blessed are the meek,
 for they will inherit the earth.
Blessed are those who hunger and thirst for righteousness,
 for they will be filled.
Blessed are the merciful,
 for they will be shown mercy.
Blessed are the pure in heart,
 for they will see God.
Blessed are the peacemakers,
 for they will be called children of God.
Blessed are those who are persecuted because of righteousness,
 for theirs is the kingdom of heaven.

"Blessed are you when people insult you, persecute you and
falsely say all kinds of evil against you because of me. Rejoice
and be glad, because great is your reward in heaven, for in the
same way they persecuted the prophets who were before you.

"You are the salt of the earth. But if the salt loses its salti-
ness, how can it be made salty again? It is no longer good for
anything, except to be thrown out and trampled underfoot.

"You are the light of the world. A town built on a hill
cannot be hidden. Neither do people light a lamp and put it
under a bowl. Instead they put it on its stand, and it gives
light to everyone in the house. In the same way, let your light

shine before others, that they may see your good deeds and glorify your Father in heaven.

New Interpretations of Jewish Laws

"Do not think that I have come to abolish the Law or the Prophets; I have not come to abolish them but to fulfill them. For truly I tell you, until heaven and earth disappear, not the smallest letter, not the least stroke of a pen, will by any means disappear from the Law until everything is accomplished. Therefore anyone who sets aside one of the least of these commands and teaches others accordingly will be called least in the kingdom of heaven, but whoever practices and teaches these commands will be called great in the kingdom of heaven. For I tell you that unless your righteousness surpasses that of the Pharisees and the teachers of the law, you will certainly not enter the kingdom of heaven.

"You have heard that it was said to the people long ago, 'You shall not murder, and anyone who murders will be subject to judgment.' But I tell you that anyone who is angry with a brother or sister will be subject to judgment. Again, anyone who says to a brother or sister, 'Raca,' is answerable to the court. And anyone who says, 'You fool!' will be in danger of the fire of hell.

"Therefore, if you are offering your gift at the altar and there remember that your brother or sister has something against you, leave your gift there in front of the altar. First go and be reconciled to them; then come and offer your gift.

"Settle matters quickly with your adversary who is taking you to court. Do it while you are still together on the way, or your adversary may hand you over to the judge, and the judge may hand you over to the officer, and you may be thrown into prison. Truly I tell you, you will not get out until you have paid the last penny.

"You have heard that it was said, 'You shall not commit adultery.' But I tell you that anyone who looks at a woman lustfully has already committed adultery with her in his heart. If your right eye causes you to stumble, gouge it out and throw it away. It is better for you to lose one part of your body than for your whole body to be thrown into hell. And if your right hand causes you to stumble, cut it off and throw it away. It is better for you to lose one part of your body than for your whole body to go into hell.

"It has been said, 'Anyone who divorces his wife must give her a certificate of divorce.' But I tell you that anyone who divorces his wife, except for sexual immorality, makes her the victim of adultery, and anyone who marries a divorced woman commits adultery.

"Again, you have heard that it was said to the people long ago, 'Do not break your oath, but fulfill to the Lord the vows you have made.' But I tell you, do not swear an oath at all: either by heaven, for it is God's throne; or by the earth, for it is his footstool; or by Jerusalem, for it is the city of the Great King. And do not swear by your head, for you cannot make even one hair white or black. All you need to say is simply 'Yes' or 'No'; anything beyond this comes from the evil one.

"You have heard that it was said, 'Eye for eye, and tooth for tooth.' But I tell you, do not resist an evil person. If anyone slaps you on the right cheek, turn to them the other cheek also. And if anyone wants to sue you and take your shirt, hand over your coat as well. If anyone forces you to go one mile, go with them two miles. Give to the one who asks you, and do not turn away from the one who wants to borrow from you.

"You have heard that it was said, 'Love your neighbor and hate your enemy.' But I tell you, love your enemies and pray for those who persecute you, that you may be children of your Father in heaven. He causes his sun to rise on the evil and the good, and sends rain on the righteous and the unrighteous. If you love those who love you, what reward will you get? Are not even the tax collectors doing that? And if you greet only your own people, what are you doing more than others? Do not even pagans do that? Be perfect, therefore, as your heavenly Father is perfect.

Charity, the Lord's Prayer, and Fasting

"Be careful not to practice your righteousness in front of others to be seen by them. If you do, you will have no reward from your Father in heaven.

"So when you give to the needy, do not announce it with trumpets, as the hypocrites do in the synagogues and on the streets, to be honored by others. Truly I tell you, they have received their reward in full. But when you give to the needy, do not let your left hand know what your right hand is doing, so that your giving may be in secret. Then your Father, who sees what is done in secret, will reward you.

"And when you pray, do not be like the hypocrites, for they love to pray standing in the synagogues and on the street corners to be seen by others. Truly I tell you, they have received their reward in full. But when you pray, go into your room, close the door and pray to your Father, who is unseen. Then your Father, who sees what is done in secret, will reward you. And when you pray, do not keep on babbling like pagans, for they think they will be heard because of their many words. Do not be like them, for your Father knows what you need before you ask him. This, then, is how you should pray:

> Our Father in heaven,
> hallowed be your name,
> your kingdom come,
> your will be done,
> on earth as it is in heaven.
> Give us today our daily bread.
> And forgive us our debts,
> as we also have forgiven our debtors.
> And lead us not into temptation,
> but deliver us from the evil one.

"For if you forgive other people when they sin against you, your heavenly Father will also forgive you. But if you do not forgive others their sins, your Father will not forgive your sins.

"When you fast, do not look somber as the hypocrites do, for they disfigure their faces to show others they are fasting. Truly I tell you, they have received their reward in full. But when you fast, put oil on your head and wash your face, so that it will not be obvious to others that you are fasting, but only to your Father, who is unseen; and your Father, who sees what is done in secret, will reward you.

Money and Wealth

"Do not store up for yourselves treasures on earth, where moths and vermin destroy, and where thieves break in and steal. But store up for yourselves treasures in heaven, where moths and vermin do not destroy, and where thieves do not break in and steal. For where your treasure is, there your heart will be also.

"The eye is the lamp of the body. If your eyes are healthy, your whole body will be full of light. But if your eyes are unhealthy, your whole body will be full of darkness. If then the light within you is darkness, how great is that darkness!

"No one can serve two masters. Either you will hate the one and love the other, or you will be devoted to the one and despise the other. You cannot serve both God and money.

"Therefore I tell you, do not worry about your life, what you will eat or drink; or about your body, what you will wear. Is not life more than food, and the body more than clothes? Look at the birds of the air; they do not sow or reap or store away in barns, and yet your heavenly Father feeds them. Are you not much more valuable than they? Can any one of you by worrying add a single hour to your life?

"And why do you worry about clothes? See how the flowers of the field grow. They do not labor or spin. Yet I tell you that not even Solomon in all his splendor was dressed like one of these. If that is how God clothes the grass of the field, which is here today and tomorrow is thrown into the fire, will he not much more clothe you—you of little faith? So do not worry, saying, 'What shall we eat?' or 'What shall we drink?' or 'What shall we wear?' For the pagans run after all these things, and your heavenly Father knows that you need them. But seek first his kingdom and his righteousness, and all these things will be given to you as well. Therefore do not worry about tomorrow, for tomorrow will worry about itself. Each day has enough trouble of its own.

Judging Others, Answers to Prayers, and the Golden Rule,

"Do not judge, or you too will be judged. For in the same way you judge others, you will be judged, and with the measure you use, it will be measured to you.

"Why do you look at the speck of sawdust in your brother's eye and pay no attention to the plank in your own eye? How can you say to your brother, 'Let me take the speck out of your eye,' when all the time there is a plank in your own eye? You hypocrite, first take the plank out of your own eye, and then you will see clearly to remove the speck from your brother's eye.

"Do not give dogs what is sacred; do not throw your pearls to pigs. If you do, they may trample them under their feet, and turn and tear you to pieces.

"Ask and it will be given to you; seek and you will find; knock and the door will be opened to you. For everyone who asks receives; the one who seeks finds; and to the one who knocks, the door will be opened.

"Which of you, if your son asks for bread, will give him a stone? Or if he asks for a fish, will give him a snake? If you, then, though you are evil, know how to give good gifts to your children, how much more will your Father in heaven give good gifts to those who ask him!

So in everything, do to others what you would have them do to you, for this sums up the Law and the Prophets.

"Enter through the narrow gate. For wide is the gate and broad is the road that leads to destruction, and many enter through it. But small is the gate and narrow the road that leads to life, and only a few find it.

False Prophets and the House
Built on Rock

"Watch out for false prophets. They come to you in sheep's clothing, but inwardly they are ferocious wolves. By their fruit you will recognize them. Do people pick grapes from thornbushes, or figs from thistles? Likewise, every good tree bears good fruit, but a bad tree bears bad fruit. A good tree cannot bear bad fruit, and a bad tree cannot bear good fruit. Every tree that does not bear good fruit is cut down and thrown into the fire. Thus, by their fruit you will recognize them.

"Not everyone who says to me, 'Lord, Lord,' will enter the kingdom of heaven, but only the one who does the will of my Father who is in heaven. Many will say to me on that day, 'Lord, Lord, did we not prophesy in your name and in your name drive out demons and in your name perform many miracles?' Then I will tell them plainly, 'I never knew you. Away from me, you evildoers!'

"Therefore everyone who hears these words of mine and puts them into practice is like a wise man who built his house on the rock. The rain came down, the streams rose, and the winds blew and beat against that house; yet it did not fall, because it had its foundation on the rock. But everyone who hears these words of mine and does not put them into practice is like a foolish man who built his house on sand. The rain came down, the streams rose, and the winds blew and beat against that house, and it fell with a great crash."

When Jesus had finished saying these things, the crowds were amazed at his teaching, because he taught as one who had authority, and not as their teachers of the law.

Source: Matthew 5:1–47; 6:1–34; 7:1–29, from the *New International Version*. (International Bible Society, 1984). Reprinted by permission.

PARABLES OF THE GOOD SAMARITAN
AND PRODIGAL SON

Of the approximately thirty parables of Jesus, the two most famous appear only in Luke: the good Samaritan and the prodigal son. Luke sets both parables in a larger narrative context. The good Samaritan parable is introduced in a dialogue between Jesus and a lawyer (adapted from Mark 12:28–34) on loving one's neighbor. Jesus then explains that the notion of one's neighbor crosses religious and social boundaries, just as a

Samaritan aids a battered Jew in spite of enmity between their two ethnic groups. The prodigal son parable is one of three that Jesus gives in response to criticisms that he associates with sinners. The parable's message is one of forgiveness. The father (representing God) forgives the younger son (representing non-Jews) who squanders his inheritance, while the dutiful older brother (representing Jews) protests.

The Good Samaritan

On one occasion an expert in the law stood up to test Jesus. "Teacher," he asked, "what must I do to inherit eternal life?"

"What is written in the Law?" he replied. "How do you read it?"

He answered, "'Love the Lord your God with all your heart and with all your soul and with all your strength and with all your mind'; and, 'Love your neighbor as yourself.'"

"You have answered correctly," Jesus replied. "Do this and you will live."

But he wanted to justify himself, so he asked Jesus, "And who is my neighbor?"

In reply Jesus said: "A man was going down from Jerusalem to Jericho, when he was attacked by robbers. They stripped him of his clothes, beat him and went away, leaving him half dead. A priest happened to be going down the same road, and when he saw the man, he passed by on the other side. So too, a Levite, when he came to the place and saw him, passed by on the other side. But a Samaritan, as he traveled, came where the man was; and when he saw him, he took pity on him. He went to him and bandaged his wounds, pouring on oil and wine. Then he put the man on his own donkey, brought him to an inn and took care of him. The next day he took out two denarii and gave them to the innkeeper. 'Look after him,' he said, 'and when I return, I will reimburse you for any extra expense you may have.'

"Which of these three do you think was a neighbor to the man who fell into the hands of robbers?"

The expert in the law replied, "The one who had mercy on him."

Jesus told him, "Go and do likewise."

The Prodigal Son

Now the tax collectors and sinners were all gathering around to hear Jesus. But the Pharisees and the teachers of the law muttered, "This man welcomes sinners and eats with them." Then Jesus told them this parable: . . .

Jesus continued: "There was a man who had two sons. The younger one said to his father, 'Father, give me my share of the estate.' So he divided his property between them.

"Not long after that, the younger son got together all he had, set off for a distant country and there squandered his wealth in wild living. After he had spent everything, there was a severe famine in that whole country, and he began to be in need. So he went and hired himself out to a citizen of that country, who sent him to his fields to feed pigs. He longed to fill his stomach with the pods that the pigs were eating, but no one gave him anything.

"When he came to his senses, he said, 'How many of my father's hired servants have food to spare, and here I am starving to death! I will set out and go back to my father and say to him: Father, I have sinned against heaven and against you. I am no longer worthy to be called your son; make me like one of your hired servants.' So he got up and went to his father.

"But while he was still a long way off, his father saw him and was filled with compassion for him; he ran to his son, threw his arms around him and kissed him.

"The son said to him, 'Father, I have sinned against heaven and against you. I am no longer worthy to be called your son.'

"But the father said to his servants, 'Quick! Bring the best robe and put it on him. Put a ring on his finger and sandals on his feet. Bring the fattened calf and kill it. Let's have a feast and celebrate. For this son of mine was dead and is alive again; he was lost and is found.' So they began to celebrate.

"Meanwhile, the older son was in the field. When he came near the house, he heard music and dancing. So he called one of the servants and asked him what was going on. 'Your brother has come,' he replied, 'and your father has killed the fattened calf because he has him back safe and sound.'

"The older brother became angry and refused to go in. So his father went out and pleaded with him. But he answered his father, 'Look! All these years I've been slaving for you and never disobeyed your orders. Yet you never gave me even a young goat so I could celebrate with my friends. But when this son of yours who has squandered your property with prostitutes comes home, you kill the fattened calf for him!'

"'My son,' the father said, 'you are always with me, and everything I have is yours. But we had to celebrate and be glad, because this brother of yours was dead and is alive again; he was lost and is found.'"

Source: Luke 10:25–37; 15:1–3, 11–32, from the *New International Version*. (International Bible Society, 1984). Reprinted by permission.

PETER RECEIVES THE KEYS

Early Christian traditions typically traced their lineage back to an original follower of Jesus. Early Gnostics viewed Jesus' brothers, James and Thomas, as their founders. For Ethiopians, the founder is the eunuch of Acts 8. For the Orthodox of Constantinople, the founder is Andrew the Apostle. The Roman Catholic Church, though, considers its foundation to be Peter, the first supreme Pope. The concept of the Petrine Papacy is based on two doctrines. First, the doctrine of apostolic succession maintains that the original Apostles had authority over specific regional churches, which they passed on to their successors. Peter established the Church of Rome, and at his death authority was passed to Linus, and so on down to the present Pope. Second, the doctrine of the primacy of Peter, forged in the third through fifth centuries, maintains that Peter was given supreme authority over all Church congregations. The argument for this latter claim is based on the following passage from Matthew. Drawing from a scene in Mark 8:27 in which Peter identifies Jesus as the Messiah, Matthew then recounts that Jesus rewarded Peter with keys to the kingdom of God. Although the language is metaphorical, Peter is clearly given sweeping authority, indicating Matthew's allegiance to the Petrine tradition. Matthew continues by foreshadowing Jesus' fate.

When Jesus came to the region of Caesarea Philippi, he asked his disciples, "Who do people say the Son of Man is?"

They replied, "Some say John the Baptist; others say Elijah; and still others, Jeremiah or one of the prophets."

"But what about you?" he asked. "Who do you say I am?"

Simon Peter answered, "You are the Messiah, the Son of the living God."

Jesus replied, "Blessed are you, Simon son of Jonah, for this was not revealed to you by flesh and blood, but by my Father in heaven. And I tell you that you are Peter, and on this rock I will build my church, and the gates of Hades will not overcome it. I will give you the keys of the kingdom of heaven; whatever you bind on earth will be bound in heaven, and whatever you loose on earth will be loosed in heaven."

Then he ordered his disciples not to tell anyone that he was the Messiah.

From that time on Jesus began to explain to his disciples that he must go to Jerusalem and suffer many things at the hands of the elders, the chief priests and the teachers of the law, and that he must be killed and on the third day be raised to life.

Peter took him aside and began to rebuke him. "Never, Lord!" he said. "This shall never happen to you!"

Jesus turned and said to Peter, "Get behind me, Satan! You are a stumbling block to me; you do not have in mind the concerns of God, but merely human concerns."

Then Jesus said to his disciples, "Whoever wants to be my disciple must deny themselves and take up their cross and follow me. For whoever wants to save their life will lose it, but whoever loses their life for me will find it. What good will it be for someone to gain the whole world, yet forfeit their soul? Or what can anyone give in exchange for their soul? For the Son of Man is going to come in his Father's glory with his angels, and then he will reward each person according to what they have done.

"Truly I tell you, some who are standing here will not taste death before they see the Son of Man coming in his kingdom."

Source: Matthew 16:13–28, from the *New International Version*. (International Bible Society, 1984). Reprinted by permission.

LAZARUS RAISED FROM THE DEAD

The Gospel of John presents an account of Jesus that is almost entirely different from that of the synoptic Gospels. In John, Jesus' ministry is three years, as opposed to one year; the subject of eternal life is emphasized, and not the kingdom of God; Jesus performs no exorcisms, refers to himself as the son of God, is the subject of his own teachings, and says little about the poor. Although Jesus performs miracles in both John and the synoptics, the purpose is different. In John, they are intentionally performed as signs indicating his divine role, whereas in the synoptics such signs are shunned and miracles are depicted mainly as acts of compassion. In the following passage, Jesus performs his most dramatic miracle by raising a dead man to life. For John, as well as the synoptics, Jesus' supernatural powers were seen by the Jewish leaders as a threat to social and religious stability, inciting them to plot against him.

Lazarus's Death

Now a man named Lazarus was sick. He was from Bethany, the village of Mary and her sister Martha. (This Mary, whose brother Lazarus now lay sick, was the same one who poured perfume on the Lord and wiped his feet with her hair.) So the sisters sent word to Jesus, "Lord, the one you love is sick."

When he heard this, Jesus said, "This sickness will not end in death. No, it is for God's glory so that God's Son may be glorified through it." Now Jesus loved Martha and her sister and Lazarus. So when he heard that Lazarus was sick, he stayed where he was two more days, and then he said to his disciples, "Let us go back to Judea."

"But Rabbi," they said, "a short while ago the Jews there tried to stone you, and yet you are going back?"

Jesus answered, "Are there not twelve hours of daylight? Anyone who walks in the daytime will not stumble, for they see by this world's light. It is when a person walks at night that they stumble, for they have no light."

After he had said this, he went on to tell them, "Our friend Lazarus has fallen asleep; but I am going there to wake him up."

His disciples replied, "Lord, if he sleeps, he will get better." Jesus had been speaking of his death, but his disciples thought he meant natural sleep.

So then he told them plainly, "Lazarus is dead, and for your sake I am glad I was not there, so that you may believe. But let us go to him."

Then Thomas (also known as Didymus) said to the rest of the disciples, "Let us also go, that we may die with him."

Jesus Arrives and Raises Lazarus

On his arrival, Jesus found that Lazarus had already been in the tomb for four days. Now Bethany was less than two miles from Jerusalem, and many Jews had come to Martha and Mary to comfort them in the loss of their brother. When Martha heard that Jesus was coming, she went out to meet him, but Mary stayed at home.

"Lord," Martha said to Jesus, "if you had been here, my brother would not have died. But I know that even now God will give you whatever you ask."

Jesus said to her, "Your brother will rise again."

Martha answered, "I know he will rise again in the resurrection at the last day."

Jesus said to her, "I am the resurrection and the life. The one who believes in me will live, even though they die;

and whoever lives by believing in me will never die. Do you believe this?"

"Yes, Lord," she replied, "I believe that you are the Messiah, the Son of God, who is to come into the world."

After she had said this, she went back and called her sister Mary aside. "The Teacher is here," she said, "and is asking for you." When Mary heard this, she got up quickly and went to him. Now Jesus had not yet entered the village, but was still at the place where Martha had met him. When the Jews who had been with Mary in the house, comforting her, noticed how quickly she got up and went out, they followed her, supposing she was going to the tomb to mourn there.

When Mary reached the place where Jesus was and saw him, she fell at his feet and said, "Lord, if you had been here, my brother would not have died."

When Jesus saw her weeping, and the Jews who had come along with her also weeping, he was deeply moved in spirit and troubled. "Where have you laid him?" he asked.

"Come and see, Lord," they replied.

Jesus wept.

Then the Jews said, "See how he loved him!"

But some of them said, "Could not he who opened the eyes of the blind man have kept this man from dying?"

Jesus, once more deeply moved, came to the tomb. It was a cave with a stone laid across the entrance. "Take away the stone," he said.

"But, Lord," said Martha, the sister of the dead man, "by this time there is a bad odor, for he has been there four days."

Then Jesus said, "Did I not tell you that if you believe, you will see the glory of God?"

So they took away the stone. Then Jesus looked up and said, "Father, I thank you that you have heard me. I knew that you always hear me, but I said this for the benefit of the people standing here, that they may believe that you sent me."

When he had said this, Jesus called in a loud voice, "Lazarus, come out!" The dead man came out, his hands and feet wrapped with strips of linen, and a cloth around his face.

Jesus said to them, "Take off the grave clothes and let him go."

Reaction of the Sanhedrin

Therefore many of the Jews who had come to visit Mary, and had seen what Jesus did, believed in him. But some of them went to the Pharisees and told them what Jesus had done.

Then the chief priests and the Pharisees called a meeting of the Sanhedrin.

"What are we accomplishing?" they asked. "Here is this man performing many signs. If we let him go on like this, everyone will believe in him, and then the Romans will come and take away both our temple and our nation."

Then one of them, named Caiaphas, who was high priest that year, spoke up, "You know nothing at all! You do not realize that it is better for you that one man die for the people than that the whole nation perish."

He did not say this on his own, but as high priest that year he prophesied that Jesus would die for the Jewish nation, and not only for that nation but also for the scattered children of God, to bring them together and make them one. So from that day on they plotted to take his life.

Therefore Jesus no longer moved about publicly among the people of Judea. Instead he withdrew to a region near the wilderness, to a village called Ephraim, where he stayed with his disciples.

Source: John 11:1–54, from the *New International Version.* (International Bible Society, 1984). Reprinted by permission.

JESUS' DEATH

LAST SUPPER

Jesus' final days took place in Jerusalem during the Jewish holiday of Passover. The four Gospels depict Jesus and his disciples gathering for a meal, known as the "Last Supper" (Luke describes this as the traditional meal of the Passover festival). At this meal, according to the synoptic Gospels, Jesus performed ritual acts with the bread and wine. This event is the basis of the Christian sacrament of the Eucharist. In Christian doctrine, a sacrament is a visible religious rite that confers special grace. The number of sacraments has varied throughout Christian history; twelfth-century theologian Hugo of St. Victor listed thirty. But baptism and the Eucharist have always been the most important within Christian traditions.

Now the Passover and the Festival of Unleavened Bread were only two days away, and the chief priests and the teachers of the law were scheming to arrest Jesus secretly and kill him. "But not during the festival," they said, "or the people may riot."

While he was in Bethany, reclining at the table in the home of Simon the Leper, a woman came with an alabaster jar of very expensive perfume, made of pure nard. She broke the jar and poured the perfume on his head.

Some of those present were saying indignantly to one another, "Why this waste of perfume? It could have been sold for more than a year's wages and the money given to the poor." And they rebuked her harshly.

"Leave her alone," said Jesus. "Why are you bothering her? She has done a beautiful thing to me. The poor you will always have with you, and you can help them any time you want. But you will not always have me. She did what she could. She poured perfume on my body beforehand to prepare for my burial. Truly I tell you, wherever the gospel is preached throughout the world, what she has done will also be told, in memory of her."

Then Judas Iscariot, one of the Twelve, went to the chief priests to betray Jesus to them. They were delighted to hear this and promised to give him money. So he watched for an opportunity to hand him over.

On the first day of the Festival of Unleavened Bread, when it was customary to sacrifice the Passover lamb, Jesus' disciples asked him, "Where do you want us to go and make preparations for you to eat the Passover?"

So he sent two of his disciples, telling them, "Go into the city, and a man carrying a jar of water will meet you. Follow him. Say to the owner of the house he enters, 'The Teacher asks: Where is my guest room, where I may eat the Passover with my disciples?' He will show you a large room upstairs, furnished and ready. Make preparations for us there."

The disciples left, went into the city and found things just as Jesus had told them. So they prepared the Passover.

When evening came, Jesus arrived with the Twelve. While they were reclining at the table eating, he said, "Truly I tell you, one of you will betray me—one who is eating with me."

They were saddened, and one by one they said to him, "Surely you don't mean me?"

"It is one of the Twelve," he replied, "one who dips bread into the bowl with me. The Son of Man will go just as it is written about him. But woe to that man who betrays the Son of Man! It would be better for him if he had not been born."

While they were eating, Jesus took bread, and when he had given thanks, he broke it and gave it to his disciples, saying, "Take it; this is my body."

Then he took a cup, and when he had given thanks, he gave it to them, and they all drank from it.

"This is my blood of the covenant, which is poured out for many," he said to them. "Truly I tell you, I will not drink again from the fruit of the vine until that day when I drink it new in the kingdom of God."

When they had sung a hymn, they went out to the Mount of Olives.

Source: Mark 14:1–25, from the *New International Version.* (International Bible Society, 1984). Reprinted by permission.

FATHER, SON, AND HOLY SPIRIT

In John's account of the Last Supper, Jesus gives a farewell discourse, presented here. Unlike the synoptic Gospels, in which Jesus speaks in short, crisp sayings and parables, in John Jesus speaks in extended discourses. The discourse topic here is the relation between God the Father and Jesus the Son. The doctrine of the Trinity, central to Christianity, holds that God is a unity of three persons: the Father, Son, and Holy Spirit. Although the term "Trinity" and its technical meaning were developed by early Church Fathers, passages that associate the Father, Son, and Holy Spirit are the scriptural basis of the doctrine. The following account is particularly important in this regard. The Holy Spirit is only briefly mentioned at the end of this passage. In the Old Testament occasional references are made to a spirit of God, but John and other New Testament writers expand on this notion and see the Holy Spirit both as a divine presence and as an agent of guidance for the Church.

"Do not let your hearts be troubled. You believe in God; believe also in me. My Father's house has many rooms; if that were not so, would I have told you that I am going there to prepare a place for you? And if I go and prepare a place for you, I will come back and take you to be with me that you also may be where I am. You know the way to the place where I am going."

Thomas said to him, "Lord, we don't know where you are going, so how can we know the way?"

Jesus answered, "I am the way and the truth and the life. No one comes to the Father except through me. If you really know me, you will know my Father as well. From now on, you do know him and have seen him."

Philip said, "Lord, show us the Father and that will be enough for us."

Jesus answered: "Don't you know me, Philip, even after I have been among you such a long time? Anyone who has seen me has seen the Father. How can you say, 'Show us the Father'? Don't you believe that I am in the Father, and that the Father is in me? The words I say to you I do not speak on my own authority. Rather, it is the Father, living in me, who is doing his work. Believe me when I say that I am in the Father and the Father is in me; or at least believe on the evidence of the works themselves. Very truly I tell you, whoever believes in me will do the works I have been doing, and they will do even greater things than these, because I am going to the Father. And I will do whatever you ask in my name, so that the Father may be glorified in the Son. You may ask me for anything in my name, and I will do it.

Jesus Promises the Holy Spirit.

"If you love me, keep my commands. And I will ask the Father, and he will give you another advocate to help you and be with you forever—the Spirit of truth. The world cannot accept him, because it neither sees him nor knows him. But you know him, for he lives with you and will be in you. I will not leave you as orphans; I will come to you. Before long, the world will not see me anymore, but you will see me. Because I live, you also will live. On that day you will realize that I am in my Father, and you are in me, and I am in you. Whoever has my commands and keeps them is the one who loves me. The one who loves me will be loved by my Father, and I too will love them and show myself to them."

Then Judas (not Judas Iscariot) said, "But, Lord, why do you intend to show yourself to us and not to the world?"

Jesus replied, "Anyone who loves me will obey my teaching. My Father will love them, and we will come to them and make our home with them. Anyone who does not love me will not obey my teaching. These words you hear are not my own; they belong to the Father who sent me.

"All this I have spoken while still with you. But the Advocate, the Holy Spirit, whom the Father will send in my name, will teach you all things and will remind you of everything I have said to you.

Source: John 14:1–26, from the *New International Version*. (International Bible Society, 1984). Reprinted by permission.

TRIAL, CRUCIFIXION, RESURRECTION

After the Last Supper, Jesus went with his disciples to a hillside graveyard to pray. There he was arrested, brought before the Jewish legal council, and accused of blasphemy. Not empowered to perform criminal executions, the council brought Jesus to the Roman governor Pilate, where they made a case for treason based on Jesus' messianic claims. Pilate pronounced the desired verdict and sentence. All four Gospels place responsibility on the Jews, first the priests and then an angry mob, although the ultimate decision rested with the governor. Jesus was then executed on a cross, in classic Roman fashion, and placed in the rock-hewn tomb of a wealthy follower. Mark's Gospel reports that after a few days the tomb was found empty, and a young man present at the tomb announced that Jesus was resurrected. The other Gospels report appearances of the resurrected Jesus.

Jesus Betrayed and Arrested

Just as he was speaking, Judas, one of the Twelve, appeared. With him was a crowd armed with swords and clubs, sent from the chief priests, the teachers of the law, and the elders.

Now the betrayer had arranged a signal with them: "The one I kiss is the man; arrest him and lead him away under guard." Going at once to Jesus, Judas said, "Rabbi!" and kissed him. The men seized Jesus and arrested him. Then one of those standing near drew his sword and struck the servant of the high priest, cutting off his ear.

"Am I leading a rebellion," said Jesus, "that you have come out with swords and clubs to capture me? Every day I was with you, teaching in the temple courts, and you did not arrest me. But the Scriptures must be fulfilled." Then everyone deserted him and fled.

A young man, wearing nothing but a linen garment, was following Jesus. When they seized him, he fled naked, leaving his garment behind.

They took Jesus to the high priest, and all the chief priests, the elders and the teachers of the law came together. Peter followed him at a distance, right into the courtyard of the high priest. There he sat with the guards and warmed himself at the fire.

The chief priests and the whole Sanhedrin were looking for evidence against Jesus so that they could put him to death, but they did not find any. Many testified falsely against him, but their statements did not agree.

Then some stood up and gave this false testimony against him: "We heard him say, 'I will destroy this temple made with human hands and in three days will build another, not made with hands.'" Yet even then their testimony did not agree.

Then the high priest stood up before them and asked Jesus, "Are you not going to answer? What is this testimony that these men are bringing against you?" But Jesus remained silent and gave no answer.

Again the high priest asked him, "Are you the Messiah, the Son of the Blessed One?"

"I am," said Jesus. "And you will see the Son of Man sitting at the right hand of the Mighty One and coming on the clouds of heaven."

The high priest tore his clothes. "Why do we need any more witnesses?" he asked. "You have heard the blasphemy. What do you think?"

They all condemned him as worthy of death. Then some began to spit at him; they blindfolded him, struck him with their fists, and said, "Prophesy!" And the guards took him and beat him.

Peter Denies Jesus

While Peter was below in the courtyard, one of the servant girls of the high priest came by. When she saw Peter warming himself, she looked closely at him.

"You also were with that Nazarene, Jesus," she said.

But he denied it. "I don't know or understand what you're talking about," he said, and went out into the entryway.

When the servant girl saw him there, she said again to those standing around, "This fellow is one of them." Again he denied it.

After a little while, those standing near said to Peter, "Surely you are one of them, for you are a Galilean."

He began to call down curses, and he swore to them, "I don't know this man you're talking about."

Immediately the rooster crowed the second time. Then Peter remembered the word Jesus had spoken to him: "Before the rooster crows twice you will disown me three times." And he broke down and wept.

Jesus before Pilate

Very early in the morning, the chief priests, with the elders, the teachers of the law and the whole Sanhedrin, made their plans. So they bound Jesus, led him away and handed him over to Pilate.

"Are you the king of the Jews?" asked Pilate.

"You have said so," Jesus replied.

The chief priests accused him of many things. So again Pilate asked him, "Aren't you going to answer? See how many things they are accusing you of."

But Jesus still made no reply, and Pilate was amazed.

Now it was the custom at the festival to release a prisoner whom the people requested. A man called Barabbas was in prison with the insurrectionists who had committed murder in the uprising. The crowd came up and asked Pilate to do for them what he usually did.

"Do you want me to release to you the king of the Jews?" asked Pilate, knowing it was out of self-interest that the chief priests had handed Jesus over to him. But the chief priests stirred up the crowd to have Pilate release Barabbas instead.

"What shall I do, then, with the one you call the king of the Jews?" Pilate asked them.

"Crucify him!" they shouted.

"Why? What crime has he committed?" asked Pilate.

But they shouted all the louder, "Crucify him!"

Wanting to satisfy the crowd, Pilate released Barabbas to them. He had Jesus flogged, and handed him over to be crucified.

The soldiers led Jesus away into the palace (that is, the Praetorium) and called together the whole company of soldiers. They put a purple robe on him, then twisted together a crown of thorns and set it on him. And they began to call out to him, "Hail, king of the Jews!" Again and again they struck him on the head with a staff and spit on him. Falling on their knees, they paid homage to him. And when they had mocked him, they took off the purple robe and put his own clothes on him. Then they led him out to crucify him.

A certain man from Cyrene, Simon, the father of Alexander and Rufus, was passing by on his way in from the country, and they forced him to carry the cross.

Jesus' Crucifixion, Death, and Burial

They brought Jesus to the place called Golgotha (which means "the place of the skull"). Then they offered him wine mixed with myrrh, but he did not take it. And they crucified him. Dividing up his clothes, they cast lots to see what each would get.

It was nine in the morning when they crucified him. The written notice of the charge against him read: The King of the Jews.

They crucified two rebels with him, one on his right and one on his left. Those who passed by hurled insults at him, shaking their heads and saying, "So! You who are going to destroy the temple and build it in three days, come down from the cross and save yourself!" In the same way the chief priests and the teachers of the law mocked him among themselves. "He saved others," they said, "but he can't save himself! Let this Messiah, this king of Israel, come down now from the cross, that we may see and believe." Those crucified with him also heaped insults on him.

At noon, darkness came over the whole land until three in the afternoon. And at three in the afternoon Jesus cried out in a loud voice, "Eloi, Eloi, lema sabachthani?" (which means "My God, my God, why have you forsaken me?").

When some of those standing near heard this, they said, "Listen, he's calling Elijah."

Someone ran, filled a sponge with wine vinegar, put it on a staff, and offered it to Jesus to drink. "Now leave him alone. Let's see if Elijah comes to take him down," he said.

With a loud cry, Jesus breathed his last.

The curtain of the temple was torn in two from top to bottom. And when the centurion, who stood there in front of Jesus, saw how he died, he said, "Surely this man was the Son of God!"

Some women were watching from a distance. Among them were Mary Magdalene, Mary the mother of James the younger and of Joseph, and Salome. In Galilee these women had followed him and cared for his needs. Many other women who had come up with him to Jerusalem were also there.

It was Preparation Day (that is, the day before the Sabbath). So as evening approached, Joseph of Arimathea, a prominent member of the Council, who was himself waiting for the kingdom of God, went boldly to Pilate and asked for Jesus' body. Pilate was surprised to hear that he was already dead. Summoning the centurion, he asked him if Jesus had already died. When he learned from the centurion that it was so, he gave the body to Joseph. So Joseph bought some linen cloth, took down the body, wrapped it in the linen, and placed it in a tomb cut out of rock. Then he rolled a stone against the entrance of the tomb. Mary Magdalene and Mary the mother of Joseph saw where he was laid.

Jesus' Resurrection

When the Sabbath was over, Mary Magdalene, Mary the mother of James, and Salome bought spices so that they might go to anoint Jesus' body. Very early on the first day of the week, just after sunrise, they were on their way to the tomb and they asked each other, "Who will roll the stone away from the entrance of the tomb?"

But when they looked up, they saw that the stone, which was very large, had been rolled away. As they entered the tomb, they saw a young man dressed in a white robe sitting on the right side, and they were alarmed.

"Don't be alarmed," he said. "You are looking for Jesus the Nazarene, who was crucified. He has risen! He is not here. See the place where they laid him. But go, tell his disciples and Peter, 'He is going ahead of you into Galilee. There you will see him, just as he told you.'"

Trembling and bewildered, the women went out and fled from the tomb. They said nothing to anyone, because they were afraid.

Source: Mark 14:43–72; 15:1–47; 16:1–8, from the *New International Version.* (International Bible Society, 1984). Reprinted by permission.

NEW TESTAMENT CHURCH

ASCENSION, PENTECOST

The book of the Acts of the Apostles, written about 85 CE, chronicles the events of the early Church after Jesus' resurrection. The book is sometimes termed the Gospel of the Holy Spirit because the author depicts the expansion of the early Church as being guided by the Holy Spirit. The opening of Acts, presented here, recounts Jesus' ascension into heaven and the arrival of the Holy Spirit a few days later, during the Jewish agricultural festival of Pentecost. The believers are directly affected by the presence of the Holy Spirit, as evidenced by their speaking in foreign tongues. Peter emerges as the leader of the Church, and thousands of believers are baptized.

Jesus' Appearance and Ascension

After his suffering, he presented himself to them and gave many convincing proofs that he was alive. He appeared to them over a period of forty days and spoke about the kingdom of God. On one occasion, while he was eating with them, he gave them this command: "Do not leave Jerusalem, but wait for the gift my Father promised, which you have heard me speak about. For John baptized with water, but in a few days you will be baptized with the Holy Spirit."

Then they gathered around him and asked him, "Lord, are you at this time going to restore the kingdom to Israel?"

He said to them: "It is not for you to know the times or dates the Father has set by his own authority. But you will receive power when the Holy Spirit comes on you; and you will be my witnesses in Jerusalem, and in all Judea and Samaria, and to the ends of the earth."

After he said this, he was taken up before their very eyes, and a cloud hid him from their sight.

They were looking intently up into the sky as he was going, when suddenly two men dressed in white stood beside them. "Men of Galilee," they said, "why do you stand here looking into the sky? This same Jesus, who has been taken from you into heaven, will come back in the same way you have seen him go into heaven." . . .

The Day of Pentecost

When the day of Pentecost came, they were all together in one place. Suddenly a sound like the blowing of a violent wind came from heaven and filled the whole house where they were sitting. They saw what seemed to be tongues of fire that separated and came to rest on each of them. All of them were filled with the Holy Spirit and began to speak in other tongues as the Spirit enabled them.

Now there were staying in Jerusalem God-fearing Jews from every nation under heaven. When they heard this sound, a crowd came together in bewilderment, because each one heard their own language being spoken. Utterly amazed, they asked: "Aren't all these who are speaking Galileans? Then how is it that each of us hears them in our native language? Parthians, Medes and Elamites; residents of Mesopotamia, Judea and Cappadocia, Pontus and Asia, Phrygia and Pamphylia, Egypt and the parts of Libya near Cyrene; visitors from Rome (both Jews and converts to Judaism); Cretans and Arabs—we hear them declaring the wonders of God in our own tongues!" Amazed and perplexed, they asked one another, "What does this mean?"

Some, however, made fun of them and said, "They have had too much wine."

Then Peter stood up with the Eleven, raised his voice and addressed the crowd: "Fellow Jews and all of you who live in Jerusalem, let me explain this to you; listen carefully to what I say. These people are not drunk, as you suppose. It's only nine in the morning! No, this is what was spoken by the prophet Joel:

"'In the last days, God says,
    I will pour out my Spirit on all people.
Your sons and daughters will prophesy,
    your young men will see visions,
    your old men will dream dreams.
Even on my servants, both men and women,
    I will pour out my Spirit in those days,
    and they will prophesy.
I will show wonders in the heavens above
    and signs on the earth below,
    blood and fire and billows of smoke.

The sun will be turned to darkness
and the moon to blood
before the coming of the great and glorious day of the Lord.
And everyone who calls
on the name of the Lord will be saved.'

"Fellow Israelites, listen to this: Jesus of Nazareth was a man accredited by God to you by miracles, wonders and signs, which God did among you through him, as you yourselves know. This man was handed over to you by God's deliberate plan and foreknowledge; and you, with the help of wicked men, put him to death by nailing him to the cross. But God raised him from the dead, freeing him from the agony of death, because it was impossible for death to keep its hold on him. . . .

With many other words he warned them; and he pleaded with them, "Save yourselves from this corrupt generation." Those who accepted his message were baptized, and about three thousand were added to their number that day.

They devoted themselves to the apostles' teaching and to fellowship, to the breaking of bread and to prayer. Everyone was filled with awe at the many wonders and signs performed by the apostles. All the believers were together and had everything in common. They sold property and possessions to give to anyone who had need. Every day they continued to meet together in the temple courts. They broke bread in their homes and ate together with glad and sincere hearts, praising God and enjoying the favor of all the people. And the Lord added to their number daily those who were being saved.

Source: Acts 1:3-11, 2:1-24, 40-47, from the *New International Version.* (International Bible Society, 1984). Reprinted by permission.

PAUL ON JUDAIZERS

After a dramatic conversion experience and a period of indoctrination, Paul soon rose in leadership to the status of an Apostle. During three missionary journeys in non-Jewish territories throughout the Mediterranean region, he established dozens of churches and corresponded with many of them. Written about 55 CE, Paul's letter to the Church of Galatia is a pivotal text in the development of early Christianity. Shortly after his visit, Church members in Galatia were persuaded by Christian Judaizers that adherence to Jewish law was a prerequisite for becoming a Christian. Paul argues vehemently that obedience to Jewish law will not absolve our sins. Righteousness comes about only through faith in Christ, and this is open to Jews and non-

Jews alike. This foreshadows a larger issue that would emerge in the decades ahead about whether Christianity is merely a Jewish sect or a distinct religion. In the first two chapters presented here, Paul describes his efforts to set Christianity apart from its Jewish framework. His account is important for its autobiographical content, and also because it is the earliest written discussion of first-century Church politics.

I am astonished that you are so quickly deserting the one who called you to live in the grace of Christ and are turning to a different gospel—which is really no gospel at all. Evidently some people are throwing you into confusion and are trying to pervert the gospel of Christ. But even if we or an angel from heaven should preach a gospel other than the one we preached to you, let them be under God's curse! As we have already said, so now I say again: If anybody is preaching to you a gospel other than what you accepted, let them be under God's curse!

Am I now trying to win the approval of human beings, or of God? Or am I trying to please people? If I were still trying to please people, I would not be a servant of Christ.

Paul Called by God

I want you to know, brothers and sisters, that the gospel I preached is not of human origin. I did not receive it from any man, nor was I taught it; rather, I received it by revelation from Jesus Christ.

For you have heard of my previous way of life in Judaism, how intensely I persecuted the church of God and tried to destroy it. I was advancing in Judaism beyond many of my own age among my people and was extremely zealous for the traditions of my fathers. But when God, who set me apart from my mother's womb and called me by his grace, was pleased to reveal his Son in me so that I might preach him among the Gentiles, my immediate response was not to consult any human being. I did not go up to Jerusalem to see those who were apostles before I was, but I went into Arabia. Later I returned to Damascus.

Then after three years, I went up to Jerusalem to get acquainted with Cephas and stayed with him fifteen days. I saw none of the other apostles—only James, the Lord's brother. I assure you before God that what I am writing you is no lie.

Then I went to Syria and Cilicia. I was personally unknown to the churches of Judea that are in Christ. They only heard the report: "The man who formerly persecuted us is now preaching the faith he once tried to destroy." And they praised God because of me.

Then after fourteen years, I went up again to Jerusalem, this time with Barnabas. I took Titus along also. I went in response to a revelation and, meeting privately with those esteemed as leaders, I presented to them the gospel that I preach among the Gentiles. I wanted to be sure I was not running and had not been running my race in vain. Yet not even Titus, who was with me, was compelled to be circumcised, even though he was a Greek. This matter arose because some false believers had infiltrated our ranks to spy on the freedom we have in Christ Jesus and to make us slaves. We did not give in to them for a moment, so that the truth of the gospel might be preserved for you.

Paul as an Apostle to the Gentiles

As for those who were held in high esteem—whatever they were makes no difference to me; God does not show favoritism—they added nothing to my message. On the contrary, they recognized that I had been entrusted with the task of preaching the gospel to the uncircumcised, just as Peter had been to the circumcised. For God, who was at work in Peter as an apostle to the circumcised, was also at work in me as an apostle to the Gentiles. James, Cephas and John, those esteemed as pillars, gave me and Barnabas the right hand of fellowship when they recognized the grace given to me. They agreed that we should go to the Gentiles, and they to the circumcised. All they asked was that we should continue to remember the poor, the very thing I had been eager to do all along.

When Cephas came to Antioch, I opposed him to his face, because he stood condemned. For before certain men came from James, he used to eat with the Gentiles. But when they arrived, he began to draw back and separate himself from the Gentiles because he was afraid of those who belonged to the circumcision group. The other Jews joined him in his hypocrisy, so that by their hypocrisy even Barnabas was led astray.

When I saw that they were not acting in line with the truth of the gospel, I said to Cephas in front of them all, "You are a Jew, yet you live like a Gentile and not like a Jew. How is it, then, that you force Gentiles to follow Jewish customs?

"We who are Jews by birth and not sinful Gentiles know that a person is not justified by the works of the law, but by faith in Jesus Christ. So we, too, have put our faith in Christ Jesus that we may be justified by faith in Christ and not by the works of the law, because by the works of the law no one will be justified.

"But if, in seeking to be justified in Christ, we Jews find ourselves also among the sinners, doesn't that mean that Christ promotes sin? Absolutely not! If I rebuild what I destroyed, then I really would be a lawbreaker.

"For through the law I died to the law so that I might live for God. I have been crucified with Christ and I no longer live, but Christ lives in me. The life I now live in the body, I live by faith in the Son of God, who loved me and gave himself for me. I do not set aside the grace of God, for if righteousness could be gained through the law, Christ died for nothing!"

Source: Galatians 1:6–24, 2:1–21, from the *New International Version*. (International Bible Society, 1984). Reprinted by permission.

PAUL ON LIFE AFTER DEATH

An immediate theological difficulty faced by Paul was the question of how Jesus could be divine despite his criminal execution. Paul's solution was to see Jesus' death on the cross and subsequent resurrection as the end of the old Jewish law and the beginning of a new era of divine grace. Through baptism, Christians symbolically participate in the cross by dying to their old lives and reemerging anew. The crucifixion and resurrection are so central to Paul's teaching that they are the only features of the life of Jesus with which he is concerned. In the following discussion from Paul's first letter to the church of Corinth, written about 55 CE, life after death is also linked to the resurrection: Because Christ resurrected, we are assured that we too will be. Unlike Greek writers, who construe life after death as the continuation of a bodiless, immortal soul, Christian doctrine holds to the bodily resurrection of the dead as found in post-exilic Jewish writings. Paul teaches that our new bodies will be heavenly and imperishable in nature, rather than earthly and perishable, and that all those who belong to Christ will be simultaneously resurrected when he returns.

Christ's Resurrection as Proof of Bodily Resurrection

But if it is preached that Christ has been raised from the dead, how can some of you say that there is no resurrection of the dead? If there is no resurrection of the dead, then not even Christ has been raised. And if Christ has not been raised, our preaching is useless and so is your faith. More than that, we are then found to be false witnesses about God, for we have testified about God that he raised Christ from the dead. But he did not raise him if in fact the dead are not raised. For if the dead are not raised, then Christ has not been raised either. And if Christ has not been raised, your faith is futile; you are still in your sins. Then those also who have fallen asleep in Christ are lost. If only for this life we have hope in Christ, we are of all people most to be pitied.

But Christ has indeed been raised from the dead, the firstfruits of those who have fallen asleep. For since death came through a man, the resurrection of the dead comes also through a man. For as in Adam all die, so in Christ all will be made alive. But each in turn: Christ, the firstfruits; then, when he comes, those who belong to him. Then the end will come, when he hands over the kingdom to God the Father after he has destroyed all dominion, authority, and power. For he must reign until he has put all his enemies under his feet. The last enemy to be destroyed is death. For he "has put everything under his feet." Now when it says that "everything" has been put under him, it is clear that this does not include God himself, who put everything under Christ. When he has done this, then the Son himself will be made subject to him who put everything under him, so that God may be all in all. . . .

Death of Natural Body followed by Resurrection of Spiritual Body

But someone will ask, "How are the dead raised? With what kind of body will they come?" How foolish! What you sow does not come to life unless it dies. When you sow, you do not plant the body that will be, but just a seed, perhaps of wheat or of something else. But God gives it a body as he has determined, and to each kind of seed he gives its own body. Not all flesh is the same: People have one kind of flesh, animals have another, birds another and fish another. There are also heavenly bodies and there are earthly bodies; but the splendor of the heavenly bodies is one kind, and the splendor of the earthly bodies is another. The sun has one kind of splendor, the moon another and the stars another; and star differs from star in splendor.

So will it be with the resurrection of the dead. The body that is sown is perishable, it is raised imperishable; it is sown in dishonor, it is raised in glory; it is sown in weakness, it is raised in power; it is sown a natural body, it is raised a spiritual body.

If there is a natural body, there is also a spiritual body. So it is written: "The first man Adam became a living being"; the last Adam, a life-giving spirit. The spiritual did not come first, but the natural, and after that the spiritual. The first man was of the dust of the earth; the second man is of heaven. As was the earthly man, so are those who are of the earth; and as is the heavenly man, so also are those who are of heaven. And just as we have borne the image of the earthly man, so shall we bear the image of the heavenly man.

I declare to you, brothers and sisters, that flesh and blood cannot inherit the kingdom of God, nor does the perishable inherit the imperishable. Listen, I will tell you a mystery: We will not all sleep, but we will all be changed—in a flash, in the twinkling of an eye, at the last trumpet. For the trumpet will sound, the dead will be raised imperishable, and we will be changed. For the perishable must clothe itself with the imperishable, and the mortal with immortality. When the perishable has been clothed with the imperishable, and the mortal with immortality, then the saying that is written will come true: "Death has been swallowed up in victory."

"Where, O death, is your victory?

Where, O death, is your sting?"

The sting of death is sin, and the power of sin is the law. But thanks be to God! He gives us the victory through our Lord Jesus Christ.

Source: Galatians 1:6–24, 2:1–21, from the *New International Version.* (International Bible Society, 1984). Reprinted by permission.

NONCANONICAL GOSPELS

INFANCY GOSPEL OF JAMES

Early Christians desired more information about Jesus' childhood than what is sparsely presented in the four Gospel narratives. Many childhood gospels circulated, but most of the information in these derive from two texts written about 150 CE: the Infancy Gospel of James *and the* Infancy Gospel of Thomas. *The* Infancy Gospel of James, *also called the* Protoevangelium, *or first gospel, is pseudonomously ascribed to James, the brother of Jesus, and scholars believe that its author was a non-Jewish Christian from outside Palestine. The text presents the oldest account of the early life of Mary, including her espousal to Joseph, and describes the virgin birth of Jesus. The tradition of Mary's lifelong virginity runs counter to statements in the gospels referring to Jesus' brothers. The* Infancy Gospel of James *reconciles these two traditions by presenting Joseph as a widower with children from his previous marriage. The feast of Mary's presentation in the temple (November 21) in Catholic and Orthodox traditions is based on events in the following selection.*

Mary Raised in the Temple and Joseph Chosen to Watch Over her

7. When Mary was two years old, Joachim said, "Let us bring her to the temple of the Lord, so that we may make good on the vow that we promised [i.e., to leave Mary with the priests], otherwise the Lord will be displeased with us, and will not receive our offering."

   Anna said, "Let us wait for the third year, so that the child will not look for her father or mother."

   Joachim replied, "Yes we will wait." When the child was three years old, Joachim said, "Invite the daughters of the Hebrews who are undefiled to join us, and have them each take a lamp. Have them stand with the lamps burning so that the child will not turn back, and her heart will not be captivated by the world outside the temple of the Lord." So, they did this until they reached the temple of the Lord.

   The priest then received her, kissed her, and blessed her, saying, "The Lord has magnified your name among all generations. Through you, the Lord will reveal his redemption to the people of Israel on the final days." The priest set her down on the third step of the altar, and the Lord God sent his grace down on her. She then danced with her feet, and the whole house of Israel loved her.

8. Amazed, her parents returned home, praising the Lord God because the child did not try to leave. Mary was in the temple of the Lord as if she were a dove that lived there, and she received nourishment from an angel's hand. When she was twelve years old a council of the priests was held, and they said, "Mary has reached the age of twelve years in the temple of the Lord. What then will we do with her, since she might defile the sanctuary of the Lord?" They then said to the high priest, "Stand near the altar of the Lord; go in, and pray concerning her, and whatever the Lord reveals to you, we will do."

   Wearing a robe with twelve bells, the high priest went into the holy of holies, and prayed concerning her.

An angel of the Lord then stood near him, and said, "Zacharias, Zacharias, go out and assemble the widowers among the people, and have each of them bring his staff. To whomever the Lord displays a sign, he will take her as his wife." The heralds went out through the region of Judaea, and when the trumpet of the Lord sounded, they all ran to them.

9. Joseph threw down his axe and went out to meet them. When assembled, they went to the high priest, taking with them their staffs. The high priest then took all of their staffs into the temple and prayed. When he finished his prayer, he left the temple with their staffs, and returned them to each. But there was no sign on any of them. When Joseph took his staff last, a dove flew out of it and landed on Joseph's head. The priest said to Joseph, "You have been chosen by lot to take the virgin of the Lord and watch after her. But Joseph refused, saying: I have children, I am an old man, and she is a young girl. I am afraid that I might become a laughing-stock to the people of Israel. . . .

Mary becomes Pregnant

13. When Mary was in her sixth month, Joseph returned from his construction work, and, entering his house, he discovered that she was with child. He hit his face, threw himself on the ground on sackcloth, and wept bitterly, saying: "With what face can I look upon the Lord my God? What prayer can I make about this maiden? I received her as a virgin from the temple of the Lord, yet I have not watched over her. Who is it that has hunted me down? Who has done this evil thing in my house, and defiled the virgin? Am I not reliving the story of Adam? When Adam was in prayer and singing praise, the serpent came, found Eve alone, and fully deceived her. This now has happened to me. Joseph stood up from the sackcloth, called Mary, and said, "You who were cared for by God, why have you done this and forgotten the Lord your God? Why have you lowered your soul, you who were brought up in the holy of holies, and received nourishment from the hand of an angel?"

She wept bitterly, saying, "I am innocent and have known no man."

Joseph said to her, "What, then, produced what is in your womb?"

She answered, "As the Lord my God lives, I do not know where it came from."

14. Joseph was afraid, and he left reflecting about what he should do with her. He thought, "If I conceal her sin, I will then be fighting against the law of the Lord. But if I expose her to the people of Israel, I fear that which is in her might be from an angel, and I will be guilty of handing over innocent blood to the doom of death. What then should I do with her? Well, I will secretly divorce her."

But when night came, an angel of the Lord appeared to him in a dream, saying: "Do not be afraid for this maiden, for that which is in her is of the Holy Spirit. She will give birth to a son, and you will call him Jesus, for he will save his people from their sins." Joseph awoke from sleep, and glorified the God of Israel, who had given him this grace. He then kept Mary.

Mary and Joseph face a Tribunal

15. Annas the scribe came to him, and said, "Why have you not appeared in our assembly?"

Joseph replied, "Because I was tired from my journey, and rested the next day."

Annas turned and saw that Mary was with child. He then went to the priest and said to him, "Joseph, whom you vouched for, has committed a grievous crime."

The priest asked, "How so?"

Annas replied, "He has defiled the virgin whom he received from the temple of the Lord. He has been involved with her and has not revealed it to the people of Israel."

The priest asked, "Has Joseph done this?

Annas replied, "Send officers, and you will find the virgin with child." The officers left, found it just as he had said, and brought her along with Joseph to the tribunal.

The priest said, "Mary, why have you done this? Why have you lowered your soul so much and forgotten the Lord your God? And you, Mary, who were raised in the holy of holies, received nourishment from the hand of an angel, heard the hymns, and danced before him. Why have you done this?"

Weeping bitterly, Mary replied, "As the Lord my God lives, I am pure before him, and have not been intimate with a man."

The priest said to Joseph, "Why have you done this?"

Joseph replied, "As the Lord lives, I am pure concerning her."

The priest said, "Do not bear false witness, but speak the truth. You were secretly intimate with her, and you have not revealed it to the people of Israel. You have not bowed your head before the strong hand of God, so that your seed might be blessed." Joseph was silent.

16. The priest said, "Hand over the virgin whom you received out of the temple of the Lord." Joseph burst into tears. The priest then said, "I will have you drink of the water of the ordeal of the Lord, and he shall reveal your sins to your eyes." The priest took the water, gave it to Joseph to drink, and sent him away to the hill-country. However, Joseph returned unharmed. He then gave it to Mary to drink and sent her away to the hill-country. But she too returned unharmed. Everyone wondered why sin did not appear in them. The priest said, "If the Lord God has not revealed your sins, then neither will I judge you." He then sent them away. Joseph took Mary and left for his house, rejoicing and glorifying the God of Israel.

Source: *Infancy Gospel of James* 7–9, 13–16, tr., Alexander Walker (adapted).

INFANCY GOSPEL OF THOMAS

Written about 150 CE, the Infancy Gospel of Thomas was among the most popular apocryphal writings in the early Church. The text deals with Jesus' childhood up to his twelfth year. The youthful Jesus is presented as having deadly divine powers, which he angrily uses to get his way. As he grows, though, his sense of moral responsibility develops, and he uses his powers to heal rather than harm. The story provides an interesting interpretation of the divine and human natures of Jesus: His power and knowledge are fully divine, but his conscience and emotions are human and require maturing. The text is reconstructed from several surviving manuscripts that vary; some scholars believe that the original included sayings, although only the story lines have survived.

Jesus Angered by his Playmates

1. I Thomas, an Israelite, write you this account so that all non-Jewish brothers may know the miracles performed by our Lord Jesus Christ in his infancy, which he did in our country after his birth. It began as follows.
2. This child Jesus, when five years old, was playing in the shallow area of a mountain stream. He collected the

flowing water into pools, and immediately made them clear. By his word alone he made them obey him. He softened some clay and molded twelve sparrows out of it. It was the Sabbath when he did this. There were also several other children playing with him. A certain Jew, seeing what Jesus was doing, playing on the Sabbath, rushed off and said to his father Joseph: "Your son is at a stream where he has taken clay and made twelve birds out of it, and thus has violated the Sabbath. Joseph, coming to the place and seeing him, shouted at him, "Why do you do something on the Sabbath that is unlawful? Jesus then clapped his hands, and called out to the sparrows, "Off you go!" and the sparrows flew off loudly. The Jews who saw this were amazed, and they left to report to their leaders what they had seen Jesus doing.

3. The son of Annas the scribe, who was standing with Joseph, took a willow branch and released the water that Jesus had collected. Seeing this, Jesus became angry and said to him, "You are wicked, impious, and foolish. What harm did the pool of water do to you? Now you will be dried up like a tree, and you will not produce leaves, roots, or fruit. Immediately the boy completely dried up. Jesus then left and headed back to Joseph's house. But the parents of the boy that had been dried up, lamenting that he died so young, picked him up and carried him to Joseph. They then blamed him saying, "It is your child that did this."

4. Later Jesus was again passing through the village when a boy ran up to him and hit him on the shoulder. Jesus became angry and said to him, "You will not go back the way you came." Immediately he fell down dead. Some who saw what had taken place said, "Where did this child come from, where every word of his is fulfilled?" The parents of the dead boy went to Joseph and blamed him saying, "Since your child behaves like this, you cannot live with us in this village, unless you teach him to bless and not to curse, for he is killing our children. . . .

Jesus Begins to Heal Others

14. Joseph saw that Jesus was energetic in mind and body, and again he was determined that Jesus should learn how to read. So he took Jesus away, and handed him over to another teacher. The teacher said to Joseph, "I will first teach him the Greek letters, then the Hebrew." The teacher was aware of the unfortunate situation that

Jesus created [for a previous teacher], and the teacher was afraid of him. Nevertheless, he wrote out the alphabet, and gave him all his attention for a long time, but Jesus said nothing. Jesus then said to him, "If you are really a teacher, and know the letters, tell me the power of the alpha, and I will tell you the power of the beta." The teacher was angered by this, and struck Jesus on the head. Jesus, being in pain, cursed him, and the teacher immediately became unconscious and fell to the ground on his face. Jesus returned to Joseph's house. Joseph was grieved, and instructed his mother, saying, "Do not let him go outside the door, because those who make him angry die."

15. After some time another teacher, who was a close friend of Joseph, said to him, "Bring your child to my school, and perhaps I will be able to flatter him into learning his letters." Joseph said, "If you have the courage, take him with you." The teacher took him in with great fear and agony, but the child went along peacefully. Walking boldly into the schoolroom, he found a book lying on the reading desk. He took it but did read not the letters that were in it; rather, opening his mouth, he spoke by the Holy Spirit, and taught the law to those that were standing around. A large crowd gathered near him and listened, wondering at the maturity of his teaching and the skill of his words, and that he, as a mere child, spoke the way he did. Joseph hearing of this, ran to the school worried that his teacher might once again be having problems with him. The teacher said to Joseph, "Understand, brother, that I have taken in your child as a student, but he is already full of much grace and wisdom. I beg you to take him home." When Jesus heard this, he laughed right at him and said, "Since you have spoken correctly, and observed correctly, for your sake I will cure the teacher that I struck down." Immediately the other teacher was cured. Joseph took Jesus and went home.

16. Joseph sent his son James to tie up wood and bring it home, and Jesus also followed him. When James was gathering the sticks, a snake bit James' hand. When he was filled with pain and at the point of death, Jesus came close and blew on the bite; the pain immediately stopped, and the creature burst, and instantly James was safe and sound.

17. After this the child of one of Joseph's neighbors fell sick and died, and his mother wept bitterly. Hearing the loud crying and commotion, Jesus ran quickly and found the

child dead. He then touched the infant's chest and said: "I say to you, child, do not be dead, but be alive, and be with your mother." Immediately the child looked up and laughed. Jesus said to the woman: Take him, give him milk, and remember me. Seeing this, the crowd that was standing by wondered and said, "This child is either God or an angel of God, for every word of his becomes a reality. Jesus left and played with the other children.

18. Sometime later there was a great commotion while a house was being constructed. Jesus got up and went to the place. Seeing a man lying dead, he took him by the hand, and said, "Sir, I say to you, arise, and go on with your work." Immediately the man stood up and glorified him. Seeing this, the crowd wondered and said, "This child is from heaven, for he has saved many people from death, and he will continue to save others during his whole life."

Source: *Infancy Gospel of Thomas* 1–4, 14–18, tr., Alexander Walker (adapted).

GNOSTIC GOSPEL OF THOMAS

The 1945 discovery of several dozen Christian Gnostic texts in Nag hammadi Egypt has redefined the study of early Christianity. The text manuscripts, written in the Coptic language, date from perhaps the Fourth Century CE, and may be derived from an original Greek text from the first or second century CE. The jewel in the crown of these texts is the Gospel of Thomas, *which broadens our understanding of the historical Jesus. The text is a sayings gospel insofar as it contains no story line and little dialogue. The 114 sayings are organized around particular catchwords but do not systematically develop themes. Although the text was ultimately compiled in the second century, it may be based on an original core of short sayings as early as those in any other Gospel. These, in turn, come from orally transmitted accounts of Jesus' teachings. The challenge for scholars is to identify that core amid embellishments penned by later writers. A Gnostic component of the text suggests that these are secret teachings of Jesus, knowledge of which will free one's spirit from the material world. Many of the sayings parallel those found in the four canonical Gospels. Some of the parables in Thomas are more concise and thus, perhaps, earlier than their canonical counterparts (8, 9, 57, 63, 64, 65). Many sayings are unique to this text, although they probably did not originate with Jesus (15, 17, 18, 19). Most interesting, however, are two sayings that some scholars believe originated with Jesus but that are absent from the canonical Gospels (97, 98).*

1. And he said, "Whoever discovers the meaning of these sayings won't taste death."
2. Jesus said, "Whoever seeks shouldn't stop until they find. When they find, they'll be disturbed. When they're disturbed, they'll be [...] amazed, and reign over the All."
3. Jesus said, "If your leaders tell you, 'Look, the kingdom is in heaven,' then the birds of heaven will precede you. If they tell you, 'It's in the sea,' then the fish will precede you. Rather, the kingdom is within you and outside of you. When you know yourselves, then you'll be known, and you'll realize that you're the children of the living Father. But if you don't know yourselves, then you live in poverty, and you are the poverty."
4. Jesus said, "The older person won't hesitate to ask a little seven-day-old child about the place of life, and they'll live, because many who are first will be last, and they'll become one."
5. Jesus said, "Know what's in front of your face, and what's hidden from you will be revealed to you, because there's nothing hidden that won't be revealed."
6. His disciples said to him, "Do you want us to fast? And how should we pray? Should we make donations? And what food should we avoid?"

   Jesus said, "Don't lie, and don't do what you hate, because everything is revealed in the sight of heaven; for there's nothing hidden that won't be revealed, and nothing covered up that will stay secret."
7. Jesus said, "Blessed is the lion that's eaten by a human and then becomes human, but how awful for the human who's eaten by a lion, and the lion becomes human."
8. He said, "The human being is like a wise fisher who cast a net into the sea and drew it up from the sea full of little fish. Among them the wise fisher found a fine large fish and cast all the little fish back down into the sea, easily choosing the large fish. Anyone who has ears to hear should hear!"
9. Jesus said, "Look, a sower went out, took a handful of seeds, and scattered them. Some fell on the roadside; the birds came and gathered them. Others fell on the rock; they didn't take root in the soil and ears of grain didn't rise toward heaven. Yet others fell on thorns; they choked the seeds and worms ate them. Finally, others fell on good soil; it produced fruit up toward heaven, some sixty times as much and some a hundred and twenty."

10. Jesus said, "I've cast fire on the world, and look, I'm watching over it until it blazes."

11. Jesus said, "This heaven will disappear, and the one above it will disappear too. Those who are dead aren't alive, and those who are living won't die. In the days when you ate what was dead, you made it alive. When you're in the light, what will you do? On the day when you were one, you became divided. But when you become divided, what will you do?"

12. The disciples said to Jesus, "We know you're going to leave us. Who will lead us then?"

    Jesus said to them, "Wherever you are, you'll go to James the Just, for whom heaven and earth came into being."

13. Jesus said to his disciples, "If you were to compare me to someone, who would you say I'm like?"

    Simon Peter said to him, "You're like a just angel."

    Matthew said to him, "You're like a wise philosopher."

    Thomas said to him, "Teacher, I'm completely unable to say whom you're like."

    Jesus said, "I'm not your teacher. Because you've drunk, you've become intoxicated by the bubbling spring I've measured out."

    He took him aside and told him three things. When Thomas returned to his companions, they asked, "What did Jesus say to you?"

    Thomas said to them, "If I tell you one of the things he said to me, you'll pick up stones and cast them at me, and fire will come out of the stones and burn you up."

14. Jesus said to them, "If you fast, you'll bring guilt upon yourselves; and if you pray, you'll be condemned; and if you make donations, you'll harm your spirits. If they welcome you when you enter any land and go around in the countryside, heal those who are sick among them and eat whatever they give you, because it's not what goes into your mouth that will defile you. What comes out of your mouth is what will defile you."

15. Jesus said, "When you see the one who wasn't born of a woman, fall down on your face and worship that person. That's your Father."

16. Jesus said, "Maybe people think that I've come to cast peace on the world, and they don't know that I've come to cast divisions on the earth: fire, sword, and war. Where there are five in a house, there'll be three against two and two against three, father against and son and son against father. They'll stand up and be one."

17. Jesus said, "I'll give you what no eye has ever seen, no ear has ever heard, no hand has ever touched, and no human mind has ever thought."

18. The disciples said to Jesus, "Tell us about our end. How will it come?" Jesus said, "Have you discovered the beginning so that you can look for the end? Because the end will be where the beginning is. Blessed is the one who will stand up in the beginning. They'll know the end, and won't taste death."

19. Jesus said, "Blessed is the one who came into being before coming into being. If you become my disciples and listen to my message, these stones will become your servants; because there are five trees in paradise which don't change in summer or winter, and their leaves don't fall. Whoever knows them won't taste death."

20. The disciples asked Jesus, "Tell us, what can the kingdom of heaven be compared to?" he said to them, "It can be compared to a mustard seed. Though it's the smallest of all the seeds, when it falls on tilled soil it makes a plant so large that it shelters the birds of heaven."

57. Jesus said, "My Fathers' kingdom can be compared to someone who had [good] seed. Their enemy came by night and sowed weeds among the good seed. The person didn't let anyone pull out the weeds, 'so that you don't pull out the wheat along with the weeds,' they said to them. 'On the day of the harvest, the weeds will be obvious. Then they'll be pulled out and burned.'"

63. Jesus said, "There was a rich man who had much money. He said, 'I'll use my money to sow, reap, plant, and fill my barns with fruit, so that I won't need anything.' That's what he was thinking to himself, but he died that very night. Anyone who has ears to hear should hear!"

64. Jesus said, "Someone was planning on having guests. When dinner was ready, they sent their servant to call the visitors. The servant went to the first and said, 'My master invites you.' They said, 'Some merchants owe me money. They're coming tonight. I need to go and give them instructions. Excuse me from the dinner.' The servant went to another one and said, 'My master invites you.' They said, 'I've just bought a house and am needed for the day. I won't have time.' The servant went to another one and said, 'My master invites you.' They said, 'My friend is getting married and I'm going to make dinner. I can't come. Excuse me from the dinner.' The servant went to another one and said, 'My master invites you.' They said, 'I've just bought a farm and am going to

collect the rent. I can't come. Excuse me.' The servant went back and told the master, 'The ones you've invited to the dinner have excused themselves.' The master said to their servant, 'Go out to the roads and bring whomever you find so that they can have dinner.' Buyers and merchants won't [enter] the places of my Father."

65. He said, "A [creditor] owned a vineyard. He leased it out to some sharecroppers to work it so he could collect its fruit. He sent his servant so that the sharecroppers could give him the fruit of the vineyard. They seized his servant, beat him, and nearly killed him. The servant went back and told his master. His master said, 'Maybe he just didn't know them.' he sent another servant, but the tenants beat that one too. Then the master sent his son, thinking, 'Maybe they'll show some respect to my son.' Because they knew that he was the heir of the vineyard, the sharecroppers seized and killed him. Anyone who has ears to hear should hear!"

97. Jesus said, "The Father's kingdom can be compared to a woman carrying a jar of flour. While she was walking down [a] long road, the jar's handle broke and the flour spilled out behind her on the road. She didn't know it, and didn't realize there was a problem until she got home, put down the jar, and found it empty."

98. Jesus said, "The Father's kingdom can be compared to a man who wanted to kill someone powerful. He drew his sword in his house and drove it into the wall to figure out whether his hand was strong enough. Then he killed the powerful one."

Source: *Gnostic Gospel of Thomas* 1–20, 57, 63–65, 97, 98, tr. Mark M. Mattison.

GNOSTIC GOSPEL OF MARY

The Gospel of Mary *(named after Mary Magdalene) was discovered in Egypt in 1896, and, like the* Gnostic Gospel of Thomas, *is in the Coptic language and might be based on a first or second century Greek original. Much of it is lost, and the surviving sections are presented below. It opens with the resurrected Jesus explaining to the disciples how sin results from attachment to the material world and our failure to see that matter will ultimately dissolve away. Jesus leaves, then Mary discusses a vision she had in which Jesus explained to her how the soul ascends from the corrupting material world to the divine realm. Along the soul's journey it is obstructed by four powers that rule the world, namely, Darkness, Desire, Ignorance, and Wrath. When finished Peter and Andrew have doubts about Mary's vision and question why Jesus would come to her, a woman. Levi, however, defends Mary's authority to speak on behalf of Jesus.*

[Pages 1 through 6 are missing.]

"Then will matter be destroyed, or not?"

The Savior said, "Every nature, every form, every creature exists in and with each other, but they'll dissolve again into their own roots, because the nature of matter dissolves into its nature alone. Anyone who has ears to hear should hear!"

Peter said to him, "Since you've explained everything to us, tell us one more thing. What's the sin of the world?"

The Savior said, "Sin doesn't exist, but you're the ones who make sin when you act in accordance with the nature of adultery, which is called 'sin.' That's why the Good came among you, up to the things of every nature in order to restore it within its root." Then he continued and said, "That's why you get sick and die, because you love what tricks you. Anyone who can understand should understand! "Matter gave birth to a passion that has no image because it came from what's contrary to nature. Then confusion arises in the whole body. That's why I told you to be content at heart. If you're discontented, find contentment in the presence of the various images of nature. Anyone who has ears to hear should hear!"

When the Blessed One said these things, he greeted them all and said, "Peace be with you! Acquire my peace. Be careful not to let anyone mislead you by saying, 'Look over here!' or 'Look over there!' Because the Son of Humanity exists within you. Follow him! Those who seek him will find him.

"Go then and preach the gospel about the kingdom. Don't lay down any rules beyond what I've given you, nor make a law like the lawgiver, lest you be bound by it." When he said these things, he left.

But they grieved and wept bitterly. They said, "How can we go up to the Gentiles to preach the gospel about the kingdom of the Son of Humanity? If they didn't spare him, why would they spare us?"

Then Mary arose and greeted them all. She said to her brothers and sisters, "Don't weep and grieve or let your hearts be divided, because his grace will be with you all and will protect you. Rather we should praise his greatness because he's prepared us and made us Humans."

When Mary said these things, she turned their hearts toward the Good and they started to debate the words of the Savior.

Peter said to Mary, "Sister, we know the Savior loved you more than all other women. Tell us the words of the Savior that you remember – the things which you know that we don't, and which we haven't heard."

In response Mary said, "I'll tell you what's hidden from you." So she started to tell them these words: "I saw the Lord in a vision and I said to him, 'Lord, I saw you in a vision today.' In response he said to me, 'You're blessed because you didn't waver at the sight of me. For where the mind is, there is the treasure.' I said to him, 'Lord, now does the one who sees the vision see it in the soul or in the spirit?' In response the Savior said, 'They don't see in the soul or in the spirit, but the mind which exists between the two is what sees the vision.' . . . [Pages 11 through 14 are missing.]

And Desire said, 'I didn't see you going down, but now I see you're going up. So why are you lying, since you belong to me?' In response the soul said, 'I saw you, but you didn't see me or know me. I was to you just a garment, and you didn't recognize me. 'When it said these things, it left, rejoicing greatly. Again, it came to the third power, which is called 'Ignorance.' It interrogated the soul and said, 'Where are you going? In wickedness you're bound. Since you're bound, don't judge!' And the soul said, 'Why do you judge me, since I haven't judged? I was bound, even though I haven't bound. They didn't recognize me, but I've recognized that everything will dissolve – both the things of the earth and the things of heaven.' When the soul had overcome the third power, it went up and saw the fourth power, which took seven forms: The first form is Darkness; The second, Desire; The third, Ignorance; The fourth, Zeal for Death; The fifth, the Kingdom of the Flesh; The sixth, the Foolish 'Wisdom' of Flesh; The seventh, the 'Wisdom' of Anger. These are the seven powers of Wrath. They ask the soul, 'Where do you come from, you murderer, and where are you going, conqueror of space?' In response the soul said, 'What binds me has been killed, what surrounds me has been overcome, my desire is gone, and ignorance has died. In a world I was released from a world, and in a type from a type which is above, and from the chain of forgetfulness which exists only for a time. From now on I'll receive the rest of the time of the season of the age in silence.'"

When Mary said these things, she fell silent because the Savior had spoken with her up to this point.

In response Andrew said to the brothers and sisters, "Say what you will about what she's said, I myself don't believe that the Savior said these things, because these teachings seem like different ideas."

In response Peter spoke out with the same concerns. He asked them concerning the Savior: "He didn't speak with a woman without our knowledge and not publicly with us, did he? Will we turn around and all listen to her? Did he prefer her to us?"

Then Mary wept and said to Peter, "My brother Peter, what are you thinking? Do you really think that I thought this up by myself in my heart, or that I'm lying about the Savior?"

In response Levi said to Peter, "Peter, you've always been angry. Now I see you debating with this woman like the adversaries. But if the Savior made her worthy, who are you then to reject her? Surely the Savior knows her very well. That's why he loved her more than us.

"Rather we should be ashamed, clothe ourselves with perfect Humanity, acquire it for ourselves as he instructed us, and preach the gospel, not laying down any other rule or other law beyond what the Savior said."

When Levi said these things, they started to go out to teach and to preach.

Source: *Gnostic Gospel of Mary,* tr. Mark M. Mattison.

GNOSTIC GOSPEL OF JUDAS

The Gospel of Judas *was discovered in Egypt in the late 1970s. The manuscript, written in the Coptic language, has been carbon dated at 280 CE, and, like the Gnostic Gospels of Thomas and Mary, may be derived from an original Greek text composed a century earlier. Until its discovery, all that was known of it was from the following brief description by early Church father Irenaeus (130–202 CE): "[The Cainite Gnostic sect] declare that Judas the traitor was thoroughly acquainted with these things, and that he alone, knowing the truth as no others did, accomplished the mystery of the betrayal; by him all things, both earthly and heavenly, were thus thrown into confusion. They produce a fictitious history of this kind, which they style the Gospel of Judas" (Against Heresies, 1.31). In* The Gospel of Thomas, *Jesus criticizes his disciples for their ignorance of spiritual matters, and he takes Judas aside to teach him the true meaning. God, depicted as a luminous cloud, created a hierarchy of lesser divine beings, including Saklas (i.e., the Gnostic demiurge), which in turn created the first human. Humans are of two races—or*

"generations": those like Judas with an immortal soul who will
return to the divine immortal realm, and those like the other dis-
ciples who will die on earth. At its close, Jesus instructs Judas to
inform the authorities about him, and Judas obediently complies.
The following is the concluding portion of the manuscript.

This is the secret message of judgment Jesus spoke with
Judas Iscariot over a period of eight days, three days before
he celebrated Passover. When he appeared on earth, he did
signs and great wonders for the salvation of humanity. Some
[walked] in the way of righteousness, but others walked in
their transgression, so the twelve disciples were called. He
started to tell them about the mysteries beyond the world
and what would happen at the end. Often he didn't reveal
himself to his disciples, but you'd find him in their midst as a
child. . . .

Jesus said, "[Come] and I'll teach you about the
[mysteries that no] human [will] see, because there exists
a great and boundless realm whose horizons no angelic
generation has seen, [in] which is a [great] invisible Spirit,
which no [angelic] eye has ever seen, no heart has ever com-
prehended, and it's never been called by any name. . . . Saklas
said to his angels, 'Let's create a human being after the likeness and the image.' And they fashioned Adam and his wife
Eve, who in the cloud is called 'Life,' because by this name
all the generations seek him, and each of them calls her by
their names. Now Saklas didn't [command . . .] give birth,
except [. . .] among the generations [. . .] which this [. . .] and
the [angel] said to him, 'Your life will last for a limited time,
with your children.'"

Then Judas said to Jesus, "[How] long can a person live?"

Jesus said, "Why are you amazed that the lifespans
of Adam and his generation are limited in the place he's
received his kingdom with his ruler?" Judas said to Jesus,
"Does the human spirit die?"

Jesus said, "This is how it is. God commanded Michael
to loan spirits to people so that they might serve. Then the
Great One commanded Gabriel to give spirits to the great
generation with no king – the spirit along with the soul. So
the [rest] of the souls [. . .] light [. . . the] Chaos [. . .] seek
[the] spirit within you which you've made to live in this flesh
from the angelic generations. Then God caused knowledge to
be brought to Adam and those with him, so that the kings of
Chaos and Hades might not rule over them."

[Then] Judas said to Jesus, "So what will those
generations do?"

Jesus said, "Truly I say to you, the stars complete all these things. When Saklas completes the time span that's been determined for him, their first star will appear with the generations, and they'll finish what's been said. Then they'll sleep around in my name, murder their children, and [they'll...] evil and [...] the realms, bringing the generations and presenting them to Saklas. [And] after that [...] will bring the twelve tribes of [Israel] from [...], and the [generations] will all serve Saklas, sinning in my name. And your star will [rule] over the thirteenth realm." Then Jesus [laughed]. [Judas] said, "Master, why [are you laughing at me?"]

[Jesus] answered [and said], "I'm not laughing [at you but] at the error of the stars, because these six stars go astray with these five warriors, and they'll all be destroyed along with their creations."

Then Judas said to Jesus, "What will those do who've been baptized in your name?"

Jesus said, "Truly I say [to you], this baptism [which they've received in] my name [...] will destroy the whole generation of the earthly Adam. Tomorrow they'll torture the one who bears me. Truly I [say] to you, no hand of a mortal human [will fall] upon me. Truly [I say] to you, Judas, those who offer sacrifices to Saklas [...] everything that's evil. But you'll do more than all of them, because you'll sacrifice the human who bears me. Your horn has already been raised, your anger has been kindled, your star has ascended, and your heart has [strayed]. Truly [I say to you], your last [... and] the [... the thrones] of the realm have [been defeated], the kings have grown weak, the angelic generations have grieved, and the evil [they sowed...] is destroyed, [and] the [ruler] is wiped out. [And] then the [fruit] of the great generation of Adam will be exalted, because before heaven, earth, and the angels, that generation from the realms exists. Look, you've been told everything. Lift up your eyes and see the cloud with the light in it and the stars around it. And the star that leads the way is your star."

Then Judas looked up and saw the luminous cloud, and he entered it. Those standing on the ground heard a voice from the cloud [...].

And Judas didn't see Jesus anymore. Immediately there was a disturbance among [the] Jews. [...] Their high priests grumbled because he'd gone into the guest room to pray. But some scribes were there watching closely so they could arrest him during his prayer, because they were afraid of the people, since they all regarded him as a prophet. And they approached Judas and said to him, "What are you doing here? Aren't you Jesus' disciple?" Then he answered them as they wished. Then Judas received some money and handed him over to them.

Source: *Gnostic Gospel of Judas,* tr. Mark M. Mattison.

EARLY STATEMENTS OF FAITH

BAPTISM, PRAYER, AND THE EUCHARIST: DIDACHE

Discovered in 1873, the Didache *is a manual of early Church doctrine from the Syrian Church of Antioch. Eusibius, a fourth-century bishop, notes the high value placed on the* Didache *by early churches. Although the original date of the work is disputed, scholars believe that some parts are of first-century origin and contemporaneous with the Gospels. The brief work can be divided into four parts. The opening lists a series of moral injunctions taken from various parts of the Bible. Instructions concerning baptism, fasting, and prayer ritual follow. Next, instructions are given on receiving new prophets, apostles, and Christians. Finally, a warning is given concerning the return of Jesus. Following are the instructions on ritual from the second division.*

7. Concerning Baptism. Concerning baptism, baptize in this way: After first saying everything in these Teachings, baptize in the name of the Father, and of the Son, and of the Holy Spirit, in living water. If you do not have living water, baptize in other water; and if you cannot in cold, in warm. If you do not have either, pour out water three times upon the head in the name of the Father, Son, and Holy Spirit. Before the baptism the baptizer should fast, as well as the baptized, and whoever else can. You should instruct the baptized to fast for one or two days prior.

8. Concerning Fasting and Prayer. Do not let your fasts be like those of the hypocrites who fast on Monday and Thursday. Instead, you should fast on Wednesday and Friday. Also do not pray as the hypocrites do. Instead, pray in this way as the Lord commanded in His Gospel: "Our Father who are in heaven blessed be your name. May your kingdom come. May your will be done, as in heaven, so on earth. Give us today our daily bread, and forgive our debt as we also forgive our debtors. And bring us not into temptation, but deliver us from the evil one. For yours is the power and the glory forever." Pray this way three times a day.

9. The Thanksgiving (Eucharist). Concerning the thanksgiving, give thanks in this way. First, concerning the cup: "We thank you, our Father, for the holy vine of David your servant, which you made known to us through Jesus your servant; may you be glorified forever." Concerning the broken bread: "We thank you, our Father, for the life and knowledge which you made known to us through Jesus your servant; may you be glorified forever. Just as this broken bread was scattered over the hills, and was gathered together and became one, so too let your Church be gathered together from the ends of the earth into your kingdom; for yours is the glory and the power through Jesus Christ forever." Let no one eat or drink of your Thanksgiving, except those who have been baptized to the name of the Lord; for concerning this also the Lord has said, do not give that which is holy to the dogs.

10. Prayer after Communion. After you are filled, give thanks in this way: "We thank you, holy Father, for your holy name which you caused to live in our hearts, and for the knowledge and faith and immortality, which you made known to us through Jesus your servant; may you be glorified forever. You, Master almighty, created all things for your name's sake; you gave food and drink to men for enjoyment, that they might give thanks to you. You freely gave to us spiritual food and drink and life eternal through your servant. Before all things we thank you, who are mighty. May you be exalted forever. Remember, Lord, your Church, to deliver it from all evil and to make it perfect in your love, and gather it from the four winds, sanctified for your kingdom which you have prepared for it; may you be glorified forever. Let grace come, and let this world pass away. Hosanna to the God (Son) of David! If anyone is holy, let him come; if anyone is not so, let him repent. Maranatha. Amen."

Source: Didache 7–10, tr. Matthew Brown Riddle (adapted).

APOSTLES' CREED

In the early Church, many controversies erupted over fine points of Christian theology. This often resulted in the creation of some creed that distinguished acceptable theological positions from unacceptable ones. Composed around 150 CE, the Apostles' Creed is perhaps the first of these. The controversy was gnosticism, the view that we should free our spirits from the evil material world by acquiring special knowledge. Christian Gnostics believed that God was not really the creator of the world and that Jesus could not have suffered and died because he was a spiritual being. The Apostles' Creed opposes both of these contentions. Below are two versions of the creed, the earliest version, often called "The Old Roman Symbol," as recorded by Rufinus of Aquileia (340–410), and the expanded version that Christians still use today, as first recorded by Pirmin (700–753). The name "Apostle's Creed" was given to it based on the mistaken assumption that the apostles themselves each contributed a phrase to it.

Earliest Version (390 CE)

I believe in God the Father Almighty, and in Jesus Christ, his only Son, our Lord; Who was born by the Holy Ghost of the Virgin Mary; Was crucified under Pontius Pilate and was buried; The third day he rose from the dead; He ascended into heaven; and sits on the right hand of the Father; From there he will come to judge the quick and the dead. And in the Holy Ghost; The Holy Church; The forgiveness of sins; The resurrection of the body.

Accepted Version (710 CE)

I believe in God the Father Almighty, maker of heaven and earth. And in Jesus Christ his only Son our Lord, who was conceived by the Holy Ghost, born of the virgin Mary. He suffered under Pontius Pilate, was crucified, died, and was buried; He descended into hell. The third day He rose again from the dead. He ascended into heaven and is seated at the right hand of God the Father Almighty. From there He will come to judge the living and the dead. I believe in the Holy Ghost, the holy catholic church, the communion of saints, the forgiveness of sins, the resurrection of the body, and the life everlasting. Amen.

Source: "The Apostles' Creed", tr. Philip Schaff (adapted).

NICENE CREED

The Nicene Creed emerged in response to the Arian controversy, a dispute involving the claims of a Christian priest named Arius (c. 250–336) that Christ was created by God and hence was not God himself. The Council of Nicaea was called in 325 to resolve the issue, which was decided against Arius. The Nicene Creed's exact date of origin is a matter of dispute, and at least some components of it were added in later centuries. Nevertheless, its content reflects the Council's decision against

Arianism. At a minor Church council in 589, the sentence "I believe in the Holy Ghost . . . who proceeds from the father" was expanded to read "who proceeds from the father and the son (filioque)." The issue involves whether the Holy Ghost originated from the father alone, or from both the father and the son. Known as the filioque *clause, its inclusion provoked discord with the Eastern Orthodox churches and became their rallying cry in the Great Schism of 1054. The* filioque *clause was definitively added to the creed by the Catholics at the Second Council of Lyons in 1274. Today, the Nicene Creed remains the most popular confession of faith in Catholic, Orthodox, and most Protestant liturgies, although Orthodox churches omit the* filioque *clause.*

I believe in one God, the Father Almighty, Maker of heaven and earth, of all things visible and invisible. And in one Lord Jesus Christ, the only-begotten Son of God, begotten of His Father before all worlds, God of God, Light of Light, Very God of very God, begotten, not made, being of one substance with the Father; by whom all things were made; who for us and for our salvation came down from heaven, and was incarnate by the Holy Spirit of the virgin Mary, and was made man; and was crucified also for us under Pontius Pilate; He suffered and was buried, and the third day He rose again according to the Scriptures, and ascended into heaven, and is seated at the right hand of the Father; and He will come again, with glory, to judge both the living and the dead; whose kingdom will have no end. And I believe in the Holy Spirit, the Lord and giver of life, who proceeds from the Father and the Son; who with the Father and the Son together is worshipped and glorified; who spoke by the Prophets; and I believe one holy catholic and apostolic church; I acknowledge one baptism for the remission of sins; and I look for the resurrection of the dead, and the life of the world to come. Amen.

Source: Nicene Creed, tr. Henry R. Percival.

CHALCEDON CREED

In 451, the Council of Chalcedon was called to address two controversial theological positions. A position called Nestorianism *denied the unity of Christ's divinity and humanity; in this view, Christ had two distinct personas. A contrasting position called* Monophysitism *held that Christ in fact had one nature, part of which was divine and the other part human. Against both of these positions, the Chalcedon council held that Christ has one substance but two natures: He is both fully human and fully God. This official view is reflected in the Chalcedon Creed.*

Following, then, the holy fathers, we unite in teaching all men to confess the one and only Son, our Lord Jesus Christ. This self-same one is perfect both in deity and in humanness; this self-same one is also actually God and actually man, with a rational soul and a body. He is of the same reality as God as far as his deity is concerned and of the same reality as we ourselves as far as his humanness is concerned; thus like us in all respects, sin only excepted. Before time began he was begotten of the Father, in respect of his deity, and now in these "last days," for us and on behalf of our salvation, this selfsame one was born of Mary the virgin, who is God-bearer in respect of his humanness.

We also teach that we apprehend this one and only Christ-Son, Lord, only-begotten—in two natures; and we do this without confusing the two natures, without transmuting one nature into the other, without dividing them into two separate categories, without contrasting them according to area or function. The distinctiveness of each nature is not nullified by the union. Instead, the "properties" of each nature are conserved and both natures concur in one "person" and in one reality. They are not divided or cut into two persons, but are together the one and only and only-begotten Word of God, the Lord Jesus Christ. Thus have the prophets of old testified; thus the Lord Jesus Christ himself taught us; thus the Symbol of Fathers has handed down to us.

Source: Chalcedon Creed, tr. Henry R. Percival (adapted).

CHURCH FATHERS, SAINTS, AND MYSTICS

THE MARTYRDOM OF POLYCARP

During the first three centuries CE, several Roman rulers systematically persecuted Christians. Some victims were outspoken leaders, and others became conspicuous for not participating in pagan religious rituals. In either case they were barbarically executed, as were Jesus and the Apostles before them. Stories of religious martyrs became an important part of early Christian writing, both to commemorate the tragic events and to instill a sense of religious bravery in those who might experience a similar fate. The most popular of all early stories of martyrs is that of Polycarp (c. 69–c. 155), bishop of Smyrna, who was arrested during a pagan festival for failing to participate. He was burnt to death after refusing to renounce his faith.

9. As Polycarp entered the stadium, a voice from heaven came to him and said, "Be strong, and show yourself as

a man, Polycarp." No one saw who it was that spoke to him, but our brothers who were present heard the voice. As he was brought forward, there was a great uproar when they heard that Polycarp was taken. When he came near, the proconsul asked him whether he was Polycarp. On his confessing that he was, [the proconsul] tried to persuade him to deny [Christ], saying, "Have respect for your old age," and similar things, according to their custom, [such as], "Swear by the fortune of Caesar; repent, and say, Away with the Atheists." But Polycarp, gazing with a stern expression at the crowd of wicked heathens in the stadium, and waving his hand toward them, while with groans he looked up to heaven, said, "Away with the Atheists." Then the proconsul urged him, saying, "Swear, and I will set you free; reject Christ." Polycarp stated, "For eighty six years I have served him, and he never did me any harm. How then can I blaspheme my king and my savior?" . . .

While he spoke these and many similar things, he was filled with confidence and joy. His expression was full of grace, so that not merely did he look troubled by the things said to him, but, on the contrary, the proconsul was astonished. He sent his herald to proclaim in the middle of the stadium three times, "Polycarp has confessed that he is a Christian." This proclamation having been made by the herald, the whole crowd—both of the heathen and Jews who lived in Smyrna—shouted out with uncontrollable fury, and in a loud voice, "This is the teacher of Asia, the father of the Christians, and the overthrower of our gods, he who has been teaching many not to sacrifice, or to worship the gods." Speaking this, they shouted out, asking Philip the Asiarch to set loose a lion on Polycarp. But Philip answered that it was unlawful for him to do this since the shows of wild beasts were already finished. Then it seemed good to them to unanimously shout out that Polycarp should be burnt alive. . . .

This, then, was carried into effect with greater speed than it was spoken. The crowd immediately gathered wood and sticks out of the shops and baths; the Jews especially, according to custom, eagerly assisted them with this. . . .

When he had pronounced this *amen,* and finished his prayer, those who were appointed for the purpose lit the fire. As the flame blazed in great fury, we, to whom it was given to witness it, saw a great miracle, and have been spared so that we might report to others what took place. The fire, shaping itself into the form of an arch, like the sail of a ship when filled with the wind, encompassed the body of the martyr like a circle. He appeared within it, not like flesh that is burnt, but like bread that is baked, or as gold and silver glowing in a furnace. Further, we smelled a sweet odor [coming from the fire], as if frankincense or some similar precious spices had been smoking there.

Eventually, when those wicked men saw that his body could not be consumed by the fire, they ordered an executioner to stab him with a dagger. When doing this, a dove came out of him, with a great quantity of blood that extinguished the fire. The people wondered why there should be such a difference between the unbelievers and the elect. This most admirable Polycarp was one of these, having in our own times been an apostolic and prophetic teacher, and bishop of the Catholic Church in Smyrna. For every word that came out of his mouth either has been or will yet be accomplished.

Source: *The Martyrdom of Polycarp,"* tr. Philip Schaff (adapted).

TERTULLIAN ON HERETICS

Early Christians were forced to defend their faith against attacks by both Jewish and Roman critics. Christianity was new and comparatively distinct from more ancient religious traditions and was thus frequently ridiculed by outsiders. Even within Christianity, theological disputes erupted between factions, resulting in defenses on both sides of the issue. One of early Christianity's most influential defenders was Tertullian (c. 160–c. 225), who emphasized the importance of nonrational faith when confronting the more perplexing doctrines of Christianity, such as the divine incarnation and the crucifixion of Jesus. In the selections here we find Tertullian's most famous anti-intellectual expressions: "What indeed has Athens to do with Jerusalem?" and "It is by all means to be believed, because it is absurd."

These [pagan philosophies] are "the doctrines" of men and "of demons" produced for itching ears of the spirit of this world's wisdom. This the Lord called "foolishness," and "chose the foolish things of the world" to confound even philosophy itself. For (philosophy) it is which is the material of the world's wisdom, the rash interpreter of the nature and the dispensation of God. Indeed heresies are themselves instigated by philosophy. . . . Whence spring those "fables and endless genealogies," and "unprofitable question," and "words which spread like a cancer?" From all these, when the apostle would restrain us, he expressly names philosophy as that which he would have us be on our guard against. Writing to the Colossians, he says, "See that no one charm you through philosophy and vain deceit, after the tradition of men, and contrary to the wisdom of the Holy Ghost." He had been at Athens, and had in his interviews [with us philosophers] became acquainted with that human wisdom which pretends to know the truth. However, it only corrupts truth, and is itself divided into its own diverse heresies, by the variety of its mutually repugnant sects. What indeed has Athens to do with Jerusalem? What agreement is there between the Academy and the Church? What between heretics and Christians? Our instruction comes from "the porch of Solomon," who had himself taught that "the Lord should be sought in simplicity of heart." Away with all attempts to produce a patchwork Christianity from Stoic, Platonic, and dialectic composition. We want no unnecessary disputation after possessing Christ Jesus, no inquiry after enjoying the gospel. With our faith, we desire no further belief. For this is our palmary faith, that there is nothing which we ought to believe besides....

There are, to be sure, other things also quite as foolish [as the birth of Christ], which have reference to the humiliations and sufferings of God. Or else, let them call a crucified God "wisdom." But Marcion will apply the knife to this doctrine [of the crucifixion] also, and even with greater reason. For which is more unworthy of God, which is more likely to raise a blush of shame, that God should be born, or that he should die? That he should bear the flesh, or the cross? Be circumcised, or be crucified? Be cradled, or be coffined? Be laid in a manger, or in a tomb? Talk of "wisdom!" You will be more arbitrary if you refuse to believe this also. But, after all, you will not be "wise" unless you become a "fool" to the world, by believing "the foolish things of God." Have you, then, cut away all sufferings from Christ, on the ground that, as a mere phantom, he was incapable of experiencing them?... The Son of God was crucified; I am not ashamed because men are ashamed of it. The Son of God died; it is by all means to be believed, because it is absurd. He was buried, and rose again; the fact is certain, because it is impossible. But how will all this be true in him, if he was not himself true—if he really had not in himself that which might be crucified, might die, might be buried, and might rise again?

Source: Tertullian, *The Prescription Against Heretics*, ch. 7, *On the Flesh of Christ*, ch. 5, tr. Peter Holmes.

JEROME'S PREFACE TO THE VULGATE

During the first few centuries, disorganized and conflicting Latin versions of the Christian scriptures circulated among churches. Hoping to finally put the matter in order, near the close of the fourth century Pope Damasus commissioned a scholar from Italy named Jerome (c. 342–420) to compile a definitive Latin text of the Old and New Testaments. The project took some time, but Jerome succeeded in translating most of it. His work became the foundation for the Latin Vulgate, the authoritative text of the Bible in the Roman Catholic world. The following is his Preface to the four Gospels, which was addressed to Pope Damasus in 383 CE. The issues Jerome raises here are precisely those that modern translators of the Bible must also face.

You urge me to revise the old Latin version, and, as it were, to sit in judgment on the copies of the Scriptures which are now scattered throughout the whole world. Inasmuch as they differ from one another, you would have me decide which of them agree with the Greek original. The labor is one of love, but at the same time both perilous and presumptuous; for in judging others I must be content to be judged by all. How can I dare to change the language of the world in its hoary old age, and carry it back to the early days of its infancy? Is there a man, learned or unlearned, who will not, when he takes the volume into his hands, and perceives that what he reads does not suit his settled tastes, break out immediately into violent language, and call me a forger and a profane person for having the audacity to add anything to the ancient books, or to make any changes or corrections therein?

Now there are two consoling reflections which enable me to bear the odium. First, the command is given by you who are supreme bishop; and secondly, even on the showing of those who revile, readings at variance with the early copies cannot be right. For if we are to pin our faith to the Latin texts, it is for our opponents to tell us *which;* for there are almost as many forms of texts as there are copies. If, on the other hand, we are to glean the truth from a comparison of *many,* why not go back to the original Greek and correct the mistakes introduced by inaccurate translators, and the blundering alterations of confident but ignorant critics, and, further, all that has been inserted or changed by copyists more asleep than awake? I am not discussing the Old Testament, which was turned into Greek by the Seventy elders, and has reached us by a descent of three steps.... I therefore promise in this short Preface the four Gospels only, which are to be taken in the following order, Matthew, Mark, Luke, John, as they have been revised by a comparison of the Greek manuscripts. Only early ones have been used. But to avoid any great divergences from the Latin which we are accustomed to read, I have used my pen with some restraint, and while I have corrected only such passages as seemed to convey a different meaning, I have allowed the rest to remain as they are.

Source: Jerome, Preface to *The Four Gospels,* tr. William Henry Fremantle (adapted).

AUGUSTINE'S CONFESSIONS

Perhaps the most important theologian in the history of Christianity is Augustine (354–430), bishop of the North African city of Hippo. Like Tertullian, Augustine defended Christianity against attacks by Roman pagans and Christian heretics alike. He wrote on a range of issues of Christian doctrine, and his views helped shape the direction of the religion. His most famous work is his autobiography, the Confessions, *which describes his struggle to find spiritual contentment through hedonism, through the Manichean religious cult, and finally through Christianity.*

Augustine and the Manicheans

Book 2. I will now call to mind my past foulness, and the carnal corruptions of my soul, not because I love them, but so that I may love you, God. . . . I had a desire to commit robbery, and did so. I was compelled neither by hunger, nor poverty, but through a distaste for doing right, and a desire for wickedness. I stole things that I already had, and much better. Nor did I desire to enjoy what I stole, but only the theft and sin itself. There was a pear tree close to our vineyard, heavily loaded with fruit, which was tempting neither for its color nor its flavor. Late one night, a few of us shameless young folk went to shake and rob it, having, according to our disgraceful habit, prolonged our games in the streets until then. We carried away large loads, not to eat ourselves, but to fling to pigs, having only eaten some of them. This pleased us all the more because it was not permitted. . . .

Book 3. I came to Carthage, where a cauldron of unholy loves bubbled up all around me. I was not in love as yet, but I was in love with love . . . . To love and to be loved was sweet to me, especially when I gained the enjoyment of the body of the person I loved. I contaminated the spring of friendship with the filth of sensuality, and I dimmed its luster with the hell of lustfulness. Foul and dishonorable as I was, through an excess of vanity, I nevertheless craved to be thought elegant and refined. I fell rashly, then, into the love in which I longed to be ensnared.... [In time] I directed my mind to the Holy Scriptures, so that I might see what they were ... [but] my inflated pride rejected their style, nor could the sharpness of my wit pierce their inner meaning.... I then fell among [Manichean] men proudly raving, very carnal, and verbose, in whose mouths were the snares of the devil—the lure being composed of a mixture of the syllables of your name, and of our Lord Jesus Christ, and of the Intercessor, the Holy Ghost, the Comforter....

Book 5. For nearly the whole of those nine years during which, with unstable mind, I had followed the Manicheans, I had been looking forward with great eagerness for the arrival of [the Manichean teacher] Faustus. The other members of the sect whom I had chanced to encounter, when unable to answer the questions I raised, always directed me to look forward to his coming. By discoursing with him, these, and greater difficulties if I had them, would be most easily and amply cleared away. When at last he arrived, I found him to be a man of pleasant speech, who spoke of the very same things as they themselves did, although more fluently, and in better language. But of what profit to me was the elegance of my cup-bearer, since he failed to offer me the more precious draught for which I thirsted?... When it became plain to me that he was ignorant of those arts [of rhetoric] in which I had believed him to excel, I began to despair of his clearing up and explaining all the perplexities that harassed me.

I came to Milan and went to Ambrose the bishop, known to the whole world as among the best of men.... I studiously listened to him preaching to the people, not with the proper motive, but, as it were, trying to discover whether his eloquence matched his reputation.... And while I opened my heart to admit how *skillfully* he spoke, gradually it became clear how *truly* he spoke. These things also began to appear to me to be defensible. The Catholic faith, for which I had felt nothing could be said against the attacks of the Manichaeans, I now conceived might be maintained without presumption.... So I earnestly bent my mind to see if I could possibly prove the Manichaeans guilty of falsehood.... Because these philosophers were without the saving name of Christ, I utterly refused to have them cure my fainting soul. I resolved, therefore, to be a catechumen in the Catholic Church, which my parents had commended to me, until something settled should exhibit itself to me toward which I might steer my course.

Augustine's Conversion

Book 6. When I had revealed to my mother that I was now no longer a Manichaean, though not yet a Catholic Christian, she did not leap for joy.... She replied to me that she believed in Christ, that before she departed this life, she would see me a Catholic believer.... Active efforts were made to get me a wife. I wooed, I was engaged, my mother taking the greatest pains in the matter, that when I was once married, the health-giving baptism might cleanse me.... A maiden came forward who was two years under the marriageable age, but, as she was pleasing, I waited for her.... Meanwhile my sins were multiplying. My mistress was torn from my side as an impediment to my marriage, and my heart, which clung to her, was racked, and wounded, and bleeding. She went back to Africa, vowing to God to never know another man, and leaving with me my natural son by her. But I unhappily could not imitate her and, impatient of delay, I took another mistress—since it would be two years until I was to marry my betrothed, and I was not so much a lover of marriage as a slave to lust....

Book 8. The very toys of toys, and vanities of vanities, my old mistresses, still enthralled me.... But when a profound reflection had, from the secret depths of my soul, drawn together and heaped up all my misery before the sight of my heart, there arose a mighty storm, accompanied by as mighty a shower of tears. So that I might pour forth fully with natural expressions, I left [my friend] Alypius; for it seemed to me that solitude was fitter for the business of weeping. So I retired to such a distance that even his presence could not be oppressive to me.... I threw myself down, how, I do not know, under a certain fig-tree, giving free course to my tears, and the streams of my eyes gushed out, an acceptable sacrifice to you. And, not indeed in these words, yet to this effect, I spoke to you: "But you, Lord, how long? How long, Lord? Will you be angry forever?"...

I was saying these things and weeping in the most bitter contrition of my heart, when suddenly I heard the voice, sounding like a boy or girl—I don't know which—coming from a neighboring house, chanting, and repeating, "Take up and read; take up and read." Immediately my expression changed, and I earnestly considered whether it was usual for children in any kind of game to sing these words. Nor could I remember ever to have heard the like. So, restraining the torrent of my tears, I got up, interpreting it no other way than as a command to me from heaven to open the book, and to read the first chapter that I should light upon. For I had heard that Anthony, accidentally coming in while the gospel was being read, received the admonition as if what was read were addressed to him: "Go and sell what you have, give to the poor, and you will have treasure in heaven, and come and follow me." To this oracle he was immediately converted to you. I quickly returned to the place where Alypius was sitting; for there had I put down the volume of the apostles, when I rose from there. I grasped, opened, and in silence read that paragraph on which my eyes first fell: "Not in rioting and drunkenness, not in chambering and wantonness, not in strife and envying; but put on the Lord Jesus Christ, and make no provision for the flesh, to fulfill the lusts there of." I did not read any further, nor did I need to; for instantly, as the sentence ended—by a light of security, so to speak, infused into my heart—all the gloom of doubt vanished away.

Source: Augustine, Confessions, tr. Joseph Green Pilkington (adapted).

THE RULE OF SAINT BENEDICT

Benedict of Nursia (480–547), an Italian monk within the Roman Catholic Church, is most remembered for the Rule, or list of precepts, that he created for a monastic community that he founded in southern Italy. Hailed for its balance and moderation, his Rule was adopted by monasteries throughout Western Europe, resulting in Benedict's designation as "the Father of Western Monasticism." The Rule consists of seventy-three sections; the three presented here deal with the varieties of monastic life, vows of silence, and vows of poverty.

Concerning the kinds of monks and their way of living. It is evident that there are four kinds of monks. The Cenobites are the first kind; that is, those living in a monastery, serving under a rule of an abbot. The second kind is that of the Anchorites; that is, the hermits. They are the ones who, not by the new fervor of a conversion but by the long probation of life in a monastery, have learned to fight against the devil, having already been taught by the comfort of many. In the army of their brothers, they have been well prepared for the solitary fight of the hermit. Being secure now without the consolation of others, with God's help they are able to fight with their own hand or arm against the vices of the flesh or of their thoughts.

The third and especially bad kind of monks are the Sarabaites, approved by no rule, experience being their teacher, as with the gold which is tried in the furnace. But, softened after the manner of lead, keeping faith with the world by their works, they are known through their shaved scalps to lie to God. Without any shepherd, they are shut up by twos or threes, or even alone, in sheepfolds of their own, not of the Lord's. Their law is the satisfaction of their desires, for whatever they think is good or superior, this they call holy. What they do not wish, they consider unlawful. The fourth kind of monks is called Gyratory. During their whole life they are guests, for three or four days at a time, in the cells of the different monasteries, throughout the various provinces. They are always wandering and never stationary, given over to the service of their own pleasures and the joys of the palate, and in every way worse than the Sarabaites. Concerning the most contemptable way of living of all of these monks, it is better to be silent than to speak. These things therefore being omitted, let us proceed, with God's help, to examine the best kind, the Cenobites.

Concerning silence. Let us do as the prophet says: "I said to myself, "I will watch what I do and not sin in what I say. I will hold my tongue. But as I stood there in silence— not even speaking of good things—the turmoil within me grew worse." Here the prophet shows that if one should at times, for the sake of silence, to refrain from good sayings; how much more, as a punishment for sin, should one to cease from evil words. And therefore, if anything is to be asked of the prior, let it be asked with all humility and subjection of reverence, unless one seem to speak more than is fitting. However, language that is abusive, idle or brings about laughter, we condemn in all places with a lasting prohibition: nor do we permit a disciple to open his mouth for such sayings.

Whether the monks should have anything of their own. More than anything else, this special vice is to be cut off from the monastery, root, and branch, namely, that one should presume to give or receive anything without the order of the abbot, or should have anything of his own. He should have absolutely nothing—neither a book, nor tablets, nor a pen— nothing at all. For indeed it is not allowed for the monks to have their own bodies or wills in their own power. But all things necessary they must not expect from the Father of the monastery. Nor is it allowable to have anything which the abbot did not give or permit. All things must be common to all, as it is written: "Let not any man presume or call anything his own." But if anyone will have been discovered delighting in this most evil vice, being warned once and again, if he does not amend, he will be subjected to punishment.

Source: The Rule of Saint Benedict, Sects. 1, 6, 33, tr. Ernest F. Henderson.

AQUINAS ON FAITH AND REASON

During the Middle Ages, one of the chief theological issues was the relation between faith and reason. Tertullian addressed this issue with his famous rhetorical question, "What does Athens have to do with Jerusalem?" implying that reason plays no role in matters of faith. Thomas Aquinas (1225–1274) argued to the contrary that reason can go a long way in establishing religious truths, such as the existence and nature of God. However, he argued, faith in divine revelation still is required for establishing the more particular truths of Christianity. In this selection, Aquinas explains the dual paths toward knowledge of God, the need for faith in addition to reason, and the compatibility of faith and reason.

3. The truths that we confess concerning God fall under two categories. [First] some things that are true of God are beyond all the competence of human reason, such as that God is three and one. There are other things to which even human reason can attain, such as the existence and unity of God, which philosophers have proved to a demonstration under the guidance of the light of natural reason. It is clear that there are points of absolute intelligibility in God that are altogether beyond the compass of human reason.... Human understanding cannot go so far with its natural power as to grasp God's substance, since, under the conditions of the present life, knowledge and understanding begin with the senses. Therefore, objects beyond the senses cannot be grasped by human understanding except so far as knowledge is gathered of them through the senses. But things of sense cannot lead our understanding to discover in them the essence of the divine substance, since they are effects inadequate to the power that caused them. Nevertheless [as to the second category] our understanding is thereby led to some knowledge of God, namely, of his existence and of other attributes that must necessarily be attributed to the first cause. There are, therefore, some points of intelligibility in God, accessible to human reason, and other points that altogether transcend the power of human reason...

4. It is an Advantage for the Truths of God, known by Natural Reason, to be Proposed to Humans to be

Believed on Faith. If a truth of this nature were left to the sole inquiry of reason, three disadvantages would follow. One is that the knowledge of God would be confined to few. The discovery of truth is the fruit of studious inquiry, and very many people are hindered from this. . . . Another disadvantage is that those who did arrive at the knowledge or discovery of the aforesaid truth would take a long time to gain it, because of the profundity of such truth and the many prerequisites to the study. . . . A third disadvantage is that, because of the infirmity of our judgment and the disquieting force of imagination, there is some mixture of error in most of the investigations of human reason. . . .

7. The Truth of Reason is not Contrary to the Truth of Christian Faith. The natural dictates of reason must certainly be quite true: it is impossible to think of their being otherwise. Nor again is it permissible to believe that the tenets of faith are false, being so evidently confirmed by God. Since therefore falsehood alone is contrary to truth, it is impossible for the truth of faith to be contrary to principles known by natural reason. Whatever is put into the disciple's mind by the teacher is contained in the knowledge of the teacher, unless the teacher is teaching dishonestly, which would be a wicked thing to say about God. But the knowledge of principles naturally known is put into us by God, since God himself is the author of our nature. Therefore these principles also are contained in the divine wisdom. Whatever therefore is contrary to these principles is contrary to divine wisdom, and cannot be of God. . . .

8. The Relation of Human Reason to the first Truth of Faith. Things of the senses, from which human reason takes its beginning toward knowledge, retain in themselves some trace of imitation of God, insofar as they exist and are good. Yet this trace is so imperfect that it proves wholly insufficient to declare the substance of God himself.

Source: Thomas Aquinas, *Summa Contra Gentiles,* Book 1, chs. 3, 4, 7, 8. tr. Joseph Ricaby (adapted).

TERESA OF AVILA ON THE PRAYER OF UNION

Teresa of Avila (1515–1582) was a Spanish mystic within the Roman Catholic Church, who at age 19, entered a Carmelite convent, a monastic order devoted to contemplation. She reported having visions and raptures; in the most famous of these, an angel pierced her heart with a flaming arrow, which, when removed, left her with a love for God. In her book Interior Castle *(1577), she explains the different stages of spiritual development with the metaphor of seven sets of mansions. The mystic enters the castle door through prayer and then roams the mansions' millions of rooms at will. The first few mansions involve ordinary prayer, but the fifth one is more mystical and involves a Prayer of Union by which one's soul is possessed by God. In the following selection, she explains the effects of this union using the analogy of a silkworm. The silkworm starts from a tiny egg that feeds on mulberry leaves, spins a cocoon, and emerges as a butterfly. The silkworm represents the soul, its nourishment is the Church, the silk house is Christ, and the spinning of the cocoon is the prayer of union. Thus, the union experience, which does not last even a half hour, transforms the mystic, and the new "butterfly" feels like a stranger in its new world.*

You have heard how wonderfully silk is made—in a way that God alone could plan—how it all comes from an egg resembling a tiny grain of pepper. Not having seen it myself, I only know of it by hearsay, so if the facts are inaccurate the fault will not be mine. When, in the warm weather, the mulberry trees come into leaf, the little egg which was lifeless before its food was ready, begins to live. The caterpillar nourishes itself on the mulberry leaves until, when it has grown large, people place near it small twigs upon which, of its own accord, it spins silk from its tiny mouth until it has made a narrow little cocoon in which it buries itself. Then this large and ugly worm emerges from the cocoon as a lovely little white butterfly.

If we had not seen this but had only heard of it as an old legend, who could believe it? Could we persuade ourselves that insects so utterly without the use of reason as a silkworm or a bee would work with such industry and skill in our service that the poor little silkworm loses its life over the task? This would be enough for a short meditation, sisters, without my adding more, for you may learn from it the wonders and the wisdom of God. Imagine if we knew the properties of all things. It is most profitable to ponder over the grandeurs of creation and to exult in being the brides of such a wise and mighty King.

Let us return to our subject. The silkworm symbolizes the soul which begins to live when, ignited by the Holy Spirit, it begins using the ordinary help given by God to everyone, and applies the remedies left by Him in His Church, such as regular confession, religious books, and sermons. These are the cures for a soul that is dead in its carelessness and sins and is liable to fall into temptation. Then it comes to life and continues nourishing itself on this food and on devout meditation until it has attained full life. This is the essential point, for I attach no importance to the rest. When the silkworm is full-grown, as I told you in the first part of this chapter, it begins to spin silk and to build the house in which it will die. By this house, when speaking of the soul, I mean Christ. I think I read or heard somewhere, either that our life is hid in Christ, or in God (which means the same thing) or that Christ is our life. It makes little difference to my meaning which of these quotations is correct.

This shows, my daughters, how much, with God's help, we can do to prepare this home for ourselves, toward making Him our dwelling-place as He is in the prayer of union. You may think that I mean that we can take away from or add something to God when I say that He is our home, and that we can make this home and dwell in it by our own power. Indeed we can. While we can neither deprive God of anything nor add anything to Him, yet we can take away from and add to ourselves, like the silkworms. The little we can do will hardly have been accomplished when this insignificant work of ours, which amounts to nothing at all, will be united by God to His greatness and thus enhanced with such immense value that our Lord Himself will be the reward of our toil. Although He has had the greatest share in it, He will join our small pains to the bitter sufferings He endured for us and make them one.

Forward then, my daughters! Hurry with your work and build the little cocoon. Let us renounce self-love and self-will, care for nothing earthly, do penance, pray, humble ourselves, be obedient, and perform all the other good works of which you know. Act as you know you should; you have been taught your responsibilities. Die! Die as the silkworm does when it has fulfilled the purpose of its creation, and you will see God and be immersed in His greatness, just as the little silkworm is enveloped in its cocoon. Understand that when I say "you will see God," I mean in the manner described, in which He displays Himself in this kind of union.

Now let us see what happens to the "silkworm," for everything I have been saying leads to this. Through this prayer, as soon as the soul has become entirely dead to the world, it emerges like a lovely little white butterfly! Oh, how great God is! How beautiful the soul is after having been immersed in God's grandeur and united closely to Him for such a short time! Indeed, I do not think it is ever as long as half an hour. Truly, the spirit will not recognize itself since it is as different from what it was as is the white butterfly from the repulsive caterpillar. It does not know how it can have deserved so great a good, or rather, from where this grace came which it well knows it does not deserve. The soul desires to praise our Lord God and yearns to sacrifice itself and die a thousand deaths for Him. It feels an unconquerable desire for great crosses and would like to perform the most severe penances. It longs for solitude and for all people to know God. It is bitterly grieved at seeing people offend Him. I will describe these things more fully in the next mansion; there they are of the same nature, yet in a more advanced state the effects are far stronger. For, as I told you, once the soul has received this assistance from God, it strives to make more progress, and it will experience great things.

Source: Teresa of Avila, *Interior Castle,* Fifth Mansion, ch. 2:1–6, tr. Benedict Zimmerman (adapted).

PROTESTANT STATEMENTS OF FAITH

LUTHERANS: AUGSBURG CONFESSION

As Protestant Christian Churches throughout Europe took issue with the Roman Catholic Church, they created confessions of faith that defined their principal theological tenets. Among the first of these was the Augsburg Confession, *written in part by Martin Luther (1483–1546) in 1530. Even today it is a foundational statement for most Lutheran denominations, and Lutheran clergy take an oath by it upon ordination. In spite of Luther's harsh attacks on core Catholic doctrine, the original twenty-one articles of the Augsburg Confession highlight the similarities between Lutheran Protestants and Catholics, rather than the differences. Seven articles added later discuss Catholic abuses. The selected articles have a distinctively Lutheran tone.*

Original Articles

Article 4. Of Justification. They [i.e., the Lutheran Churches] also teach that men cannot be justified before God by their own strength, merits, or works, but are freely justified for Christ's sake, through faith, when they believe that they are received into favor, and that their sins are forgiven for Christ's sake, who, by His death, has made satisfaction for our sins. This faith God imputes for righteousness in His sight. Rom. 3 and 4.

Article 7. Of the Church. Also they teach that one holy Church is to continue forever. The Church is the congregation of saints, in which the Gospel is rightly taught and the Sacraments are rightly administered. And to the true unity of the Church it is enough to agree concerning the doctrine of the Gospel and the administration of the Sacraments. Nor is it necessary that human traditions, that is, rites or ceremonies, instituted by men, should be everywhere alike. As Paul says: One faith, one Baptism, one God and Father of all, etc. Eph. 4, 5, 6.

Article 10. Of the Lord's Supper. Of the Supper of the Lord they teach that the Body and Blood of Christ are truly present, and are distributed to those who eat the Supper of the Lord; and they reject those that teach otherwise.

Article 11. Of Confession. Of Confession they teach that Private Absolution ought to be retained in the churches, although in confession an enumeration of all sins is not necessary. For it is impossible according to the Psalm: Who can understand his errors? Ps. 19, 12.

Article 21. Of the Worship of the Saints. Of the Worship of Saints they teach that the memory of saints may be set before us, that we may follow their faith and good works, according to our calling, as the Emperor may follow the example of David in making war to drive away the Turk from his country. For both are kings. But the Scripture teaches not the invocation of saints or to ask help of saints, since it sets before us the one Christ as the Mediator, Propitiation, High Priest, and Intercessor. He is to be prayed to, and has promised that He will hear our prayer; and this worship He approves above all, to wit, that in all afflictions He be called upon, 1 John 2, 1: If any man sin, we have an Advocate with the Father, etc.

Added Articles Against Catholic Abuses

Article 23. Of the Marriage of Priests. There has been common complaint concerning the examples of priests who were not chaste. For that reason also Pope Pius is reported to have said that there were certain causes why marriage was taken away from priests, but that there were far weightier ones why it ought to be given back; for so Platina writes. Since, therefore, our priests were desirous to avoid these open scandals, they married wives, and taught that it was lawful for them to contract matrimony.

Article 27. On Monastic Vows. What is taught on our part concerning Monastic Vows, will be better understood if it be remembered what has been the state of the monasteries, and how many things were daily done in those very monasteries, contrary to the Canons. In Augustine's time they were free associations. Afterward, when discipline was corrupted, vows were everywhere added for the purpose of restoring discipline, as in a carefully planned prison. Gradually, many other observances were added besides vows. And these fetters were laid upon many before the lawful age, contrary to the Canons.

Article 28. Of Ecclesiastical Power. There has been great controversy concerning the Power of Bishops, in which some have awkwardly mixed up the power of the Church and the power of the sword. From this confusion very great wars and disorders have resulted, while the Pontiffs, emboldened by the power of the Keys, not only have instituted new services and burdened consciences with reservation of cases and ruthless excommunications, but have also undertaken to transfer the kingdoms of this world, and to take the Empire from the Emperor. These wrongs have long since been rebuked in the Church by learned and godly men. Therefore our teachers, for the comforting of men's consciences, were constrained to show the difference between the power of the Church and the power of the sword, and taught that both of them, because of God's commandment, are to be held in reverence and honor, as the chief blessings of God on earth.

Source: Augsburg Confession, in *Triglot Concordia: The Symbolical Books of the Evangelical Lutheran Church* (St. Louis: Concordia Publishing House, 1921).

ANGLICANS: THIRTY-NINE ARTICLES OF RELIGION

Between 1534 and 1563—a particularly volatile period of British history—the Church of England moved toward Protestantism. In 1571, during the reign of Queen Elizabeth, Parliament enacted Thirty-Nine Articles of Religion, which, influenced by Calvinist theology, defined the new denomination. Clergy today in the Church of England are required to assent to the Thirty-Nine Articles, and the Articles of Religion in other Anglican churches— such as the Episcopalian Church in the United States—are based on these. Since 1784, Methodist churches have followed Twenty-Four Articles of Religion taken from these. The selections here reflect Anglican views of Church hierarchy, rejecting the papacy and establishing the British monarch as the Church's head.

Article 19: Of the Church. The visible Church of Christ is a congregation of faithful men, in which the pure word of God is preached and the sacraments be duly ministered according to Christ's ordinance in all those things that of necessity are requisite to the same. As the Church of Jerusalem, Alexandria, and Antioch have erred: so also the Church of Rome hath erred, not only in their living and manner of ceremonies, but also in matters of faith.

Article 23: Of Ministering in the Congregation. It is not lawful for any man to take upon him the office of public preaching or ministering the sacraments in the congregation, before he be lawfully called and sent to execute the same. And those we ought to judge lawfully called and sent, which be chosen and called to this work by men who have public authority given unto them in the congregation to call and send ministers into the Lord's vineyard.

Article 37: Of the Civil Magistrates. The Queen's Majesty hath the chief power in this realm of England and other her dominions, unto whom the chief government of all estates of this realm, whether they be ecclesiastical or civil, in all causes doth appertain, and is not nor ought to be subject to any foreign jurisdiction.

Where we attribute to the Queen's Majesty the chief government, by which titles we understand the minds of some slanderous folks to be offended, we give not to our princes the ministering either of God's word or of sacraments, the which thing the Injunctions also lately set forth by Elizabeth our Queen doth most plainly testify: but only that prerogative which we see to have been given always to all godly princes in Holy Scriptures by God himself, that is, that they should rule all estates and degrees committed to their charge by God, whether they be temporal, and restrain with the civil sword the stubborn and evil-doers.

The Bishop of Rome hath no jurisdiction in this realm of England. The Laws of the realm may punish Christian men with death for heinous and grievous offences.

It is lawful for Christian men at the commandment of the Magistrate to wear weapons and serve in the wars.

Source: "Articles of Religion," from The Book of Common Prayer (London: Bagster, 1855).

PRESBYTERIANS: WESTMINSTER CONFESSION

At the beckoning of the British Parliament, the Westminster Confession was created in 1646 by churches in England that followed the reformed theology of John Calvin (1509–1546). Although the Anglican Church abandoned it shortly afterward, the Confession was adopted by the Scottish Parliament in 1649, making it a cornerstone of Presbyterianism. The Confession also was adopted in modified form by other Protestant denominations throughout Europe and America. The chapters presented here reflect the distinctively Calvinistic points of the Confession.

Chapter 6. Of the Fall of Man, of Sin, and of the Punishment Thereof. 1. Our first parents, being seduced by the subtlety and temptation of Satan, sinned in eating the forbidden fruit. This their sin God was pleased, according to his wise and holy counsel, to permit, having purposed to order it to his own glory. 2. By this sin they fell from their original righteousness, and communion with God, and so became dead in sin, and wholly defiled in all the faculties and parts of soul and body. 3. They being the root of all mankind, the guilt of this sin was imputed, and the same death in sin and corrupted nature conveyed to all their posterity, descending from them by ordinary generation. 4. From this original corruption, whereby we are utterly indisposed, disabled, and made opposite to all good, and wholly inclined to all evil, do proceed all actual transgressions. 5. This corruption of nature, during this life, doth remain in those that are regenerated: and although it be through Christ pardoned and mortified, yet both itself, and all the motions thereof, are truly and properly sin. 6. Every sin, both original and actual, being a transgression of the righteous law of God, and contrary thereunto, doth, in its own nature, bring guilt upon the sinner, whereby he is bound over to the wrath of God, and curse of the law, and so made subject to death, with all miseries spiritual, temporal, and eternal. . . .

Chapter 10. Of Effectual Calling. 1. All those whom God hath predestinated unto life, and those only, he is pleased, in his appointed and accepted time, effectually to call, by his Word and Spirit, out of that state of sin and death, in which they are by nature, to grace and salvation by Jesus Christ; enlightening their minds spiritually and savingly, to understand the things of God; taking away their heart of stone, and giving unto them a heart of flesh; renewing their wills, and by his almighty power determining them to that which is good, and effectually drawing them to Jesus Christ, yet so as they come most freely, being made willing by his grace. 2. This effectual call is of God's free and special grace alone, not from any thing at all foreseen in man, who is altogether passive therein, until, being quickened and renewed by the Holy Spirit, he is thereby enabled to answer this call, and to embrace the grace offered and conveyed in it. 3. Elect infants, dying in infancy, are regenerated and saved by Christ through the Spirit, who worketh when, and where, and how he pleaseth. So also are all other elect persons, who are incapable of being outwardly called by the ministry of the Word. 4. Others, not elected, although they may be called by the ministry of the Word, and may have some common operations of the Spirit, yet they never truly come to Christ, and therefore cannot be saved; much less can men, not professing the Christian religion, be saved in any other way whatsoever than by Christ, be they never so diligent to frame their lives according to the light of nature, and the law of that religion they do profess; and to assert and maintain that they may is without warrant of the World of God. . . .

Chapter 17. Of the Perseverance of the Saints. 1. They whom God hath accepted in his Beloved, effectually called and sanctified by his Spirit, can neither totally nor finally fall away from the state of grace; but shall certainly persevere therein to the end, and be eternally saved. 2. This perseverance of the saints depends, not upon their own free will, but upon the immutability of the decree of election, flowing from the free and unchangeable love of God the Father; upon the efficacy of the merit and intercession of Jesus Christ; the abiding of the Spirit and of the seed of God within them; and the nature of the covenant of grace: from all which ariseth also the certainty and infallibility thereof. 3. Nevertheless they may, through the temptations of Satan and of the world, the prevalency of corruption remaining in them, and the neglect of the means of their preservation, fall into grievous sins; and for a time continue therein: whereby they incur God's displeasure, and grieve his Holy Spirit; come to be deprived of some measure of their graces and comforts; have their hearts hardened, and their consciences wounded; hurt and scandalize others, and bring temporal judgments upon themselves.

Source: *The Westminster Confession of Faith* (Edinburgh: T&T Clark, 1882).

BAPTISTS: FIRST LONDON BAPTIST CONFESSION OF FAITH

In sixteenth-century England, a group of independent churches emerged based on the conviction that local congregations should be free from the authority of larger governing bodies. By their very nature, these congregations were diverse, formulating their own practices and theology. In 1608, former

Anglican minister John Smyth (1554–1612) founded the first Baptist church in Amsterdam. Smyth and his followers moved back to England, establishing Baptist churches there. After his untimely death from tuberculosis, Baptists split into two groups: General Baptists, who believed that Christ died for all people, and Particular Baptists, who held that he died only for the elect. In 1643, Particular Baptists in London created a confession of faith. Unlike later Baptist confessions, which were modifications of the Westminster Confession, this one has a distinct content. The following selections, taken from the 1646 edition of this Confession, highlight key points of Baptist theology, and Article 21 specifically articulates the position of the Particular Baptists.

21. Jesus Christ by His death did purchase salvation for the elect that God gave unto Him: These only have interest in Him, and fellowship with Him, for whom He makes intercession to His Father in their behalf, and to them alone doth God by His Spirit apply this redemption; as also the free gift of eternal life is given to them, and none else. . . .

25. The preaching of the gospel to the conversion of sinners, is absolutely free; no way requiring as absolutely necessary, any qualifications, preparations, or terrors of the law, or preceding ministry of the law, but only and alone the naked soul, a sinner and ungodly, to receive Christ crucified, dead and buried, and risen again; who is made a prince and a Savior for such sinners as through the gospel shall be brought to believe on Him. . . .

36. Being thus joined, every [local] church hath power given them from Christ, for their well-being, to choose among themselves persons for elders and deacons, being qualified according to the word, as those which Christ hath appointed in His testament, for the feeding, governing, serving, and building up of His Church; and that none have any power to impose on them either these or any other. . . .

39. Baptism is an ordinance of the New Testament, given by Christ, to be dispensed upon persons professing faith, or that are made disciples; who upon profession of faith, ought to be baptized, and after to partake of the Lord's Supper. . . .

42. Christ hath likewise given power to His Church to receive in, and cast out, any member that deserves it; and this power is given to every congregation, and not to one particular person, either member or officer, but in relation to the whole body, in reference to their faith and fellowship.

Source: *Confession of Faith of Seven Congregations or Churches of Christ in London* (London: 1646).

CONGREGATIONALISTS: SAVOY DECLARATION OF FAITH AND ORDER

In addition to the Baptists, another group of independent churches in England was the Congregationalists. In 1658, representatives from about 120 of these churches met in Savoy Palace in an effort to unify their congregations. Modifying the Westminster Confession, they created the Savoy Declaration of Faith and Order. The selection here is one of their two principal additions to the Westminster Confession, which asserts the right of a congregation to govern itself.

The Institution of Churches, and the Order Appointed in Them by Jesus Christ. 1. By the appointment of the Father all power for the calling, institution, order, or government of the Church, is invested in a supreme and sovereign manner in the Lord Jesus Christ, as King and Head thereof. 2. In the execution of this power wherewith he is so entrusted, the Lord Jesus calleth out of the world unto communion with himself, those that are given unto him by his Father, that they may walk before him in all the ways of obedience, which he prescribeth to them in Word. 3. Those thus called (through the ministry of the Word by his Spirit) he commandeth to walk together in particular societies or churches, for their mutual edification, and the due performance of that public worship, which he requireth of them in this world. 4. To each of these churches thus gathered, according to his mind declared in his Word, he hath given all that power and authority, which is any way needful for their carrying on that order in worship and discipline, which he hath instituted for them to observe, with commands and rules for the due and right exerting and executing of that power. 5. These particular churches thus appointed by the authority of Christ, and entrusted with power from him for the ends before expressed, are each of them as unto those ends, the seat of that power which he is pleased to communicate to his saints or subjects in this world, so that as such they receive it immediately from himself. 6. Besides these particular churches, there is not instituted by Christ any church more extensive or catholic entrusted with power for the administration of his ordinances, or the execution of any authority in his name. 7. A particular church gathered and completed according to the mind of Christ, consists of officers and members. The Lord Christ having given to his called ones (united according to his appointment in church-order) liberty and power to choose persons fitted by the Holy Ghost for that purpose, to be over them, and to minister to them in the Lord. . . .

Source: *Declaration of Faith and Order* (London: J. P., 1659).

RESTORATIONISTS: CAMPBELL'S THIRTEEN PROPOSITIONS

Restoration Movement emerged in America in the early nineteenth century during the Second Great Awakening. The movement's founders, Barton Stone (1772–1844) and Thomas Campbell (1763–1854), shared the conviction that the entire christian church needs to be restored to function of the early church as described in the New Testament. Congregations that were part of this movement go by various names, such as Churches of Christ, Christian Churches, and Disciples of Christ. While these churches resist creeds, believing that they divide Christians, Thomas Campbell devised a list of thirteen propositions to help modern christian communities return to the original ways of the early church, and "take up things just as the Apostles left them" as Campbell words it. The following from Declaration and Address (1809).

Proposition 1. That the church of Christ upon earth is essentially, intentionally, and constitutionally one; consisting of all those in every place that profess their faith in Christ and obedience to him in all things according to the scriptures, and that manifest the same by their tempers and conduct, and of none else as none else can be truly and properly called christians.

2. That although the church of Christ upon earth must necessarily exist in particular and distinct societies, locally separate one from another; yet there ought to be no schisms, no uncharitable divisions among them. . . .
3. That in order to this, nothing ought to be inculcated upon christians as articles of faith; nor required of them as terms of communion; but what is expressly taught, and enjoined upon them, in the word of God. . . .
4. That although the scriptures of the Old and New Testament are inseparably connected, . . . the New Testament is as perfect a constitution for the worship, discipline, and government of the New Testament church, and as perfect a rule for the particular duties of its members; as the Old Testament was for the worship discipline and government of the Old Testament church, and the particular duties of its members.

5. That with respect to the commands and ordinances of our Lord Jesus Christ, where the scriptures are silent, as to the express time or manner of performance, if any such there be; no human authority has power to interfere, in order to supply the supposed deficiency, by making laws for the church . . . .

6. That although inferences and deductions from scripture premises, when fairly inferred, may be truly called the doctrine of God's holy word: yet are they not formally binding upon the consciences of christians farther than they perceive the connection, and evidently see that they are so; for their faith must not stand in the wisdom of men; but in the power and veracity of God. . . .

7. That although doctrinal exhibitions of the great system of divine truths, and defensive testimonies in opposition to prevailing errors, be highly expedient; and the more full and explicit they be, for those purposes, the better; yet as these must be in a great measure the effect of human reasoning, and of course must contain many inferential truths, they ought not to be made terms of christian communion. . . .

8. That as it is not necessary that persons should have a particular knowledge or distinct apprehension of all divinely revealed truths in order to entitle them to a place in the church; . . . the way of salvation thro' Jesus Christ, accompanied with a profession of their faith in, and obedience to him, in all things according to his word, is all that is absolutely necessary to qualify them for admission into his church.

9. That all that are enabled, thro' grace, to make such a profession, and to manifest the reality of it in their tempers and conduct, should consider each other as the precious saints of God, should love each other as brethren. . . .

10. That division among christians is a horrid evil, fraught with many evils. It is anti-christian, as it destroys the visible unity of the body of Christ. . . . In a word, it is productive of confusion, and of every evil work. . . .

Source: Thomas Campbell, *Declaration and Address* (Washington PA: Brown and Sample, 1809).

ASSEMBLIES OF GOD: STATEMENT OF FUNDAMENTAL TRUTHS

The Pentecostal movement began around 1900 through the ministry of Charles Parham (1873–1929), who emphasized baptism of the Holy Spirit and speaking in tongues. In 1974, several independent Pentecostal congregations formed the Assemblies of God denomination. Pentecostals initially resisted creeds, but theological disputes prompted the General Council of the Assemblies of God to create a Statement of Fundamental Truths *in 1916. Of the seventeen statements, the more uniquely Pentecostal ones are presented here.*

5. The Promise of the Father. All believers are entitled to, and should ardently expect, and earnestly seek the promise of the Father, the baptism in the Holy Ghost and fire, according to the command of the lord Jesus Christ. This was the normal experience of all in the early Christian church. With it comes the enduement of power for life and service. The bestowment of the gifts and their uses in the work of the ministry. Luke 24:49; Acts 1:4, 1:8; 1 Cor. 12:1–31.

6. The Full Consummation of the Baptism in the Holy Ghost. The full consummation of the baptism of believers in the Holy Ghost and fire, is indicated by the initial sign of speaking in tongues, as the spirit of God gives utterance. Acts 2:4. This wonderful experience is distinct from and subsequent to the experience of the new birth. Acts 10:44–46; 15:8,9.

12. Divine Healing. Deliverance from sickness is provided for in the atonement, and is the privilege of all believers. Isa. 53:4,5; Matth. 8:16,17.

14. The Blessed Hope. The Resurrection of those who have fallen asleep in Christ. The rapture of believers, which are alive and remain, and the translation of the true church, this is the blessed hope set before all believers. 1 Thess. 4:16–17; Rom. 8:23; Tit. 2:13.

15. The Imminent Coming and Millennial Reign of Jesus. The premillennial and imminent coming of the Lord to gather his people unto himself, and to judge the world in righteousness while reigning on the earth for a thousand years is the expectation of the true church of Christ.

16. The Lake of Fire. The devil and his angles, the beast and false prophet, and whosoever is not found written in the book of Life, the fearful and unbelieving, and abominable, and murderers and whoremongers, and sorcerers, and idolators and all liars shall be consigned to everlasting punishment in the lake which burneth with fire and brimstone, which is the second death.

17. The New Heavens and New Earth. We look for new heaven and a new earth wherein dwelleth righteousness. 2 Pet. 3:13; Rev. 1 and 22.

Source: "A Statement of Fundamental Truths," General Council of the Assemblies of God, October 2–7, 1916.

CATHOLIC DOCUMENTS

THE COUNCIL OF TRENT

Held between the years 1545 and 1563, the Council of Trent was the nineteenth ecumenical council recognized by the Catholic Church, and was initiated at the insistence of Holy Roman Emperor Charles V to help bridge the gap between Catholics and Protestants. Although Protestant representatives attended some of the sessions, the end result of the Council was the reaffirmation of Catholicism's doctrines that had triggered the Protestant Reformation to begin with. The Council of Trent marks the beginning of a period of Church history known as the Counter-Reformation during which time the Catholic Church combated the Protestant doctrine and the advance of Protestantism in Europe and elsewhere. The selections that follow address several of the most central issues that divide Catholicism from Protestantism, namely, transubstantiation, purgatory, religious images, and indulgences.

> *On Transubstantiation.* Because Christ, our Redeemer, declared that which He offered under the species of bread to be truly His own body, therefore has it ever been a firm belief in the Church of God, and this holy Synod does now declare it anew, that, by the consecration of the bread and of the wine, a conversion is made of the whole substance of the bread into the substance of the body of Christ our Lord, and of the whole substance of the wine into the substance of His blood. This conversion is, by the holy Catholic Church, suitably and properly called Transubstantiation.
>
> *On Purgatory.* The Catholic Church, instructed by the Holy Ghost, has, from the sacred writings and the ancient tradition of the Fathers, taught, in sacred councils, and very recently in this ecumenical Synod, that there is a Purgatory, and that the souls there detained are helped by the prayers of the faithful, but principally by the acceptable sacrifice of the altar. Accordingly, the holy Synod commands to bishops that they diligently endeavor that the sound doctrine concerning Purgatory, transmitted by the holy Fathers and sacred councils, be believed, maintained, taught, and everywhere proclaimed by the faithful of Christ. But let the more difficult and subtle questions, which tend not to edification, and from which for the most part there is no increase

of piety, be excluded from popular discourses before the uneducated multitude. In like manner, such things as are uncertain, or which labor under an appearance of error, let them not allow to be made public and so treated. While those things which tend to a certain kind of curiosity or superstition, or which savor of filthy lucre, let them prohibit as scandals and stumbling-blocks of the faithful. But let the bishops take care that the prayers of the faithful who are living, that is, the sacrifices of masses, prayers, alms, and other works of piety, which have been customarily performed by the faithful for the other faithful departed, be piously and devoutly performed, in accordance with the institutes of the church. Whatever is due on their behalf, from the endowments of testators, or in other ways, shall be discharged, not in a thoughtless manner, but diligently and accurately, by the priests and ministers of the church, and others who are bound to render this service.

On Sacred Images. The images of Christ, of the Virgin Mother of God, and of the other saints, are to be had and retained particularly in temples. Due honor and veneration are to be given them, not that any divinity or virtue is believed to be in them on account of which they are to be worshipped; or that anything is to be asked of them; or, that trust is to be reposed in images, as was of old done by the Gentiles who placed their hope in idols. But [honor and veneration are given to them] because the honor which is shown them is referred to the prototypes which those images represent. Accordingly, by the images which we kiss, and before which we uncover the head, and prostrate ourselves, we adore Christ. And we venerate the saints, whose likeness they bear, as, by the decrees of Councils, and especially of the second Synod of Nicaea, has been defined against the opponents of images.

On Indulgences. The power of conferring Indulgences was granted by Christ to the Church, and she has, even in the most ancient times, used that power, delivered to her by God. The sacred Holy Synod teaches, and commands, that the use of Indulgences, for the Christian people most salutary, and approved of by the authority of sacred Councils, is to be retained in the Church. It condemns with anathema those who either assert that they are useless, or who deny that there is in the Church the power of granting them. In granting them, however, it desires that, in accordance with the ancient and approved custom in the Church, moderation be observed to help prevent ecclesiastical discipline from being weakened by excessive practice. And being desirous that the abuses which have crept therein, and by occasion of which this honorable name of Indulgences is blasphemed by heretics, be amended and corrected, it ordains generally by this decree, that all evil gains for the obtaining thereof (from which source a most prolific cause of abuses among the Christian people has been derived) be wholly abolished. But as regards the other abuses which have proceeded from superstition, ignorance, irreverence, or from whatever other source, since, by reason of the manifold corruptions in the places and provinces where the said abuses are committed, they cannot conveniently be specially prohibited. It commands all bishops, diligently to collect, each in his own church, all abuses of this nature, and to report them in the first provincial Synod, that, after having been reviewed by the opinions of the other bishops also, they may forthwith be referred to the Sovereign Roman Pontiff, by whose authority and prudence that which may be expedient for the universal Church will be ordained; that this the gift of holy Indulgences may be dispensed to all the faithful, piously, holily, and incorruptly.

Source: Council of Trent, Sessions 13, 25, tr. James Waterworth.

POPE LEO XIII ON THE CONDITION OF LABOR: RERUM NOVARUM

Papal encyclicals are letters written by Popes of the Roman Catholic Church to their bishops on issues of theological importance, and in recent times they have become the most frequently used venues for Papal teaching. Although the Catholic Church does not recognize encyclicals as infallible statements of papal authority, it nevertheless expects believers to give internal religious assent to their teachings. One of the most famous Papal encyclicals is by Pope Leo XIII (1810–1903), on the issue of social justice and inequality. Issued in 1891, the encyclical is titled "Rerum Novarum," Latin for "of revolution," which are its opening two words. Its subtitle is "On the Condition of Labor." In this work, Pope Leo acknowledges the radical economic inequality between business owners and laborers, and the oppressive conditions that workers are often forced to face. He argues that, contrary to socialist views of total equality, "capital cannot do without labor, nor labor without capital" and the two must coexist. The Church must remind both sides of their respective duties, particularly that of justice and treatment of workers with dignity. He writes that, in matters of social inequality, "the poor and helpless have a claim to special consideration," a view that anticipates the more recent Catholic social principle of "preferential option for the poor."

1. It is not surprising that the spirit of revolutionary change, which has so long been predominant in the nations of the world, should have passed beyond politics and made its influence felt in the cognate field of practical economy. The elements of a conflict are unmistakable: the growth of industry, and the surprising discoveries of science; the changed relations of masters and workmen; the enormous fortunes of individuals, and the poverty of the masses; the increased self-reliance and the closer mutual combination of the working population; and, finally, a general moral deterioration. The momentous seriousness of the present state of things just now fills every mind with painful apprehension; wise men discuss it; practical men propose schemes; popular meetings, legislatures, and sovereign princes, all are occupied with it—and there is nothing which has a deeper hold on public attention.

2. Therefore, venerable brethren, as on former occasions, when it seemed opportune to refute false teaching, we have addressed you in the interests of the Church and of the common weal; and have issued letters on "Political Power," on "Human Liberty," on the "Christian Constitution of the State," and on similar subjects, so now we have thought it useful to speak on the "Condition of Labor."

3. It is a matter on which we have touched once or twice already. But in this letter the responsibility of the Apostolic office urges us to treat the question expressly and at length in order that there may be no mistake as to the principles which truth and justice dictate for its settlement. The discussion is not easy, nor is it free from danger. It is not easy to define the relative rights and the mutual duties of the wealthy and of the poor, of capital and of labor. And the danger lies in this, that crafty agitators constantly make use of these disputes to pervert men's judgments and to stir up the people to sedition.

4. But all agree, and there can be no question whatever, that some remedy must be found, and quickly found, for the misery and wretchedness which press so heavily at this moment on the large majority of the very poor. The ancient workmen's guilds were destroyed in the last century, and no other organization took their place. Public

institutions and the laws have repudiated the ancient religion. Hence by degrees it has come to pass that workingmen have been given over, isolated and defenseless, to the callousness of employers and the greed of unrestrained competition. The evil has been increased by rapacious usury, which, although more than once condemned by the Church, is nevertheless, under a different form but with the same guilt, still practiced by avaricious and grasping men. And to this must be added the custom of working by contract, and the concentration of so many branches of trade in the hands of a few individuals, so that a small number of very rich men have been able to lay upon the masses of the poor a yoke little better than slavery itself. . . .

20. Let it be laid down, in the first place, that humanity must remain as it is. It is impossible to reduce human society to a level. The Socialists may do their utmost, but all striving against Nature is vain. There naturally exist among mankind innumerable differences of the most important kind; people differ in capability, in diligence, in health, and in strength; and unequal fortune is a necessary result of inequality in condition. Such inequality is far from being disadvantageous either to individuals or to the community; social and public life can only go on by the help of various kinds of capacity and the playing of many parts; and each man, as a rule, chooses the part which peculiarly suits his case. As regards bodily labor, even had man never fallen from the state of innocence, he would not have been wholly unoccupied; but that which would then have been his free choice and his delight, became afterwards compulsory, and the painful expiation of sin. . . .

21. The great mistake that is made in the matter now under consideration is to possess oneself of the idea that class is naturally hostile to class; that rich and poor are intended by Nature to live at war with one another. So irrational and so false is this view that the exact contrary is the truth. Just as the symmetry of the human body is the result of the disposition of the members of the body, so in a State it is ordained by Nature that these two classes should exist in harmony and agreement, and should, as it were, fit into one another, so as to maintain the equilibrium of the body politic. Each requires the other; capital cannot do without labor, nor labor without capital. Mutual agreement results in pleasantness and good order; perpetual conflict necessarily

produces confusion and outrage. Now, in preventing such strife as this, and in making it possible, the efficacy of Christianity is marvelous and manifold. First of all, there is nothing more powerful than Religion (of which the Church is the interpreter and guardian) in drawing, rich and poor together, by reminding each class of its duties to the other, and especially of the duties of justice. Thus Religion teaches the laboring man and the workman to carry out honestly and well all equitable agreements freely made; never to injure capital, or to outrage the person of an employer; never to employ violence in representing his own cause, or to engage in riot or disorder; and to have nothing to do with men of evil principles, who work upon the people with artful promises and raise foolish hopes which usually end in disaster and in repentance when too late. Religion teaches the rich man and the employer that their workpeople are not their slaves; that they must respect in every man his dignity as a man and as a Christian; that labor is nothing to be ashamed of, if we listen to right reason and to Christian philosophy, but is an honorable employment, enabling a man to sustain his life in an upright and creditable way; and that it is shameful and inhuman to treat men like chattels to make money by, or to look upon them merely as so much muscle or physical power....

30. Neither must it be supposed that the solicitude of the Church is so occupied with the spiritual concerns of its children as to neglect their interests, temporal and earthly. Its desire is that the poor, for example, should rise above poverty and wretchedness, and should better their condition in life; and for this it strives. By the very fact that it calls men to virtue and forms them to its practice, it promotes this in no slight degree. Christian morality, when it is adequately and completely practiced, conduces of itself to temporal prosperity, for it merits the blessing of that God who is the source of all blessings; it powerfully restrains the lust of possession and the lust of pleasure—twin plagues, which too often make a man without self-restraint miserable in the midst of abundance: it makes men supply by economy for the want of means, teaching them to be constant with frugal living, and keeping them out of the reach of those vices which eat up not merely small incomes, but large fortunes, and dissipate many a good inheritance.

31. Moreover, the Church intervenes directly in the interest of the poor by setting on foot and keeping up many things which it sees to be efficacious in the relief of poverty. Here again it has always succeeded so well that it has even extorted the praise of its enemies. . . .

39. Whenever the general interest or any particular class suffers, or is threatened with evils which can in no other way be met, the public authority must step in to meet them. . . . [If] health were endangered by excessive labor, or by work unsuited to sex or age—in these cases, there can be no question that, within certain limits, it would be right to call in the help and authority of the law. The limits must be determined by the nature of the occasion which calls for the law's interference—the principle being this, that the law must not undertake more, or go further, than is required for the remedy of the evil or the removal of the danger.

40. Rights must be religiously respected wherever they are found; and it is the duty of the public authority to prevent and punish injury, and to protect each one in the possession of his own. Still, when there is question of protecting the rights of individuals, the poor and helpless have a claim to special consideration. The richer population have many ways of protecting themselves, and stand less in need of help from the State; those who are badly off have no resources of their own to fall back upon, and must chiefly rely upon the assistance of the State. And it is for this reason that wage-earners, who are undoubtedly among the weak and necessitous, should be specially cared for and protected by the commonwealth.

Source: From Pope Leo XIII, *The Condition of Labor* (Staten Island: Press of the Mission of the Immaculate Virgin, 1891).

RECENT SECTARIAN MOVEMENTS

UNITARIANISM: WILLIAM ELLERY CHANNING

Denominations emerging from the Protestant Reformation initially shared basic theological assumptions with the older Catholic and Orthodox traditions. Foremost among these were the notion of the Trinity and the idea that the Bible was the unique word of God. Growing political freedom in Europe and America permitted some Christian groups to step outside these traditional theological boundaries. One of the first such groups was the Unitarians, who, as their name implies, denied the Trinity in favor of a unified conception of God. Jesus, in their view, was a divinely appointed prophet and teacher, but not God himself. In America, Unitarianism became more formally organized through the efforts of William Ellery Channing (1780–1842), a former Congregationalist pastor. Though denying the Trinity, Channing remained committed to other tenets of Christianity. Some later Unitarians departed not only from Christian theology, but from all traditional religion, adopting instead a scientific humanism. The following selections are from Channing's seminal sermon Unitarian Christianity, *delivered in 1819 at an ordination ceremony in Baltimore, Maryland.*

I. We regard the Scriptures as the records of God's successive revelations to mankind, and particularly of the last and most perfect revelation of his will by Jesus Christ. Whatever doctrines seem to us to be clearly taught in the Scriptures, we receive without reserve or exception. We do not, however, attach equal importance to all the books in this collection. Our religion, we believe, lies chiefly in the New Testament. The dispensation of Moses, compared with that of Jesus, we consider as adapted to the childhood of the human race, a preparation for a nobler system, and chiefly useful now as serving to confirm and illustrate the Christian Scriptures. Jesus Christ is the only master of Christians, and whatever he taught, either during his personal ministry, or by his inspired Apostles, we regard as of divine authority, and profess to make the rule of our lives.

This authority, which we give to the Scriptures, is a reason, we conceive, for studying them with peculiar care, and for inquiring anxiously into the principles of interpretation, by which their true meaning may be ascertained. The principles adopted by the class of Christians in whose name I speak, need to be explained, because they are often misunderstood. We are particularly accused of making an unwarrantable use of reason in the interpretation of Scripture. We are said to exalt reason above revelation, to prefer our own wisdom to God's. Loose and undefined charges of this kind are circulated so freely, that we think it due to ourselves, and to the cause of truth, to express our views with some particularity.

Our leading principle in interpreting Scripture is this, that the Bible is a book written for men, in the language of men, and that its meaning is to be sought in the same manner as that of other books. We believe that God, when he speaks to the human race, conforms, if we may also say, to the established rules of speaking and writing. How else would the Scriptures avail us more, than if communicated in an unknown tongue? . . .

II. Having thus stated the principles according to which we interpret Scripture, I now proceed to the second great head of this discourse, which is, to state some of the views which we derive from that sacred book, particularly those which distinguish us from other Christians.

1. In the first place, we believe in the doctrine of God's unity, or that there is one God, and one only. To this truth we give infinite importance, and we feel ourselves bound to take heed, lest any man spoil us of it by vain philosophy. The proposition, that there is one God, seems to us exceedingly plain. We understand by it, that there is one being, one mind, one person, one intelligent agent, and one only, to whom underived and infinite perfection and dominion belong. We conceive, that these words could have conveyed no other meaning to the simple and uncultivated people who were set apart to be the depositaries of this great truth, and who were utterly incapable of understanding those hair-breadth distinctions between being and person, which the sagacity of later ages has discovered. We find to intimation, that this language was to be taken in an unusual sense, or that God's unity was a quite different thing from the oneness of other intelligent beings.

   We object to the doctrine of the Trinity, that, whilst acknowledging in words, it subverts in effect, the unity of God. According to this doctrine, there are three infinite and equal persons, possessing supreme divinity, called the Father, Son, and Holy Ghost. Each of these persons, as described by theologians, has his own particular consciousness, will, and perceptions. They love each other, converse with each other, and delight in each other's society. They perform different parts in man's redemption, each having his appropriate office, and neither doing the work of the other. The Son is mediator and not the Father. The Father sends the Son, and is not himself sent; nor is he conscious, like the Son, of taking flesh. Here, then, we have three intelligent agents, possessed of different consciousness, different wills, and different perceptions, performing different acts, and sustaining different relations; and if these things do not imply and constitute three minds or beings, we are utterly at a loss to know how minds or beings are to be formed. It is difference of properties, and acts, and consciousness, which leads us to the belief of different intelligent beings, and, if this mark fails us, our whole knowledge fall; we have no proof, that all the agents and persons in the universe are not one and the same mind. When we attempt to conceive of three Gods, we can do nothing more than represent to ourselves three agents, distinguished from each other by similar marks and peculiarities to those which separate the persons of the Trinity; and when common Christians hear these persons spoken of as conversing with each other, loving each other, and performing different acts, how can they help regarding them as different beings, different minds? ...

Source: William Ellery Channing, *Unitarian Christianity,* in *The Works of William E. Channing* (Boston: American Unitarian Association, 1882).

MORMONISM: JOSEPH SMITH

Mormonism encompasses a few historically related denominations, the largest of which is the Church of Jesus Christ of Latter-Day Saints. Mormon belief is founded on the work of Joseph Smith (1805–1844), who maintained that an angelic vision revealed to him the location of gold plates buried during a previous age. Smith's translation of these plates comprises the Book of Mormon, *first published in 1830. The work chronicles the history and religious practices of a band of Israelites who migrated to America in 600 BCE. Under two leaders, two distinct conflicting cultures emerged: the civilized Nephites, and the nomadic and warring Lamanites. Ostensibly the forefathers of the Native Americans, the Lamanites exterminated the Nephites. Anticipating their demise, Moroni, a Nephite chronicler, buried a golden copy of the* Book of Mormon *to preserve their story. A twenty-page section of the* Book of Mormon *describes how Jesus visited the Nephites and gave them Christian doctrine, much of which is paraphrased from the New Testament Gospels. Selections from this are below.*

11. ... And it came to pass, as they understood they cast their eyes up again toward heaven; and behold, they saw a Man descending out of heaven; and he was clothed in a white robe; and he came down and stood in the midst of them; and the eyes of the whole multitude were turned upon him, and they durst not open their mouths, even one to another and wist not what it meant, for they thought it was an angel that had appeared unto them.

And it came to pass that he stretched forth his hand and spake unto the people, saying:

Behold, I am Jesus Christ, whom the prophets testified shall come into the world. . . .

Behold, verily, verily, I say unto you, I will declare unto you my doctrine. And this is my doctrine, and it is the doctrine which the Father hath given unto me; and I bear record of the Father, and the Father beareth record of me, and the Holy Ghost beareth record of the Father and me; and I bear record that the Father commandeth all men, everywhere, to repent and believe in me. And whoso believeth in me, and is baptized, the same shall be saved; and they are they who shall inherit the kingdom of God. And whoso believeth not in me, and is not baptized, shall be damned.

Verily, verily, I say unto you, that this is my doctrine, and I bear record of it from the Father; and whoso believeth in me believeth in the Father also; and unto him will the Father bear record of me, for he will visit him with fire and with the Holy Ghost. And thus will the Father bear record of me, and the Holy Ghost will bear record unto him of the Father and me; for the Father, and I, and the Holy Ghost are one.

And again I say unto you, ye must repent, and become as a little child, and be baptized in my name, or ye can in nowise receive these things. And again I say unto you, ye must repent, and be baptized in my name, and become as a little child, or ye can in nowise inherit the kingdom of God. Verily, verily, I say unto you, that this is my doctrine, and whoso buildeth upon this buildeth upon my rock, and the gates of hell shall not prevail against them. And whoso shall declare more or less than this, and establish it for my doctrine, the same cometh of evil, and is not built upon my rock; but he buildeth upon a sandy foundation, and the gates of hell stand open to receive such when the floods come and the winds beat upon them. Therefore, go forth unto this people, and declare the words which I have spoken, unto the ends of the earth. . . .

17. Behold, now it came to pass that when Jesus had spoken these words he looked round about again on the multitude, and he said unto them: Behold, my time is at hand. I perceive that ye are weak, that ye cannot understand all my words which I am commanded of the Father to speak unto you at this time. Therefore, go ye unto your homes, and ponder upon the things which I have said, and ask of the Father, in my name, that ye may understand, and prepare

your minds for the morrow, and I come unto you again. But now I go unto the Father, and also to show myself unto the lost tribes of Israel, for they are not lost unto the Father, for he knoweth whither he hath taken them.

And it came to pass that when Jesus had thus spoken, he cast his eyes round about again on the multitude, and beheld they were in tears, and did look steadfastly upon him as if they would ask him to tarry a little longer with them. And he said unto them: Behold my bowels are filled with compassion toward you. Have ye any that are sick among you? Bring them hither. Have ye any that are lame, or blind, or halt, or maimed, or leprous, or that are withered, or that are deaf, or that are afflicted in any manner? Bring them hither and I will heal them, for I have compassion upon you; my bowels are filled with mercy....

18. ... Therefore, keep these sayings which I have commanded you that ye come not under condemnation; for woe unto him whom the Father condemneth. And I give you these commandments because of the disputations which have been among you. And blessed are ye if ye have no disputations among you. And now I go unto the Father, because it is expedient that I should go unto the Father for your sakes.

And it came to pass that when Jesus had made an end of these sayings, he touched with his hand the disciples whom he had chosen, one by one, even until he had touched them all, and spake unto them as he touched them. And the multitude heard not the words which he spake, therefore they did not bear record; but the disciples bare record that he gave them power to give the Holy Ghost. And I will show unto you hereafter that this record is true. And it came to pass that when Jesus had touched them all, there came a cloud and overshadowed the multitude that they could not see Jesus. And while they were overshadowed he departed from them, and ascended into heaven. And the disciples saw and did bear record that he ascended again into heaven.

Source: *Book of Mormon,* Third Nephi 11:8–10, 31–41; 17:1–7; 18:33–39.

JEHOVAH'S WITNESSES: CHARLES TAZE RUSSELL

The Jehovah's Witnesses denomination is based on the views of Charles Taze Russell (1852–1916), who, though not ordained, spent his life preaching about the second coming of Jesus. Russell believed that the Bible provided clues for the end times, and based on this belief he made an unsuccessful prediction of Jesus' return. Attracting many followers, he formed an independent church in 1878, and the following year founded a periodical called The Watchtower, *which became a major outlet for his theological views. Since 1931, the movement he started has gone by the name Jehovah's Witnesses. In the selection below, Russell emphasizes Jesus' messianic role and the ability of the church to partake in the divine nature.*

The word Christ or *Kristos* is a Greek word, introduced into our English language, but not *translated* into it. Its translation is, ANOINTED.

"Unto us a child is born," etc., and "they shall call his name Jesus." The name Jesus means Deliverer or Savior, and the child was named in view of a work he was to do; for we are told, "he *shall* save his people from their sins." Jesus was always his name, but from the time of his baptism, when the Holy Ghost descended upon him and *anointed* him as the High Priest, preparatory to his making "the sin offering" on the cross, and thus accomplishing what is indicated by his *name,* his *title* has been "The Anointed,"—Jesus "the *Christ* (anointed) of God."—Lu 9:20. Jesus was frequently called by this *title* instead of by his name; as English people oftenest speak of their sovereign as "the Queen," instead of calling her by her name—*Victoria.*

But, as Jesus was in God's plan as the *anointed one,* before the foundation of the world, so too THE CHURCH of Christ, was recognized in the same plan; that is, God purposed to take out of the world a "little flock," whom he purposed raising above the condition of the *perfect human nature,* to make them "partakers of the *Divine nature."* The relationship of Jesus toward these, is that of "*Head* overall, God blessed forever," "for he hath given him to head over *the church* (of the first-born) which is his body." As Jesus was foreordained to be *the anointed one,* so we, also, were chosen to the same anointing of the Spirit, as members in his body and under him as our head. And so we read (Eph 1:3:) "God hath blessed us with all spiritual blessings *in Christ* according as he hath chosen us *in him* before the foundation of the world, that we should be holy and without blame before him in love; having predestinated us unto the adoption of children by Jesus Christ to himself... wherein he hath made us accepted *in the beloved."* (See also *vs. 20–23.*) Again, (Ro 8:29) "Whom he did foreknow he also did predestinate to be conformed to the image of his Son, that he (head and body) might be the *first-born* (heir) among many brethren."

God's plan of saving *the world* by a "restitution of all things," waits until first, this bride of Jesus—these members of the Spirit-anointed body, shall be gathered out from the world according to his purpose. . . .

Source: Charles Taze Russell, "The Christ of God," *Food for Thinking Christians,* part 5, in Zion's Watchtower, 1881.

CHRISTIAN SCIENCE: MARY BAKER EDDY

The Christian Science movement was founded by Mary Baker Eddy (1821–1910), who believed that the central message of Christianity is healing. In her most influential work, Science and Health *(1875), she argues that the material world and all illness associated with it are unreal and illusory. Healing comes after prayer when God simply removes the afflicted person's false belief in the illusion. Selections from this work are below.*

> *Chapter 2. Healing Primary.* First in the list of Christian duties, he [i.e., Jesus] taught his followers the healing power of Truth and Love. He attached no importance to dead ceremonies. It is the living Christ, the practical Truth, which makes Jesus "the resurrection and the life" to all who follow him in deed. Obeying his precious precepts—following his demonstration so far as we apprehend it—we drink of his cup, partake of his bread, are baptized with his purity; and at last we shall rest, sit down with him, in a full understanding of the divine Principle which triumphs over death. For what says Paul? "As often as ye eat this bread, and drink this cup, ye do show the Lord's death till he come."
>
> *Healing Early Lost.* The proofs of Truth, Life, and Love, which Jesus gave by casting out error and healing the sick, completed his earthly mission; but in the Christian Church this demonstration of healing was early lost, about three centuries after the crucifixion. No ancient school of philosophy, *materia media,* or scholastic theology ever taught or demonstrated the divine healing of absolute Science.
>
> *Chapter 4. Real and Unreal Identity.* The divine Mind maintains all identities, from a blade of grass to a star, as distinct and eternal. The questions are: What are God's identities? What is Soul? Does life or soul exist in the thing formed? Nothing is real and eternal—nothing is Spirit—but God and His idea. Evil has no reality. It is neither person, place, nor thing, but is simply a belief, an illusion of material sense.

The identity, or idea, of all reality continues forever; but Spirit, or the divine Principle of all, is not in Spirit's formations. Soul is synonymous with Spirit, God, the creative, governing, infinite Principle outside of finite form, which forms only reflect.

Real Life Is God. When being is understood, Life will be recognized as neither material nor finite, but as infinite—as God, universal good; and the belief that life, or mind, was ever in a finite form, or good in evil, will be destroyed. Then it will be understood that Spirit never entered matter and was therefore never raised from matter. When advanced to spiritual being and the understanding of God, man can no longer commune with matter; neither can he return to it, any more than a tree can return to its seed. Neither will man seem to be corporeal, but he will be an individual consciousness, characterized by the divine Spirit as idea, not matter. Suffering, sinning, dying beliefs are unreal. When divine Science is universally understood, they will have no power over man, for man is immortal and lives by divine authority.

Chapter 6. Christian Science Discovered. In the year 1866, I discovered the Christ Science or divine laws of Life, Truth, and Love, and named my discovery Christian Science. God had been graciously preparing me during many years for the reception of this final revelation of the absolute divine Principle of scientific mental healing.

Causation Mental. Christian Science explains all cause and effect as mental, not physical. It lifts the veil of mystery from Soul and body. It shows the Scientific relation of man to God, disentangles the interlaced ambiguities of being, and sets free the imprisoned thought. In divine Science, the universe, including man, is spiritual, harmonious, and eternal. Science shows that what is termed *matter* is but the subjective state of what is termed by the author *mortal mind*.

Mind the Only Healer. Science not only reveals the origin of all disease as mental, but it also declares that all disease is cured by divine Mind. There can be no healing except by this Mind, however much we trust a drug or any other means toward which human faith or endeavor is directed. It is mortal mind, not matter, which brings to the sick whatever good they may seem to receive from materiality. But the sick are never really healed except by means of the divine power. Only the action of Truth, Life, and Love can give harmony.

Source: Mary Baker Eddy, *Science and Health,* from chs. 2, 4, and 6 (Boston: Christian Science Publishing Company, 1875).

NEW AGE CHRISTIANITY: LEVI H. DOWLING

The New Age religious movement is based on the astrological concept that the current Piscean age is closing and will be followed by a new age of Aquarius. With the coming of this new age, a new conception of the world and religious truth will also take hold, emphasizing the unity of all things, individual freedom, and the relativity of truth. New Age religion intentionally lacks the formal institutional and doctrinal structure of the major world religions and draws liberally from many religious sources—including astrology, Wicca, and paganism, as well as the major religions themselves. Among the influential New Age writings distinctly in the Christian tradition is the Aquarian Gospel of Jesus the Christ, *which first appeared in 1907. Its author, Levi H. Dowling (1844–1911), was a pastor and physician who claimed to have transcribed this book from the universal Akashic records. The work amplifies the account of Jesus' life and teachings in the New Testament, describing Jesus' childhood and trips to the Far East. Like the New Age movement itself, the religious views expressed here are highly eclectic, influenced particularly by Hinduism, Buddhism, Taoism, Gnosticism, and Zoroastrianism. The New Testament book of Matthew states that Joseph fled to Egypt with Mary and the infant Jesus, thereby avoiding Herod's efforts to kill the newborn king of the Jews. Developing this plot, Dowling describes Jesus' early childhood in Egypt under the tutelage of Elihu and Salome. Although the Elihu character does not appear in the New Testament, the book of Mark mentions a woman named Salome who was present at Jesus' crucifixion. In this selection, Elihu lectures Mary and Jesus about the unity of all things, the higher and lower human selves, and the nature of God.*

> *Chapter 8.* Again Elihu met his pupils in the sacred grove and said, No man lives unto himself; for every living thing is bound by cords to every other living thing. Blest are the pure in heart; for they will love and not demand love in return. They will not do to other men what they would not have other men do unto them. There are two selfs; the higher and the lower self. The higher self is human spirit clothed with soul, made in the form of God. The lower self, the carnal self, the body of desires, is a reflection of the higher self, distorted by the murky ethers of the flesh. The lower self is an illusion, and will pass away; the higher self is God in man, and will not pass away. The higher self is the embodiment of truth; the lower self is truth reversed, and so is falsehood manifest. The higher self is justice, mercy, love and right; the lower self is what the higher self is not. The lower self breeds

hatred, slander, lewdness, murders, theft, and everything that harms; the higher self is mother of the virtues and the harmonies of life. The lower self is rich in promises, but poor in blessedness and peace; it offers pleasure, joy and satisfying gains, but gives unrest and misery and death. It gives men apples that are lovely to the eye and pleasant to the smell; their cores are full of bitterness and gall. If you would ask me what to study I would say, your selfs; and when you well had studied them, and then would ask me what to study next, I would reply, your selfs. He who knows well his lower self, knows the illusions of the world, knows of the things that pass away; and he who knows his higher self, knows God; knows well the things that cannot pass away. Thrice blessed is the man who has made purity and love his very own; he has been ransomed from the perils of the lower self and is himself his higher self. Men seek salvation from an evil that they deem a living monster of the nether world; and they have gods that are but demons in disguise; all powerful, yet full of jealousy and hate and lust; whose favors must be bought with costly sacrifice of fruits, and of the lives of birds, and animals, and human kind. And yet these gods possess no ears to hear, no eyes to see, no heart to sympathize, no power to save. This evil is myth; these gods are made of air, and clothed with shadows of a thought. The only devil from which men must be redeemed is self, the lower self. If man would find his devil he must look within; his name is self. If man would find his savior he must look within; and when the demon self has been dethroned the savior, Love, will be exulted to the throne of power. The David of the light is Purity, who slays the strong Goliath of the dark, and seats the savior, Love, upon the throne.

Source: Levi H. Dowling, *The Aquarian Gospel of Jesus the Christ,* ch. 8 (Los Angeles: Cazenove, 1908).

Islam

INTRODUCTION

Islam's basic tenets are expressed in its most holy creed: "There is no God but Allah, and Muhammad is his messenger." *Islam* means surrender, and adherents to the religion are called *Muslims,* meaning those who surrender. Staunchly monotheistic, Islam sees Allah as the omnipotent creator God who, through a series of prophets, has called people to obedience. At the end of time, Allah will resurrect the dead, condemn the wicked to hell, and entrust believers to eternal peace in his garden. Following prophets such as Moses and Jesus, Muhammad is the final and greatest prophet, who delivered the definitive expression of Allah's voice in the Qur'an, Islam's holiest book. Drawing on Jewish narratives, Muslims trace their religious heritage from Adam to Noah to Abraham and, finally, to Ishmael, Abraham's first son. Muslim faith is embodied not only in religious practice but in a social order governed by Islamic law.

TIME OF INGRATITUDE

The cradle of Islam was the Arabian Peninsula, during a period Muslims contemptuously refer to as the *time of ingratitude (al-jahiliyyah),* that is, ingratitude toward God. Economically, desert conditions of the peninsula did not allow for widespread agriculture, so inhabitants depended on trade with the surrounding empires. When the Arabs later lost their spice monopoly, trading cities such as Petra died. As a convenient stopping place on well-traveled trade routes, though, Mecca survived as the prosperous center of trading in the Arab world. Politically, Mecca was plagued by warring factions involving its two main tribes, the Quraysh and the Khuza'a, each with divisive clans.

Religiously, inhabitants believed in a range of spiritual forces and deities. Belief in polydemonism prevailed, involving supernatural *jinn,* sprites, and demons—some good and others evil—that inhabited special objects or locations. Tapping into their ancient Semitic heritage, the people set up shrines to various nature gods and goddesses. Hubal, god of the moon, was the principal deity of the Meccans, and before his idol people would cast lots and divining arrows. Three chief goddesses of Mecca—Al-Lat, Al-Manat, and Al-Uzza—were worshipped. There was widespread belief in a creator deity, named Allah, who was high god of the regional pantheon. Sacred shrines with carved and uncarved stones were thought to be the dwelling places of these spirits and deities, and they became the focus of offerings and prayers. There was also a significant Jewish and Christian monotheistic presence. Large numbers of Diaspora Jews, fleeing enemies for over a thousand years, settled in Arabia's desert. The Jews interacted well with their new neighbors, and many Arabs converted to Judaism. Hermit Christian monks settled in the desert regions, along with heretical Christian sects escaping the authority of the Roman Church. Muslim tradition also notes the presence of pre-Islamic monotheists, known as *Hanif*, who carried the torch of Abraham's religion through the time of ingratitude.

Festivals and pilgrimages dominated the religious activities of the Meccans. Annual festivals lasting weeks drew inhabitants from throughout the peninsula to the two cities of Mina and Ukaz. With its 365 shrines, one for each day of the year, Mecca was a constant attraction to pilgrims. Meccan religious activity centered on the Ka'bah, an austere cubical structure housing idols, murals of the gods, and the Black Stone. The stone, believed to have fallen from heaven, was the object of a special ritual in which naked pilgrims would circle it seven times and then kiss it. Muslim tradition maintains that the Ka'bah was originally built by Abraham.

EARLY YEARS OF MUHAMMAD

Even a brief survey of world religions indicates that the lives of the religious founders are shrouded in legend, often to the point that their historical lives can no longer be recovered. Although many accounts of Muhammad are also legendary, Islam has the advantage of early written sources, written not just by early Muslims, but by Muhammad himself.

Born about 570 CE, Muhammad was from the Hashimite family clan of Mecca, part of the Quraysh tribe. The clan's founder, from whom Muhammad descended, traced his lineage back to Ishmael, Abraham's first son according to Jewish legend. Muhammad's birth name is unknown, although his honorific title, *Muhammad,* means "highly praised." Tragedy marked his infant and childhood years. His father died before he was born, and as a minor under pre-Islamic law he was unable to acquire inheritance. He was entrusted to his grandfather, who, according to one tradition, had him raised by a Bedouin foster mother. His natural mother died when he was six, and his grandfather two years later. Under the care of his uncle, he became involved with caravans. A story relates that the 12-year-old Muhammad accompanied his uncle to Syria on a caravan, where he met a Christian monk who recognized him as the future great prophet. Because of his reputation for honesty, Muhammad was soon entrusted with the leadership of caravans. A pivotal moment in his life arrived when, at age 25, he led a caravan for a wealthy widow named Khadija. Although she was fifteen years his senior, the two married, and for years she became an important source of encouragement for Muhammad. She bore him four daughters, as well as three sons who died in infancy. Fatima, the best-known daughter, later married his cousin Ali.

According to his tribal custom, during one month of every year Muhammad retreated for religious reflection. He reflected on the good fortune given him by Allah, in view of his family and successful caravan career. He also thought about Jews and Christians who had a book, the Bible, by virtue of which they were prospering more than his own people. This moved him toward monotheism. Islam was born on the *Night of Power* (Laylat al-Qadr) when, on retreat in a cave outside Mecca, the 40-year-old Muhammad had a life-changing vision. In a voice like reverberating bells, the angel Gabriel approached him, commanding him to recite a phrase: "And the Lord is most generous, who by the pen has taught mankind things they knew not." He went through a period of doubt for a few months, even contemplating suicide, fearing he was an ecstatic visionary—a position not held in high esteem in his society. He also considered that he might be mad or that he had heard the voice of a *jinn*. Eventually his doubts dispersed and his wife became his first convert, believing that he was a prophet.

Visions and revelations of this kind continued throughout his life. They were recorded or memorized by others as they occurred and then were compiled into the text of the Qur'an. The moments of revelation began with Muhammad becoming entranced while shaking and sweating. Then, in rhymed prose, rhapsodies in Arabic flowed from his mouth. During his early prophetic career, the main points of his message were that Allah is the only God, that the dead will resurrect, and that Allah will judge all. After his wife, his next converts included his cousin Ali and a merchant named Abu Bakr, both of whom assumed leadership positions after Muhammad's death. As his following grew, the first Muslims were subjected to verbal attacks, threats, and later physical violence. The opposition was in part economically motivated by those whose livelihoods depended on religious pilgrimages to the Ka'bah; they assumed that Muhammad's message of a single God would draw fewer pilgrims than did the many idols housed in their city.

For protection, Muhammad first sent a band of his followers to Ethiopia, where they were warmly received by local

Christians. He and about fifty followers were then placed under siege in their Meccan neighborhood in an attempt to starve them into submission. Under pressure, Muhammad strangely reported a new revelation: Along with Allah, the three key Meccan goddesses were acknowledged. The siege was lifted, and the exiles returned from Ethiopia. Later, Muhammad announced that the new revelation was inspired by the devil, and the relevant passages were removed from his record of revelations. Hostility increased when his wife and uncle died. He tried to establish himself in an oasis town named Taif, about sixty miles southeast of Mecca, but failed.

LATER YEARS OF MUHAMMAD

The turning point in Muhammad's mission occurred during a pilgrimage festival. He met residents of the northern city Yathrib who suggested that their people would be more receptive to him, in part because the city had many Jews who were awaiting the arrival of a prophet. The city was in political turmoil, and the residents believed that they could benefit from Muhammad's administrative skills. A period of negotiations followed. It was agreed that Muhammad would be the final arbiter of all disputes and that the various religious groups, including the Jews and Muslims, would be autonomous. The migration to Yathrib, called the *hijrah* (flight), began with around a hundred of his followers' families. In 622 CE, at age 52, Muhammad joined them, fleeing Meccan authorities as he made the journey. This migration is so momentous for Islam that it marks the starting point of the Muslim calendar.

Muhammad quickly became a successful administrator and statesman, an accomplishment that even his enemies acknowledged. He renamed the city *Medina,* city of the prophet. Living unpretentiously in a clay house and milking goats, he was ever available for consultation. He punished the guilty but was merciful toward his personal enemies. Of his several diplomatic marriages, his primary wife, A'isha, daughter of Abu Bakr, had particular influence over him and is the source of many of the traditions later ascribed to him.

Although he was successful in Medina, hostilities with Mecca continued. Believing that he had a responsibility to provide for the Meccan emigrant followers living in Medina, Muhammad intercepted a caravan to Mecca for its booty. Attempting this a second time, his band of 300 encountered an army of 1,000 Meccans at a site called Badr. The ensuing battle was a victory for Muhammad. Not dissuaded, a few years later the Meccans launched a military offensive against Muhammad's army. In what is known as the Battle of Uhud, the Muslims were badly outnumbered and forced to retreat, and Muhammad himself was slightly wounded. Even so, the battle was a moral victory because the Meccans failed to eradicate Muhammad. Two years later the Meccans attacked Medina directly with a confederate army of inhabitants of surrounding cities and nomads. On the recommendation of a Persian soldier in his camp, Muhammad ordered a trench dug around the entire city, a strategy that resulted in victory.

With each military victory (and moral victories like Uhud), his converts increased, and his control over Medina became more firm. The Jewish population, which had attracted him to the city, ironically failed to accept him as God's prophet. Some even aided the Meccans in their attack. Now with increased authority, Muhammad drove them out. His disappointment with the Jews had theological consequences as well. The Jewish and Christian elements of his religion were suppressed, and the traditional Arab elements were emphasized. No longer would Muslims pray facing Jerusalem; they would face toward Mecca. Qur'anic passages of this period urged Muslims to make pilgrimages to Mecca, which included circumambulation of the Ka'bah and kissing its Black Stone. Friday became the official day of rest, not Saturday or Sunday. During his rule in Medina, other central Muslim doctrines were established, such as fasting, almsgiving, and ritual prayer. Social laws involving marriage, divorce, inheritance, and treatment of slaves and prisoners were also formalized.

In the fifth year of the migration, Muhammad and his followers approached Mecca with the intention of making a pilgrimage, but they were met with resistance from the city leaders. The two sides reached a face-saving compromise in which Muhammad and his followers withdrew, with the understanding that the next year they would return and the city would be open to them for a pilgrimage. However, in the intervening year a Meccan broke the truce, and Muhammad responded by marching on the city. Realizing that they were unable to resist his force, the leaders of the city surrendered and bloodshed was avoided. Riding into the Ka'bah on his camel, with his own hands he smashed its 360 idols, declaring, "Truth has come and falsehood has vanished." Thus, he reclaimed the shrine for God. All of Mecca converted, giving no resistance. The territory around the Ka'bah was declared sacred *(haram)*, and non-Muslims were prohibited from entering the area. Muhammad then returned to Medina.

In the tenth year after his migration, he made a final announcement at the Ka'bah: "Today I have completed my religion for you and I have fulfilled the extent of my favor toward you. It is my will that Islam be your religion. I have completed my mission. I have left you the Book of Allah and clear commandments. If you keep them you will never go wrong." Shortly thereafter, reporting severe headaches, he died while in A'isha's house and was buried on that spot.

THE CALIPHATE

Muhammad founded both a new religion and a new social order. Although he believed that his mission as a religious prophet was complete at the time of his death, plans for a larger Muslim social community *(umma)* were not as yet realized. He had planned to conquer Syria and Iraq but died too soon. Upon his death, key political decisions were made by Muhammad's early companions *(Sahaba)*, many of whom were his first converts. Their first task was to appoint a successor, or Caliph, who would fill Muhammad's political leadership role, but not his prophetic role. From the start, however, there was political dissent. To the consternation of Ali, Muhammad's cousin who expected to step into the leadership role, the early companions selected Abu Bakr as the first Caliph. For the sake of unity, Ali deferred to his rival. Plans were drawn for military expansion, but the aged Caliph died only two years into his rule.

For the next ten years, the newly appointed Caliph Umar expanded Muslim territory far into the Persian and Byzantine empires. Non-Arab converts were denied equal political rights, and it would be almost a hundred years before a unified Muslim political order would emerge. Umar was stabbed to death by a Persian slave, and Uthman became the third Caliph. According to legend, trouble started for Uthman when he lost Muhammad's seal ring in a well. He prompted further negative reaction by favoring his family clan, the Umayyads, which originally had opposed Muhammad in Mecca. A small rebellion erupted in Medina, in which a disaffected faction (which later became the Kharajites) laid siege to his house. Civil war later erupted, and, twelve years into his rule, Uthman was assassinated by rebel Muslim troops from Egypt. The early companions finally elected Ali as the fourth Caliph, but he was immediately opposed by Syrian governor Mu'awiyah, who sought to avenge the death of Uthman, his cousin. War broke out between Ali and Mu'awiyah, and on the eve of the decisive battle Ali was killed by a soldier from a rebel group that had split with him as a result of disagreement with his policies. The Caliphate fell to Ali's son, Husan, but he quickly ceded it to Mu'awiyah.

Under the first wave of Muslim expansion by the first four Caliphs, Arabia, Persia, and North Africa were conquered. For the next ninety years the Caliphate was held by the secular Umayyad Dynasty (661–750), established by Mu'awiyah. After Mu'awiyah's death, the Caliphate was passed to his unpopular son Yazid. In 680 an insurrection against Yazid was launched by Ali's son, Husayn. Husayn and his followers were massacred in what is now the Iraqi city of Kerbala (a tragedy that became the rallying cry of the Shi'i Muslims). Centered in Damascus, the Umayyads continued to push Muslim boundaries. Moving across North Africa and into Spain, expansion into Europe was halted at the French border in the Battle of Tours in 732. The Caliphate was next held by the Abbasid Dynasty (750–1285), centered in Baghdad, and then by the Ottoman Empire (1300–1922), centered in Istanbul. In 1924 the Caliphate was abolished by the Turkish National Assembly, inheritors of the Ottoman Empire. To justify this controversial decision, the Assembly maintained that "the idea of a single caliph, exercising supreme religious authority over all the peoples of Islam, is an idea taken from fiction, not from reality."

SUNNI AND SHI'A

Just as political factions divided early Islam, so did theological differences, the key issue being whether Ali and his successors had a special spiritual status. Islam today is divided into two main groups over this issue. The Sunni, or Sunnite, attribute no special function to Ali, whereas the Shi'a, or Shi'ite, do. Sunnis make up approximately 90 percent of Muslims worldwide. Their full name is *Ahl al-Sunnah wa 'l-Hadith,* that is, followers of the path laid out by the prophet in his sayings. In addition to rejecting the special spiritual status of Ali, Sunnis recognize the first four Caliphs as political successors to Muhammad and acknowledge the political authority of the Caliphate in general. Sunnis must also follow one of the four schools of Islamic law *(madhahib),* developed in the eighth and ninth centuries.

Prior to the emergence of the four Sunni schools of law, Muslims used several guides to determine proper conduct. After the Qur'an was consulted for guidance, appeals were made to practices of Muhammad *(sunna)* as compiled by scholars into texts called *Hadith*. When these avenues failed to achieve a solution, decisions were made in one of three ways: analogical deductions from existing laws *(qiyas),* consensus of the Muslim community or its leading scholars *(ijma),* or independent decisions of a single jurist *(ijtihad).*

The four schools of Islamic law not only systematized the above appeal routes, but developed their own codes of behavior from these. The methodological differences between the four schools are subtle, although their geographical domains are more distinct. The *Hanafite* school, which provides the greatest scope of reasoning, predominates in former Turkish empire areas (Turkey, Palestine, Egypt) and India. The *Malikite* school, which focuses more on the traditions of Muhammad's companions rather than on Muhammad, is dominant in West Africa. The *Shafi'ite* school, which developed the standard hierarchy of appeals, is most prominent in Indonesia. Finally, the *Hanbalite* school, the most literalist in adhering to the letter of the Qur'an, is found in Saudi Arabia and Qatar.

Shi'a Muslims, consisting of 10 percent of the Muslim population, are located primarily in Iran. Shi'a origins are difficult to trace because of negative Sunni chronologies and biased reports by later Shi'as. However, with the assassination of Ali and the creation of the Umayyad Caliphate in 661, a faction loyal to the memory of Ali emerged. Devotion to Ali and his selected descendants became the test of true faith. Early Shi'as were in continual opposition to the ruling Caliph, with some groups advocating armed resistance.

About 40 factions of Shi'as have emerged over the years. The most numerous are the Twelvers *(Ithna 'Asha-Riyyah)*, who comprise about 80 percent of their number. The central Twelver doctrine is that of the Imam, or leader. Twelvers believe that Muhammad's spiritual abilities *(wilaya)* were passed on to a series of Imams, beginning with Ali. Twelver theology holds that human beings require inspired leadership in order to adhere faithfully to the dictates of Islam and that successive Imams are clearly designated by predecessors *(nass)*. Imams are also thought to be guided by Allah and to be infallible *(isma)*. Eleven Imams have appeared so far, and they await the appearance of the twelfth and final, named Mahdi, who is alive but hidden from view. More precisely, the Mahdi is in a state called *occultation,* in which he can see others but others cannot see him; at age four, Allah placed him in that state for protection after the death of his father, the eleventh Imam, in 873 CE. It is believed that the Mahdi made four representations *(wakils)* between 873 and 940, a period called the *lesser occultation*. He will return at the end of time, take vengeance on unbelievers, and initiate an era of peace. Until then, leaders called the *Mujtahid* make decisions of canon law on behalf of the hidden Imam. In recent times, the Ayatollahs have this function.

Two other Shi'a factions deserve mentioning. The Fivers *(Zaydis)* split from Twelver tradition by recognizing Zaydis as the fifth Imam (as opposed to Muhammad al-Baqir). Concentrated in Yemen, they do not assert the necessity of Imams and accept some of the early Caliphs. The Seveners

(Isma'ili) split from Twelver tradition by recognizing Isma'il as the seventh Imam (rather than Musa-l-Kazim). They see Isma'il as the final Imam, Mahdi, who will return for the day of judgment.

THE QUR'AN

Islam's most holy scripture, The Qur'an is the collected revelations of Muhammad, written during the last twenty-three years of his life. It is the primary sacred text for all sects of Islam. The work is divided into 114 sections called *surahs,* varying in length from 3 verses to almost 300. The term Qur'an means "to recite," in the sense that Muhammad is verbally delivering Allah's message to the people. The traditional arrangement of the *surahs* is neither chronological nor topical but rather according to length, beginning with the longest and ending with the shortest. *Surah* titles are derived from a prominent or recurring word, such as Cow, Abraham, Mary, Angels, Muhammad, Divorce, Infidels. Every *surah* (except one) begins with the phrase "In the name of God, the Merciful, the Compassionate," which was probably the original indicator of the *surah* divisions.

The exact chronology of the *surahs* was forgotten even during Muhammad's life, and many short revelations from different periods were joined together to form longer *surahs.* Modern scholars have offered several chronological schemes for organizing the *surahs,* although traditional Muslims believe that such attempts compromise the inherent beauty of the nonhistorical arrangement. Nevertheless, each *surah* is associated with either the Meccan or the Medinan period of Muhammad's life. The Meccan *surahs* are the earliest and reflect Muhammad's struggle to persuade his skeptical Meccan listeners to abandon polytheism and idolatry. They are shorter and more poetic than the Medinan sections and are characterized by vivid imagery. Meccan *surahs* describe the world's cataclysmic end and emphasize Allah's omnipotence and active role in history.

Within the Meccan period itself the style and content of the *surahs* developed. The earliest use short sentences and particularly powerful imagery and are the most lyrical. The later ones, by contrast, are longer, more direct and sermonizing, and less heated. Stories of the early prophets become more developed. When Muhammad and his followers migrated to Medina, political circumstances were considerably more favorable, and the *surahs* reflect the confident voice of a lawgiver concerned with social and political issues. These are the longest *surahs* in the Qur'an and deal with the giving of the law.

Stylistically, most of the Qur'an is written in the voice of Allah, addressing believers, unbelievers, or Muhammad. The first person is used when God describes his divine attributes, and the second when describing actions in which humans participate. Passages not in the voice of Allah are prefaced by "Say," indicating that they are to be recited by believers. Most of the Qur'an is written in rhymed prose, as opposed to poetry with meter. The latter approach was typical of poets who were thought to be guided by *jinn,* an association which Muhammad strongly resisted. Phrases are repetitive and well suited for reciting; indeed, several traditional Qur'anic division schemes break the text into sections for daily reading. Muslims believe that the literary quality of the Qur'an itself validates Muhammad's claims of prophethood, for, though illiterate, he produced a literary work of great merit.

The initial compilation of the Qur'an is a remarkable story. After each of Muhammad's revelations, efforts were made to record their content, through either writing or memorization by specially assigned reciters. Although Muhammad may have done some editing of the earlier *surahs* when in Medina, no definitive "book" existed at the time of his death. A year after Muhammad's death, many of the original reciters were killed in battle. Fearing that the Qur'an's contents would be lost through time, the first Caliph, Abu Bakr, ordered the compilation of the first complete text of the Qur'an. The task was assigned to Zayd ibn Thabit, an aide of Muhammad, who pieced the text together from oral and written sources in Medina. Variant Qur'an fragments continued to circulate for twenty-four more years, until the third Caliph, Uthman, ordered the creation of a definitive text. Again Zayd supervised the compilation. He gathered all existing manuscript fragments and met with those original reciters accompanying Muhammad who had the complete contents memorized. When the compilation was finished, all previous written versions were destroyed, ensuring that only one version of the Qur'an would remain. Although variant editions appeared later, the definitive text of the Qur'an we have today is the work of Zayd. Diacritical marks were later introduced to fix proper vocalization for recitation.

The content of the Qur'an covers a variety of subjects. Many stories parallel accounts in the Old Testament and some in the New Testament, especially those of Adam, Noah, Abraham, Joseph, and Jesus. It is unlikely that Muhammad had access to Arabic translations of Jewish or Christian texts; instead, he probably relied on oral traditions of the local Jewish and Christian populace. Other narratives are of Arabian origin. Large sections of the Qur'an provided legislation for the newly formed Muslim community in Medina.

For Muslims, the Qur'an records more, they believe, than the words of Muhammad; it is Allah's eternal speech. The Torah and Bible, they believe, are earlier and incomplete revelations of Allah. Most Muslims believe that the Qur'an is uncreated, existing from eternity, with an original engraved tablet of the Qur'an in heaven. This eternal Qur'an is written in the Arabic language, so authentic copies of the Qur'an will also be only in Arabic. The first unofficial translation appeared in 1141 in Latin and was loathed by Muslims for its disparaging renderings. The physical book itself is sacred, and copies of the Qur'an are touched only after ceremonial cleansing of the handler.

THE HADITH

After the Qur'an, the second most authoritative group of texts in Islam is the *Hadith* canons. The term *Hadith* means "talk" or "speech," and it refers to collected narratives reporting actions and sayings of Muhammad recounted by his companions. These monumental collections are the principal basis for interpreting the Qur'an and were used to develop early Islamic legal systems.

While Muhammad was alive, his companions took note of his life events and his sayings. Within the first hundred years after Muhammad's death, individual sayings were transmitted both orally and in written form from teachers of *Hadith* to their students. Within the second hundred years, booklets of *Hadith* appeared on single topics, and later on several topics. The number of *Hadith* canons grew to about three quarters of a million, most being duplicates with only slight variations as generated by the continually growing number of teachers and students of *Hadith*. Finally, they were systematically compiled in the ninth and tenth centuries into no fewer than twelve multivolume collections.

The Sunnis have nine collections, six of which are particularly revered. The most widely accepted of these are referred to as the *Two Sahih* (authentic): *Sahih al-Bukhari* and *Sahih Muslim*. The first of these, compiled by al-Bukhari (d. 875), is the more important. A prominent teacher of *Hadith,* al-Bukhari examined 600,000 sayings, the majority being duplicate versions, and sifted them down to 7,275 authentic ones. Of these, about 2,700 are nonrepetitious. Limited by space constraints, he remarked that he left out other sayings that he believed were authentic. The sayings are topically categorized into ninety-seven books, with some longer sayings split and categorized into two distinct topical divisions. The second most revered collection is that by Muslim ibn al-Hajjaj (d. 875), who examined 300,000 traditions and reduced them to 4,000.

A student of al-Bukhari, al-Hajjaj is thought to have been more critical in deeming a saying "authentic" and, unlike his teacher, presents the longer sayings in their integrated form. The remaining four collections (or *Sunan*) were compiled by Abu Dawud (d. 886), at-Tirmidhi (d. 892), an-Nasa'i (d. 915), and Ibn Majah (d. 886). Of the six *Hadith* collections, those by al-Bukhari, Muslim al-Hajjaj, and Dawud have been made available in English translation. Three Shi'a collections, called *akhbar* (as opposed to *Hadith*), are traditionally thought to originate with Ali and the Imams (Ja'far al-Sadiq in particular). Larger than the Sunni collections, they were compiled by al-Kulini (d. 939) (whose collection is the most widely respected), al-Qummi (d. 991), and al-Tusi (d. 1067).

Hadith sayings are in two parts. First is the story itself *(matn),* and second is a list of names constituting the chain of sources that establish the story's authenticity *(isnad).* The stories themselves are of two types. The first type, called sacred *Hadith (Hadith qudsi),* contains divine revelations similar to those in the Qur'an. The second, called noble *Hadith (Hadith sharif),* relates to Muhammad's personal life and nonprophetic utterances. For *Hadith* compilers, a story's authenticity rested on the integrity of each person mentioned in the chain of sources. A discipline emerged that critically scrutinized the lives of the transmitters. According to the norms of this field of study, even an otherwise authentic statement that bears a faulty chain of transmitters should be regarded as inauthentic. Muslims agree that many of the *Hadith* were invented in the early days of Islam to answer questions of law, to support religious factions, or to serve political needs in struggles for power. Thousands were rejected early on for this very reason. An early *Hadith* scholar was even executed for confessing that he fabricated 4,000 sayings for financial gain. Critical *Hadith* scholarship is still in its infancy, however, and judgment regarding the extent of their authenticity must be postponed.

SECTARIAN WRITINGS

Muslim sectarian writings are voluminous, and the lines distinguishing sacred texts from works of mere theology are often blurry. Writings from the various schools of Islamic law are particularly respected. Foundational works in the *Hanafite* school are *The Book of Roots* by Muhammad ibn al-Hasan al-Shaybani (d. 805) and the *Hidaya* by Burhan al-Din al-Marghinani (d. 1197). From the Malikite school is the *Muwatta* by Malik ibn Anas (712–795), the school's founder. From the Shafi'ite tradition is the *Rasala* by al-Shafi'i (767–820), founder of the school. Finally, from the Hanbalite school is the *Musnad* by founder ibn Hanbal (780–855) and the *Kitab-al-'Umada* by Ibn Qudama (1146–1223).

There are also a number of important writings by Sufis, that is, Islamic mystics whose writings emphasize mystical union with Allah. Key writers among the Sufis include Rabi'a al-'Adawiya (717–801), a freed slave girl whose writings stress the intense love of Allah; al-Ghazali (1058–1111), a scholar of Islamic Law; and ibn-al-Arabi (1165–1240), a Spanish-born metaphysician. The most widely influential Sufi writer is Jalal ad-Din ar-Rumi (1207–1273). Rumi's six-book *Masnawi,* sometimes referred to as the "Qur'an in Persian," is a compendium of lyric poetry and stories allegorizing Sufi doctrine.

HOLIDAYS

Friday *(jum'ah)* Weekly day of prayer established by Muhammad.

New Year's Day (Al-Hijra; first day of first Islamic month) Commemorates Muhammad's migration to Medina.

Ashura (literally, "the tenth day"; tenth day of first Islamic month) Commemorates the death of Husain, Muhammad's grandson.

Muhammad's birthday (Mawlid; twelfth day of third Islamic month) Commemorates Muhammad's birth.

Night of Ascent (Lailat al Miraj; twenty-seventh day of seventh Islamic month) Commemorates Muhammad's spiritual ascent to heaven.

Ramadan (ninth Islamic month) Month of fasting.

Night of Power (Lailat al-Qadr; last ten days of Ramadan) Commemorates Muhammad's first revelation of the Qur'an.

Feast of Breaking the Fast (Id al-Fitr; first day of tenth Islamic month) Commemorates the end of Ramadan.

Feast of Sacrifice (Eid ul-Adha; tenth day of twelfth Islamic month) Commemorates Abraham's attempt to sacrifice his son Ishmael.

TIMELINE

570 CE	Birth of Muhammad
610	Muhammad's first vision in a cave near Mecca
622	Muhammad and followers flee to Medina (Hijira)
630	Muhammad captures Mecca
632	Death of Muhammad; Abu Bakr chosen as Caliph
633–642	Muslim conquests of Fertile Crescent and North Africa
650	Qur'an written down
656	Ali becomes fourth Caliph
661	Ali murdered; Mu'awiyah becomes Caliph
680	Shi'a sect emerges
710–732	Muslim armies enter Spain from North Africa, halted at Battle of Tours
765	Shi'a sect divided between Twelvers and Seveners
800	Efforts begun to compile the *Hadith*
1100–1200	Sufism founded
1299	Ottoman Empire founded
1918	Fall of Ottoman Empire

GLOSSARY

Allah Literally, "God"; the Muslim name for the single Deity who is creator and judge.

Caliph Literally, "Successor." The political successors to Muhammad according to the Sunni tradition.

Companions *Sahaba* in Arabic; Muhammad's closest followers during his life who assumed leadership roles after his death.

Hadith Literally, "Speech"; sacred collections of short narratives about Muhammad that are thought to have originated with his early companions.

Imam Literally, "He" who stands before; spiritual leaders of the Shi'a tradition beginning with Ali and continuing through a line of his descendants.

Ka'bah Literally, "Cube"; a cubelike building in the open-air Mosque of Mecca, which is the central shrine of Islam.

Mahdi Literally, "The Guided One"; the final and awaited Imam in Shi'a tradition who will establish an era of peace.

Muslim Literally, "One Who Surrenders"; a follower of Islam.

Qur'an Literally, "to recite"; Islam's holiest text, consisting of Muhammad's collected revelations.

Shi'a Literally, "Separate Party"; branch of Islam, comprising 10 percent of all Muslims, whose members honor the spiritual leadership of Ali and the other Imams.

Sufi Literally, "Wool Clad"; practitioners of Sufism, Islam's mystical tradition, which emphasizes the mystical union of the believer with God.

Sunni From the Arabic *sunnah,* meaning "custom"; branch of Islam, comprising 90 percent of all Muslims, whose members accept the leadership role of the Caliphate.

Twelver From the Arabic *Ithna 'Ashariyya,* meaning "followers of the twelve Imams"; division of Shi'a Islam, comprising 80 percent of its number, whose members acknowledge the leadership of twelve specific Imams.

QUR'AN: MUHAMMAD IN MECCA

NIGHT OF POWER

Muhammad's first revelation occurred on the Night of Power while on retreat in a cave near Mecca. It is recorded in "The Clot" (surah 96). An early sequel to this surah, called "The Power" (surah 97), celebrates Muhammad's call to prophethood on the Night of Power. Both appear below.

Clots of Blood (96)

Read: In the name of your Lord, who created man from clotted blood.
Read: Your Lord is most generous. He taught men through the pen what they did not know.
Man is outrageous for thinking that he is self-sufficient. All things return to your Lord.
Have you considered him who criticizes a servant when he prays?

Have you considered whether he was in proper guidance or embraced piety?
Have you considered how he does not believe and turns his back? Does he not know that God can see?
No, surely, if he does not stop, we will drag him by his hair—his lying sinful hair.
So let him call his supporters: we in turn will call the guards of hell.
No, do not obey him, but kneel and come closer.

The Power (97)

We revealed it on the Night of Power. What will help you understand what the Night of Power is?
The Night of Power is better than a thousand months.
The angels and the Spirit descend in it, by the permission of their Lord with every command.
Peace it is until the break of the dawn.

Source: *Surahs* 96, 97. This and the following selections from the *Qur'an* are adapted from translations by George Sale and Edward H. Palmer.

DIVINE JUDGMENT

After his call to prophethood, Muhammad lived in Mecca for about twelve years, trying to convince his fellow citizens to worship only Allah. His efforts are illustrated in the following four early Meccan surahs: "The Calamity" (surah 101), "Worldly Gain" (surah 102), "Time" (surah 103), and "The Slanderer" (surah 104). Muhammad's earliest revelations were short, poetic declamations about punishment in hell for unbelievers. Because the context of most of the Meccan revelations was quickly lost, we do not know who the specific offenders were who provoked these harsh condemnations.

The Calamity (11)

The calamity: what is the calamity?
What will help you understand what the calamity is?
On that day men will be like scattered moths, and the mountains will be like tufts of fluffed wool.
For him whose scale is heavy, he will be in a blissful life. But as for him whose scale is light, he will live in the pit of hell.
What will help you understand what it is? It is a burning Fire.

Worldly Gain (102)

The preoccupation with worldly gain deceives you until you are in your grave.
Ultimately you will know, and certainly you will know.

If you knew with certainty, you would surely see hell. Then you will see
it with the certainty of your own eyes.
Then you will surely be questioned about your bliss.

Time (103)

As sure as the sun sets, man is in a condition of loss—except for those
who believe and do right, and encourage each other to be true, and
encourage each other to be patient.

The Slanderer (104)

Punishment awaits every slanderous backbiter who hoards his wealth
and counts it. He thinks that his wealth can immortalize him.
Not so. He will be thrown into consuming Fire.
What will help you understand what this consuming Fire is?
It is the Fire ignited by God, which rises above the hearts. It is an
archway over them on long-drawn columns.

Source: *Surahs 101–104.*

THE OPENING

*The first surah of the Qur'an, titled "The Opening," contains the
most commonly repeated prayer in Islam and is an integral part
of Muslim worship. Scholars give it an early date, from about the
fourth year of Muhammad's Meccan mission.*

Praise belongs to God, the Lord of the worlds, the merciful, the compassionate, the ruler of the Day of Judgment.
We worship you and we ask help from you.
Guide us in the right path, the path of those You are gracious to, but
not of those You are angry with, or of those who err.

Source: *Surah 1:1–7.*

EVILS OF IDOLATRY

*The overriding theme of Muhammad's message while in Mecca
was commitment to Allah and the rejection of idolatry. The following selection from "Jonah" (surah 10), a late Meccan surah,
describes how idolaters forfeit paradise and are blind to the
powers of the creator.*

God calls to the home of peace, and guides whoever He will
to the right path. To those who do what is good, goodness
and more is their reward. Darkness or shame will not cover
their faces. These are the inhabitants of Paradise, where they
will live forever.

As for those who have done evil, their reward is a similar evil. Shame will cover them. They will have nothing to defend them against God, as though their faces were covered with the deep darkness of the night. These are the inhabitants of the Fire, where they will live forever.

On the day We gather all the idolaters together, We will say to them "Off to your places, you and your idols" for we will separate them from each other. Their idols will then say to you, "It was not us that you worshipped. As God is our ever-sufficient witness between us and you, we were unaware of you worshipping us."

Every soul will understand what it had done before; they will then be returned to God, their true Lord, and that which they contrived before will abandon them.

Say: "Who provides for you from the heaven and the earth? Who rules over sound and sight? Who brings forth the living from the dead, and the dead from the living? Who governs all affairs?"

They will then say, "God."

Say: "Do you not then show reverence?"

That is God, your true Lord. What is there after the truth but error? How then can you turn away from him?

Thus is the word of your Lord proved true against those who disobeyed; they will not believe.

Say: "Are there any of your idols who can produce a creation and do it again?" Say: "God produces a creation, then does it again; how then can you be so deceived?"

Say: "Are there any of your idols who can guide you to the truth?" Say: "God guides you to the truth." Is then He who guides you to the truth more worthy to be followed, or he that cannot guide you but must be himself guided? What is the problem with you? How can you judge so?

But most of them follow only speculation, but speculation has no advantage at all against the truth. God surely knows what they do.

Source: *Surah* 10:25–36.

EARLY PROPHETS

The Qur'an states that every nation has its prophet (surah 13:7), and it mentions about thirty prophets by name preceded Muhammad. Most of these are also mentioned in the Bible. The prophets typically spoke to unreceptive idolatrous people, and Allah subsequently destroyed the idolaters for their continued disbelief. The hillsides are scattered with the ruins of the idolaters' cities as monuments to their recalcitrance. As Muhammad's own prophetic message was met with disbelief and hostility, he warned the Meccans of the consequences. During Muhammad's late Meccan period of revelation, detailed accounts of early prophets are prominent. Surah 11, titled "Hud," recounts the stories of Noah, Hud, Salih, Abraham, Lot, Shu'aib, and Moses. Noah, Abraham, Lot, and Moses are from Jewish tradition. The Qur'an's account of these prophets differs from biblical accounts, explaining in surah 6:91 that the Jews suppressed much of Moses' revelation and that Muhammad is revealing new information. Hud, Salih, and Shu'aib, unique to Qur'anic tradition, are prophets sent by Allah to the Arabs.

Hud and the People of Ad

To the people of Ad we sent their kinsman Hud. Hud said, "My people, you must serve God; you have no god but Him. You have constructed a lie. My people, I do not ask you for any payment in return; my compensation is only from Him who created me. Have you no understanding?

My people, you must ask forgiveness from your Lord, and then turn to Him. He will open the skies with abundant rain for you, and add strength to your strength. Do not then return to your sin."

The people replied, "Hud, you have not given us a clear revelation, so will we not leave our gods at your word, nor will we believe you. We can only assume that some of our gods have infected you with evil."

Hud said, "God is my witness, and you too bear witness, that I am free from your sin of associating with other gods. So do not hesitate to plot against me, all of you. I rely upon God, my Lord and your Lord. By their hair He holds every beast that walks. My Lord's path is straight. But if you turn your backs toward him, then I have communicated to you what I was sent to do, and my Lord will replace you with another people. You cannot harm Him at all, for my Lord is guardian over all."

When our judgment was fulfilled, through our mercy We rescued Hud, and those who believed with him. We saved them from great suffering.

Thus was the tribe of Ad. They denied the signs of their Lord, and rebelled against His messengers, and followed the command of every headstrong degenerate. They were cursed in this world, and will also be on resurrection day. Did not Ad disbelieve their Lord? Yes. Away with Ad, the people of Hud.

Salih and the People of Thamud

To the people of Thamud we sent their kinsman Salih. Salih said, "My people, you must worship God and have no god but Him. He is the one that made you from the earth, and provided for you to live in it. Ask forgiveness from Him and return to Him, for my Lord is nearby and answers."

The people answered, "Salih, we set our hopes in you until now. Do you forbid us to worship what our fathers worshipped? We are in serious doubt about what you are now asking of us."

Salih said, "My people, consider: if I am indeed acting on a clear sign from my Lord through mercy he has shown me, then who will save me against God if I rebel against Him? You will add only to my loss. My people, here is a she-camel from God as a sign for you. Allow her to feed in God's earth, and do not harm her, otherwise you will immediately be inflicted with punishment."

But they killed her and Salih said, "Enjoy yourselves in your houses for three days, after which you will be destroyed."

When our judgement was fulfilled, through our mercy we saved Salih, and those who believed with him, from disgrace on that day. Your Lord is powerful and mighty. A dreadful cry struck those who had done wrong, and by morning they were lying dead in their houses, as though they had never lived in them. Did not Thamud disbelieve their Lord? Yes. Away with Thamud.

Abraham and Lot's People

Our messengers came to Abraham with good news and they said, "Peace." He said, "Peace" and quickly brought them a roasted calf. When he saw that they did not reach out their hands for any of it, he became uneasy and feared them. They said, "Do not be afraid, for we were sent to the people of Lot."

His wife was standing by, laughing, and we gave her the good news of Isaac, and of Jacob after Isaac.

She said, "Unfortunately for me, how can I bear a son when I am an old woman, and this husband of mine an old man? This is surely an unusual thing."

They said, "Do you wonder at the decree of God? God's mercy and blessings are upon you and your house. He is to be praised and glorified."

When Abraham's fear subsided and he heard the good news, he argued with us about Lot's people. Abraham was gentle, compassionate, and contrite.

"Do not do this, Abraham, for the judgment of your Lord is here. A punishment is coming to them that cannot be delayed."

When our messengers came to Lot, he was grieved for the people, but unable to protect them, and he said, "This is a terrible day." His people came rushing toward him, as they had a history of doing this evil. He said, "My people, here are my daughters who are purer for you. Fear God, and do not disgrace me with my guests. Is there not one rational man among you?"

They said, "You know that we have no interest in your daughters; you know exactly what we want."

He said, "If only I had power over you, or could rely on help from some strong support."

The guests said, "Lot, we are the messengers of your Lord, they will certainly not touch you. Escape with your people in the darkness of the night, and let none of you look back. As to your wife, her outcome will be the same as theirs. The morning is their appointed time, and is not the morning approaching?"

When our judgement was fulfilled, we turned everything upside down. We rained down stones of baked clay upon them, one after another, bearing marks from your Lord. They are never very far from the unjust.

Shu'aib and the People of Midian

To the people of Midian we sent their kinsman Shu'aib. He said, "My people: serve God; you have no god but Him, and do not give short measure and weight. I see you well off now, I fear for you the torments of a coming day. My people, be fair when giving measure and weight, and do not cheat men of their things. Do not spread evil over the earth, thereby corrupting it. What God leaves for you is better if you are believers. But I am not a guardian over you."

The people replied, "Shu'aib, do your prayers tell you that we should abandon what our fathers served, or that we should not do as we please with our wealth? You are, indeed, a mild yet straight-forward one."

He said, "My people. Do you not see? If I have a clear revelation from my Lord, and if He has supplied me with abundant things, and if I will not follow you in that which I myself forbid you, then do I seek anything but your improvement so far as I am capable? My sole help is in God. I rely on Him and I turn to him. My people, do not let your opposition to me bring down upon you the same thing that happened to the people of Noah, or the people of Hud, or the people of Salih. Nor are the people of Lot far distant from you. "

Ask forgiveness from your Lord and turn to Him. My Lord is merciful and loving.

They said, "Shu'aib, we do not understand much of what you say, and we see that you are weak among us. We would stone you if it were not for your tribe. You have no power over us."

He said, "My people, do you value my tribe more than you do God? Do you treat him as something to throw behind you? My Lord understands whatever you do. My people, act as you see fit, and so will I. But eventually you will know who is punished, and be disgraced, and is a liar. Watch, then, and I will be watching with you."

When our judgment was fulfilled, through our mercy we saved Shu'aib, and those who believed with him. A dreadful cry struck those who had done wrong, and by morning they were lying dead in their houses, as though they had never lived in them. So, away with Midian, just as it was away with Thamud.

Moses and the Egyptians

We sent Moses with our signs and incontestable power to Pharaoh and his chiefs, but they followed Pharaoh's command, and Pharaoh's command was wicked. He will lead his people on resurrection day, and lead them down into the Fire, an evil place to be brought to.

In this world they were followed by a curse, and, on resurrection day, evil will be the help that they will receive.

These are the stories of the cities, which we relate to you. Some of them are still standing, some are now gone. We did not wrong them: they wronged themselves. Their gods, who they called on instead of God, gave them no advantage whatsoever, but only added to their downfall.

This is your Lord's grasp when He takes hold of cities that have done wrong. His grasp is terrible and effective.

Surely this is a sign for those who fear the torment of the last day, the day when men will be gathered. It will be a day to witness.

We will not delay it, except to an appointed time. On the day when it comes no soul will speak except by His permission. Some will be miserable, others happy. As for those who are miserable, there in the Fire they will groan and weep for as long as the heavens and the earth endure, unless your Lord wills otherwise. Your Lord is one who does what he wills. As for those who are happy, they will live in paradise for as long as the heavens and the earth endure, unless the Lord wills otherwise—an endless blessing.

Have no doubt about what these men worship: they only worship what their fathers worshipped before. We will pay them back their portion in full.

We gave Moses the Book before, and then they disagreed with it, and, had it not been for a word that had already been pronounced by your Lord, their status would have already been decided. But they are still in suspicious doubt concerning it.

Source: *Surah* 11:50–110.

RESURRECTION OF THE DEAD

Muhammad met with resistance concerning the concept of the bodily resurrection of the dead. In the following, from two late Meccan surahs, "Pilgrimage" (surah 22) and "Believers" (surah 23) he makes this doctrine more palpable by offering analogies to bodily resurrection. He also graphically describes Allah's power, which implies Allah's ability to resurrect even dead bodies.

Pilgrimage (22)

People, if you are in doubt about the resurrection of the dead: consider that we created you from earth, then from a clot, then from congealed blood, then from a piece of flesh, partly formed and partly unformed. We did so that we may demonstrate to you our power.

We make what we please rest in the womb until an appointed time. We then bring you forth babies and let you reach your full age. Some of you will die, but others are kept back until the most decrepit age when he no longer knows anything.

You see the earth parched, and when we send down water on it, it stirs and swells, and brings forth herbs of every beauteous kind. This is because God is the truth, He brings life to what is dead, and He has power over all things.

The Hour is coming, there is no doubt in this or that He will raise up those who are in their graves.

Some people dispute about God, without having knowledge or guidance or illuminating scripture. He turns his head away from God in scorn to mislead others from the path of God. He will be disgraced both in this world and on the day of the resurrection. We will make him experience the torment of burning.

It will be said: "This is because of the deeds which your hands have done before, for God is not unjust to His servants."

Believers (23)

[Once born], you will surely die; then you will be raised on the day of resurrection. We have created seven heavens above you; we are not careless with our creation.

We send down water from the heaven water in the right quantity, and we make it fall into the ground; but, we are still able to take it away. Through this we produce orchards of palms and grapes where you have much fruit, and from which you eat. A tree growing out of Mount Sinai produces oil and a condiment to eat.

Cattle also provide you with an example. We give these to you to drink from what is in their bellies. You have other benefits from them: you eat them and ride on them as you do ships.

Source: *Surahs* 22:5–10, 23:12–22.

REVEALED QUR'AN

As Muhammad's revelations grew to a sizable collection within a few years, the Qur'an itself frequently became a subject of further revelation. A middle Meccan surah recounts, "We have divided the Qur'an into sections so that you may recite it to the people with deliberation. We have imparted it by gradual revelation" (surah 17:106). Another states, "We have revealed the Qur'an in the Arabic tongue so that you may understand its meaning. It is a transcript of the eternal book in our keeping, sublime, and full of wisdom" (surah 43:3–4). In a late Meccan surah, Muhammad's illiteracy is offered as proof that the Qur'an was divinely revealed (surah 29:48). The following from "Jonah" (surah 10), of the late Meccan period, discusses the fate of those who deny the divine authority of the Qur'an.

Is it a surprise to mankind that we inspired a man from among them, saying "Warn mankind, and give good news to those who believe that the Lord favors them because of their devotion?" Unbelievers say that this man [i.e., Muhammad] is clearly a sorcerer.

Your Lord is God, who created the heavens and the earth in six days. He then took his throne to govern the affair. No one can plead with him unless he first gives permission. This is your God, your Lord, so worship Him. Do you not understand?

To Him you will all return, God's promise is true. He makes his creatures, then He has them return again to him so that He may reward those who believe and do what is right and just. But for those who disbelieve, they will drink boiling water and be severely punished for their disbelief. . . .

But when our clear revelations are recited to them, those who do not hope to meet us say, "Bring us a different Qur'an, or change this." Say, "It is not for me to change it of my own will; I only follow what has inspired me. If I defy my Lord, I will fear the torment of a terrible day."

Say: "If God had pleased, I would not have recited it to you, nor would he have made you aware of it. I had lived a lifetime with you prior to this. Can you not understand?"

Who is more sinful than the person who creates lies about God, or denies His revelations? These sinners will not succeed. . . .

This Qur'an could not have been created by anyone except God. It confirms what came before it and it clarifies the Scriptures from the Lord of the worlds. There is no doubt about this.

If they say, "He created it himself," say "If what you are saying is true, then find a chapter like it, and call on whoever you can besides God." They deny that which their understanding cannot grasp, while the clarification of it has not yet come to them. Others before them also disbelieved, and see what has happened to those evil ones.

Some believe in this, and others do not. But your Lord knows best who the evil ones are.

Source: *Surah* 10:2–4, 16–18, 37–41.

QUR'AN: MUHAMMAD IN MEDINA

LAWS

In 622, Muhammad and his early followers migrated to Medina, where he became the city administrator. The focus of his revelations soon shifted from that of a lone defender of monotheism to that of a lawgiver. The following selections from "The Cow" (surah 2) present laws concerning drinking, gambling, orphans, divorce, weaning, widows, and dowries.

Various Laws

If they ask you about wine and gambling, say, "There is both sin and benefit with them, but the sin outweighs the benefit."

If they ask you how much they should spend on charity, say "Give what you can spare." Thus God makes clear his revelations so that you may happily reflect on this world and the next.

If they ask you about orphans, say, "It is best to be fair to them." If you interact with them, remember that they are your brothers. God knows the evildoer from the well doer, and if he wishes He can surely punish you. God is mighty and wise.

Do not marry idolatrous women until they first become believers, for surely a believing slave girl is better than an idolatrous woman, even if she pleases you. Do not wed idolatrous men until they first become believers, for a believing slave is better than an idolater, even if he pleases you. They invite you to the Fire, but God invites you to paradise and forgiveness. Through His grace, he makes clear His revelations to everyone, which they may remember.

If they ask you about menstruation, say, "It is an uncleanliness, so keep away from women during menstruation, and do not be intimate with them until they are clean. When they are clean, be intimate with them in the manner that God has directed you. God loves those who turn to Him, and those who keep themselves clean.

Your women are your land to cultivate, so cultivate whenever you choose. Do good deeds and fear God. Know that you are going to meet Him, and give good news to believers.

Do not make oaths in God's name that will prevent you from being virtuous and from promoting peace among people. God hears and knows. He will not punish you for mistakes in your oaths, but He will punish you for what your hearts have earned. God is gracious and merciful.

Marriage and Divorce

Those who abstain from intimacy with their wives must wait four months; but if they break their vow, God is forgiving and merciful. If they intend to divorce their wives, God hears and knows.

Divorced women [before remarrying] must keep to themselves for three menstrual cycles and wait for the results [of possible pregnancy]. It is unlawful for them to hide what God has created in their wombs, assuming they believe in God and the last day. In this case [where the woman is pregnant from her husband] it is best for their husbands to take them back and reconcile. In all fairness, women must act toward their husbands as their husbands act toward them. But men have precedence over them. God is mighty and wise.

Divorce is permitted twice. After that, they should stay together or separate with kindness. It is not lawful to take from them anything that you have given them, unless both fear that they cannot keep within God's bounds. So if you fear that you cannot keep within God's bounds, it is no crime in you both if she ransoms herself. These are God's bounds, do not transgress them. Those who transgress against God's bounds are evil doers.

If a husband divorces his wife, it is unlawful for him to remarry her until she first marries another husband; if he too then divorces her, it is lawful for them both to come together again, assuming they think that they can keep within God's bounds. These are God's bounds which He makes clear to a people of understanding.

When you divorce your wives, and they have reached the required waiting time, then either retain them kindly, or let them go kindly. But do not retain them by force to harm them, for whoever does that is unjust in his soul. Do not take God's revelation lightly. Remember God's favors to you, and that He has sent down to you a Scripture and wisdom to warn you. Fear God, and know that God knows everything.

When you divorce your wives, and they have reached their required waiting time, do not prevent them from marrying their new husbands when they have made reasonable terms of agreement with each other. This is a warning against those of you who believe in God and the last day. This is better and more proper for you. God knows, but you do not know.

Mothers must nurse their children two whole years if the father wishes the nursing term to be complete. Fathers must provide food and clothing for them, but within reason for no one is obliged beyond his capacity. A mother will not be treated unfairly because of her child; nor the child's father. The same obligation is required of the father's heir. If upon counseling the parents mutually consent to wean that child, then doing so will not be unlawful. And if you wish to provide a wet-nurse for your infant, it is permitted if you promise to pay her reasonably. Fear God, and know that God sees what you do.

Those of you who die and leave wives behind, they must wait by themselves for four months and ten days. When they have reached their required time, it is no dishonor to you for them to do whatever they will with themselves, within reason. God is well aware of what you do. It is permissible for you to make them an offer of marriage, or secretly consider doing so within your hearts. God knows that you will remember them. Do not meet with them in secret, unless you speak honorably. Do not decide on marriage until the waiting period is reached. God sees what is in your souls, so beware, and know that God is forgiving and merciful.

It is permissible for you to divorce your wives if you have not yet touched them, or settled on their dowry. But compensate them, the wealthy according to his circumstance and the poor according to his. A reasonable compensation is a duty in this situation.

If you divorce them before you have touched them, but you have already settled on their dowry, then give them back half of the dowry unless they relinquish it. But it is more honorable for the husband to relinquish it. Remember to be generous with each other. God sees what you do.

Observe the prayers, especially the middle prayer, and stand attentive before God. If you are fleeing an enemy, then pray on foot or on horseback. But when you are in safety, remember God. He taught what you did not previously know.

If you die and leave widows, you should bequeath to them maintenance for a year, without making them leave their homes. But it is no dishonor to you if they leave voluntarily for any purpose. God is mighty and wise.

Source: *Surah* 10:2–4, 16–18, 37–41.

TREATMENT OF WOMEN

In spite of contemporary criticism of the treatment of women in Muslim societies, Islam introduced women's rights where few existed previously. Before Muhammad, women were more like property, with no inheritance rights, and female infants often were buried alive. Marriage contracts were loose and often temporary. Muhammad condemned infanticide and required that daughters be given a share of inheritance. In matters of marriage, adultery was denounced, women were allowed the right of consent for marriage, and divorce became more difficult. Written about 626, the following selections from "Women" (surah 4) are laws pertaining to women and include some of these reforms.

God instructs you concerning your children. The son should inherit the same portion as two daughters, and if there are more than two daughters, then they should inherit two-thirds of what the deceased leaves. If there is only one daughter, then she should inherit half. Concerning the man's parents, each of them should inherit a sixth of what he leaves, if the man had children. But if the man has no children, and his parents inherit, then his mother should inherit one third. If the man has brothers, his mother should inherit a sixth of what is left after other bequests and debts. Between your parents and your children, you do not know which is closest to you in usefulness. This is a law from God. God is knowing and wise.

Husbands will inherit half of what their wives leave, if they have no children. But if they have children, then husbands will inherit a fourth of what is left after other bequests and debts. Wives will inherit one fourth of what husbands leave if you have no children. If they have children, wives will inherit one eighth of what is left after other bequests and debts. If a man or woman has no children or parents, but has two siblings, then each will inherit one sixth. If there are additional siblings, they will inherit equal shares of one third of what is left after other bequests and debts, without prejudicing others. This is a law from God. God is knowing and wise.

These are God's bounds, and whoever obeys God and His Messenger, God will allow him to enter gardens watered by flowing rivers, and to live there forever. That is a mighty achievement. But those who rebel against God and His Messenger, and violate His bounds, God will send him to a Fire where he will live forever. For him this is a shameful tragedy.

If your women commit adultery, call in four witnesses from among yourselves. If they confirm this, then keep those women in houses until death releases them, or God finds another way for them.

If two men commit indecency, then punish them both. But if they repent and change their ways, leave them alone. God is forgiving and compassionate.

God forgives those who do evil through ignorance but then quickly repent. God is all-knowing, wise. But God does not forgive those who do evil and on their deathbeds finally say "Now I repent." Nor does he forgive those who die in disbelief. For each of these We have prepared a severe punishment.

Believers it is unlawful for you to inherit women of your deceased kinsmen against their will. Do not prevent them from remarrying with the intention of keeping part of the dowry that you have given them, unless it is proven that they have committed adultery. Live with them with gentleness, for if you disfavor them, it may be that you disfavor something in which God has placed much good for you.

If you wish to replace one wife for another, and have given one of them a something of great value, then do not take anything from it. That would be wrong and clearly unjust. How can you take it back when one of you have slept with each other and have made a firm contract?

Do not marry women that your fathers had married, except from previous marriages. It is detestable, hateful, and an evil thing. It is unlawful for you to marry your mothers, your daughters, your sisters, your paternal aunts, your maternal aunts, your brother's daughters, your sister's daughters, your foster mothers, your foster sisters, and your wives' mothers. Nor may you marry your step daughters who are your wards and born of your wives with whom you have been intimate, but if you have not been intimate with them, it is permissible. Nor may you marry the lawful spouses of your sons from your own production, and two sisters—unless you have already done so, for God is forgiving and merciful. Nor may you marry a woman who is already married, except if she is your slave. God's Book against you.

It is lawful for you to marry anyone else besides this, so long as you provide for them with your wealth, act properly, and do not marry them for fornicating. For the pleasure you have enjoyed of them, give them their lawful dowry as you are obligated. For it is no crime for you to make any other agreement between yourselves after you have fulfilled your obligation. God is knowing and wise.

If you do not have sufficient means of marrying a free woman who is a believer, then marry a slave girl who is a believer. God best knows about your faith, for you come one from the other. Marry them, then, with the permission of their masters, and give them their fair dowry, assuming they are chaste, and do not receive lovers. Once married to you, if they commit adultery, then inflict on them half the penalty for a free married women. This is permitted for you who fear sinning by marrying free unbelieving women, but it is better for you if you can avoid marrying slaves. God is forgiving and merciful.

Men have authority over women because of those advantages that God has given the one of them to excel the other, and for the expense it takes in maintaining their wives. Good women are obedient and, in the absence of their husbands, guard what God would have them guard. But those who you fear may be disloyal, reprimand them, move them to separate rooms, and hit them. But if they are obedient, do not look for a reason to quarrel with them. God is high and great.

If they fear a split between husband and wife, get a mediator from his family and one from hers, assuming they desire reconciliation. God will reunite them; God is knowing and wise....

If they ask your advice about women, say "God gives you instructions about them, and so does that which is revealed to you in Scripture, such as about widowed women that you are opposed to marrying and do not wish to give what is owed to them, or about helpless children, or about dealing fairly with orphans. God knows the good that you do."

If a woman fears abuse or desertion from her husband, it is permissible for them both to reconcile with each other, for reconciliation is better than separation. Souls are prone to selfishness, so act kindly and know that God is aware of what you do.

You may not be able to treat your wives equally, even though you want to. However, do not be overly partial to one while leaving the other in suspense. If you act properly and fear wrongdoing, then God is forgiving and merciful. But if they separate, God can satisfy both out of His wealth, for God is abundant and wise.

Source: *Surah* 4:11–25, 34–35, 127–130.

JESUS THE PROPHET

According to the Qur'an, Jesus is a highly exalted prophet who was born of a virgin, performed miracles, delivered God's message, and will return at the end of time. However, the Qur'an denies the reality of the crucifixion, implying either that it was an illusion or that someone else was crucified as a substitute for Jesus. It also denies the Trinity and the divine nature of Jesus. The following selections, from two surahs, express these views about Jesus. The first, from "Mary" (surah) 19 describes how the infant Jesus miraculously spoke to Mary's relatives about his divinely appointed role as a prophet. The second, from "The Table" (surah 5), describes some of Jesus' miracles and how Jesus denied ever claiming to be God.

Infant Jesus Speaks

Mary brought the child Jesus to her people, carrying him in her arms. They said to her, "Mary, have you done something awful? Sister of Aaron, your father was not a bad man, and your mother was not a prostitute." She then signaled to the child to answer them. They said, "How can we speak to him? He is only an infant in the cradle."

Then the infant said, "I am the servant of God. He has given me the Book of the Gospel, and has appointed me a prophet. He has made me blessed wherever I will be; and has required me to observe prayer and to give to charity, as long as I live. He has required me to be kind to my mother, and not be disobedient or unpleasant. Peace is on me the day I was born, the day I will die, and the day I will be raised to life."

Such was Jesus, the son of Mary. It is the word of truth, concerning which they dispute.

Jesus Denies being God

On the day that God will assemble the Messengers, he will say to them, "What response did you receive when you preached to the people where you were sent?" They will answer, "We do not know, you are the knower of secrets."

When God said, "Jesus, son of Mary, remember my kindness toward you and toward your mother. I strengthened you with the Holy Ghost so you could speak to men in the cradle and when grown up. I taught you the Scripture, wisdom and the law and the gospel. It was with my power that you created the likeness of a bird out of clay which, when you blew on it, became a bird. It was by my permission that you healed the blind from birth and the leprous. It was by my permission that you brought forth the dead. I protected you from the children of Israel when you came to them with clear signs, and the disbelievers among them said 'this is nothing but sorcery.' I inspired the disciples to believe in me and my Messenger, they said, 'We believe, bear witness that we submit.'"

The disciples asked, "Jesus, son of Mary, is your Lord able to send down to us a banquet table from heaven?"

Jesus replied, "Fear God, if you believe."

They then said, "We desire to eat from that table so that our hearts may be content, and we know that what you have told us is true, and that we may be thereby among the witnesses."

Jesus the son of Mary replied, "God, our Lord, send down to us a table from heaven so it may be a feast for all of us, and a sign from You. Provide for us, for You are the best of providers."

God said, "Yes, I will send it down to you; but whoever disbelieves among you after that, I will punish with a severity which I have not imposed on anyone before." Then God said, "Jesus, son of Mary, did you ever say to men, worship me and my mother as two gods, beside God?"

Jesus replied, "Praise to you. But it is not my place to say what I have no right to say. If I had said it, You would have known it; You know what is in my heart, but I do not know what is in Your heart. You are one who knows the unseen. I never told them anything except what You instructed me, namely, worship God, my Lord and your Lord. I was a witness of their actions while I lived among them. But now that you have taken me away to yourself, You watch over them, for You are witness over all. If You desire, punish them, for they are Your servants. If You desire, forgive them. You are mighty and wise."

God said, "Today they will benefit from the truth of their confession, for they will have gardens beneath flowing rivers to live in forever and ever." God is well pleased with them, and they are well pleased with Him; this is the greatest happiness.

Source: *Surah* 19:29-34; 5:109–119.

UNBELIEVING PEOPLE OF THE BOOK

According to the Qur'an, certain groups of people had received revealed scriptures prior to Muhammad. These "people of the book" include the Jews, Christians, Zoroastrians, and Sabians. The Qur'an acknowledges the legitimacy of these religions, maintaining a place for such believers in the afterlife. However, he argues, many people of the book have abandoned their revealed teachings by adopting false gods and denying God's true prophets. The following selection from "The Table" (surah 5) criticizes the unbelieving people of the book.

People of the Book, Our Messenger has come to you to clarify many things that you concealed and passed over in the scriptures. A light and a clear Book of revelation now comes to you from God. . . .

We revealed the Torah which contains guidance and light. The prophets, who professed true religion, used it to judge those who were Jews. The Rabbis and Scholars also judged others by the Scriptures, which were committed to their care and of which they were witnesses.

Do not fear men, but fear me, and do not sell my revelations for a trivial purpose. Those who fail to judge according to what God has revealed are unbelievers.

We commanded them in Scripture to give life for life, eye for eye, nose for nose, ear for ear, and tooth for tooth, and wound for wound. But whoever declines retaliation out of charity, that should be accepted as compensation for him. Those who fail to judge according to what God's revelations are unjust.

We also had Jesus the son of Mary to follow in the footsteps of the messengers, confirming the Torah which was sent down before him. We gave him the Gospel, containing guidance and light, confirming also the Scripture which was given before it, and also giving direction and warnings to those who fear God. Thus, those who received the gospel should judge according to what God has revealed in it; those who fail to judge according to what God has revealed are transgressors. . . .

True believers, do not take Jews or Christians for your friends. Some are friends of each other, but if you befriend them, you become one of them. God does not direct you to unjust people. . . .

Moreover, if the People of the Book believe and fear God, we will surely acquit them from their sins, and we will lead them into gardens of pleasure. If they observe the Torah, the Gospel, and the other Scriptures which have been sent down to them from their Lord, they will surely eat good things both from above them and from under their feet. There are people among them who act properly; but evil is what many of them do.

Messenger, circulate the entirety of what your Lord has sent down to you. If you do not, then you will have failed to deliver His message. God will protect you from everyone. God does not guide the unbelievers.

Say, "People of the Book, you are not grounded on anything, until you observe the Torah and the Gospel, and that which has been sent down to you from your Lord." That which has been sent down to you from your Lord will surely increase the transgression and disbelief of many of them: but do not be concerned for the unbelieving people. Believers, Jews, Sabians, and Christians: whoever among them believes in God and the last day, will have nothing to fear or nor be grieved about.

We previously made a covenant with the children of Israel, and sent messengers to them. When a messenger visited them with a message that they did not want to hear, they accused some of them of deceiving them, and they killed others. They presumed that there should be no punishment for those crimes, and they became blind and deaf. God turned to them with forgiveness, but afterwards many of them again became blind and deaf. God saw what they did.

They are surely unbelievers who say "God is the Messiah, the son of Mary." The Messiah himself said, "Children of Israel, serve God, my Lord and your Lord." Whoever elevates other gods to God's level, God will exclude him from paradise, and his home will be hell fire. The evil ones will have no one to help them.

They are certainly unbelievers who say "God is the third of three." For there is no God besides the one God. If they continue saying these things, a severe punishment will surely be inflicted those unbelievers.

Will they not therefore turn to God, and ask forgiveness from him? God is gracious and merciful.

The Messiah, the son of Mary, was only a messenger. Other messengers had preceded him, and his mother, though virtuous, was only a woman. They both ate normal food. See how we declare to them the revelations of God's unity; and see how they turn away from the truth.

Say, "Will you worship, besides God, something that has no power to harm or help you?" God hears and sees everything.

Say, "People of the Book, do not go beyond the proper boundaries of your religion by speaking what is not true. Do not follow the views of those who have erred, seduced many, and strayed from the strait path."

The disbelievers among the children of Israel were cursed by the tongue of David, and of Jesus the son of Mary. This happened to them because they were rebellious and transgressed. They did not stop one another from the evil which they committed. What they did was wrong.

Source: *Surah* 5:15, 44–47, 51, 65–78.

FIVE PILLARS OF ISLAM

The primary ritual requirements of Islam are known as the Five Pillars of Islam (arkan ad-din). They are (1) sincerely uttering the creed, "There is no God but Allah, and Muhammad is his messenger" (shahada), (2) praying five times a day facing Mecca (salat), (3) paying an alms tax for the needy (zakat), (4) fasting during the month of Ramadan (sawm), and (5) making a pilgrimage to Mecca once in one's life, if possible (hajj). Each of these has its foundation in the Qur'an. Elements of the first pillar—the creed—are found in surahs 37:35, 47:19, and 48:29. The remaining four pillars are discussed in the following selections from "The Cow" (surah 2), from the late Medinan period.

Prayer

We have seen you turn about your face toward heaven with uncertainty, but we will make you turn yourself toward a direction that will please you. Turn your face toward the Sacred Mosque, and wherever you are, turn toward it. Those who were given Scripture know this to be truth from their Lord. God is not ignorant of what they do.

Even if you would show them every kind of proof, they would still not follow your direction, and neither would you follow their direction. Nor will any of them follow the direction of each other. If you follow their desires, after receiving the knowledge which has been given you, then you will become an evil one.

Those to whom we have given Scripture know our messenger, just as they know their own children. But some of them hide the truth against their own knowledge. Truth is from your Lord, so do not doubt it.

Everyone has a goal toward which God turns him. Strive to run toward good things. Wherever you are, God will bring you all back together, for God is almighty.

Wherever you come from, face toward the Sacred Mosque, and wherever you are, face toward it, so that men may have no argument against you, except only those among them who are unjust. Do not fear them, but fear me so that I may fulfil my favors to you, and you may be properly guided.

Fasting

Believers, fasting is required of you, just as it was required of those before you, so that you may avoid evil. You should fast for a certain number of days. But for those among you who are sick or on a journey, fast an equal number of other days.

Those who cannot do it, they may make up for their neglect by feeding a poor man. But if he voluntarily does what is good, this will be better for him. But to fast is better for you, if you only knew it.

The month of Ramadhan is when the Qur'an was revealed as a guide for everyone, with clear signs for guidance and judgment. If you are home on this month, then fast during it. But if you are sick or on a journey, then do so on other days. God desires for you what is easy, not what is difficult, so you may complete the number of days, glorify God for having guided you, give him thanks.

When my servants ask you about me, then I am near; I will hear the prayer of him that prays, when he prays to me. Let them listen to me, and believe in me, that they may be properly directed. It is lawful for you on the night of the fast to be intimate with your wives: they are a garment to you, and you to them. God knows that you cheat yourselves otherwise, but he turns toward you and forgives you. So, be intimate with them, and earnestly desire that which God ordains for you. Also, eat and drink until you can plainly distinguish a white thread from a black thread by dawn's light. Then keep the fast until night, but do not be intimate with your wives, but constantly praying in the mosques. These are the required boundaries of God, so do not go near them to break them. Thus God clarifies his revelations to everyone, that you may obey him. . . .

Alms Giving

Contribute from your means to cause of the religion of God, and do not let your hands cause your downfall. Do good, for God loves those who do good.

Pilgrimage

Make the Great Pilgrimage *(hajj)* or Little Pilgrimage *('umra)* to Mecca for God. If you are prevented from doing so, then send the offering that will be the easiest, and do not shave your heads until your offering reaches the place of sacrifice. But if any of you is sick or afflicted with a head injury, then you must substitute the shaving of your head by fasting, alms giving, or some offering. When secure, if you continue by doing both the Little and Great Pilgrimages, bring whatever offering is the easiest. If you do not have anything to give, then fast three days during the pilgrimage, and seven when you return, totaling ten days. This pertains to him whose house is not in the region of the Sacred Mosque. Fear God, and know that God punishes severely.

The Great Pilgrimage is during known months. For those who decide to go on the Great Pilgrimage, during that time they must not be intimate with women, misbehave, or quarrel. God knows the good that you do. Take provision for your journey, but the best provision is piety. Fear me, you who have understanding.

It is permissible for you to seek profit from your Lord by trading during the pilgrimage. When you proceed from Mount Arafat [on your way to the Sacred Mosque], remember God near the Sacred monument. Remember him for he has guided you, although before this you were among those who went astray. Then proceed from the place where the people go in procession. Ask forgiveness from God, for God is gracious and merciful.

When you have finished your sacred obligations, remember God as you remember your parents, but with more reverence.

Source: *Surah* 2:144–150, 183–187, 195–200.

JIHAD

Often called the sixth pillar of Muslim obligation, jihad, or holy war, is struggling for Allah's cause. Islam divides the world into two homes: the home of submission, encompassing Muslim territories (Dar al-Islam), and the home of struggle, encompassing non-Islamic territories (Dar al-Harb). The obligation of jihad is to extend the home of submission through missionary activities or, when necessary, through armed force. Jihad aims at political control over societies, to govern them by the principles of Islam. In theory, forced conversion of individuals is not intended. It was originally the responsibility of the Caliphs. Traditionally, jihad should be undertaken only when success is likely. Although the explicit obligation of jihad first appears in the Hadith, its foundations are laid in the Qur'an. The following selection from "The Women" (surah 4), written just after the unsuccessful battle of Uhud, advises Muslims who fight for Allah.

Believers, take the necessary precautions against your enemies, and either go to war in separate parties, or go all together in one body.

Among you are some who linger behind the others. If a misfortune occurs to you in battle, the lingerer will say, God has been gracious to me, since I was not killed with them. But if success comes to you from God, the lingerer will say (as if there was no friendship between you and him), I wish to God that I had been with them, for I would have gained great merit.

Let them therefore fight for the cause of God, who give up the present life in exchange for the afterlife. For whoever fights for the cause of God, whether killed or victorious, We will surely give him a great reward.

What reason do you have for not fighting for God's true religion, to help defend vulnerable men, women, and children? The vulnerable say, Lord, remove us from this city of wicked people, give us a protector, and provide us with a defender.

Those who believe will fight for the religion of God; but those who disbelieve will fight for the religion of Evil. So, fight against the friends of the Devil, for the Devil's strategy is weak.

Have you not observed those who were told, Hold back your hands from war, be constant at prayers, and pay the required charity? Then, when they were called to war, observe how some of them fear men the way they should fear God, or even with a greater fear. They say, Lord, why have you commanded us to go to war and have not permitted us to wait for our natural end? Say to them, The enjoyments of this life are small, but the future will be better for these who fear God, and you will not be injured at all on the day of judgment....

They wish that you would become disbelievers, just as they are disbelievers, and that you should be like them. Therefore, do not become friends with any of them, until they travel to the religion of God. If they then turn back from the faith, take hold of them and kill them wherever you find them. Do not take friends or helpers from among them, except those who are in alliance with you, or who come to you with their hearts forbidding them either to fight against you or against their own people.

If God desired, he could have made them more powerful than you, and they would have fought against you.

But if they retreat from you, do not fight against you, and offer you peace, God will not allow you to attack them. . . .

When you march to war on the earth, it is permissible for you to shorten your prayers, if you are afraid that the disbelievers might attack you, for disbelievers are your open enemy. When you, Prophet, are with them and lead them in prayer, let a group of them stand to prayer with you, and let them hold their weapons. When they have completed their prostrations, let them move behind you, and let another group come that has not prayed, and let them pray with you, taking precautions and holding their weapons. The unbelievers hope that you will neglect your weapons and equipment while you pray, so that they can immediately attack you. It is permissible for you to put down your weapons if you are inconvenienced by rain or illness, but still take the necessary precautions. God has prepared for the unbelievers a horrible punishment.

Source: *Surah* 4:71–77, 89–90, 101–102.

MUHAMMAD'S WIVES

The selection below from "The Clans" (surah 33), revealed in about 629, presents the domestic side of Muhammad in his final years. At the time he had nine wives, several previously widowed, and additional slave girls. This surah advises his wives on proper conduct and discusses his relations with them. Recommendations are also made on etiquette when visiting Muhammad.

Wives of the prophet, if you commit a clear indecency, the punishment for it will be doubled to you, and this is easy with God. But if you are obedient to God and his Messenger, and will do that which is right, We will give you twice the reward, and we have prepared for you a generous provision in paradise.

Wives of the prophet, you are not like other women. If you fear God, do not be too free in your speech, in case someone with a heart infected with lust should desire you. Speak in a way that is appropriate. Stay quietly in your houses, and do not display yourselves with the flamboyance of the earlier time of ignorance. Observe the appointed times of prayer, give to charity, and obey God and his Messenger. God desires to remove vanity from you and make you perfectly pure, you who are Members of the Prophet's Family. Remember what is recited to you in your homes concerning the signs of God and the wisdom revealed in the Koran. God is clear-sighted, and well acquainted with your actions.

For Muslim men and women, believing men and women, devout men and women, truthful men and women, patient men and women, humble men and women, charitable men and women, fasting men and women, chaste men and women, praiseful men and women: for you God has prepared forgiveness and a great reward.

When God and his Messenger have decreed something, it is not proper for a true believer of either gender to have the liberty of choosing a different matter of their own. Whoever disobeys God and his Messenger have surely erred.

Remember when you [i.e., Muhammad] said to the man [i.e., Zayd, Muhammad's adopted son] to whom both God and you favored, "Keep your wife to yourself, and fear God." You attempted to keep secret something that God was about to reveal [i.e., that Muhammad intended to marry Zayd's wife]. You did so because you feared others, while it would have been better for you to rear God. When Zayd finally divorced her with the necessary procedure, We joined her with you in marriage. We did so to remove any accusation against true believers who marry the wives of their adopted sons when the divorce followed procedure. God's commends must be performed. Therefore, no crime is to be charged against the Prophet for doing what God allowed him to do. This is just as it was with prophets before him that have since passed away, who delivered God's message and feared only Him. God takes an account of all things.

Muhammad is not the father of any man among you [i.e., he left no male heirs]. He is the Messenger of God, and the Seal of the Prophets. God knows all things. . . . . .

Prophet, we have allowed you your wives to whom you have given dowries; also your slave girls that God granted you as rewards; also the daughters of your paternal uncles and aunts, and the daughters of your maternal uncles and aunts who have fled with you from Mecca; also any other believing woman, if she gives herself to the Prophet and the Prophet desires to marry her. This is a unique privilege granted to you, above the rest of the true believers.

We know what we have instructed other believers concerning their wives and slave girls. So that no one can criticize you, we granted you this privilege. God is gracious and merciful.

You may postpone intimacy with any of your wives or be intimate with them as you see fit. It is permissible for you to desire and take out of turn those whom you have temporarily postponed. This will be easier so that they may be content and pleased with what you give to them all, and not grieve them.

God knows what is in your hearts. He is knowing and gracious.

It will be unlawful for you [i.e., Muhammad] to marry other women after this, or to exchange any of your wives for others, even though their beauty pleases you, except for your slave girls. God observes all things.

Believers, do not enter the houses of the Prophet unless you are given permission to eat with him. Do not wait for its preparation. When you are invited, enter, and when you have eaten, leave. Do not linger and enter into familiar conversation, for this inconveniences the Prophet. It is awkward to ask you to leave, but God is not awkward about the truth. When you ask of the Prophet's wives what you may have occasion for, ask from behind a curtain. This will be purer for your hearts and their hearts.

It is also not appropriate for you to offend the Messenger of God, or to marry his wives after him. This would be a grievous thing in the sight of God.

Whether you divulge something, or conceal it, truly God knows all things.

It is permissible for their fathers, sons, brothers, brothers' sons, sisters' sons, their wives, or their slaves, to speak with them unveiled. But they should fear God; for God is the witness of all things.

Source: *Surah* 33:30–40, 50–55.

IDOLATRY ABOLISHED

By 630, the tables had clearly turned against idolatry in Mecca in favor of Islam. Muhammad rode into the Ka'bah and destroyed its idols. In the following selection from "The Repentance" (surah 9), a declaration of immunity is announced: Muslims would no longer be bound by obligations to idolatrous tribes that repeatedly broke agreements with Muslims. Idolaters would also be barred from the Ka'bah.

A declaration of immunity from God and his Messenger, to the idolaters with whom you have made treaties: Travel safely back and forth across the land four months. Know that you cannot evade God, and that God will disgrace the unbelievers.

A proclamation from God and his Messenger to the people, on the day of the Greater Pilgrimage: God and his Messenger end all agreements with the idolaters. If you repent, this will be better for you; but if you turn back on God, know that you will not evade God.

Warn unbelievers of a painful punishment from God, except the idolaters with whom you have made agreements and who afterwards keep those agreements and not nor assist others against you. Keep these agreements that you have made with them, until their time elapses. God loves those who fear him.

When the months in which you are not allowed to attack them have passed, kill the idolaters wherever you find them. Take them as prisoners, surround them, and ambush them in every convenient place. But if they repent, observe the appointed times of prayer, and pay the required charity, dismiss them freely, for God is gracious and merciful.

If any idolater seeks protection of you, grant him protection so that he may hear the word of God. Afterwards let him reach the place of his security. This will be sufficient since they are people which do not know the excellence of the religion you preach.

How can idolaters make an agreement with God and his Messenger unless they do so at the Sacred Mosque? As long as they are loyal to you, be loyal to them. God loves those who fear him.

How can there be such an agreement when, if they triumph over you, they will not acknowledge the bonds of either blood relationship or treaty? They will please you with their words, but their hearts will oppose you, for most of them are wicked doers.

They sell God's revelations for a small price and obstruct his way. It is certainly evil that they do. They do not acknowledge with believers either blood relationship or treaty. They are disobedient.

Yet if they repent, observe the appointed times of prayer, and give to charity, they will become your brothers in religion. We distinctly proposed our signs to people who understand.

But if they violate their agreements after making treaties, and insult your religion, then you should oppose the leaders of infidelity (for there is no trust in them) so that they may stop their treachery.

Will you not fight against people who have violated their agreements, conspired to banish the Messenger of God, and attacked you first of their own will? Will you fear them? It is better for you to fear God, if you are true believers.

So, attack them. God will punish them by your hands, cover them with shame, and give you the victory over them. He will heal the hearts of the people who believe, and take away the anger in their hearts. God will show mercy to whom he pleases. God is knowing and wise.

Did you think that God will abandon you, even though you fought for his religion, took no friends except God, his Messenger and believers? God knows well what you do.

It is inappropriate for idolaters to visit the mosques of God while persisting in their disbelief. The works of these men are worthless, and they will remain in hell fire forever.

No one should visit the mosques of God except those who believe in God and the last day, pray continually, pay the required charity, and fear God alone. . . .

Believers: the idolaters are unclean; do not let them come near the Sacred Mosque after this year.

Source: *Surah* 9:1–18, 28.

FINAL REVELATION

In 632, just months before his death, Muhammad delivered his final revelation while on pilgrimage to Mecca. Set within the context of dietary regulations from "The Table" (surah 5), Muhammad proclaimed the completion of Islam.

You are allowed to eat animals, except those that you are commanded to abstain from, but not wild animals while you are on pilgrimage to Mecca. God ordains that which he pleases.

True believers, do not violate the holy rites of God, nor the sacred month, nor the animal offering, nor the garlands hung about the animals, nor those who are travelling to the Sacred House, seeking God's favor and pleasure. But when you will have finished your pilgrimage, then you may hunt. Do not let your hatred toward those who prevent you from entering the Sacred House, provoke you to disobey God, by taking revenge on them in the sacred months. Assist each other according to justice and piety, but do not assist each other in injustice and malice. Fear God; for God is severe in punishing.

You are forbidden to eat decayed meat, blood, swine's flesh, and animals that have been dedicated in the name of any besides God. You are forbidden to eat that which has been killed through strangling, violent attack, falling, gorging by the horns of another animal, devoured by wild animal (except what you rescue and then kill yourselves), and that which has been sacrificed to idols. You are forbidden from dividing meat through divination arrows. This is an impiety.

Today the unbelievers have abandoned their religion. Therefore do not fear them, but fear me. Today I have perfected your religion for you, and have completed my mercy on you. I have chosen Islam to be your religion.

But whoever is forced by necessity through hunger to eat of what we have forbidden, not designing to sin, surely God will be indulgent and merciful to him.

They will ask you what they are lawfully permitted to eat. Answer, You may eat things that are good and pure, and also what you have taught birds of prey and dogs to catch, teaching them as God has taught you. So, eat what they will catch for you, and commemorate it in the name of God. Fear God, for God is swift in taking an account.

Today you are allowed to eat things that are good. The food of the People of the Book is also lawfully permitted for you; and your food is lawfully permitted for them.

Source: *Surah* 5:1–5.

HADITH

CALL TO PROPHETHOOD

The Hadith *are collections of reports of events in the life of Muhammad or quotations by him. Within Muslim tradition, they have varying degrees of authenticity, and in their authority the Hadith is second to that of the Qur'an. The story of Muhammad's call to prophethood on the night of power is recorded in the following* Hadith *selection.*

Narrated A'isha the mother of the faithful believers: The commencement of the Divine Inspiration to Allah's Apostle was in the form of good dreams which came true like bright day light, and then the love of seclusion was bestowed upon him. He used to go in seclusion in the cave of Hira' where he used to worship (Allah alone) continuously for many days before his desire to see his family. He used to take with him the journey food for the stay and then come back to (his wife) Khadija to take his food like-wise again till suddenly the Truth descended upon him while he was in the cave of Hira'. The angel came to him and asked him to read. The Prophet replied, "I do not know how to read."

The Prophet added, "The angel caught me (forcefully) and pressed me so hard that I could not bear it any more. He then released me and again asked me to read and I replied, 'I do not know how to read.' Thereupon he caught me again and pressed me a second time till I could not bear it any more. He then released me and again asked me to read but again I replied, 'I do not know how to read (or what shall I read?)' Thereupon he caught me for the third time and pressed me, and then released me and said, 'Read in the name of your lord, who has created (all that exists) and has created man from a clot. Read! And your Lord is the Most Generous.'" (96: 1, 2, 3) Then Allah's Apostle returned with the Inspiration and with his heart beating severely. Then he went to Khadija bint Khuwailid and said, "Cover me! Cover me!" They covered him till his fear was over and after that he told her everything that had happened and said, "I fear that something may happen to me." Khadija replied, "Never! By Allah, Allah will never disgrace you. You keep good relations with your Kith and kin, help the poor and the destitute, serve your guests generously and assist the deserving calamity-afflicted."

Khadija then accompanied him to her cousin Waraqa ibn Naufal ibn Asad ibn 'abdul 'Uzza, who, during the Pre-Islamic Period, became a Christian and used to write the writing with Hebrew letters. He would write from the Gospel in Hebrew as much as Allah wished him to write. He was an old man and had lost his eyesight. Khadija said to Waraqa, "Listen to the story of your nephew, O my cousin!" Waraqa asked, "O my Nephew! What have you seen?" Allah's Apostle described whatever he had seen. Waraqa said, "This is the same one who keeps the secrets (angel Gabriel) whom Allah had sent to Moses. I wish I were young and could live up to the time when your people would turn you out." Allah's Apostle asked, "Will they drive me out?" Waraqa replied in the affirmative and said, "Anyone (man) who came with something similar to what you have brought was treated with hostility; and if I should remain alive till the day when you will be turned out then I would support you strongly." But after a few days Waraqa died and the Divine Inspiration was also paused for a while.

Source: *Sahih al-Bukhari* 1:3, from *The Translation of the Meanings of Sahih al-Bukhari,* tr. Muhammad Muhsin Khan (Chicago: Kazi Publications, 1979), 9 vols. Reprinted by permission.

NIGHT JOURNEY

Surah 17:1 of the Qur'an, written in the middle Meccan period, reads, "Glory be to him who made his servant go by night from the sacred temple [of Mecca] to the farther temple [of Jerusalem] whose surroundings we have blessed, that we might show him some of our signs." In what is referred to as the Night Journey, Muhammad was carried by Gabriel to the temple of Jerusalem (isra) *and brought through the seven heavens to God* (mi'raj). *Although some Muslims interpret this as a vision, most see it as a literal journey. In commemoration of this event, a Muslim shrine called the Dome of the Rock stands on the place of Muhammad's ascent, the former site of the Jewish temple of Jerusalem. It is Islam's third most holy place, after Mecca and Medina. The story of the Night Journey from the* Hadith *is recounted here.*

Narrated Anas ibn Malik from Malik ibn Sa'sa'a that Allah's Apostle described to them his Night Journey saying, While I was lying in Al-Hatim or Al-Hijr, suddenly someone came to me and cut my body open from here to here [across the chest]. He then took out my heart. Then a gold tray full of Belief was brought to me and my heart was washed and was filled (with Belief) and then returned to its original place. Then a white animal which was smaller than a mule and bigger than a donkey was brought to me. . . . The animal's step (was so wide that it) reached the nearest heaven. When he asked for the gate to be opened it was asked, "Who is it?" Gabriel answered, "Gabriel." It was asked, "Who was accompanying you?" Gabriel replied, "Muhammad." It was asked, "Has Muhammad been called?" Gabriel replied in the affirmative. Then it was said, "He is welcomed. What an excellent visit his is!" The gate was opened, and when I went over to the first heaven, I saw Adam there. Gabriel said (to me), "This is your father, Adam; pay him your greetings." So I greeted him and he returned the greeting to me and said, "You are welcomed, o pious son and pious Prophet." Then Gabriel ascended with me till we reached the second heaven. . . . There I saw

Yahya (i.e., John) and 'Isa (i.e., Jesus) who were cousins of each other.... Then Gabriel ascended with me to the third heaven and...there I saw Joseph.... Then Gabriel ascended with me to the fourth heaven and...there I saw Idris....

Then Gabriel ascended with me to the fifth heaven and ... there I saw Harun (i.e., Aaron). Then Gabriel ascended with me to the sixth heaven and...there I saw Moses.... When I left him (i.e., Moses) he wept. Someone asked him, "What makes you weep?" Moses said, "I weep because after me there has been sent (as Prophet) a young man whose followers will enter Paradise in greater numbers than my followers." Then Gabriel ascended with me to the seventh heaven and...there I saw Abraham.... Then I was made to ascend to Sidrat-ul-Muntaha (i.e., the Lote Tree of the farthest limit). Behold! Its fruits were like the jars of Hajr (i.e., a place near Medina) and its leaves were as big as the ears of elephants. Gabriel said, "This is the Lote Tree of the farthest limit." Behold! There ran four rivers, two were hidden and two were visible. I asked, "What are these two kinds of rivers, O Gabriel?" He replied, "As for the hidden rivers, they are two rivers in Paradise and the visible rivers are the Nile and the Euphrates." Then Al-Bait-ul-Ma'mur (i.e., the Sacred House) was shown to me and a container full of wine and another full of milk and a third full of honey were brought to me. I took the milk. Gabriel remarked, "This is the Islamic religion which you and your followers are following." Then the prayers were enjoined on me: They were fifty prayers a day.

When I returned, I passed by Moses who asked (me), "What have you been ordered to do?" I replied, "I have been ordered to offer fifty prayers a day." Moses said, "Your followers cannot bear fifty prayers a day, and by Allah, I have tested people before you, and I have tried my level best with Bani Israil (in vain). Go back to your Lord and ask for reducing your followers' burden." So I went back, and Allah reduced ten prayers for me. Then again I went back to Allah and he reduced ten more prayers. When I came back to Moses he said the same. I went back to Allah and he ordered me to observe ten prayers a day. When I came back to Moses, he repeated the same advice, so I went back to Allah and was ordered to observe five prayers a day. When I came back to Moses, he said "...go back to your Lord and ask for reducing your followers' burden." I said, "I have requested so much of my Lord that I feel ashamed, but I am satisfied now and surrender to Allah's Order." When I left, I heard a voice saying, "I have passed My Order and have reduced the burden of My Worshippers."

Source: *Sahih al-Bukhari* 5:227, tr. Kahn, from *The Translation of the Meanings of Sahih al-Bukhari,* tr. Muhammad Muhsin Khan (Chicago: Kazi Publications, 1979), 9 vols. Reprinted by permission.

CHARITY

Almsgiving (zakat) *is one of the five pillars of Islam and involves a mandatory tax upon those who can afford it. This is often contrasted with deeds of generosity* (sadaqah) *that are voluntary beyond the almsgiving tax. The spirit behind both of these is charity, which is discussed in these* Hadith *selections.*

Abu Musa reported, The Prophet said: "*Sadaqah* is incumbent on every Muslim." They (his companions) said, "O Prophet of Allah! And (what about him) who has not got (anything to give)?" He said: "He should work with his hand and profit himself and give in charity." They said, "What if he has nothing (in spite of this)?" He said: "He should help the distressed one who is in need." They said, "What if he is unable to do this." He said: "He should do good deeds and refrain from doing evil—this is charity on his part."(Bukhari 24:31.)

Abu Hurairah reported, The Prophet said: "On every bone of the fingers charity is incumbent every day: One assists a man in riding his beast or in lifting his provisions to the back of the animal, this is charity; and a good word and every step which one takes in walking over to prayer is charity; and showing the way (to another) is charity."(Bukhari 56:72.)

Abu Hurairah reported, The Prophet said: "Removal from the way of that which is harmful is charity." (Bukhari 46:24.)

Jabir said, The Messenger of Allah said: "Every good deed is charity, and it is a good deed that you meet your brother with a cheerful countenance and that you pour water from your bucket into the vessel of your brother." (*Musnad* of Ahmad Miskhat 6:6.)

Abu Hurairah said, The Prophet said, "The man who exerts himself on behalf of the widow and the poor one is like the one who struggles in the way of Allah, or the one who keeps awake in the night (for prayers) and fasts during the day." (Bukhari 69:1.)

Abu Hurairah said, The Messenger of Allah said, "A prostitute was forgiven—she passed by a dog, panting with its tongue out, on the top of a well containing water, almost dying with thirst; so she took off her boot and tied it to her head-covering and drew forth water for it; she was forgiven on account of this." It was said: Is there a reward for us in (doing good to) the beasts? He said: "In every animal having a liver fresh with life there is a reward." (Bukhari and Muslim Miskhat 6:6.)

Abu Hurairah said on the authority of the Prophet (who said): "There is a man who gives a charity and he conceals it so much so that his left hand does not know what his right hand spends." (Bukhari 24:11.)

Zubair reported, The Prophet said: "If one of you should take his rope and bring a bundle of fire-wood on his back and then sell it, with which Allah should save his honor, it is better for him than that he should beg of people whether give him or do not give him." (Bukhari 24:50.)

Fatimah bint Qais said, The Messenger of Allah said: "In (one's) wealth there is a due besides the zakat"; then he recited: "It is not righteousness that you turn your faces toward the East and the West." (Tirmidhi Miskhat 6:6.)

Ibn Abbas reported, The Prophet sent Mu'adh to Yaman and said: "Invite them to bear witness that there is no god but Allah and that I am the Messenger of Allah; if they accept this, tell them that Allah has made obligatory on them five prayers in every day and night; if they accept this, tell them that Allah has made obligatory in their wealth a charity which is taken from the wealthy among them and given to the poor among them." (Bukhari 24:1.)

Abu Hurairah said, When the Messenger of Allah died and Abu Bakr became (his successor), and those of the Arabs who would disbelieve disbelieved, Umar said, "How do you fight people (who profess Islam)?" and the Messenger of Allah said, "I have been commanded to continue fighting against people until they say, There is no god but Allah; whoever says this will have his property and his life safe unless there is a due against him and his reckoning is with Allah." (Abu Bakr) said, "By Allah! I will fight those who make a difference between prayer and zakat, for zakat is a tax on property; By Allah! If they withhold from me even a she-kid which they used to make over to the Messenger of Allah, I will fight against them for their withholding it." Umar said, "By Allah! Allah opened the heart of Abu Bakr (to receive the truth), so I know that it was true." (Bukhari 24:1.)

Source: Adapted from Maulana Muhammad Ali, *A Manual of Hadith.*

PILGRIMAGE

One of the Five Pillars of Islam is pilgrimage (haj) to the holy city of Mecca, which Muslims are expected to do at least once in their lifetime. The official pilgrimage takes place during one week in the final month of the Islamic calendar. In preparation, the pilgrim must enter a sacred state of ihram, which consists of restrictions in clothing, hygiene, and behavior. Upon arrival in Mecca, the pilgrim performs various rituals that commemorate the lives of Abraham and his wife Hagar, who, according to Muslim tradition, are the founding ancestors of the Arabic people. Chief among these is a visit to the Ka'bah for the ritual of tawaf. This consists of circumambulating the Ka'bah counterclockwise seven times and, if there is no crowd, kissing the corner of the Black Stone on each circuit. The selections that follow are from Hadith passages that discuss pilgrimages during the time of Muhammad.

Ibn 'Abbas reported, Al-Aqra' asked the Messenger "Is the pilgrimage to be performed every year or only once?" He said: "Only once; and whoever does it more than once, it is supererogatory." (Abu Dawud 11:1.)

Ibn 'Abbas said, Fadzl was riding behind the Messenger when a woman of (the tribe of) Khath'am came . . . and she said, "O Messenger of Allah. The ordinance regarding pilgrimage made obligatory by Allah for His servants found my father a very old man unable to sit firmly on a riding camel, shall I perform a pilgrimage on his behalf?" He said, "Yes." And this happened in the Farewell Pilgrimage. (Bukhari 25:1.)

Ibn 'Abbas said, The people of Yaman used to go to pilgrimage while they had no provisions with them and they said, "We are those who trust [in Allah]." But when they came to Mecca they begged of people, so Allah revealed: "And make provision, for the benefit of provision is the guarding oneself." (Bukhari 25:6.)

Ibn 'Umar said, The months of pilgrimage are Shawwal and Dhul-l-Qa'dah and (the first) ten days of Dhu-l-Hijjah. And Ibn 'Abbas said, "It is the Sunnah that a man shall not enter the state of ihram [i.e., a sacred state] except in the months of pilgrimage." (Bukhari 25:34.)

Ibn 'Umar reported about the Prophet, a man asked him, What should a man wear in the state of ihram? He said: "He shall not wear shirt, nor turban, nor trousers, nor head-gear, nor any cloth dyed with wars or saffron; and if he does not find shoes, let him wear leather stockings, and he should cut them off so that they may be lower than the ankles." (Bukhari 3:51.)

Urwah said, A'ishah informed me that when the Prophet entered (Mecca on pilgrimage), the first thing that he did was that he performed ritual washing, then circumambulated [around the Ka'bah], and there was no visit to the Ka'bah. (Bukhari 25:62.)

Ibn 'Abbas said, The Prophet circumambulated the House riding on a camel, and every time that he came to the corner [of the black stone], he made a sign with something which he had with him and said, Allahu Akbar. (Bukhari 25:61.)

Ibn 'Abbas reported, The Prophet said: "The making of circumambulations round the House is like prayer except that you talk in it; and whoever talks in it, let him not talk anything but good."

A'ishah said, We went out with nothing in view but pilgrimage, and when we reached Sarif, I menstruated. The Messenger of Allah entered upon me and I was weeping. He said, "What is the matter? Have you menstruated?" I said, "Yes." He said: "This is a matter that Allah has ordained for the daughters of Adam, so do what the pilgrims do, except that you shall not circumambulate round the House." (Bukhari 6:l.)

'Ali said. The Prophet appointed me, so I superintended the sacrifice of camels; and he ordered me so I distributed their flesh; then he ordered me and I distributed their coverings and their skins. (Bukhari 25:120.)

Jabir said, We used not to eat of the flesh of our sacrifices beyond the three days of Mina; then the Prophet gave us permission and said: "Eat and take it as a provision (for the journey)." So we ate and took it as a provision.

'Abd Allah said, The Prophet, and a party of his companions, had their heads shaven, and some of them had their hair clipped. (Bukhari 25:127.)

Ibn 'Abbas reported, Dhu-l-Majaz and 'Ukaz were markets for trade (during the pilgrimage) in the days of Ignorance. When Islam came, they [i.e., the Muslims] disliked this until it was revealed: "There is no blame on you if you seek bounty from your Lord" at the time of pilgrimage. (Bukhari 25:150.)

Source: Adapted from Maulana Muhammad Ali, *A Manual of Hadith* (Lahore: Ahmadiyya, 1944).

JIHAD

The foundation of jihad—or holy war—was laid down in the Qur'an and Hadith and refined in later legal discussions. The tradition that emerged contends that believers can fulfill jihad in four possible ways: through one's heart, tongue, hand, or sword. Jihad through one's heart—a practice sometimes called greater jihad—*involves overcoming temptation or some personal evil. Islam can next be advanced through the tongue and the hand by defending what is right and rectifying what is wrong. Finally, through the sword, Islam can be militarily advanced—a practice sometimes called* lesser jihad. *The selections here from the* Hadith *are often associated with different types of jihad.*

Abu Hurairah said, A man came to the Messenger of Allah and said, "Guide me to a deed which is equal to jihad." He said, "I do not find it." Then he said: "Is it in your power that when the one engaged in jihad goes forth, you should enter your mosque and stand in prayer and have no rest, and that you should fast and break it not?" He said, "Who can do it?" (Bukhari 56:1.)

Mughirah reported, The Prophet said, "Some people from among my community will remain in the ascendant, until the command of Allah comes to them and they will be triumphant." (Bukhari 61:28.)

Imran ibn Husain said, The messenger of Allah said, "A party of my community will not cease fighting for the Truth—they will be triumphant over their opponents." (Abu Dawud Mishkat 18.)

Abu Hurairah reported, The Messenger of Allah said: "Surely Allah will raise for this community at the beginning of every century one who will revive for it its faith." (Abu Dawud 36:1.)

Ibn Abbas reported, . . . And this (letter) ran as follows: "In the name of Allah, the Beneficent, the Merciful. From Muhammad, the servant of Allah and His Messenger, to Heraclius, the Chief of the Roman Empire. Peace be with him who follows the guidance. After this, I invite you with invitation to Islam. Become a Muslim and you will be in peace— Allah will give you a double reward; but if you turn away, on you will be the sin of your subjects. And, O followers of the Book! Come to an equitable proposition between us and you that we will not serve any but Allah, and that we will not associate aught with Him, and that some of us will not take others for lords besides Allah; but if they turn back, then say: Bear witness that we are Muslims." (Bukhari 1:1.)

Salamah said, "I swore allegiance to the Prophet, then I turned to the shade of a tree." When the crowd diminished, he (the Prophet) said, "O Ibn al-Akwa! Will you not swear allegiance?" He said, "I said, I have already sworn allegiance, O Messenger of Allah!" He said, "And do it again." So I swore allegiance to him a second time. I (the reporter) said to him, "O Abu Muslim! For what did you swear allegiance (to him) then?" He said, "For death." (Bukhari 56:110.)

Abd Allah ibn Aufa reported, The Messenger of Allah said: "And know that paradise is beneath the protection of the swords." (Bukhari 56:22.)

Abu Hurairah said, I heard the Prophet say, "By him in Whose hand is my soul, were it not that there are men among the believers who cannot bear to remain behind me—and I do not find that on which to carry them—I would not remain behind an army that fights in the way of Allah; and by Him in whose hand is my soul. I love that I should be killed in the way of Allah then brought to life, then killed again then brought to life, then killed again then brought to life, then killed again." (Bukhari 56:7.)

Abu Hurairah said, The Messenger of Allah said, "Whom do you count to be a martyr among you?" They said, "O Messenger of Allah! Whoever is killed in the way of Allah is a martyr." He said: "In that case the martyrs of my community will be very few—he who is killed in the way of Allah is a martyr; he who dies a natural death in the way of Allah is a martyr; he who dies of the plague (in the way of Allah) is a martyr; he who dies of cholera (in the way of Allah) is a martyr." (Muslim Miskhat 18.)

Abu Allah reported, "A women was found among the killed in one of the battles of the Prophet so the Messenger of Allah forbade the killing of women and children." (Bukhari 56:147.)

Ibn Umar reported, The Messenger of Allah said: "I have been commanded that I should fight these people till they bear witness that there is no god but Allah and keep up prayer and pay zakat. When they do this, their blood and their property will be safe with me except as Islam requires, and their reckoning is with Allah." (Bukhari 2:16.)

Source: Adapted from Maulana Muhammad Ali, *A Manual of Hadith* (Lahore: Ahmadiyya, 1944).

THE ESSENCE OF ISLAM

Travelers frequently paid visit to Muhammad, sometimes asking to know more about Islam. The following selection is a famous hadith that describes one such visitor and the advice that Muhammad gave him.

Omar Ibn al-Khattab said, one day several companions and I were sitting with the Prophet when suddenly a man appeared before us, whose clothes were very white and hair very black. We could see no indication that he was travelling, and none of us recognized him. Eventually he sat down so close to the Prophet that his knees were near the Prophet's knees, and he placed the palms of his hands on the Prophet and said, "Muhammad, teach me about Islam."

The Prophet said, "Islam is that you testify that there is no God but God, and that Muhammad is his messenger. You should be unwavering in prayer, be charitable, fast during the month of Ramadan and make a pilgrimage to the Ka'ba if you have the ability to do so." The man replied, "You have answered correctly." We wondered at his questioning the Prophet and then telling him that he spoke the truth. Then the man said, "Teach me about faith *(iman)*." The Prophet said, "You should believe in God and in his Angels, in his Books, in his Prophets, in the day of resurrection, and that every virtue and vice is by the will of God." The man said, "You have answered correctly". He then said, "Teach me about proper conduct *(ishan)*." The Prophet said, "You should worship God as if you saw him, for though you do not see him know that he sees you." The man said, "You have answered correctly." He then said, "Teach me about the resurrection." The Prophet said, "I am no wiser than you about this." The man then said, "Then tell me about its signs." The Prophet said, "When a female slave gives birth to her master, and when you see the barefooted, the naked, the homeless and shepherds possessing houses."

Omar then said, after that the man left and I remained sitting along time. The Prophet then said to me, "Do you know who he was?" I replied, "Only God and his prophets know." The Prophet said, "It was the angel Gabriel, and he came here to instruct you about your faith."

Source: Khatib al-Tibrizi, *Mishkat al-Masabih,* 1.1, tr. Arnold N. Matthews (adapted).

RECITING THE QUR'AN

Many Hadith *passages indicate that the memorization and recitation of Qur'anic verses was an expected form of piety for Muslims during Muhammad's life. Muhammad himself ritually recited its passages. Special reciters memorized the Qur'an's entirety and recited it daily. At least one function of recitation was to preserve its content, as illustrated in the following* Hadith *passage: "The Prophet heard a reciter reciting the Qur'an in the mosque at night. The Prophet said, May Allah bestow his mercy on him, as he has reminded me of such-and-such verses of such-and-such surahs, which I missed!" (Sahih al-Bukhari 6:562). Recitation was also a daily ritual for laypeople: "The Prophet said, If one recites the last two verses of surah-al-Baqara at night, it is sufficient for him (for that night)" (Sahih al-Bukhari, 6:560). In Qur'anic recitation, not only the words were memorized, but the tonal songlike vocalizations as well.*

The following describes the variety of vocalizations that were permitted.

> Narrated Umar ibn Al-Khattab: I heard Hisham ibn Hakim reciting *surah* Al-Furqan during the lifetime of Allah's Apostle and I listened to his recitation and noticed that he recited in several different ways which Allah's Apostle had not taught me. I was about to jump over him during his prayer, but I controlled my temper, and when he had completed his prayer, I put his upper garment around his neck and seized him by it and said, "Who taught you this Surah which I heard you reciting?" He replied, "Allah's Apostle taught it to me." I said, "You have told a lie, for Allah's Apostle has taught it to me in a different way from yours." So I dragged him to Allah's Apostle and said (to Allah's Apostle), "I heard this person reciting Surah Al-Furqan in a way which you haven't taught me!" On that Allah's Apostle said, "Release him (O 'Umar)! Recite, O Hisham!" Then he recited in the same way as I heard him reciting. Then Allah's Apostle said, "It was revealed in this way," and added "Recite, O'Umar!" I recited it as he had taught me. Allah's Apostle then said, "It was revealed in this way. This Koran has been revealed to be recited in seven different ways, so recite of it whichever is easier for you."

Source: *Sahih al-Bukhari* 6:514, tr. Kahn, from *The Translation of the Meanings of Sahih al-Bukhari,* tr. Muhammad Muhsin Khan (Chicago: Kazi Publications, 1979), 9 vols. Reprinted by permission.

STONING OF ADULTEROUS JEWS

The Hadith *provides a narrative context for many Qur'anic passages, the meanings of which would otherwise be lost. For example,* surah *17:81 states, "Truth has come and falsehood vanished. Falsehood is ever bound to vanish." Although the surrounding verses provide no context, the* Hadith *does: "Allah's Apostle entered Mecca (in the year of the conquest) and there were three-hundred and sixty idols around the Ka'bah. He then started hitting them with a stick in his hand and said, Truth has come and falsehood vanished. Falsehood is ever bound to vanish" (Sahih al-Bukhari 6:244). The following* Hadith *narrative gives the context for another equally obscure Qur'anic passage: "Bring the Torah and read it, if what you say be true" (surah 3:93). The* Hadith *story, from about the fourth year of the migration to Medina, highlights the interaction between the Jews and early Muslims, Muhammad's administrative function in settling legal questions, and the prohibition against adultery.*

Narrated Abdullah ibn Umar: The Jews brought to the Prophet a man and a woman from among them who had committed illegal sexual intercourse. The Prophet said to them, "How do you usually punish the one among you who has committed illegal sexual intercourse?" They replied, "We blacken their faces with coal and beat them." He said, "Don't you find the order of Ar-Rajm (i.e., stoning to death) in the Torah?" They replied, "We do not find anything in it." 'Abdullah ibn Salam (after hearing this conversation) said to them, "You have told a lie! Bring here the Torah and recite it if you are truthful." (So the Jews brought the Torah.) And the religious teacher who was teaching it to them put his hand over the Verse of Ar-Rajm and started reading what was written above and below the place hidden with his hand, but he did not read the Verse of Ar-Rajm. 'Abdullah ibn Salam removed his (i.e., the teacher's) hand from the Verse of Ar-Rajm and said, "What is this?" So when the Jews saw that Verse, they said, "This is the Verse of Ar-Rajm." So the Prophet ordered the two adulterers to be stoned to death, and they were stoned to death near the place where biers are placed near the Mosque. I saw her companion (i.e., the adulterer) bowing over her so as to protect her from the stones.

Source: Sahih al-Bukhari 6:79, tr. Kahn, from The Translation of the Meanings of Sahih al-Bukhari, tr. Muhammad Muhsin Khan (Chicago: Kazi Publications, 1979), 9 vols. Reprinted by permission.

DEATH OF MUHAMMAD

After complaining of severe headaches, Muhammad died in the house of his favorite wife, A'isha. The Hadith narratives surrounding his death describe his companions' concern about a possible successor to Muhammad and their fear that Muhammad might become an object of worship. The following account of Muhammad's death, attributed to A'isha, maintains that Muhammad appointed no successor.

A'isha, the wife of the Prophet, said, When the ailment of Allah's Apostle became aggravated, he requested his wives to permit him to be treated in my house, and they gave him permission. He came out (to my house), walking between two men with his feet dragging on the ground. . . . When Allah's Apostle entered my house and his disease became aggravated, he said, "Pour on me the water of seven waterskins, the mouths of which have not been untied, so that I may give advice to the people." So we let him sit in a big basin . . . and then started to pour water on him from these waterskins till he started pointing to us with his hands intending to say "You have done your job".... Then he went out to the people and led them in prayer and preached to them....

When Allah's Apostle became ill seriously, he started covering his face with his woolen sheet, and when he felt short of breath, he removed it from his face and said, "That is so! Allah's curse be on the Jews and the Christians, as they took the graves of their prophets as (places of worship)," intending to warn (the Muslims) of what they had done.... I argued with Allah's Apostle repeatedly about the matter (i.e., his order that Abu Bakr should lead the people in prayer in his place when he was ill), and what made me argue so much was that it never occurred to my mind that after the Prophet, the people would ever love a man who had taken his place, and I felt that anybody standing in his place would be a bad omen to the people, so I wanted Allah's Apostle to give up the idea of choosing Abu Bakr (to lead his people in prayer).

Narrated A'isha: It was one of favors toward me that Allah's Apostle expired in my house on the day of my turn while leaning against my chest and Allah made my saliva mix with his saliva at his death. 'Abdur-Rahman entered upon me with a Siwak in his hand and I was supporting (the back of) Allah's Apostle (against my chest). I saw the Prophet looking at the Siwak and I knew that he loved the Siwak, so I said (to him), "Shall I take it for you?" He nodded in agreement. So I took it and it was too stiff for him to use, so I said, "Shall I soften it for you?" He nodded his approval. So I softened it and he cleaned his teeth with it. In front to him there was a jug or a tin containing water. He started dipping his hand in the water and rubbing his face with it. He said, "None has the right to be worshipped except Allah. Death has its agonies." He then lifted his hands (toward the sky) and started saying, "With the highest companion," till he expired and his hand dropped down.

Narrated Al-Aswad: It was mentioned in the presence of A'isha that the Prophet had appointed Ali as successor by will. Thereupon she said, "Who said so? I saw the Prophet while I was supporting him against my chest. He asked for a tray, and then fell on one side and expired, and I did not feel it. So how [do the people say] he appointed Ali as his successor?"

Source: *Sahih al-Bukhari* 5:727, 730, 736, tr. Kahn, from *The Translation of the Meanings of Sahih al-Bukhari,* tr. Muhammad Muhsin Khan (Chicago: Kazi Publications, 1979), 9 vols. Reprinted by permission.

FIRST COMPILATION OF THE QUR'AN

During Muhammad's life, isolated Qur'anic verses were preserved in writing, but the only complete copies existed in the memories of the reciters. The following passage describes the circumstances surrounding the first written compilation of the Qur'an, initiated by the first Caliph, Abu Bakr, a year after Muhammad's death.

Narrated by Zayd ibn Thabit: Abu Bakr As-Siddiq sent for me when the people of Yama-ma had been killed (i.e., a number of the Prophet's Companions who fought against Musailama). [I went to him] and found Umar ibn Al-Khattab sitting with him. Abu Bakr then said [to me], "Umar has come to me and said, 'Casualties were heavy among the Qurra of the Koran (i.e., those who knew the Koran by heart) on the day of the Battle of Yamama, and I am afraid that more heavy casualties may take place among the Qurra on other battlefields, whereby a large part of the Koran may be lost. Therefore I suggest you (Abu Bakr) order that the Koran be collected.' I said to Umar, 'How can you do something which Allah's Apostle did not do?' Umar said, 'By Allah, that is a good project.' Umar kept on urging me to accept his proposal till Allah opened my chest for it and I began to realize the good in the idea which Umar had realized." Then Abu Bakr said [to me], "You are a wise young man and we do not have any suspicion about you, and you used to write the Divine Inspiration for Allah's Apostle. So you should search for [the fragmentary scripts of] the Koran and collect it [in one book]." By Allah! If they had ordered me to sift one of the mountains, it would not have been heavier for me than this ordering me to collect the Koran.... So I started looking for the Koran and collecting it from [what was written on] palm-leaf stalks, thin white stones and also from the men who know it by heart, till I found the last verse of Surah At-Tauba (Repentance) Abi Khuzaima Al-Ansari.... Then the complete manuscripts [copy] of the Koran remained with Abu Bakr till he died, then with Umar till the end of his life, and then with Hasfa, the daughter of Umar.

Source: *Sahih al-Bukhari* 6:509, tr. Kahn, from *The Translation of the Meanings of Sahih al-Bukhari,* tr. Muhammad Muhsin Khan (Chicago: Kazi Publications, 1979), 9 vols. Reprinted by permission.

DEFINITIVE COMPILATION OF THE QUR'AN

In spite of the existence of Abu Bakr's single written compilation of the Qur'an, the Qur'an was still principally transmitted through memorized accounts and scattered written verses. As conflicting versions arose, the third Caliph, Uthman, authorized a definitive written edition twenty-four years after Muhammad's death. The following excerpt recounts the story of Uthman's edition.

Narrated Anas ibn Malik: Hudhaifa ibn Al-Yaman came to 'Uthman at the time when the people of Sha'm and the people of Iraq were waging war to conquer Arminya and Adharbijan. Hudhaifa was afraid of their (the people of Sha'm and Iraq) differences in the recitation of the Koran, so he said to 'Uthman, "O the chief of the Believers! Save this nation before they differ about the Book (Koran) as Jews and the Christians did before." So 'Uthman sent a message to Hafsa saying, "Send us the manuscripts of the Koran so that we may compile the Koranic materials in perfect copies and return the manuscripts to you." Hafsa sent it to 'Uthman. 'Uthman then ordered Zayd ibn Thabit, 'Abdullah ibn Az-Zubair, Sa'id ibn Al-As and 'Abdur-Rahman ibn Harith ibn Hisham to rewrite the manuscripts in perfect copies. 'Uthman said to the three Quaishi men, "In case you disagree with Zayd ibn Thabit on any point in the Koran, then write it in the dialect of Quraish as the Koran was revealed in their tongue." They did so, and when they had written many copies, 'Uthman returned the original manuscripts to Hafsa. 'Uthman sent to every Muslim province one copy of what they had copied, and ordered that all the other Qur'anic materials, whether written in fragmentary manuscripts or whole copies, be burnt. Zayd ibn Thabit added, "A verse from Surah Ahzab was missed by me when we copied the Koran, and I used to hear Allah's Apostle reciting it. So we searched for it and found it with Khuzaima ibn Thabit Al-Ansari. [That verse was]: "Among the believers are men who have been true in their covenant with Allah" (22:23).

Source: *Sahih al-Bukhari* 6:510, tr. Kahn, from *The Translation of the Meanings of Sahih al-Bukhari,* tr. Muhammad Muhsin Khan (Chicago: Kazi Publications, 1979), 9 vols. Reprinted by permission.

SUNNI AND SHI'I WRITINGS

SUNNI ISLAMIC LAW

Ibn Idris al-Shafi'i (767–820) was the foremost scholar of early Islamic law. He is best known for his analysis of the "four roots of jurisprudence." That is, legal questions are resolved by appealing first to the Qur'an, second to the Sunna, third to consensus, and last to analogical reasoning. After his death, Shafi'i's disciples founded the Shafi'ite school; his penetrating analysis of the four roots was also adopted by the other schools of Islamic Law. The following from Shafi'i's Risala *discusses the use of consensus, analogy, and personal reasoning in resolving legal questions.*

Chapter 11. On Consensus (Ijma).

480. Shafi'i said: Some asked me: I have understood your doctrine concerning God's commands and His Apostle's orders that he who obeys God obeys His Apostle, [for] God has imposed [on men] the duty of obeying His Apostle, and that the proof for what you held has been established that it would be unlawful for a Muslim who has known the Book [of God] and the sunna [i.e., Hadith tradition of the Prophet] to give an opinion at variance with either one, for I know that this [i.e., acceptance of the Book and the sunna] is a duty imposed by God. But what is your proof for accepting the consensus of the public [on matters] concerning which no explicit command of God nor any [sunna] related on the authority of the Prophet is to be found? Do you assert, with others, that the consensus of the public should always be based on an established sunna even if it were not related [on the authority of the Prophet]?

481. [Shafi'i] replied: That on which the public are agreed and which, as they assert, was related from the Apostle, that is so. As to that which the public do not relate [from the Prophet], which they may or may not relate as a tradition from the Prophet, we cannot consider it as related on the authority of the Prophet—because one may relate only what he has heard, for no one is permitted to relate [on the authority of the Prophet] information which may or may not be true. So we accept the decision of the public because we have to obey their authority, and we know that wherever there are sunnas of the Prophet, the public cannot be ignorant of them, although it is possible that some are, and we know that the public can neither agree on anything contrary to the sunna of the Prophet nor on an error....

484. He asked: What is the meaning of the Prophet's order to follow the community? ....

487. [Shafi'i] replied: When the community spread in the lands [of Islam], nobody was able to follow its members who had been dispersed and mixed with other believers and unbelievers, pious and impious. So it was meaningless to follow the community [as a whole], because it was impossible [to do so], except for what the [entire] community regarded as lawful or unlawful [orders] and [the duty] to obey these [orders].

He who holds what the Muslim community holds shall be regarded as following the community, and he who holds differently shall be regarded as opposing the community he was ordered to follow. So the error comes from separation: but in the community as a whole, there is no error concerning the meaning of the Qur'an, the sunna, and analogy.

Chapter 12. On Analogy (Qiyas).

488. He asked: On what ground do you hold that [on matters] concerning which no text is to be found in the Book, nor a sunna or consensus, recourse should be had to analogy? Is there any binding text for analogical deduction?
489. [Shafi'i] replied: If analogy were [stated] in the text of the Book or the sunna, such a text should be called either God's command or the Apostle's order rather than analogy.
490. He asked: What is analogy? Is it personal reasoning [ijtihad], or are the two different?
491. [Shafi'i] replied: They are two terms with the same meaning. . . .
493. On all matters touching the [life of a] Muslim there is either a bonding decision or an indication as to the right answer. If there is a decision, it should be followed; if there is no indication as to the right answer, it should be sought by personal reasoning, and personal reasoning is analogy [qiyas]. . . .
496. [He asked]: If [legal] knowledge is derived through analogy—provided it is rightly applied—should [the scholars] who apply analogy agree on most [of the decision], although we may find them disagreeing on some?
497. [Shafi'i replied]: Analogy is of two kinds: the first, if the case in question is similar to the original meaning [of the precedent], no disagreement on this kind [is permitted]. The second, if the case in question is similar to several precedents, analogy must be applied to the precedent nearest in resemblance and most appropriate. But those who apply analogy are likely to disagree [in their answers]. . . .

Chapter 13. On Personal Reasoning (Ijtihad).

534. He asked: On what ground do you hold that [the exercise of] personal reasoning [ijtihad] is permitted in addition to what you have already explained?
535. [Shafi'i] replied: It is on the basis of God's saying: "from whatever place thou issuest, turn thy face in the

direction of the Sacred Mosque; and wherever you may be, turn your faces in its direction" [Koran. II. 145]. Regarding him who [wishes to] face the Sacred Mosque [in prayer] and whose residence is at a distance from it, [legal] knowledge instructs [us] that he can seek the right direction through ijtihad on the basis of certain indications [guiding] toward it. For he who is under an obligation to face the Sacred House and does not know whether he is facing the right or wrong direction may be able to face the right one through certain indications known to him [which helps him] to face it as accurately as he can, just as another person may know other indications which help to orient him [in the right direction], although the direction sought by each person may be different from that sought by the other.

Source: Ibn Idris al-Shafi'i, *Risala*, 480, 481, 484, 487, 488–491, 493, 496, 497, 534, 535, from *Islamic Jurisprudence: Shafi'i's Risala,* tr. Majid Khadduri (Baltimore: Johns Hopkins Press, 1961). Reprinted by permission.

SUNNI CREED

Born in Basra, in what is now Iraq, al-Ash'ari (873–935) was a prominent theologian in the Sunni Hanbalite school of Islamic law. He argued that God's acts are utterly beyond rational comprehension and that, if God willed, He could send devout believers to hell. Al-Ash'ari is credited with having formulated the first systematic creed of Islam, which is presented below. Bracketed references are to passages in the Qur'an.

The essence of our belief is that we confess faith in Allah, His angels, His Books, His Messengers, the revelation of Allah, and what the trustworthy have handed down on the authority of Allah's Messenger, rejecting none of them.

We confess that Allah is One—There is none worthy of worship but He—unique, eternal, possessing neither consort nor child; and that Muhammad is His servant and Messenger, who He sent with the guidance and the real Religion; and that Paradise is real and Hell is real; and that there is no doubt regarding the Coming Hour; and that Allah will raise up all those who are in the graves; and that Allah is on His throne (as He has said, "The Merciful is on the Throne"—[20:4]); and that He has a face (as He has said, "but the Face of your Lord shall abide resplendent with majesty and glory"—[55:27]); and that He has two hands, bila kaifa (without asking how?) (as He has said, "I have created with my two hands,"—[38:75] and he has said, "nay! Outstretched are both His hands"—[5:69]); and that He has an eye, without asking how (as He said, "under Our eyes it floated on"—[54:14]), and that anybody who thinks that the names of Allah are other than He is in error; and that Allah has Knowledge (as He has said, "in His knowledge He sent it down,"—[4:164]), and (as He said, "And no female conceives and brings forth without His knowledge"—[35:12]), we also assert that Allah has hearing and sight, and we do not deny it as the Mu'tazila, the Jahmiyyah, and the Khaarijites deny it; and we assert that Allah has Prowess (Quwwah) (as He has said, "saw they not that Allah Who created them was mightier than they in Prowess?"—[41:14]); and we believe that the Word of Allah is uncreated, and that He has created nothing without first saying to it, "Be!," And it is (as He has said, "Our word to a thing when we will it is but to say, 'Be!,' and it is"—[16:42]), and that there is no good or evil on earth save what Allah wishes: and that things exist by Allah's wish; and that not a single person has the capacity to do anything until Allah causes him to act, and we are not independent of Allah, nor can we pass beyond the range of Allah's knowledge; and that there is no creator save Allah, and the works of human beings are things created and decreed by Allah (as He had said, "Allah has created you and what you make"—[37:94]); and that human beings have not the power to create anything, but are themselves created (as He has said, "Is there a creator other than Allah?"—[35:3], and as He has said, "they create nothing, but are themselves created,"—[16:20] and as he said, "Shall He who creates be as He who creates not?,"—[16:17] and as He has said, "were they created by nothing or were they themselves the creators?,"—[52:35] for this is mentioned in Allah's Book frequently); and that Allah favors the Believers by granting them obedience to Him, is gracious to them, considers them, does what is salutary for them, guides them; whereas He causes the Disbelievers to stray, does not guide them, does not give them the grace to believe.

As the deviators and rebels think for if He were gracious to them and did what is salutary for them they would be sound; and if He guided them, they would be guided; as He has said, "He whom Allah guides is the guided and they whom he misleads will be the lost"—[7:177], and that Allah has power to do what is salutary for the infidels and be gracious to them, that they may become believers, nevertheless He wills that they be infidels, as He knows; and that He forsakes them and seals up their hearts; and that good and evil are dependent upon the general and the particular decrees of Allah, His sweet and His bitter; and we know that what passes us by was not to befall us, and what befalls us was not to pass us by; and that human beings do not control for themselves what is hurtful or what is helpful, except what Allah wishes; and that we ought to commit our affairs to Allah and assert our complete need of and dependence upon Him.

We believe, too, that the Qur'an is the uncreated word of Allah, and that he who believes that the Qur'an is created is an infidel.

We hold that Allah will be seen in the next world by sight (as the moon is seen on the night it is full, so shall the faithful see Him, as we are told in the traditions that come down on the authority of Allah's Messenger); and we believe that the infidels will be veiled from Him when the faithful see Him in Paradise (as Allah has said, "Yea, they shall be shut out as by a veil from their Lord on that day"—[83:15], and that Musa asked Allah for the sight of Him in this world, and "Allah manifested Himself to the mountain" and "turned it to dust,"—[7:139], and taught Musa by it that he should not see Him in this world).

It is opinion that we ought not to declare a single one of the people of the Qibla an infidel for a sin of which he is guilty, such as fornication or theft or the drinking of wine, as the Kharijites hold, thinking that such people are infidels; but we believe that he who commits any of these mortal sins, such as fornication or theft or the like presumptuously declaring it lawful and not acknowledging that forbidden is an infidel.

We believe that Islam is more extensive than faith, and that faith is not the whole of Islam.

We hold that Allah changes men's hearts, and that their hearts are between two of Allah's fingers, and that Allah will place the heavens on a finger and the earth on a finger, as we are told in the tradition that comes down on the authority of Allah's Messenger.

We hold that we ought not to relegate any of the Monotheists, or those who hold fast to the faith, to Paradise or to Hell, save him in whose favor the Messenger of Allah has borne witness concerning Paradise; and we hope that sinners will attain to Paradise, but we fear that they will be punished in Hell.

We believe that Allah, by the intercession of Muhammad, Allah's Messenger, will bring forth a people from Hell after they have been burned to ashes, in accordance with what we are told in the traditions related on the authority of Allah's messenger.

We believe in the punishment of the grave, and the Pool, and hold that the Scales are real, and the Bridge is real, and the resurrection after death is real, and that Allah will line up human beings at the Station, and settle the account with the faithful.

We believe that faith consists of words and deeds, and is subject to increase and decrease; and we receive the authentic traditions regarding it related on the authority of the Messenger of Allah, which the trustworthy have transmitted, one just man from another, until the tradition goes back to the Messenger of Allah.

We believe in affection toward our forebears in faith, whom Allah chose for the company of His Prophet, we praise them with the praise wherewith Allah praised them, and are attached to them all.

We believe that the excellent Imam, after the Messenger of Allah, is Abu Bakr the Veracious, and that Allah strengthened the Religion by him and gave him success against the renegades, and the Muslims promoted him to the imamate just as the Messenger of Allah made him leader of prayer, and they all named him the caliph of Allah's Messenger; then after him came 'Umar Ibn Al-Kattab; then Uthmaan bin Affaan (those who fought with him wrongfully and unrighteously); then 'Ali Ibn Abi taalib; wherefore these are the Imams after the Messenger of Allah, and their caliphate of Prophecy.

We bear witness concerning Paradise in favor of the ten in whose favour the Messenger of Allah bore witness to it, and we are attached to all the Companions of the Prophet and avoid what was disputed among them.

We hold that the four Imam are orthodox, divinely guided, excellent caliphs, unmatched by others in excellence.

We accept all the traditions for which the traditionalists vouch: the descent in to the lower heavens, and the Lord's saying, "Is there any who has a request? Is there any who ask forgiveness?" and the other things they relate and vouch for; dissenting from what the deviators and followers of error assert.

We rely, in that wherein we differ, upon our Lord's book, and the sunnah of our Prophet and the unanimous consent (ijma) of the Muslims and what it signifies; and we do not introduce into Allah's religion innovations that Allah does not allow, nor do we believe of Allah what we do not know.

We believe that Allah will come in the day of resurrection (as He has said, "and thy Lord shall come and the Angels rank"—[80:23]); and that Allah is near His servants, even as He wishes (as He has said, "We are nearer to him than his Jugular vein,"—[50:15] and as He said, "He came nearer and approached and was at the distance of two bows or even closer"—[53:8,9]).

It belongs to our religion to observe the Friday Assembly, and the feasts, and the remaining prayers and public devotions under the leadership of every pious man or impious (as it is related of 'Abd Allah ibn Umar that he used to pray behind al-Hajjaj ibn-yusuf); and we believe that the wiping of the sandals is a sunnah at home and in travel, contrarily to the belief of anybody who denies it; and we approve prayer for the welfare of the imams of the Muslims, and the confession of their imamate; and we regard it as error on anybody's part to "going out" against them when they have clearly abandoned rectitude; and we believe in abstinence from "going out" against them with the sword, and abstinence from fighting in civil commotions.

We confess the going forth of Antichrist (ad-Dajjaal), as it is contained in the tradition related on the authority of Allah's Messenger.

We believe in the punishment of the grave, and in Munkar and Nakir, and their interrogation of those who are buried in the graves.

We accept the Hadith of Ascension (mi'raj) and regard as authentic many of the visions of sleep, and confess there are interpretations to them.

We approve alms on behalf of the Muslim dead, and prayer for their welfare; and we believe that Allah helps them by it.

We accept it as true that there are sorcerers and sorcery in the world, and that sorcery exists in the world.

We believe in praying for those of the people of the Qibla who are dead, the pious and the impious, and in the lawfulness of being their heirs.

We confess that Paradise and Hell are created; and that he who dies or is slain is at his appointed term; and that sustenance is from Allah who gives it to His creatures in the permitted and the forbidden; and that Satan Whispers to man and causes him to doubt and infects him, contrarily to the belief of the Mu'tazilah and the Jahmiyyahh (as Allah has said, "they who swallow down usury shall arise in the resurrection only as he arises who Satan hath infected by his touch,"—[2:276] and as he has said, "against the mischief of the stealthily withdrawn whisperer, who whispers in man's breast against jinn and men."—[114:46]).

We believe that Allah can design particularly for the just signs he manifests to them.

Our belief regarding the children of the polytheists is that Allah will kindle a fire for them in the next world, and then will say to them, "rush into it!" as the tradition tells us concerning it.

We hold that Allah knows what human beings are doing, and they are going to do, what has been, what is, and how what is not would have been if it had been.

We believe in obedience to the Imams and in the sincere counsel of the Muslims.

We approve separation from every innovation tendency, and the avoidance of the people of straying impulses.

Source: Islamicweb.com. Reprinted by permission.

SHI'I CREED

Eighty percent of Shi'i Muslims belong to the Twelver sect (Ithna 'Asha-Riyyah). *The most distinctive feature of Twelver theology is the belief in the twelve Imams (Ali and eleven of his descendants) who intermediate between God and humans. The Imams carried both a spiritual and a civil authority derived from and virtually paralleling that of Muhammad. The following selections concerning the Imam are from one of the earliest Shi'i creeds, the* Risalatu'l-I'tiqadat, *compiled by Shi'i theologian ibn Babawayhi al-Qummi (918–991). Ibn Babawayhi was also a collector of* Hadith *and assembled one of the Four Books of Shi'i* Hadith.

35. Our belief concerning the number of the prophets is that there have been one hundred and twenty-four thousand prophets and a like number of representatives. Each prophet had a representative to whom he gave instructions by the command of God. And concerning them we believe that they brought the truth from God and their word is the word of God, their command God's command, and obedience to them obedience to God. . . .

    The leaders of the prophets are five on whom all depends: Noah, Abraham, Moses, Jesus, and Muhammad. Muhammad is their leader; he confirmed the other apostles.

    It is necessary to believe that God did not create anything more excellent than Muhammad and the Imams. After his prophet, the proofs of God for the people are the Twelve Imams. . . . Our belief regarding them is that they are in authority. It is to them that God has ordained obedience, they are the witnesses for the people and they are the gates of God. They are the road to Him and the guides thereto, and the repositories of

His knowledge and the interpreters of His revelations and the pillars of His unity. They are immune from sins and errors. They are those from whom "God has removed all impurity and made them absolutely pure." They are possessed of the power of miracles and of irrefutable arguments; and they are for the protection of the people of this earth just as the stars are for the inhabitants of the heavens. They may be likened, in this community, to the Ark of Noah: he who boards it obtains salvation or reaches the Gates of Repentance....

We believe that the Proof of Allah in His earth and representative among His slaves in this age of ours is the Upholder of the laws of God, the Expected One, Muhammad ibn al-Hasan al-Askarī (i.e., the Twelfth Imam). He it is concerning whose name and descent the Prophet was informed by God, and he it is who *will fill the earth with justice and equity just as it is now full of oppression and wrong*. He it is whom God will make victorious over the whole world until from every place the call to prayer is heard and religion will belong entirely to God, exalted be He. He is the rightly guided Mahdi about whom the prophet gave information that when he appears, Jesus, son of Mary, will descend upon the earth and pray behind him. We believe there can be no other upholder of the true religion than him; he may live in the state of occultation (as long as he likes); were it the space of the existence of this world, there would be no upholder of the true religion other than him.

36. Our belief concerning prophets, apostles, Imams and angels is that they are infallible and do not commit any sin, minor or major. He who denies infallibility to them in any matter is an infidel....

37. Our belief concerning those who exceed the bounds of belief [such as those who ascribe divinity to Ali or the other Imams] and those who believe in delegation [that is, God delegated his rule to Muhammad and Ali] is that they are deniers of God. They are more wicked than the Jews, the Christians, the Fire Worshippers or any heretics; none have belittled God more....

Our belief concerning the Prophet is that he was poisoned during the expedition to Khaybar. The poison continued to be noxious until it cut his aorta and he died of its effects....

38. Our belief concerning the evildoers is that they are accursed and dislocation from them is necessary.... And our belief regarding those who killed the prophets and

the Infallible Imams is that they are unbelievers and polytheists, who will forever remain in the lowest stage of fire. . . .

39. Our belief concerning permissible concealing of one's true beliefs *(taqiya)* is that it is obligatory, and he who forsakes it is in the same position as he who forsakes prayer. . . . Now until the time when the Imam al-Qa'im appears, such concealing is obligatory and it is not permissible to dispense with it. He who does . . . has truly gone out of the religion of God. And God has described the showing of friendship to unbelievers as being possible only in the state of concealing. . . .

   And the Imam Ja'far said . . . "Mix with enemies openly but oppose them inwardly, so long as the authority is a matter of question." He also said, "Diplomacy with a true believer is a form of polytheism, but with a hypocrite in his own house, it is worship." And he said, "He who prays with hypocrites [that is, the Sunnis], standing in the first row, it is as though he prayed with the Prophet standing in the first row." And he said, "Visit their sick and attend their funerals and pray in their mosques." . . .

40. Our belief concerning the ancestors of the Prophet, contrary to the Sunnis, is that they were Muslims from Adam down to 'Abdallah, father of the Prophet. . . .

41. Our belief concerning the descendants of Ali is that they are the offspring of the Messenger of God and devotion to them is obligatory reward for his apostleship . . .

Source: Ibn Babawayhi al-Qummi, *Risalatu'l-I'tiqadat,* chs. 35–41; adapted from A Shi'ite Creed, tr. Asaf A. A. Fyzee (London: Oxford University Press, 1942).

JESUS AND ISLAM: THE GOSPEL OF BARNABAS

Muslim theology, both Sunni and Shi'i, rejects the view that Jesus is God or the Messiah and that he was crucified; rather, Jesus was a prophet whom his followers wrongly deified. The Gospel of Barnabas is an account of the life of Jesus from the Muslim perspective. Although the exact origins of this work are unclear, it appears to have been written in the fourteenth or fifteenth century and survives in an Italian and a Spanish version. The work is pseudonymously attributed to Barnabas, the New Testament figure from the Book of Acts. The lengthy text reworks the New Testament account of Jesus into a Muslim-friendly narrative in which Jesus foretells the coming of Muhammad and in which Judas is mistaken for Jesus and crucified in his place.

Who Is Jesus?

42. [The Priests] sent the Levites and some of the scribes to question Jesus, saying: "Who are you?"

    Jesus confessed and said the truth: "I am not the Messiah."

    They said: "Are you Elijah or Jeremiah, or any of the ancient prophets?"

    Jesus answered: "No."

    Then they said: "Who are you? Tell us so that we may report back to those who sent us."

    Jesus answered: "I am a voice that cries through all Judaea, and proclaims: 'Prepare the way for the Messenger of the Lord,' just as it is written in Isaiah." ...

43. James said: "Master, tell us in whom this promise regarding the Messiah was made: the Jews say 'in Isaac,' and the Ishmaelites say 'in Ishmael.'"

    Jesus then said: ... "Believe me, for truly I tell you that the promise was made in Ishmael, not in Isaac." ...

70. Jesus departed from Jerusalem after the Passover, and entered into the borders of Caesarea Philippi. Then, the angel Gabriel having told him of the agitation which was beginning among the common people, he asked his disciples, saying: "What do men say of me?"

    They said: "Some say that you are Elijah, others Jeremiah, and others one of the old prophets."

    Jesus answered: "And you; what say you that I am?"

    Peter answered: "You are Christ, son of God."

    Jesus was angry and reprimanded him saying: "Get out and depart from me, because you are the devil and try to cause me offense!" He threatened the eleven, saying: "Misfortune to you if you believe this, for I have won from God a great curse against those who believe this." He was glad to send Peter away. Then the eleven pleaded with Jesus for him; he did not send Peter away, but rather rebuked him again saying, "Beware that never again you say such words, because God would condemn you!"

    Peter wept and said: "Lord, I have spoken foolishly; ask God to pardon me."

    Then said Jesus: "If our God willed not to show himself to Moses his servant, nor to Elijah whom he so loved, nor to any prophet, will you think that God should show himself to this faithless generation? Do you not know that God has created all things of nothing with one single word, and all people have had their origin out of a piece of clay? Now, how shall God have likeness to man? Misfortune to those who permit themselves to be deceived by Satan!"

Having said this, Jesus pleaded with God for Peter; the eleven and Peter wept and said: "So be it, so be it, holy Lord our God."

Afterwards Jesus left and went into Galilee in order to extinguish this foolish view which the common folk began to hold concerning him. . . .

JUDAS CRUCIFIED IN PLACE OF JESUS

215. When the soldiers with Judas drew near to the place where Jesus was, Jesus heard the approach of many people, and then withdrew into the house in fear. The eleven disciples were sleeping. Then God, seeing the danger of his servant Jesus, commanded his ministers Gabriel, Michael, Rafael, and Uriel, to remove Jesus from the world. The holy angels came and took Jesus out through the window that faced toward the South. They carried him and placed him in the third heaven in the company of angels, praising God forevermore.

216. Judas suddenly entered before everyone else into the chamber from which Jesus had been taken up. The disciples were still sleeping. God then acted magnificently changing Judas in his speech and face to be like Jesus so that we believed him to be Jesus. Having awakened us, he was seeking where Jesus was. Perplexed, we answered "You, Lord, are our master. Have you now forgotten us?"

Judas smiled and said "Now you are foolish since you do not recognize me as Judas Iscariot!" As he was saying this, the soldiers entered and grabbed Judas since he appeared in every way like to Jesus.

217. . . . So they led Judas to Mount Calvary, where they hanged criminals, and there they crucified him naked for even greater humiliation. Judas did nothing but cry out: "God, why have you forsaken me, since the criminal has escaped and I die unjustly?"

I say in all truth that the voice, the face, and the character of Judas were so like that of Jesus that his disciples and believers entirely believed that he was Jesus. Thus some abandoned the doctrine of Jesus, believing that Jesus had been a false prophet, and that he performed his miracles through magic.

Jesus had said that he would not die until near the end of the world, and at that time he would be taken away from the world. But those who stood firm in the doctrine of Jesus were so overcome with sorrow, seeing him die who looked entirely like Jesus, that they did not remember what Jesus had said. So in company with the mother of Jesus they went to Mount Calvary. . . . They took Judas down from the cross crying unbelievably, and buried him in the new tomb of Joseph, having wrapped him up in a hundred pounds of precious ointments. . . .

218. Each man then returned to his house. . . . Those disciples who did not fear God went at night, stole the body of Judas and hid it, spreading a report that Jesus was risen again. Great confusion then arose. . . .

219. Jesus [while in heaven] prayed that God would give him power to see his mother and his disciples. Then merciful God commanded his four favorite angels—Gabriel, Michael, Rafael, and Uriel—to carry Jesus to his mother's house, and keep watch over him there continually for three days, permitting him only to be seen by them that believed in his doctrine. . . .

220. The four angels then explained to the Virgin Mary how God had sent for Jesus and transformed Judas so that he would suffer the punishment to which he had sold another. . . .

Then I, Barnabas, said: "Master, seeing that God is merciful, why has he tormented us, making us believe that you were dead? . . ."

Jesus answered: "Believe me, Barnabas, every sin, however small, God severely punishes, because God is offended by sin. Since my mother and my faithful disciples that were with me loved me a little with earthly love, God in his righteousness has chosen to punish this love with the present grief, in order that it may not be punished in the flames of Hell. I have been innocent in the world, even though people have called me "God," and "Son of God." To prevent me from being mocked by demons on the Day of Judgment, God has willed that I should be mocked by people in this world through the death of Judas, making all people believe that I died on the cross. This mocking will continue until the coming of Mohammed, the messenger of God, who will reveal this deception to those who believe in God's law."

Source: Adapted from *The Gospel of Barnabas,* tr. Lonsdale Ragg (Oxford: Clarendon Press, 1907), chs. 42, 43, 70, 215–220.

SUFI WRITINGS

RABI'A: UNCONDITIONAL LOVE OF GOD

Almost as old as Islam itself, Sufism is the mystical tradition of Islam that emphasizes mystical union with God. Rabi'a al-'Adawiya (717–801) was one of the earliest and most admired Sufis and is sometimes referred to as the Muslim St. Teresa. She was kidnapped as a girl, sold into slavery, and later freed because of her piety. Thereafter she lived as an ascetic with a small group of followers. Although she did not write systematic treatises on Sufism, her sayings were passed down to later generations of Sufis who recorded them and used them as sounding boards for their own mystical ideas. Her key theological contribution is the notion of the unconditional love of God (mahabbah), which parallels the Hindu notion of bhakti *or the Christian notion of* agape. *Following are anecdotes about Rabi'a from* Memorial of the Saints *by twelfth-century Sufi poet Attar of Nishapur.*

Once during Spring Rabi'a went into her chamber and bowed her head in meditation. Her handmaid said, "Mistress, come outside so that you can see the phenomenal works of God." "No," she answered, "you come inside, so you can see the maker of those works. Contemplation of the maker has turned me away from contemplating that which he has made."

It is related that Rabi'a once fasted seven days and nights, never sleeping, but passed every night in prayer. When she was nearly starving, someone came in and left a bowl of food. She went to get a lamp, but on returning found that a cat had spilled the bowl. "I will go," she said, "and get a jug of water and break my fast." While she was getting it, the lamp went out. She tried to drink in the dark, but the jug slipped from her hand and broke into pieces. She wailed and heaved such a sigh that the room was in danger of catching fire [from her burning heart]. "Lord," she cried, "what is this you are doing to pitiful me?" She heard a voice saying, "If you wish, I will give you the wealth of all the world, but I will remove your love for me from your heart, for heavenly love and earthly wealth cannot meet in one heart. You have a desire and I have a desire, but my and your desire cannot live together in a single heart." Rabi'a said: "When I heard this warning, I cut off my heart from every worldly hope. For thirty years I have prayed as though every prayer that I performed were the last prayer of all, and I have become so detached from mankind that, for fear that someone might distract my mind from God, I pray at sunrise, 'God, make me busy with you, so that they may not make me busy with them.'"

One day Hasan of Basra and Malik son of Dinar and Shakik of Balkh came to see Rabi'a when she was ill. Hasan said, "No one is sincere in his claim [to love God] unless he patiently endures the misfortunes from his Lord." Rabi'a said, "This sounds too selfish." Shakik said, "No one is sincere in his claim unless he gives thanks for the misfortunes from his Lord." Rabi'a said, "You still can do better." Malik said, "No one is sincere in his claim unless he delights in the misfortunes of his Lord." Rabi'a said, "This still needs improvement." They said, "Maybe you should just tell us." She said, "No one is sincere in his claim unless he forgets the misfortune when seeing his Lord."'

Abdu 'l-Wahid son of 'Amir relates that he and Sufyan Thauri went to ask after Rabi'a in her illness. "She inspired me," he said, "with such awe that I dare not speak, so I begged Sufyan to begin. Sufyan said to Rabi'a, "If you would say a prayer, He would relieve your pain." Rabi'a turned her face toward him and replied, "Sufyan, do you not know who has willed this pain on me? Hasn't God willed it?" Sufyan said, "Yes." "Then," said she, "knowing this, aren't you suggesting that I ask of Him something contrary to His will? It is not right to oppose one's beloved."

Sufyan said, "What do you desire, Rabi'a?" She replied, "Why do you ask me this question, considering that you are one of the learned? By the glory of God, for twelve years I have desired fresh dates and never tasted them, although dates, as you know, are very cheap in Basra. I am a servant, and what has a servant to do with desire? If I will something and my Lord does not will it, that is infidelity. You must will that which He wills so that you may be His true servant. If He gives you nothing, that is another thing."

Rabi'a said: "He that worships his Lord either from fear of punishment or in hope of reward is a bad servant." "Why, then," they asked, "Do you worship him? Do you have no hope of Paradise?" She answered, "Is it not enough that we are permitted to worship him? Should we not obey him, even if there were no paradise and hell? Is he not worthy of our pure devotion?"

Rabi'a used to say, "God, if I worship you from fear of hell, then burn me in hell, and if I worship you in hope of paradise, then exclude me from Paradise. But if I worship you for your own sake; do not withhold your everlasting beauty."

A man said to Rabi'a, "I have committed many sins; if I were to repent, would God turn toward me?" She replied, "No, but if he turned toward you, you would repent."

Source: Attar of Nishapur, *Memoirs of the Saints (Tadhkirat-ul-Awliya),* tr. Reynold Nicholson (adapted).

UNVEILING THE QUR'AN'S SECRETS: SANA'I OF GHAZNI

Born in the city of Ghazni, in what is now Afghanistan, Sufi poet Sana'i (d. c. 1150) composed The Enclosed Garden of the Truth upon his return from a pilgrimage to Mecca and Medina. In the selections here from that work, he explains the urgency of disciplining oneself to be receptive to Allah's message. He warns, though, not to confuse the words of the Qur'an with its hidden and secret meaning. As beautiful as the words themselves are, there is a deeper content that can only be grasped by the soul, and not through the intellect.

Parable of the Schoolboy. If a boy is unable to learn his task, hear at once what it is that he wants; be kind to him and treat him tenderly; do not make him grieve in helpless expectation; at such a time give him sweetmeats in his lap to comfort him, and do not treat him harshly. But if he will not read, at once send for the strap. Take hold of his ears and rub them hard. Threaten him with the schoolmaster and say that he will have strict orders to punish him—that he will shut him up in a rat-house, and the head rat will strangle him. In the path that leads to the life to come, do not be less apt than a boy to receive admonition. Eternity is your sweetmeat. Hurry, then, and you can obtain paradise for the price of two rak'ahs [i.e., a cycle in the Salah prayer ritual]. Otherwise the rat-house will for you be Hell. It will be your tomb which meets you on your way to that other mansion. Go to the writing-school of the prophets for a time. Do not choose this folly for yourself, this affliction. Read just one tablet of the religion of the prophets. Since you know nothing about this, go, read and learn, that happily you may become their friend and may happily escape from this stupidity. In this corrupt and baleful world do not think that there is anything worse than stupidity.

The Secret Qur'an. The tongue cannot tell the secret of the Qur'an, for His intimates keep it concealed. The Qur'an indeed knows its own secret; hear it from itself, for itself

knows it. Except by the soul's eye no one knows the mea-
surer of words from the true reader of the Qur'an. I will
not take upon myself to say that you truly know the Qur'an
though you are Uthman [the third Caliph]. The world is like
the summer's heat, its people like drunkards in it, all wandering in the desert of indifference. Death is the shepherd, and
men his flock. In this waste of desire and wretchedness, the
hot sand appears to be running water. The Qur'an is like the
cool water of the Euphrates, while you are like a thirsty sinner on the plain of the Judgment. You should hold the letter
and Qur'an as a cup and its water. Drink the water, but do
not gaze on the vessel.... In a cry of anguish, the suffering of a pure heart will tell the secret of the pure Qur'an.
How can reason discover its interpretation? Take a delight
in it and you will discover its inmost secret.... The letter
may be uttered by the tongue, its soul can only be read by
the soul. The letter is like the shell, and the true Qur'an
is the pearl; the heart of the free-born does not desire the
shell.... When the soul recites the Qur'an, it enjoys a lus-
cious morsel. Whoever hears it, mends his ragged robe. The
words, the voice, and the letters of the verses are like three
stalks in bowls of vegetables. Though the husk is neither fair
nor sweet, it still guards the kernel.... When the day of true
religion dawns, the night of thought, fancy and sense will fly
away. When the veiled ones of the unseen world see that you
are stainless, they lead you to the invisible abode and reveal
to you their faces.

Disclosing to you the secret of the Qur'an, they will withdraw the veil of letters. The earthy will have a reward of earth,
but the pure will see purity. An understanding of the Qur'an
does not dwell in the brain where pride starts up. The ass is
as dumb as a mere stone, and does not lend his ear to the
secret of God's word; he turns away from hearing the Qur'an
and pays no heed to the sura's secret. But if your mind is disciplined toward God, it will discover in the sura the secret of the
Qur'an.

Source: Adapted from Sana'i of Ghazni, *The First Book of the
Hadiquatu' l-haqiqat; or, The Enclosed Garden of the Truth,* tr. J.
Stephenson (Calcutta: Baptist Mission Press, 1910).

SUFI PATH: AL-GHAZALI

*Abu Hamid al-Ghazali (1058–1111) was a scholar of Islamic law
and philosopher who ultimately rejected academic approaches
to truth in favor of immediate mystical experience. The following*

is from al-Ghazali's biography, Deliverer from Error, in which he describes his initial acquaintance with Sufism.

When God in the abundance of his mercy had healed me of this malady, I ascertained that those who are engaged in the search for truth may be divided into three groups. (1) Scholastic theologians, who profess to follow theory and speculation. (2) The philosophers, who profess to rely upon formal logic. (3) The sufis, who call themselves the elect of God and possessors of intuition and knowledge of the truth by means of ecstasy. "The truth," I said to myself, "must be found among these three classes of men who devote themselves to the search for it. If it escapes them, one must give up all hopes of attaining it...." Determined to follow these paths and to search out these systems to the bottom, I proceeded with my investigation in the following order: Scholastic theology; philosophical systems; and, finally Sufism....

When I had finished my examination of these doctrines [of the philosophers], I applied myself to the study of Sufism. I saw that in order to understand it thoroughly one must combine theory with practice. The aim which the Sufis set before them is as follows: to free the soul from the tyrannical yoke of the passions, to deliver it from its wrong inclinations and evil instincts, in order that in the purified heart there should only remain room for God and for the invocation of his holy name.

As it was more easy to learn their doctrine than to practice it, I studied first of all those of their books which contain it.... I acquired a thorough knowledge of their researches, and I learned all that was possible to learn of their methods by study and oral teaching. It became clear to me that the last stage could not be reached by mere instruction, but only by transport, ecstasy, and the transformation of the moral being.

Ten years passed in this manner. During my successive periods of meditation there were revealed to me things impossible to recount. All that I shall say for the edification of the reader is this: I learned from a sure source that the Sufis are the true pioneers on the path of God. There is nothing more beautiful than their life, nor more praiseworthy than their rule of conduct, nor purer than their morality.... In a word, what can one criticize in them? To purge the heart of all that does not belong to God is the first step in their cathartic method. The drawing upon of the heart by prayer is the keystone of it, as the cry "God is great" is the keystone of prayer, and the last stage of being lost in God.

I say the last stage, with reference to what may be reached by an effort of will; but, to tell the truth, it is only the first stage in the life of contemplation, the vestibule by which the initiated enter.

From the time that they set out on this path, they begin to have revelations. They come to see in the waking state angels and souls of prophets. They hear their voices and wise counsels. By means of this contemplation of heavenly forms and images they rise by degrees to heights which human language cannot reach, which one cannot even indicate without falling into great and inevitable errors. The degree of proximity to Deity which they attain is regarded by some as intermixture of being *(haloul),* by others as identification *(ittihad),* by others as intimate union *(wasl).* But all these expressions are wrong. . . . In short, he who does not arrive at the intuition of these truths by means of ecstasy, knows only the *name* of inspiration. The miracles done by the saints are, in fact, merely the earliest forms of prophetic manifestation. Such was the state of the Apostle of God when, before receiving his commission, he retired to Mount Hira to give himself up to such intensity of prayer and meditation that the Arabs said, "Muhammad has become captivated of God."

This state, then, can be revealed to the initiated in ecstasy, and to him who is incapable of ecstasy, by obedience and attention, on condition that he frequents the society of Sufis till he arrives, so to speak, at the imitative initiation. Such is the faith which one can obtain by remaining among them, and intercourse with them is never painful.

Source: Abu Hamid al-Ghazali, *Deliverer from Error,* sects. 78, 122–125, 132–135; adapted from *The Confessions of Al Ghazali,* tr. Claud Field (New York: E. P. Dutton and Company, 1909).

UNION AND SEPARATION: RUMI

The most widely acclaimed Sufi writer is Jalal ad-Din ar-Rumi (1207–1273), whose poetic work the Masnawi *is often referred to as the Qur'an in Persian. Central to Rumi's writings are the paired notions of union and separation; that is, moments of the mystic's life consist of blissful union with God, whereas, of necessity, other moments involve separation. Separation frequently manifests itself in human pain and suffering. Rumi argues that such suffering must be understood in a larger context: The spiritual happiness we achieve in the state of union is accentuated by the suffering we experience while in separation. The following selections are from Rumi's* Masnawi *and his other epic writing, the* Diwan.

Only the imagination that has contemplated Unification, and then, after direct vision, has undergone separation;

Not a definitive separation, but one for a good purpose, since that station is secure from all separation;

In order to preserve the spiritualized body, the Sun pulls back from the snow for a moment. (*Masnawi* 6:4012–15)

At the time of union, only God knows what that Moon is! For even during separation, what incredible joy and expansion of spirit! (*Diwan* 30321)

Separation and parting from Thee is difficult, oh Beloved, especially after Thy embrace! (*Diwan* 13901)

If man should see himself at all, if he should see that his wound is deadly and gangrenous,

Then from such looking within, pain would arise, and pain would bring him out from behind the veil.

Until mothers feel the pain of childbirth, the child finds no way to be born.

The trust is within the heart and the heart is pregnant; all the exhortations of the saints act as a midwife.

The midwife says, "The woman has no pain. Pain is necessary, for it will open a way for the child."

He that is without pain is a brigand, for to be without pain is to say "I am God."

To say "I" at the wrong time is a curse, but to say it at the right time is a mercy. (*Masnawi* 2:2516–22)

The body is pregnant with the spirit, the body's suffering is the pain of childbirth—the coming of the embryo brings pain and torment for the woman.

Look not at the wine's bitterness, look at the joy of drunkards! Look not at the woman's affliction, look at the hope of the midwife! (*Diwan* 5990)

How much the Beloved made me suffer before this work settled into the eye's water and the liver's blood!

A thousand fires and smokes and heartaches—and its name is Love! A thousand pains and regrets and afflictions—and its name is Beloved!

Let every enemy of his own spirit set out to work! Welcome to the spirit's sacrifice and a pitiful death!

My heart keeps saying, "I suffer because of Him," and I keep laughing at its weak hypocrisy. (*Masnawi* 1:1773–82)

Union with this world is separation from that world. The health of this body is the sickness of the spirit.

It is hard to be separated from this caravanserai—so know that separation from that permanent abode is harder!

Since it is hard for you to be separated from the painting, think what it will be to be parted from the Painter!

Oh you who cannot bear to be without this despicable world! How can
   you bear to be without God, oh friend, how?
Since you cannot bear to be without this black water, how can you bear
   to be without God's fountain? . . .
If you should see the Beauty of the Loving God for one instant and
   throw your soul and existence into the fire,
Then having seen the glory and splendor of His proximity, you would
   see these sweet beverages as carrion. . . .
Strive quickly to find Self in selflessness—and God knows best the right
   course. (*Masnawi* 4:3209-13, 15-16, 18)

Source: Jalal ad-Din ar-Rumi, *Diwan* and *Masnawi selections*, *from The Sufi Path of Love: The Spiritual Teachings of Rumi*, tr. William C. Chittick (Albany: State University of New York Press, 1983), pp. 235–236. Reprinted by permission.

Baha'i Faith

INTRODUCTION

The Baha'i Faith began in mid-nineteenth-century Persia, a Shi'i Islamic society, and is now widely recognized as an independent world religion. It was founded by Baha'u'llah and his forerunner the Bab, and developed and guided by his son, Abdu'l-Baha, and great-grandson, Shoghi Effendi. The Baha'i Faith emphasizes the unity of all religions and world peace. "To be a Baha'i," according to Abdu'l-Baha, "simply means to love all the world; to love humanity and try to serve it; to work for universal peace and universal brotherhood." Baha'i doctrine is sometimes expressed in the "three onenesses." (1) The oneness of God: There is a single and ultimately unknowable God who is given different names. The knowledge we do have of God derives from his various prophets who instruct us. (2) The oneness of humankind: There is a single human race, and we are all members of it. (3) The oneness of religion: All religions are unified insofar as they are each stages in God's revelatory plan.

BAHA'I FOUNDERS

The Baha'i Faith is historically founded on the Babi religion, which in turn rests on the Shi'i Muslim doctrine of the Hidden Imam. According to this doctrine, the Mahdi, the final Imam—or spiritual successor to Ali—is alive but was placed by God in a condition of occultation in which he can see others but others cannot see him (or at least they cannot recognize him). He will return at the end of time, take vengeance on the wicked, and initiate an era of peace. Shi'i Islam has numerous denominations and sects that have differing views of the status of the Imams in general and of the Mahdi. The nineteenth-century Shaykhi sect, founded by Shaykh (Sheik) Ahmad al-Ahsa'i (1753–1826), maintained that Imams have an almost divine status and that each generation needs a gate (Bab) as an intermediary between the Hidden Imam and believers. Although one of the Shaykhi leaders claimed to be guided by the Mahdi in his dreams, no one initially claimed to be the Bab himself.

The forerunner to the Baha'i Faith was affiliated with the Shaykhi sect—either formally or as a sympathizer. Sayyid Ali-Muhammad Shirazi (1819–1850) was born into a merchant family in south Persia; his father died soon after his birth, and he was raised by his uncle. He married at age 22 and subsequently joined the Shaykhi. In 1844, while on a pilgrim-age to Mecca, he claimed to be the Bab, which was a more extreme claim than his Shaykhi predecessors had made. It is this event that Baha'is designate as the beginning of their religion. Scholars believe that the Bab privately announced to his followers that he was the Mahdi himself; the public declaration of Babhood, though, was politically safer to make. Even so, his declaration quickly attracted followers, but it also raised political concerns, and for the next six years—the remainder of his life—he was exiled or imprisoned. After his announcement, the Bab formed a religious group called the Babis. The first eighteen of his followers were sent out as proselytizers. Later the Bab publicly claimed to be the Imam Mahdi himself, and in 1848, in an important work called the *Bayan,* he declared that he was a manifestation of God, superseding Muhammad. The *Bayan* also presents a constitution for the coming Babi state and a series of laws. In perhaps the most controversial section, it maintains that believers can take all possessions of nonbelievers. The severity of some of the Bab's laws dramatized his messianic role and rhetorically underscored his legislative authority. However, these laws were counterbalanced by others that prohibit harming or offending others, especially nonbelievers. In any event, only a few of the Bab's laws were ever implemented.

He summoned the Shah of Persia to acknowledge his authority, and in 1848 the Babis distanced themselves from Islam. The same year about 300 Babis set off on a march that prompted armed confrontation. They defended themselves but were quickly crushed by the Persian government. Massive persecution of Babis followed, and the Bab was executed by a firing squad in 1850. Witnesses reported that he and a follower were suspended by rope. The first volley only severed their ropes, and they dropped to the ground. Seeing this as a divine sign, the commander of the regiment withdrew the troops, but a new group of soldiers was brought in, and they finished the task. The Bab's body was secretly retrieved by his followers and, after a number of years, transported to its final resting place at the Mausoleum of the Bab in Haifa, Israel. His immediate successor as Babi leader was Mirza Yahya (Subh-i-Azal), who resided in Baghdad. Before the Bab died, he foretold of a leader, greater than himself, who would finish his work.

The Baha'i Faith's second founder was Baha'u'llah (1817–1892), an honorific title that means "Glory of God." Baha'u'llah, originally named Mirza Husayn-Ali Nur, was born in Tehran, the capital of Persia. He had no formal education and was the eldest son of a distinguished minister of state. When he was 22, his father died and he was left to manage the estate and care for his family. At age 26 (1844), he espoused Babism and became one of the Bab's earliest followers, although, as some Baha'i historians maintain, he never personally met the Bab. In 1852, a Babi named Sadiq attempted to assassinate the Iranian Shah in retaliation for the execution of the Bab. Sadiq and eighty others were killed, and many more were imprisoned or exiled. Baha'u'llah's property was confiscated and he was imprisoned for four months, after which he was exiled to Baghdad. Mirza Yahya (the Bab's provisional successor) went into hiding and made his way to Baghdad when he heard that Baha'u'llah was there. This initial period of exile lasted until 1863 and was relatively peaceful. Baha'u'llah retreated to the desert for two years (1854–1856), and when he returned he ably met challenges by the Muslim Mullahs in defense of Babism. He wrote several books while in Baghdad, the most important of these being *The Book of Certitude (Kitab-i-Iqan),* which explained how prophets from one dispensation anticipate the prophets of the next.

In 1863, Baha'u'llah was summoned to Constantinople (Istanbul). While he was preparing for the journey, his house overflowed with well-wishers, and for twelve days he and later his family were compelled to camp in a garden, later named Ridvan (paradise). At this time he privately announced that he was the leader foretold by the Bab. As such, he declared himself to be the manifestation or appearance of God. This announcement, known to Baha'is as the Declaration at Ridvan, is the basis of their most important festival, celebrated each year from April 21 to May 2. Baha'u'llah, his family, and twenty-six followers went to Constantinople, where they were confined to squalid conditions for four months, and then they moved to Adrianople (Edirne), Turkey, where they remained until 1868. There he attracted more followers and openly announced his mission. He wrote letters to the Shah and other world leaders, including Napoleon III, Pope Pius IX, Czar Nicholas II, and Queen Victoria. In 1868, a long-standing tension between Baha'u'llah and Mirza Yahya culminated in division, principally owing to Baha'u'llah's claim of a new dispensation and universal religion. Contrary to Baha'u'llah's wishes, their quarreling led to violence between the two factions. Mirza Yahya was deported to Cyprus, where ultimately his followers abandoned him. Baha'u'llah was deported to Acre, Palestine (then part of Syria), which was a prison city for criminals of the Turkish Empire. For two years he and eighty followers were confined to army barracks; the conditions were so harsh that several of the followers died. When the barracks were needed to house troops, Baha'u'llah was moved to a small house in the city in which he stayed for six years. During these years his followers grew substantially in number.

At this time he wrote *The Most Holy Book (Kitab-i-Aqdas)*, his most important work, which lays out the basic laws and principles for his followers and establishes the basis of Baha'i administration. In 1877, he was released from the prison city, although the prison sentence was never removed. After a two-year stay in a house north of Acre, Baha'u'llah moved to a more regal estate, known as Bahji, secured through donations from his followers. He spent the remaining years of his life writing and teaching while administrative functions were taken over by his eldest son, Abdu'l-Baha (1844–1921). Upon Baha'u'llah's death in 1892, Abdu'l-Baha was appointed successor, as designated in Baha'u'llah's will. Baha'u'llah's burial site—a garden building near the main mansion at Bahji—is the holiest site for the Baha'i Faith.

Abdu'l-Baha ("servant of Baha") was born in Tehran and was only nine when his father was first imprisoned (1852). He was a dutiful companion to his father, attending him throughout his years of exile and closely guarding him. After Baha'u'llah's death, the transition of leadership was not smooth, particularly as Abdu'l-Baha was opposed by several family members. After Baha'u'llah's death, Abdu'l-Baha built the shrine on Mount Carmel as a burial site for the Bab. Abdu'l-Baha's dissenting relatives reported to the Turkish government that he was constructing a fortress, and beginning in 1901 he was confined to Acre for seven years. There he lived an austere life, teaching and visiting the sick. In 1907, a tribunal met to determine his fate. Coincidentally, a revolution broke out in the Ottoman Empire, and the tribunal members were called to Istanbul. The new leaders of the Empire (the Young Turks) released all political and religious prisoners in the Empire. Thus, after a total of forty years of imprisonment in Palestine, Abdu'l-Baha too was released (1908). From 1911 to 1913, he traveled to Great Britain, France, Germany, Hungary, the United States, Canada, and Egypt, where he met with religious and political leaders, scientists, and philosophers. He spoke at universities, to charitable organizations, and at institutions of various religions. Through these efforts, Abdu'l-Baha was responsible for spreading the Baha'i Faith beyond the Middle East and into the Western world. He continued adapting the Baha'i Faith to modern social ideas. In his role as a spiritual leader, he maintained exclusive authority in interpreting scripture, as appointed to him by Baha'u'llah, although he did not consider his own writings to be equally authoritative. During the years of World War I, Abdu'l-Baha and the Baha'is in Palestine were under wartime restrictions and had only limited contact with outside pilgrims. Their efforts focused on securing food supplies for the Baha'is and the surrounding poor. After the war, Palestine was occupied by the British and Abdu'l-Baha was officially honored with knighthood. He died in 1921, stating in his will that leadership should be passed to his 24-year-old grandson, Shoghi Effendi (1897–1957), whom he appointed "Guardian of the Cause."

Studying abroad at the time, Shoghi Effendi was surprised at the news of his position. During his tenure as leader, he established the administrative structure of the Baha'i Faith and became responsible for the subsequent formalized organization of Baha'is around the world. He established teaching plans to spread the Baha'i Faith worldwide, including in North America. His definitive English translations and clarifications of Baha'u'llah's writings helped secure the Baha'i Faith in non-Islamic Western countries. Perhaps most important, he arranged for the long-awaited election of members to the Universal House of Justice (Bayt al-Adl al-Azam), which would succeed him after his death by overseeing the Baha'i community and elucidating doctrine. The plan for this task was Abdu'l-Baha's Will and Testament, which, in turn, draws from the *Aqdas*. The first election of the members of the Universal House of Justice took place in 1963, six years after Shoghi Effendi's death. Members reside in Haifa, Israel, meet almost daily, and are reelected every five years. Today, the Baha'i Faith has more than 5 million followers who reside in virtually every country throughout the world. It remains the largest religious minority in Iran, the cradle of the Baha'i Faith, with more than a quarter million believers. However, since the Iranian Islamic revolution of 1979, more than 200 Baha'is have been executed, and thousands more persecuted.

BAHA'I TEACHING

The Baha'i Faith now reflects little of its original Imami theology, although Shi'i elements have a greater presence in Iranian Baha'i traditions. Because of Baha'u'llah's appearance, the function of the Bab is no longer considered primary. A central tenet of Baha'i teaching is that God's nature is unknowable. Everything around us, though, exhibits different attributes of the divine, as each is created by God and endowed with different sets of attributes. Most generally, God is a single infinite power, which implies the nonexistence of evil: Evil is only the absence of good, just as darkness is the absence of light. Neither darkness nor evil has a reality; these are only names we give to the absence of the reality in question. The most striking aspect of Baha'i theology is its notion of the unity of religions. Revelation is thought to be progressive, and prophets deliver messages appropriate to their own times. All true prophets from the various religions should be acknowledged as genuine—including Moses, Zoroaster, Jesus, Muhammad, Krishna, and Buddha. The prophets are *manifestations* of God and have special insight into the spiritual realm. Baha'i revelation is seen as the fulfillment of all previous revelations.

In its eschatological teachings, the Baha'i Faith holds that there is life after death through the continuation of a disembodied soul. However, heaven, hell, and final judgment are symbolic. Baha'u'llah is the messianic figure spoken of by previous prophets, and the "final judgment" is the appearance of each new manifestation/prophet of God. Institutionally, the Baha'i Faith has no official priests and no monastic component, and all Baha'is are expected to participate in teaching. Local spiritual assemblies assist with life-cycle rites such as weddings and funerals, plan community events, counsel members, and coordinate Baha'i education programs. Nine Baha'is are elected annually (April 21) by secret ballot to help supervise the local assemblies. National spiritual assemblies oversee the local spiritual assemblies, and the Universal House of Justice oversees these. Baha'is follow a nineteen-month calendar, each month having nineteen days with four intercalary days between the last two months. One month is designated for fasting.

In their social and moral beliefs, Baha'is teach racial and gender equality, monogamy, abstinence from alcohol and narcotics, and the voluntary sharing of property. Strong emphasis is placed on world peace and the unity of all humankind, as indicated in the statement by Baha'u'llah that "you are all fruits of one tree, the leaves of one branch, the flowers of one garden." The Baha'i founders and the Universal House of Justice have variously advocated a universal language, a universal league of nations, and an international court of arbitration. Although Baha'is believe in the doctrine of a just war, military aggression is rejected.

BAHA'I SCRIPTURES

The most sacred body of Baha'i texts are the writings of the Bab and Baha'u'llah, which are considered to be revelations. Second to those are the writings of Abdu'l-Baha, which, while not revealed, are considered to be inspired. The writings of Shoghi Effendi are not on a par with either of these groups, but are still considered authoritative. The letters of the Universal House of Justice are also authoritative, but also are not scriptural. The complete corpus of Baha'i sacred texts is perhaps 200 volumes, although some writings are still in manuscript form. The Bab, Baha'u'llah, and Abdu'l-Baha were imprisoned and exiled for much of their lives, and because they were prohibited from public speaking under these conditions, they devoted their time to writing.

The Bab composed about fifty volumes of writings. His most important work is the *Qayyum al-Asma'* (1844), a commentary on the Surah of Joseph in the Qur'an, which Baha'is consider to be the Bab's first revealed work. The foremost doctrinal works of the Bab are the Persian and Arabic *Bayan* ("exposition"). Although they share the same title, they are two independent works with some overlapping themes. The Persian *Bayan* (1848) is larger, though intentionally left incomplete, and is his principal doctrinal work. The Arabic *Bayan* (1850) was composed during the last few months of the Bab's life.

Baha'u'llah penned over a hundred volumes of writings, including letters to world leaders, prayers, and laws. Many of these are published as compilations. His most important writings are *The Book of Certitude (Kitab-i-Iqan), Most Holy Book (Kitab-i-Aqdas), The Hidden Words, The Seven Valleys, Tablet of the Holy Mariner,* and *Tablet of Glad-Tidings.* Abdu'l-Baha's writings include *Tablets of the Divine Plan, A Traveler's Narrative, Memorials of the Faithful,* and *Secret of Divine Civilization.* Important talks were also published, including *Promulgation of Universal Peace* and *Some Answered Questions.* Abdu'l-Baha composed about fifty volumes of text, some of which are in the form of letters to Baha'is as well as to those outside the faith. Shoghi Effendi composed about thirty-five volumes of text. His key works are *The Dispensation of Baha'u'llah, The Advent of Divine Justice, The Promised Day Is Come,* and *The World Order of Baha'u'llah.* His book *God Passes By* is his interpretation of Baha'i history. His writings also include letters and translations of the writings of the Bab, Baha'u'llah, and Abdu'l-Baha. *The Baha'i World,* an ongoing series of volumes founded by Shoghi Effendi, is a compilation of official Baha'i writings since 1925. It includes religious calendars, festival descriptions, poetry, music, administrative information, articles on theological topics, maps, bibliographies, transliterations, and definitions.

HOLIDAYS

Nineteen Day Fast (March 2–20) Parallels Muslim Ramadan.

New Year's Day (Naw Ruz; March 21) The day of the Spring equinox.

(Continued)

HOLIDAYS *(Continued)*

Ridvan (April 21–May 2) Commemorates Baha'u'llah's prophethood; days 1, 9, and 12 are particularly important.

Declaration of the Bab (May 23) Commemorates the Bab's foretelling of the Messenger.

Ascension of Baha'u'llah (May 29) Commemorates the death of Baha'u'llah.

Martyrdom of the Bab (July 9) Commemorates the death of the Bab.

Birth of the Bab (October 20)

Birth of Baha'u'llah (November 12)

Day of the Covenant (November 26) Commemorates the birth of Abdu'l-Baha.

Ascension of Abdu'l-Baha (November 28) Commemorates the death of Abdu'l-Baha.

TIMELINE

1795	Shaykhi sect started by Shaykh Ahmad, advancing the notion of "the Bab" who mediates between believers and the Hidden Imam
1844	Sayyid Ali-Muhammad Shirazi claims to be the Bab
1848	Babi march, followed by persecution of Babis
1850	The Bab publicly executed
1854	Baha'u'llah writes *The Book of Certitude (Kitab-i-Iqan)*
1863	Baha'u'llah announces that he is the promised one foretold by the Bab
1868	Baha'u'llah and group of followers sent to the penal colony of Acre, Palestine
1873	Baha'u'llah writes *The Most Holy Book (Kitab-i-Aqdas)*

TIMELINE *(Continued)*

1892	Death of Baha'u'llah, succeeded by his son Abdu'l-Baha
1908	Abdu'l-Baha released from a lifetime of exile and imprisonment at age 64
1921	Death of Abdu'l-Baha, who appoints his grandson Shoghi Effendi the Guardian of the Cause
1957	Shoghi Effendi dies without children and without appointing a successor
1963	First Baha'i World Congress and election of first Universal House of Justice

---

GLOSSARY

Bab Arabic for "gate"; the term refers to a person who is an intermediary between the Hidden Imam and believers. This is the title adopted by Sayyid Ali-Muhammad Shirazi (d. 1850), who declared himself to be the Bab.

Babi religion (babism) The religion founded by the Bab (Sayyid Ali-Muhammad Shirazi), which was the precursor to the Baha'i Faith.

Baha Literally, "Glory" or "Splendor"; a title that designates Baha'u'llah. The phrase "People of Baha" refers to followers of Baha'u'llah (superseding People of the Bayan). This designation of *Baha'i* as a follower of Baha'u'llah became current during the later years of Baha'u'llah's residence in Adrianople.

Baha'u'llah Literally, "Glory of God." Founder of the Baha'i Faith, born Mirza Husayn-Ali Nuri (d. 1892). Baha'is believe him to be the *Manifestation of God,* commissioned by God to unify the modern world through a theory and practice of unity.

Bayan Literally, "exposition"; the title of two distinct books by the Bab (one in Persian, the other in Arabic). The term "Bayan" is also used by the Bab as a reference to the whole of his revelation in a generic sense.

Dispensation A divinely appointed age in which God reveals himself through a prophet.

House of Justice (Bayt al-Adl al-Azam) Internationally elected Baha'i administrative institution that oversees the Baha'i community. First described by Baha'u'llah and officially elected in 1963.

Manifestation Appearance of God; a prophet of God's revelation in a given dispensation.

Point, Primal Symbol of the Bab. In Persian mysticism, all knowledge originates from a single dot, or point.

Qa'im Literally, "He who shall arise" from a descendant of Muhammad; also known as the Mahdi, "The Guided One."

THE BAB

IMPRISONMENT

In 1844, Sayyid Ali-Muhammad Shirazi announced that he was indeed "The Bab," and for the next six years, until the end of his life, he was imprisoned or exiled. In the following selections from an "Epistle to Muhammad Shah," the Bab recounts his plight from 1844 to 1848.

God beareth Me witness, I was not a man of learning, for I was trained as a merchant. In the year sixty [i.e., 1844] God graciously infused my soul with the conclusive evidences and weighty knowledge which characterize Him Who is the Testimony of God—may peace be upon Him—until finally in that year I proclaimed God's hidden Cause and unveiled its well-guarded Pillar, in such wise that no one could refute it. "That he who should perish might perish with a clear proof before him and he who should live might live by clear proof." [Qur'an 8:44.]

In that same year I despatched a messenger and a book unto thee, that thou mightest act toward the Cause of Him Who is the Testimony of God as befitteth the station of thy sovereignty. But inasmuch as dark, dreadful, and dire calamity had been irrevocably ordained by the Will of God, the book was not submitted to thy presence, through the intervention of such as regard themselves the well-wishers of the government. Up to the present, when nearly four years have passed, they have not duly presented it to Your Majesty. However, now that the fateful hour is drawing nigh, and because it is a matter of faith, not a worldly concern, therefore I have given thee a glimpse of what hath transpired.

I swear by God! Shouldst thou know the things which in the space of these four years have befallen Me at the hands of thy people and thine army, thou wouldst hold thy breath from fear of God, unless thou wouldst rise to obey the Cause of Him Who is the Testimony of God and make amends for thy shortcomings and failure.

While I was in Shiraz the indignities which befell Me at the hands of its wicked and depraved Governor waxed so grievous that if thou wert acquainted with but a tithe thereof, thou wouldst deal him retributive justice. For as a result of his unmitigated oppression, thy royal court hath become, until the Day of Resurrection, the object of the wrath of God. Moreover, his indulgence in alcohol had grown so excessive that he was never sober enough to make a sound judgement. Therefore, disquieted, I was obliged to set out from Shiraz with the aim of attaining the enlightened and exalted court of Your Majesty. The Mu'tamidu'd-Dawlih then became aware of the truth of the Cause and manifested exemplary servitude and devotion to His chosen ones. When some of the ignorant people in his city arose to stir up sedition, he defended the divine Truth by affording Me protection for a while in the privacy of the Governor's residence. At length, having attained the good-pleasure of God, he repaired to his habitation in the all-highest Paradise. May God reward him graciously....

Following his ascension to the eternal Kingdom, the vicious Gurgin, resorting to all manner of treachery, false oaths and coercion, sent Me away from Isfahan with an escort of five guards on a journey which lasted seven days, without providing the barest necessities for My travel (Alas! Alas! For the things which have touched Me!), until eventually Your Majesty's order came, instructing Me to proceed to Mah-ku....

I swear by the Most Great Lord! Wert thou to be told in what place I dwell, the first person to have mercy on Me would be thyself. In the heart of a mountain is a fortress [Mah-ku]...the inmates of which are confined to two guards and four dogs. Picture, then, My plight...I swear by the truth of God! Were he who hath been willing to treat Me in such a manner to know Who it is Whom he hath so treated, he, verily, would never in his life be happy. Nay—I, verily, acquaint thee with the truth of the matter—it is as if he hath imprisoned all the Prophets, and all the men of truth and all the chosen ones....

When this decree was made known unto Me, I wrote to him who administereth the affairs of the kingdom, saying: "Put Me to death, I adjure thee by God, and send My head wherever thou pleasest. For surely an innocent person such as I, cannot reconcile himself to being consigned to a place reserved for criminals and let his life continue." My plea remained unanswered. Evidently His Excellency the Haji is not

fully aware of the truth of our Cause. It would be far more heinous a deed to sadden the hearts of the faithful, whether men
or women, than to lay waste the sacred House of God....

In brief, I hold within My grasp whatsoever any man
might wish of the good of this world and of the next. Were
I to remove the veil, all would recognize Me as their Best
Beloved, and no one would deny Me. Let not this assertion astound Your Majesty; inasmuch as a true believer in
the unity of God who keepeth his eyes directed toward Him
alone, will regard aught else but Him as utter nothingness.
I swear by God! I seek no earthly goods from thee, be it as
much as a mustard seed. Indeed, to possess anything of this
world or of the next would, in My estimation, be tantamount
to open blasphemy. For it ill beseemeth the believer in the
unity of God to turn his gaze to aught else, much less to hold
it in his possession. I know of a certainty that since I have
God, the Ever-Living, the Adored One, I am the possessor of
all things, visible and invisible....

In this mountain I have remained alone, and have come to
such a pass that none of those gone before Me have suffered
what I have suffered, nor any transgressor endured what I have
endured! I render praise unto God and yet again praise Him.
I find Myself free from sorrow, inasmuch as I abide within the
good-pleasure of My Lord and Master. Methinks I am in the
all-highest Paradise, rejoicing at My communion with God, the
Most Great. Verily this is a bounty which God hath conferred
upon Me; and He is the Lord of unbounded blessings.

Source: Ali Muhammad Shirazi, "Epistle to Muhammad Shah,"
from *Selections from the Writings of the Bab* (Haifa: Baha'I
World Centre, 1976).

THE QAYYUMU'L-ASMA': A NEW QUR'AN

The Qayyumu'l-Asma', *a commentary on the* Surah of Joseph *in
the Qur'an, was composed in 1844 and is the first book the Bab
wrote after his Declaration. The first chapter was written in the
presence of his first believer, Mulla Husayn, and, according to
the Bab, the whole book was written in forty days. Baha'is consider it his first revealed text and his most important work. He
declares a new day, comparing the book itself to the Qur'an, and
thereby announcing a new revelation from God. The* Qayyumu'l-
Asma' *continually draws on passages and themes from the
Qur'an, replicating many of its laws. It is also in the literary
style of the Qur'an—even to the point that the Bab intended it
to be recited like the Qur'an. The following passages establish a*

fundamental theme in the Baha'i faith: The Bab is a continuation in the line of the prophets acknowledged by Islam, most notably Moses, Jesus, and Muhammad.

1. All praise be to God Who hath, through the power of Truth, sent down this Book unto His servant, that it may serve as a shining light for all mankind....Verily this is none other than the sovereign Truth; it is the Path which God hath laid out for all that are in heaven and on earth. Let him then who will, take for himself the right path unto his Lord. Verily this is the true Faith of God, and sufficient witnesses are God and such as are endowed with the knowledge of the Book. This is indeed the eternal Truth which God, the Ancient of Days, hath revealed unto His omnipotent Word—He Who hath been raised up from the midst of the Burning Bush. This is the Mystery which hath been hidden from all that are in heaven and on earth, and in this wondrous Revelation it hath, in very truth, been set forth in the Mother Book by the hand of God, the Exalted....

61. Verily, Christ is Our Word which We communicated unto Mary; and let no one say what the Christians term as "the third of three," inasmuch as it would amount to slandering the Remembrance Who, as decreed in the Mother Book, is invested with supreme authority. Indeed God is but one God, and far be it from His glory that there should be aught else besides Him. All those who shall attain unto Him on the Day of Resurrection are but His servants, and God is, of a truth, a sufficient Protector. Verily I am none other but the servant of God and His Word, and none but the first one to bow down in supplication before God, the Most Exalted; and indeed God witnesseth all things.

62. O People of the Qur'an! Ye are as nothing unless ye submit unto the Remembrance of God and unto this Book. If ye follow the Cause of God, We will forgive you your sins, and if ye turn aside from Our command, We will, in truth, condemn your souls in Our Book, unto the Most Great Fire. We, verily, do not deal unjustly with men, even to the extent of a speck on a date-stone.

63. O Peoples of the earth! Verily the resplendent Light of God hath appeared in your midst, invested with this unerring Book, that ye may be guided aright to the ways of peace and, by the leave of God, step out of the darkness into the light and onto this far-extended Path of Truth. [Qur'an 5:15–18.]...O peoples of the earth! Verily His Remembrance is come to you from God after an

interval during which there were no Messengers, that He may purge and purify you from uncleanliness in anticipation of the Day of the One true God; therefore seek ye whole-heartedly divine blessings from Him, inasmuch as We have, in truth, chosen Him to be the Witness and the Source of wisdom unto all that dwell on earth. . . .

Whenever the faithful hear the verses of this Book being recited, their eyes will overflow with tears and their hearts will be deeply touched by Him Who is the Most Great Remembrance for the love they cherish for God, the All-Praised. He is God, the All-Knowing, the Eternal. They are indeed the inmates of the all-highest Paradise wherein they will abide for ever. Verily they will see naught therein save that which hath proceeded from God, nothing that will lie beyond the compass of their understanding. There they will meet the believers in Paradise, who will address them with the words "Peace, Peace" lingering on their lips. . . .

68. Say, O peoples of the world! Do ye dispute with Me about God by virtue of the names which ye and your fathers have adopted for Him at the promptings of the Evil One? God hath indeed sent down this Book unto Me with truth that ye may be enabled to recognize the true names of God, inasmuch as ye have strayed in error far from the Truth. Verily We have taken a covenant from every created thing upon its coming into being concerning the Remembrance of God, and there shall be none to avert the binding command of God for the purification of mankind, as ordained in the Book which is written by the hand of the Bab.

Source: Ali Muhammad Shirazi, Qayyumu'l-Asma', chs. 1, 61–63, 68, from *Selections from the Writings of the Bab.* Reprinted by permission.

THE BAYAN: A BOOK FOR A NEW DISPENSATION

The Persian Bayan *is the central book of the Babi religion insofar as it establishes a new system of laws and religious principles. The Bab here declares himself to be the independent manifestation of God, whereas in his previous writings he refers to himself as the Mahdi or the Promised One. The following selection explains the relation of the* Bayan *to previous divine books, particularly the* Qur'an.

True knowledge, therefore, is the knowledge of God, and this is none other than the recognition of His Manifestation in each Dispensation. Nor is there any wealth save in poverty in all save God and sanctity from aught else but Him—a state that can be realized only when demonstrated toward Him Who is the Dayspring of His Revelation. This doth not mean, however, that one ought not to yield praise unto former Revelations. On no account is this acceptable, inasmuch as it behooveth man, upon reaching the age of nineteen, to render thanksgiving for the day of his conception as an embryo. For had the embryo not existed, how could he have reached his present stage? Likewise had the religion taught by Adam not existed, this Faith would not have attained its present stage. Thus consider thou the development of God's Faith until the end that hath no end. . . .

Twelve hundred and seventy years have elapsed since the declaration of Muhammad, and each year unnumbered people have circumambulated the House of God [Mecca]. In the concluding year of this period He Who is Himself the Founder of the House went on pilgrimage. Great God! There was a vast concourse of pilgrims from every sect. Yet not one recognized Him, though He recognized every one of them—souls tightly held in the grasp of His former commandment. The only person who recognized Him and performed pilgrimage with Him is the one round whom revolve eight Vahids [i.e., sections of the Bayan], in whom God hath gloried before the Concourse on high by virtue of his absolute detachment and for his being wholly devoted to the Will of God. This doth not mean that he was made the object of a special favour, nay, this is a favour which God hath vouchsafed unto all men, yet they have suffered themselves to be veiled from it. . . .

Everyone is eagerly awaiting His appearance, yet since their inner eyes are not directed toward Him sorrow must needs befall Him. In the case of the Apostle of God—may the blessings of God rest upon Him—before the revelation of the Qur'an everyone bore witness to His piety and noble virtues. Behold Him then after the revelation of the Qur'an. What outrageous insults were levelled against Him, as indeed the pen is ashamed to recount. Likewise behold the Point of the Bayan. His behavior prior to the declaration of His mission is clearly evident unto those who knew Him. Now, following His manifestation, although He hath, up to the present, revealed no less than five hundred thousand verses on different subjects, behold what calumnies are uttered, so unseemly that the pen is stricken with shame at the mention of them. But if all men were to observe the ordinances of God no sadness would befall that heavenly Tree.

Source: Ali Muhammad Shirazi, Bayan 5:4, 18; 6:11, from *Selections from the Writings of the Bab.*

A COMING LEADER

In the Bayan, *the Bab announced the coming of a future prophet—the Sun of Truth, or more generally described as "He Whom God Will Manifest." The Bab depicts him in eschatological terms and notes that his nature is reflected in the* Bayan. *Baha'is believe that the Bab is foretelling the coming of Baha'u'llah.*

If at the time of the appearance of Him Whom God will make manifest all the dwellers of the earth were to bear witness unto a thing whereunto He beareth witness differently, His testimony would be like unto the sun, while theirs would be even as a false image produced in a mirror which is not facing the sun. For had it been otherwise, their testimony would have proved a faithful reflection of His testimony.

I swear by the most sacred Essence of God that but one line of the Words uttered by Him is more sublime than the words uttered by all that dwell on earth. Nay, I beg forgiveness for making this comparison. How could the reflections of the sun in the mirror compare with the wondrous rays of the sun in the visible heaven? The station of one is that of nothingness, while the station of the other, by the righteousness of God—hallowed and magnified be His Name—is that of the Reality of things. . . .

If in the Day of His manifestation a king were to make mention of his own sovereignty, this would be like unto a mirror challenging the sun, saying: "The light is in me." It would be likewise, if a man of learning in His Day were to claim to be an exponent of knowledge, or if he who is possessed of riches were to display his affluence, or if a man wielding power were to assert his own authority, or if one invested with grandeur were to show forth his glory. Nay, such men would become the object of the derision of their peers, and how would they be judged by Him Who is the Sun of Truth! . . .

It is not permissible to ask questions from Him Whom God will make manifest, except that which well beseemeth Him. For His station is that of the Essence of divine Revelation. . . . Whatever evidence of bounty is witnessed in the world, is but an image of His bounty; and every thing owes its existence to His Being. . . . The Bayan is, from beginning to end, the repository of all of His attributes, and the treasury of both His fire and His light. Should anyone desire to ask questions, he is allowed to do so only in writing, that he may derive ample understanding from His written reply and that it may serve as a sign from his Beloved. However, let no one ask aught that may prove unworthy of His lofty station. For instance, were a person to inquire the price of straw from a merchant of rubies, how ignorant would he be and how unacceptable. Similarly unacceptable would be the questions of the highest-ranking people of the world in His presence, except such words as He Himself would utter about Himself in the Day of His manifestation.

Source: Ali Muhammad Shirazi, Bayan 3:12, 13, from *Selections from the Writings of the Bab.*

DAY OF RESURRECTION

The Bab believed that the resurrection, judgment, heaven, and hell were to be understood metaphorically. In the following selection, he explains that the "day of resurrection" refers to the advent of a new dispensation that "resurrects" the previous one. For example, the Qur'an is resurrected in the Bayan, *and the* Bayan *ultimately will be resurrected in the advent of "He whom God will manifest."*

The substance of this chapter is this, that what is intended by the Day of Resurrection is the Day of the appearance of the Tree of divine Reality, but it is not seen that any one of the followers of Shi'ih Islam hath understood the meaning of the Day of Resurrection; rather have they fancifully imagined a thing which with God hath no reality. In the estimation of God and according to the usage of such as are initiated into divine mysteries, what is meant by the Day of Resurrection is this, that from the time of the appearance of Him Who is the Tree of divine Reality, at whatever period and under whatever name, until the moment of His disappearance, is the Day of Resurrection.

For example, from the inception of the mission of Jesus—may peace be upon Him—till the day of His ascension was the Resurrection of Moses. For during that period the Revelation of God shone forth through the appearance of that divine Reality, Who rewarded by His Word everyone who believed in Moses, and punished by His Word everyone who did not believe; inasmuch as God's Testimony for that Day was that which He had solemnly affirmed in the Gospel. And from the inception of the Revelation of the Apostle of God—may the blessings of God be upon Him—till the day of His ascension was the Resurrection of Jesus—peace be upon Him—wherein the Tree of divine Reality appeared in the person of Muhammad, rewarding by His Word everyone who was a believer in Jesus, and punishing by His Word everyone who was not a believer in Him. And from the moment when the Tree of the Bayan appeared until it disappeareth is the Resurrection of the Apostle of God, as is divinely foretold in the Qur'an; the beginning of which was when two hours and eleven minutes had passed on the eve of the fifth of Jamadiyu'l-Avval, 1260 A.H. [May 22, 1844], which is the year 1270 of the Declaration of the Mission of Muhammad. This was the beginning of the Day of Resurrection of the Qur'an, and until the disappearance of the Tree of divine Reality is the Resurrection of the Qur'an. The stage of perfection of everything is reached when its resurrection occurreth. The perfection of the religion of Islam was consummated at the beginning of this Revelation; and from the rise of this Revelation until its setting, the fruits of the Tree of Islam, whatever they are, will become apparent. The Resurrection of the Bayan will occur at the time of the appearance of Him Whom God shall make manifest. For today the Bayan is in the stage of seed; at the beginning of the manifestation of Him Whom God shall make manifest its ultimate perfection will become apparent. He is made manifest in order to gather the fruits of the trees He hath planted; even as the Revelation of the Qa'im [He Who ariseth], a descendant of Muhammad— may the blessings of God rest upon Him—is exactly like unto the Revelation of the Apostle of God Himself [Muhammad]. He appeareth not, save for the purpose of gathering the fruits of Islam from the Qur'anic verses which He [Muhammad] hath sown in the hearts of men. The fruits of Islam cannot be gathered except through allegiance unto Him [the Qa'im] and by believing in Him. At the present time, however, only adverse effects have resulted; for although He hath appeared in the midmost heart of Islam, and all people profess it by reason of their relationship to Him [the Qa'im], yet unjustly have they consigned Him to the Mountain of Maku, and this notwithstanding that in the Qur'an the advent of the Day of Resurrection hath been promised unto all by God. For on that Day all men will be brought before God and will attain His Presence; which meaneth appearance before Him Who is the Tree of divine Reality and attainment unto His presence; inasmuch as it is not possible to appear before the Most Holy Essence of God, nor is it conceivable to seek reunion with Him. That which is feasible in the matter of appearance before Him and of meeting Him is attainment unto the Primal Tree.

Source: Ali Muhammad Shirazi, Bayan 2:7, from *Selections from the Writings of the Bab.*

CALL TO BELIEF

Acceptance of the Bab's message was not as widespread as he had hoped. The Bab compared his situation to the initial disbelief Muhammad's contemporaries had demonstrated toward Muhammad—just as Muhammad had compared his situation to those of the rejected prophets from the past. The following selections are from "An Address to a Muslim Divine" (Abdu's-Sahib). And again, like Muhammad, the Bab warns of divine punishment for disbelievers.

Thy vision is obscured by the belief that divine revelation ended with the coming of Muhammad, and unto this We have borne witness in Our first epistle. Indeed, He Who hath revealed verses unto Muhammad, the Apostle of God, hath likewise revealed verses unto Ali-Muhammad. For who else but God can reveal to a man such clear and manifest verses as overpower all the learned? Since thou hast acknowledged the revelation of Muhammad, the Apostle of God, then there is no other way open before thee but to testify that whatever is revealed by the Primal Point hath also proceeded from God, the Help in Peril, the Self-Subsisting. Is it not true that the Qur'an hath been sent down from God and that all men are powerless before its revelation? Likewise these words have also been revealed by God, if thou dost but perceive. What is there in the Bayan which keepeth thee back from recognizing these verses as being sent forth by God, the Inaccessible, the Most Exalted, the All-Glorious? . . .

Thou contendest, "How can we recognize Him when we have heard naught but words which fall short of irrefutable proofs?" Yet since thou hast acknowledged and recognized Muhammad, the Apostle of God, through the Qur'an, how canst thou withhold recognition from Him Who sent thee the Book, despite thy calling thyself "His servant"? Verily He doth exercise undisputed authority over His revelations unto all mankind. . . .

We enjoin thee to save thyself and all the inhabitants of that land from the fire, then to enter the peerless and exalted Paradise of His good-pleasure. Otherwise the day is approaching when thou shalt perish and enter the fire, when thou shalt have neither patron nor helper from God. We have taken compassion on thee, as a sign of Our grace, inasmuch as thou hast related thyself unto Us. Verily We are aware of all things. We are cognizant of thy righteous deeds, though they shall avail thee nothing; for the whole object of such righteousness is but recognition of God, thy Lord, and undoubted faith in the Words revealed by Him.

Source: Ali Muhammad Shirazi, "An Address to a Muslim Divine," from *Selections from the Writings of the Bab.*

BAHA'U'LLAH

DIFFERENT MANIFESTATIONS IN DIFFERENT DISPENSATIONS

Between 1861 and 1862, while exiled in Baghdad, Baha'u'llah composed the Kitab-i-Iqan (The Book of Certitude), *perhaps the most influential Baha'i scripture. The work explains how different periods of time had their own prophets who subtly anticipated future prophets in future dispensations. Followers of these prophets invariably misinterpreted their messages. Baha'u'llah believes that special attention to key passages in their writings and symbolic terms will show that each prophet indeed announced the coming of the next. The work was composed one or two years prior to his Declaration at Ridvan, and thus he does not include himself in the chain of prophets.*

Consider the past. How many, both high and low, have, at all times, yearningly awaited the advent of the Manifestations of God in the sanctified persons of His chosen Ones. How often have they expected His coming, how frequently have they prayed that the breeze of divine mercy might blow, and the promised Beauty step forth from behind the veil of concealment, and be made manifest to all the world. And whensoever the portals of grace did open, and the clouds of divine bounty did rain upon mankind, and the light of the Unseen did shine above the horizon of celestial might, they all denied Him, and turned away from His face—the face of God Himself. Refer ye, to verify this truth, to that which hath been recorded in every sacred Book.

Ponder for a moment, and reflect upon that which hath been the cause of such denial on the part of those who have searched with such earnestness and longing. Their attack hath been more fierce than tongue or pen can describe. Not one single Manifestation of Holiness hath appeared but He was afflicted by the denials, the repudiation, and the vehement opposition of the people around Him. Thus it hath been revealed: "O the misery of men! No Messenger cometh unto them but they laugh Him to scorn." [Qur'an 36:30]. . . .

Again He saith: "Each nation hath plotted darkly against their Messenger to lay violent hold on Him, and disputed with vain words to invalidate the truth." [Qur'an 40:5]. . . .

Among the Prophets was Noah. For nine hundred and fifty years He prayerfully exhorted His people and summoned them to the haven of security and peace. None, however, heeded His call. Each day they inflicted on His blessed person such pain and suffering that no one believed He could survive. How frequently they denied Him, how malevolently they hinted their suspicion against Him! ...And after Noah the light of the countenance of Hud shone forth above the horizon of creation. For well-nigh seven hundred years, according to the sayings of men, He exhorted the people to turn their faces and draw nearer unto the Ridvan of the divine presence. What showers of afflictions rained upon Him, until at last His adjurations bore the fruit of increased rebelliousness, and His assiduous endeavours resulted in the wilful blindness of His people.... "And their unbelief shall only increase for the unbelievers their own perdition." [Qur'an 35:39]. ...

And after Him there appeared from the Ridvan of the Eternal, the Invisible, the holy person of Salih, Who again summoned the people to the river of everlasting life. For over a hundred years He admonished them to hold fast unto the commandments of God and eschew that which is forbidden. His admonitions, however, yielded no fruit, and His pleading proved of no avail. Several times He retired and lived in seclusion. All this, although that eternal Beauty was summoning the people to no other than the city of God.

Later, the beauty of the countenance of the Friend of God [i.e., Abraham] appeared from behind the veil, and another standard of divine guidance was hoisted. He invited the people of the earth to the light of righteousness. The more passionately He exhorted them, the fiercer waxed the envy and waywardness of the people, except those who wholly detached themselves from all save God, and ascended on the wings of certainty to the station which God hath exalted beyond the comprehension of men. It is well known what a host of enemies besieged Him, until at last the fires of envy and rebellion were kindled against Him. And after the episode of the fire came to pass, He, the lamp of God amongst men, was, as recorded in all books and chronicles, expelled from His city.

And when His day was ended, there came the turn of Moses. Armed with the rod of celestial dominion, adorned with the white hand of divine knowledge, and proceeding from the Paran of the love of God, and wielding the serpent of power and everlasting majesty, He shone forth from the Sinai of light upon the world. He summoned all the peoples and kindreds of the earth to the kingdom of eternity, and invited them to partake of the fruit of the tree of faithfulness. ...

And when the days of Moses were ended, and the light of Jesus, shining forth from the dayspring of the Spirit, encompassed the world, all the people of Israel arose in protest against Him. They clamoured that He Whose advent the Bible had foretold must needs promulgate and fulfill the laws of Moses, whereas this youthful Nazarene, who laid claim to the station of the divine Messiah, had annulled the law of divorce and of the Sabbath day—the most weighty of all the laws of Moses. Moreover, what of the signs of the Manifestation yet to come? These people of Israel are even unto the present day still expecting that Manifestation which the Bible hath foretold! How many Manifestations of Holiness, how many Revealers of the light everlasting, have appeared since the time of Moses, and yet Israel, wrapt in the densest veils of satanic fancy and false imaginings, is still expectant that the idol of her own handiwork will appear with such signs as she herself hath conceived!

...There is yet another verse in the Gospel wherein He saith: "Heaven and earth shall pass away: but My words shall not pass away" [Luke 21:33]. Thus it is that the adherents of Jesus maintained that the law of the Gospel shall never be annulled, and that whensoever the promised Beauty is made manifest and all the signs are revealed, He must needs re-affirm and establish the law proclaimed in the Gospel, so that there may remain in the world no faith but His faith. This is their fundamental belief. And their conviction is such that were a person to be made manifest with all the promised signs and to promulgate that which is contrary to the letter of the law of the Gospel, they must assuredly renounce him, refuse to submit to his law, declare him an infidel, and laugh him to scorn. This is proved by that which came to pass when the sun of the Muhammadan Revelation was revealed. Had they sought with a humble mind from the Manifestations of God in every Dispensation the true meaning of these words revealed in the sacred books—words the misapprehension of which hath caused men to be deprived of the recognition of the Sadratu'l-Muntaha, the ultimate Purpose—they surely would have been guided to the light of the Sun of Truth, and would have discovered the mysteries of divine knowledge and wisdom.

From all that We have stated it hath become clear and manifest that before the revelation of each of the Mirrors reflecting the divine Essence, the signs heralding their advent must needs be revealed in the visible heaven as well as in the invisible, wherein is the seat of the sun of knowledge, of the moon of wisdom, and of the stars of understanding and utterance. The sign of the invisible heaven must needs be revealed in the person of that perfect man who, before each Manifestation appeareth, educateth, and prepareth the souls of men for the advent of the divine Luminary, the Light of the unity of God among men.

Source: Baha'u'llah, *Kitab-I-Iqan* (Wilmette: Baha'i Publishing Trust, 1989). Reprinted by permission.

BAHA'I LAWS

In around 1873, ten years after his declaration at Ridvan and midway into his ministry, Baha'u'llah penned the Kitab-i-Aqdas (Most Holy Book), *which is principally a compendium of Baha'i law. Although the* Bayan *also contains laws, Baha'is believe that the* Bayan *has been superseded by the* Aqdas. *Accordingly, the* Aqdas *follows some of the* Bayan's *laws and ignores others. Section 42 describes the function of the Universal House of Justice, which is the ruling body of the Baha'i Faith.*

1. The first duty prescribed by God for His servants is the recognition of Him Who is the Dayspring of His Revelation and the Fountain of His laws, Who represen- teth the Godhead in both the Kingdom of His Cause and the world of creation. Whoso achieveth this duty hath attained unto all good; and whoso is deprived thereof hath gone astray, though he be the author of every righ- teous deed. It behoveth every one who reacheth this most sublime station, this summit of transcendent glory, to observe every ordinance of Him Who is the Desire of the world. These twin duties are inseparable. Neither is acceptable without the other. Thus hath it been decreed by Him Who is the Source of Divine inspiration. . . .

12. It hath been ordained that obligatory prayer is to be per- formed by each of you individually. Save in the Prayer for the Dead, the practice of congregational prayer hath been annulled. He, of a truth, is the Ordainer, the All-Wise.

13. God hath exempted women who are in their courses from obligatory prayer and fasting. Let them, instead, after performance of their ablutions, give praise unto God, repeating ninety-five times between the noon of one day and the next "Glorified be God, the Lord of Splendour and Beauty." Thus hath it been decreed in the Book, if ye be of them that comprehend.

14. When travelling, if ye should stop and rest in some safe spot, perform ye—men and women alike—a single prostra- tion in place of each unsaid Obligatory Prayer, and while prostrating say "Glorified be God, the Lord of Might and Majesty, of Grace and Bounty." Whoso is unable to do this, let him say only "Glorified be God"; this shall assuredly suffice him. He is, of a truth, the all-sufficing, the ever- abiding, the forgiving, compassionate God. Upon complet- ing your prostrations, seat yourselves cross-legged—men and women alike—and eighteen times repeat "Glorified be God, the Lord of the kingdoms of earth and heaven." Thus doth the Lord make plain the ways of truth and guidance,

ways that lead to one way, which is this Straight Path. Render thanks unto God for this most gracious favour; offer praise unto Him for this bounty that hath encompassed the heavens and the earth; extol Him for this mercy that hath pervaded all creation. . . .

16. O Pen of the Most High! Say: O people of the world! We have enjoined upon you fasting during a brief period, and at its close have designated for you Naw-Ruz as a feast. Thus hath the Day-Star of Utterance shone forth above the horizon of the Book as decreed by Him Who is the Lord of the beginning and the end. Let the days in excess of the months be placed before the month of fasting. We have ordained that these, amid all nights and days, shall be the manifestations of the letter Ha, and thus they have not been bounded by the limits of the year and its months. It behoveth the people of Baha, throughout these days, to provide good cheer for themselves, their kindred and, beyond them, the poor and needy, and with joy and exultation to hail and glorify their Lord, to sing His praise and magnify His Name; and when they end—these days of giving that precede the season of restraint—let them enter upon the Fast. Thus hath it been ordained by Him Who is the Lord of all mankind. The traveler, the ailing, those who are with child or giving suck, are not bound by the Fast; they have been exempted by God as a token of His grace. He, verily, is the Almighty, the Most Generous. . . .

30. The Lord hath ordained that in every city a House of Justice be established wherein shall gather counsellors to the number of Baha, and should it exceed this number it doth not matter. They should consider themselves as entering the Court of the presence of God, the Exalted, the Most High, and as beholding Him Who is the Unseen. It behoveth them to be the trusted ones of the Merciful among men and to regard themselves as the guardians appointed of God for all that dwell on earth. It is incumbent upon them to take counsel together and to have regard for the interests of the servants of God, for His sake, even as they regard their own interests, and to choose that which is meet and seemly. Thus hath the Lord your God commanded you. Beware lest ye put away that which is clearly revealed in His Tablet. Fear God, O ye that perceive.

31. O people of the world! Build ye houses of worship throughout the lands in the name of Him Who is the Lord of all religions. Make them as perfect as is possible in the world of being, and adorn them with that which befitteth

them, not with images and effigies. Then, with radiance and joy, celebrate therein the praise of your Lord, the Most Compassionate. Verily, by His remembrance the eye is cheered and the heart is filled with light.

32. The Lord hath ordained that those of you who are able shall make pilgrimage to the sacred House, and from this He hath exempted women as a mercy on His part. He, of a truth, is the All-Bountiful, the Most Generous.

33. O people of Baha! It is incumbent upon each one of you to engage in some occupation—such as a craft, a trade, or the like. We have exalted your engagement in such work to the rank of worship of the one true God. Reflect, O people, on the grace and blessings of your Lord, and yield Him thanks at eventide and dawn. Waste not your hours in idleness and sloth, but occupy yourselves with what will profit you and others. Thus hath it been decreed in this Tablet from whose horizon hath shone the day-star of wisdom and utterance. The most despised of men in the sight of God are they who sit and beg. Hold ye fast unto the cord of means and place your trust in God, the Provider of all means. . . .

37. Whoso layeth claim to a Revelation direct from God, ere the expiration of a full thousand years, such a man is assuredly a lying impostor. We pray God that He may graciously assist him to retract and repudiate such claim. Should he repent, God will, no doubt, forgive him.

   If, however, he persisteth in his error, God will, assuredly, send down one who will deal mercilessly with him. Terrible, indeed, is God in punishing! Whosoever interpreteth this verse otherwise than its obvious meaning is deprived of the Spirit of God and of His mercy which encompasseth all created things. Fear God, and follow not your idle fancies. Nay, rather, follow the bidding of your Lord, the Almighty, the All-Wise. Erelong shall clamorous voices be raised in most lands. Shun them, O My people, and follow not the iniquitous and evil-hearted. This is that of which We gave you forewarning when We were dwelling in Iraq, then later while in the Land of Mystery, and now from this Resplendent Spot. . . .

42. Endowments dedicated to charity revert to God, the Revealer of Signs. None hath the right to dispose of them without leave from Him Who is the Dawning-place of Revelation. After Him, this authority shall pass to the Aghsan, and after them to the House of Justice—should it be established in the world by then—that they may use

these endowments for the benefit of the Places which have been exalted in this Cause, and for whatsoever hath been enjoined upon them by Him Who is the God of might and power. Otherwise, the endowments shall revert to the people of Baha who speak not except by His leave and judge not save in accordance with what God hath decreed in this Tablet—lo, they are the champions of victory betwixt heaven and earth—that they may use them in the manner that hath been laid down in the Book by God, the Mighty, the Bountiful. . . .

49. God hath imposed a fine on every adulterer and adulteress, to be paid to the House of Justice: nine mithqals of gold, to be doubled if they should repeat the offence. Such is the penalty which He Who is the Lord of Names hath assigned them in this world; and in the world to come He hath ordained for them a humiliating torment. Should anyone be afflicted by a sin, it behoveth him to repent thereof and return unto his Lord. He, verily, granteth forgiveness unto whomsoever He willeth, and none may question that which it pleaseth Him to ordain. He is, in truth, the Ever-Forgiving, the Almighty, the All-Praised. . . .

63. God hath prescribed matrimony unto you. Beware that ye take not unto yourselves more wives than two. Whoso contenteth himself with a single partner from among the maidservants of God, both he and she shall live in tranquillity. And he who would take into his service a maid may do so with propriety. Such is the ordinance which, in truth and justice, hath been recorded by the Pen of Revelation. Enter into wedlock, O people, that ye may bring forth one who will make mention of Me amid My servants. This is My bidding unto you; hold fast to it as an assistance to yourselves. . . .

65. It hath been laid down in the Bayan that marriage is dependent upon the consent of both parties. Desiring to establish love, unity and harmony amidst Our servants, We have conditioned it, once the couple's wish is known, upon the permission of their parents, lest enmity and rancour should arise among them. And in this We have yet other purposes. Thus hath Our commandment been ordained. . . .

149. Recite ye the verses of God every morn and eventide. Whoso faileth to recite them hath not been faithful to the Covenant of God and His Testament, and whoso turneth away from these holy verses in this Day is of those who throughout eternity have turned away from God. Fear ye

God, O My servants, one and all. Pride not yourselves on much reading of the verses or on a multitude of pious acts by night and day; for were a man to read a single verse with joy and radiance it would be better for him than to read with lassitude all the Holy Books of God, the Help in Peril, the Self-Subsisting. Read ye the sacred verses in such measure that ye be not overcome by languor and despondency. Lay not upon your souls that which will weary them and weigh them down, but rather what will lighten and uplift them, so that they may soar on the wings of the Divine verses toward the Dawning-place of His manifest signs; this will draw you nearer to God, did ye but comprehend. . . .

155. Gambling and the use of opium have been forbidden unto you. Eschew them both, O people, and be not of those who transgress. Beware of using any substance that induceth sluggishness and torpor in the human temple and inflicteth harm upon the body. We, verily, desire for you naught save what shall profit you, and to this bear witness all created things, had ye but ears to hear.

Source: Baha'u'llah, *Kitab-I-Aqdas*, 1, 12–14, 16, 30–33, 37, 42, 49, 63, 65, 149, 155 (Haifa: Baha'i World Centre, 1992). Reprinted by permission.

PROMOTING PEACE

Many of Baha'u'llah's writings focus on the place of the Baha'i Faith in God's scheme of revelation, and also on laws that govern the Baha'i community. Some writings, though, focus on the larger issue of world peace—a distinguishing feature of the Baha'i Faith. Such themes are seen in the following excerpt from the Lawh-i-Dunya (Tablet of the World).

Whilst in the Prison of Akka, We revealed in the Crimson Book that which is conducive to the advancement of mankind and to the reconstruction of the world. The utterances set forth therein by the Pen of the Lord of creation include the following which constitute the fundamental principles for the administration of the affairs of men:

First: It is incumbent upon the ministers of the House of Justice to promote the Lesser Peace so that the people of the earth may be relieved from the burden of exorbitant expenditures. This matter is imperative and absolutely essential, inasmuch as hostilities and conflict lie at the root of affliction and calamity. Second: Languages must be reduced to one common language to be taught in all the schools of the world. Third: It behoveth man to adhere tenaciously unto that which will promote fellowship, kindliness, and unity. Fourth: Everyone, whether man or woman, should hand over to a trusted person a portion of what he or she earneth through trade, agriculture, or other occupation, for the training and education of children, to be spent for this purpose with the knowledge of the Trustees of the House of Justice. Fifth: Special regard must be paid to agriculture. Although it hath been mentioned in the fifth place, unquestionably it precedeth the others. Agriculture is highly developed in foreign lands, however in Persia it hath so far been grievously neglected. It is hoped that His Majesty the Shah—may God assist him by His grace—will turn his attention to this vital and important matter.

Were men to strictly observe that which the Pen of the Most High hath revealed in the Crimson Book, they could then well afford to dispense with the regulations which prevail in the world. Certain exhortations have repeatedly streamed forth from the Pen of the Most High that perchance the manifestations of power and the dawning-places of might may, sometime, be enabled to enforce them. Indeed, were sincere seekers to be found, every emanation of God's pervasive and irresistible Will would, for the sake of His love, be revealed. But where are to be found earnest seekers and inquiring minds? Whither are gone the equitable and the fair-minded? At present no day passeth without the fire of a fresh tyranny blazing fiercely, or the sword of a new aggression being unsheathed. Gracious God! The great and the noble in Persia glory in acts of such savagery that one is lost in amazement at the tales thereof.

Source: Baha'u'llah, *Lawh-i-Dunya,* from *Tablets of Baha'u'llah Revealed after the Kitab-i-Aqdas* (Haifa: Baha'i World Centre, 1978). Reprinted by permission.

PARADISE

Just as the Bab reinterpreted the traditional notion of the "Day of Judgment," so too does Baha'u'llah give a broader interpretation to the notion of "paradise" and "hell." They are partly experienced here on earth, although they are more vast in the afterlife. The following selection is from the Suriy-i-Vafa (Tablet to Vafa).

As to Paradise: It is a reality and there can be no doubt about it, and now in this world it is realized through love of Me and My good-pleasure. Whosoever attaineth unto it

God will aid him in this world below, and after death He will enable him to gain admittance into Paradise whose vastness is as that of heaven and earth. Therein the Maids of glory and holiness will wait upon him in the daytime and in the night season, while the day-star of the unfading beauty of his Lord will at all times shed its radiance upon him and he will shine so brightly that no one shall bear to gaze at him. Such is the dispensation of Providence, yet the people are shut out by a grievous veil. Likewise apprehend thou the nature of hell-fire and be of them that truly believe. For every act performed there shall be a recompense according to the estimate of God, and unto this the very ordinances and prohibitions prescribed by the Almighty amply bear witness. For surely if deeds were not rewarded and yielded no fruit, then the Cause of God—exalted is He—would prove futile. Immeasurably high is He exalted above such blasphemies! However, unto them that are rid of all attachments a deed is, verily, its own reward. Were We to enlarge upon this theme numerous Tablets would need to be written.

Source: Baha'u'llah, *Suriy-I-Vafa,* from *Tablets of Baha'u'llah Revealed after The Kitab-i-Aqdas.*

ABDU'L-BAHA

BAHA'U'LLAH'S TEACHINGS

Several of Abdu'l-Baha's writings are formal religious texts and resemble the style of the Bayan *or* Kitab-i-Iqan. *Other texts, though, are more informal in nature, such as those based on public lectures. The effect of these is the communication of Baha'i doctrine to a wider circle of people. Such is the case with the following summary of Baha'u'llah's teachings from Abdu'l-Baha's "Discourse at the London Theosophical Head Quarters," September 30, 1911.*

[Baha'u'llah] declared the most human virtues; He manifested the Spiritual powers, and put them into practice in the world around Him.

Firstly: He lays stress on the search for Truth. This is most important, because the people are too easily led by tradition. It is because of this that they are often antagonistic to each other, and dispute with one another. But the manifesting of Truth discovers the darkness and becomes the cause of Oneness of faith and belief: because Truth cannot be two! That is not possible.

Secondly: Baha'u'llah taught the Oneness of humanity; that is to say, all the children of men are under the mercy of the Great God. They are the sons of one God; they are trained by God. He has placed the crown of humanity on the head of every one of the servants of God. Therefore all nations and peoples must consider themselves brethren. They are all descendants from Adam. They are the branches, leaves, flowers and fruits of One Tree. They are pearls from one shell. But the children of men are in need of education and civilization, and they require to be polished, till they become bright and shining. Man and woman both should be educated equally and equally regarded. It is racial, patriotic, religious, and class prejudice, that has been the cause of the destruction of Humanity.

Thirdly: Baha'u'llah taught that Religion is the chief foundation of Love and Unity and the cause of Oneness. If a religion become the cause of hatred and disharmony, it would be better that it should not exist. To be without such a religion is better than to be with it.

Fourthly: Religion and Science are inter-twined with each other and cannot be separated. These are the two wings with which humanity must fly. One wing is not enough. Every religion which does not concern itself with Science is mere tradition, and that is not the essential. Therefore science, education, and civilization are most important necessities for the full religious life.

Fifthly: The Reality of the divine Religions is one, because the Reality is one and cannot be two. All the prophets are united in their message, and unshaken. They are like the sun; in different seasons they ascend from different rising points on the horizon. Therefore every ancient prophet gave the glad tidings of the future, and every future has accepted the past.

Sixthly: Equality and Brotherhood must be established among all members of mankind. This is according to Justice. The general rights of mankind must be guarded and preserved. All men must be treated equally. This is inherent in the very nature of humanity.

Seventhly: The arrangements of the circumstances of the people must be such that poverty shall disappear, and that every one as far as possible, according to his position and rank, shall be comfortable. Whilst the nobles and others in high rank are in easy circumstances, the poor also should be able to get their daily food and not be brought to the extremities of hunger.

Eighthly: Baha'u'llah declared the coming of the Most Great Peace. All the nations and peoples will come under the shadow of the Tent of the Great Peace and Harmony—that is to say, by general election a Great Board of Arbitration shall be established, to settle all differences and quarrels between the Powers; so that disputes shall not end in war.

Ninthly: Baha'u'llah taught that hearts must receive the Bounty of the Holy Spirit, so that Spiritual civilization may be established. For material civilization is not adequate for the needs of mankind and cannot be the cause of its happiness. Material civilization is like the body and spiritual civilization is like the soul. Body without soul cannot live.

This is a short summary of the Teachings of Baha'u'llah. To establish this Baha'u'llah underwent great difficulties and hardships. He was in constant confinement and He suffered great persecution. But in the fortress (Akka) He reared a spiritual palace and from the darkness of His prison He sent out a great light to the world. It is the ardent desire of the Baha'is to put these teachings into common practice: and they will strive with soul and heart to give up their lives for this purpose, until the heavenly light brightens the whole world of humanity.

Source: Abdu'l-Baha, "Discourse at the London Theosophical Head Quarters," from *Abdu'l-Baha in London* (London: Baha'i Publishing Trust, 1982). Reprinted by permission.

THE UNITY OF EXISTENCE

In another informal work, Some Answered Questions (written between 1904 and 1906), Abdu'l-Baha considers the issue of the unity of existence, sometimes called pantheism, which is the theological position that God is identical to the universe as a whole. He distinguishes between two types of unity of existence: that of the Sufis and that of the prophets. The unity of existence of the Sufis maintains that individual beings (people, animals) are subcomponents of God's essence. This he rejects because it implies that God becomes a lower form of existence. The unity of existence of the prophets sees the world as an emanation of God, distinct from yet illuminated by God's being. This maintains the immanence of God's attributes, while still conserving God's transcendence. Baha'u'llah endorses this view as the true unity of existence.

Question: What is the nature of the "unity of existence" propounded by the Theosophists and the Sufis, and what in reality do they intend by it? Is this belief true or not?

Answer: Know that the idea of the unity of existence is ancient and is not restricted to the Theosophists and the Sufis alone. Indeed, it was espoused by some of the Greek philosophers, such as Aristotle, who said: "The uncompounded Reality is all things, but it is not any single one of them." "Uncompounded" stands here in contrast to "composed"—that is to say, that solitary Reality, which is sanctified and exalted above composition and division, has resolved itself into countless forms. Thus, real Existence is all things, but it is not any single one of them.

The proponents of the unity of existence hold that real Existence is even as the sea, and that all created things are like unto its waves. These waves, which signify the created things, are the countless forms which that real Existence assumes. Hence, that sanctified Reality is the pre-existent sea, and the countless forms of created things are its originated waves....

In summary, the Sufis speak only of God and creation, and believe that God has resolved Himself into, and manifested Himself through, the infinite forms of His creation, even as the sea which appears in the infinite forms of its waves. These originated and imperfect waves are identical to the pre-existent Sea, which is the sum of all the divine perfections. The Prophets, however, hold that there are the world of God, the world of the Kingdom, and the world of creation: three things. The first emanation is the outpouring grace of the Kingdom, which has emanated from God and has appeared in the realities of all things, even as the rays emanating from the sun are reflected in all things. And that grace—the rays—appears in infinite forms in the realities of all things, and is specified and individuated according to their capacity, receptivity, and essence. But the assertion of the Sufis would require that absolute wealth descend into poverty, that the Pre-existent be confined to originated forms, and that the very quintessence of power be reflected in the mirror of powerlessness and be subjected to the inherent limitations of the contingent world. And this is a self-evident error, for we observe that the reality of man, who is the noblest of all creatures, cannot descend to the reality of the animal; that the essence of the animal, which is endowed with the power of sensation, does not abase itself to the degree of the plant; and that the reality of the plant, which is the power of growth, does not degrade itself to the reality of the mineral.

In brief, superior realities do not descend or abase themselves to the degree of inferior realities. How, then, could the universal Reality of God, which transcends all descriptions and attributes, resolve itself, notwithstanding its absolute sanctity and holiness, into the forms and realities of the contingent world, which are the very source of imperfections? This is pure fantasy and untenable conjecture. On the contrary, that Essence of sanctity is the sum of all divine and lordly perfections, and all creatures receive illumination from His emanational appearance and partake of the lights of His celestial perfection and beauty, in the same way that all earthly creatures acquire the grace of light from the rays of the sun, without any descent or abasement of the latter into the recipient realities of these earthly beings.

Source: Abdu'l-Baha, *Some Answered Questions* (Haifa: Baha'i World Centre, 2014). Reprinted by permission.

UNIVERSAL LOVE

A key theme in the Baha'i Faith is a love of humanity. One of the most dramatic statements of this doctrine is from Abdu'l-Baha's public talk in Paris, October 24, 1911, on the subject of "The Universal Love."

An Indian said to Abdu'l-Baha: "My aim in life is to transmit as far as in me lies the message of Krishna to the world."

Abdu'l-Baha said: The Message of Krishna is the message of love. All God's prophets have brought the message of love. None has ever thought that war and hate are good. Every one agrees in saying that love and kindness are best. Love manifests its reality in deeds, not only in words—these alone are without effect. In order that love may manifest its power there must be an object, an instrument, a motive. There are many ways of expressing the love principle; there is love for the family, for the country, for the race, there is political enthusiasm, there is also the love of community of interest in service. These are all ways and means of showing the power of love. Without any such means, love would be unseen, unheard, unfelt—altogether unexpressed, unmanifested! Water shows its power in various ways, in quenching thirst, causing seed to grow, etc. Coal expresses one of its principles in gas-light, while one of the powers of electricity is shown in the electric light. If there were neither gas nor electricity, the nights of the world would be darkness! So, it is necessary to have an instrument, a motive for love's manifestation, an object, a mode of expression.

We must find a way of spreading love among the sons of humanity. Love is unlimited, boundless, infinite! Material things are limited, circumscribed, finite. You cannot adequately express infinite love by limited means. The perfect love needs an unselfish instrument, absolutely freed from fetters of every kind. The love of family is limited; the tie of blood relationship is not the strongest bond. Frequently members of the same family disagree, and even hate each other. Patriotic love is finite; the love of one's country causing hatred of all others, is not perfect love! Compatriots also are not free from quarrels among themselves. The love of race is limited; there is some union here, but that is insufficient. Love must be free from boundaries! To love our own race may mean hatred of all others, and even people of the same race often dislike each other. Political love also is much bound up with hatred of one party for another; this love is very limited and uncertain. The love of community of interest in service is likewise fluctuating; frequently competitions arise, which lead to jealousy, and at length hatred replaces love. A few years ago, Turkey and Italy had a friendly political understanding; now they are at war! All these ties of love are imperfect. It is clear that limited material ties are insufficient to adequately express the universal love.

The great unselfish love for humanity is bounded by none of these imperfect, semi-selfish bonds; this is the one perfect love, possible to all mankind, and can only be achieved by the power of the Divine Spirit. No worldly power can accomplish the universal love. Let all be united in this Divine power of love! Let all strive to grow in the light of the Sun of Truth, and reflecting this luminous love on all men, may their hearts become so united that they may dwell evermore in the radiance of the limitless love.... The animal creation is captive to matter, God has given freedom to man. The animal cannot escape the law of nature, whereas man may control it, for he, containing nature, can rise above it. The power of the Holy Spirit, enlightening man's intelligence, has enabled him to discover means of bending many natural laws to his will. He flies through the air, floats on the sea, and even moves under the waters. All this proves how man's intelligence has been enabled to free him from the limitations of nature, and to solve many of her mysteries. Man, to a certain extent, has broken the chains of matter. The Holy Spirit will give to man greater powers than these, if only he will strive after the things of the spirit and endeavour to attune his heart to the Divine infinite love.

When you love a member of your family or a compatriot, let it be with a ray of the Infinite Love! Let it be in God, and for God! Wherever you find the attributes of God love that person, whether he be of your family or of another. Shed the light of a boundless love on every human being whom you meet, whether of your country, your race, your political party, or of any other nation, color or shade of political opinion. Heaven will support you while you work in this ingathering of the scattered peoples of the world beneath the shadow of the almighty tent of unity. You will be servants of God, who are dwelling near to Him, His divine helpers in the service, ministering to all Humanity. All Humanity! Every human being! Never forget this! Do not say, he is an Italian, or a Frenchman, or an American, or an Englishman, remember only that he is a son of God, a servant of the Most High, a man! All are men! Forget nationalities; all are equal in the sight of God!

Source: Abdu'l-Baha, "The Universal Love," *Paris Talks* (London: Baha'i Publishing Trust, 1979). Reprinted by permission.

ABDU'L-BAHA'S WILL

Abdu'l-Baha died in 1921, and in his will he appointed Shoghi Effendi to succeed him as the Guardian of the Cause of the Baha'i Faith. The following selections, from the conclusion of his will, describe this appointment.

O ye the faithful loved ones of Abdu'l-Baha! It is incumbent upon you to take the greatest care of Shoghi Effendi, the twig that hath branched from and the fruit given forth by the two hallowed and Divine Lote-Trees, that no dust of despondency and sorrow may stain his radiant nature, that day by day he may wax greater in happiness, in joy and spirituality, and may grow to become even as a fruitful tree.

For he is, after Abdu'l-Baha, the Guardian of the Cause of God, the Afnan, the Hands (pillars) of the Cause and the beloved of the Lord must obey him and turn unto him. He that obeyeth him not, hath not obeyed God; he that turneth away from him, hath turned away from God and he that denieth him, hath denied the True One. Beware lest anyone falsely interpret these words, and like unto them that have broken the Covenant after the Day of Ascension (of Baha'u'llah) advance a pretext, raise the standard of revolt, wax stubborn and open wide the door of false interpretation. To none is given the right to put forth his own opinion or express his particular conviction. All must seek guidance and turn unto the Center of the Cause and the House of Justice. And he that turneth unto whatsoever else is indeed in grievous error.

Source: Abdu'l-Baha, *The Will and Testament of Abdu'l-Baha* (Wilmette, IL: Baha'i Publishing Trust, 1971). Reprinted by permission.

SHOGHI EFFENDI

POSSIBILITIES FOR THE FUTURE

A principal achievement of Shoghi Effendi's leadership was the establishment of the formal Baha'i administrative structure. As a visionary, in many of his writings and talks he mapped out achievement goals and multiyear plans to accomplish these. Some of his goals, such as the establishment of the Universal House of Justice, did not come into being until after his death. The following selection from The Advent of Divine Justice, a December 25, 1938, address to American and Canadian Baha'is, lists goals for the future.

I can only for the moment cite at random certain of these opportunities which stand out preeminently, in any attempt to survey the possibilities of the future: The election of the International House of Justice and its establishment in the Holy Land, the spiritual and administrative center of the Baha'i world, together with the formation of its auxiliary branches and subsidiary institutions; the gradual erection of the various dependencies of the first Mashriqu'l-Adhkar of the West, and the intricate issues involving the establishment and the extension of the structural basis of Baha'i community life; the codification and promulgation of the ordinances of the *Most Holy Book* [Kitab-i-Aqdas], necessitating the formation, in certain countries of the East, of properly constituted and officially recognized courts of Baha'i law; the building of the third Mashriqu'l-Adhkar of the Baha'i world in the outskirts of the city of Tihran, to be followed by the rise of a similar House of Worship in the Holy Land itself; the deliverance of Baha'i communities from the fetters of religious orthodoxy in such Islamic countries as Persia, Iraq, and Egypt, and the consequent recognition, by the civil authorities in those states, of the independent status and religious character of Baha'i National and Local Assemblies; the precautionary and defensive measures to be devised, coordinated, and carried out to counteract the full force of the inescapable attacks which the organized efforts of ecclesiastical organizations of various denominations will progressively launch and relentlessly pursue; and, last but not least, the multitudinous issues that must be faced, the obstacles that must be overcome, and the responsibilities that must be assumed, to enable a sore-tried Faith to pass through the successive stages of unmitigated obscurity, of active repression, and of complete emancipation, leading in turn to its being acknowledged as an independent Faith, enjoying the status of full equality with its sister religions, to be followed by its establishment and recognition as a State religion, which in turn must give way to its assumption of the rights and prerogatives associated with the Baha'i state, functioning in the plenitude of its powers, a stage which must ultimately culminate in the emergence of the worldwide Baha'i Commonwealth, animated wholly by the spirit, and operating solely in direct conformity with the laws and principles of Baha'u'llah.

Source: Shoghi Effendi, *The Advent of Divine Justice* (Wilmette, IL: Baha'i Publishing Trust, 1990). Reprinted by permission.

UNITY OF RELIGIONS, RACES, AND GOD

The writings of the Bab and Baha'u'llah reflect the fact that their initial audience was Muslim. The unity of religions, races, and God is indeed a pervasive theme of their writings; however, this theme is often presented in contexts that defend the Bab's and Baha'u'llah's roles as legitimate prophets in the line of Moses, Jesus, and Muhammad. In Shoghi Effendi's writings, the Muslim context is less important and the theme of unity is brought to the fore on its own merits. This is evident in the following selections from the Preface to The Promised Day Is Come *(1941).*

The fundamental principle enunciated by Baha'u'llah ... is that religious truth is not absolute but relative, that Divine Revelation is a continuous and progressive process, that all the great religions of the world are divine in origin, that their basic principles are in complete harmony, that their aims and purposes are one and the same, that their teachings are but facets of one truth, that their functions are complementary, that they differ only in the nonessential aspects of their doctrines, and that their missions represent successive stages in the spiritual evolution of human society....

. . . His mission is to proclaim that the ages of the infancy and of the childhood of the human race are past, that the convulsions associated with the present stage of its adolescence are slowly and painfully preparing it to attain the stage of manhood, and are heralding the approach of that Age of Ages when swords will be beaten into plowshares, when the Kingdom promised by Jesus Christ will have been established, and the peace of the planet definitely and permanently ensured. Nor does Baha'u'llah claim finality for His own Revelation, but rather stipulates that a fuller measure of the truth He has been commissioned by the Almighty to vouchsafe to humanity, at so critical a juncture in its fortunes, must needs be disclosed at future stages in the constant and limitless evolution of mankind.

The Baha'i Faith upholds the unity of God, recognizes the unity of His Prophets, and inculcates the principle of the oneness and wholeness of the entire human race. It proclaims the necessity and the inevitability of the unification of mankind, asserts that it is gradually approaching, and claims that nothing short of the transmuting spirit of God, working through His chosen Mouthpiece in this day, can ultimately succeed in bringing it about. It, moreover, enjoins upon its followers the primary duty of an unfettered search after truth, condemns all manner of prejudice and superstition, declares the purpose of religion to be the promotion of amity and concord, proclaims its essential harmony with science, and recognizes it as the foremost agency for the pacification and the orderly progress of human society. . . .

Mirza Husayn-Ali, surnamed Baha'u'llah (the Glory of God), a native of Mazindaran, whose advent the Bab [Herald and Forerunner of Baha'u'llah] had foretold, . . . was imprisoned in Tihran, was banished, in 1852, from His native land to Baghdad, and thence to Constantinople and Adrianople, and finally to the prison city of Akka, where He remained incarcerated for no less than twenty-four years, and in whose neighborhood He passed away in 1892. In the course of His banishment, and particularly in Adrianople and Akka, He formulated the laws and ordinances of His Dispensation, expounded, in over a hundred volumes, the principles of His Faith, proclaimed His Message to the kings and rulers of both the East and the West, both Christian and Muslim, addressed the Pope, the Caliph of Islam, the Chief Magistrates of the Republics of the American continent, the entire Christian sacerdotal order, the leaders of Shi'ih and Sunni Islam, and the high priests of the Zoroastrian religion. In these writings He proclaimed His Revelation, summoned those whom He addressed to heed His call and espouse His Faith, warned them of the consequences of their refusal, and denounced, in some cases, their arrogance and tyranny. . . .

The Faith which this order serves, safeguards and promotes is . . . essentially supernatural, supranational, entirely non-political, non-partisan, and diametrically opposed to any policy or school of thought that seeks to exalt any particular race, class, or nation. It is free from any form of ecclesiasticism, has neither priesthood nor rituals, and is supported exclusively by voluntary contributions made by its avowed adherents. Though loyal to their respective governments, though imbued with the love of their own country, and anxious to promote at all times, its best interests, the followers of the Baha'i Faith, nevertheless, viewing mankind as one entity, and profoundly attached to its vital interests, will not hesitate to subordinate every particular interest, be it personal, regional, or national, to the over-riding interests of the generality of mankind, knowing full well that in a world of interdependent peoples and nations the advantage of the part is best to be reached by the advantage of the whole, and that no lasting result can be achieved by any of the component parts if the general interests of the entity itself are neglected.

Source: Shoghi Effendi, *The Promised Day Is Come* (Wilmette, IL: Baha'i Publishing Trust, 1980). Reprinted by permission.

THE UNIVERSAL HOUSE OF JUSTICE

PROMISE OF WORLD PEACE

Shoghi Effendi died in 1957. One of his principal concerns was to establish the Universal House of Justice to succeed him when he died. The Universal House of Justice was officially elected in 1963, and since then it has overseen Baha'i administration, interpreted Baha'i scripture, and produced its own authoritative Baha'i texts. The following selections are from one such text, The Promise of World Peace, addressed to the world in October 1985.

The Great Peace toward which people of good will throughout the centuries have inclined their hearts, of which seers and poets for countless generations have expressed their vision, and for which from age to age the sacred scriptures of mankind have constantly held the promise, is now at long last within the reach of the nations. For the first time in history it is possible for everyone to view the entire planet, with all its myriad diversified peoples, in one perspective. World peace is not only possible but inevitable. It is the next stage in the evolution of this planet—in the words of one great thinker, "the planetization of mankind."...

A candid acknowledgement that prejudice, war, and exploitation have been the expression of immature stages in a vast historical process and that the human race is today experiencing the unavoidable tumult which marks its collective coming of age is not a reason for despair but a prerequisite to undertaking the stupendous enterprise of building a peaceful world. That such an enterprise is possible, that the necessary constructive forces do exist, that unifying social structures can be erected, is the theme we urge you to examine....

No serious attempt to set human affairs aright, to achieve world peace, can ignore religion. Man's perception and practice of it are largely the stuff of history. An eminent historian described religion as a "faculty of human nature." That the perversion of this faculty has contributed to much of the confusion in society and the conflicts in and between individuals can hardly be denied. But neither can any fair-minded observer discount the preponderating influence exerted by religion on the vital expressions of civilization. Furthermore, its indispensability to social order has repeatedly been demonstrated by its direct effect on laws and morality....

Banning nuclear weapons, prohibiting the use of poison gases, or outlawing germ warfare will not remove the root causes of war. However important such practical measures obviously are as elements of the peace process, they are in themselves too superficial to exert enduring influence. Peoples are ingenious enough to invent yet other forms of warfare, and to use food, raw materials, finance, industrial power, ideology, and terrorism to subvert one another in an endless quest for supremacy and dominion. Nor can the present massive dislocation in the affairs of humanity be resolved through the settlement of specific conflicts or disagreements among nations. A genuine universal framework must be adopted....

The emancipation of women, the achievement of full equality between the sexes, is one of the most important, though less acknowledged prerequisites of peace. The denial of such equality perpetrates an injustice against one half of the world's population and promotes in men harmful attitudes and habits that are carried from the family to the workplace, to political life, and ultimately to international relations. There are no grounds, moral, practical, or biological, upon which such denial can be justified. Only as women are welcomed into full partnership in all fields of human endeavor will the moral and psychological climate be created in which international peace can emerge.

Source: Universal House of Justice, *The Promise of World Peace, to the Peoples of the World, a Statement* (Haifa: Baha'i World Centre, 1985). Reprinted by permission.

Indigenous Religions

INTRODUCTION

Indigenous religions are ones that were developed and practiced by native tribal people in their particular geographical areas. Prior to the formation of cities, nations and empires, all human religious practices were indigenous. But with the rise of world urbanization, indigenous tribes have greatly declined, and with them their languages, rituals, and religious myths. Today perhaps 300 million people—4% of the world's population—practice traditional indigenous religion. These are largely people who live in remote regions that for centuries have had minimal contact from colonizers or modern nations.

Indigenous religions are as varied as the thousands of native tribes within their respective regions. Generally speaking, these tribes were nomadic, wandering from place to place in search of food and water, and many of their religious myths encoded information regarding where to find the necessities of life and instructions for constructing tools or temporary buildings, or hunting. Others myths took the form of stories that recounted the deeds of ancestral beings with many containing ethical codes for present behavior. They also encoded complex rituals, many of which were linked with human life cycle such as rites of passage and special events. Still other myths were more metaphysical in nature and involved spirits and gods with hymns to those beings. Many indigenous people had no writing systems, nor did they build permanent structures or monuments. Thus, tribal religions were perpetuated in oral tradition, often passed from generation to generation. Because of both the uniqueness of various tribal practices and the rarity of firsthand documents, religions from these regions lack the kind of official sacred texts that we find in major world religions such as Hinduism or Judaism. Our knowledge of them rests largely on the secondhand written accounts of travelers, missionaries and, more recently, social science researchers. In this chapter we will focus on three geographical regions of indigenous religion: Africa, the Americas, and Oceania.

AFRICA

Africa is a large and culturally diverse continent, which makes it difficult to generalize about its religious practices. About one-third of the African people follow traditional African religions, and the remaining two-thirds are Muslim or Christian.

Traditional African religions are restricted to specific tribal regions; there are as many as 700 languages in Africa, and each represents a different cultural group and religion. The various traditional religions are unique insofar as they developed from within their respective cultures and no attempt was made to send out missionaries or to convert people of other tribal religions. Nevertheless, these tribal religions have some shared features. First, many African religions hold a common belief in a high god—a supreme being in the sky and creator of all. However, because they believe that the high god is remote, religious rituals often focus on specialized tutelary gods, ancestral spirits, and animal spirits. Second, African religions have dramatic rituals involving ecstatic dances, chants, the wearing of masks, and the use of other fetish objects. So prominent are these visual worship practices in African religion that, for some time, the term *fetishism* designated African religion in general. Third, although African religions have some belief in an afterlife, their primary concern is with living well in this life. Fourth, African religions frequently hold that individual people are composed of numerous souls of their ancestors, which were handed on to them by their parents. The ancestral spirits inhabit all parts of a person's body, such as blood or bones, and make their wishes known. The ancestral spirits are particularly offended when living family members quarrel with each other or are immoral. This might prompt a particular ancestral spirit to rise up from within a living family member, take possession of her, and make her vocalize the ancestral spirit's discontent. Spirit possession and trances of this type, it is believed, are important for helping heal and integrate an individual.

For more distinct features of African religions, we must look to regional tribal practices. For simplicity, we can divide the African continent into four geographical regions that designate distinct cultural and religious traditions. One region is the northern portion, dominated by the Sahara desert. This area has seen much Christian and Muslim missionary activity, especially along the well-traveled trade routes; thus, when scholars speak of traditional African religion, they typically refer to the remaining three sub-Saharan areas. A second geographical area is eastern Africa, which contains 200 distinct tribal societies. The religious practices of the Nuer—herdspeople from the grasslands and swamps of southern Sudan—have attracted special attention. A third area is central and southern Africa, which is marked off by its regionally shared language group called *Bantu*. A fourth and final area is West Africa, which accounts for half of Africa's total population.

AMERICA

The term "Native American" designates the indigenous peoples of the Western Hemisphere, including the peoples of both North and South America. Unlike African religion, which does contain some common themes, few generalizations can be made about indigenous American religion beyond what is central to most religions—namely, belief in the supernatural, the use of religious symbols, and ritual practices. There is no single concept of a high god or nature gods. In some tribes religious symbols are sometimes modeled after natural objects, and in others they tend to be abstract. Religious practices are sometimes formalized and other times integrated into daily activity. When Europeans first arrived in the Americas, there were around 240 tribal groups in North America alone. Anthropologists have classified these into the following nine groups based on geographical location and language:

Arctic: Aleut, Inuit

Subarctic (Alaska to Labrador): Chipewyan, Mountain, Tanana, Yellowknife

Northwest Coast (Alaska to northern California): Chinook, Haida, Nootka, Tlingit

California: Chumash, Esselen, Mojave, Pomo, Wappo

Western Plateau and Great Basin (east of California): Flathead, Nez Perce, Paiute, Shoshoni, Umatilla, Ute

Southwest (Arizona, New Mexico, Texas, northern Mexico): Apache, Hopi, Navajo, Pueblo, Zuni

Plains (north of Texas): Arapaho, Cheyenne, Comanche, Dakota, Kiowa, Lakota, Pawnee

Eastern Woodlands (northeast of Mississippi): Delaware, Iroquois, Ojibwa, Shawnee, Susquehanna, Winnebago

Southeast (Louisiana to Florida): Cherokee, Chickasaw, Choctaw, Creek, Seminole

Though Mexico and South America were no less varied in their regional tribes, these areas are most distinguished by major empires. Among the oldest of these is the *Maya*, which flourished between 250 and 900 CE in Mesoamerica (southern Mexico, Guatemala, and Belize). They developed a complex calendar and a hieroglyphic form of writing that has recently been translated. Their religion focused on a collection of nature gods, such as the sun, moon, rain, corn, and double-headed snake. For reasons not entirely clear, the civilization went into decline, its major cities being overtaken with jungle growth. Following on the heels of the Maya, just to the north in central Mexico, arose the *Toltec* empire, which peaked from the tenth to the twelfth centuries. Toltecs practiced human sacrifice in religious ceremonies, and, drawing on earlier mythology, they developed a cult of *Quetzalcoatl*, the "Feathered Serpent." They declined with the invasion of northern Mexican tribes into this region, giving rise to the *Aztec* empire. The Aztecs perpetuated both the practice of human sacrifice and the cult of Quetzalcoatl. Like the Maya, they too developed a system of writing, which gives us a direct avenue to understanding their religion. By the fifteenth century the Aztecs ruled central and southern Mexico; their expansion was finally halted in 1521 by Spanish explorers. During the rise of the Aztecs in Mexico, Peru saw the emergence of the *Inca* empire, which, like the Aztec, was crushed by Spanish conquest in 1532. With the Spanish invasion came Roman Catholic Christianity, which was quickly imposed on the conquered people. In rural areas, though, vestiges of the ancient religions remain, often intermingled with Catholic elements.

The selections here sample the religious mythology of African, Native American, and Oceanic tribes. They explore the cause of death, the structure of the spiritual realm, the creation of the world, and the source of human suffering. In each case the myths express anguish about the human predicament and offer some statement about our place in the spiritual nature of things.

OCEANIA

"Oceania" is a loosely defined term that refers to the islands of the south and central Pacific. Historically, it consists of three principal regions: (1) Polynesia (including Samoa, New Zealand, Hawaii, Easter Island); (2) Melanesia (including New Guinea, Fiji, and New Caledonia); (3) Micronesia (including Guam and the Marshall Islands). Australia and Tasmania are often associated with Oceania as a fourth region, as we will do here. There is great cultural and historical diversity among the people of these regions, with hundreds of distinct languages and each tribal group having its own myth and ritual cycles. At the same time, however, they share histories of migration, early settlement, dependence on sea travel, and similar types of myths and deities that spread throughout the island regions.

Like many indigenous religions from other parts of the world, the earliest inhabitants of Oceania developed complex religious systems that included myths for explaining how the world came to be as it is, and ritual practices for manipulating natural forces. These include stories about how the world emerged along with its land formations and variety of animals, especially vicious creatures like sharks. There are stories about the first humans, the discovery of fire, the creation of social codes, and acts of vengeance that the gods take on disobedient humans. The uniqueness of these stories rests on their tropical island settings, and the role that the sea plays both for navigation and food.

Australia, because of its sheer size and distinct geography, is a special case. At the time of white settlement in Australia, there were an estimated 300,000 Aborigines, divided among around 500 tribes. Today their population is around twice that number. Australian Aborigines have traditionally viewed themselves as custodians of the land, and much of their religious lore and practice is concerned with how the world came to be as it is, and the role of humans in maintaining it. In Aboriginal culture, there is a strong sense of a common life force that pervades the entire world, with humans, animals, and spirits all manifestations of it. They see themselves as fundamentally linked to the land they inhabit, and as having a primordial connection with other humans and animals. Their ancestors were also aware of the fragility of their environment and so attempted to avoid damaging it by their actions. This concern continues today among those Aboriginal peoples who maintain their traditions, but white settlement has led many to lose this sense of connection with the land.

TIMELINE: AFRICA

200,000 BCE	Earliest true humans in Africa
4000–1000 BCE	Ancient African civilizations of the Nile Valley
1000 BCE	Spread of Bantu migration through sub-Saharan Africa
300–700 CE	Expansion of Christianity across northern Africa
600–1000	Spread of Bantu migration to southern Africa
700–800	Expansion of Islam across northern Africa
700	Beginning of Arab slave trade in Africa
1000	Spread of Islam into sub-Saharan Africa
1441	Beginning of European slave trade in Africa
1900	Peak of European colonization of Africa

TIMELINE: AMERICA

20,000 BCE	Arrival of first settlers in the Americas
250–900 CE	Classical Mayan civilization
1200–1519	Aztec civilization
1350–1533	Inca Empire in Peru
1492	Discovery of America by Columbus
1830	Indian Removal Act passed by U.S. Congress
1979	U.S. American Indian Religious Freedom Act

TIMELINE: OCEANIA

50,000 BCE	Human habitation in Australia
40,00 BCE	Human habitation in New Guinea
30,000 BCE	Bread baking in Australia, oldest in the world
3,500 BCE	Human habitation in Fiji
1,500 BCE	Human habitation in New Caledonia
300 CE	Human habitation in Hawaii
1000	Habitation in Easter Island
1300	Human habitation in New Zealand
1521	Magellan lands in Mariana Islands
1770	James Cook lands in New Zealand and Australia
1800	European colonization and missionary activity begins

GLOSSARY

Aborigine Indigenous people of a particular region, often used in reference to the indigenous people of Australia.

Baiame The creator god and sky father in Australian aboriginal mythology.

Bantu Region and language group of central and southern Africa.

Cherokee Indigenous North American people of the Iroquois group of the southeastern United States.

Dreamtime (The Dreaming) Ancient time period in Australian aboriginal mythology when creation took place.

Fetishism Use in worship practices of special objects that contain spiritual power, such as masks.

High God A supreme being in the sky and creator of all.

Hopi Indigenous North American people of the Pueblo group in the southwestern United States.

Maui Trickster god in Polynesian mythology.

Maya Indigenous pre-Columbian people and civilization of southern Mexico and Guatemala.

Nature Deity A divine being in charge of a force within nature, such as the sky, the sun, water, fire.

Oceania: Pacific Island regions of Polynesia, Melanesia, and Micronesia, sometimes also including Australia and Tasmania.

Olofat Malicious trickster god in Micronesian mythology.

Popol Vuh Mayan religious text composed around 1550.

Quetzalcoatl Mythical priest-king of the Toltec people.

San Indigenous people of southern Africa, also called Bushmen; prior to and distinct from Bantu inhabitants.

Tezcatlipoca Mythical evil wizard of the Toltec people.

Toltec Indigenous pre-Columbian people and civilization of central Mexico in the tenth to twelfth centuries CE.

Trickster Supernatural figure or cultural hero who appears in various guises and uses cunning for mischievous activities.

AFRICA

CAUSE OF DEATH

One of the most distinctive and pervasive themes in African religious myth is that death is unnatural: God originally intended humans to live forever, but there was some misunderstanding that prevented this. The plots, human characters, and gods differ, but there is an unmistakable thread tying these myths together throughout Africa's diverse regions. Three such stories are presented here.

Unkulunkulu [the High God of the Zulu people of the Bantu] sent a chameleon; he said to it, "Go, chameleon, go and say, 'Let not men die!'" The chameleon set out; it went slowly, it loitered in the way; and as it went it ate of the fruit of a bush which is called Ubukwebezane. At length Unkulunkulu sent a lizard after the chameleon, when it had already set out for some time. The lizard went; it ran and made great haste, for Unkulunkulu had said, "Lizard, when you have arrived say, 'Let men die!'" So the lizard went, and said, "I tell you, it is said, 'Let men die!'" The lizard came back again to Unkulunkulu before the chameleon had reached his destination, the chameleon, which was sent first—which was sent and told to go and say, "Let not men die!" At length it arrived and shouted, saying, "It is said, 'Let not men die!'" But men answered, "Oh, we have accepted the word of the lizard; it has told us the word. It is said 'Let men die!' We cannot hear your word. Through the word of the lizard men will die."

Imana [the High God of the Bantu tribes in Rwanda] used to talk with men. One day he said to a man, "Do not go to sleep to-night; I am coming to give you some good news." There was a serpent hidden in the hut, who overheard these words. The man kept awake till cockcrow, after which he was overpowered by sleep, and did not hear when Imana came and called him. The serpent was on the watch and answered the call. Imana thought the man was speaking, and said, "You will die, but you will rise again; you will grow old, but you will get a new skin, you, your children, and your grandchildren." Next morning the man went to see Imana, and complained that he had not received any message. Imana asked, "It was not you, then, to whom I spoke in the night?" "No." "Then it must have been the snake, who is forever accursed. If a Tusi ever comes across that snake let him kill it—likewise the Hutu and the Twa. Let them kill one wherever they find it. But as for you, you will die, you and your children and your children's children."

In the beginning of the world when the Creator had made men and women and the animals, they all lived together in the creation land. The Creator was a big chief, past all men, and being very kindhearted, was very sorry whenever anyone died. So one day he sent for the dog, who was his head messenger, and told him to go out into the world and give his word to all people that for the future whenever anyone died the body was to be placed in the compound, and wood ashes were to be thrown over it; that the dead body was to be left on the ground, and in twenty-four hours it would become alive again.

When the dog had traveled for half a day he began to get tired; so as he was near an old woman's house he looked in, and seeing a bone with some meat on it he made a meal of it, and then went to sleep, entirely forgetting the message which had been given him to deliver. After a time, when the dog did not return, the Creator called for a sheep, and sent him out with the same message. But the sheep was a very foolish one, and being hungry, began eating the sweet grasses by the wayside. After a time, however, he remembered that he had a message to deliver, but forgot what it was exactly. So as he went about among the people, he told them that the message the Creator had given him to tell the people, was that whenever anyone died they should be buried underneath the ground.

A little time afterwards the dog remembered his message, so he ran into the town and told the people that they were to place wood ashes on the dead bodies and leave them in the compound, and that they would come to life again after twenty-four hours. But the people would not believe him, and said, "We have already received the word from the Creator by the sheep, that all dead bodies should be buried." In consequence of this the dead bodies are now always buried, and the dog is much disliked and not trusted as a messenger. If he had not found the bone in the old woman's house and forgotten his message, the dead people might still be alive.

Source: Adapted from Alice Werner, *Myths and Legends of the Bantu* (London: G. G. Harrap and Co., Ltd., 1933), chs. 2 and 3; Elphinstone Dayrell, *Folk Stories from Southern Nigeria, West Africa* (London; New York: Longmans, Green and Co., 1910).

KING OF DEATH: ANGOLAN MYTH

The myths about the cause of death express a frustration with the boundaries that separate the living from the dead. This theme plays out in a variety of myths in which a dejected person attempts to cross over this boundary. The following legend from the Bantu Ambundu tribe of Angola describes a heartbroken king's efforts to retrieve his dead wife from the realm of death— which is presided over by Lord Kalunga-ngombe. The king enlists the aid of a medicine man who makes the journey.

Kitamba was a chief who lived at Kasanji. He lost his head-wife, Queen Muhongo, and mourned for her many days. Not only did he mourn himself, but he insisted on his people sharing his grief. "In my village, too, no man will do anything. The young people will not shout; the women will not pound; no one will speak in the village." His headmen argued with him, but Kitamba was inflexible, and declared that he would neither speak nor eat nor allow anyone else to do so till his queen was restored to him. The headmen consulted together, and called in a medicine man. Having received his fee—first a gun, and then a cow—hearing their statement of the case, he said, "All right," and set off to gather herbs. He pounded these in a medicine-mortar, and, having prepared a potion, ordered the king and all the people to wash themselves with it. He next directed some men to dig a grave in his guest-hut at the fireplace, which they did. He entered it with his little boy, giving two last instructions to his wife: to leave off her girdle [i.e., to dress negligently, as if in mourning] and to pour water every day on the fireplace. Then the men filled in the grave.

The medicine man saw a road open before him. He walked along it with his boy till he came to a village, where he found Queen Muhongo sitting, sewing a basket. She saw him approaching, and asked, "Where do you come from?" He answered, in the usual form demanded by native politeness, "I have sought you, yourself. Since you have been dead, King Kitamba will not eat, drink, or speak. In the village they do not pound food; they do not speak. He says, 'fetch my head-wife and I will talk and eat.' That is what brought me here. I have spoken." The queen then pointed out a man seated a little way off, and asked the doctor who he was. As he could not say, she told him, "He is the King of Death, Lord Kalunga-ngombe. He is always consuming us, us all." Directing his attention to another man who was chained, she asked if he knew him, and he answered, "He looks like King Kitamba, whom I left where I came from." It was indeed Kitamba, and the queen further informed the messenger that her husband had not many years to live, and also that "anyone who comes here in the realm of Death never returns again." She gave him the armlet which had been buried with her, to show to Kitamba as a proof that he had really visited the abode of the dead. She urged him, though, not to tell the king that he had seen him there. And he must not eat anything in Kalunga; otherwise he would never be permitted to return to earth.

Meanwhile, the medicine man's wife had kept pouring water on the grave. One day she saw the earth beginning to crack; the cracks opened wider, and, finally, her husband's head appeared. He gradually made his way out, and pulled his small son up after him. The child fainted when he came out into the sunlight, but his father washed him with some herbal medicine, and soon brought him to.

Next day the medicine man went to the headmen and presented his report; he was repaid with two slaves and returned to his home. The headmen told Kitamba what he had said, and produced the token. The only comment he is recorded to have made, on looking at the armlet, is "Truth, it is the same." We do not hear whether he countermanded the official mourning, but it is to be presumed he did so, for he made no further difficulty about eating or drinking. Then, after a few years, he died. They wailed at the funeral, then dispersed.

Source: Adapted from Alice Werner, *Myths and Legends of the Bantu*, ch. 2.

WOMAN'S SEARCH FOR THE HIGH GOD: ZAMBIAN MYTH

Religious traditions around the world struggle with explaining why God allows human suffering. The next story from a Bantu tribe of Zambia is about an old woman who, having suffered miserably through her life, attempts to find the High God and have him explain the meaning of her ordeal. Her efforts, though, fail.

An old woman, whose parents had died when she was a child, lost all her sons and daughters, one after another, and was left with no one belonging to her. When she was very old and weary she thought she must be about to follow them. But instead of that she found herself growing younger, and was seized with a strong desire to find Leza [the High God] and ask him the meaning of it all. Thinking that he had his abode in the sky, she began to cut down trees and make a scaffolding by which she could climb up.

But when she had built it up to a considerable height, the lower poles rotted away, and the whole fell down, she falling with it. She was not hurt, and tried again, but with no better success. At last she gave up in despair, and set out to reach the place where, as she believed, the sky joins the earth. So she wandered through one country after another, and when the people asked her what she wanted she said, "I am seeking Leza." "What do you want of him?" "My brothers, you ask me? Here in the nations is there one who has suffered as I have suffered? I am alone. As you see me, a solitary old woman, that is how I am!"

The people answered, "Yes, we see! That is how you are! Bereaved of friends and kindred? In what do you differ from others? Shikakunamo [High God of the Baila tribe] sits on the back of every one of us, and we cannot shake him off!"

Source: Adapted from Alice Werner, *Myths and Legends of the Bantu*, ch. 3.

TREE TO THE UPPER WORLD: TANZANIAN MYTH

The previous myth expresses the belief that the spiritual realm is located physically above the world in which we live. Just as the old woman attempts to build a scaffolding to breach the gulf, other myths describe similar mechanisms for climbing up to the heavens. The following myth from the Wachagga people of Tanzania's Kilimanjaro region describes a mysterious tree that leads to the world above.

> A girl named Kichalundu went out one day to cut grass. Finding it growing very luxuriantly in a certain place, she stepped on the spot and sank into a quagmire. Her companions took hold of her hands and tried to pull her out, but in vain; she vanished from their sight. They heard her singing, "The ghosts have taken me. Go and tell my father and mother," and they ran to call the parents. The whole countryside gathered about the place, and a diviner advised the father to sacrifice a cow and a sheep. This was done, and they heard the girl's voice again, but growing fainter and fainter, till at last it was silent, and they gave her up for lost. But after a time a tree grew up on the spot where she had disappeared. It went on growing, until at last it reached the sky. The herd-boys, during the heat of the day, used to drive their cattle into its shade, and themselves climbed up into the spreading branches. One day two of them ventured higher than the rest, and called out, "Can you see us still?" The others answered, "No, come down again!" but the two daring fellows refused. "We are going on into the sky to *Wuhu*, the World Above!" Those were their last words, for they were never seen again. And the tree was called *Mdi Msumu*, "the Story-tree."

Source: Adapted from Alice Werner, *Myths and Legends of the Bantu,* ch. 5.

DEAD PEOPLE BECOME CLOUDS: SAN MYTH

The San—or Bushmen—are an indigenous people of southern Africa. Their social composition consists of autonomous groups of families totaling around fifty people, typically with no dominant leader. Although at one point they occupied about one-third of the African continent, their numbers now are greatly diminished and total less than 100,000. The following San myth describes how, upon death, nature covers over the footprints that we made while alive and then carries us away to become clouds. Unlike the previous myths, which are presented in a somewhat stylized form, the one here conveys the unedited utterances of a specific tribesperson.

> The wind does thus when we die, our [own] wind blows; for we, who are human beings, we possess wind; we make clouds when we die. Therefore, the wind does thus when we

die, the wind makes dust, because it intends to blow, taking away our footprints, with which we had walked about while we still had nothing the matter with us. And our footprints, which the wind intends to blow away, would [otherwise still] lie plainly visible. For, the thing would seem as if we still lived. Therefore, the wind intends to blow, taking away our footprints. And, our gall, when we die, sits in the sky; it sits green in the sky, when we are dead.

Therefore, mother was wont to do thus when the moon lying down came, [when] the moon stood hollow. Mother spoke, she said: "The moon is carrying people who are dead. For, you are those who see that it lies in this manner; and it lies hollow, because it is killing itself [by] carrying people who are dead. This is why it lies hollow. It is not threatening; for, is it a moon of badness? You may [expect to] hear something, when the moon lies in this manner. A person is the one who has died, he whom the moon carries. Therefore, you may [expect to] hear what has happened, when the moon is like this."

The hair of our head will resemble clouds when we die, when we in this manner make clouds. These things are those which resemble clouds; and we think that [they] are clouds. We, who do not know, we are those who think in this manner, that [they] are clouds. We, who know, when we see that they are like this, we know that [they] are a person's clouds; [that they] are the hair of his head. We, who know, we are those who think thus, while we feel that we seeing recognize the clouds, how the clouds do in this manner form themselves.

Source: Wilhelm Heinrich Immanuel Bleek et al., *Specimens of Bushman Folklore* (London: G. Allen and Company, 1911).

WAR OF THE GODS: YORUBA MYTH

The myth that follows, from the Yoruba city of Ife, describes an epic war between the gods that engulfed the earth. The Father of the Gods (Aramfe) had two sons: the Creator of Men (Orisha) and the King of Men (Oduwa). At creation the Father of the Gods gave the Creator of Men a bag containing the wisdom and craftsmanship for the advancement of human civilization. But when the Creator of Men was sleeping, his brother, the King of Men, stole the bag. Although the King of Men then possessed the bag, he nevertheless did not have the power to teach its secrets. The Creator of Men asked for the bag back, but the King of Men refused. This in turn brought catastrophic war to the city of Ife between armies of the two gods and their human followers. The Father of the Gods tried to stop the conflict by punishing the gods and humans alike with great floods, but that failed. The God of Iron (Ogun)—son of the King of Men—grew weary of the war and asked the King of Men to return the bag to the Creator of Men. But the King of Men still refused and, transforming into stone, he sank beneath the soil, forever taking the bag with him.

When the God of Iron and other gods first made known their handicrafts, men learned to patiently acquire thatch, food, and wine in forests and rivers. So man thrived. But in those days strife and turmoil came to the gods. For out of jealousy and pride, the King of Men [had stolen and] held the bag [of knowledge and wisdom] that the Father of the Gods gave to the great Creator of Men. Often the Creator of Men made a plea, and often a petitioner came before his brother the King of Men. But it was in vain. But then once the King of Men sat with the God of Iron in that same palace where the ancestors reign. The sound of drums was heard and the great Creator of Men approached with a skilled brass worker, and said: "The time has come to teach the art of the Father of the Gods to men. Give back the bag, for it is mine, so that I may do our father's bidding. Otherwise, beware: is it not told how caution slept in the still woods when the proud leopard fell, lured on by silence, beneath the monster's foot?" Then the King of Men was greatly angered: "Am I not king? Did not the Father of the Gods make me lord of gods and men? Go away! Who dares to speak inappropriate words before the king is preparing to travel."

The gods and their followers of men took up arms, and on that day the first wars began in Ife and the forest. Such was the fall of the gods from divine ways, and such was the despair for men that the King of Men created through his theft. But the gods cared little about their deep guilt until darkness fell and everything was quiet. For then they remembered their heritage, the calm of heaven that was born and destined for the world. Gloom, too, came down with the still night. A sense of unholy wrong and ungodly sin weighed down the weary warriors, and everything was changed. All around, the forest seemed dead, and its branches were still. The quiet air was also dead amidst the forest's strangling and knotted growth. While in that hush, the storm's silent messenger, there came the distant thunderous voice of the old Father of the Gods. He thought: "In vain did I send my sons—the children of my happy valley— into the waste beneath to make a world of amusement. For the homes of Ife are held in desolation, and women with their babies are outcast in the naked woods." But when the whirling clouds were wheeling in the sky and the great trees were smitten by the wind, the thunderous Father of the Gods in his anger reprimanded his erring sons: "At my command you came to darkness, where the evil of the void—lifeless violence—had made its home, to shape in the abyss a world of joy and lead creation in the ways of heaven. Why, then, this fighting? Did the void's black soul outmatch you, or possess your hearts to come again into that void? I grieve for man's misfortune. But you have carried them on the wave of your wrong-doing, and your punishment is theirs to share. For now I hurl my thunderbolts, with floods upon the land to fill the marshes and lagoons, and stop forever your unholy war."

Dawn came, the storm was gone, and in his grief the old Father of the Gods departed on black clouds. But still the wrath and anger of his sons continued, and the rebel gods fought on in the dripping forests and the marshes. In the clouds far away the Father of the Gods reasoned to himself: "I spoke in thunders, and my deluge filled the marshes that a priest had once dried. But still they fight. Punish them as I may, what can I achieve? Maybe something in all-powerful heaven, but what about here? What does this mean? I cannot tell. In the unknown, beyond the sky where I have set the sun, is he-who-speaks-not. He knows all. Can this be truth that the world was withdrawn amidst the unnatural strife of brothers, and by strife it must continue?"

Scribe, your pen has written about how the first wars began, and how the old Father of the Gods tried to stop the flow of blood. But of the weary days of all that war, what mouth can speak? It is said the anger of the gods endured two hundred years. We know a priest made strange amulets for all the mortal soldiers of the gods: one charm could turn a spear aside, a second robbed the wounding sword of all its sting, another made one so terrible that twenty must flee. But not one word is handed down of the great deeds, of hopes and fears, of imminent defeat or victory snatched away. No legend has survived, and no voice has called through the dimness of those mysterious years. But when an end came to the terrible days that were foreknown to him-who-speaks-not, memories of the calm of heaven came upon the sleepless gods. For while the moon lay soft with all her spell on Ife of the many battles; while with sorrowful reproach the wise trees stood and gazed upon the gods who made the soil the voices of the forest sang their dreams of peace: "sleep, sleep" all weary nature craved, and "sleep" the slumberous reed-folk urged, and between the shadow and the silvered leaf, for sleep the drowsing breezes yearned.

With the break of dawn, the God of Iron, the warrior, with his comrades stood before the King, and thus he spoke: "King of Men, we weary of the battle, and its agony weighs heavy on our people. Have you forgotten the effortless hours of the Father of the Gods' realm? What is the point of this war, this empty war between one mother's sons? You may say that the Creator of Men willed it so. It was said of old "he who has no house will buy no broom." Why then did the great Creator of Men bring plagues on those he made in love? In heaven afar the Father of the Gods gave to you the empire, but to the Creator of Men knowledge of the ways of mysteries and hidden things. You stole the bag, but not the clues to its use— the skill, the wisdom of great the Creator of Men which alone could wake the sleeping wisdom. The nations of the world are yours: give back the bag, and the great Creator of Men will trouble us no more."

But neither the God of Iron nor the soft voices of the night could loosen the King of Men from the bondage of envy. The rule of men and empire were of no influence when the hot thought of the Father of the Gods' wisdom newly roused his black anger. He held the bag, but all the faithless years had not revealed its promised treasures. Bitterly he answered: "these many years my brother, the Creator of Men, has made war upon me; while for the crown, its power and greatness, I have continuously labored for. Today my son (i.e., the King of Iron) [who is the hope of my cause and my cause itself] now tires of war, and joins my enemies. Weak son, the scepter you were born to hold and hand down strengthened to a line of kings could not uphold your will and be your encouragement until the end. Is it not said, "shall one priest bury, and immediately his mate dig up the corpse?" You have undone more than a brief day's work, which all my heart has longed for through a life of labor. So let it be, God of Soft Iron! Upon your royal brow descends this day the crown of a diminished chieftaincy, with the sweet honors of a king only in name. For I go back to the Father of the Gods' hills and the calm realm about which you babble on and on." Then the King of Men transformed to stone and sank beneath the soil, taking away the fateful bag. And thus, beneath, through all the ages of the world a voiceless wisdom and arts which found no teacher have lain in bondage.

Source: John Wyndham, *Myths of Ife* (London, 1921).

AMERICA

CREATION: MAYAN MYTH

The Popol Vuh *is one of the more important documents of pre-Columbian Mayan religion. Composed around 1550 by an unknown Mayan author, it was written in the Quiché language of Mayan Guatemala, using Spanish letters. In the early 1700s, it was translated into Spanish by a Catholic priest, and, although the original Quiché has since been lost, the translation survives. The work chronicles the formation of the world of the Quiché people and lists their kings up to the year 1550. The following selection is the account of creation, which describes the gods' efforts to create humans; dissatisfied with their early productions, though, they resolve to destroy the immoral and arrogant creatures.*

The god Hurakan, the mighty wind, passed over a universe wrapped in the gloom of a dense and primeval night. He called out "earth," and the solid land appeared. The chief gods took counsel; they were Hurakan, Gucumatz, the serpent covered with green feathers, and Xpiyacoc and Xmucane, the mother and father gods. As the result of their deliberations, animals were created. But as yet man was not. To supply the deficiency the divine beings resolved to create manikins carved out of wood. But these soon incurred the displeasure of the gods, who, irritated by their lack of reverence, determined to destroy them. Then by the will of Hurakan, the Heart of Heaven, the waters were swollen, and a great flood came upon the manikins of wood. They were drowned and a thick resin fell from heaven. The bird Xecotcovach tore out their eyes; the bird Camulatz cut off their heads; the bird Cotzbalam devoured their flesh; the bird Tecumbalam broke their bones and sinews and ground them into powder. Because they had not thought on Hurakan, therefore the face of the earth grew dark, and a pouring rain commenced, raining by day and by night. Then all sorts of beings, great and small, gathered together to abuse the men to their faces. The very household utensils and animals jeered at them, their mill-stones, their plates, their cups, their dogs, their hens. Said the dogs and hens, "Very badly have you treated us, and you have bitten us. Now we bite you in turn." Said the mill-stones, "Very much were we tormented by you, and daily, daily, night and day, it was *squeak, screech, screech,* for your sake. Now you will feel our strength, and we will grind your flesh and make meal of your bodies." And the dogs upbraided the manikins because they had not been fed, and tore the unhappy images with their teeth. And the cups and dishes said, "Pain and misery you gave us, smoking our tops and sides, cooking us over the fire burning and hurting us as if we had no feeling. Now it is your turn, and you will burn." Then ran the manikins hither and thither in despair. They climbed to the roofs of the houses, but the houses crumbled under their feet; they tried to mount to the tops of the trees, but the trees hurled them from them; they sought refuge in the caverns, but the caverns closed before them. Thus was accomplished the ruin of this race, destined to be overthrown. And it is said that their posterity are the little monkeys who live in the woods.

After this catastrophe, before the earth was yet quite recovered from the wrath of the gods, there existed a man "full of pride," whose name was Vukub-Cakix. The name signifies "Seven-times-the-color-of-fire," or "Very brilliant," and was justified by the fact that its owner's eyes were of silver, his teeth of emerald, and other parts of his anatomy of precious metals. In his own opinion Vukub-Cakix's existence rendered unnecessary that of the sun and the moon, and this egoism so disgusted the gods that they resolved upon his overthrow. His two sons, Zipacna and Cabrakan (earth-heaper and earthquake), were daily employed, the one in heaping up mountains, and the other in demolishing them, and these also incurred the wrath of the immortals. Shortly after the decision of the deities the twin hero-gods Hun-Ahpu and Xbalanque came to earth with the intention of chastising the arrogance of Vukub-Cakix and his progeny.

Now Vukub-Cakix had a great tree of the variety known in Central America as "nanze" or "tapal," bearing a fruit round, yellow, and aromatic, and upon this fruit he depended for his daily sustenance. One day on going to partake of it for his morning meal he mounted to its summit in order to seek out the choicest fruits, when to his great indignation he discovered that Hun-Ahpu and Xbalanque had been before him, and had almost stripped the tree of its produce. The hero-gods, who lay concealed within the foliage, now added injury to theft by hurling at Vukub-Cakix a dart from a blow-pipe, which had the effect of precipitating him from the summit of the tree to the earth. He arose in great wrath, bleeding profusely from a severe wound in the jaw. Hun-Ahpu then threw himself upon Vukub-Cakix, who in terrible anger seized the god by the arm and wrenched it from the body. He then proceeded to his dwelling, where he was met and anxiously interrogated by his spouse Chimalmat. Tortured by the pain in his teeth and jaw he, in an excess of spite, hung

Hun-Ahpu's arm over a blazing fire, and then threw himself down to bemoan his injuries, consoling himself, however, with the idea that he had adequately avenged himself upon the interlopers who had dared to disturb his peace.

But Hun-Ahpu and Xbalanque were in no mind that he should escape so easily, and the recovery of Hun-Ahpu's arm must be made at all hazards. With this end in view they consulted two venerable beings in whom we readily recognize the father-mother divinities, Xpiyacoc and Xmucane, disguised for the nonce as sorcerers. These personages accompanied Hun-Ahpu and Xbalanque to the abode of Vukub-Cakix, whom they found in a state of intense agony. The ancients persuaded him to be operated upon in order to relieve his sufferings, and for his glittering teeth they substituted grains of maize. Next they removed his eyes of emerald, upon which his death speedily followed, as did that of his wife Chimalmat. Hun-Ahpu's arm was recovered, re-affixed to his shoulder, and all ended satisfactorily for the hero-gods.

But their mission was not yet complete. The sons of Vukub-Cakix, Zipacna and Cabrakan, remained to be accounted for. Zipacna consented, at the entreaty of four hundred youths, incited by the hero-gods, to assist them in transporting a huge tree which was destined for the roof-tree of a house they were building. While assisting them, he was beguiled by them into entering a great ditch which they had dug for the purpose of destroying him, and when once he descended was overwhelmed by tree-trunks by his treacherous acquaintances, who imagined him to be slain. But he took refuge in a side-tunnel of the excavation, cut off his hair and nails for the ants to carry up to his enemies as a sign of his death, waited until the youths had become intoxicated with pulque because of joy at his supposed demise, and then, emerging from the pit, shook the house that the youths had built over his body about their heads, so that all were destroyed in its ruins. But Hun-Ahpu and Xbalanque were grieved that the four hundred had perished, and laid a more efficacious trap for Zipacna. The mountainbearer, carrying the mountains by night, sought his sustenance by day by the shore of the river, where he lived upon fish and crabs. The hero-gods constructed an artificial crab which they placed in a cavern at the bottom of a deep ravine. The hungry titan descended to the cave, which he entered on all fours. But a neighboring mountain had been undermined by the divine brothers, and its bulk was cast upon him. Thus at the foot of Mount Meavan perished the proud "Mountain Maker," whose corpse was turned into stone by the catastrophe.

Of the family of boasters only Cabrakan remained. Discovered by the hero-gods at his favorite pastime of overturning the hills, they enticed him in an easterly direction, challenging him to overthrow a particularly high mountain. On the way they shot a bird with their blow-pipes, and poisoned it with earth. This they gave to Cabrakan to eat. After partaking of the poisoned fare his strength deserted him, and failing to move the mountain he was bound and buried by the victorious hero-gods.

Source: *The Popol Vuh,* Book I, from Lewis Spence, *The Popol Vuh, the Mythic and Heroic Sagas of the Kichés of Central America* (London: David Nutt, 1908).

QUETZALCOATL AND TEZCATLIPOCA: MEXICAN MYTH

Quetzalcoatl and Tezcatlipoca were major rival deities in pre-Columbian Mesoamerica. Quetzalcoatl, the feathered serpent, was the deity of a religious cult among the Toltec people of central Mexico in the tenth to twelfth centuries CE. Several myths depict Quetzalcoatl as a priest-king of Tollan, the urban center of the Toltec region. Sacrificing only animals, he runs into conflict with the evil wizard Tezcatlipoca, who prefers human sacrifice. Tezcatlipoca then expels Quetzalcoatl. In the following myth, Tezcatlipoca tricks Quetzalcoatl and usurps his power. The dejected Quetzalcoatl then leaves for his homeland.

In the days of Quetzalcoatl there was abundance of everything necessary for subsistence. The maize was plentiful, the calabashes were as thick as one's arm, and cotton grew in all colors without having to be dyed. A variety of birds of rich plumage filled the air with their songs, and gold, silver, and precious stones were abundant. In the reign of Quetzalcoatl there was peace and plenty for all men.

But this blissful state was too fortunate, too happy to endure. Envious of the calm enjoyment of the god and his people the Toltecs, three wicked "necromancers" plotted their downfall—the deities Huitzilopochtli, Tezcatlipoca, and Tlacahuepan. These laid evil enchantments upon the city of Tollan, and Tezcatlipoca in particular took the lead in these envious conspiracies. Disguised as an aged man with white hair, he presented himself at the palace of Quetzalcoatl, where he said to the pages in-waiting: "Pray present me to your master the king. I desire to speak with him."

The pages advised him to retire, as Quetzalcoatl was indisposed and could see no one. He requested them, however, to tell the god that he was waiting outside. They did so, and procured his admittance.

On entering the chamber of Quetzalcoatl the wily Tezcatlipoca simulated much sympathy with the suffering god-king. "How are you, my son?" he asked. "I have brought you a drug which you should drink, and which will put an end to the course of your malady."

"You are welcome, old man," replied Quetzalcoatl. "I have known for many days that you would come. I am exceedingly indisposed. The malady affects my entire system, and I can use neither my hands nor feet."

Tezcatlipoca assured him that if he partook of the medicine which he had brought him he would immediately experience a great improvement in health. Quetzalcoatl drank the potion, and at once felt much revived. The cunning Tezcatlipoca pressed another and still another cup of the potion upon him, and as it was nothing but *pulque,* the wine of the country, he speedily became intoxicated, and was as wax in the hands of his adversary. . . .

The Toltecs were so tormented by the enchantments of Tezcatlipoca that it was soon apparent to them that their fortunes were on the wane and that the end of their empire was at hand. Quetzalcoatl, chagrined at the turn things had taken, resolved to leave Tollan and go to the country of Tlapallan, from which he had come on his civilizing mission to Mexico. He burned all the houses which he had built, and buried his treasure of gold and precious stones in the deep valleys between the mountains. He changed the cacao-trees into mesquites, and he ordered all the birds of rich plumage and song to quit the valley of Anahuac and to follow him to a distance of more than a hundred leagues. On the road from Tollan he discovered a great tree at a point called Quauhtitlan. He rested there, and requested his pages to hand him a mirror. Regarding himself in the polished surface, he exclaimed, "I am old," and from that circumstance the spot was named Old Quauhtitlan. Proceeding on his way accompanied by musicians who played the flute, he walked until fatigue arrested his steps, and he seated himself upon a stone, on which he left the imprint of his hands. This place is called Temacpalco (The Impress of the Hands). At Coaapan he was met by the Nahua gods, who were inimical to him and to the Toltecs.

"Where do you go?" they asked him. "Why do you leave your capital?"

"I go to Tlapallan," replied Quetzalcoatl, "from which I came."

"For what reason?" persisted the enchanters.

"My father the Sun has called me thence," replied Quetzalcoatl.

"Go, then, happily," they said, "but leave us the secret of your art, the secret of founding in silver, of working in precious stones and woods, of painting, and of feather-working, and other matters."

But Quetzalcoatl refused, and cast all his treasures into the fountain of Cozcaapa (Water of Precious Stones). At Cochtan he was met by another enchanter, who asked him where he was bound, and on learning his destination proffered him a draught of wine. On tasting the vintage Quetzalcoatl was overcome with sleep. Continuing his journey in the morning, the god passed between a volcano and the Sierra Nevada (Mountain of Snow), where all the pages who accompanied him died of cold. He regretted this misfortune exceedingly, and wept, lamenting their fate with most bitter tears and mournful songs. On reaching the summit of Mount Poyauhtecatl he slid to the base. Arriving at the seashore, he embarked upon a raft of serpents, and was wafted away toward the land of Tlapallan.

Source: Lewis Spence, *The Myths of Mexico and Peru* (New York: T. Y. Crowell Co., 1913).

CREATION: HOPI MYTH

The Hopi people of North America are part of the Pueblo Indian group, located in what is now the southwestern United States. Their villages were often cliff dwellings and contained at least two dominant kivas, or underground social chambers. The best-known of their rituals is the Snake Dance, in which performers danced with live snakes in their mouths. The following Hopi creation myth describes how two principal goddesses—the Hard-Being Women of the east and west—dried the land, created animals, and then created one race of people. Another goddess—Spider Woman—created other races, which introduced discord into society.

A very long time ago there was nothing but water. In the east, the Hard-Being Woman (Huruing Wuhti), the deity of all hard substances, lived in the ocean. Her house was a kiva like the kivas of the Hopi of today. To the ladder leading into the kiva were usually tied a skin of a gray fox and one of a yellow fox. Another Hard-Being Woman lived in the ocean in the west in a similar kiva, but to her ladder was attached a turtle-shell rattle.

The Sun also existed at that time. Shortly before rising in the east, the Sun would dress up in the skin of the gray fox, whereupon it would begin to dawn—the so-called white dawn of the Hopi. After a little while the Sun would lay off the gray skin and put on the yellow fox skin, whereupon the bright dawn of the morning—the so-called yellow dawn of the Hopi— would appear. The Sun would then rise, that is, emerge from an opening in the north end of the kiva in which the Hard-Being Woman lived. When arriving in the west again, the sun would first announce his arrival by fastening the rattle on the point of the ladder beam, whereupon he would enter the kiva, pass through an opening in the north end of the kiva, and continue his course eastward under the water, and so on.

By and by these two deities caused some dry land to appear in the midst of the water, the waters receding eastward and westward. The Sun passing over this dry land constantly took notice of the fact that no living being of any kind could be seen anywhere, and mentioned this fact to the two deities. So one time the Hard-Being Woman of the west sent word through the Sun to the Hard-Being Woman in the east to come over to her as she wanted to talk over this matter. The Hard-Being Woman of the east complied with this request and proceeded to the West over a rainbow. After consulting each other on this point the two concluded that they would create a little bird; so the deity of the east made a wren of clay, and covered it up with a piece of native cloth. Hereupon they sang a song over it, and after a little while the little bird showed signs of life. Uncovering it, a live bird came forth, saying: "Why do you want me so quickly?" "Yes," they said, "we want you to fly all over this dry place and see whether you can find anything living." They thought that as the Sun always passed over the middle of the earth, he might have failed to notice any living beings that might exist in the north or the south. So the little Wren flew all over the earth, but upon its return reported that no living being existed anywhere. Tradition says, however, that by this time Spider Woman (Kohk'ang Wuhti) lived somewhere in the south-west at the edge of the water, also in a kiva, but this the little bird had failed to notice.

Hereupon the deity of the west proceeded to make very many birds of different kinds and form, placing them again under the same cover under which the Wren had been brought to life. They again sang a song over them. Presently the birds began to move under the cover. The goddess removed the cover and found under it all kinds of birds and fowls. "Why do you want us so quickly?" the latter asked. "Yes, we want you to inhabit this world." Hereupon the two deities taught every kind of bird the sound that it should make, and then the birds scattered out in all directions.

Hereupon the Hard-Being Woman of the west made of clay all different kinds of animals, and they were brought to life in the same manner as the birds. They also asked the same question: "Why do you want us so quickly?" "We want you to inhabit this earth," was the reply given them, whereupon they were taught by their creators their different sounds or languages, after which they proceeded forth to inhabit the different parts of the earth. They now concluded that they would create people. The deity of the east made of clay first a woman and then a man, who were brought to life in exactly the same manner as the birds and animals before them. They asked the same question, and were told that they should live upon this earth and should understand everything. Hereupon the Hard-Being Woman of the east made two tablets of some hard substance, whether stone or clay tradition does not say, and drew upon them with the wooden stick certain characters, handing these tablets to the newly created man and woman, who looked at them, but did not know what they meant. So the deity of the east rubbed with the palms of her hands, first the palms of the woman and then the palms of the man, by which they were enlightened so that they understood the writing on the tablets. Hereupon the deities taught these two a language. After they had taught them the language, the goddess of the east took them out of the kiva and led them over a rainbow, to her home in the east. There they stayed four days, after which the Hard-Being Woman told them to go now and select for themselves a place and live there. The two proceeded forth saying that they would travel around a while and wherever they would find a good field they would remain. Finding a nice place at last, they built a small, simple house, similar to the old houses of the Hopi. Soon the Hard-Being Woman of the west began to think of the matter again, and said to herself: "This is not the way yet that it should be. We are not done yet," and communicated her thoughts to the Hard-Being Woman of the east. By this time Spider Woman had heard about all this matter and she concluded to anticipate the others and also create some beings. So she also made a man and woman of clay, covered them up, sang over them, and brought to life her handiwork. But these two proved to be Spaniards. She taught them the Spanish language, also giving them similar tablets and imparting knowledge to them by rubbing their hands in the same manner as the woman of the East had done with the "White Men." Hereupon she created two burros, which she gave to the Spanish man and woman. The latter settled down close by. After this, Spider Woman continued to create people in the same manner as she had created the Spaniards, always a man and a woman, giving a different language to each pair. But all at once she found that she had forgotten to create a woman for a certain man, and that is the reason why now there are always some single men.

She continued the creating of people in the same manner, giving new languages as the pairs were formed. All at once she found that she had failed to create a man for a certain woman, in other words, it was found that there was one more woman than there were men. "Oh my!" she said, "How is this?" and then addressing the single woman she said: "There is a single man somewhere, who went away from here. You try to find him and if he accepts you, you live with him. If not, both of you will have to remain single. You do the best you can about that." The two finally found each other, and the woman said, "Where will we live?" The man answered: "Why here, anywhere. We will remain together." So he went to work and built a house for them in which they lived. But it did not take very long before they commenced to quarrel with each other. "I want to live here alone," the woman said. "I can prepare food for myself." "Yes, but who will get the wood for you? Who will work the fields?" the man said. "We had better remain together." They made up with each other, but peace did not last. They soon quarreled again, separated for while, came together again, separated again, and so on. Had these people not lived in that way, all the other Hopi would now live in peace, but others learned it from them, and that is the reason why there are so many contentions between the men and their wives. These were the kind of people that Spider Woman had created. The Hard-Being Woman of the west heard about this and commenced to meditate upon it. Soon she called the goddess from the east to come over again, which the latter did. "I do not want to live here alone," the deity of the west said, "I also want some good people to live here." So she also created a number of other people, but always a man and a wife. They were created in the same manner as the deity of the east had created hers. They lived in the west. Only wherever the people that Spider Woman had created came in contact with these good people, there was trouble. The people at that time led a nomadic life, living mostly on game. Wherever they found rabbits or antelope or deer they would kill the game and eat it. This led to a good many contentions among the people. Finally the Woman of the west said to her people: "You remain here; I am going to live, after this, in the midst of the ocean in the west. When you want anything from me, you pray to me there." Her people regretted this very much, but she left them. The Hard-Being Woman of the east did exactly the same thing, and that is the reason why at the present day the places where these two live are never seen.

Those Hopi who now want something from them deposit their prayer offerings in the village. When they say their wishes and prayers they think of those two who live in the far distance, but of whom the Hopi believe that they still remember them.

The Spanish were angry at the Hard-Being Woman and two of them took their guns and proceeded to the abiding place of the deity. The Spaniards are very skillful and they found a way to get there. When they arrived at the house of the Hard-Being Woman, the latter at once surmised what their intentions were. "You have come to kill me," she said; "don't do that; lay down your weapons and I will show you something; I am not going to hurt you." They laid down their arms, whereupon she went to the rear end of the kiva and brought out a white lump like a stone and laid it before the two men, asking them to lift it up. One tried it, but could not lift it up, and what was worse, his hands adhered to the stone. The other man tried to assist him, but his hands also adhered to the stone, and thus they were both prisoners. Hereupon the Hard-Being Woman took the two guns and said: "These do not amount to anything," and then rubbed them between her hands to powder. She then said to them: "You people ought to live in peace with one another. You people of Spider Woman know many things, and the people whom we have made also know many, but different, things. You ought not to quarrel about these things, but learn from one another; if one has or knows a good thing he should exchange it with others for other good things that they know and have. If you will agree to this I will release you." They said they did, and that they would no more try to kill the deity. Then the latter went to the rear end of the kiva where she disappeared through an opening in the floor, from where she exerted a secret influence upon the stone and thus released the two men. They departed, but the Hard-Being Woman did not fully trust them, thinking that they would return, but they never did.

Source: Heinrich Richert Voth, *The Traditions of the Hopi,* in *Field Columbian Museum,* Publication, Anthropological Series (Chicago: The Museum, 1895–1905), vol. 8.

CREATION: CHEROKEE MYTH

The Cherokee people of North America are of the Iroquois language group and lived in what is now the southeastern United States. In the 1830s, the United States government forced them to relocate to Oklahoma. The following Cherokee creation myth emphasizes the role of animals in the creation process. While the world was covered with water, they existed in a realm above the earth, slowly inhabiting it as it became dry. Vegetation followed, and finally humans appeared.

The earth is a great island floating in a sea of water, and suspended at each of the four cardinal points by a cord hanging down from the sky vault, which is of solid rock. When the world grows old and worn out, the people will die and the cords will break and let the earth sink down into the ocean, and all will be water again. The Indians are afraid of this. When all was water, the animals were above, in the place Beyond the Arch; but it was very much crowded, and they were wanting more room. They wondered what was below the water, and at last "Beaver's Grandchild," the little Water-beetle, offered to go and see if it could learn. It darted in every direction over the surface of the water, but could find no firm place to rest. Then it dived to the bottom and came up with some soft mud, which began to grow and spread on every side until it became the island which we call the earth. It was afterwards fastened to the sky with four cords, but no one remembers who did this.

At first the earth was flat and very soft and wet. The animals were anxious to get down, and sent out different birds to see if it was yet dry, but they found no place to land and came back again to the place Beyond the Arch. At last it seemed to be time, and they sent out the Buzzard and told him to go and make ready for them. This was the Great Buzzard, the father of all the buzzards we see now. He flew all over the earth, low down near the ground, and it was still soft. When he reached the Cherokee country, he was very tired, and his wings began to flap and strike the ground, and wherever they struck the earth there was a valley, and where they turned up again there was a mountain. When the animals above saw this, they were afraid that the whole world would be mountains, so they called him back, but the Cherokee country remains full of mountains to this day.

When the earth was dry and the animals came down, it was still dark, so they got the sun and set it in a track to go every day across the island from east to west, just overhead. It was too hot this way, and the "Red Crawfish" had his shell scorched a bright red, so that his meat was spoiled; and the Cherokee do not eat it. The conjurers put the sun another hand-breadth higher in the air, but it was still too hot. They raised it another, until it was seven handbreadths high and just under the sky arch. Then it was right, and they left it so. This is why the conjurers call the highest place "The Seventh Height," because it is seven hand-breadths above the earth.

Every day the sun goes along under this arch, and returns at night on the upper side to the starting place.

There is another world under this, and it is like ours in everything—animals, plants, and people—save that the seasons are different. The streams that come down from the mountains are the trails by which we reach this underworld, and the springs at their heads are the doorways by which we enter it, but to do this one must fast and go to water, and have one of the underground people for a guide. We know that the seasons in the underworld are different from ours, because the water in the springs is always warmer in winter and cooler in summer than the outer air.

When the animals and plants were first made—we do not know by whom—they were told to watch and keep awake for seven nights, just as young men now fast and keep awake when they pray to their medicine. They tried to do this, and nearly all were awake through the first night, but the next night several dropped off to sleep, and the third night others were asleep, and then others, until, on the seventh night, of all the animals only the owl, the panther, and one or two more were still awake. To these were given the power to see and to go about in the dark, and to make prey of the birds and animals which must sleep at night. Of the trees only the cedar, the pine, the spruce, the holly, and the laurel were awake to the end, and to them it was given to be always green and to be greatest for medicine, but to the others it was said: "Because you have not endured to the end you will lose your hair every winter."

Men came after the animals and plants. At first there were only a brother and sister until he struck her with a fish and told her to multiply, and so it was. In seven days a child was born to her, and thereafter every seven days another, and they increased very fast until there was danger that the world could not keep them. Then it was made that a woman should have only one child in a year, and it has been so ever since.

Source: James Mooney, *Myths of the Cherokee, from Nineteenth Annual Report of the Bureau of American Ethnology: To the Secretary of the Smithsonian Institution*, 1897–98 (Washington, DC: U.S. Government Printing Office, 1900).

ORIGIN OF DISEASE AND MEDICINE: CHEROKEE MYTH

The following myth illustrates the close relationship that the Cherokee people had to their natural surroundings. According to the myth, as human population increased and became insensitive toward the animal world, the animals rose up against them. They afflicted humans with rheumatism, fears, nightmares, and diseases. Only the plants were sympathetic to the humans and thus provided cures for their ailments.

In the old days the beasts, birds, fishes, insects, and plants could all talk, and they and the people lived together in peace and friendship. But as time went on the people increased so rapidly that their settlements spread over the whole earth, and the poor animals found themselves beginning to be cramped for room. This was bad enough, but to make it worse humans invented bows, knives, blowguns, spears, and hooks, and began to slaughter the larger animals, birds, and fishes for their flesh or their skins, while the smaller creatures, such as the frogs and worms, were crushed and trodden upon without thought, out of pure carelessness or contempt. So the animals resolved to consult upon measures for their common safety.

The Bears were the first to meet in council in their town-house under Kuwahi Mountain, the "Mulberry Place," and the old White Bear chief presided. After each in turn had complained of the way in which humans killed their friends, ate their flesh, and used their skins for their own purposes, it was decided to begin war at once against them. Someone asked what weapons humans used to destroy them. "Bows and arrows, of course," cried all the Bears in chorus. "And what are they made of?" was the next question. "The bow of wood, and the string of our entrails," replied one of the Bears. It was then proposed that they make a bow and some arrows and see if they could not use the same weapons against humans themselves. So one Bear got a nice piece of locust wood and another sacrificed himself for the good of the rest in order to furnish a piece of his entrails for the string. But when everything was ready and the first Bear stepped up to make the trial, it was found that in letting the arrow fly after drawing back the bow, his long claws caught the string and spoiled the shot. This was annoying, but some one suggested that they might trim his claws, which was accordingly done, and on a second trial it was found that the arrow went straight to the mark. But here the chief, the old White Bear, objected, saying it was necessary that they should have long claws in order to be able to climb trees. "One of us has already died to furnish the bowstring, and if we now cut off our claws we must all starve together. It is better to trust to the teeth and claws that nature gave us, for it is plain that human weapons were not intended for us."

No one could think of any better plan, so the old chief dismissed the council and the Bears dispersed to the woods and thickets without having concerted any way to prevent the increase of the human race. Had the result of the council been otherwise, we should now be at war with the Bears, but as it is, the hunter does not even ask the Bear's pardon when he kills one.

The Deer next held a council under their chief, the Little Deer, and after some talk decided to send rheumatism to every hunter who should kill one of them unless he took care to ask their pardon for the offense. They sent notice of their decision to the nearest settlement of Indians and told them at the same time what to do when necessity forced them to kill one of the Deer tribe. Now, whenever the hunter shoots a Deer, the Little Deer, who is swift as the wind and cannot be wounded, runs quickly up to the spot and, bending over the blood-stains, asks the spirit of the Deer if it has heard the prayer of the hunter for pardon. If the reply be "Yes," all is well, and the Little Deer goes on his way; but if the reply be "No," he follows on the trail of the hunter, guided by the drops of blood on the ground, until he arrives at his cabin in the settlement, when the Little Deer enters invisibly and strikes the hunter with rheumatism, so that he becomes at once a helpless cripple. No hunter who has regard for his health ever fails to ask pardon of the Deer for killing it, although some hunters who have not learned the prayer may try to turn aside the Little Deer from his pursuit by building a fire behind them in the trail.

Next came the Fishes and Reptiles, who had their own complaints against humans. They held their council together and determined to make their victims dream of snakes coiling about them in slimy folds and blowing foul breath in their faces, or to make them dream of eating raw or decaying fish, so that they would lose appetite, sicken, and die. This is why people dream about snakes and fish.

Finally the Birds, Insects, and smaller animals came together for the same purpose, and the Grubworm was chief of the council. It was decided that each in turn should give an opinion, and then they would vote on the question as to whether or not humans were guilty. Seven votes should be enough to condemn them. One after another denounced human cruelty and injustice toward the other animals and voted in favor of their death. The Frog spoke first, saying: "We must do something to check the increase of the race, or people will become so numerous that we will be crowded from off the earth. See how they have kicked me about because I'm ugly, as they say, until my back is covered with sores"; and here he showed the spots on his skin. Next came the Bird—no one remembers now which one it was—who condemned humans "because he burns my feet off," meaning the way in which the hunter barbecues birds by impaling them on a stick set over the fire, so that their feathers and tender feet are singed off. Others followed in the same strain. The Ground-squirrel alone ventured to say a good word for humans, who seldom hurt him because he was so small, but this made the others so angry that they fell upon the Ground-squirrel and tore him with their claws, and the stripes are on his back to this day.

They began then to devise and name so many new diseases, one after another, that had not their invention at last failed them, no one of the human race would have been able to survive. The Grubworm grew constantly more pleased as the name of each disease was called off, until at last they reached the end of the list, when someone proposed to make menstruation sometimes fatal to women. On this he rose up in his place and cried: "Thanks! I'm glad some more of them will die, for they are getting so thick that they tread on me." The thought fairly made him shake with joy, so that he fell over backward and could not get on his feet again, but had to wriggle off on his back, as the Grubworm has done ever since.

When the Plants, who were friendly to humans, heard what had been done by the animals, they determined to defeat the latter's evil designs. Each Tree, Shrub, and Herb, down even to the Grasses and Mosses, agreed to furnish a cure for some one of the diseases named, and each said: "I will appear to help humans when they call upon me in their needs." Thus came medicine; and the plants, every one of which has its use if we only knew it, furnish the remedy to counteract the evil wrought by the revengeful animals. Even weeds were made for some good purpose, which we must find out for ourselves. When the medicine man does not know what medicine to use for a sick person, the spirit of the plant tells him.

Source: James Mooney, *Myths of the Cherokee, from Nineteenth Annual Report of the Bureau of American Ethnology: To the Secretary of the Smithsonian Institution*, 1897–98 (Washington, DC: U.S. Government Printing Office, 1900).

ORIGIN OF CORN: CREEK MYTH

Many Native American myths concern the origin of corn, a staple in Native American diets. One account from the Creek Indians of the southeastern United States attributes it to the

Corn Woman. The myth takes many forms, but the central theme is this: An old woman of mysterious origins enters a village and secretly provides the inhabitants with corn, which they all enjoy. They discover, though, that she produces the corn from scabs on her body, her feces, or some other disgusting source. Repulsed by this, they can no longer eat what she supplies. Versions of the myth have the Corn Woman solve the problem in different ways. In one account she instructs her sons to kill and decapitate her and drag her body around, and corn then grows where her blood has seeped into the soil. The Corn Woman's solution in the version here is much more humane.

It is said that corn was obtained by one of the women of a local clan. She had a number of neighbors and friends, and when they came to her house she would serve some corn into an earthen bowl and they would eat it. They found it delicious, but did not know where she got the stuff of which to make it. Finally they noticed that she washed her feet in water and rubbed them, whereupon what came from her feet was corn. She said to them, "You may not like to eat from me in this way, so build a corncrib, put me inside and fasten the door. Don't disturb me, but keep me there for four days, and at the end of the fourth day you can let me out." They did so, and while she was there they heard a great rumbling like distant thunder, but they did not know what it meant. On the fourth day they opened the door as directed and she came out. Then they found that the crib was well stocked with corn. There was corn for making bread, hard flint corn for making other kinds. She instructed them how to plant grains of corn from what she had produced. They did so, the corn grew and reproduced and they have had corn ever since.

Source: Adapted from John R. Swanton, *Myths and Tales of the Southeastern Indians, Smithsonian Institution Bureau of American Ethnology*, Bulletin 88 (Washington, DC: U.S. Government Printing Office, 1929).

OCEANIA

THE WISE AND FOOLISH TWINS: MELANESIAN MYTH

A popular theme in Melanesian mythology is the contrast between two celestial twin brothers, one wise, the other foolish. Both were created by a primal deity who traced two images into the dirt, and covered them with droplets of his blood. The wise brother, To-Kabinana, is the sun; the foolish, To-Karvuvu, is the

moon. The following myths, from New Guinea, describe how the
stupid blunders of To-Kabinana result in bad things, such as can-
nibalism and man-eating sharks.

In the beginning, a deity drew two male figures on the
ground, and then, cutting himself with a knife, he sprinkled
the two drawings with his blood and covered them over with
leaves. They came to life as To-Kabinana and To-Karvuvu.
The former then climbed a coconut tree which produced light
yellow nuts, and picked two unripe ones. He threw them to
the ground, where they burst and changed into two women,
whom he took as his wives. His brother asked him how
he had gotten the two women, and To-Kabinana told him.
Accordingly, To-Karvuvu also climbed a tree and likewise
threw down two nuts. But they fell so that their underside
struck the ground, and from them came two women with
depressed, ugly noses. So To-Karvuvu was jealous because
his brother's wives were better looking than his, and he
took one of To-Kabinana's spouses, abandoning the two ugly
females who were his own.

To-Kabinana and To-Karvuvu were one day walking in
the fields when the former said to the latter, "Go, and look
after our mother." So To-Karvuvu went, filled a bamboo vessel with water, poured it over his mother, heated stones in
the fire, killed her, and laid her in the oven to roast, after
which he returned to To-Kabinana, who asked him how their
mother was and if he had taken good care of her. To-Karvuvu
replied, "I have roasted her with the hot stones," whereupon
his brother demanded, "Who told you to do that?" "Oh," he
answered, "I thought you said to kill her!" But To-Kabinana
declared, "You fool, you will die before me. You never cease
doing foolish things. Our descendants now will cook and eat
human flesh."

One day To-Kabinana carved a Thum-fish out of wood and
let it float on the sea and made it alive so that it might always
be a fish. The Thum-fish drove the Malivaran-fish ashore in
great numbers so that they could be caught. Now To-Karvuvu
saw them, and asked his brother where were the fish that
forced the Malivaran-fish ashore, saying that he also wished
to make some. Accordingly, To-Kabinana told him to make
the figure of a Thum-fish. However the stupid fellow instead
carved the image of a shark and put it in the water. The
shark, however, did not drive the other fish ashore, but ate
them all up. To-Karvuvu went crying to his brother and said,
"I wish I had not made my fish, for he eats all the others."
To-Kabinana then asked, "What kind of a fish did you make?"

and he replied, "A shark." Then ToKabinana said, "You are indeed a stupid fellow. You have brought it about that our descendants will suffer. That fish will eat all the others, and he will eat people as well."

Source: Adapted from Roland B. Dixon, *The Mythology of All Races: Oceanic* (Boston: Marshall Jones Company, 1916).

MAUI THE TRICKSTER-GOD: POLYNESIAN MYTH

In Polynesian mythology, Maui is the creator god of the islands and people of the region. Maui is a trickster who uses his cunning to accomplish his desires by breaking the rules of society. The following are three popular Maui myths: how he fished up the land, how he discovered the source of fire, and how he restrained the sun. The first two are from New Zealand, and the third from Hawaii.

Maui had a sorcerer grandmother to whom it was the duty of the elder brothers to carry food, but they neglected her and ate it themselves. Maui offered to take their place, but when he came to his grandmother, he found her ill, one half of her body being already dead, whereupon he wrenched off her lower jaw, made from it a fish-hook, which he concealed about him, and then returned to his home. His brothers did not like to have him accompany them on their fishing trips, but Maui hid in their canoe, and when they were out at sea next day, he revealed himself. At first they were going to put him ashore, but finally they agreed to let him stay, since they thought that he could not fish if they did not give him a hook. Not dismayed, Maui took out his magic hook, struck his nose with his fist until it bled, and baited his hook with the blood. Lowering his line, he soon got a tremendous bite and at last hauled in the land from the bottom of the sea, which was a giant fish. Telling his brothers not to cut up the fish-land, he went away. But they disobeyed him and began to hack it with their knives, thus causing the great fish-land to struggle, break the canoe, and kill the brothers. From the cuts made by them, the land became rough and rugged, thus making the mountains and valleys.

Maui and his brothers lived with their mother, but every morning she disappeared before they awoke, and none knew where she went. Determining to solve the mystery, Maui stopped up every chink and cranny in the house, thus preventing the morning light from coming in, so that his mother overslept. Maui, waking in time, saw her leave the house, pull up a clump of tall grass, and disappear down an opening that it covered. Adopting his favorite disguise of a bird, he followed, flying down the hole to the world below, where he revealed himself to his mother and demanded food. The fire being out, his mother was about to send a servant to secure some, when Maui volunteered to bring it. Accordingly, he went to the house of his ancestor Mafuike, an old woman who was the owner and guardian of fire. He asked her for a piece of smoldering wood, and she gave him one of her fingers, in which fire was contained. He left, but when out of sight, extinguished it in a stream and returned for more. She gave him another finger, which he extinguished in a similar manner, and thus got from her in succession all her fingers and toes, except the last. In anger, she set the world afire. Maui fled, but was pursued by the flames, which threatened to consume everything. In distress he called upon rain, snow, and hail to aid him, and they, coming to his assistance, succeeded in putting out the conflagration and thus saved the world.

Maui's mother was very troubled by the shortness of the day, occasioned by the rapid movement of the sun. Since it was impossible to dry properly the sheets of bark paper used for clothing, Maui determined to cut off the legs of the sun so that it could not travel so fast. His mother, accordingly, made strong ropes for him and sent him to his blind old grandmother to get more assistance. He found her cooking bananas, and as she laid them down one after the other, Maui stole them. At length discovering her loss, but unable to see the culprit, she sniffed about angrily until she smelt a man. She asked who it was, and when Maui told her that he was her grandson, she forgave him and presented him with a magic club to aid him in his attack on the sun. Maui now went off eastward to where the sun climbed daily out of the underworld. As the sun rose, Maui roped its legs one after the other and tied the ropes strongly to great trees. Suitably caught, the sun could not get away, and Maui gave it a tremendous beating with his magic weapon. To save its life, the sun begged for mercy, and on promising to go more slowly ever after, it was released from his bonds.

Source: Adapted from Roland B. Dixon, *The Mythology of All Races: Oceanic* (Boston: Marshall Jones Company, 1916).

OLOFAT THE TRICKSTER-GOD: MICRONESIAN MYTH

In Micronesian mythology, Olofat is a trickster-god, fire-god, and god of death. The following story, from the Caroline Islands, describes how Olofat maliciously created sharks to harm people.

In response to Olofat's malice, his father, Luk, unsuccessfully attempts to kill him.

Olofat saw that one of his brothers was better than he and also more beautiful, and he became angry at this. He looked down from the sky-world and saw two boys who had caught a couple of sharks, with which they were playing in a fishpond. He descended to earth and gave the sharks teeth, so that they bit the hands of the children. When the boys ran home crying with pain and told their troubles to their mother, Ligoapup, who was the sister of Olofat. She asked the boys if they had seen anyone around; they said that they had, and that he was more handsome than any man whom they had ever seen. Knowing that this must be her brother, Olofat, Ligoapup asked her sons where he was, and they answered, "Close by the sea." She then told them to go and get him and bring him to her. But when they reached the place where they had seen him, they found only an old, grey-haired man, covered with dirt. Returning to their mother, they informed her that the man whom they had seen was no longer there. But she instructed them to go back and bring whoever they might find.

Accordingly they set off, but this time they saw only a heap of filth in place of a man, and so once more they went home to their mother. She told them to return a third time. Obeying her, they questioned the filth, saying, "Are you Olofat? For if you are, you must come to our mother." Then the pile of filth turned into a handsome man who accompanied them to Ligoapup. She said to him, "Why are you such a deceiver?" And Olofat replied, "How so?" She replied, "First, you turned yourself into a dirty old man, and then into a pile of filth." Olofat answered, "I am afraid of my father." Ligoapup said, "You are afraid because you gave teeth to the shark." Olofat replied, "I am angry at our father Luk, since he created my brother handsomer than I am, and with greater power. I will give teeth to all sharks, so that they may eat men whenever canoes tip over." When Luk, who was in the sky-world, became aware of these things, he said to his wife Inoaeman, "It would be best if Olofat came back to heaven, since he is only doing evil on earth"; His wife said, "I think so, too. Otherwise he will destroy mankind, for he is an evil being." . . .

When Luk saw Olofat, he said, "We have tried in every possible way to kill you, but it seems that you cannot die. Bring me Samenkoaner." After Samenkoaner had come and sat down, Luk asked him, "How is it that Olofat cannot die? Can you kill him?" To this Samenkoaner replied, "No, not even if I thought about it for a whole night long, could I find a means; for he is older than I." Luk said, "But I do

not wish that he should destroy all men upon the earth."
Then the Rat, Luk's sister, advised that they should burn
Olofat. Accordingly they made a great fire, to which they
brought Olofat; but he had with him a roll of coconut fiber,
and when Luk ordered them to throw him into the flames,
he crept through the roll and came out safely on the other
side of the fire. Then Luk said, "Rat, we have tried everything to kill him, but in vain"; and the Rat answered, "He
cannot die; so make him the lord of all who are evil and
deceitful."

DIVISION OF LABOR BETWEEN THE SEXES: AUSTRALIAN MYTH

*The most pervasive shared aspect of Australian Aboriginal reli-
gion is "The Dreaming" or "Dreamtime," which is the ancient
time of the creation of all things by sacred ancestors, whose
spirits continue into the present. The Dreaming has a beginning,
but it has no real end because it continues to affect and shape
the present. The overall concern in most myths of the Dreaming
is how the world came to be inhabitable by humans, and the
power of the ancestors is thought to be available still to those
with the proper ritual knowledge. In some cases the ancestors
were transformed into features of the landscape, and in others
they died or passed beyond tribal lands. In most cases, however,
their spirits survive, and they continue to be as alive as they
were during the primordial Dreaming, although in altered form.
They are eternal, and many are said to be self-created. Unlike
the gods of other peoples, however, the ancestors are portrayed
as living much like humans: They hunt their food with spears or
other hand weapons, they require water in order to survive, and
even the most powerful build shelters in order to protect themselves from the elements. The following story from tribes living
near the Murray River in New South Wales tells of how men
and women came to cohabit and describes how each has certain
duties and obligations.*

During the Dreaming the Raven ancestor wanted to cross
a river, but since he could not swim he decided to build a
canoe. After searching for suitable bark, he fashioned one
and began to carry it to the water. As he walked, he began to
hear a rhythmic tapping in the air above his head, and after
searching around determined that it was coming from his
canoe. He set it down and discovered to his surprise that a
woman was sitting in it. He had never before seen a female,
and so he stared at her, fascinated by the differences in their
respective physiques.

The woman said nothing to him, but stepped from the canoe and helped him to carry it to the bank of the river. After they were both in the small craft, he handed her the paddle, but she shook her head and sat in the back of the canoe. Her actions indicated that she expected him to do the hard work of paddling. Because he had never before met a woman, he was unfamiliar with the proper relationships between the sexes, but she began to teach him his role and what sort of work was appropriate for her. He found many of her lessons difficult to accept, and the learning process was fraught with conflicts, but at the same time he realized that there were unexpected compensations. Many things he had had to do by himself were now shared, and they developed a mutually satisfactory partnership. Later they had children, and raising them presented more challenges and rewards. One day when the two were searching for food their young wandered from the tree in which they sheltered. When they reached the ground they adapted by taking on human form, and thus they became the first Aborigines. All of Australia's original people are descended from these two ancestors.

THE FIRST DEATH: AUSTRALIAN MYTH

Death is a central concern of Australian Aboriginal religion. There is a great deal of speculation regarding how it first entered the world and whether it is final. In this story from the Kamilroi tribe, Baiame, the all-father, finished creating the world, and after extensive travels around the land he was well satisfied with his work. Subsequently he returned to his abode in the sky along with his wife Birrahgnooloo, whom some tribes regard as the Mother-of-All and his partner in creation.

As Baiame walked the world, he fashioned various animals and plants, along with important features of the landscape such as rivers and mountains. Finally he created humans out of the dust of the mountains, intending that they would be custodians of the land. The first people began to reproduce, and Baiame's world became increasingly filled with various species. The sun and rain he provided sustained both plant and animal life, and sustenance was plentiful.

Long after his departure to heaven, however, the land was afflicted by the first great drought, which is still today a recurrent problem in Australia. Although humans had been ordered by Baiame not to eat certain species, a man driven to desperation began to kill and eat some of them and shared the food with his wife. They offered a forbidden kangaroo-rat to a friend who was afflicted by hunger, but mindful of Baiame's prohibition he refused the meat and went away.

As he walked he became steadily weaker, until he collapsed at the base of a large tree. The man and woman who had offered him food saw him from a distance and called out to him, but he was too weak to respond. As they watched, a large black shape emerged from the tree and picked up his dying body and carried it up into the high branches. The monster who carried him was Yowee, the spirit of death, and the man became the first human to die. Baiame had intended that his creation would be perfect and that all of his creatures would have plenty of food and water, but in his absence they experienced severe privation, which allowed death to enter the world and claim its first victim. Since that time death has been the fate of all creatures.

HOW FIRE BECAME WIDELY AVAILABLE: AUSTRALIAN MYTH

A number of Australian Aboriginal myths concern the origins of fire. In some the ancestors jealously guard the secrets of how to make and maintain fire, and there is a general sense that such a wondrous lore would not freely be shared. Fire is often obtained by trickery or theft, and those who acquire it generally want to keep it for themselves. In the following story from the Northern Territory, two men acquire the secret of fire and refuse to share it with their tribe.

Before fire was widely available, people made their food more edible by leaving it to dry in the sun. One day Bootoolgah the crane ancestor was rubbing two sticks together and noticed that this action produced a spark. He showed this to his wife Goonur, the kangaroo rat, who realized that this technique could be used to make fire whenever they wanted. They fashioned two sticks that could be carried in a pouch, which they carried with them at all times. They first used fire to cook some fish they had caught, and marveled at how much better it tasted than sun-dried flesh. They decided to keep the secret of fire for themselves, and they always went to hidden places to make their fires and cook their food. When other members of their tribe noticed that their meat looked different from theirs, Bootoolgah and Goonur claimed that they had dried it in the sun like everyone else, but the others became suspicious. One day Boolooral, the night owl, followed them silently and saw them making fire to cook their food, and he reported back to the elders of the tribe. Rather than try to take the secret by force, they decided to trick the two. They announced that a huge *corroboree* (tribal gathering) would be held, the largest in living memory, and that all the surrounding tribes would participate.

Each group arrived decorated with its distinctive symbols. Some painted their whole bodies, while others had elaborate costumes made with feathers. All performed dances unique to their tribes, and no one had ever seen such a wondrous display. During the celebrations Bootoolgah and Goonur became so entranced by the spectacle that they forgot to guard their fire sticks. When their guard was down, a man who had been pretending to be sick grabbed the bag in which the fire sticks were hidden and brought them to the tribal elders. They learned how to use them to make fire, and subsequently shared the lore with the rest of the tribe, so that everyone could make use of it.

THE RAINBOW SERPENT: AUSTRALIAN MYTH

Different ancestors figure in myths of the various regions of Australia. One of the most widely dispersed ancestral characters is the Rainbow Serpent, named Ngaljod in Northern Arnhem Land and known by other names in other parts of the continent. He is an enormous snake who commonly lives in lakes and rivers. When he moves from one place to another, he makes rivers and water holes. His voracious appetite often brings him into conflict with other ancestors. He is essentially an amoral character, whose actions created important aspects of the landscape, but he has no particular love for humans. Rather, he eats them whenever he can, and many myths about the Rainbow Serpent focus on how dangerous he is.

Before going off to hunt, the men of a tribe in the Northern Territory warned their boys not to venture near the sea because a giant snake lived there, waiting to eat unwary children. After they left the boys began to play, but after becoming bored decided to follow the sound of the surf to the beach. As they drew near, they saw a beautiful rainbow in the sky, but they failed to realize that it was caused by the Rainbow Serpent, who had arched his coils up from the water. The colors of the rainbow were caused by the light reflecting off his scales.

When the boys reached the water, they were so enraptured by the beauty of the landscape that they failed to notice the serpent, who swam toward them swiftly and silently. He swallowed them whole. When the hunters returned to their camp, they immediately noticed that the boys had disappeared, and when they followed their tracks to the beach they found that they ended at the water's edge. There were two black rocks in the ocean that had not been there before, and the men realized that the rainbow serpent had swallowed the boys and turned them into rocks. There was nothing they could do about this situation, and so they sadly returned to their camp. The rocks are still visible today between Double Island Point and Inship Rock. When a rainbow appears in the sky, the elders of the tribe tell this story to the younger members in order to illustrate the importance of obedience and the dangers of wandering by themselves.